A Worldly Christian

Photo of Neill from WCC archives.

A Worldly Christian
The Life and Times of Stephen Neill

Dyron B. Daughrity

The Lutterworth Press

The Lutterworth Press

P.O. Box 60
Cambridge
CB1 2NT
United Kingdom

www.lutterworth.com
publishing@lutterworth.com

Hardback ISBN: 978 0 7188 9584 6
Paperback ISBN: 978 0 7188 9585 3
PDF ISBN: 978 0 7188 4847 7
ePub ISBN: 978 0 7188 4846 0

British Library Cataloguing in Publication Data
A record is available from the British Library

First published by The Lutterworth Press, 2021
Copyright © Dyron B. Daughrity, 2021

All rights reserved. No part of this edition may be reproduced, stored electronically or in any retrieval system, or transmitted in any form or by any means, electronic, mechanical, photocopying, recording, or otherwise, without prior written permission from the Publisher (permissions@lutterworth.com).

This book is dedicated to Sunde, my wife.
She has provided complete support for me as I hunted down every little note and scribble pertaining to Stephen Charles Neill. She supported me in my pursuits abroad, sometimes months at a time, as I chased the ghost of Neill. She helped me transcribe his terrible handwriting into something comprehensible. For nearly thirty years she has stood by me in my aim to be
a better scholar and person.

Thank you, dear Sunde.

Contents

List of Illustrations	viii
Acknowledgements	ix
1. Introduction	1
2. Childhood, Youth and Education: 1900-24	17
3. Amy Carmichael and Neill's Early Years in South India: 1924-28	58
4. An Educator in South India: 1928-39	91
5. Neill's Years as Bishop of Tinnevelly: 1939-45	124
6. Loss of a Bishopric: 1944-45	162
7. Return to Europe and Ecumenical Labour: 1944-62	208
8. A Professorship in Hamburg: 1962-68	266
9. The Nairobi Years: 1969-73	297
10. Final Years in Oxford: 1973-84	334
Afterword	369
Appendix	372
Bibliography	377
Index	389

List of Illustrations

Photo of Neill from WCC archives	ii
Stephen Neill's birth certificate	21
Dedication to Neill with wrong date for his birth (Palayamkottai Cathedral)	22
Stephen, Henry, Gerald in tennis gear (courtesy of Penny Golby)	37
Dean Close School's 'Officers Training Corp'	41
Young Neill (courtesy of Trinity College, Cambridge)	46
Amy Carmichael with children	62
Anglican delegates at Tambaram, Madras, 1938	122
Plaque commemorating all bishops of Tirunelveli diocese up to 1999 (Holy Trinity Cathedral)	129
Stephen Neill, newly enthroned as Bishop of Tinnevelly, 1939	138
Bishop Stephen Neill in his prime, c. 1943	140
Tirunelveli Diocesan Offset Press, initiated by Neill	149
Neill as bishop (Bishopstowe, Palayamkottai)	157
Bishop Stephen Neill Centre	158
Bishop Stephen Neill, Dr W.A. Visser't Hooft, Dr Henry Smith Leiper, Dr R.C. Mackie, Oliver Tomkins, Frederick Nolde (from WCC, World Council of Churches website)	213
Stephen Neill, c. 1948	216
Stephen Neill, 1953	248
Bishop Stephen Neill and U. Kyaw Than, 1958	252
Grave marker for Stephen Neill (photo by Randy Chesnutt)	362

Acknowledgments

I must first acknowledge Adrian Brink, Debora Nicosia, and the helpful staff of The Lutterworth Press. It has been a pleasure to work with you. I am deeply grateful to Adrian for the opportunity to publish my biography of Stephen Neill with a company that published numerous of Neill's own works in the past.

I want to acknowledge three students who helped me during the proofreading stages of the present work: Tara Brandenberger, Diana Keester, and Jackson Nichols. Thanks to all three of you for your careful look at the manuscript. I wish you the very best as you continue your studies. I am especially thankful to Tara for her excellent work on the Index; it will be helpful to scholars for years to come.

I have several close colleagues at Pepperdine who have been a constant support for my research: Randy Chesnutt, Ron Highfield, Nick Cumming, and Dan Rodriguez. I must also thank my dear friend, Jay Brewster, who is a continuous source of strength and friendship. I also acknowledge Jim Gash and Lee Kats for their unflagging support of my scholarly pursuits.

As always, I acknowledge my loving family: my wife Sunde, my son Ross, and my daughters Clare, Mande Mae, and Holly Joy. Sunde. Your stable, cheerful, supportive presence keeps us all connected through thick and thin. Thank you for all you do. Kids, I cannot wait to see you each night after I get home from work. Thank you for all those summer nights down at the beach listening to Dua Lipa, Machine Gun Kelly, and Van Halen.

Mom and Dad – thank you for being such close friends to me. I appreciate you more and more with each passing day. The Covid era has been painful, especially the loss of Uncle G.C.. Let us hope that the worst of it is behind us.

I acknowledge the Pasadena Church of Christ, a group of Christians who continue to lovingly embrace my family and me, and minister to me as much as I minister to them.

I want to acknowledge Stephen Neill. I never knew you, but I am grateful for the life you lived. I think you fully understood your imperfections, as when you called yourself 'the chief of sinners'. However, you had so many gifts as well. I am deeply grateful for the honor it was for me to study your life carefully, for over twenty years now.

As I have done for every book I have written, I humbly acknowledge Jesus Christ as my Lord and Savior with the following passage from Scripture:

Now unto him that is able to do exceeding abundantly above all that we ask or think, according to the power that worketh in us, Unto him be glory in the church by Christ Jesus throughout all ages, world without end. Amen.
(Ephesians 3:20–21 KJV)

Dyron Boyce Daughrity
Malibu, California
23 April 2021

Chapter One
Introduction

Stephen Charles Neill (1900-84) was one of the most important figures on the world Christian scene during the twentieth century. Neill's stellar student career and his turbulent tenure as an Anglican missionary in South India provide a touchstone for investigating his times. Neill's was a remarkable life, useful for exploring the larger contexts of which he was a part. As historian Robert Eric Frykenberg has written:

> Here and there, and every once in a while, some story about an individual emerges and we learn about actions, circumstances, and events that are more than ordinary. Placed in a position of special worth or advantage, with special recognition or significance, the story of the life of such a personality serves to illuminate many things around it, both near and far.[1]

Neill's life was indeed one of those life-stories that was 'more than ordinary'. Stephen Neill's life was a tumultuous one, beginning with his missionary service to India, from 1924 to 1945. During this period Gandhi's nationalist movement was challenging fiercely the massive British colonial enterprise, raising serious quandaries for Indians, for example, why they should fight for the independence of others while still under foreign rule. Traditional

---
1. Robert Eric Frykenberg, *History and Belief: The Foundations of Historical Understanding* (Grand Rapids, MI: Eerdmans, 1996), p. 72.

Indian ways of life were being subverted economically, governmentally, culturally and religiously. This was all reaching a head during Neill's tenure as a missionary in South India. In 1947, only two years after Neill's departure, India gained its independence. Neill was caught up in all of this and in many ways was a casualty of these tensions.

Stephen Neill was loved by most of the Indian Christians he served. Christianity and British imperialism meant emancipation for many of them, especially Dalits. Lower-caste people received education and benefits unimaginable under Brahmin rule. However, Neill was still a part of this massive imperial machine that was clearly in decline. Both Indians and Britons knew that collapse and withdrawal were inevitable; it was only a question of when.[2] Neill's bishopric in India, 1939-45, was right in the middle of this maelstrom, and he knew it. Later in life, he reflected:

> During these days, stirring events were taking place in India, and it was impossible to remain unaffected by the rising tide of nationalism. . . . This was an unpleasant time at which to be at work in India; and, the deeper one's affection for the Indian people, the more unpleasant it was certain to become.[3]

The maelstrom was not just about Indian politics; there was tremendous conflict going on in Neill's various personal and professional associations as well and many of the problems that surfaced during his India years would remain with him to the end.

Neill was an extremely competent, even brilliant, man but he was also a man of fragile health – both physical and psychological. He was able to hide it fairly well, and for long periods. Eventually, however, it would surface and occasionally his fragile health led to breakdowns. For example, Neill dealt with two severe crises during his time in South India which led him into serious conflict with people within his circle. During both of them he questioned whether he could go on as a missionary. In the first case he persevered; the second one nearly killed him, however. He did manage to make it through with therapy but it completely derailed his career.

While Stephen Neill's intellectual gifts were obvious to all, he was also a classic case of what Peter Berger has called a 'homeless mind'.[4] Intense

2. Neill lamented the fact that 'the independence of India was to be achieved by revolution and not by gradual progress'. See Stephen Neill, *God's Apprentice: The Autobiography of Bishop Stephen Neill*, ed. by Eleanor Jackson, with a Foreword by C.F.D. Moule (London: Hodder & Stoughton, 1991), p. 128.
3. Ibid., pp. 128, 131.
4. See Peter Berger, Brigitte Berger and Hansfried Kellner, *The Homeless Mind: Modernization and Consciousness* (New York: Random House, 1973). This is

struggles punctuated his life. His conflicts were not always with other people; they were often battles with his own inner demons. Neill was never satisfied; he was constantly trying to improve himself and fix the people around him. He was a perfectionist. When in power, he could be dictatorial and exacting. He carried himself with an air of authority that propelled him into positions of leadership but throughout his life a dark side was never far away.

Those who knew Neill tended to recognise his issues. Christopher Lamb wrote:

> [There was] perhaps a sense that he had never fulfilled the superlative promise of his youth. The reasons for that are not yet fully clear, though his autobiography speaks of internal struggles commensurate with the powers of mind that everyone recognized in him.[5]

Lamb speculates on the origin of these struggles:

> [As a boy] He . . . experienced the temptation to contract out of society in a world of books and imagination. . . . The precocious teenager, teaching himself Hebrew by torchlight under the bedclothes, found it difficult to share what he was learning with his contemporaries, and may have taken early refuge in a kind of lonely stoicism. Religion, as well as nature and circumstance, may have conspired to mold him this way. . . . Perhaps a less austere religion would have given the church a servant less deeply damaged.[6]

Signs of greatness were never distant, however. For example, 'Neill's academic career was spectacularly untroubled.'[7]

Richard Pierard once commented upon Neill's teen years:

> As a teenager he began to display the psychological symptoms that would plague him throughout his life – insomnia, deep depression, and outbursts of temper. . . . [Some] have suggested he suffered

---

touched on later in the final chapter of the present work.

5. Christopher Lamb, 'Stephen Neill 1900-1984, Unafraid to Ask Ultimate Questions', in *Mission Legacies: Biographical Studies of Leaders of the Modern Missionary Movement*, ed. by Gerald Anderson, Robert Coote, Norman Horner and James Phillips (Maryknoll, NY: Orbis Books, 1994), p. 445.
6. Ibid.
7. Ibid., p. 446.

from repressed sexuality (one even said homosexuality), since he never married and had a negative attitude toward women involved professionally in Christian work.[8]

However, Pierard, too, recognised the powerful gifts within:

> Neill distinguished himself as an Anglican churchman, biblical scholar, missionary theorist, ecumenical leader, and historian. . . . He possessed competence in biblical and classical languages as well as several modern European and Indian languages, and was the author, co-author, or editor of at least sixty-five books, as well as innumerable essays, reviews, addresses, and sermons.[9]

Eleanor Jackson knew Neill and edited his autobiography seven years after his death. She, too, noticed a certain dissonance:

> It is now possible to see more clearly which parts of Neill's legacy will have abiding value, while the issues involved in Neill's work, and his heroic struggle with his personal problems, remain highly relevant today. If one may sum up his life in a single verse of Scripture, the most appropriate text would seem to be, 'But we have this treasure in earthen vessels, to show that the transcendent power belongs to God and not to us' (2 Cor. 4:7).[10]

Renowned New Testament scholar, C.F.D. Moule, a contemporary of Neill, wrote the Foreword to Neill's published autobiography. In a passage of sympathetic candor, Moule contrasted Neill's many strengths with his crippling weaknesses:

> A born linguist with a fastidious 'feel' for words, blessed with a tenacious memory full of anecdotes and circumstantial detail, he could lay a spell on any audience. [His] is . . . a story of contrasts. There is the pathos of frustrated ambition, the dogging of ill-health, insomnia, psychological imbalance and bouts of depression; but also a childlike enjoyment of praise . . . and the elation of wielding

---

8. Richard Pierard, 'Stephen Neill', in *Historians of the Christian Tradition: Their Methodology and Influence on Western Thought*, ed. by Michael Bauman and Martin Klauber, (Nashville, TN: Broadman Holman, 1995), p. 532.
9. Ibid., p. 531.
10. Eleanor Jackson, 'The Continuing Legacy of Stephen Neill', *International Bulletin of Missionary Research*, Vol. 19, no. 2 (April 1995), p. 77.

1. Introduction

> a formidable intellect and the polyglot gift to hold huge audiences spellbound with lucid expositions in their own languages.... There is a fresh and ever-curious mind, but also a reactionary streak.... An ingratiating charm lives next door to an Irish temper, controlled with difficulty; the apostolic asceticism is no stranger to a relish for good cuisine. Vanity threatens to spoil one who is conscious of exceptional talents ... [but] Stephen Neill's constant desire was to place his remarkable abilities at the disposal of God.... India was his first and last love. The premature termination of his ministry there (whatever its real cause or circumstances) was traumatic. Everything else that he did was pushed at him by circumstances – the toilsome years of ecumenical organizing and drafting, the Chairs at Hamburg and Nairobi; even the very active last years in Oxford.... Readers [of Neill's autobiography] ... will want to give thanks ... for the extraordinary achievements of this much-tempted, brilliant, enigmatic man.[11]

Owen Chadwick and Kenneth Cragg, two well-known historians and also contemporaries of Neill, wrote an article on him shortly after his death, pointing out his contrasting forces within:

> Neill was the most powerful intellectual force which the Church of India had seen since W.H. Mill in the earlier nineteenth century.... To friends he always gave the impression of a man without strain or worry who could work longer hours than most.... Behind the scenes [however] his health was still troublesome.... Perhaps he had a little sense of frustration.[12]

Neill's internal struggles, frequent illnesses, and occasional unbalance were somewhat well-known. In his obituary in *The Times*, it was written:

> His death removes one of the most striking and gifted figures from the world church scene, the variety of whose gifts at one time seemed certain to ensure him one of the highest offices in the church.... [However] Many will regret that Neill's breakdowns precluded the offices of leadership for which he was otherwise so well fitted.[13]

---

11. Moule, 'Foreword', in Neill, *God's Apprentice*, pp. 7-8.
12. Kenneth Cragg and Owen Chadwick, 'Stephen Charles Neill, 1900-1984', *Proceedings of the British Academy*, Vol. 71 (1985), pp. 606-8.
13. *The Times*, 24 July 1984.

Neill's breakdown in 1944, and the ensuing events which led to the termination of his office as bishop, were the reasons his career would take a sudden turn. He never would hold a high office in the Church again. While he never fully recovered from that devastation, he did move on to become one of the most important figures of twentieth-century Christianity. His international fame came from his many books, his lectures on nearly every continent and an enormous breadth of scholarship that wowed audiences everywhere he went. He served the global church in many capacities, leaving a mark nearly everywhere he went.

After a stellar academic career in England, Neill surprised those around him by becoming a missionary to South India. He spent two decades there (1924-45), eventually becoming bishop of the Tinnevelly (Tirunelveli) diocese in 1939.[14] It was not his tenure in South India that made him a Christian celebrity; rather, it was his writings. C.F.D. Moule called him an 'indefatigable reader and writer', noting in particular, 'the astonishing number and the consistently high quality of books Stephen Neill wrote'.[15]

Although Neill died in 1984, many of his 65 books are still read and cited.[16] Some of the books he either wrote or edited are classics.[17] His *History of the Ecumenical Movement* is a standard reference work to this day. He was an expert in the history of New Testament criticism. His treatment

---

14. Tinnevelly is the name the British gave to the region; today the diocese is known in its Tamil form 'Tirunelveli'.
15. Moule, 'Foreword', in Neill, *God's Apprentice*, pp. 7-8.
16. *A History of Christianity in India: The Beginnings to AD 1707* (Cambridge: University Press, 1984) was republished in 2004; with John Goodwin and Arthur Dowle, *Concise Dictionary of the Bible* (London: Lutterworth Press, 1966) was republished in 2004; *A History of Christianity in India: 1707-1858* (Cambridge: University Press, 1985) was republished in 2002; *Jesus Through Many Eyes: Introduction to the Theology of the New Testament* (Philadelphia, PA: Fortress Press, 1976) was republished in 2002 (Cambridge: James Clarke & Co.); *Christian Faith and Other Faiths: The Christian Dialogue with Other Religions* (London: Oxford University Press, 1961) was republished in 1999.
17. *A History of Christian Missions* (Harmondsworth,: Penguin Books, 1964) has gone through several editions, most recently in revised form under the editorship of Owen Chadwick (London: Penguin, 1986). This book made *Christian History*'s '100 Great Books for Christian History Buffs' (Fall 2001). *The Interpretation of the New Testament: 1861-1961* (London: Oxford University Press, 1964) was republished and brought up to 1986 (second edition) by N.T. Wright (*The Interpretation of the New Testament: 1861-1986* [Oxford: University Press, 1988]). *A History of the Ecumenical Movement 1517-1948*, edited by Ruth Rouse and Neill (Philadelphia, PA: Westminster Press, 1954) is the standard reference work on the ecumenical movement's history. The substantial *Concise Dictionary of the Christian World Mission*, edited by Neill, Gerald Anderson and John Goodwin (New York: Abingdon Press, 1971) is still an important reference work in Christian mission studies.

1. Introduction

of Anglicanism is still one of the best.[18] Perhaps his greatest contributions were in the area of Christian missions. His *History of Christian Missions* is still used in university and seminary courses. His investigation of the relationship between colonialism and Christian missions gained him admittance to the British Academy.[19] Missions historian Timothy Yates wrote that Neill's books on the Apostle's Creed, entitled *Beliefs* (1939) and *Foundation Beliefs* (1941), 'deserve to be reprinted'.[20] Indeed, it was his seemingly ubiquitous publications which prompted Yates to write, 'Stephen Neill must be regarded as one of the intellectual giants of his generation.'[21]

Neill was a ubiquitous presence on the world church scene over several decades. His prominence can be accredited to several factors. First, at 83 years his life was a long and productive one. His career intersected with the important discussions and debates that occurred throughout the twentieth-century Church.

Second, he often found himself in the middle of important developments in church history. He lived in six different countries throughout his life: the United Kingdom, India, Switzerland, Germany, Kenya and the United States.[22] He was in India during the decline of colonialism and played a role in the establishment of the Church of South India.[23] He was in Geneva when the World Council of Churches was born in 1948. He was a professor in West Germany during the 1960s, right smack in the middle of the Cold War. He was a professor at the University of Nairobi during the early 1970s, when African colonial resentment was erupting.

A third reason for Neill's prominence was that he was able to communicate with a broad cross-section of people and cultures because of

---

18. Stephen Neill, *Anglicanism* (Harmondsworth: Penguin Books, 1958). This book was still being published into the 1980s and later citations in this present volume are from the 4th edn, published in 1982 by Oxford University Press.
19. This is according to Cragg and Chadwick in 'Stephen Charles Neill: 1900-1984', pp. 602-14. Neill's book *A History of Christian Missions* launched his study of this topic. Following that book (first published in 1964), Neill authored a volume that deals more specifically with these ideas called *Colonialism and Christian Missions* (London: Lutterworth Press, 1966). In 1970 he published *Call to Mission* (Philadelphia, PA: Fortress Press), a work that proposes five crucial issues surrounding missions and imperialism.
20. Timothy Yates, *Christian Mission in the Twentieth Century* (Cambridge: University Press, 1994), p. 144.
21. Ibid., p. 143.
22. Neill spent significant time in Connecticut, New Jersey, and North Carolina. While he never held a long-term position in the US, he often visited for extended periods, particularly for research.
23. Neill left India just before the Church of South India (CSI) was formed in 1947.

his facility in languages; he could read or speak around fifteen of them.[24] This afforded him the rare opportunity to communicate with prominent members of the Christian world scene in their native language.

A fourth reason for Neill's wide popularity was his strategic goal of writing for laypeople as well as for scholars. Many of his books were directed at the laity, and they returned the favour by reading his writings and inviting him to lecture, affording him the privilege of travelling all over the world as an invited guest of numerous ecclesial and educational establishments.

Overview of Neill's Life and Career

Stephen Neill was born in Edinburgh on 31 December 1900, the last day of the nineteenth century. During his early childhood, his parents were missionary doctors in India. In 1912 Neill began studies at Dean Close School, an evangelical boarding school in Cheltenham, where he studied until 1919, excelling in classical languages. He attended Trinity College, Cambridge, from 1919 to 1924. Neill was a brilliant student in classics, theology and New Testament studies.

In 1924 Neill entered the South Indian mission field. He joined with his parents and a sister to help the Dohnavur mission, famously associated with Amy Carmichael. In 1927 he moved back to England for a short time but returned to India in 1928 as a missionary for the Church Missionary Society (CMS).[25] He served the Tinnevelly (now Tirunelveli) and Travancore dioceses in various ways until 1930 when he became Warden of Tirumaiur, a theological college in the Tinnevelly diocese. He became bishop of that diocese in 1939. When he suffered a breakdown in 1944, his bishopric abruptly ended, as did his residence in India.

Between 1946 and 1961 Neill was an active contributor to the worldwide ecumenical movement – a grand initiative of the mainline Protestant churches and many of the Eastern Orthodox churches to foster Christian unity. He served in the role of Assistant Bishop to the Archbishop of Canterbury and served as a liaison between the Archbishop and the World Council of Churches in Geneva from 1947 to 1950. He was there when the World Council of Churches became a reality. That institution

---

24. Neill spoke English, German, French, Spanish, Tamil and Malayalam. He studied Latin, Greek, Hebrew, Icelandic, Portuguese, Sanskrit, Urdu, Italian and Swahili. Neill was aware of this gift. In his autobiography, he wrote 'My one gift is that I understand words. . . . From the age of five I read voraciously.' See Neill, *God's Apprentice*, pp. 34-35.
25. The Church Missionary Society changed its name in 1995 to the Church Mission Society.

has accomplished immeasurable good on behalf of Christianity worldwide. Once again, due to poor health and interpersonal conflicts, Neill abruptly resigned in 1950, although he remained a resident of Geneva.

During the years 1950 to 1962 Neill started a new publishing venture called World Christian Books. He was perfect for this job because he was so adept at writing and in foreign languages. He was able to recruit authors from all over the world in order to publish books for the global church. Neill was a key person in bringing together the Western churches with the churches in the Global South. At that time, the Global South churches were often called the 'younger churches'. This time proved very productive for Neill and he published dozens of 'simple' books in 35 different languages. He also edited a couple of major dictionaries that would greatly assist the emerging, global, Christian consciousness. In 1954, with Ruth Rouse, he edited the landmark book, *A History of the Ecumenical Movement 1517-1948*. His literary output during this period was impressive.

In 1962 Neill moved to Germany and served as the Chair of Missions at the University of Hamburg, a post he held until 1967. He produced an important trilogy of books that investigated European colonialism's impact on the Church, and vice versa. The writings he produced during the 1960s were major contributions to the scholarly community and won him election to the British Academy in 1969.[26] Some of the books Neill produced in the 1960s enjoyed great success and had far-reaching impact, such as *Christian Faith and Other Faiths* (1961) and *The Interpretation of the New Testament 1861-1961* (1964). He frequently preached at St Thomas a' Becket Anglican Church in Hamburg during this period, and seemed to achieve a level of mental stability that allowed his prodigious academic gifts to flourish.

In 1969 Neill moved to East Africa and founded a Department of Philosophy and Religious Studies at the University of Nairobi. He taught philosophy, religious education, Old Testament, Koine Greek, Religion in the modern world, Hinduism and several other subjects. He had to contend with the anti-colonial movement that was in full steam at the time and wrote of this period, 'The minds of all our students had been deeply influenced and thoroughly conditioned by the anti-missionary myth.'[27] Not only did he contend with a lack of sympathy and a lack of resources, he also dealt with a lack of personnel. Nevertheless, Neill's years in Nairobi were not in vain, as the Department of Philosophy and Religious Studies exists to the present day and is one of the leading centres in Africa of the study of religion. Some of Neill's mentees during

---

26. Cragg and Chadwick, 'Stephen Charles Neill: 1900-1984', p. 610.
27. Neill, *God's Apprentice*, p. 304.

that time, such as Jesse Mugambi, went on to become internationally known in their discipline. In 1973 Neill made one final move: back home to the United Kingdom.

The last decade of Neill's life was spent at Wycliffe Hall, Oxford, where he served as an assistant bishop and held the academic title of 'Senior Scholar'. He kept a busy schedule of travelling and lecturing. During this period he began writing his magnum opus, a three-volume history of Christianity in India. He died in 1984, having just published the first volume and completed the research for the second. It was organised by Alister McGrath of Oxford and published a year later.[28] Alas, his untimely death robbed us of what would have been an extremely helpful third volume.

Neill was a constant presence on the world church scene in the twentieth century. It was never his intention to be a wandering missionary statesman, ecumenist or religious studies professor. Neill believed his calling was to be a missionary and he was hurt deeply when that door shut. He never fully recovered from the trauma of losing his bishopric in India in 1944-45 but, through faith and sheer determination, he bounced back and made substantial contributions to the faith that had sustained him throughout.

A Word on Sources

Written near the end of his life, the most significant published primary source on Neill's life is his autobiography, *God's Apprentice*, published by Hodder & Stoughton in 1991. His autobiography provides a valuable glimpse into how he perceived his life story. Nevertheless, this source is not without problems for the researcher. Neill, the expert historian, was unable to be candid about certain chapters of his life. Undoubtedly, some would agree with Jocelyn Murray that Neill's autobiography 'conceals more than it tells us about the author'.[29] Similarly, Bishop Richard Holloway argues that, while revealing in some places, the autobiography 'hides more than it discloses'.[30]

For example, in his autobiography Neill never mentions the name of Amy Carmichael who was in charge of his first mission when he arrived in India for the first time in 1924 and with whom he fell into conflict. He neglects to acknowledge the death of his sister Marjorie Penelope in 1929. They were both in India at the time and this loss, no doubt, would have

---

28. *A History of Christianity in India: The Beginnings to AD 1707* and *A History of Christianity in India: 1707-1858*.
29. Jocelyn Murray, 'Book Review: *God's Apprentice: The Autobiography of Bishop Stephen Neill*', *International Bulletin of Missionary Research*, Vol. 17, no. 3 (July 1993), p. 142.
30. Richard Holloway, 'The Mystery in Stephen Neill', *Church Times*, no. 6717 (8 November 1991), p. 13.

affected Neill. Neill provides a lopsided account of the way in which he lost his bishopric. To the end of his life, he never acknowledged the core reason why in 1944 he came under fire from Indian villagers and church authorities. He minimises conflicts with others and typically takes the safer route: a breakdown in his health. Certainly, his health was precarious but his mental challenges often led him to snap and lash out at others, further isolating someone who struggled for deep and lasting friendships. This happened repeatedly in his career. Neill never married, so his friends, students and co-workers were particularly important to him. However, with enough lapses in his behaviour, Neill could become insufferable to those around him, forcing him to move to another country and start all over again. Why did Neill, in the words of one, 'airbrush' his own memoirs, knowing the disservice that was being done to history?[31] Was he even aware of what he was doing? Were there things he wanted to hide? We gain a small glimpse into Neill's methodology near the end of his autobiography, a glimpse that sheds some light on these questions:

> I have come to the conclusion that I have the wrong kind of memory. I remember and feel as vividly and acutely as though they were happening today all the fears and anxieties, the frustrations and failures, the absurdities and contradictions, the feelings of exasperation and near despair. I do not forget the occasional successes and achievements, the moments of happiness in which it has seemed as though something really had got done that was worthwhile; but these things come to me with far less immediacy and vividness than the others. As a result I tend to take a rather dark view of the past, to question what appears to be achievement, and to wonder whether anything has been done that will stand the test of time or even the censure of my own conscience.[32]

Neill began his writing his autobiography on 31 December 1970.[33] The latest date mentioned in that work is 1980.[34] He died rather suddenly in 1984.

Neill began to ponder writing an autobiography during a visit to India in 1970. He had been invited to preach the Christmas Day service at All Saints Church in Coonoor – in the Nilgiri Hills of Tamil Nadu.[35] One can

---

31. Letter from Eleanor Jackson to the author dated 28 November 2002.
32. Neill, *God's Apprentice*, p. 317.
33. Ibid., p. 27.
34. Ibid., p. 331.
35. Neill had several connections in the area. He had spent time there during his

only speculate that it was the nostalgia of being in South India, preaching in Tamil, visiting the graves of his parents, and spending time with his sister that prompted him to consider writing his life story.

Neill's autobiography was published in 1991 under the editorship of Eleanor Jackson. According to Jackson, less than half of the complete manuscript was actually published; it was pared down to meet the publishers' length requirement.[36] The published autobiography is at times difficult to read, due to its patchy coverage of some events. One reviewer writes:

> Although the editor has done her best to present the text in a faithful and orderly fashion, it still reads like the transcript of an oral history full of gaps and digressions, weak on dates, sometimes pompous and self-serving, often harsh in its judgment of others, clearly not the book Neill would have published if he had lived to revise it and edit it himself.[37]

As an editor, Neill realised his autobiographical ruminations would have to be given more coherence if a book were to be made. At the end of the published version of his autobiography, he wrote:

> There are a number of books which I still hope to write. If I manage to complete in ten years all that I have in mind to do, I may then perhaps sit down to write my autobiography, and that would be a far more difficult and exacting task than the setting down of these somewhat random recollections of grace abounding to the chief of sinners over a period of rather more than seventy years.[38]

---

missionary days in order to escape the gruelling summer heat, a habit of many Western missionaries. He had a sister in Coonoor, Isabel, who was a missionary to Muslims. She had lived there since 1928. Isabel Neill contributed an article for a book entitled *Debate on Missions*, ed. by Herbert E. Hoefer (Chennai: Gurukul Lutheran Theological College, 1979). The 'Contributors' section in the book contains the following quotation (p. xviii): 'Miss Neill has been a missionary in India since 1928, especially among the Muslim women. Presently she is running a girls' boarding school in Coonoor.' Neill's parents had gone to live with Isabel in 1947. His father worked as the chaplain of All Saints Church almost until his death in 1948. Neill's mother died there in 1951. Both of them are buried in the churchyard. Neill and Isabel owned property in Coonoor, and Neill visited there about every two years after he left India. See Neill, *God's Apprentice*, pp. 26-27, 330-31.

36. Jackson gave the author extensive correspondence between herself and the editors at Hodder & Stoughton.
37. Charles Henry Long, 'Review of *God's Apprentice*, by Stephen Neill', *Anglican Theological Review*, Vol. 75, no. 3 (Summer 1993), pp. 423-25.
38. Neill, *God's Apprentice*, p. 336.

Nevertheless, the 'random recollections' left behind are invaluable for the study of Stephen Neill.

Neill interpreted his own life in less than critical terms. For example, in his interpretation of his skirmish with Amy Carmichael, the famous missionary to India, he exonerated himself, yet blamed others.[39] In other places he explains away his quick temper: 'I lost my temper in public in one of the committees which followed on the diocesan council. . . . But it is not easy, as tiredness grows, to have everything under control.'[40]

Again, when Neill was clearly in the wrong during the downfall of his bishopric, he was accused by his boss, Foss Westcott, the Metropolitan of India, Burma and Ceylon, of refusing to acknowledge any wrongdoing:

> You must have realized the scandal which your action had caused and serious injury to the Church and her work which they had entailed, but in not one of your letters has there been any acknowledgment of this fact, or expression of sorrow for having been the cause of it.[41]

Neill, however, interpreted the situation differently, choosing to place the blame on a series of events such as exhaustion, an infection in his hand and the loss of his reading glasses, which could not be replaced because of the war.[42]

In reading the autobiography, one gets the impression that Neill was often surrounded with incompetence and he had to come onto the scene and straighten things out. This happens repeatedly.

Neill's autobiography 'reveals a curiously complex personality'.[43] At a few points he speculated candidly on his shortcomings. One writer wrote the following:

> Insofar as an autobiography is intended to reveal the person, Neill comes through as a rather tragic figure, lonely, restless and unfulfilled, suffering from insomnia and frequent bouts of deep depression. There is no doubt of his courage, creativity and unwavering faith.

---

39. Ibid., p. 93. It must be noted that Neill never did mention Carmichael's name in his autobiography. However, it is clear that he was referring to their intense argument that led to Neill's dismissal from the Dohnavur mission.
40. Ibid., p. 200.
41. Archbishop Westcott to Stephen Neill, 26 June 1945, Westcott Papers, Bishops Box 4, Special Collections, Bishop's College, Kolkata, India.
42. Neill, *God's Apprentice*, pp. 197, 200.
43. Anonymous, '"Bishop, Scholar, Missionary", Review of *God's Apprentice*, by Stephen Neill', *Expository Times*, no. 103 (April 1992), p. 224.

But there is doubt that his long list of accomplishments really reflected the extraordinary promise with which his career began. He seemed always to be getting ready, always the accomplished apprentice, in one field after another, to the end.[44]

What comes through loud and clear in Neill's autobiography is ambivalence. He felt a tremendous need for people, yet was reluctant to reveal too much of himself. He was proud and often boastful, countered by a recourse to self-effacing humility. There are many emotional highs and lows throughout the account, inevitably leading the reader to question the emotional stability of the man. By the end of his life, Neill was keenly aware of his psychological problems, for example, when he wrote: 'My fierce temper, the outward expression of so many inward frustrations.'[45]

In Stephen Neill there are clear signs of brilliance, soaring brilliance, and it is doubtful that Neill stretched the truth in this regard. Neill's contemporaries often described him in the loftiest of terms:

> Apart from William Temple, Stephen Neill may have been the outstanding Anglican of his generation. He was certainly the most versatile: classicist, linguist, historian, missionary statesman, ecumenical pioneer, popular preacher and lecturer, author, innovator in theological education on four continents, teaching in fluent Tamil, German and Swahili as well as English. His intellectual gifts were legendary. His record as a student at Cambridge is said never to have been surpassed.[46]

Yet there are instances in his autobiography where Neill, in almost Pauline fashion, confessed his simple faith:

> I had every reason to believe that Christ had died for my sins; the rest of my life could not be spent in any other way than in grateful and adoring service of the One who had wrought that inestimable benefit. Even now, I see no way of improving on that discovery. . . . Then, as now, the thing that I cared about far more deeply than anything else was that men and women should be brought to know Jesus Christ.[47]

---

44. Long, 'Review of *God's Apprentice*, by Stephen Neill', pp. 424-25.
45. Neill, *God's Apprentice*, p. 36.
46. Long, 'Review of *God's Apprentice*, by Stephen Neill', pp. 423-24.
47. Neill, *God's Apprentice*, pp. 35-36, 72.

1. Introduction

Both Neill's published and unpublished autobiographies are used at length in this work. However, his autobiography is only one among many primary sources I have used. Neill's interpretation of his life is only one possible interpretation. The biographer must cross-check and approach all sources with a degree of distrust.

Those who are familiar with the scholarship on Stephen Neill know that I have published numerous writings about him. In fact, my first published book, which stemmed from my PhD dissertation at the University of Calgary in Canada, was entitled *Bishop Stephen Neill: From Edinburgh to South India* and was published by Peter Lang in 2008 as part of its Theology and Religion series. That book dealt with the first half of Neill's life. Since my PhD years (1999-2005), however, I have continued to research Neill's years in Geneva, Hamburg, Nairobi, Oxford and various places in the United States. I still travel regularly to India in search of more Stephen Neill leads. I believe I have visited all of the major archives in the world that have a significant amount of Neill material.

Here I should point out a wonderfully fortuitous event regarding Stephen Neill's autobiography. In 2003 I was invited by Brian Stanley to the Henry Martyn Centre, University of Cambridge, to deliver a lecture on Stephen Neill. It so happened that Bishop N.T. (Tom) Wright was also there giving a lecture. I attended his lecture and introduced myself afterwards, knowing that he and Stephen Neill were acquainted and even published a book together. Tom was happy to hear that someone was finally doing serious work on Neill and he divulged some information that brought me up short. He told me he had a copy of Neill's *unedited* autobiography in manuscript form. This was particularly important for me to hear because I had just visited Eleanor Jackson's home and found that her version of the manuscript was in bad shape and missing large sections.

I finally got around to e-mailing Bishop Wright in 2005 and asked him whether he would lend me the Neill manuscript he had in his possession. About a year later, on 30 July 2006, he wrote back to let me know it was hidden somewhere in his garage and I would be welcome to visit him to try to find it.

On 22 May 2010 he wrote to me again to let me know that he was moving from Durham to St Andrews and would have to go through all of the boxes in his garage; he wanted me to know that he believed the Neill manuscript would probably surface during the move. He wrote to me again on 26 July 2010 to let me know the good news:

> The typescript has at last shown up, as I thought it would once we went through all the boxes in the store room. (I did invite you to perform this task some while ago, I recall!) . . . I will get my

secretary to photocopy and send it to you. It's quite bulky so it may need two or more parcels. We'll see. Warm greetings and good wishes, Tom Wright.

His secretary e-mailed me on 16 September 2010 to let me know she had shipped it to me and that I should receive it in four to five weeks: 'Better late than never', she wrote. It was a wonderful day when the two parcels arrived in my office at my university in California.

The unedited autobiography is indeed bulky and difficult to work with. However, it is complete – and it has served me well in writing this full biography of Stephen Neill. There are many passages that were edited out of the published version and I am supremely grateful to Tom Wright for sending me this valuable work.

I consulted countless primary sources for this work: the Church Missionary Society archives held at the University of Birmingham, the Dean Close School archives in Cheltenham, the University of Cambridge archives and many collections in India, including those held by Bishop's College in Kolkata, Gurukul Lutheran Theological Seminary in Chennai and the Bishop Stephen Neill Study and Research Centre in Palayamkottai, Tamil Nadu. I researched the World Council of Churches (WCC) archives in Geneva, the Divinity Library Special Collections at Yale University and the archives of St Thomas à Becket Anglican Church in Hamburg. I conducted myriad interviews in Africa, the UK, the US, India, Germany, Switzerland and probably a few other countries along the way.

I have been researching Stephen Neill since the year 1999. This book is probably not the last time I will write on him but it is certainly my most important contribution. I am deeply grateful to Adrian Brink at The Lutterworth Press for the opportunity to write it. It is the perfect press to publish the Neill biography, as he published numerous books with the company, including the *Concise Dictionary of the Bible*, *Salvation Tomorrow*, *The Unfinished Task*, *Colonialism and Christian Missions* and the *Concise Dictionary of the Christian World Mission*. It is my hope that this biography will be a meaningful addition to Lutterworth's line-up of books by and about Bishop Stephen Neill.

Chapter Two
Childhood, Youth and Education: 1900-24

Neill's childhood was unstable. His father was generally absent, he was placed into a boarding school at an early age and he was frequently ill. He began showing signs of emotional imbalance during his late teenage years, resulting in a complete breakdown in 1919. However, in other ways, his early years were quite successful. He gained frequent recognition for his intellectual gifts, winning numerous academic awards at both Dean Close and Cambridge. He mastered his subjects much more rapidly than his peers but he also began to show signs of imbalance, tension and dissonance. What resulted, in the words of C.F.D. Moule, is 'disturbing reading – a story of contrasts . . . of this much-tempted, brilliant, enigmatic man'.[1]

Neill's Familial Background

Neill's paternal grandfather was Henry James Neill.[2] In the middle of the nineteenth century, Henry started a provisioning service for goldminers in Australia. After he was married and had made a fortune, he returned

---

1. Moule, 'Foreword', in Neill, *God's Apprentice*, pp. 7-8.
2. Christopher Lamb writes, 'The Neill family came originally from Ulster.' See Lamb, "Stephen Neill 1900-1984, Unafraid to Ask Ultimate Questions," p. 445. Ulster is a historic area of the island of Ireland, which includes the province of Northern Ireland (part of the UK) and includes the counties of Antrim and Down and the city of Belfast.

to his homeland of Northern Ireland and bought a beautiful property at Rockport, Craigavad, near Belfast.[3] Shortly thereafter, he and his wife started a family. Twelve children were born, six boys and six girls. Henry James, who was not a very religious man,[4] then bought a dilapidated wine and spirits business; it soon became a financial success.

Although Neill never met this grandfather, he listened carefully to the family stories. Henry James Neill was 'capricious' with a sometimes 'violent temper'.[5] He was a savvy businessman; Neill records, 'everything that he touched turned to gold under his hands'.[6] Having been 'a very wealthy man when he died', a dribble of inheritance came to Stephen in 1968.[7] While Henry James was adept in making money, he was not very generous with his boys as they were growing up. As soon as they entered university, however, their father gave them 'as much money as they wanted'.[8] When Henry James died in 1894, he left his fortune to his surviving eleven children, allowing the boys to have their fair share with no strings attached. It was a different matter for the girls, however, who 'could not touch their capital, and were debarred by the will from leaving anything outside the family'.[9] The children stood in awe of their father and they all adored their virtuous mother, of whom Neill writes almost nothing.[10] All in all, according to Neill, the family was 'a typical prosperous middle-class Victorian family'.[11]

Henry's sons proved to be successful people, although Neill points out their questionable spending habits. They managed 'to get through a great deal of money without having very much to show for it at the end of the day'. One of the boys became a successful lawyer in London, one moved to Madras and succeeded in the wine business, one was a doctor, one was born with only three fingers on his right hand and 'never succeeded in overcoming this disability', one died young, and one, Charles, became a doctor-missionary. This doctor-missionary, Charles Neill, was Stephen Neill's father. 'It is the aunts, however, who made the most lasting impression on an observant small boy', Neill writes, pointing to 'an element

---

3. There is an error in *God's Apprentice* here. *God's Apprentice* uses the name 'Craigaird'. However, such a town does not exist. Neill means 'Craigavad', where a well-known preparatory school to which Neill refers is located.
4. Neill, *God's Apprentice*, p. 15.
5. Ibid., p. 14.
6. Ibid., p. 13.
7. Ibid.
8. Ibid., p. 15.
9. Ibid., p. 13.
10. Neill rarely discussed the women of the family in his autobiography; it focuses almost entirely on the men and their careers.
11. Neill, *God's Apprentice*, p. 14.

2. Childhood, Youth and Education: 1900-24

of [psychological] instability in the family' that he believes was quite evident in one of his aunts in particular. 'Defects the Neills had in many directions', he wrote of his paternal heritage. However, he emphasised the tendency of all the Neills towards 'making supremely happy marriages'.[12]

Stephen Neill's father, Charles, was born on 12 November 1868.[13] He was a 'naturally religious person', according to Neill, and 'had from an early age a strong desire to enter the ordained ministry of the Church'.[14] Henry James, however, had other plans and Charles became a doctor. Charles' schooldays were spent in England studying Greek prose and participating in athletics. He went up to Gonville and Caius College, University of Cambridge, excelling in his medical studies, liberally supported by his wealthy father. Throughout his life he maintained a devout, evangelical faith.

Stephen Neill's mother's maiden name was Monro. James Monro of Edinburgh was Neill's wealthy maternal grandfather.[15] James Monro was a brilliant child. By the age of eighteen he had completed his studies at the University of Edinburgh, receiving the gold medal in philosophy along the way. In 1857 he took the examination for the Indian Civil Service, being placed third overall. However, he was a bit too young to join their ranks immediately, so he spent a year studying law in Berlin. In 1858 he left for India with the words of Micah written in the front of his Bible: 'to do justice, to love mercy and to walk humbly with thy God' (Micah 6.8). In 1862, while on leave, James Monro married Ruth Littlejohn. She was the daughter of an Aberdeen minister and scholar, James Bentley, who became Professor of Hebrew and Oriental Languages at the University of Aberdeen in 1797. Neill claimed there was also a distant connection to Richard Bentley, of Trinity College, Cambridge, whom Neill describes as 'the greatest of all English classical scholars'.[16]

The Monros would return to northern India in 1858 'at a fortunate moment for anyone engaged in the service of the government of India'.[17] This was the year Queen Victoria took control of India away from the East India

---

12. Ibid., p. 14. By the time his father died, Neill's parents had been married 52 years and, once, after his father's death, Neill's mother said to him, 'Of course, you know, we were really sweethearts right up to the end.' See Neill, *God's Apprentice*, p. 14. Neill concluded this discussion on Neill marriages with the statement, 'as far as I can recall, there has been only one divorce in the family in seventy years' (p. 15).
13. According to *God's Apprentice*, p. 165, Neill's father was baptized in 1868 at the 'little parish church of Glencraig... which stands just outside the old family estate of Rockport'.
14. Neill, *God's Apprentice*, p. 15.
15. Lamb writes, 'His maternal grandfather was successively distinguished in the Indian Civil Service, as the commissioner of the Metropolitan Police, and a missionary in Bengal.' See Lamb, 'Stephen Neill 1900-1984, Unafraid to Ask Ultimate Questions', p. 445.
16. Neill, *God's Apprentice*, p. 16.
17. Ibid.

Company, 'resolving India's anomalous status within the empire'.[18] No doubt the Monros were well taken care of in their 'palatial establishment' tended by many Indian servants.[19] James Monro found himself at home in India, learning the Bengali language and spending much time interacting with the villagers. He would often say to missionaries, 'The life of India is in the villages.'[20] Stephen Neill, much later, acquired precisely this same conviction.

The Monros were successful in every sense. As James' career headed rapidly upwards, children also came along quickly, two girls – Jessye, a brilliant woman who would never marry, and Margaret Penelope, or, 'Daisy', Stephen Neill's mother, who was born in 1870 – and two boys – Charles, who would become a doctor-parson, and the other, William, a scholar of Indian languages.

'Then', writes Neill, 'disaster struck.'[21] All of the district officers were required to submit reports. James' report did not go over favourably, a scandal ensued and he resigned. Returning to England, he joined the Criminal Investigation Department at Scotland Yard, rising rapidly to the office of Commissioner. However, 'Then in 1890 disaster struck once again. I have never quite understood what occurred.'[22] Allegedly, James gave in to a bribe over whether or not to go along with a government plan of some sort. He was also accused of leaking information during the debacle. Again, he resigned before formal charges were brought against him. In his autobiography, it is clear that Neill believed his grandfather Monro did nothing wrong in either case, for it 'is inconceivable in a man of his integrity' to have been guilty of any of the charges.[23]

Neill's grandfather Monro, then 52 years of age and with his entire family of six, decided to head back to his beloved India as an independent missionary.[24] He took along with him other volunteers, including four who were medically trained. His daughter Daisy and son Charles had also studied medicine. In addition, Charles Monro had recently introduced

18. Thomas R. Metcalf, *Ideologies of the Raj* (Cambridge: Cambridge University Press, 1998), p. 60. This was a momentous time for the relationship between India and Britain; an attempt to heal the breaches that had resulted in the Indian Mutiny of 1857.
19. Neill, *God's Apprentice*, p. 16.
20. Ibid., p. 17.
21. Ibid., pp. 17-18.
22. Ibid., p. 18.
23. Ibid.
24. In *God's Apprentice*, pp. 20-21, Neill wrote that his grandfather had originally offered to go to India as a CMS missionary, but withdrew his offer when it seemed to him that the CMS was dragging its feet. According to Neill, the CMS begged that he might reconsider his withdrawal but he refused. Instead, he supported himself via his Indian Civil Service pension of £1,000 a year and some support from various friends.

Stephen Neill's birth certificate: 31 December 1900.

one of his fellow medical students at Cambridge to his sister Daisy. This young man, who was by now (1892) courting Daisy, was Charles Neill – Stephen Neill's father.[25] The entire group, which included both of Neill's parents, moved to India in 1892 and settled at a town called Ranaghat, a railway junction located about fifty miles north of Calcutta (now Kolkata), to begin their medical/missionary work.

Stephen Neill made an insightful observation about his parents: 'It would be hard to imagine any greater contrast than that which existed between my parents – in background, tradition, gifts, and temperament.'[26] There was one thing they did have in common, however: Charles Neill and Daisy Monro were both very shy people.[27] They began working closely together in 1892 while in India. They believed they were in love, but neither of them had the courage to articulate the depth of this love. Neill commented that for a very long time neither was willing to admit 'the hard word [presumably "love"]' to the other.[28] On 5 November 1896, four years after they met, Charles Neill and Daisy Monro married in the little mud church at the hospital-missionary compound in Ranaghat known as Doyabari, 'the house of mercy'.

Childhood

The Neills produced seven children between 1898 and 1909, although the youngest died in infancy. In order, they were: Marjorie Penelope (1898), Henry Christopher (1899), Stephen Charles (1900), Gerald Monro

---

25. Daisy had also invited one of her friends, named Mary Simpson, who was trained as a doctor.
26. Neill, *God's Apprentice*, p. 13.
27. Neill wrote that he believed his parents passed on a 'double portion' of that shyness to their children. Neill claimed that, of all the children, he had probably been the most successful in overcoming this menace, although even he struggled with self-confidence throughout his life. See *God's Apprentice*, p. 24, for this discussion.
28. Neill, *God's Apprentice*, p. 23.

(1902), Eric James (1904) and Isabel Ruth (1906).[29] Stephen was born in Edinburgh, while his parents were on leave from their missionary work in India.[30] Both of his parents, according to Neill, suffered from ill health during this era of their lives. The illnesses and climate eventually took their toll and, by 1902 or 1903, it was clear the Neills would have to leave India. So, they returned to England and Stephen's father decided to change careers and enter the ministry, something he would have done earlier had it not been for the overriding determination of his father.

Stephen's father, Charles, attended the Clergy Training School (now Westcott House, where Stephen Neill studied for ordination) at Cambridge. He was ordained as a deacon and priest in Durham Cathedral and began parish work nearby at Haughton-le-Skerne. Stephen's earliest memories took place there: green fields, tranquil flowing water and a garden. His companions were his two older siblings and he worked hard to keep up with them in all ways. Neill wrote, 'I certainly never learned to read, I simply found that I could at some point before my fifth birthday. . . . From the age of five I read voraciously.'[31]

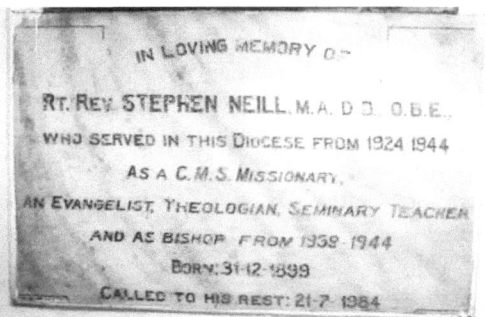

This commemoration to Bishop Neill is in Holy Trinity Cathedral, Palayamkottai, and features the wrong year for Neill's birth – a fairly common mistake that Neill took delight in explaining.

---

29. The seventh child was a daughter, born and deceased in 1909. She goes unnamed in Neill's autobiography. Neill claimed the other children never saw her. See *God's Apprentice*, p. 25.

30. Pierard, 'Stephen Neill', p. 532. Neill's birthday fell on the very last day of the nineteenth century and he delighted in the telling of this fact throughout his life. In his later years, many recall him saying that his only remaining ambition was to live to his third century. An obituary of Neill recorded Charles Neill's words, 'Uncle Stephen was born on the last day of the nineteenth century. He liked to tell people that. He seemed especially pleased when they misunderstood and supposed that he had been born in 1899. It was not that he took pleasure in the mistakes of others. He found a scholarly satisfaction in getting things right and the delight of a natural teacher in explaining things to others. He would patiently point out that each century ends at the end of the hundredth year.' *The Decanian*, no. 264, January 1985, pp. 50-51. *The Decanian* is the school newspaper of Dean Close School. The full collection is available at Special Collections, Dean Close School, Cheltenham.

31. Neill, *God's Apprentice*, pp. 25, 35.

2. Childhood, Youth and Education: 1900-24

Charles was a restless man, moving many times while the children were young.[32] The stint near Durham did not last long and, in hopes that the clean Swiss air might help Charles to recover his health, the family packed up and moved to Switzerland near Lac Leman. Shortly thereafter, they moved to Glion, and then to Lausanne, where Neill, at the age of five, began his school career, receiving all of his Swiss education in French. In 1907, the year Charles' health began to improve, he set his sights on India again.[33] One can witness here the seeds of Stephen Neill's peripatetic career. His moves were not nearly as frequent as his father's but they were in general more profound. It seems not to have bothered Stephen when he would relocate to India, Switzerland, Germany, or Africa, and even be forced to gain fluency in a different language.

Stephen's parents decided to go to India for a nine-month period, leaving the children in the care of Daisy's parents, Aunt Jessye (Daisy's sister), a Swiss governess and four girl cousins, three of them older than Stephen, from the Monro side of the family. The parents returned after nine months and then went back to India one more time, only to return with the realisation that 'their children needed them, and that until we were grown up and able to stand on our own, India must be out of the picture'.[34]

---

32. During Neill's childhood, the family lived in many different places. For the sake of clarity, the places of residence are presented here in order: Edinburgh (where Neill was born); India (at least a few times and in various places); Cambridge (for Charles' ministerial study); Haughton-le-Skerne in County Durham; Switzerland (three different towns); Liskeard in Cornwall; Ussher Greer in Lisburn, Northern Ireland; Cheltenham (where Stephen and the other children began attending Dean Close School); and Nutley on the southern edge of Ashdown Forest in East Sussex.
33. Dr Charles Neill to CMS Secretary General, 6 February 1907, CMS/G2 I1/O1907/42, CMS Archives, Special Collections, University of Birmingham, Birmingham. Dr Neill reported his arrival at Ranaghat. He wrote that he would be helping Dr Archer by taking over his medical duties so Dr Archer could enter into language studies. This date is also confirmed in an article by 'Rev. Dr. C. Neill' in the 1907 edition of the journal, *Mercy and Truth*. The article was written by Charles Neill in April 1907, while he was in Ranaghat; Dr C. Neill, 'Some Ranaghat Jottings', *Mercy and Truth: A Record of CMS Medical Missions*, no. 11 (1907), pp. 176-78. The article begins, 'You may be interested to hear something of our doings during the last few weeks.' By then he had been in India over two months; his arrival in India was probably late January 1907. Dr Neill was a general practitioner in India but he seemed to spend much of his time working on the eyes of the Indians. Neill testified to this in *God's Apprentice*, 'my father became well known as an eye-surgeon', p. 22.
34. Neill, *God's Apprentice*, p. 26. Lamb, 'Stephen Neill 1900-1984, Unafraid to Ask Ultimate Questions', p. 445, writes, 'His father became a doctor and then a missionary, but during the years of Stephen's childhood his restless temperament kept the family home moving around.'

It was probably 1908 when the family moved to a parish at Liskeard in Cornwall, where Stephen Neill's father, Charles, resumed pastoral work.[35] This ministry was cut short, however, as the nomadic cleric decided to 'try his luck among his own people in Northern Ireland'.[36] That venture did not last long either. Again itching to move, in September 1910 Charles picked up his family and moved to Cheltenham, where he became Vicar of St Mark's Church.

The parents put Stephen and Henry into a small private school called Suffolk Hall.[37] Neill's recollections of Suffolk Hall are scant. He wrote that the school was owned by a Liberal MP named Arthur Lancelot Soames. Apparently, Soames recognised the Neill boys' abilities because he tried to get them into schools of 'greater renown'.[38] Neill remembered that the teaching, particularly in Latin and Greek, was 'exceptionally good', thus launching his interest in these languages.[39]

One episode at Suffolk Hall affected Neill profoundly. Apparently, Neill had been accused of cheating during a test. Neill's classmates hounded him for weeks about the incident. Neill vehemently denied the charges: 'I am not one who has ever needed to cheat in examinations.' The rancour continued for three weeks because the headmaster 'failed to rise to the occasion and to stamp on the absurdity at the very start.' Neill concluded, 'I think that this experience did me permanent harm; it made it harder for me than it should have been to put my trust in my fellow men, and undermined my belief in the rationality of my species.'[40]

Whether the accusations of cheating were a factor or not, Neill's destiny would take a significant turn when his father contacted a local evangelical boarding school: Dean Close Memorial. Charles Neill had

---

35. The year must have been 1908, although Neill in *God's Apprentice* puts the year at 1906. According to Stephen Neill (*God's Apprentice*, p. 15), his father was born on 12 November 1868. Neill's father was forty years old during the family's time in Switzerland (*God's Apprentice*, p. 26) and the parents had decided during their most recent India trip, which occurred while the children were in Switzerland, that this would be their last. Thus, they returned to Switzerland to collect the children, then moved to Cornwall (*God's Apprentice*, p. 27). Additional evidence for the 1908 date is contained in a letter of Dr Charles Neill. Dated 23 July 1906, the letter expresses regret that he cannot go to Ranaghat this year, due to family reasons; Dr C. Neill to CMS Secretary General, 23 July 1906, CMS/G2 I1/O1906/149, CMS Archives, University of Birmingham.
36. Neill, *God's Apprentice*, p. 27.
37. Neill recorded that they were at first 'day-boys' but eventually, when he was eight years old, he and Henry became boarders for a brief time. See *God's Apprentice*, p. 28.
38. Ibid., p. 28.
39. Ibid.
40. Ibid.

2. Childhood, Youth and Education: 1900-24

become convinced of the excellence of evangelical education, particularly as exhibited at Dean Close. The school was within his parish and he was promptly appointed secretary to the governors.[41] The parents enrolled Henry in 1911 and Stephen in 1912.[42] Both of them lived at home and attended the school as day boys. Young Stephen's life would begin to find some sense of stability there, partly because he now had a consistent place to call home and partly because of the welcome presence of his brother and best friend, Henry.[43] Henry Christopher Neill was at Dean Close from 1911 to 1918. He was just older than Stephen and lived much longer; he was born on 12 October 1899 and died on 20 February 1993, at the age of 94.[44] His obituary reads:

> Henry was the oldest and longest lived of the four Neill brothers. At school from 1911-18 he was Senior Prefect, an all-round sportsman (Cricket; Hockey-Captain; Gym) and, like Bishop Stephen, an outstanding classical scholar. After Caius, Cambridge, he returned to teach at DCS for five years (1922-26) before moving to Achimota College in what was then The Gold Coast, where he became Headmaster in 1945. During the Second War he was a Captain in the Gold Coast Regt. In 1950 [to 1956] he again joined the DCS staff for a further ten years, before finishing with a stint (1957-67) at Sandroyd. In recent years in retirement with his family near Liverpool he had not enjoyed the best of health.

---

41. Ibid., p. 27. 'The Dean Close Memorial School Annual Report and Abstract of Accounts for Year Ending Dec. 31, 1910' also testifies to this, as Rev. Charles Neill appears for the first time as a member of the Executive Committee and also as a Life Governor, a post he actively maintained at least until 1918, according to the Annual Reports; 'The Dean Close Memorial School Annual Report and Abstract of Accounts for Year Ending Dec. 31, 1910', Special Collections, Dean Close School.
42. Neill, *God's Apprentice*, pp. 27-28, 'Henry went there one year ahead of me. I entered in January of 1912.' This is confirmed by the school's 'Large Registry' (which contains records from 7 May 1886 to August 1924), Special Collections, Dean Close School. Stephen Neill is listed as entering the school in 1912 and his older brother, Henry Christopher, in 1911. See 'Old Decanian Newsletter, 1993', Special Collections, Dean Close School.
43. Lamb, 'Stephen Neill 1900-1984, Unafraid to Ask Ultimate Questions', p. 445, writes, '[Neill] was educated at Dean Close School, Cheltenham, a place that earned his affection for . . . providing him with the geographical roots of which his father's roving nature had deprived him.'
44. For Henry's obituary, see the 'Old Decanian Newsletter, 1993', Special Collections, Dean Close School. Another helpful source for basic biographical information on the early part of Henry's life is the 'Old Decanian Register, 1886-1948', Special Collections, Dean Close School.

Richard Padfield told the author in an interview at Dean Close School that Henry lived as an amnesiac for many years.[45] Mr Padfield was the only non-family mourner in attendance at Henry's funeral on 20 February 1993.[46]

An abrupt move in 1913 took the Neills out of Cheltenham and into another parish at Nutley in East Sussex. Neill remarked that the move occurred because the workload was likely to be less strenuous, for Charles had experienced 'a fairly comprehensive breakdown' earlier that year.[47] Henry and Stephen both moved with the family to Nutley, where the brothers enjoyed riding their bicycles and listening to Handel's *Messiah*, which first revealed to Neill 'what music can be, and what it can do to a man's heart'.[48] Nevertheless, the boys were by that time plugged into Dean Close School. It would have been difficult for them to adjust elsewhere and there were no other evangelical schools in the Nutley area. Thus, it was determined that it would be best for the boys to become full-time boarders at Dean Close, and Charles sent Henry and Stephen back to Cheltenham in 1913. Young Stephen and his brother finally had the opportunity to settle. The parents, however, continued their roving ways.[49] Of this perambulatory tendency, Neill wrote:

> My father was just forty years old, and embarked on a family Odyssey which never really ended until his death. India was in his heart and his blood, and he could never settle down to life in England. It would be unendurably tedious to chronicle all the family moves. . . . Throughout these years, my father continued his peripatetic career. It was his practice to take over some derelict parish, work it up almost frenziedly for a couple of years or so, and then feel the urge to move on, probably to some entirely different

---

45. Richard Padfield described it as 'short-term amnesia'; Richard Padfield, interview by author, 21 January 2003.
46. This was according to Mr Padfield. He and Henry Neill were friends. One day Henry Neill and Padfield walked through Caius College together. Henry pointed out his former room with tears in his eyes; Padfield, interview by author, 21 January 2003.
47. Neill, *God's Apprentice*, p. 32.
48. Ibid.
49. It must be noted here that Neill actually lived with his parents until they moved to Nutley. However, he had attended Dean Close since 1912. His parents did not decide to check him in as a permanent boarder at Dean Close until 1913. The Dean Close 'Large Registry' confirms that the Neills moved to Nutley around this time, as Neill's brother Eric listed his parents' residence as 'Nutley Vicarage, Uckfield, Sussex'.

part of England. The result was that we never had anywhere that we could call home. We had no roots, no opportunity to make permanent friends in any of the places where we lived. He returned to India a number of times, more than once for considerable periods . . . follow[ing] impulses which at times could hardly be described as rational.[50]

Neill would find the closest thing to a permanent home for himself in Cheltenham at Dean Close School.[51]

Despite a 'capricious' father and a nomadic childhood, Neill continued to adore both of his parents.[52] Fond memories pour forth from his autobiography. Neill considered his parents 'utterly devoted . . . in every respect' to his welfare. Neill recalled his father's frugality at one point: '[I]f a hapless child had left the electric light on all night, one might have thought that the whole family was teetering on the verge of bankruptcy.' His father was also prone to having 'paralysing headaches'. Quick to defend the goodness of his father, however, Neill remarked, 'I now realise how intolerable he must sometimes have found the noise of children and the incessant problems they create.'[53]

Neill described his early years with his parents as thoroughly evangelical: family prayers, Bible memorisation and recitation, unwavering faithfulness in attending church services every Sunday morning. Up to his settlement at

---

50. Neill, *God's Apprentice*, pp. 26, 40. Neill's father worked until his eightieth birthday, finally retiring from All Saints Church, Coonoor, India (near Bangalore). According to Neill's autobiography, the year was 1947, p. 26. Even in retirement, Charles worked as a medical doctor to the community. He died a few months after retirement and was buried in that community, just outside the church. Of this incessant activity, Neill wrote, 'Driven on, perhaps, by some deep inner uncertainty about himself, he found it hard to cease from work' (*God's Apprentice*, p. 25). Neill's mother died three years later (probably 1950) and was laid to rest next to Charles. This was the church in Coonoor where Neill preached Christmas Day 1970. The experience of visiting his parents' final resting place may just have been one of the factors that prompted the writing of his autobiography, because six days after that sermon, on 31 December 1970, Neill began writing his autobiography. See *God's Apprentice*, pp. 24-27.
51. In *God's Apprentice*, p. 40, Neill wrote, 'I see now that [Dean Close School] supplied the elements of stability and continuity in our lives. . . . We had no roots, no opportunity to make permanent friends in any of the places where we lived. But the school was always there.'
52. *God's Apprentice*, p. 30. Neill's book, *Out of Bondage: Christ and the Indian Villager* (London: Edinburgh House, 1930), is dedicated to his parents: 'To My Parents who have made it impossible for their children to think highly of anything in comparison with the Cross of Christ.'
53. All quotations in this paragraph are from Neill, *God's Apprentice*, p. 30.

Dean Close, young Stephen was trained in the faith by his father's sermons. Neill wrote, 'Father was rather a good preacher, pleasant and easy to listen to.'[54] Neill commented on the faith of his parents:

> My parents were to the end of their days fundamentalists, to use a term unknown in those days. Incidentally, my father's library contained the only copy I remember ever having seen of the twelve small volumes entitled *The Fundamentals*, from which the term 'fundamentalism' is derived. I knew (by 1922 or so) that I no longer saw things as my parents saw them, but my views only changed slowly, without any violent explosion, by the patient absorption of new ideas. There was no breach of affection, though there were times of tension, but it has never seemed to me right or good to shock those whose Christian faith is expressed in terms other than those that I can accept.[55]

Neill claimed his parents had come under the influence of the Keswick movement with its more intense spirituality and greater emphasis on the Holy Spirit.[56] His parents were also very missionary-minded, displayed in their frequent travels to India. There was great missionary fervour amongst evangelical Christians at the time, epitomised by John Mott's famous declaration, 'The evangelisation of the world in this generation.'[57]

---

54. Ibid., p. 31.
55. Ibid., p. 65.
56. The Keswick movement was mainly geared towards increasing personal devotion in the Christian life through prayer, meditation and pious devotion to one's faith. It was known largely for its international conventions. These conventions are still in existence – for example, in Kolkata in early February each year. The movement was founded in the 1870s with the motto, 'All One in Christ Jesus'. Ruth Rouse claims that the Keswick movement, while not directly producing any ecumenical movements, certainly inspired ecumenism. Kevin Ward claims that Keswick spirituality arose in response to a new climate of imperialism, possibly producing 'conditions for the open display of racism on the Niger'. See Ruth Rouse, 'Voluntary Movements and the Changing Ecumenical Climate', Chapter 7 of *A History of the Ecumenical Movement 1517-1948*, ed. by Rouse and Neill. See also Kevin Ward, '"Taking Stock": The Church Missionary Society and Its Historians', Chapter 1 of *The Church Mission Society and World Christianity, 1799-1999*, ed. by Kevin Ward and Brian Stanley (Grand Rapids, MI: Eerdmans, 2000). For an entire work on the movement, see Steven Barabas, *So Great Salvation: The History and Message of the Keswick Convention* (Westwood, NJ: Revell, 1952).
57. Mott is probably the best-known ecumenist of the early twentieth century. His famous declaration recurs in Rouse and Neill, eds, *A History of the Ecumenical Movement 1517-1948*. Mott was largely responsible for the Edinburgh World Missionary Conference of 1910, which is considered the origin of the modern

Boarding School

The foundation stone for 'The Dean Close Memorial School' was laid in Cheltenham on 11 November 1884. The school opened less than two years later on 7 May 1886, with nine boarders and three day boys.[58] Dean Close School was part of the revival of public education in Britain that took place between 1840 and 1890 and saw no less than 62 schools founded.[59]

Dean Close School was named after Francis Close, Dean of Carlisle. His death on 17 December 1882 made a great impression on the citizens of Cheltenham, where he had served as a curate from 1824 until 1856.[60] Close was, apparently, quite conservative in his theology and, according to the 1 May 1853 edition of the *The Sunday Times*, he could be autocratic. In a short article entitled 'Clerical Tyranny at Cheltenham', an anonymous writer blasted the methods of discipline he observed in Dean Francis Close:

> There is no species of tyranny so intolerable as priestly tyranny. Cheltenham, more than any other town, is 'a close borough' where it is forbidden to act, speak, or think except in accordance with the views of the reverend 'rooster' who regulates the conscience of the pious ladies who sit under him. In fact Mr. Close has become

---

ecumenical movement. For Mott's call to evangelisation, see his *The Decisive Hour of Christian Missions* (New York: Student Volunteer Movement for Foreign Missions, 1910).

58. M.A. Girling and Sir Leonard Hooper, eds., *Dean Close School: The First Hundred Years* (Oxford: Holywell Press, 1986), p. 206. See also R.F. McNeile, *A History of Dean Close School* (Shrewsbury: Wilding, 1966), p. 9.

59. It should be noted that 'public education' in this case meant the establishment of many new private schools. Until the Education Act 1870 all schools in England and Wales were charitable or private institutions; the 1870 act permitted local governments to complement the existing elementary schools. (Scotland has a separate education system.) During this period, resources were also provided to help the older schools recover from decades of decline. See S.J. Curtis, *History of Education in Great Britain* (London: University Tutorial Press, 1968), and Richard J. Aldrich, *School and Society in Victorian Britain: Joseph Payne and the New World of Education* (New York: Garland Publishing, 1995).

60. Francis Close was born in 1797 to a wealthy cleric. He went to the University of Cambridge and became a favourite pupil of Charles Simeon, a famous evangelical leader. He first went to the parish of St Mary's, Cheltenham, as a curate, suddenly becoming in charge two years later when the rector died. R.J.W. Evans notes, 'Francis Close was soon being widely spoken of as "Pope of Cheltenham".' Close went on to serve as Dean of Carlisle from 1856 until 1882. He retired to Cornwall and, that same year, died there on 17 December. See Evans, 'Town, Gown and Cloth: An Essay on the Foundation of the School', in Girling and Hooper, *Dean Close School: The First Hundred Years*, pp. 9-13.

more despotic than the autocrat of Russia amongst the wealthy and dyspeptic inhabitants, the liverless nabobs and the rickety valetudinarians by whom the town is chiefly supported. Under the pretext of protecting public morality he has successfully laboured to abolish theatricals in the town and succeeded in suppressing the annual races. Some spirited individuals have introduced steeple chases and the success of these has stirred up the rooster's bile. He now threatens he can no longer recommend Cheltenham as a safe place to send children to school.[61]

Dean Close was also an educator, being one of the founders of Cheltenham College and of St Paul's Training College. He was an important voice in the movement to promote a national elementary education in England.[62] Memorialising his name with a school in Cheltenham seemed fitting. It also seemed right that the school was evangelical in its outlook,[63] as Dean

---

61. *The Sunday Times*, 1 May 1853.
62. T.H. Clark, 'The Late Dean Close', 21 November 1883, Special Collections, Dean Close School. This obituary testifies that Dean Close died on 17 December 1882.
63. The Evangelical awakening was in full tilt in mid-nineteenth-century England. It had given birth to the Church Missionary Society in 1799 and had grown rapidly by the 1850s. According to Kevin Ward, '"Taking Stock": The Church Missionary Society and Its Historians', p. 21, the distinctive theological emphases of the Evangelical movement were: 'The sinfulness of human beings and their justification by faith in the work of Christ on the Cross; the need for conversion of each individual; the supreme authority of the Bible as God's word; and an activism based on optimism about what converted men and women can achieve when inspired by God's Spirit.' Stephen Neill argued that it is a common misconception that the Anglican Evangelicals are a comparatively small group of Methodists who remained within the Church of England when the others moved out. He countered this misconception by stating, 'Anglican Evangelicalism was a distinct movement, with its own marked characteristics, which have continued to be the characteristics of the Evangelical wing of the Church of England till the present day. Some of the Evangelicals had come under the influence of Wesley, others had not; and on the whole they spent a great deal more of their time in criticizing the great man than in agreeing with him.' See Neill, *Anglicanism*, p. 190. Neill provides an excellent discussion on the matter, pp. 190-94. For an important work here, see D.W. Bebbington's *Evangelicalism in Modern Britain: A History from the 1730s to the 1980s* (London: Unwin Hyman, 1989), which is one of the most thorough treatments to date. See also John Wolffe, ed., *Evangelical Faith and Public Zeal: Evangelicals and Society in Britain, 1780-1980* (London: SPCK, 1995). It is also important to note that the rise of the Evangelical movement in England was tied to the abolition of slavery, often a rally point for Evangelical groups. See Andrew Porter, 'Trusteeship, Anti-Slavery, and Humanitarianism', in Andrew Porter, ed., *The Oxford History of the British Empire: The Nineteenth Century* (Oxford: University Press, 1999), pp. 198-221.

2. Childhood, Youth and Education: 1900-24   31

Close was religiously conservative.[64] The school's founding objective was to, 'educate boys of parents of limited means for the spheres they are to occupy upon Scriptural, Evangelical and Protestant principles in conformity with the Articles of the Church of England as now by law established'.[65]

Dean Close School achieved remarkable success in the early years. By the second year the school's enrolment had risen from twelve to 70. By the third year there was an enrolment of 150 and the school roll had reached 200 by 1890, only four years after its foundation.[66] One reason the school experienced such impressive growth was the exceptional leadership provided by Dr W.H. Flecker, the Headmaster, who remained with Dean Close from its inception until 1924.[67] Stephen was a pupil under this dominating personality, of whom one historian wrote, '[The boys'] attitude towards him was in general one of admiration and respect, but not of affection.'[68]

During Neill's time in the school, Dr Flecker was in the last years of his 38- year tenure (1886 to 1924). Neill characterised this competent man as having 'brilliant intellectual gifts and [an] inexhaustible capacity for hard work. . . . [H]e could teach any subject at a moment's notice.'[69] However, there was another side to Flecker:

> Yet for all that, I cannot hold any other opinion than that Flecker was a bad headmaster. I do not think that he ever understood boys, and his nervous rages made him terrifying to the more timid among them. . . . I think that the great majority of boys left the school with no feeling of affection for the man who had guided their destinies in their formative years.[70]

---

64. Dean Close once 'preached a sermon of great vigour against the annual Cheltenham horserace meeting . . . [and] issued a pamphlet which sold like hot cakes in the summer of 1827' that referred to the races as a 'Heathen festival'. He also prevented the town theatre from being re-erected after a fire burned it down in 1839. He railed against a choir festival which he characterised a 'perversion of God's house' and spoke out against tobacco use, as well. See Evans, 'Town, Gown and Cloth: An Essay on the Foundation of the School', p. 9.
65. McNeile, *A History of Dean Close School*, p. 4.
66. Evans, 'Town, Gown and Cloth: An Essay on the Foundation of the School', p. 20.
67. On Flecker, see L.M.J. Kramer, 'Another Look at Dr. W.H. Flecker', pamphlet, undated, R.F. McNeile, 'Three Decanian Worthies', pamphlet, 1951, C. Williams, 'Flecker of Dean Close', pamphlet, 1946, and John Sherwood, 'No Golden Journey', pamphlet, 1973, all held in Special Collections, Dean Close School.
68. McNeile, *A History of Dean Close School*, p. 13. It must be noted that Dean Close School was exclusively for boys until the early 1970s, when girls began to be admitted. It became fully co-educational in 1974. Padfield, interview by author, 21 January 2003.
69. Neill, *God's Apprentice*, p. 29.
70. Ibid. Evans depicts Flecker as somewhat iron-fisted, disallowing a sharing of

Perhaps one reason Neill presented this other side of Flecker is because Flecker in his later years began punishing the boys with a cane. Although the canings tended to be fairly light, there were occasions when a boy would get hurt. However, caning was acceptable practice in his time.[71] Neill remarked of Flecker's penchant for punishment, 'Flecker, in his furious rages, could lay into boys with a vigour in which moderation played no part.' Neill admitted, 'My own rare encounters with the law certainly did me no harm.'[72] An interesting point arises here. Stephen Neill adopted some of the exact same behaviour as his former headmaster, including use of the cane.

Neill found boarding at Dean Close School to be 'unpleasant and disagreeable'.[73] He was annoyed at the 'absurd and pedantic rules about silence in the dormitories'.[74] He found the amount of food inadequate: 'The school, no doubt, counted on the parents to supplement fairly lavishly the regular rations of the boys.'[75]

It was also at Dean Close that Neill began to learn about sex, although not formally. In his autobiography, he wrote that children should understand sex by the age of fourteen.[76] Neill eventually learned about 'the birds and the bees' from clergymen as his mother once tried to bring up the subject but 'seeing that I had not the least idea what she was talking about, let the subject drop'.[77] He realised there was a good deal of 'irregular sexual

---

any of the responsibilities of leadership: 'Town, Gown and Cloth: An Essay on the Foundation of the School', p. 25. McNeile agrees, 'One marked trait in his character was an unwillingness to decentralise or delegate authority': *A History of Dean Close School*, p. 14. McNeile also writes of Flecker, 'He dominated the School in every detail, and in fact he *was* the school. . . . To the ordinary boy he was rather terrifying': ibid., p. 13. Kramer agrees, 'All agree that "Flecker was the school and the school Flecker"': 'Another Look at Dr. W.H. Flecker', p. 9.

71. Ibid., p. 10. Kramer writes, 'He strove for strict discipline and is said to have suppressed homosexuality among boys, although vulgar talk did occur in some circles. Yet in the main [previous students] became intensely loyal and grateful.'
72. Neill, *God's Apprentice*, p. 33.
73. Ibid., p. 32. Verrier Elwin, a schoolmate of Neill at Dean Close, wrote at length about his years at the school in his autobiography, *The Tribal World of Verrier Elwin: An Autobiography* (Oxford: Oxford University Press, 1964). Elwin had somewhat similar sentiments about Dean Close, 'As I look back I feel mostly a certain regret . . . that I could have had so much better an education if I had been put in a different kind of school': *The Tribal World of Verrier Elwin*, p. 17.
74. Neill, *God's Apprentice*, p. 33.
75. Ibid.
76. Ibid., p. 34.
77. Ibid.

activity' among the boys at Dean Close School, although he stopped short of discussing any events in particular.[78] Verrier Elwin, a schoolmate of Neill and later an anthropologist, commented on these 'irregularities':

> Dean Close school was riddled, as the headmaster put it, with 'impurity' and though I left school without ever knowing exactly what he meant, I think masturbation and certainly 'little boys' must have been in his mind.[79] Official opposition naturally developed interest in our pretty juniors into what was almost a cult; so far as I know, and certainly in my own case, nothing ever 'occurred', but there was a sweetness and charm, all the attraction of forbidden fruit.[80]

Elwin seemed to have had in mind homosexual tendencies. Neill pointed out that this 'irregular activity' was, in fact, homosexuality.[81] He stated that in those days the only way for a boy to deflect the 'unwelcome attentions of older boys' was to make known his principles and, further, make it known that he was 'not likely to budge from them'.[82] Neill wrote, 'Far more harm is done in the preparatory schools than is generally recognized.'[83]

---

78. Ibid., p. 33.
79. Neill alluded to Flecker's reluctance to discuss issues related to sex in *God's Apprentice*, p. 34. He wrote, 'In confirmation class Flecker made some guarded references [to sex] but closed the subject down with the remark, "Well, perhaps the less I say about that the better."'
80. Elwin, *The Tribal World of Verrier Elwin*, p. 15.
81. Neill, *God's Apprentice*, pp. 33-34.
82. Ibid., p. 33.
83. Ibid., p. 33. Neill claimed that his two younger brothers, who had gone to Dean Close for a while but then attended St Paul's, another private school, told him that St Paul's was far worse in this area than Dean Close. See *God's Apprentice*, p. 33. C. S. Lewis encountered similar things in his school days, which Neill pointed out in *God's Apprentice*, p. 33: 'I think that what C.S. Lewis has written in *Surprised by Joy* is widely true.' See C.S. Lewis, Chapter 6 in *Surprised by Joy: The Shape of My Early Life* (New York: Harcourt, Brace & World, 1955). Lewis recounted in detail the 'fagging system', wherein an older boy would lord over a younger 'tart', demanding of him menial tasks, including sexual favours in many cases. Lewis explained, p. 87, 'A Tart is a pretty and effeminate-looking small boy who acts as a catamite to one or more of his seniors.' Lewis recounted that pederasty (an older boy having sex with a younger boy) was a characteristic trait of being a 'Normal Boy' in those days (p. 89). Lewis denied having a part in these 'games'. Malcolm Muggeridge, in his autobiography *Chronicles of Wasted Time – Number 1: The Green Stick* (London: St James's Place, 1972), recorded these types of practices during his schoolboy days. He recounted, 'for instance, their acceptance of sodomy as more or less normal behaviour. When I went to Cambridge . . . a similar atmosphere of homosexuality

Speculation has occurred in recent years regarding Neill's sexual orientation. In his biographical article on Neill, Richard Pierard writes:

> As a teenager [Neill] began to display the psychological symptoms that would plague him throughout his life – insomnia, deep depression, outbursts of temper. . . . Others have suggested he suffered from repressed sexuality (one even said homosexuality), since he never married and had a negative attitude toward women involved professionally in Christian work.[84]

Eleanor Jackson was probably the person who mentioned Neill's possible homosexual tendencies. In an unpublished version of Jackson's article, entitled 'The Continuing Legacy of Stephen Neill', she wrote,

> It could also be argued that had [Neill] admitted to himself he was homosexual, and had a lasting friendship, a stable relationship with a man to whom he could confide his loneliness, depression and frustration, and by whom he was loved, whether in a physical sense or not, he would have been happier and more successful. . . . It is impossible to say whether it was ill-health, rumours of homosexuality or his courageous criticism of colonial administrators which caused his path to preferment to be blocked after 1944.[85]

Interviews by the author provide little evidence that would firmly establish Neill's sexual orientation. He was fond of being with young men, which will be discussed later when the scandal surrounding the loss of his bishopric occurs. However, to maintain that Neill was homosexual would be to go beyond the evidence. Neill himself provided the following brief discussion of homosexuality in *A Genuinely Human Existence*, his major work on psychology:

> It is the principle of creativity that has led the Christian consciousness at all times to disapprove of certain manifestations of the sexual impulse in which the creative impulse either is not present at all, or in which it can never find more than a very imperfect outlet.

---

tended to prevail. . . . I emerged unscathed', p. 78.
84. Pierard, 'Stephen Neill', p. 532.
85. This article was later edited and published in the *International Bulletin of Missionary Research*, Vol. 19, no. 2 (April 1995). See Eleanor Jackson's personal collection. This quotation comes from p. 9 of the unpublished version of the article. The published version was less candid on issues relating to Neill's sexuality.

2. Childhood, Youth and Education: 1900-24

> The most obvious examples are homosexuality and masturbation. It is probable that neither of these activities is as harmful as popular estimation has supposed, or as we have been given to understand by the slightly hysterical denunciations of Christian moralists. But each falls below the level of genuinely human activity. . . . To exaggerate the wrongfulness of such acts may defeat itself by producing a state of nervous tension in which the impulse which it is intended to control may acquire compulsive power, and the last state is worse than the first.[86]

Another quotation from *A Genuinely Human Existence* is strikingly close to being a personal confession about what homosexuality can do to a career:

> There is reason to think that in certain cases, though by no means in all, homosexuality may be the result of some grave and early injuries, and in such cases it is hardly possible to hope for the full restoration of normal emotional development. In other cases, the needed help has come too late; mental health has been restored, but the precious years, in which a career could have been planned or emotional fulfilment sought, have passed and cannot be given back. There is a reality of permanent and irreparable loss.[87]

Neill's views on homosexuality are inconclusive. However, the possibility that he was a closeted gay man should not be ruled out.

Neill's social development began slowly. Early on, he had to make a decision about whether he wanted to exist almost entirely in the world of books or get acquainted with his peers. He did become quite a socialite at Dean Close but, had his father not prodded him, the temptation was to focus on what he considered his one true gift:

> My one gift is that I understand words. Since my earliest childhood I have been fascinated by the sight and sound of words, by the patterns in which they can be arranged and by the subtleties of meaning that they can express.[88]

---

86. Neill, *A Genuinely Human Existence: Towards a Christian Psychology* (Garden City, NY: Doubleday, 1959), p. 145.
87. Ibid., p. 205.
88. Neill, *God's Apprentice*, p. 35.

By the age of fourteen Neill was intrigued by foreign languages. He began reading a chapter of the New Testament in Greek every day.[89] He knew French from his years in Switzerland. He had learned a great deal of Hebrew by the age of fifteen.[90] Nevertheless, Neill broke through the introverted tendencies he inherited and became broadly involved at Dean Close. No doubt this was due to the family atmosphere that existed for the Neill boys at the school.[91] Neill's older brother Henry Christopher began at Dean Close in 1911, Stephen in 1912 and the two youngest brothers in 1913 and 1914, respectively. Gerald Monro attended Dean Close from 1913 to 1917 and Eric James attended from 1914 to 1917.[92]

Neill experienced a religious conversion in 1914 when, along with forty or fifty others, he came down with the mumps.[93] His ten-day Easter

89. Ibid., p. 36. He claimed that, by the time he went to Cambridge in 1919, he had 'read through the New Testament five times, and carried off the Carus prize in my first term'. This is verified in *Crockford's Clerical Directory, 1957-58* (London: Oxford University Press). However, it was the Junior Carus Greek Testament Prize that Neill won in 1919. The 'Historical Register of the University of Cambridge, 1921-1930' and *Crockford's Clerical Directory, 1957-58* both verify that Neill won the Senior Carus Greek Testament Prize in 1923; 'Historical Register of the University of Cambridge, 1921-1930', Special Collections, Wren Library, Trinity College, Cambridge.
90. In *God's Apprentice*, p. 35, Neill claimed that he learned Hebrew with the aid of A.B. Davidson's *Hebrew Grammar* (unrevised) and an unnamed book by the Rev. Peter Mason.
91. In addition to the four Neill boys attending Dean Close, their father was also quite involved, giving several donations and even, in 1913, chairing the distribution of prizes. See 'Occasional Notes', *The Decanian, 1913*, Special Collections, Dean Close School.
92. Like his brother, Stephen, Gerald Monro entered the ministry. He attended Gonville and Caius College, Cambridge, and received his BA in 1925 and MA in 1929. He was ordained deacon in 1926 and priest in 1928. He served various parishes throughout his life and was for a time the Warden of Gonville and Caius College. He died in the early 1990s. See *Crockford's Clerical Directory, 1991-92*.Eric James also attended Gonville and Caius College. He died in 1957. The details of Eric James' life are conspicuous in their absence from Stephen Neill's published autobiography. Eleanor Jackson's personal correspondence with the editors at Hodder & Stoughton sheds some light on Eric James, as she was able to access the complete version of Neill's unpublished autobiography. In a letter, dated 13 December 1990, Jackson wrote that the death of his brother was 'clearly an event of major importance to him'. In another letter to the editorial director at Hodder & Stoughton, dated 2 August 1991, Jackson wrote, 'I am still a little worried that we missed out the pages about his brother's death in 1957, but I can't think what could be done unless one wrote half a paragraph in the appropriate place in the chapter "Professor in Germany". One might tie it in with his comments on the effects of war, as he considered his brother a war casualty – his war work having turned him into a very heavy smoker, and hence his death from lung cancer. But it is a bit late for this now.'
93. Verrier Elwin also discussed this outbreak, 'Later the influenza epidemic struck the school with great force. It seemed to break out simultaneously in every dormitory and,

Stephen Neill and his brothers Henry and Gerald, in tennis gear, 1920.

holiday was spent at the school and he was miserable at not being able to go home. On Tuesday evening of Holy Week, Neill converted to Christianity:

> As I was lying in bed, it occurred to me that, if it was true, as I had every reason to believe, that Christ had died for my sins, the rest of my life could not be spent in any other way than in

---

even more disastrously, in the servants' quarters so that for the first two days there was no one to look after us and no proper food'; *The Tribal World of Verrier Elwin*, p. 13.

grateful and adoring service of the One who had wrought that inestimable benefit. . . . I can recall no emotional accompaniment. All that happened was that I got out of bed and said my prayers, a ceremony which had been neglected for a considerable period. At that time I had heard the word 'conversion' used of Hindus who had become Christians; as far as I knew, I had never heard it used of something that could happen to one brought up in so Christian an atmosphere as I, but, up to that point, so totally unaware of the inner meaning of the gospel. Only after much later reflection did I come to the conclusion, which I have never seen reason to modify, that this extremely unromantic occurrence constituted my conversion. . . . I have the impression that many people who deny ever feeling 'born again' are singularly lacking in awareness of the heights and depths of the Christian revelation, and of its effects on the human personality. I did not speak to anyone of what had happened to me; nor do I imagine that my family noticed any great change in me. . . . I did myself notice certain changes that were gradually taking place. I found that I now said the General Confession with a good deal of feeling.[94]

The conversion experience motivated Neill to enter 'fully into the religious life of the school'.[95] He received Confirmation in 1915 when the bishop of

---

94. Neill, *God's Apprentice*, p. 36. Neill wrote two articles on conversion later in life: 'Conversion', *Scottish Journal of Theology*, Vol. 3, no. 4 (1950), pp. 352-62, and 'Conversion', *The Expository Times*, Vol. 89 (April 1977), pp. 205-8. Based on these articles, Neill considered conversion the seminal event in the Christian faith. He believed conversion was often mis-perceived as an ecstatic experience. Neill believed, rather, that, 'Emotion is largely irrelevant to the significance of conversion.' For Neill, 'the central factor is always in the will. Conversion always involves acceptance of the will of God as that which determines the life of men". Neill believed God's will was revealed in 'the Word and promises of God', which for Neill meant the Bible; 'Conversion', *Scottish Journal*, p. 355. In both of the journal articles, Neill cited William James' *Varieties of Religious Experience* (London: Longmans, Green & Co., 1903) as an important source, although he believed the discussion had moved well beyond James. In the latter article, he called for a scientific study of conversion that would do for more recent scholarship what James did for his readers. In both articles, Neill strongly opposed what he believed to be a widespread assumption that conversion is merely 'an adolescent emotional experience'; 'Conversion', *The Expository Times*, p. 205. Clearly, Neill took his conversion seriously and considered it a momentous turning point in his Christian development. While his conversion was devoid of emotion, Neill was very careful not to diminish the conversion experience in others; he knew how important the event could be in a life.
95. Neill, *God's Apprentice*, p. 37.

Gloucester, Sumner Gibson, came and spoke at Dean Close.[96] Timothy Yates wrote about Neill's conversion: 'Although brought up in a devoutly evangelical home, it was to this conversion experience that Neill looked as the beginning of his conscious Christian life, the deep knowledge that he was "in Christ".'[97]

The outbreak of the Great War in 1914 was a momentous time for Neill, as well as for many others at Dean Close.[98] Neill wrote, 'It had not occurred to us that the murder of an obscure Austrian Archduke far away could affect the destiny of all of us for ever and a day.'[99] What was most surprising of all was that war was breaking out, not 'with the less enlightened peoples of the Sudan' but right in the middle of Europe! Neill wrote, 'This indoctrination explains the almost frenetic hatred felt for Germany when the curse of war was let loose upon the world in 1914.'[100] Neill blamed the outbreak of war on Germany for 'the deliberate breaking of a promise. . . . It was they who pointed the way to that degeneracy of public morality with which we have lived in the later years of this deplorable century.'[101]

The first months of the war had little bearing on life at Dean Close. However, 'It was not long before casualty lists began to come in, and we found in them the names of boys we had known and who seemed little older than ourselves.'[102] Neill remembered a boy who came back to the school minus an eye. He also remembered the rationing that was enforced late in the war, debilitating the boys with malnutrition, 'four small half-slices of grey bread and a large ration of stodgy boiled rice was not enough. . . . I, for one, could not run or play any kind of game.'[103]

---

96. Ibid., pp. 40-41. Gibson's lecture introduced Neill to the poet Robert Browning, whose work Neill never ceased to relish. Of Browning, Neill wrote, 'Browning seems today to be almost forgotten, which perhaps is symptomatic of the astonishing flabbiness of a great deal that passes for Christian faith today.' *God's Apprentice*, p. 41. It is also interesting to note that Robert Browning was considered one of William Temple's (the former Archbishop of Canterbury) 'three great teachers', according to Neill, along with Plato and the Apostle John. *God's Apprentice*, p. 41. Neill was a personal friend of the Archbishop and held him in the highest esteem.
97. Timothy Yates, 'Stephen Neill: Some Aspects of a Theological Legacy', *Anvil*, Vol. 5, no. 2 (1988), p. 153.
98. Verrier Elwin also recorded detailed recollections of life at Dean Close during the war. In his autobiography he wrote, 'I was only twelve years old. But gradually . . . the names of old boys began to appear in the casualty lists and the food steadily got worse, some idea of the realities of war began to come home to us. As the days went by we finally found ourselves eating horseflesh and jealously watching our rations of sugar, butter and bread.' See *The Tribal World of Verrier Elwin*, p. 13.
99. Neill, *God's Apprentice*, p. 38.
100. Ibid.
101. Ibid., pp. 38-39.
102. Ibid., p. 39.
103. Ibid. Verrier Elwin's autobiography concurs, 'the "four for tea" referred to the

Since 1914 extensive reports were routinely given about Dean Close alumni who were in battle. Many of them were actually in the trenches and some even wrote letters to Headmaster Dr Flecker. One of them reads:

> I am writing this in a concrete dugout on top of a hill, from which I am supposed to be watching the enemy; but it is much too misty to be able to see anything, so that it is not a very difficult job; the only drawback is the cold.[104]

Some of these letters, published in the school paper, are quite detailed. For example, a letter from Captain A.D. Macdonald, the commander of one former pupil named Philip E. Moon (from the graduating class of 1914) who was killed in action on 28 April 1915, reads:

> The Germans exploded a series of mines under our sector of the line on the morning of the 28th of April, about 8 o'clock, and your boy, along with many of his comrades, was at his post in the fire trench. They were all killed instantaneously. . . . Philip was a brave soldier and a good lad – one of the very best – and he has, for a long time, had our admiration and love. I will always treasure the memory of him – his great love of nature and his knowledge of flowers was so wonderful to us all. . . . I shall be very glad to have a photograph of him if you can spare one.[105]

Stories such as these, printed often in the school paper, captured the emotions and imagination of the pupils. During the war, every issue of *The Decanian* began with a list of names of Dean Close alumni who had gone to war, been wounded or killed in action. Another letter, referring to former Dean Close pupil, Lieutenant E.E. Brown, reads:

> He was a great favourite with us all, while his almost reckless bravery was the cause of much comment. He hardly knew what fear was, and it was owing to his contempt for the enemy that he met his death, instantaneously by a bullet through his head while looking over the parapet.[106]

---

number of slices of dry and tasteless bread that one had managed to consume during the high tea which was the main meal of the day'. See *The Tribal World of Verrier Elwin*, p. 11.
104. *The Decanian*, March 1917, p. 214.
105. *The Decanian*, June 1916, p. 130.
106. Ibid., p. 131.

Dean Close School's "Officer Training Corp," 1918.
Stephen Neill is in the bottom row, second from right.

These letters and descriptions of the war in *The Decanian* are very graphic. No doubt they inspired a sense of patriotism, however. They were always followed in the school newspaper by a section that discussed the Officers Training Corps (OTC).[107]

By 1918 Neill's time at Dean Close was drawing to a close and, with his eighteenth birthday rapidly approaching (31 December 1918), it appeared that he might be called to defend his country. News from the warfront did not seem to be getting any better[108] and, standing solemnly before the Roll of Honour in the chapel with his brother Henry, this proved to make the war that much more real:

---

107. Verrier Elwin wrote, 'The war naturally gave a great stimulus to the Officers' Training Corps. I was never very keen on games and used the OTC as an outlet for my surplus energies. . . . It never occurred to anyone that there was the least inconsistency between the Scripture classes, where we were taught to love our enemies, and the Bombing classes, where we were taught to kill them.' See *The Tribal World of Verrier Elwin*, pp. 13-14.

108. Neill wrote, '1918 had destroyed our hopes of Russian victories, and seen the greatest defeats for the French and British armies since the first days of the war.' See *God's Apprentice*, p. 42.

> The casualty lists grew longer and longer. Henry and I were startled to see how many of the names were those of boys with whom we had studied and played and fought not so long before the day of their death. It seemed at the time there would be no end to all that.[109]

Then, finally, just in time to spare Stephen from the worry of potential service in the war, the Germans sued for peace and the armistice was signed.

> I know exactly where I was on 11 November 1918 when the sirens sounded and told us it was all over – reading Plato's *Theatetus* in the big schoolroom. We all went into chapel and sang the *Te Deum*; but I could not sing. The sense of relief and deliverance was too deep. As Siegfried Sassoon put it, 'My heart was shaken with tears and laughter. . . . The singing will never be done.'[110]

The school had done its best to foster a sense of patriotism in its pupils. The OTC was a highly popular extracurricular activity for the boys. The corps was for a time led by the headmaster's son, the famous novelist and poet James Elroy Flecker, who had been wounded in Mesopotamia and returned to Dean Close to help out his father. Neill felt the younger Flecker imposed 'the maximum of military effort on himself and on us'.[111] Neill considered the long hours in corps training to be 'practically all futile, wasted effort'.[112]

Neill was involved in many activities during his time at Dean Close.[113] He was Senior Prefect in 1917, a distinguished office at the school. He was an exceptional athlete, participating in gymnasium, track, football, tennis and cricket. He was often recognised for his intellectual achievements, receiving many awards and honours throughout his school career. Reading *The Decanian* newsletters from those years, one can see the assiduousness of this over-achiever during his years at Dean Close, 1912-19.

Clearly, Stephen was a tremendous pupil; the question was which direction would he take in life? He excelled in several areas: New Testament, history, literature, classical languages and modern European languages. He

---

109. Neill, *God's Apprentice*, p. 42.
110. Ibid.
111. Ibid., p. 39-40.
112. Ibid., p. 40.
113. For a comprehensive list of Neill's activities and accomplishments while at Dean Close, see Dyron Daughrity, *Bishop Stephen Neill: From Edinburgh to South India* (New York: Peter Lang, 2008), pp. 251–255.

2. Childhood, Youth and Education: 1900-24

was proficient in Latin and Greek, could read Hebrew and was competent in German and French.[114] He secured a good scholarship to study the classics at Trinity College, Cambridge. The story surrounding this event deserves telling.[115]

Stephen went to Cambridge for a week with his father in December 1918 to compete for a major scholarship in classics. It was the first time Neill had ever been to Cambridge. He roomed with a young man who caused Neill a bit of anxiety when he realised that this chap was better read in the classics than he was. Neill befriended this intimidating intellect, who was none other than A.D. (Arthur Darby) Nock, later a Fellow of Clare College and, by the age of 28, the Frothingham Professor of the History of Religions at Harvard University. Neill suffered intensely during that 'gruelling' week and ended up with a stye in his right eye, due to his anxiety. After one week, the results of the competition arrived by telegram, which only mentioned that Neill had received a scholarship and not which one. A day later Neill discovered that he and A.D. Nock had both won prestigious entrance scholarships to study classics at Trinity College.

Following the stress of the exam and of meeting a superior intellect in A.D. Nock, Neill was diagnosed with a severe case of the shingles and had to miss an entire term at Dean Close. This was also the time when Neill became aware of two afflictions that would remain with him for the greater part of his life: insomnia and depression. Of his insomnia, Neill wrote:

> My insomnia appears to have a purely physical cause or causes. It began after a teenage illness and persisted until a course of massage in Geneva made me realise that it was related to circulatory problems, and my body's apparent inability to regulate its temperature properly in certain climatic conditions. Since worrying about not sleeping makes the condition worse, I soon learned to get up and do some work, usually writing or reviewing books. For years, I never got a good night's sleep, but my output shows I really was awake, and not imagining it. Nevertheless, natural sleep would have been better for me.[116]

Neill's more traumatic affliction was depression. Regarding his frequent bouts with this nagging enemy, Neill wrote:

---

114. Stephen's father did not like the idea of him learning German. However, Neill's grandfather, who had studied in Berlin in 1858, 'overruled' his son. Stephen did not enter his German studies through the beginners' class; he was placed in the advanced class and received private tutoring from the teacher. It wasn't long before he was working through Goethe's *Faust*. See Neill, *God's Apprentice*, p. 41.
115. Ibid., pp. 43-44.
116. Ibid., p. 44.

It was as though all the lights went out in the world. This could happen suddenly, like a bolt from heaven; or it could start as a grey patch somewhere on the horizon, which would gradually spread until the whole heaven was blotted out by this grey blankness. The experience was accompanied by a total lack of interest in anything. . . . Prayer became a mere formula, with no sense that it was being addressed to anyone in particular or that there was any possibility of its being heard. As far as I remember, attacks in those distant days never lasted for more than three days at a time, and recovery could vary in the same way as the onset of the trouble. I might be in the depths at one moment, and entirely free the next; or the clouds might slowly and gradually dissipate themselves until the zenith was clear again. I diagnosed this affliction as the malaise which often beset medieval monks, *daemonium meridianum*; later I learned to call it *accidie*. I knew therefore that this darkness had nothing to do with being cut off from God, but it was only in later years that I became fully aware of the extent to which misfortune can fall.[117]

After taking his Cambridge entrance exams, Neill had a comprehensive breakdown in health. He took an entire term off – January to March 1919 – before completing his final term at Dean Close. It was neither his last nor most severe encounter with these ailments.[118]

Neill finally completed his studies at Dean Close, spending the summer there relaxing, riding his bike and enjoying a brief hiatus from the rigours of school life.[119] Neill stayed in touch with the school to the very end of his life.[120] After winning the prestigious scholarship, Neill must have been

---

117. Ibid., pp. 44-46. Neill claimed his depression miraculously improved on 25 January 1956, while he was kneeling for communion at Trinity College. However, in time it returned. Neill experienced other short periods of improvement in December 1965 and December 1970.
118. In his autobiography Neill lamented his frequent bouts with poor health, 'I have from time to time asked myself where I should have been and what I might have done if I had been gifted with better health. But this is a futile and meaningless question. . . . I would have been an entirely different person, and the story that follows would have been an entirely different story. At times I have been tempted to wish that there could have been a little less suffering on the way that I have trodden. . . . In any case, to look across the river and suppose that the grass is greener on the other side is an absurd and futile waste of time.' Neill, *God's Apprentice*, p. 46.
119. Ibid.
120. Neill and his brother Henry were both life governors of Dean Close. See *God's Apprentice*, p. 27. This fact was corroborated by Richard Padfield, interview by author, 21 January 2003.

aware that he had been well-prepared at Dean Close, 'though, it does seem to me odd that when I went to Cambridge I had never heard the name of Karl Marx'.[121] Nevertheless, from the close-knit, 220-pupil world of Dean Close, he was now ready to move on to the study of classics at Cambridge – with a student body of 6,000.[122]

Trinity College, Cambridge

It was surprising that Neill chose Trinity College, as Gonville and Caius was the 'family college'.[123] He never regretted the decision, however. In the autumn of 1919, with his father there to help with the move, he took residence in room D3 in the Victorian New Court.[124] He and his father went to a used furniture shop and bought 'the minimum on which a man could live'.[125] His father made him a promise of 37.10 pounds per quarter which would be deposited into his bank account.[126] His first impression of the students he met was very positive. He felt well-treated by the older students and enjoyed the acquaintance of his tutor, Ernest Harrison. The members of the Classical Reading Society elected him into their group for weekly study and translation. The transition from Cheltenham to Cambridge was quite fluid.

Neill knew he was in the right place for studying classics. Along with Harrison, an 'impeccable' Latin and Greek scholar, Neill studied under Donald Robertson (Professor of Greek), Francis Cornford (scholar of Greek Philosophy), Professor Sheppard of King's College (expert in Greek Literature), Franklin Angus of Trinity Hall (scholar of Ancient Philosophy, especially Lucretius) and also, the one Neill felt 'towered above them all', A.E. Housman (the great Latinist).[127] His first year was heavy, as he took many examinations. In January 1920 he wrote twelve papers within six days and ended up taking third place, earning himself the Davies Scholarship.

---

121. Neill, *God's Apprentice*, p. 47.
122. Ibid., pp. 28 and 58.
123. Ibid., p. 42. Neill's father, his uncle Charles and his brother Henry all went to Caius, as did his two younger brothers and a nephew. Neill remarked, 'for some reason Caius never attracted me'.
124. Stephen Charles Neill was admitted in 1919. His father is listed as Rev. Charles Neill MA (Arts), MB (Medicine), BCh (Surgery). Neill listed as his permanent residence, 15 Boulton Rd, Chiswick, London. His birth is listed as Edinburgh, 31 December 1900; status: Entrance Scholar. His tutor is listed as Mr Harrison. See 'Trinity College Admissions Book', Special Collections, Wren Library, Trinity College, Cambridge.
125. Neill, *God's Apprentice*, p. 48.
126. Ibid., p. 68. Neill remarked, 'Only once did I have to ask for more.'
127. Ibid., p. 50.

Stephen Neill while at Trinity College, Cambridge, c. 1923.

2. Childhood, Youth and Education: 1900-24

His new friend A.D. Nock finished first, taking home the Waddington Scholarship. In March Neill won a Senior Scholarship, worth £100 a year for five years. He wrote the first part of the Classical Tripos later that year. Neill was thriving, and he knew it:

> I have in fact singularly few memories of doing any work at Cambridge. . . . I had worked so hard at (Dean Close) school that it was only rarely that I had to exert myself really hard at Cambridge. So I amused myself by working for the university prizes.[128]

And win prizes he did. Neill attributed this to the fact that he was an 'extremely good examination candidate'.[129] According to the Historical Register of the University of Cambridge, 1921-30, Neill's penchant for winning prizes was remarkable indeed.[130]

Richard Padfield, a friend of the Neill family, remarked that the people at Dean Close were not surprised when they began to get word that Stephen was 'mopping up' the awards at Cambridge.[131] However, his plethora of awards began to cause a bit of a problem. At Dean Close School, Dr Flecker would always give the pupils a free half-day holiday when one of their own received a great reward at Cambridge or Oxford. When Stephen began to win habitually, Dr Flecker was forced to add an extra week's holiday onto the regular school break in order to honour the agreement. Soon, however, Flecker announced that the extra week was all that would be given, no matter how many prizes Neill happened to be awarded.[132]

While at Cambridge Neill maintained his close association with Dean Close. The school archives reveal Neill and his brother Henry came back on several occasions, once for the Old Decanians soccer match against the Dean Close team.[133] In March 1923 Neill returned to lecture about life

---

128. Ibid., p. 52.
129. Ibid., p. 67.
130. For a comprehensive list of Neill's prizes and awards he won while at Cambridge, see Daughrity, pp. 255–256.
131. Padfield, interview by author, 21 January 2003.
132. Padfield, interview by author, 21 January 2003. The Dean Close school paper, *The Decanian*, closely followed Neill's awards at Cambridge. It recorded him winning the Carus, the Davies, 'First Class' in the Classical Tripos – Part I, the Jeremie, Evans, Members', 'First Class' in the Classical Tripos – Part II, Distinction in Philosophy and History, 'Second Class' in the Modern Languages Tripos, Chancellor's Medal, 'First Class' in the Theological Tripos – Part II, the Crosse Scholarship, another Carus and a Winchester Prize. This story is also recounted by Mary Paterson, 'Bishop Stephen Neill: School Days, Latter Days, Plus a Few Days Here and There', unpublished paper (ca. 2000), Bishop Stephen Neill Study and Research Centre, Palayamkottai, India.
133. *The Decanian*, March 1923.

at Cambridge. In June that same year he returned to read a paper on the poems of A.E. Housman.[134] Both Henry and Stephen were present at the dedication of the new Dean Close School chapel on 1 November 1923.[135]

Henry and Stephen were also members of the Old Decanian Society (ODS) during the early 1920s as well. The ODS usually met at Trinity College, Cambridge, in Stephen's room and Stephen usually recorded the notes of their meetings.[136] On 28 November 1921, at one of these meetings, a toast was proposed by one of the members to Stephen's health, commending his 'latest success in the world of learning, which were too numerous to be entered fully'. True to form, Neill responded 'in a graceful speech'.[137]

Stephen served as President of the Cambridge ODS in 1923.[138] Interestingly, another figure who was also to become famous served as the Oxford ODS President at the same time: Verrier Elwin. Elwin was two years behind Neill at Dean Close and, in spite of Elwin's gifted intellect, he was unable to escape the long shadow of Neill's legacy at the school. Ramachandra Guha, Elwin's biographer, writes:

> Two classes ahead of Verrier Elwin was Stephen Neill, regarded as the school's star student. . . . Neill had a phenomenal aptitude for languages and a near-photographic memory. He was also very pious. For years after he left school – with a scholarship to Trinity College, Cambridge – the Classics teacher would correct answers by saying, 'Stephen Neill would never have written this.' In school, Verrier shadowed Neill honour for honour,

---

134. *The Decanian*, July 1923, p. 50, 'On Saturday, June 16th, Mr. S.C. Neill read a paper on the poems of A.E. Housman. Dr. Flecker was present and opened the meeting with a short speech, in which he congratulated Mr. Neill on his recent success in the Theological Tripos, and the Society on having such a distinguished visitor to speak to them. Mr. Neill's paper was heard with great interest; and the discussion which followed showed how much the Society valued this latest act of kindness from its first Secretary.'
135. See 'The History of Dean Close School Chapel', pamphlet produced at Dean Close School, Special Collections, Dean Close School.
136. See 'Old Decanian Society Notes 1904-1927', Special Collections, Dean Close School. Neill was the primary recorder of these notes during this period; his signature is always at the end of these documents.
137. The 'Old Decanian Society Notes 1904-1927' provide an interesting glimpse into the social aptitude of Neill. On one occasion, 6 May 1923, Stephen 'proposed the Toast of the King, and later the Toast of the School, delivering a most graceful speech'.
138. See 'Old Decanian Society Notes 1904-1927'. There are several examples of Neill's signature on the minutes, e.g. 'S.C. Neill, President, 6.5.23'.

2. Childhood, Youth and Education: 1900-24

winning . . . three prestigious prizes for history, literature, and scripture. But the divergences in their paths were also becoming apparent.[139]

The divergences that Guha is referring to is the fact that, as Neill became increasingly pious, Elwin was going the other way. According to Guha, Neill embodied everything that Dean Close wanted in an alumnus. He writes:

> Stephen Neill is still venerated in Dean Close as the prize pupil whose future career most fully embodied the aspirations of the Evangelical party of the Church of England. . . . There now hangs a portrait of Stephen Neill in the school, the only Old Decanian so honoured, the pupil described by a loving *alma mater* as 'Evangelist, Missionary, Statesman, Scholar, Teacher and Benefactor'.[140]

In contrast, Elwin is something of a black sheep at Dean Close according to his biographer: 'The school, unsurprisingly, had long been embarrassed by Elwin's career. . . . The school continues to regard Elwin as something of a black sheep in comparison with his near contemporary Bishop Stephen Neill, whose career they would rather more willingly memorialize.'[141]

There was an incident involving these two that made headlines, literally, in one of Britain's national newspapers, *The Times*, in October 1924. At a meeting of the annual Church Congress at Oxford University, there was a public discussion on the topic 'What the youth ask of the Church'. Both Neill and Elwin presented papers. Elwin argued that the war had turned the young more towards their faith and that young people were still inclined to be religious. He is quoted as saying, 'Youth want to know how to keep straight; the fact of sex is becoming very real and not too clearly understood.' He argued that the youth were looking for true religion 'that really functions in people's lives. . . . If the Church would lead the way, the youth would follow.' His comments received cheers from the crowd.

Neill argued differently. He said young people just need to feel loved. He called for church leaders to talk informally with young men. According to *The Times*, Neill then became emotional and asked, 'Can the Church

---

139. Ramachandra Guha, *Savaging the Civilized: Verrier Elwin, His Tribals, and India* (Chicago: University of Chicago Press, 1999), p. 10. Elwin abandoned his Christianity for Hinduism during his time in India in the 1930s and 1940s. He eventually became a polygamist, marrying two Gond tribal women in India and shocking many of the British.
140. Ibid., pp. 11-12.
141. Ibid., p. 316.

not show us something of the spirit of the Cross?' Neill urged his audience to practice more self-sacrifice.[142] While Neill does not mention the incident in his autobiography, Elwin does in his:

> In my fourth year the annual Church Congress was held in Oxford. . . . [O]n the subject: 'What Youth asks of the Church' I was chosen to represent Oxford and an old classmate, S.C. Neill, represented Cambridge. Neill was not exactly a 'fellow-student', for at school he had always been in quite a different class to me, earning scholarships and prizes with rather intimidating brilliance. He is now a bishop but still, I believe, a very learned man. Shortly before the Congress he wrote to me asking for a copy of my speech and in all innocence I sent it to him. He did not return the compliment, with the result that when the day came he was in a very favourable position to make some carefully prepared cracks at my expense. I still remember his referring to 'the warm streams of oratory that had descended on the audience from Oxford' (loud laughter) and his going on to say that he spoke for 'the sheep that had no shepherd', which was exactly what I thought I had been doing myself. This speech of mine got me into the headlines and for the first time in my life I saw myself in big type.[143]

Neill was an extremely competitive person.[144] He was willing to go to great lengths to win an argument; this trait would surface often in his life. The incident also shows Neill's tendency to become emotional. An excellent public speaker, Neill virtually always won over his audience using whatever techniques he could.[145]

---

142. See *The Times*, 29 September 1924.
143. Elwin, *The Tribal World of Verrier Elwin*, pp. 24-25. Neill mentioned Elwin in *God's Apprentice*, but only in the context that Elwin was a former classmate at Dean Close and was active in the Oxford Inter-Collegiate Christian Union, p. 55. Elwin's biographer briefly mentions the public debate; Guha, *Savaging the Civilized*, pp. 23-24. He remarks that both Neill and Elwin were successful in their 'first public appearance'.
144. The entire incident was also recounted at Dean Close in *The Decanian*, December 1924: 'For a day or two Neill and Elwin were public characters. We hope to be able, in a future number, to give some account of their speeches. Meanwhile we offer them our hearty congratulations and even our sincere thanks for what they did in the great meeting at Oxford.'
145. Neill was an outstanding public speaker. Owen Chadwick, in his *Michael Ramsey: A Life* (Oxford: Clarendon Press, 1990), writes, 'Stephen Neill . . . had lately dazzled the university [Cambridge] by his lecturing and preaching power', p. 68.

2. Childhood, Youth and Education: 1900-24

If we take as an example a book review he wrote in 1934 on one of Neill's books, Elwin was clearly personally hurt by Neill,. In a bitter critique of Neill's *Builders of the Indian Church*, Elwin wrote that Neill's book was 'written in the awkward and borrowed phraseology of another age'. He chastised Neill for 'still preaching in a black gown':

> We do not expect an ex-Fellow of Trinity, Cambridge, and a former leader of the Student Christian Movement, which is supposed to teach its members better things, to refer to the non-Christians in India as a *heathen*, or to fill his pages with such trite missionary clichés as 'work in *virgin soil* usually has to be carried on for a generation *without harvest*,' 'On an average a convert is baptised *every five minutes throughout the year*,' 'Every city staked out in the name of Christ *the front line of advance*,' 'Women have in the Civil Disobedience Movement undergone imprisonment *for what they believe to be the cause of their country*,' 'The spread of the Good News.' While of village children he can write, 'These unkempt, shy creatures must be *caught* and *tamed*.'[146]

Clearly, Neill and Elwin did not see eye to eye when it came to working in India. Neill was a tireless learner and he continued to progress in his study of languages. Under the inspiration of Alexander Nairne, at that time Dean of Jesus College, he studied Italian and began reading Dante, one of his lifelong joys. He continued in his German studies, wearing out his Cassell's dictionary in the process.[147] He began a study of Sanskrit.[148] He continued to read the Greek New Testament daily. In addition to languages, in his fourth year he embarked on a year's reading of theology, eventually winning the Crosse Scholarship. It was while sitting this series of examinations that Neill showed his mastery of biblical Hebrew. A legend persisted for some time around Trinity that he knew Hebrew as well as he knew Greek.[149]

---

146. Guha, *Savaging the Civilized*, p. 91.
147. Neill, *God's Apprentice*, p. 64.
148. Neill would return to his study of Sanskrit a few years later during his first leave from India. Eleanor Jackson's personal collection, p. 82. Jackson has some notes from the original, unedited autobiography which did not make it into the published version, *God's Apprentice*. During her editorship of *God's Apprentice*, she was able to access the original manuscript version of Neill's unpublished autobiography. There are a few pieces of information from her notes that are cited in the present work. This information is not found in *God's Apprentice*. Hereafter, these notes will be cited as 'Eleanor Jackson's personal collection'.
149. Neill, *God's Apprentice*, p. 67.

Neill stayed busy with church activities and other avocations, although he remained a 'convinced Sabbatarian' with a strict observance of the Christian Sabbath.[150] He frequently met with friends for tea, he rowed often for exercise and he participated in the 'Magpie and Stump' political society.[151] He bought a motorcycle with the extra money from his many scholarships and awards.[152]

What mattered most to Stephen Neill during these years was his evangelical faith. He worshipped regularly at the College chapel, preferring early Communion and Evensong, which still exist at Trinity – and, indeed, at most of the Cambridge colleges. He joined the Cambridge Inter-Collegiate Christian Union (CICCU) where he made several friends, including Carey Francis (later missionary to Africa) and Clifford Martin (later bishop of Liverpool).[153] With these and about 50 others, he formed the Cambridge Missionary Band in 1920.[154] This experience would point his career compass in the direction of India.

In 1921 Neill was invited to become President of the Cambridge branch of the Student Christian Movement (SCM).[155] This came as a total surprise to him, as the CICCU and the SCM had split in 1910. However, to the chagrin of his fellow CICCU members, Neill agreed. The SCM opened up many opportunities for Neill, not least of which was meeting the famous Presbyterian missionary and ecumenist, William Paton, who was then serving as the Secretary of the National Christian Council of India, Burma

---

150. Ibid., p. 52. Another dimension of his Sabbatarian conviction was that he never missed Church services and he always read outside of his current field. For example, when studying the classics, he read theology on the Sabbath; but, when studying theology, he read detective stories on the Sabbath.
151. Eleanor Jackson's personal collection, p. 55. It is interesting to note that Malcolm Muggeridge was a friend of Neill's during this time. See Neill, *God's Apprentice*, p. 95. Magpie and Stump is the name of a long-established debating society at Trinity College, Cambridge.
152. Neill, *God's Apprentice*, p. 68.
153. The CICCU was founded in 1877 under the influence of the American revivalism of Dwight Moody and Ira Sankey. It split away from the Student Christian Movement in 1910 and carried with it a distaste of higher criticism in favour of a conservative evangelical view of the Bible. For a history of the CICCU, see David Goodhew, 'The Rise of the Cambridge Inter-Collegiate Christian Union, 1910-1971', *The Journal of Ecclesiastical History*, Vol. 54, no. 1 (January 2003), pp. 62-89.
154. Neill maintained contact with surviving members of this group his entire life. See *God's Apprentice*, p. 55.
155. See Tissington Tatlow, *The Story of the Student Christian Movement* (London: SCM Press, 1933), and John Eric Fenn, *Learning Wisdom: Fifty Years of the Student Christian Movement* (London: SCM Press, 1939). In Tatlow's history, Neill appears simply as one in attendance at the 1924 COPEC conference, p. 670. Fenn's book is only a cursory history of 125 pages and includes nothing on Neill.

2. Childhood, Youth and Education: 1900-24

and Ceylon.[156] In addition to his SCM work, Neill participated in various ecumenical campaigns in the city of Cambridge, as well as helping to lead a youth camp each year. In April 1924 he participated in a Conference on Politics, Economics and Citizenship (COPEC), held in Birmingham under the chairmanship of William Temple, the future Archbishop of Canterbury.

One other activity of Neill's must be mentioned here. Neill had not decided by early 1924 whether or not he would give his life to ordained ministry in the Church. He knew he wanted to go to India later that year but was not sure whether to go as an ordained minister or as a layman. Thus, he decided to 'get all the preliminaries out of the way, so that if I decided to be ordained, my work would not be interrupted by a period of residence at a theological college'.[157] Neill enrolled as an associate at Westcott House, where his father had trained for ministry.[158] Stephen passed the General Ordination Examination (GOE) of the Church of England easily without preparation and developed a very negative view of that exam:

> The GOE seems to me to be one of the gravest misfortunes that has ever befallen the Church of England. Much of the training for the ministry in that ancient Church seems to me deplorably bad, and I believe that the GOE is somewhere near the heart of the trouble. It is one of those examinations which can be passed without having ever read a single theological book. . . . One does not go to heaven because one has heard of Schleiermacher, but it is sad that so many Anglican ordinands have never even heard the name of the father of modern theology.[159]

With the examination and ordination requirements out of the way, Neill could suspend his decision on whether or not to become ordained, and focus on other things, including his upcoming future career as a missionary and his last days as a Cambridge scholar.

Toward the end of his time at Cambridge, Neill was advised by some to try for a Trinity fellowship, awarded to three or four students a year and based mainly on a dissertation.[160] This would require a year of further

---

156. See Paton's biography by Eleanor M. Jackson, *Red Tape and the Gospel: A Study of the Significance of the Ecumenical Missionary Struggle of William Paton (1886-1943)* (Birmingham: Phlogiston, 1980).
157. Neill, *God's Apprentice*, p. 72.
158. The author went to Westcott House to obtain a history of the college but none was available, other than that found at the college's official website: www.westcott.cam.ac.uk.
159. Neill, *God's Apprentice*, p. 73.
160. The fellowship competition is also based on a general exam. Fellowships are

research and writing. He was undecided at first, as his father could no longer provide him with an allowance because one of Neill's younger brothers, Gerald, also now at university, had not been awarded any scholarship and Charles Neill decided to fully support him. In addition to the financial predicament, Neill had by now become convinced that he must follow in his father's footsteps as a missionary to the people of India. However, the challenge to become a Fellow proved too tempting. Thus, Neill applied for a Burney Studentship in the Philosophy of Religion, worth £200 a year. Again, he was successful, affording him the ability to 'live on in modest comfort' during this final year.[161] He had about ten months in which to produce a work worthy of a fellowship.

After searching for a topic, he settled on an analysis of the influence of Plotinus on the three Cappadocian Fathers: Basil of Caesarea, Gregory of Nyssa and Gregory of Nazianzus.[162] He gathered up several doctoral dissertations in the field done by Roman Catholics, poured himself into the actual texts themselves, took copious amounts of notes and in the end placed his notes neatly into five piles, providing him with an outline for his dissertation.[163]

Even for an intellect as keen as Neill's, the dissertation was a colossal undertaking. He began writing on 10 July 1924.[164] He described this extremely challenging task in his autobiography:

---

difficult to explain, according to Neill, 'It is almost impossible to explain to anyone who does not know Oxford or Cambridge the meaning of election to a fellowship. Long ago groups of learned men agreed to live together as a family – to think together, to eat together, to pray together and to play together . . . and in course of time admitted young students into the intimacy of the common life . . . much of the intimate familial character of the common life has disappeared, but much still remains. And once a member of the family, one has entered into a fellowship which can never be dissolved. . . . This system has changed, and I knew that by going to India I would lose my fellowship within a few years. But a past fellow is still in a very real sense a member of the foundation, and retains certain rights and privileges until the end of his days.' See Neill, *God's Apprentice*, p. 76.

161. Ibid., p. 68.
162. The Cappadocian Fathers were fourth-century Christian bishops who made substantial contributions to the doctrine of the Trinity. The location of Neill's dissertation is unknown to the author. An inquiry was sent to the archivist, Jonathan Smith, at Trinity College, Cambridge, with the following reply, dated 19 May 2003: 'Successful Trinity Fellowship dissertations are now kept in the Library here, but unfortunately Neill's, which we know was entitled *Plotinus and the Cappadocians* is a little too early to have been saved.' It was uncommon in those days, according to Smith, to maintain dissertations unless they were for the doctoral degree. Neill's dissertation was not for a doctoral degree; it was in competition for a fellowship.
163. Neill, *God's Apprentice*, p. 73.
164. Ibid., pp. 72-73.

I hope that I shall never again have to work as hard as I did in those two months. For the first and last time in my life, my work pursued me into my dreams, and this was a danger signal. I owe much to Geoffrey Eley (now Sir Geoffrey), who saw what was happening and insisted that I sometimes get out and play tennis. Then I fell untimely ill. . . . Most of those illnesses could be easily explained as the result of underfeeding and overwork. . . . Nock became troubled about the amount of aspirin I was consuming. . . . I know I was earnestly prayed for in Westcott House Chapel. B. K. came to me to comfort me, knowing how much the loss of even a few days could mean to my dissertation, but after three days I rose from my bed. . . . In less than two months I had written 100,000 words. . . . No one ought to write so much so fast; in later years I have tried . . . to avoid writing more than a thousand words in a day. The mind grows tired. . . . It is not surprising that on 28 August 1924 I felt drained of knowledge, of energy, and of everything else that makes life human. I felt that I knew what Angus meant when he told me that . . . there was no sin which he could not have committed.[165]

The dissertation was due on 31 August. By 28 August Neill had written all he could, had carefully revised and edited and handed it in 'with a profound distrust of what is commonly called research, and a grave disinclination ever to be engaged in it again'.[166]

In addition to the dissertation, the candidates for a fellowship, of which there were 24 that year,[167] had to write two papers: one on 'General Aspects of Literature and History' and the other on 'General Aspects of Philosophy and Science'.[168] Neill sat the exams and waited for the date when the results would be announced. In October, when word came that results were available, Neill 'passed through the Great Gate [of Trinity College]' where the porter must have accidentally broken the news to Neill for the first time when he said, 'I think I have to congratulate you, Sir.' Neill chose not to discuss his emotional response in his autobiography, choosing only to describe it as 'indecorous'.[169]

---

165. Ibid., pp. 73-74.
166. Ibid., p. 75.
167. Neill claimed that there were 24 candidates for fellowships 'representing a wide range of faculties and disciplines'. See Neill, *God's Apprentice*, p. 75.
168. Ibid. Neill wrote, 'There was only one thing certain about this examination: that absolutely anything could be asked.'
169. See Neill, *God's Apprentice*, p. 76. It should be noted here that Neill's old school, Dean Close, praised the awarding of his fellowship as well, 'Mr. S.C. Neill . . . has been elected to a Fellowship at Trinity College, Cambridge, a fitting conclusion to

Neill was the first person ever elected to a Trinity prize fellowship on a theological dissertation.[170] There were three other Cambridge fellows admitted that year: an Australian mathematician by the name of Thomas (who was later knighted); Henry Salt, a lawyer; and a Jewish biochemist by the name of Questal. The four of them were honoured in a chapel service and welcomed into the distinguished community of Cambridge fellows.[171] Among them was the classicist and poet A.E. Housman, whom Neill greatly admired but had never met. Housman, with a smile, remarked to Neill that night, 'If there is any crime which ought absolutely to debar a man from being elected to a fellowship at Trinity, it is that of going to India as a missionary.'[172]

Neill's decision was shocking to the people around him. However, Neill had been determined to go since the year before after a candid conversation with his father: 'I had discussed the matter with my father the year before [in 1923], weighing the claims of Cambridge, and . . . the mission field. . . . He remarked, "Knowing you as I do, I have very little doubt as to the way in which you will decide."'[173] Actually, it was in June 1924 that Neill purchased his ticket to India, a month before he had even begun to write his dissertation.[174] The success of the fellowship was for Neill simply another challenge. He knew he would end up in the mission field. He knew his decision of 'turning his back' on a very distinguished opportunity at Cambridge was no doubt 'peculiar' in the eyes of his peers.[175] However, he was resolute.

Neill decided to depart for India in late November 1924 as a lay missionary, opting not to become ordained just yet. That would come later.

Neill cherished his time at Cambridge. 'It is impossible to set down on paper what I owe to Trinity', he wrote, 'The very stones are dear to me!'[176] Nevertheless, he was soon to board a ship for India via Marseilles, France. He had to leave England with little time to focus on anything other than his new life as a missionary. He managed one last trip to his beloved Dean Close School:

---

that long list of academical successes which has been recorded in previous numbers of the Magazine. This is the first time that a past member of this School has obtained a Fellowship at the College in which he was formerly Scholar.' See *The Decanian*, December 1924, p. 78.
170. Neill, *God's Apprentice*, p. 76.
171. Eleanor Jackson's personal collection, p. 99.
172. Neill, *God's Apprentice*, pp. 76-77.
173. Ibid., p. 71.
174. Ibid., p. 72.
175. Ibid., p. 77.
176. Eleanor Jackson's personal collection, p. 100.

2. Childhood, Youth and Education: 1900-24

> On Saturday, November 18th, Mr. S.C. Neill paid a short farewell visit to the School and preached an impressive sermon in the Chapel on the following Sunday. He sailed on the 22nd of that month for South India, where he is engaged in missionary work in a school at Dohnavur. We offer him our sincerest wishes for his health and for his success in his difficult work.[177]

Stephen Neill departed Victoria Station for Marseilles on 22 November 1924, feeling 'very forlorn and lonely', with his brother Henry running after him to bid a final farewell.[178]

---

177. *The Decanian*, March 1925, p. 97. This is a very important piece of information, as it is the only reference known to the author that contains the precise date of Neill's departure.
178. Neill, *God's Apprentice*, p. 78.

Chapter Three
Amy Carmichael and Neill's Early Years in South India: 1924-28

Neill's first year in India was a disaster. He had a major falling out with the famous missionary Amy Carmichael, an individual every bit as strong-willed as he was. The results were so personally damaging to Neill that he never did mention the events of 1924-25 after they happened.

Neill's Arrival in 1924

The name of Neill's Bibby Line vessel was the S.S. *Warwickshire*.[1] His travel companions included two lay missionaries and the rest were 'fairly rough types'.[2] Neill remembered playing the game 'skittles' and passing through the Suez Canal during his long trip.[3] While on the Red Sea, he came down with a fever that lasted all the way to Colombo, the capital of Ceylon, now Sri Lanka. One week of waiting in Colombo was followed by a one-night trip to Tuticorin (now called Thoothukudi), a port city on the coast of southeast India. Neill's sea journey was followed by an 'excruciatingly uncomfortable Ford eight-seater' drive to Tinnevelly

---

1. Neill, *God's Apprentice*, p. 79. Bibby is a British shipping company founded in 1807 by the Bibby family and based in Liverpool.
2. Ibid.
3. Skittles is a form of bowling, in which a wooden disk or ball is thrown to knock down the pins.

3. Amy Carmichael and Neill's Early Years in South India: 1924-28   59

Junction.⁴ Finally, Neill took a three-mile bullock-cart ride to the Dohnavur mission, located in the Tinnevelly diocese. This was his first home in India.

By the time of Neill's arrival in South India in 1924 the diocese was well established; former CMS missionary Norman H. Tubbs was the fourth occupant of the bishopric. The mission work was thriving. The official Annual Reports of the CMS provide insight into the inner workings and daily life of the diocese. The 1923-24 Annual Report shows that Tinnevelly had twenty Europeans working as missionaries: four clergymen, one layman and fifteen women. Native leadership was well-established: there were 51 clergymen, 572 laymen and 260 women working in conjunction with the CMS. Tinnevelly had more churches and members than any of the ten dioceses or districts in India and Ceylon with 1,135 'organised congregations' and over 80,000 'adherents'. The diocese was second (after Telugu, in southern central India) in baptisms with 3,334 that year. Education had for many years been a central concern in the Tinnevelly district. The diocese had more teachers (1,056) and the second highest number of schools (555) in all of India and Ceylon. Tinnevelly ranked third in the number of pupils for a district in India with 23,828.⁵

---

4. Neill, *God's Apprentice*, p. 80. The British name for the district 'Tinnevelly' will be used more often than the Tamil 'Tirunelveli'. The diocese was known by the British as Tinnevelly during Neill's time as a missionary and the English records that cover Neill's dates in India always use the Tinnevelly spelling. Indian scholars use the two words interchangeably, however, they normally use Tinnevelly when referring to the period of British rule and Tirunelveli since independence. Tirunelveli is in the southeast of India and is separated from the state of Tranvancore by the Western Ghat mountains which extend down to Cape Comorin. The word 'Tirunelveli' is composed of three Tamil words: *thiru* which means sacred; *nel* which means paddy; and *veli* which means hedge. The town of Tirunelveli has been the capital of the province since the time of the Nayakan rulers. The Nayakans had ruled this area of India at least since 1600 when the British East India Company was established. This information and much more can be found in Samuel Jayakumar's *Dalit Consciousness and Christian Conversion: Historical Resources for a Contemporary Debate* (Chennai: Mission Educational Books, 1999). See especially pp. 48-70 for an historical discussion of the land and the people. Other important resources include Henrietta Bugge, *Mission and Tamil Society: Social and Religious Change in South India* (Richmond: Curzon Press, 1994); Franklyn J. Balasundaram, *Dalits and Christian Mission in the Tamil Country* (Bangalore: Asian Trading Corporation, 1997); and D. Dennis Hudson, *Protestant Origins in India: Tamil Evangelical Christians, 1706-1835* (Grand Rapids, MI: Eerdmans, 2000). The most authoritative account of the birth of the Tirunelveli Diocese is George Muller, *The Birth of a Bishopric: Being the History of the Tirunelveli Church from Early Beginnings to 1896* (Palayamkottai: Diocesan Offset Press, 1980). For a history of Christian missions in south India, see Daughrity, *Bishop Stephen Neill: From Edinburgh to South India*, Chapter 3.

5. *Annual Report of the Committee of the Church Missionary Society for Africa and*

There is evidence that the Tinnevelly diocese was fast becoming an autonomous entity, paving the way for the Church of South India which would be founded in September 1947. By 1924 Tinnevelly had adopted a diocesan constitution which received approval from both the Society for the Propagation of the Gospel in Foreign Parts (SPG) and the CMS.[6] This, effectively, transferred control of the diocese from the CMS offices in England to the local level.

One major factor for the burgeoning Church in South India was mass conversion from the depressed classes, in the main, the untouchables or 'dalits'. The nearby Telugu Mission, for example, had seen its Christian population almost double from about 45,000 in 1918 to about 80,000 in 1924.[7] These great successes in the eyes of the missionaries did not come without problems, however. For example, one difficult question was what kind of education the missionaries should offer the new converts who were destined by caste to live a life of subsistence. European education tended to foster 'an attitude of superiority towards manual labour, and thus does not make for the good of the community'.[8] Thus, the missionaries realised they needed to establish vocational schools and labour-training programmes in addition to the book-learning model that was common in European society. The missionaries offered an alternative livelihood – particularly to individuals who were handicapped in some way – through weaving courses and cloth-making. The goal was to save people from having to beg for a living.

Upper-class Hindus were very intrigued by the Christian faith. Some Hindus were able to quote the teachings of Jesus with great precision. One Brahmin lawyer said:

> Though there have been Moslems in India for a thousand years, you never hear a Hindu say to a Moslem: 'I wish you were more like the Prophet.' We have only known of Christianity for a quarter of that time, but there is no educated Hindu who would not say to any Christian: 'I wish you were more like Jesus Christ.'[9]

---

the East, 1923-4 (London: Church Missionary Society, 1924), pp. xii-xv, lvi. The Tinnevelly diocese here is compared with nine other dioceses in the region: 1. Punjab/Northwest Frontier/Sindh; 2. Western India; 3. United Provinces; 4. Central Provinces and Rajputana; 5. Bengal and Bihar; 6. Madras; 7. Telugu; 8. Tranvancore and Cochin; and 9. Ceylon.

6. *Annual Report of the Committee of the CMS, 1923-4*, pp. 32-33.
7. Ibid., p. 34.
8. Ibid., p. 34.
9. Ibid., p. 36. Severe and often deadly feuds took place between Muslims and Hindus during this time, leading to statements such as this one. Disastrous

3. Amy Carmichael and Neill's Early Years in South India: 1924-28

In Tinnevelly all classes were at least somewhat receptive to Christianity. The increase in Christians between 1913 and 1924 was fifteen per cent, coming predominantly from the lower castes.[10]

All was not good, however. In 1924, a crisis hit the Tinnevelly Church. The third bishop of the diocese, Bishop Waller, had tried to unite the two missionary organisations: the CMS and the SPG.[11] His plan backfired and caused a schism in the diocese. According to one Tinnevelly scholar, 'The hiccups grew into a schism which ultimately led to the birth in 1925 of a new organization called the Tinnevelly CMS Evangelical Church.'[12] Neill referred to the incident in his autobiography as 'the Alvaneri schism' and described it as 'a lamentable situation'.[13]

In 1924 Stephen Neill was entering a bustling context of missionary activity. Regardless of the internal problems taking place within the mission societies, Christianity was growing rapidly and the opportunities must have appeared boundless to him.[14] Neill's parents were in South India at the time, making the transition easier. Everything seemed to be coming together for his first missionary experience.

Amy Carmichael of Dohnavur

From the moment Neill arrived to his mission post at Dohnavur, tensions were palpable. Pierard comments: 'Neill completely omits any mention of this phase of his life.'[15] Eleanor Jackson wrote that Neill 'was forced to leave [Dohnavur] after a number of clashes with Amy Carmichael.'[16]

---

rioting at Kohat caused Gandhi to impose upon himself a 21-day fast during this time.
10. Ibid., p. 49.
11. Waller was Bishop of Tinnevelly from 1915-22.
12. P. Kanagaraj, 'Tirunelveli Diocese: A Spiritual Laboratory in the Evolution of Bishop Stephen Neill', research paper, Bishop Stephen Neill Study and Research Centre, Palayamkottai. See also Hugald Grafe, *History of Christianity in India: Vol. IV, Part 2: Tamilnadu in the Nineteenth and Twentieth Centuries* (Bangalore: Church History Association of India, 1990), pp. 78-79. Grafe claims that this schism was known as the 'Alvaneri schism'.
13. Neill, *God's Apprentice*, p. 86. Neill wrote, 'It was impossible for me not to be drawn into all these events. I was living just on the edge of the disturbed area, and was all too well aware of the whirlpools of emotion by which I was surrounded. As a very raw recruit, I had no standing in the matter, and there was nothing that I could do about it", p. 80.
14. It should be noted that Neill was not yet a part of the CMS. That did not happen until 1928.
15. Pierard, 'Stephen Neill', p. 534.
16. Eleanor Jackson, 'The Continuing Legacy of Stephen Neill', p. 78.

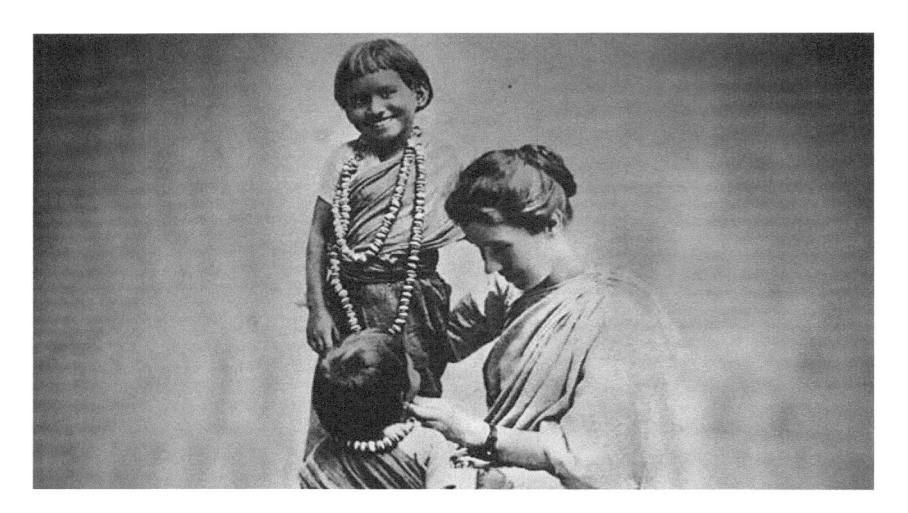

Amy Carmichael with children in South India.

Dohnavur has become famous through the work of the long-time missionary there, Amy Carmichael. The story of Dohnavur begins in the 1820s.[17] It was founded as a mission station by the German CMS missionary C.T.E. Rhenius in 1827. He named it after a pious and wealthy Prussian, Count Dohna of Scholodin. Count Dohna had made a generous gift to the local Christians who were from the Nadar caste. They built a church building in 1824. The previous name of the area was Pooliyurkurichi. The community now bears Count Dohna's name and the church still stands.[18]

The history of mission activity at Dohnavur is difficult to construct. What is known is that a missionary by the name of P.C.F. Winckler[19] was stationed in Dohnavur in 1827. He was succeeded by several CMS missionaries throughout the rest of the nineteenth century.[20] In 1834 two

17. For the official history of the Dohnavur Fellowship, see Amy Carmichael, *Gold Cord: The Story of a Fellowship* (London: SPCK, 1932).
18. The People of Dohnavur to the Home Secretary, CMS, Touring the Tinnevelly Diocese, 1 February 1947, Tinnevelly Box 1, Special Collections, Bishop's College. See also Frank Houghton, *Amy Carmichael of Dohnavur* (London: SPCK, 1953), p. 130ff. Houghton lived for some time at Dohnavur and had access to Carmichael's letters and papers, something rarely allowed today. The author went to Dohnavur and was able to talk with the senior administrators there, as well as spend time in the Carmichael library, but access to the private papers was denied.
19. Outside this brief reference, P.C.F. Winckler is unknown to the author.
20. The names of these missionaries are listed by surname and in chronological succession: P.P. Schaffter, West, Dent, Pickford and Dibb. See letter 'The People of Dohnavur to The Home Secretary'). The history of the Dohnavur mission prior to

funds were established at Dohnavur: a widow's fund and 'the Gospel fanam' (a fanam was a silver coin of southern India issued up until independence in 1947). In 1868 Lord Napier, Governor of Madras, paid a visit to Dohnavur and was amazed at the generosity of the local Christians.[21]

Dohnavur's history becomes much more accessible with the arrival of 'Walker of Tinnevelly'. The fiery preacher Thomas Walker was active in the Dohnavur mission from 1900 to 1912 and was known all over Tamil-speaking South India as a great missionary and communicator, as he spoke Tamil fluently.[22] It was Walker of Tinnevelly who lured Amy Carmichael to the Tinnevelly district by offering to teach her Tamil. In 1900 Walker managed to persuade her to remain in Dohnavur; and Dohnavur remained her home, without leave, until her death in 1951.[23] There is no scholarly biography on Amy Carmichael yet but many hagiographies.[24] The main

Carmichael is difficult to find. Neill barely mentions it. Graffe mentions Dohnavur only a few times. Gibbs excludes it, as does the Ward and Stanley volume on the history of the CMS. Elisabeth Elliot, in her biography of Carmichael, *A Chance to Die: The Life and Legacy of Amy Carmichael* (Grand Rapids, MI: Fleming H. Revell, 1987) claims it was Rhenius who began Dohnavur in 1827, p. 165. 'The People of Dohnavur' letter mentions that Sri Paul Appaswamy has researched it at some point, but the author is not familiar with this work.

21. A curious statement appears in this letter of 'The People of Dohnavur' that may shed light on the history of the offertory in South India, 'Kalasams or collecting pots were brought into use during this decade (1860-69), 300 of them being out in Dohnavur alone.'
22. Walker and his wife were CMS missionaries; they arrived in India in 1885. See Elliot, *A Chance to Die*, p. 127.
23. See Amy Carmichael, *This One Thing: The Story of Walker of Tinnevelly* (London: Oliphants Ltd, 1916). Amy arrived in India on 9 November 1895 and never left. She died in Dohnavur on 18 January 1951. Houghton, *Amy Carmichael of Dohnavur*, p. 90.
24. Houghton, *Amy Carmichael of Dohnavur*; Elliot, *A Chance to Die*; J. Hans Kommers, *Triumphant Love: The Contextual, Creative and Strategic Missionary Work of Amy Beatrice Carmichael in South India* (Durbanville: AOSIS, 2017); D. Arthur Jeyakumar, 'Amy Carmichael of Dohnavur 1867-1951', *Indian Church History Review*, Vol. 36, no. 1 (2002), pp. 5-11. The Jeyakumar article was written 'to highlight the contribution of Christian women missionaries in general and that of Amy Carmichael in particular', p. 5. The article is somewhat helpful but provides little beyond Carmichael's basic biographical information. See also John Pollock, 'Amy Carmichael', in *Concise Dictionary of the Christian World Mission*, ed. by Neill, Anderson and Goodwin; and Ruth Tucker, 'Biography as Missiology: Mining the Lives of Missionaries for Cross-Cultural Effectiveness', *Missiology: An International Review*, Vol. 27, no. 4 (October 1999), pp. 429-40. This last article deals with Stephen Neill, Amy Carmichael and Sherwood Eddy and does show an awareness of the Neill-Carmichael incident, but only because Tucker had read the Elliot biography.

reason for this absence is the inaccessibility of the primary sources. Two biographers, Frank Houghton and Elisabeth Elliot, were permitted to see Carmichael's private papers for their biographies; however, both of them used the sources uncritically and for the purpose of exhibiting Carmichael's impressive Christian faith. Today, the Houghton biography is published and promoted at Dohnavur. Elliot's biography, however, is regarded with fury by the nuns who run the compound.

This is curious, for there is little in the Elliot biography to depict Carmichael as anything less than heroic. The nuns at Dohnavur do not appreciate the Elliot biography and told the author that they feel betrayed by Elliot's attempt to make Carmichael 'more human'. For these reasons, it is doubtful that the Carmichael and Dohnavur private papers will be seen by scholars for some time; my own requests in 2003 to see the private papers at Dohnavur were declined. Ruth Tucker's insight remains true today:

> Carmichael . . . was very careful to shield from public view any negative aspects of her private life or life inside Dohnavur Fellowship. She has remained shielded since her death by a wall of privacy and an aura of holiness. The wall is very real – the gate to her private papers and letters being guarded by Dohnavur Fellowship. The aura also is maintained by a biographer such as Elisabeth Elliot – permitted to enter the gate but ending her book with a threat of sorts – daring others not to tamper with the holiness of her hero.[25]

Amy Beatrice Carmichael was born in Millisle, County Down, Northern Ireland on 16 December 1867. She was the eldest of seven children in a well-to-do, devout Presbyterian family.[26] As a girl, Amy attended a Wesleyan Methodist boarding school in Harrogate, North Yorkshire.[27] Her father died in 1885 causing Carmichael to spend some of her later teenage years and early twenties in Cumberland in the care of a Quaker, Robert Wilson, one of the founders of the Keswick Convention.[28] In 1886 and 1887 Amy

---

25. Tucker, 'Biography as Missiology', p. 434.
26. Jeyakumar, 'Amy Carmichael of Dohnavur 1867-1951', p. 5, notes that Amy had four brothers and two sisters.
27. Ibid., p. 6, Jeyakumar notes that Amy went to school there at least until 1883.
28. The Keswick Convention is a movement founded in 1875 to promote 'Scriptural holiness'. Keswick conventions can still be found in England and in countries that were formerly part of the British empire, e.g. Kolkata, where there is an evangelical-style missionary presence. See John Pollock, *The Keswick Story: The Authorized History of the Keswick Convention* (London: Hodder & Stoughton, 1964), and Barabas, *So Great Salvation*. There is a brief discussion of the Keswick movement in Chapter 2 of the present work. Stephen Neill's parents were also

attended Keswick conventions in Glasgow and Belfast. Jeyakumar says that these experiences 'intensified her thirst for winning persons to Christ'.[29] In 1892 she was sent out as the first Keswick missionary to Japan. She served there only briefly and decided to return to England on grounds of ill health. On her return trip, she stayed over in Ceylon, feeling she was able to work again. This lasted only a few months and she returned home.

In 1895 Carmichael went as a missionary to Bangalore, sponsored jointly by the Keswick Mission Committee and the Church of England Zenana Missionary Society (CEZMS).[30] It was while in the nearby hills of Ootacamund or 'Ooty' (as it was known) that Carmichael met Walker of Tinnevelly. He convinced her to come to Tinnevelly to learn Tamil from him in December 1896, the same year that Tinnevelly had become a full-blown diocese with a bishop. Amy moved to Pannaivilai and joined an evangelistic 'Itinerant Women's Band' about that time, as by then she could speak Tamil. She spent time in Dohnavur in 1900, intending only to stay for a few months to assist Walker and his wife in the teaching of Indian divinity students.

While at Dohnavur, Carmichael discovered the widespread practice of temple prostitution. Children, primarily girls, would be 'dedicated to the gods' by their families, i.e. sold to the temples, if they were unwanted, or the family needed extra money and fewer mouths to feed. The temple children would then be forced into prostitution to earn money for the priests. She began rescuing the young girls and this became her life's work. Her biographer Elisabeth Elliot writes, 'The overwhelming desire to save the children became a fire in her bones.'[31] In 1901 Carmichael began this ministry, with four abandoned children in her care.[32]

---

        influenced by the Keswick movement.
29.   Jeyakumar, 'Amy Carmichael of Dohnavur 1867-1951', p. 6.
30.   Regarding the CEZMS, Jocelyn Murray writes, 'The *zenana* was the curtain behind which the high-caste and high-status Indian women were secluded, and by extension enclosure for all women. *Zenana* missions worked within the social system with regard to women, providing home education and developing concern for women's issues from within that environment and using these as evangelistic opportunities to influence women, to the extent that this was possible without compromising the trust that permitted entry to the *zenana*.' Murray, 'The Role of Women in the CMS, 1799-1917,' in *The Church Mission Society and World Christianity, 1799-1999*, ed. by Kevin Ward and Brian Stanley (Grand Rapids, MI: Eerdmans, 2000). Jeyakumar, 'Amy Carmichael of Dohnavur 1867-1951', p. 70, notes that Carmichael was sponsored by the CEZMS until 1925.
31.   Elliot, *A Chance to Die*, p. 171.
32.   Ibid., p. 174; Houghton, *Amy Carmichael of Dohnavur*, p. 127. These two sources are openly hagiographical. They both describe the beginning of Carmichael's ministry as the triumphant moment when Carmichael begins to save the sexually

On 1 March 1904 Carmichael's work at Dohnavur began to expand. On that day Carmichael accepted a baby into her compound that had been rescued from the Hindu temple by a local Indian pastor. Another baby followed shortly thereafter. 'Soon there were fifteen Dohnavur babies there', writes Elliot.[33] Disaster struck in 1907 when Amy retired to the mountains of Ooty for a period of time. During her absence, ten of the babies contracted 'a particularly virile kind of dysentery' and died.[34] Nevertheless, in spite of overcrowding in the compound, and diseases related to overcrowding, the babies continued to arrive at Dohnavur. Amy needed help. Various missionaries came her way, but her standards were very high:

> Usually they had to be returned . . . [because] not one person did she want who was not *meant* for them. Two Indian teachers came who seemed to be the answer to prayer. Both foundered on the rock of truth and had to be sent back. . . . And so the parting of the ways began. Amy Carmichael was marching to a different drummer. There was no getting around that fact. . . . She had had a vision of holy living. She would not deviate from that no matter how well-established, rational, and practical the ways of older missions seemed to be.[35]

Carmichael's somewhat secretive, puritanical approach to her mission began to garner enemies. Elliot records, 'There arose during the early years of the Dohnavur work a fairly strong, "Get-Amy-Carmichael-out-of-India" movement among missionaries and Indian Christians.'[36] Amy's stern approach was conspicuous when she disciplined the children for sinning. Elliot records:

> Love, therefore, requires self-discipline, self-denial, and courage. It took all of those for Amy to use a cane or a leather strap on a child's wrists. Like her own mother, she expected the child to hold out her

---

exploited children from a life of misery and spiritual hopelessness.
33. Elliot, *A Chance to Die*, pp. 182-88; Houghton, *Amy Carmichael of Dohnavur*, pp. 142-43.
34. Elliot, *A Chance to Die*, p. 195; Houghton, *Amy Carmichael of Dohnavur*, pp. 161-62. Both Elliot and Houghton confirm that ten babies died during the dysentery outbreak of 1907.
35. Elliot, *A Chance to Die*, p. 198.
36. Ibid. Interestingly, this is not recorded in Houghton, nor is it the sort of thing that he *would* have recorded. This reluctance to explain perceptions of Carmichael that were unfavourable are probably one of the reasons why Houghton's biography is reprinted often and sold at Dohnavur. The Elliot biography, as noted earlier, does not meet the approval of the Dohnavur nuns.

3. Amy Carmichael and Neill's Early Years in South India: 1924-28

arm without flinching. Often the spanking was followed by a kiss and a piece of candy. Amy took the responsibility of administering these punishments herself. . . . She, after all, was the mother.[37]

Elliot continues:

> Other punishments were more imaginative. A child who lied might have quinine put on her tongue or a sign that said LIE hung round her neck for half a day. One little girl who lied habitually had her mouth inked and was kept out of school for a day or so. After the second or third time she was taken to Amma's room. 'I was shaking. She sent me to the bathroom for the strap, took me on her lap in front of a mirror, and read to me from Isaiah 53 – "He was wounded for our transgressions, he was bruised for our iniquities. . . . All we like sheep have gone astray; we have turned every one to his own way and the Lord hath laid on him the iniquity of us all." Then she beat her own arm instead of mine and explained salvation to me.'[38]

Amma was also known to tie girls' pigtails together when they quarrelled.[39] She was criticised for making young teenagers in the mission to take care of the babies.[40]

In 1912 Carmichael's two mentors died, Mrs Hopwood from Ooty,[41] with whom she stayed each summer, and her beloved Walker

---

37. Ibid., p. 213.
38. Ibid. It is important to point out that Houghton records nothing of this nature. Nevertheless, Elliot's descriptions of Carmichael's behaviour are never frowned upon or even considered awkward. Carmichael is certainly beyond suspicion to Elliot. For example, Elliot claims in the first sentence in the book, p. 15, 'To Amy Carmichael, I owe what C.S. Lewis said he owed to George MacDonald: as great a debt as one can owe another.'
39. Elliot, *A Chance to Die*, p. 213.
40. Ibid., p. 215.
41. Malcolm Muggeridge knew the Hopwoods and became close friends with Miss Hopwood. See *Chronicles of Wasted Time – Number 1: The Green Stick*, pp. 122, 125. See also Ian Hunter, *Malcolm Muggeridge: A Life* (Nashville, TN: Thomas Nelson, 1980), pp. 46, 54. Stephen Neill's sister Isabel lived with Miss Hopwood, the daughter of Mrs Hopwood. Amy Carmichael spent many summers at Ooty with the Hopwood family. See Houghton, *Amy Carmichael of Dohnavur*, pp. 105, 174. Stephen Neill knew the Hopwood family as well. See Neill, *God's Apprentice*, pp. 94-95, 202. Neill points out, p. 95, 'Like many elderly women, she had a penchant for young men; I was fortunate in enjoying her favour; but undoubtedly her favourite was Malcolm Muggeridge.'

of Tinnevelly, her 'spiritual father'. Amy was forever grateful that he had recruited her to Dohnavur.[42] In addition, in July 1913 Carmichael received word that her mother had died. She was very upset but had to continue to minister to the, by now, 140 children in the compound. She was more distraught by Walker's death, however. She wrote a biography of him in 1916 entitled *This One Thing: The Story of Walker of Tinnevelly*. Carmichael was astonished upon seeing a copy of the published version:

> When her biography of Walker was published, a blurb on the dust jacket – praise she was sure she did not deserve – made her 'too ashamed to take any pleasure in the book. O my God, I am ashamed before Thee.' The same motive of self-effacement must have been at least part of what inspired the periodic binges of 'covering her tracks' by destroying diaries, a habit which creates tantalizing gaps in the story.[43]

Until 14 January 1918, Carmichael's work at Dohnavur had been almost exclusively with girls. On that day, the first boy arrived.[44] It was the boys' ministry that brought Stephen Neill to the Carmichael compound.

To this day Dohnavur is functional and successful. The compound has expanded and now supports many ministries: a large orphans' home, a hospital,[45] a home for handicapped children, a fibre-work cottage industry pavilion, a co-ed English-medium boarding school, a publishing firm, a nunnery called 'Sisters of the Common Life',[46] as well as other, smaller

---

42. Elliot, *A Chance to Die*, pp. 219-23; Houghton, *Amy Carmichael of Dohnavur*, p. 97. Elliot describes Carmichael as being irritable and abrupt towards the people who tried to console her over the death of Walker. Houghton, however, barely mentions the death of Walker, preferring to point out that Carmichael, while shocked by the suddenness of his death, was mainly concerned with his widow who was in England at the time. Certainly, I think it seems likely that Carmichael struggled significantly with Walker's death, as four years later she published his biography.
43. Elliot, *A Chance to Die*, p. 235; Houghton, *Amy Carmichael of Dohnavur*, pp. 198-99. On Carmichael's tendency to tear up her diaries, see Houghton, *Amy Carmichael of Dohnavur*, p. 197.
44. Elliot, *A Chance to Die*, p. 246; Houghton, *Amy Carmichael of Dohnavur*, p. 219.
45. According to the Dohnavur Fellowship official brochure, the hospital assists 60,000 out-patients per year and 1,800 in-patients per year. It contains a dental clinic that assists 9,000 patients per year. It has a clinic for leprosy patients. 'Dohnavur Fellowship' brochure.
46. The nuns run the entire Fellowship today.

ministries.[47] Carmichael's legacy continues, notably through her writings. She produced about 35 books during her life and some of them sold extremely well. Many are still in print.

Opinions of Amy Carmichael vary. On the one hand, she was described by the missionary Sherwood Eddy as 'the most Christlike character I ever met.' On the other hand, she was noticeably autocratic.[48] By far the more common is the laudatory perspective of Carmichael.[49] Tucker writes:

> Elliot uses the terms *purity* and *superiority* in reference to Amy Carmichael – terms that one could easily imagine would have corresponded with Carmichael's own image of herself. . . . Carmichael found few missionaries who met her standards of separation from the world. . . . [Carmichael once wrote] 'O to be delivered from half-hearted missionaries! Don't come if you mean to turn aside for anything – for the "claims of society". . . . Don't come if you haven't made up your mind to live for *one thing* – the winning of souls.'[50]

Carmichael was the ruler of her fiefdom and went to extremes to keep 'worldly' ideas out of her compound by being distrustful of others. At Dohnavur she had created a group perspective that was completely lacking in self-criticism. For example, on one occasion she ran over a missionary while riding on her horse. She reflected on the incident, 'I did not mean to, he wouldn't get out of the way and one can't stop short in mid-gallop.'[51]

While the enormous amount of charity that poured forth from the Fellowship cannot be denied, the historian cannot help but to be perplexed

---

47. 'Dohnavur Fellowship' brochure. Jeyakumar, 'Amy Carmichael of Dohnavur 1867-1951', writes that the legal formation of Dohnavur Fellowship did not occur until 1926 and it did not become officially registered in India until 1927.
48. Tucker, 'Biography as Missiology', p. 431.
49. Ibid., p. 434, Tucker writes, 'her biographers have elevated her to super-sainthood'. There are several popular, 'devotional' biographies of Amy Carmichael, such as those by Lois Dick (1984), Sam Wellman (1998), Janet and Jeff Benge (1998) and Ruth Graham Bell (2000), but only Houghton's and Elliot's are historically useful, as they had the official archives at their disposal.
50. Tucker, 'Biography as Missiology', p. 435. The author agrees with Tucker's assessment that there is a 'wall of privacy'. Dohnavur is not open to sharing the archives at all. There is a strong reluctance among the administrators to sharing any sort of historical information other than laudatory stories. Historical research, it seems, causes discomfort among the nuns at Dohnavur. As the author was leaving the compound, the nuns continued to point out that Carmichael was a 'saint' and any attempt to make her 'human' was wrong.
51. Ibid., p. 435.

by the profoundly sheltered life Carmichael created at Dohnavur. Elliot speculated that these tendencies came from Carmichael's own sheltered childhood:

> There is some question as to whether the most elementary facts of life had ever been explained to Amy Carmichael. . . . A missionary who worked with her many years later insisted that Amy not only did not then know the truth about sex, but never learned. . . . It is clear enough that her Victorian mind refused to admit thoughts which were so unpleasant and certainly unnecessary.[52]

Carmichael refused to utter the word 'leg' due to its salaciousness. Rather, she referred to it as 'that unspeakable limb'.[53] An Indian scholar has pointed out that girls raised in the Dohnavur Fellowship are often criticised for being overly attached to the mission; they seem unable to adjust once they reach adulthood and leave the compound. He noted that they are always very rigid in their view of celibacy, as 'Amma discouraged "her girls" to get married'.[54]

Carmichael also had a rigid view of missionary work. She did not allow the missionaries to take leave; she never took a furlough during her 55 years of service. According to Elliot, the criticisms of Carmichael were at some points baleful: 'She was a dictator, she opposed marriage, her Indian girls worshipped her.'[55] The most prominent theme in her diary is self-sacrifice. She wrote, 'My Joy: To do Thy will, O God. . . . Teach us to serve . . . to give and not to count the cost . . . to toil and not to seek for rest . . . to labour and not to ask for any reward.'[56]

It was into this context that Stephen Neill arrived in December 1924. His initiation to Dohnavur was a wet one. He wrote: '[We] arrived in the time of the south-east monsoon, when the greater part of the year's rain falls in six weeks or less.'[57] Nevertheless, Neill immediately fell in love with the area:

> At early dawn my eyes awoke to the splendid panorama of the Western Ghats, which at that point rise abruptly from the plains to about six thousand feet, clothed to their summits in everlasting

---

52. Elliot, *A Chance to Die*, pp. 270, 297.
53. Tucker, 'Biography as Missiology', pp. 435-436.
54. Jeyakumar, 'Amy Carmichael of Dohnavur 1867-1951', p. 11.
55. Elliot, *A Chance to Die*, p. 201.
56. Ibid., p. 242.
57. Ibid., p. 81.

3. Amy Carmichael and Neill's Early Years in South India: 1924-28

forest. Away to the left was the nose of Comorin, the great cliff in which the mountains finally break down to the plain, and which from the beginning of time has been a great landmark for sailors making the somewhat perilous voyage round the tip of India. In twenty years I never grew weary of the sight of these mountains. Hidden away among them were glens and valleys of unbelievable beauty; and in the monsoon season the sun used to go down behind them in rivers of molten gold.[58]

At the time of Neill's arrival, Amy Carmichael was 57 years old and had already led Dohnavur for about 23 years.

It is curious that in his autobiography Stephen Neill failed to acknowledge his brief period of time at Dohnavur. Among the few historians who have studied Neill's life seriously, there is a consensus that Neill deliberately airbrushed this information out of his life story. He only refers to 'the remote village which was to be my first Indian home'.[59] Eleanor Jackson wrote, 'It is striking that in a MS of over one thousand pages, Neill makes no mention of Amy Carmichael.'[60]

Neill's service at Dohnavur is well-established, however. The primary sources show Neill lived there and that he did not get on well with Carmichael. In other places Neill did mention his residence at Dohnavur. For example, Neill's first published work, *How Readest Thou? A Simple Introduction to the New Testament* shows he was there. It was published in November 1925.[61] The Preface to that book holds the answer:

> As I write, I can look out over the plain of Tinnevelly as far as the sea; in the foreground of the picture is the tower of a Hindu temple. I would not press any of my views in matters of scholarship and criticism; but I have made no attempt to conceal my own acceptance of the historic faith of the Church, and of the revelation of God in Jesus Christ our Lord. (S.N. Dohnavur, S. India, St Mark's Day, 1925.)[62]

---

58. Neill, *God's Apprentice*, p. 80.
59. Ibid.
60. Jackson, 'The Continuing Legacy of Stephen Neill', pp. 77-78.
61. Stephen Neill, *How Readest Thou? A Simple Introduction to the New Testament* (London: Student Christian Movement, 1925). The cover of this book points out Neill's status as a 'Fellow of Trinity College, Cambridge'. The book is dedicated to A. Nairne and E.A. Willis and begins with a quotation by Brooke Foss Westcott.
62. Something very interesting occurs in this Preface. The author has a copy of the first edition of this book and the portion that says Dohnavur etc., has been

A second primary source establishing Neill's time at Dohnavur is a letter in the CMS archives at Birmingham, dated 7 January 1926. This letter, to Neill from CMS Secretary E.F.E. Wigram, states, 'I have just heard that you are not likely to remain much longer at Dohnavur.' The letter demonstrates not only that Neill was at Dohnavur but that he was also being lured to work in the CMS.

Another source that demonstrates Neill's time at Dohnavur is the Elliot biography of Carmichael. Although it is a secondary source, it is highly significant. Elliot discusses the Neills' residence in Dohnavur at length in one section.[63] She was the last person on the 'outside' who was able to consult the Dohnavur archives and that was in 1987. Another source that substantiates Neill's time in Dohnavur came from the mission's administrators. In an interview with the author, they verified that Neill spent his first year of missionary work there. The interview transcript reads: 'Neill came here immediately after his Cambridge time. He was here for a year and a half. He was a teacher to the DF boys and he taught David's father geography and history. Neill came as a missionary staff worker.'[64] These sources prove that Neill definitely spent time in the Dohnavur compound. However, why did Neill go to Dohnavur? The answer is simple: his parents were there. Several sources mention this.[65]

---

covered up with a sticker. The sticker can be pulled back, even seen through, but it would be highly interesting to find out if this is the case for all first editions to the book. It just might demonstrate Neill's decision to block this information out of the book right after it was published, yet prior to its distribution.

63. Elliot, *A Chance to Die*, pp. 267-70, 275-76.
64. Miss Nesaruthina Carunia (Former President of the Dohnavur Fellowship, 1989-2001; associated with Dohnavur since 1932) and Mr David Rajamanian (Secretary of the Dohnavur Fellowship since 1986; associated with Dohnavur since 1933; his father was the Secretary of the Dohnavur Fellowship for a few years and lived there during the same time as Neill), interviews by author, transcribed and approved by interviewees, Palayamkottai, 17 February 2003.
65. See Pierard, 'Stephen Neill', p. 534. He writes, 'After finishing his studies in 1924, Neill decided to delay assuming his Trinity College fellowship and go with his parents and sister to South India to take up the life of a missionary. Reaching India in late 1924, they settled in the Tirunelveli (known to Europeans as Tinnevelly) region. Although he later claimed he had gone out under the CMS, in fact he did not join this group until four years later. The Neill family went to Dohnavur and resided in the compound of the celebrated Amy Carmichael.' See also Jackson, 'The Continuing Legacy of Stephen Neill', pp. 77-78: 'Neill in fact joined his parents and one of his sisters in Dohnavur but was forced to leave the following summer after a number of clashes with Amy Carmichael.' Ruth Tucker goes into some detail, drawing from the Elliot biography in her article, 'Biography as Missiology'. Jocelyn Murray mentions Neill joining his parents at

3. Amy Carmichael and Neill's Early Years in South India: 1924-28

An article in *The Times*, dated 29 September 1924,[66] places the Neills in India: 'Rev. C. Neill, vicar of Baddow, Chelmsford, is leaving to take up work as a missionary in India. He was presented with a wallet of bank notes by his parishioners.'

Elliot describes the many different people who came and went in the Dohnavur compound.[67] Many were asked to leave, many left because of illness and many left because the very unglamorous work could become overwhelming. Elliot records:

> Probably no recruits were more promising than a family of four who arrived in 1924 – the parents, both of them physicians, along with their daughter and their son, a twenty-four-year-old Cambridge graduate. . . . With a fellowship from Trinity College which gave him every prospect for a brilliant career in the academic field, he opted for missionary work – to the astonishment of at least one of his classmates, Malcolm Muggeridge.[68] The presence of the Neills in 'little Dohnavur' lent a new respectability in the eyes of some who thought of it as an eccentric backwater. There must be more than met the eye if it attracted such distinguished people as the Neills.[69]

      Dohnavur in a personal letter to Eleanor Jackson, dated 21 June 1992. This letter is in Eleanor Jackson's personal collection.

66. *The Times*, 29 September 1924, p. 15.
67. Houghton, *Amy Carmichael of Dohnavur*, p. 257, agreed: 'The nineteen-twenties were years of rapid expansion . . . the Light that shone in Dohnavur . . . and was attracting men and women to it.'
68. Neill mentioned Muggeridge in his autobiography, although in a different context. He pointed out that he knew Muggeridge while at Cambridge and he also mentioned that Muggeridge, too, served as a missionary to India for three years, although, 'Even then his Christian faith was somewhat patchy.' See *God's Apprentice*, p. 95. Like Neill, Muggeridge worked at Union Christian College, in Alwaye (now Aluva), South India. Muggeridge recounted his years in India in his autobiography, *Chronicles of Wasted Time – Number 1: The Green Stick*, Chapter 3, 'Twilight of Empire', pp. 92-130. Muggeridge does not mention Neill in his autobiography. For more on Muggeridge's time in India, see Hunter's biography, *Malcolm Muggeridge: A Life*, Chapter 3, 'India', pp. 37-55. On 17 April 2004 the author received a letter from Keith Call, archivist at Wheaton College, where many of Muggeridge's papers are located. The brief letter reads, 'In a transcribed 2/12/25 photocopied letter to Vidler, MM writes that he is "going to stay with Stephen Neill (?) who was a friend of mine at Cambridge (I seem to remember that you knew him too) who's in Tinnivally (?) a place about two days' journey from here."' Thus. it can be established that Neill and Muggeridge were in contact in South India.
69. Elliot, *A Chance to Die*, p. 267.

The earliest biography of Carmichael, written in 1953 by Frank Houghton, records this coming of the Neills as a great relief to the compound.[70]

It is very strange that Neill wanted the readers of his autobiography to think that he was alone during his first year of mission work. It is true that his parents left Dohnavur before he did but he seems to disguise the fact that he went to Dohnavur because his parents were already there. Whatever the case, 'It was a bad mix. Within six months the senior Neills left.'[71]

A curious episode occurs in Neill's autobiography at this point. While at Dohnavur, Neill decided to take a trip to Suviseshapuram, 'one of the old classic stations of the CMS, where Bishop Sargent had lived for a number of years'.[72] At first reading, it appears Neill was simply going to 'the village of the good news' (English translation) as sort of a tourist opportunity. However, in the autobiography it becomes clear that Neill was more plugged in to this community at Suviseshapuram than he leads on, indicating that his stay was more than just a brief tourist experience. In the middle of describing the visit, Neill mentions, 'It happened that my parents were staying in Suviseshapuram . . .'[73] Thus, it is very likely that the Neills left Dohnavur for Suviseshapuram shortly after 30 May 1925, when they had a major falling out with Carmichael. Elliot records Carmichael's journal entry on that night, 'May 30, 1925, the most painful night of my life.'[74]

Upon arrival at Dohnavur, Neill's first goal was to learn the ancient language of Tamil. At that time Indians involved in the missionary institutions spoke a good amount of English, as many of those institutions – especially the schools – were often English-medium. However, Neill responded:

> But this was not the way in which I had been brought up. In our family it is taken for granted that wherever you are you learn the language of the people. . . . I made up my mind that I would learn Tamil or die. I nearly did both, but by a narrow margin both I and the Tamil survived."[75]

---

70. Houghton, *Amy Carmichael of Dohnavur*, pp. 270-71.
71. Elliot, *A Chance to Die*, p. 268.
72. Neill, *God's Apprentice*, p. 89. Suviseshapuram is about 50 km from Dohnavur.
73. Ibid., p. 94.
74. Elliot, *A Chance to Die*, p. 269. Jocelyn Murray concurs. In a letter she records that it was probably May 1925 when the senior Neills left Dohnavur for Suviseshapuram. Murray to Eleanor Jackson, 21 June 1992, Eleanor Jackson's personal collection. Carunia and Rajamanian testify to this, 'Father Charles Neill being here is confirmed. Suviseshapuram, where Dr. Charles Neill worked, is about 50 km from Dohnavur. The visit [to Dohnavur] lasted six months.' Interviews by author.
75. Neill, *God's Apprentice*, p. 87.

Neill's teacher was a high-caste man; and he also relied on a Tamil grammar book written by G.U. Pope. Neill studied with his teacher twice each day, from 7.30-9 a.m. and from 3-4.30 p.m., at the cost of sixpence an hour.[76] Neill also interacted with people, giving him the ability to practice. Six months later, he was speaking Tamil. Elliot speculates that the flashing brilliance of Neill's intellect may have proven a threat to Carmichael: 'This threat was exacerbated by a (perhaps unwitting) feeling of rivalry, not only with the dashing father but with the scintillating son, who far outdistanced all other struggling students by learning Tamil in six months.'[77]

Neill claims that he preached his first Tamil sermon in church, 'exactly nine months after my arrival in the country. . . . My text was Galatians 5:22, and I kept going for twenty minutes.'[78]

Neill's primary ministry was working with the boys. Dohnavur had a long history of working with girls. The boys' work actually did not begin until 14 January 1918, when a woman turned up in the grounds of Dohnavur with a baby boy.[79] In June a second boy arrived. By 1926 the number of boys had increased to 80. The first male worker to come and take supervision of the boys is not named, although we know he arrived in 1922. Houghton writes, 'He was a true gift of God, and did valuable work in many directions, but he would have been the first to admit that he lacked the special qualities that were needed for leadership on the boys' side.'[80] The precise date of this unnamed man's departure is not mentioned but it is clear that Stephen Neill took over that work when he arrived in 1924.

On one occasion in October 1925 Neill took a trip to visit his parents in Suviseshapuram. He was playing hockey with some boys in the nearby town of Ittamoti and injured his shin bone.[81] The injury was quite severe, as Neill's father decided that Stephen should take a train to Ooty, in the Nilgiri Hills, to stay with Edith Hopwood, a missionary to the Muslims in the area. (The connection with Hopwood would strengthen three years later when Isabel, Stephen's sister, began working with her.[82]) Neill's father

---

76. Ibid., p. 88.
77. Elliot, *A Chance to Die*, p. 268.
78. Neill, *God's Apprentice*, p. 93. It is a well-known fact among the Tinnevelly Christians that Stephen Neill learned Tamil extraordinarily quickly. It was also well-known that he could speak Tamil without an accent. The author has a tape of one of Neill's Tamil sermons and his fluency is obvious.
79. This episode is recorded in Chapter 24 of Houghton's biography, *Amy Carmichael of Dohnavur*.
80. Ibid., p. 222.
81. Neill, *God's Apprentice*, p. 94.
82. Of Isabel, Neill remarked, 'My sister Isabel can speak three Indian languages (though

advised him to go to Ooty because he had come down with a serious fever and he felt he would do better in the higher, cooler climate. In addition, Stephen could rest better if he were away from his work.

In addition to teaching Bible lessons and attending all of the various faith meetings, Neill was engaged in the task of teaching the boys the regular school curriculum. David Rajamanian mentions that Neill taught geography and history. It is in this context that an episode occurred during a lesson on Indian geography. Neill mentioned a particular channel of the Ganges called the Hooghly. David Rajamanian's father, named Rajappan, was in the class and began to laugh at the word 'Hooghly'. Neill became angry and caned Rajappan on the hand.[83] This would not be the last time Neill would cane a student.

The precise moment when Neill and Carmichael began to come into conflict is unknown. The earliest evidence comes from Elisabeth Elliot's work in the Carmichael archives. However, Elliot so rarely uses documentation in her work that one is not always precisely sure how she came by the information – whether from Carmichael's diary, from other primary sources at Dohnavur, from interviews at Dohnavur in the 1980s or from other Tinnevelly Christians.[84] For example, Elliot writes, 'One contemporary of Amy's claimed that the Neills came with the idea of "doing a take-over".'[85] It is never mentioned who this contemporary could be. In another place in her book, she quotes Stephen Neill as saying, 'I gave my whole soul to Dohnavur.'[86] There is no indication as to the source of this quotation.

---

      she knows well that there are things about her Tamil that I deplore).' Neill, *God's Apprentice*, p. 87. Isabel began working in the Ooty-Coonoor area in 1928. See Herbert E. Hoefer, ed., *Debate on Mission* (Madras: Gurukul Lutheran Theological College, 1979), p. xviii. To this volume Isabel contributed an article entitled, 'My Experience with Non-Baptized Believers in Christ'. Neill remained close to Isabel throughout his entire life even purchasing two properties with her near Coonoor in the hills of South India later in life. See Neill, *God's Apprentice*, p. 331.

83. Carunia and Rajamanian, interviews by author. While in South India the author heard many stories similar to this one that demonstrate Stephen Neill's stern approach to discipline.
84. The author attempted to contact Elisabeth Elliot on two occasions and both times was only able to talk to her husband who said that Elisabeth was not able to assist in any way. Nevertheless, the information that comes out of the archives and into Elliot's book is immense. Without Elliot's work, the Neill episode would be virtually unknown. It appears certain that Elliot interviewed Stephen Neill before his death in 1984 to obtain some of these statements. She quotes him often regarding these events.
85. Elliot, *A Chance to Die*, p. 267.
86. Ibid.

3. Amy Carmichael and Neill's Early Years in South India: 1924-28

According to Elliot, the Neill family caused real trouble at Dohnavur. One observer claimed that Dr Charles Neill 'made a hit with the girls'.[87] Amy was upset that the Neills were compromising her standards of strict separation between the sexes. According to two administrators of Dohnavur, Stephen followed in his father's footsteps in this regard. 'He didn't realise that in Indian culture boys and girls had to be brought up separately. Amy had to be careful not to offend the surrounding Indian people in the villages. Even today they are separated.'[88] Carmichael even proposed that Neill take a few of the boys elsewhere and 'bring them up outside of DF; but he refused the offer'.[89] Thus, part of the tension was due to differences in opinion over how boys should be brought up.

Things only got worse. It is very likely that Neill's parents left Dohnavur shortly after 30 May 1925. Already by 21 May Carmichael's diary points to her 'anxieties' regarding the Neill family. She wrote, 'A dreadful time of distress never such known here before. I am beginning to sink. Lord save me.'[90] The night of 30 May would prove particularly painful for Carmichael – she characterised it, 'The most painful night of my life.'[91] Likely, this was the moment when it was decided that the senior Neills would have to leave.

In July, there was another incident that occurred at a prayer meeting when someone began to pray for an end to the present friction at the compound.[92] Amy was shocked and disheartened. By August, things must have been excruciating for Carmichael as she wrote to a close friend, 'I do trust no one will ever know how difficult things are now – not even you dear.'[93] It was on the night of 28 November that Carmichael wrote in her diary, 'One of the very saddest nights of my life.'[94] On 29 November 1925, 'the severance took place'.[95] This is in all probability the moment

---

87. Ibid., p. 268.
88. Carunia and Rajamanian, interviews by author.
89. Ibid.
90. Houghton, *Amy Carmichael of Dohnavur*, p. 260; Elliot, *A Chance to Die*, p. 268. According to Elliot, p. 268, Neill seemed to exacerbate the tensions between them when he referred to her informants as 'spies'. Houghton, p. 260, presents a much more dignified description of the whole situation, which he refers to as 'the severance'. In Houghton's version, Carmichael remained above the fray, constantly praying through her distress. Elliot presents a more volatile situation, with descriptions such as, p. 268, 'Amy was in a state of anguish over Stephen.' Elliot presents a much more troubled Carmichael than Houghton does.
91. Houghton, *Amy Carmichael of Dohnavur*, p. 260; Elliot, *A Chance to Die*, p. 269.
92. Houghton, *Amy Carmichael of Dohnavur*, p. 260; Elliot, *A Chance to Die*, p. 269.
93. Elliot, *A Chance to Die*, p. 269. Houghton chose to leave this out of his record of the incident.
94. Houghton, *Amy Carmichael of Dohnavur*, p. 260; Elliot, *A Chance to Die*, p. 270.
95. Houghton, *Amy Carmichael of Dohnavur*, p. 260.

Stephen Neill was told he would soon have to leave. He would not completely disassociate himself from Dohnavur, however, until at least January 1926.[96]

What could possibly have happened to cause such restlessness and wounded feelings? There are a few things to consider here. First, Neill had just come out of Cambridge and may have exposed some of his liberal education while at Dohnavur. The Preface to his first book certainly indicates that this was an issue: 'With such deep matters as the possibility of revelation, the relation of the natural to the supernatural, the credibility of the Gospel narratives I have not attempted to deal here. . . . I would not press any of my views in matters of scholarship and criticism.'[97]

According to contemporary administrators at Dohnavur, Carunia and Rajamanian, Neill 'couldn't believe some of the miracles that the Lord Jesus did'.[98] Elliot's interviews in the 1980s turned up similar information. She writes:

> No European or Indian worker who was there at the time seemed to know the exact nature of the problem. One suggested that his writings were perhaps not always in theological harmony with her beliefs, but it seems unlikely that Neill wrote much in Dohnavur. He categorically stated that theology had nothing to do with his dismissal, but declined to mention any other reason.[99]

Frank Houghton speculates that this may have been what caused the Dohnavur Fellowship to establish its 'Principles' in 1926, shortly after these experiences. Included among these Principles was that the Old and New Testaments are divinely inspired and historically reliable.[100]

---

96. CMS Secretary E.F.E. Wigram to Neill, 7 January 1926, CMS/G2 I10/L1, CMS Archives, University of Birmingham: 'My dear Neill . . . I do not think that I am betraying Miss Bradshaw's confidence in mentioning that it is from her that I have just heard that you are not likely to remain much longer at Dohnavur, but, as I understand, have still every intention of serving India at least for some time to come. I want, therefore, at once to get in touch with you to see whether it may not be possible for you to throw in your lot with the CMS and come to the rescue in one or other of our great fields of opportunity.'
97. Neill, *How Readest Thou?*, pp. 5-6.
98. Carunia and Rajamanian, interviews by author.
99. Elliot, *A Chance to Die*, pp. 269-270.
100. Houghton, *Amy Carmichael of Dohnavur*, p. 270. Elliot goes further here, *A Chance to Die*, p. 269. She provides a fascinating paragraph that just might illuminate the incident, 'Stephen Neill was, according to one laconic colleague, "temperamentally unsuited to the situation." Dohnavur was a long way from Cambridge. Working under Amy Carmichael was at best difficult for him (he

3. Amy Carmichael and Neill's Early Years in South India: 1924-28

Another real possibility for Neill's dismissal was that he was indeed 'temperamentally unsuited to the situation', words attributed to one of his colleagues.[101] Elliot describes an incident that reinforces this: 'Neill was known to have given way to several violent explosions of temper during which he beat some of Amma's [Carmichael's] boys, yet in his opinion some of the punishments customarily used in Dohnavur, which he did not name, were "rather severe".'[102]

This was not out of character for Neill. Using the cane as a form of discipline was something he had learned at Dean Close School and he utilised it throughout his life when he thought someone needed to be corrected.

Nearly a year later, Carmichael was still wounded from the encounter with Stephen. She wrote to a friend, 'I long over him still, miss him and want him and long to be one in affection. The stab is not even beginning to skin over. It's just red raw.'[103] One journal entry reads, 'Poor, poor S., it was his spoiling mother and the silly Christian public chiefly. My heart is all one ache for him.'[104] Houghton wrote that, while 'Satan may have gained a temporary advantage' in Neill, Carmichael prayed for him to the very end of her life.[105]

Neill and Carmichael seem to have had temperaments destined to clash. At one point, when Neill felt he could not handle any more, he wrote a letter of resignation, although he threw it away after his mother convinced him that the boys he was working with would be devastated.[106] Had it not been for his parents, he most certainly would have left Dohnavur earlier than he did. He records:

---

remembered his first meeting with her as "an impression of power"). Apart from her oracular mystique, she had been influenced, he believed, by strong Plymouth Brethren nonconformism, a bitter pill for an Anglican to swallow. She made veiled reference later to this time when "English worship services became impossible because – no, I must not embark on the reasons."' This quotation provides more evidence that Elliot probably did interview Neill during her research, unfortunately, she rarely provides any sort of documentation. Predictably, and immediately following the preceding paragraph in the biography, Elliot seemed to express her ideas as to whom was at fault in the matter, 'Neill was known to have given way to several violent explosions of temper during which he beat some of Amma's boys.' While this probably did occur, it is interesting where Elliot chose to place it in her narrative.

101. Elliot, *A Chance to Die*, p. 269. Again, the source is not disclosed.
102. Ibid. These are issues Houghton avoids altogether.
103. Ibid., p. 270. This statement shows vulnerability, something Houghton seems reluctant to reveal in Carmichael.
104. Ibid.
105. Houghton, *Amy Carmichael of Dohnavur*, p. 270. This is a typical explanation for Houghton.
106. Neill, *God's Apprentice*, p. 94.

> My parents were staying in Suviseshapuram and knew something of my troubles. My mother said to me, 'Are you quite sure that you are right to go? These young men love and trust you; you can understand them and they can understand you. They have given you their complete confidence. Are you sure that it would be right to leave them?'[107]

Although Neill's mother persuaded him to stay at that moment of crisis, it is clear that things never panned out between Neill and Carmichael. Years later, while reflecting on that tumultuous period at Dohnavur, Neill comments:

> Some of the experiences of my first year in India were so excessively painful that by January 1926 the darkness was complete. During that first year, fellow Christians had brought into my life such darkness and suffering that it took me many years to recover from the injuries, and the scars are still there. A year in England helped, but this time of trouble did not really clear itself up until 1933.[108]

One missions historian who knew Neill quite well remarked, "Whatever happened there hurt him so deeply that he could never mention it."[109]

Whether Neill and Carmichael ever patched things up is unclear. The records differ here. Elliot claims that years later he revisited the compound and, according to one who worked there at the time, 'Amma refused to see him.' However, another worker claimed that 'Amy spoke with him kindly.'[110] Whatever the case, Neill did come back for a visit once again in 1974, long after Carmichael's death. My interviewees told me this:

> In 1974 at the Azariah centenary he visited Dohnavur on a Saturday for one day. Miss Carunia went around with him. It is documented.[111] Miss Carunia walked with him. She didn't know him. She was staring at him, wondering why he left Dohnavur. They brought up the issue as to why he left, but then the issue was

---

107. Ibid.
108. Ibid., pp. 45, 93.
109. Jocelyn Murray to Eleanor Jackson, 21 June 1992, Eleanor Jackson's personal collection.
110. Elliot, *A Chance to Die*, p. 270.
111. This information is verified in the Guest Book. It reads, 'Arrival: August 24, 1974, 5:00 pm, Stephen Neill (2 Eaton Gate, London, SW1). Departure: August 25, 1974, 4:00 pm, to Palayamkottai.' Dohnavur Guest Book, Dohnavur Fellowship.

abruptly dropped. He did mention that he had spent time here, 'It has grown and it is beautifully built up.' He was very impressed with the House of Prayer. He was impressed by Dohnavur's expansion. He quietly prayed at the House of Prayer. Neill hugged Rajappan and was glad to see him.[112]

Carmichael's feelings apparently never did fully heal. Carunia and Rajamanian claim that, when Neill was bishop, she did not allow him to come and confirm candidates. Jackson writes that Carmichael 'severed her mission's connection with the Diocese of Tirunelveli when Neill was elected bishop in 1939'.[113] This might explain why, in 1947, Christians from the Dohnavur district, but outside the Carmichael compound, wrote to the CMS claiming that Carmichael 'pretended' herself as the rightful successor to Reverend Walker of Tinnevelly:

> As the pretender to succeed Walker, Miss Carmichael got in possession of the CMS Compound and its buildings. . . . Therefore, we request you, the Secretary of the Missionary Society that bore us and nourished us, to do all that you can possibly do to make the Dohnavur Fellowship hand over the CMS Compound and buildings back to the Dohnavur Congregation so that they may use it in tune with the holy aims of those early missionaries. . . . Whenever such a move is made for Justice, the [Dohnavur] Fellowship people create a counter move with the help of their paid Servants and mission agents who are under their influence.[114]

The author brought the matter up with the Dohnavur administrators and it was clearly a sensitive issue. The following statement was issued: 'Amy Carmichael bought the land with her private funds. She asked the CMS to hold the land for the time being until DF was registered as a charitable society. It was finally registered in 1927. All the property went back into her hands in 1927.'[115] In all probability, neither Carmichael nor Neill was able to put the events of 1925 out of mind.

---

112. Carunia and Rajamanian, interviews by author.
113. Jackson, 'The Continuing Legacy of Stephen Neill', pp. 77-78.
114. The People of Dohnavur to The Home Secretary, CMS, Touring the Tinnevelly Diocese, 1 February 1947, Tinnevelly Box 1, Special Collections, Bishop's College. According to the letter, Dohnavur covered at the time over 400 acres of land and the church was requesting ten acres to use to expand the school area.
115. Carunia and Rajamanian, interviews by author.

Neill had only been in India a year when his first crisis in the mission field occurred. These events troubled him severely and, in his words, he did not fully heal until 1933. What was at the root of all this conflict? Was it Neill's 'spoiling mother', as Carmichael put it? Was it his intellectual prowess? After all, he was a Fellow of Cambridge, he was already an author at the age of 25 and he had learned an extremely difficult language in a matter of months, far quicker than most. Perhaps it was his familiarity with New Testament criticism and modern scholarship that bred resentment at the compound. Furthermore, what about Neill's explosive temper? Carmichael probably found it disconcerting. The caning issue was probably another cause for concern and it surfaced again when he lost the bishopric. Overall, Neill's time at Dohnavur was a disaster. Both he and Carmichael acknowledged that the only solution was their separation.

An Itinerant Evangelist

In January 1926 Neill ended his year of service at the Dohnavur mission. His next Indian home was in Palamcottah (now Palayamkottai) – the mission headquarters for the Tinnevelly diocese.[116] He lived with a missionary named G.T. Selwyn, who would later become his successor to the bishopric of Tinnevelly diocese.[117] Selwyn was born in 1887 and educated at Corpus Christi College, Cambridge, receiving his MA in 1908. He arrived at Tinnevelly in 1912 as a CMS missionary.[118] In 1923 he was appointed to supervise both the CMS Training School and High School in Palamcottah.[119] During this time he assisted the bishop. In his autobiography, Neill described Selwyn, a man he knew well for many years:

> Selwyn was a remarkable man and a far better missionary than I ever had it in me to become. Shy, awkward, not intellectually gifted, a hesitating preacher, if he had stayed in England he would probably have ended up as the much-respected vicar of a country town. In India he grew in stature . . . and ended up as my successor in the

---

116. Palamcottah (Palayamkottai) is where the bishop of the Tinnevelly diocese has his residence. Today it is almost a twin of the nearby city of Tirunelveli, due to the expansion of both cities.
117. Neill, *God's Apprentice*, p. 99. See also M.J. Sargunam, *Bishop Selwyn of Tirunelveli: A Biography of the Rt Rev. George T. Selwyn, Faithful Missionary and Bishop of Tirunelveli, 1945-53* (London: Christian Literature Society, 1966).
118. George Muller, *The Tirunelveli Bishopric: A Centenary Survey* (Palayamkottai: Diocesan Offset Press, 1996), p. 71.
119. Ibid., p. 77. The Bishop Sargent Training School for Teachers was new and Selwyn was Principal.

bishopric. . . . Selwyn made himself an Indian to the Indians. . . . [H]e had taken into his house a remarkable group of high-caste converts, with whom he lived as an elder brother, sharing their lives, eating all meals with them . . . and completely adopting Indian ways. . . . The one drawback in this great achievement was that Selwyn had so far Indianised himself as to lose that slight distance which gives the missionary an objectivity such as the Indian Christian finds it hard to attain. . . . To live with such a man was an education in itself.[120]

Neill moved in with Selwyn and helped out in the high school and training school; thus beginning a long acquaintance. While Neill enjoyed teaching at the schools, he was becoming increasingly frustrated, for what he really wanted to do at the time was to be an evangelist in the villages, 'where I would be talking Tamil day and night, and have contact with Hindus more than with Christians'.[121] Neill's wish was granted when shortly thereafter he was appointed head of an evangelistic band, known as the Itinerancy. The job description, according to Neill was to tour 'from place to place to make the gospel known in areas where no Christians lived'.[122]

However, just before joining the evangelistic band, a grand opportunity came Neill's way in 1926 – one that would have been foolish to decline.[123] Dr Stanley Jones was in Palamcottah for a brief visit, conducting one of his mission campaigns.[124] Neill expressed – and was granted – his desire

---

120. Neill, *God's Apprentice*, pp. 99-100. According to Tirunelveli Christians today, Selwyn is remembered as by far the most Indianised of the white bishops.
121. Neill, *God's Apprentice*, p. 100. Neill recorded, p. 81, 'In my heart of hearts, I am a *pattikkatt'al*, a dweller in small villages; this India, more than any other India, is my home.'
122. Ibid., p. 100.
123. The year 1926 can be discovered by a careful reading of Neill, *God's Apprentice*, p. 101. See also p. 105 where Neill recorded that during his years in the Itinerancy he was not yet 26 years old.
124. Stanley Jones may have influenced Neill's later 'dialogical attitude' to non-Christians. Grafe writes, 'the dialogical attitude of thinkers like J.N. Farquhar and evangelists like Stanley Jones more and more won the day, at least in the "main line" Churches.' See Grafe, *History of Christianity in India*, p. 143. Jones became quite famous through his associations with Mahatma Gandhi. He wrote a famous biography of Gandhi, *Gandhi: A Portrayal of a Friend* (Nashville, TN: Abingdon, 1948), as well as his immensely popular book, *The Christ of the Indian Road* (London: Hodder & Stoughton, 1925), which was translated into more than 20 languages and sold more than 700,000 copies. See 'Jones, E. Stanley', *New 20th Century Encyclopedia of Religious Knowledge*, 2nd ed., ed. by J.D. Douglas (Grand Rapids, MI: Baker Book House, 1991) See also E. Stanley

to assist Jones for a month. Neill was spellbound by the famous American missionary who was then 40 years old and, according to Neill, 'at the height of his powers. . . . His fame as a lecturer had travelled everywhere.'[125] Neill's job description was 'to follow Dr. Jones round and to do everything that he did not want to do himself'.[126] Neill also was given the opportunity to speak in Tamil at some of the mission campaigns headed by Jones.

After a month of assisting Jones, Neill began his job as head of the Itinerancy in June 1926.[127] The Itinerancy hailed from an idea of Thomas Gajetan Ragland (1815-1858), a graduate of the University of Cambridge and then a tutor at Corpus Christi College. Ragland took up mission work India under the auspices of the CMS in the mid-1800s.[128] Ragland was especially concerned about the disparity that existed between the state of Christian missions in the north and south of Tinnevelly. The south had a flourishing Christian presence, while the north had no missionary and only two or three priests. Ragland envisaged the solution to this in the form of a band of evangelists who would pledge themselves to spreading the good word in the villages. The band would spend its time on the road, except during the rainy season, and visit each village in the diocese at least once per year. Careful notes and documentation were to be kept regarding every village and every Christian community. Ragland established the ministry but after his death in 1858 it began to lose some of its effectiveness. It continued to decline until by the time Neill came on the scene it was 'a somewhat rickety organisation'.[129]

Life in the Itinerancy was quite regimented. The group would go out into the countryside for periods of 20 days at a time. Neill recorded the precision with which they functioned.[130] Early prayers at 4.45 a.m. Departure at 5.00 a.m. Visit two villages and then home around 8.00 a.m. From 8.30 a.m. to noon the evangelists would bathe, breakfast, study and have personal time. At noon there was a session of instruction by Neill and then prayers. At 5.00 p.m. there began another round of visits to villages. They were back home and in bed by 9.00 p.m. Neill's chronic insomnia was apparent as he needed to nap in the afternoon just to get by.

Jones, *A Song of Ascents: A Spiritual Autobiography* (Nashville, TN: Abingdon Press, 1968).
125. Neill, *God's Apprentice*, p. 100-1.
126. Ibid., p. 101.
127. Neill, *God's Apprentice*, pp. 102-3; Muller, *The Tirunelveli Bishopric*, p. 54.
128. Thomas Ragland was one of Stephen Neill's heroes. He was a highly gifted missionary who died suddenly, crippling what was a promising itinerancy work. Neill writes admiringly of Ragland in *A History of Christianity in India 1707-1858* (Cambridge: Cambridge University Press, 1985), pp. 234–235.
129. Neill, *God's Apprentice*, p. 103.
130. Ibid.

3. Amy Carmichael and Neill's Early Years in South India: 1924-28   85

Neill remembered one major frustration he had during his time as the leader of the evangelistic band.[131] Some of the members of his band were 20 years older than him. Neill did not feel that he could protest against them when something was done against his judgement. However, on one occasion, his frustration grew to such a point that he felt he had to speak out. According to Neill, members of the band were advertising Christianity as a way towards material prosperity and improvement in caste status. Indeed, this could and did happen in South India, but Neill had reservations about using this as the primary tool to persuade a villager or a village community to convert. The elder missionaries often cited examples of individuals or communities who had improved their lot in life through conversion to Christianity, which often meant a new-found affiliation with the Europeans, as well as their many institutions. Neill was more comfortable preaching about having to bear your cross if you converted to Christianity. Neill emphasised that sooner or later persecution would come to Christian converts. He argued, 'Prosperity is the blessing of the Old Testament, and adversity of the New.' After much discussion, the disagreement was resolved. Neill records, 'in the end they had come to the conclusion that my view was correct and biblical'.[132]

The work of Neill's evangelistic band bore fruit. One of his converts actually spoke to me about Neill:

> I personally owe [much] to this great man of God . . . as he was the architect of my father's family in which I stand first of its offspring.[133] My father . . . was led to Christ at his eleventh year by Stephen Neill . . . in North Tirunelveli. My father was baptized, for which he was under persecution of his grandfather who was then a staunch Hindu leader of the village. . . . Stephen Neill's service as a missionary was not ended with the baptism of my father, but it continued in building up my father's family through the marriage with my mother. My mother's father . . . was an Evangelist in the Diocesan Evangelistic Band for which Stephen Neill was the superintendent and thus the marriage was arranged. As a result of this missionary enterprise, I have the privilege of bearing his first name 'Stephen' and my younger brother 'Neill' and in turn my second grandson is christened 'Stephen'. I am also blessed by

---

131. Ibid., p. 105.
132. Ibid.
133. The author met with this man at his house in Palayamkottai and he has a picture of Stephen Neill hanging in his home with the words 'Stephen Neill: Architect of our Family' underneath.

bishop Stephen Neill being my Godfather. Being his Godson, I had the privilege to serve the Diocesan Evangelistic Band for seventeen years as superintendent and Director.[134]

It was during the years of this Itinerancy that Selwyn and Bishop Norman Tubbs came to the decision that Neill ought to be ordained. As mentioned earlier, Neill had fulfilled the academic requirements for ordination while still a student at Cambridge. Nevertheless, he decided to go to India as a layman. Neill now decided to go ahead with ordination. He explains his response to their feelings:

> I was totally committed to the service of the Indian Church; if that Church, through its constituted leaders, told me that I could serve it more usefully as a clergyman than as a layman, it seemed to me that I must pay most careful attention to this advice. I pondered, prayed, and agreed. I have never regretted the decision.[135]

The diaconal ordination service was held in Tamil at the Holy Trinity Cathedral in Palamcottah and Neill was the only candidate. Willy Holland from Travancore, a friend of Neill's, preached the sermon.[136] This first ordination into the deaconate took place on 21 December 1926.[137] Neill would be ordained a priest two years later while in England.

Another activity in which Neill was involved during his time in the evangelistic band was an annual educational camp for the outcaste Tamil boys.[138] Neill had fond memories of the camp. The days were spent studying the Bible, playing games and hiking, while the evening was arranged around an important meeting designed to explain the Christian faith to the boys. Baptism by immersion took place and was fairly common. With humour, Neill records one baptism of a good Indian friend that was administered by his then-roommate George Selwyn:

> As Selwyn put him under the first time, 'in the name of the Father', he lost his footing, struggled to the surface, only to be ruthlessly

---

134. G. Stephen Lionel, 'Bishop Stephen Neill as Missionary Statesman with Special Reference to His Contribution to the Church in Tirunelveli', research paper, Bishop Stephen Neill Study and Research Centre.
135. Neill, *God's Apprentice*, p. 105.
136. The sermon was on the text Mark 3:14: 'And he appointed twelve, that they might be with him, and that he might send them forth to preach.' Neill, *God's Apprentice*, p. 106.
137. Muller, *The Tirunelveli Bishopric*, p. 54.
138. The camp experiences are recorded by Neill in *God's Apprentice*, p. 108.

plunged under again 'in the name of the Son'; and by the time he had completed the third immersion in the name of the Holy Spirit, he struggled to the shore very thoroughly baptized inside and out.[139]

Everything at the camp was done in Tamil, which, given Neill's competence in the language, only enhanced his status and credibility among the people. A letter from E.F.E. Wigram, Secretary of the CMS, dated 10 March 1927, was sent to Neill commending him for his work in these camps.[140]

It was during the year 1927 that Neill began to think about his fellowship at Trinity which would expire in October of 1928.[141] At first Neill was ambivalent about returning to England. However, when he considered that he had already been ill on several occasions and was physically exhausted, he opted to return for a time and enjoy his prize fellowship. In addition, he felt he could benefit from studying Sanskrit and Classical Hinduism at Cambridge.

On 'Furlough' at Cambridge

Neill's Cambridge fellowship lasted from October 1927 to August 1928.[142] Neill considered this year a 'furlough'.[143] He poured himself into learning Sanskrit and Hinduism, wrote a commentary on the Gospel of John and worked on another book entitled *Out of Bondage: Christ and the Indian Villager*. Both of these books were published in 1930.[144] Concerning his Sanskrit lessons Neill writes:

---

139. Ibid.
140. CMS Secretary, E.F.E. Wigram to Neill, 10 March 1927, CMS/G2 I10/L1, CMS Archives, University of Birmingham.
141. Neill, *God's Apprentice*, p. 106.
142. The earliest witness to Neill being in England this time is an Old Decanian Society meeting. 'Old Decanian Society Notes, 1904-1927', Special Collections, Dean Close School. The date of Neill's departure for India again is established by a letter to Wigram, dated 12 August 1928, in which Neill writes that he was currently 'Sailing for Alwaye' which was to be his next work; Neill to Wigram, 12 August 1928, CMS/G2 I5/ O1928/45, CMS Archives, University of Birmingham.
143. In the Preface to Neill's book *Builders of the Indian Church* (London: Edinburgh House, 1934), Neill wrote, '*Out of Bondage* was planned during a very happy year of furlough spent at Cambridge.'
144. *The Gospel According to St John* (Cambridge: University Press, 1930) was Neill's second book after *How Readest Thou*. Neill left the *St John* manuscript with his old teacher, Alexander Nairne, as he left again for India. This book was part of a series of small commentaries Cambridge University published for use in schools. Neill's theological prowess was showcased in this text, as it was his first scholarly publication. He exhibited an acquaintance with the various Greek manuscripts and demonstrates competence on the context of this Gospel. Nairne, who served as the

> While on furlough, I spent many happy and absorbed hours learning Sanskrit at Cambridge; but I did practically nothing else, and even then the intellectual effort was considerable. . . . Sanskrit is not as difficult as Greek, but it is still a difficult language; a man cannot hope to become really proficient in it unless he starts with considerable linguistic ability and good training. Most missionaries have neither of these qualifications; nor are they given the necessary leisure for intensive study of Sanskrit.[145]

This was also the time when Neill was ordained a priest in the Church of England in Trinity College chapel by White-Thomson, the Bishop of Ely, on 24 March 1928. The sermon was preached by Neill's old friend, John Parry. Neill said the most memorable part of the ordination was that J.C. Wyatt, a prominent teacher of Tamil and Telugu at the University of Cambridge, took part in the laying on of hands; he was 87 years old. Wyatt had served as a missionary in India alongside the famous scholar of Indian languages, Robert Caldwell.

Shortly after Neill's ordination, he was given the opportunity to preach in Westminster Abbey and he chose the topic 'No man having put his hand to the plough and looking back is fit for the kingdom of God'.[146]

Another important event during that year at Cambridge was Neill's encounter with W. Wilson Cash, General Secretary of the CMS from 1926 to 1942: 'I interviewed the Rev. Stephen Neill on 29 June 1928. He came to tell me that he had decided to offer to CMS and would be willing to go to Alwaye. He referred to money received from Canon Garfield Williams. He hoped to sail in August for South India.'[147] Records confirm that Neill was accepted as a CMS missionary with 'full status' on 16 October 1928.[148]

General Editor of the series, spoke highly of Neill in the Preface, referring to him as a friend and a fine scholar. *Out of Bondage* will be discussed in the next chapter.

145. Stephen Neill, 'Missionaries and the Vernacular', *The National Christian Council Review* (formerly *The Harvest Field*), Vol. 49, no. 11 (November 1929), pp. 598-603, p. 598.

146. For details of Neill's ordination, see *Crockford's Clerical Directory*. For Neill's ordination and sermon in Westminster Abbey, see pp. 285-87 in the unpublished autobiography, 'Chapter III, Apprentice Missionary' (Chapter III begins on p. 208). For some reason, Eleanor Jackson chose not to include this section in *God's Apprentice*. See also Pierard, 'Stephen Neill', p. 534; and Anneliese Vahl, 'Stephen C. Neill: Im Einsatz für die Ökumene', in *Ökumenische Gestalten: Brückenbauer der einen Kirche*, ed. by Günter Gloede (Berlin: Evangelische Verlagsanstalt, 1974), pp. 275-83, p. 277.

147. CMS Secretary, E.F.E. Wigram to Neill, 29 June 1928, CMS/G/AH4, CMS Archives, University of Birmingham.

148. E.F.E. Wigram, 'Resolution of India Committee of 16 October 1928', CMS/G2 I5/L4, CMS Archives, University of Birmingham. The records indicate that

3. Amy Carmichael and Neill's Early Years in South India: 1924-28

Not only did Neill become a CMS missionary during this time, but he was also given a new appointment to which he would return when he arrived back in India. Discussions between the CMS and Neill had been ongoing since early 1926 regarding the possibility of Neill returning to India to teach at a CMS school. A letter from E.F.E. Wigram, Secretary of the CMS, dated 7 January 1926, reveals that Neill had been sought by them very early in his missionary career.[149] The letter demonstrates the strong desire of the CMS to have Neill's services in one of their colleges:

> My dear Neill, . . . May I pick out three typical needs as suggesting the kind of work that you may have the choice of if you feel the call to throw in your lot with the Society which no doubt has far the largest burden to bear in the missionary work of our Church in India. 1. I believe that I heard when you went to India that you were not primarily attracted by the higher educational work which naturally many who knew of your brilliant degree would have expected to have the first claim upon you. . . . 2. On the other hand one cannot ignore the fact that your degree at Cambridge pre-eminently suits you also for leadership in some of our higher educational work in India, and at present more than one of our colleges is really languishing for the need of an increased European staff. . . . First there is St John's College, Agra. . . . 3. The other college I have in mind is St Paul's College, Calcutta, which W.E.S. Holland raised to such high eminence a few years ago. . . . I need say no more about the opportunity there, because Holland is so near to you at Alwaye, and you can pretty easily talk it all over with him. In fact I do not think I could wish anything better than that you should pay a visit to him and talk out the whole question of where you can use your life to the best advantage under present conditions. . . . I need not say with what joy I should welcome the news that you were going to join our ranks.

Neill took Wigram's advice to talk to W.E.S. (Willy) Holland, who was at that time (1926) serving as Principal of Union Christian College in Alwaye. At some point after meeting with Holland and discussing these matters, Neill learned that Holland had been asked to become Principal at St John's College in Agra, which was one of the positions Wigram had

---

this was only the formal ruling and the decision had actually been made by the time of Neill's departure. The area of Travancore and Cochin is today known as Kerala. The language spoken there is Malayalam.

149. E.F.E. Wigram to Neill, 7 January 1926, CMS/G2 I10/L1, CMS Archives, University of Birmingham.

offered to Neill. Holland, in turn, asked Neill whether he would consider replacing him at Alwaye. While Neill was in Cambridge between 1927 and 1928, he made the decision to accept the position. It was agreed that his salary would be paid by the Warren Trust Fund at the rate of £50 a quarter, or £200 a year.[150]

Neill had been a 'jack of all trades' during his first few years in India: leader of the boys at Dohnavur; teacher at the High School with George Selwyn; evangelistic band leader; a stint with Stanley Jones; and brief periods with his parents. The picture we get is of a man without direction. Certain CMS leaders recognised his dazzling talents and reckoned they could channel them in an appropriate direction. That direction was in the field of education. However, Neill soon discovered his new job and his new colleagues to be less than ideal, once again, causing him many frustrations.

---

150. Neill's salary is confirmed in a letter from E.F.E. Wigram to W.S. Hunt, 20 September 1928, CMS/G2 I5/L4, CMS Archives, University of Birmingham.

Chapter Four
An Educator in South India: 1928-39

Neill worked as an educator in South India for eleven years. He began with a very short period of service (1928-29) at the Union Christian College in Alwaye, Travancore. Then, he went out on a second itinerancy campaign (1929-30) in the northern part of the Tinnevelly diocese. This was followed by work as Warden of the Nazareth Seminary in Tinnevelly from 1930 to 1939. This chapter also addresses Neill's role in the formation of the Church of South India, an important ecumenical initiative that occupied South India's Christians for years. Neill's reputation in South India grew during these years, evidenced in several calls for him to become bishop.

Educator at Alwaye

Neill left Britain for India on 12 August 1928.[1] He was not looking forward to his new post in the town of Alwaye (nowadays known as Aluva) as it was not Tinnevelly, it was not Tamil-speaking[2] and he did not care for the humidity of the area. Alwaye is located in the Travancore and Cochin region

---
1. Neill to Wigram, 12 August 1928, CMS/G2 I5/ O1928/45, CMS Archives, University of Birmingham.
2. In *God's Apprentice*, pp. 109, 112, Neill remarks, 'I was aware of a strong instinctive dislike of the idea of going there. . . . I got to the point at which I could speak [Malayalam – the language of the region] fairly fluently, and could read intelligibly, but I never got to the point at which I could preach without an interpreter.' (pp. 109, 112)

in southwest India, in present-day Kerala.[3] Neill had been to Alwaye before for the baptism of his goddaughter and godson: Mary and Michael Holland, the twin children of Willy Holland.[4] However, Holland had moved to Agra to take up his new position as Principal of St John's College in Agra and Neill was to be his successor as Principal of Union Christian College. Neill arrived to Alwaye on 17 September 1928.[5] Two young Oxford scholars had just arrived to help with the college and Neill developed good relations with them. Unfortunately, Neill just did not like the job from day one.[6] He claimed that most of the 333 students[7] would only memorise rather than think critically about the material. He wrote, 'students just scrape through'.[8] Only about half of the students and fewer than half of the lecturers were Christians. This occasionally caused conflict between Hindus and Christians in the college. On two occasions, Neill wrote to the CMS about this.[9] In addition to being disappointed in the students, Neill was frustrated by the lack of conversions that had occurred in the area:

> Christianity appears to them simply as a matter of birth and politics, and it is very hard to get them to face seriously its religious claims. I am afraid, the attitude of many of the Christians supports their point of view; quite a number of the ablest Christian students think that Christianity is better for simple people, and Hinduism better philosophically. The extent to which our Christian students are undermined by the propaganda of theosophy is alarming.[10]

For one who was at heart a missionary, this proved to be a significant drawback. Alwaye was not nearly as open to Christianity as Neill had expected. Nearly half of the area was Muslim and the villages were virtually untouched by Christian missions. Neill maintained hope but witnessed

---

3. Malcolm Muggeridge served at the Alwaye Union Christian College for three years early in his career. He discussed that part of his life at length in his autobiography, *Chronicles of Wasted Time – Number 1: The Green Stick*, Chapter 3, 'Twilight of Empire'. Muggeridge does not mention Stephen Neill in that context, however.
4. Neill, *God's Apprentice*, p. 109.
5. Neill, Annual Letter to the CMS, 1929-30, CMS/G2 AL, CMS Archives, University of Birmingham.
6. The discussion of Neill's time in Alwaye is in *God's Apprentice*, pp. 109-15.
7. Neill, Annual Letter to the CMS, 1929-30, CMS/G2 AL, CMS Archives, University of Birmingham.
8. Ibid.
9. Ibid. See also Wigram to Neill, 7 March 1929, CMS/G2 I5/L4, CMS Archives, University of Birmingham.
10. Neill, Annual Letter to the CMS, 1929-30, CMS/G2 AL, CMS Archives, University of Birmingham.

no baptisms.[11] During the time that Neill was at Alwaye, he turned his mind towards the book he had previously agreed to write while he was in England. A mere three months after arriving at this post in Travancore, Neill was already discussing 'at length a proposal that he should have leave of absence from Alwaye for a time in order to write a book on Indian villages for the United Council for Missionary Education'.[12] On 15 January 1929 the CMS India Committee approved Neill's request.[13]

However, the CMS Secretary, E.F.E. Wigram, had reservations about Neill's leave of absence. In one letter he described Neill as 'a sort of non-regulation man'.[14] Wigram wrote to Neill on 24 January 1929, explaining he had reservations about a poor precedent being set. First, books were almost always written during regular furlough or during ordinary 'hill leave', that time when the missionaries headed to the mountains during the very hot season. Neill was proposing to write the book during active duty. Second, 'It was realized that in most . . . cases the writer had probably already spent a good long time abroad, whereas you have undertaken the book after comparatively small actual experience.'[15] Third, Wigram was concerned that Neill might 'be tackling the subject in a way which would be over the heads of the majority of those for whom the book is to be written'.[16]

Neill eventually got his way, replying on 12 February 1929 to thank the committee for permission to take a leave of absence in order to write.[17]

Neill claimed to have written the book 'under the strain of College work'.[18] First published in May 1930, it was already on its third impression by January 1931.[19] He chose as its title, *Out of Bondage: Christ and the Indian Villager*.

---

11. Ibid.
12. Neill to Wigram, 5 November 1928 and 18 December 1928, CMS/G2 I5/O1929/7, CMS Archives, University of Birmingham. In these letters Neill expressed his desire to have a break in order to write his book.
13. Wigram, 'Resolution of India Committee of 15 January 1929', CMS/G2 I5/L4, CMS Archives, University of Birmingham.
14. Wigram to Rev. W.S. Hunt, 24 January 1929, CMS/G2 I5/L4, CMS Archives, University of Birmingham.
15. Wigram to Neill, 24 January 1929, CMS/G2 I5/L4, CMS Archives, University of Birmingham.
16. Ibid.
17. Neill to Wigram, 12 February 1929, CMS/G2 I5/O1929/17, CMS Archives, University of Birmingham.
18. Neill, Annual Letter to the CMS, 1929-30, CMS/G2 AL, CMS Archives, University of Birmingham.
19. See Neill, *Out of Bondage*. The Foreword to the book was written by E.A.L. Moore, the bishop of Travancore and Cochin diocese. It is interesting that Neill submitted a 60,000- word draft, but the press cut it to 35,000 words, showing that the book could have been a lot more substantive than it eventually was.

In this book Neill gave a picture of Indian life. He provided a vivid introduction to the history of India, both religious, social and political. He covered topics such as Indian houses, the terrain, crime, the Indians' penchant for travelling around their country and the caste system. The majority of the book was devoted to explaining Indian beliefs and practices and the need for the Gospel to penetrate this religion of shrines, idol-worship, spiritualism, dark and rhythmic music and strong belief in magic. In the book, Neill was quick to point out the great philanthropic contributions of Christians to the health of the Indian people, the plentiful schools and the penetration of the ignorance of typical Indian worship by the great gospel of Christ.

Neill was sympathetic to Hinduism's contributions as well, albeit when they exhibited teachings similar to Christianity such as confronting idol-worship. This early book showcases Neill's knowledge of the Hindu pantheon, discussing various gods and how individuals relate to them. One of his concerns was the poverty and despair among the villagers. He wrote, 'The three great hindrances to prosperity, which the villager himself can largely overcome, *if he will*, are disease, drink and debt.'[20]

Neill also discussed the reluctance of educated Indians to engage in manual labour. Furthermore, while the tendency of Indians to beg seemed somewhat honourable in their own eyes, Neill clearly did not share this view.[21]

The book concluded with a lengthy discussion of the desperate need for Christian missions in India. Neill provided stories that challenged his readers with the fact that Christianity needed greater investment if it was going to deal effectively with the many problems in India. Neill cautioned that the Indians who converted to Christianity were often under intense persecution and would in many cases require adoption by a Christian community, as they would become outcasts within their own. A section at the end of the book provides an early insight into Neill's missionary fervour: 'What is the Church's task in India to-day?'[22] Neill answered with a series of six discussions:

(1) The steady and systematic occupation of all the unoccupied areas within the next thirty years.
(2) The development of all work on Indian lines and the making over of control to the Indian Church at the earliest possible moment.

---

20. Neill, *Out of Bondage*, p. 62 (Neill's italics).
21. Ibid., p. 82.
22. Ibid., p. 129.

4. An Educator in South India: 1928-39

(3) An intensive campaign over thirty years to remove the evil of illiteracy in the Church.
(4) The missionary must come determined to make the land of his adoption his home.
(5) The missionary must lay aside before he comes every trace of racial prejudice and pride.
(6) Those who come to India must come knowing clearly what they have come to do, and what it is that they have to give to India.[23]

Neill was always of the opinion that India needed more from England: more missionaries, more financial commitment, more literature. In his 1929-30 Annual Letter to the CMS, he wrote, 'the College should never be left without European help'.[24] However, he also believed that the Indians would have to play the decisive role if the conversion of the subcontinent were to become a reality.

From his letters, it is evident that Neill gave considerable thought to education in India. He wrote an article in 1929, 'Missionaries and the Vernacular', that discussed some of the concerns that he would elaborate upon in the following year.[25] This article begins with Neill considering his experiences in studying Hinduism, which occupied the majority of his recent time in Cambridge. Then he proceeded to argue why Western scholars of Hinduism will never be plentiful and why there is not a need for many of them. His argument rests on the fact that in South India only a tiny percentage of the people actually understand Sanskrit. Modern translations are the medium through which literate Indians learn the Hindu classics.

The article then moves to its primary consideration: missionaries and the vernacular. Neill argued that missionaries needed to learn the vernacular of their people. For example, when teaching Indians, something that might take twenty minutes or more to explain in English, due largely to their imperfect understanding, could be quickly explained in their own language. Neill wrote, 'Let us get rid, once for all, of the pernicious idea that Indian students would rather talk English.' Indians, like Europeans, will always prefer their mother tongue.

It was not surprising when Neill's colleagues began to enquire as to his future status at Alwaye. Neill realised this was not a long-term situation for him, and he was never fond of Kerala.[26] Indian languages, particularly in

---

23. Ibid., pp. 129-36.
24. Neill, Annual Letter to the CMS, 1929-30, CMS/G2 AL, CMS Archives, University of Birmingham.
25. Neill, 'Missionaries and the Vernacular', pp. 598-603.
26. Neill, *God's Apprentice*, p. 114.

the South, are very difficult to learn. Over the mountains, in Tamil Nadu, Neill had taken great pains to become a fluent speaker. Even with his great linguistic gifts, Malayalam would require a lot of work before he could be considered fluent. On this, he wrote, 'I have been very much hampered at every turn by my ignorance of the vernacular; although Malayalam is very much like Tamil.'[27] Additionally, Neill's friends were in Tamil country and that was pulling him. He made the decision to leave when Willy Holland, the former principal, recruited Brian Crowley and his wife to take charge of the work in Alwaye.[28] Holland was by now at his new post in Agra. Neill wrote: 'If there had been any great urgency of need, I would have stayed, but . . . [when] Brian Crowley . . . arrived with his admirable wife Eileen, they at once took the students to their hearts, made a home for them . . . and conferred innumerable benefits on the life of the College.'[29]

Upon leaving Alwaye, Neill reasoned, 'I think the greatest service I ever rendered Alwaye College was in leaving it.'[30]

CMS Secretary E.F.E. Wigram knew that Neill had been itching to get out of Alwaye, but he had no place in mind for Neill to go. He urged Neill to talk with the bishop of Tinnevelly about his return to that diocese.[31] Neill and the new bishop, F.J. Western, decided that Neill should return to the itinerancy work he had been doing prior to his furlough in Cambridge.[32]

Neill left Alwaye in September of 1929 and returned to Tamil country. The conclusion of his 1929-30 Annual Letter to the CMS summarises his attitude, 'I look forward to rejoining the Tinnevelly diocese in September, and shall rejoice to be speaking Tamil again.'[33]

Another Itinerancy Campaign

From September 1929 to June 1930 Neill worked in the northern part of the Tinnevelly diocese again as a leader of an evangelistic band, with eleven men under his supervision.[34] The men were required to serve for a year as evangelists, which was to be the final chapter of their three-year

---

27. Neill, Annual Letter to the CMS, 1929-30, CMS/G2 AL, CMS Archives, University of Birmingham.
28. Wigram to Rev. W. S. Hunt, 24 January 1929, CMS/G2 I5/L4, CMS Archives, University of Birmingham.
29. Neill, *God's Apprentice*, p. 115.
30. Ibid.
31. Wigram to Neill, 7 March 1929.
32. Neill, *God's Apprentice*, p. 116.
33. Neill, Annual Letter to the CMS, 1929-30, CMS/G2 AL, CMS Archives, Special Collections, University of Birmingham.
34. Neill, *God's Apprentice*, pp. 115-18.

4. An Educator in South India: 1928-39

theological training course. Neill was able to select the location and he chose Sachiapuram in northern Tinnevelly (modern Satchiyapuram in Tamil Nadu), where the missionary Thomas Gajetan Ragland had served in the 1840s and 1850s.

The band's schedule was as rigid as it was the first time Neill had led an itinerancy. Twenty days a month were spent in the remote villages. The other ten days were spent at Sachiapuram, from where Neill would send the men out to gather the children for teaching. Following the practice of Stanley Jones, Neill would lecture to the educated Hindus and Muslims. This was Neill's passion, taking the Christian message to remote areas. It tugged at Neill's emotions when he rode his bicycle out to the villages to ask if they knew anything of the Christian gospel. Their reply was normally, 'Yes, years ago Christians used to come round here, and talk to us; they were very good people, and used to give us very good advice, to do good and not to do evil; but for a good many years we have not seen them.'[35]

At some point near the end of this period, a church council was held at Sachiapuram. The bishop attended and told Neill he needed him at Nazareth in the South to serve at the theological school. Neill was reluctant to go. In his Annual Letter to the CMS of 1930-31, he wrote, 'I came to Nazareth on June 10, 1930. I cannot pretend that I was very willing to come. It meant leaving the North of the Diocese, of the terrible needs of which I have written before.'[36] However, Neill trusted Bishop Western to make the right decision, while commenting on the common trend to disrupt the work in the north to accommodate the well-Christianized South:

> This is what had always happened. As soon as any attempt had been made to get active work going again in the north, the south would exercise its pull, and in general the pull of the south would prevail. I had no wish at all to exchange the way I was living for the far more comfortable conditions of the south. It had been my aim to sink myself deeper and deeper into the Tamil language, and into a knowledge and understanding of Hinduism and the Hindu way of life, and so to qualify myself to be an effective witness for Christ to the educated and high-caste Hindu; I had no wish to become a missionary to Christians. Least of all did I wish to settle down in an old mission-station where, as in Nazareth, the gospel had been proclaimed for more than a hundred years and where everyone was at least in name a Christian.

---

35. Ibid., p. 117.
36. Neill, Annual Letter to the CMS, 1931-32, CMS/G2 AL, CMS Archives, University of Birmingham.

> On the other hand, though always an adventurer at heart, I have always believed that the voice of the Church is a voice to which the Christian must listen with the most careful attention. . . . If the Church thought that the training of the ordained ministry was the task which at the moment I was best qualified to carry out, probably I ought to set that considered opinion above my own desires.[37]

Given Neill's questionable health, his emotional struggles and his frequent exhaustion, North India was not ideal for him in the long run; the conditions were too harsh for him.[38]

Educator at Nazareth

Nazareth's history begins in 1796. It was originally a land grant for Christians who had been cast out of their villages. When Neill arrived to live there in 1930, it was a village of about 2,000 inhabitants, who were all Christian and, due to British influence, who enjoyed a rather high level of prosperity for South India.[39] Neill described his new context:

> Nazareth has always been the centre of many mission activities. There was a high school and training school for girls. . . . There was a middle school for boys. . . . There was the largest mission hospital in the diocese. . . . There was an industrial school, . . . a large church . . . [and] sandwiched on a narrow strip of ground between the hospital and the industrial school, the Seminary over which I was to preside – a two-storeyed building with a classroom below and a chapel above, a shabby side room . . . and a street of ten small houses.[40]

---

37. Neill, *God's Apprentice*, p. 118.
38. In *God's Apprentice*, it is clear that Neill's life was plagued by health problems and emotional struggles, such as depression (pp. 9, 44-46), insomnia (pp. 9, 44), a 'fierce temper, the outward expression of so many inward frustrations' (p. 36), sciatica (pain in the sciatic nerve, p. 39), anxiety (p. 43), eye problems (p. 43), rashes ('eczema', p. 44), frequent fevers (pp. 74, 79, 167), exhaustion (pp. 131, 197, 206), a 'septic throat' (p. 164) and dysentery (p. 206). Those who knew Neill were aware of his ill-health. In the Foreword to *God's Apprentice*, p. 7, C.F.D. Moule shows he was familiar with Neill's precarious health. Cragg and Chadwick knew of Neill's constant health problems, commenting, 'Behind the scenes his health was still troublesome'; Cragg and Chadwick, 'Stephen Charles Neill, 1900-1984', p. 608.
39. Neill, *God's Apprentice*, p. 119.
40. Ibid., 119-20. The seminary was established in 1819. See Constance M.

4. An Educator in South India: 1928-39

Early on, Neill pressed the CMS for the seminary to move; he felt the facility was no longer conducive. His wish was not granted until 1937, nearly the end of his time there.

The seminary building was dilapidated; it had been closed for two years prior to Neill's arrival in 1930. Neill had to start nearly from scratch. He had to create a curriculum, organise his staff and recruit students. Neill had two teaching colleagues who had been training catechists. One he described as 'already past the retiring age'. The other was a young 'fiery nationalist, temperamental and over-sensitive. . . . [H]e had been thrust into a position for which his gifts and his knowledge were grossly inadequate.'[41] The first term drew only ten students. Neill's description of the students is unflattering:

> It is not easy to make them see the advantages of an intellectual approach of any subject connected to religion. What they would like to have would be an endless series of devotional studies of the Bible, with copious notes, which would afford material for endless sermons after they are ordained. I think after a year's work we are beginning to get over that difficulty; but they are still constitutionally incapable, partly from inherited conservation, partly from lack of background, to profit much from the critical approach to the study of the Bible.[42]

Neill's curriculum was heavy on church history and biblical studies.[43] He began with the ecumenical movement that was in full swing at the time and

---

Millington, *Led by the Spirit: A Biography of Bishop Arthur Michael Hollis, Onetime Anglican Bishop of Madras, and Later First Moderator of the C.S.I.* (Bangalore: Asian Trading Corporation, 1996), p. 13.

41. Neill, *God's Apprentice*, pp. 120-21.
42. Neill, Annual Letter to the CMS, 1931-32, CMS/G2 AL, CMS Archives, University of Birmingham.
43. Stephen Neill, 'A Curriculum for a Theological School', a paper written for *The National Christian Council Review* (May 1933), pp. 1-9. This article can also be obtained under the title of the article with the following publishing information, Mysore: Wesley House Press and Publishing House, 1933. In this important article Neill proposed the following nine subjects for the programme he would supervise: 1. The Old Testament; 2. The New Testament; 3. Church History; 4. Christian Doctrine; 5. Christian Worship; 6. Greek; 7. Tamil; 8. Non-Christian Religions; and 9. Pastoralia, which Neill defined, pp. 8-9, as 'a carpet bag into which to stuff all the remains of subjects of which we think the students should know something, . . . Christian Ethics, . . . Church Accounts, Church Law, Marriage, Moral Hygiene, Preaching, Religious Education, Practical Problems of Christian Work, Systems of Church Government, History and Constitution of Individual Churches, and Problems of Church Re-union'.

moved backwards to the Early Church. Neill's approach to Bible study was most unconventional for the students. He wanted to study 'critically', while the students were in no way familiar with this approach. They viewed the Bible as 'the absolutely reliable source of knowledge on every conceivable subject'.[44] Neill wrote, 'I knew that all our students would be dyed-in-the-wool fundamentalists . . . because they had never been told anything else.'[45] He felt Hebrew and Greek should not be required and only the most gifted students attempted these languages. All, however, were required to engage upon 'an elementary study of the Greek manuscripts'.[46]

Neill required his students to be bilingual. If lectures were in English, the examinations would be in Tamil and, if the lectures were in Tamil, the examinations would be in English. The students resented this, feeling 'that they were being very badly treated'.[47]

While critical study was foundational for the syllabus, the practical dimension was equally significant. Frequently Neill would take the students on evangelistic campaigns and to missionary conferences.[48] He also matched the students with local pastors as mentors.[49] It was important for Neill that the students overcome their lacklustre interest in the non-Christians of the area. Neill was determined that the students must be equipped to convert Hindus. This proved problematic as almost all of the students' families had been Christian for four or five generations; they knew next to nothing about Hinduism. Neill was also insistent that daily quiet time be a regular part of the course.

Neill's relations with the students were 'very stiff'.[50] This was due largely to the traditional teacher-student relationship, but certainly also had

---

44. Neill, *God's Apprentice*, p 121.
45. Ibid. In Neill's article, 'A Curriculum for a Theological School', p. 3, he wrote that many of the students were suspicious of his approach to the Bible and some of them had their faith shaken to the core by the critical approach.
46. Eleanor Jackson's personal collection, p. 208.
47. Neill, *God's Apprentice*, p 121.
48. In his Annual Letter to the CMS, 1931-32, CMS/G2 AL, CMS Archives, University of Birmingham, Neill recorded that students went to Coonoor for a Sunday School training course, to a Student Christian Association Camp for Tamils and to Alwaye to attend a Mar Thoma Church convention. In October 1933 he spoke at a CEZMS conference on 'India To-day and To-morrow'. This address was published in the CEZMS journal, *Here and There with the CEZMS*, November 1933, pp. 215-17. Neill wrote an encouraging article to the CEZMS in the same journal the following month, entitled 'Consecrated – Satisfied', December 1933, pp. 245-46.
49. Neill, *God's Apprentice*, p. 122. Neill took it upon himself to be pastor 'in sole charge' of the Nazareth parish. However, this arrangement lasted only two years.
50. Neill, Annual Letter to the CMS, 1931-32, CMS/G2 AL, CMS Archives, University of Birmingham.

something to do with Neill's disposition. However, Neill was most pleased when surrounded by young men. He remarked 'the contact with boys has given me a new lease of life'.[51] An ambivalent tendency begun at Dohnavur, continued during his itinerancy days and persisted throughout Neill's career: he maintained authoritative yet intimate relations with the young men with whom he was entrusted. His teacher at Cambridge, Alexander Nairne, who edited Neill's commentary on John, remarked in the Preface to that book, '[This book] is written for plain men and, especially, for boys, with whom Mr. Neill has a rare sympathy.'[52]

Neill's responsibilities in the seminary were manifold and demanding.[53] There were times that he gave thirteen lectures a week on topics such as Greek, Old Testament, Religions of India and Church History. The library was insufficient for teachers and students alike, prompting Neill to pursue a grant from the Warren Trust for the purchase of books. There was no secretarial help, so Neill took charge of all accounts and correspondence.

In addition to his work at the seminary, Neill was pastor of the church in Nazareth, he was in charge of a nearby Art Industrial School for training craftsmen[54] and he took bi-monthly trips in order to supervise the work of the nearby Megnanapuram High School. Neill was careful to 'keep an eye on everything, and to see that the quality of the work keeps up'.[55] He was most anxious for the arrival of an SPG (Society for the Propagation of the Gospel) man named Michael Hollis who eventually became a cornerstone of missionary work in South India. Neill was well aware that Hollis would offer a significant addition to the work as he had been a fellow and chaplain of Hereford College, Oxford.

During Neill's first year at Nazareth, he had to spend considerable time dealing with problems of immorality. He was particularly bothered by the many couples who were 'living in sin'.[56] The reasons for this behaviour were various. For example, some of the elderly couples had begun to live together after their original spouses died and they were ashamed to attempt remarriage through the Church. Others could not afford the four rupees required for a wedding fee. Neill consulted the bishop and temporarily banned those unlawfully coupled, yet the bans would be lifted as soon as they submitted to a proper Christian ceremony.

51. Ibid.
52. Alexander Nairne, Preface, in Neill, *The Gospel According to St John*, p. vii.
53. Neill, *God's Apprentice*, pp. 132-33.
54. The Industrial School trained men to make 'beautiful rosewood furniture'. See Millington, *Led by the Spirit*, p. 13.
55. Neill, Annual Letter to the CMS, 1931-32, CMS/G2 AL, CMS Archives, University of Birmingham.
56. Neill, *God's Apprentice*, p 123.

Another problem with which Neill had to deal was a leading Christian man who maintained a 'toddy shop', a makeshift liquor store, in the churchyard.[57] Neill's second year saw the arrival of Reverend A.P. Randle, who had worked at Tinnevelly before taking a lengthy period away.[58] He was a welcome addition; however, Neill was *most* pleased by the arrival of Michael Hollis from Oxford. Neill's annual letters to the CMS are usually written with a frustration evident in the many complaints of overwork and unsatisfactory conditions, necessity for more help and disappointment at the slow progress in all areas. However, Neill's Annual Letter to the CMS of 1932-33 shows exuberance: 'Far and away the most important event has been the arrival of Hollis. He has a good academic view, and seven years of teaching theology in Oxford; so really for a little corner like this, we are not badly staffed.'[59] Neill's positive outlook in his annual letters continued until Hollis' departure for furlough in 1936. When Neill heard that Hollis would not be coming back to India because his wife had had a miscarriage, Neill wrote:

> When I heard the news, I felt just for a moment that I could not possibly face the work without him. Even now I feel like a man who has lost his right arm. I do not know whether the CMS has ever realized how extraordinarily fortunate it was in having associated in this work a man of such intellectual distinction, deep evangelical conviction, and spiritual power.[60]

Michael Hollis had a 'Tractarian' background which initially caused Neill some concern,[61] but his intense focus on the conversion of Hindus

---

57. Neill, Annual Letter to the CMS, 1931-32, CMS/G2 AL, CMS Archives, University of Birmingham.
58. Little is known of Rev. Randle outside the scant information revealed about him in Neill's annual letters to the CMS. Neill recorded Randle taking two furloughs in 1932 and 1937. It is also known that he was something of a 'buildings expert' according to Neill, meaning he knew what it would take to move the seminary to a new location and how the new building should be constructed to suit the needs of the students and educators. Based on a comment by Neill in his Annual Letter to the CMS, 1931-32, it seems to be the case that Randle was an SPG missionary.
59. Neill, Annual Letter to the CMS, 1932-33, CMS/G2 AL, CMS Archives, University of Birmingham.
60. Neill, Annual Letter to the CMS, 1937-38, CMS/G2 AL, CMS Archives, University of Birmingham.
61. Neill's initial concern about Hollis would have been common for one of Evangelical, and CMS, sympathies. The 'Tractarian' movement is also known as the 'Anglo-Catholic' or 'Oxford' movement, based on the influence of John Henry Newman. Neill wrote on this movement in his widely read work, *Anglicanism*, 4th edn, pp. 254-61, 267-69.

4. An Educator in South India: 1928-39

impressed Neill greatly. They shared a house for a short time until Hollis' marriage in 1935.[62] Neill helped Hollis by doing most of the lecturing at the seminary while Hollis learned Tamil.[63] They were an excellent match: highly competent intellectuals with a strong missionary zeal. Millington writes: 'It was a remarkable occurrence that on the staff of this small rural theological college in South India, two such able men as Stephen Neill and Michael Hollis should serve at the same time. . . . These two academics must have provided a welcome stimulus for each other.'[64]

There were differences between the two men, however. Hollis was eager for unity among the various denominations and mission societies in the area; Neill was more reticent.[65] Hollis was more congenial with the students. Hollis' biographer writes:

> He admired Neill's scholarship and his fluency in Tamil but recognised his defects. Writing to England he said he got on excellently with Neill, who 'doesn't realise how autocratic he is with Indians and cannot conceal how much abler he is.' Neill was a colourful character but perhaps not always the easiest person with whom to work.[66]

Hollis must have been of an extraordinary character. Neill consistently wrote of him in high regard in his annual letters to the CMS.[67]

Neill departed India for his second leave of absence on 18 April 1933.[68] He was out of the country for just over a year.[69] He spent his time in England at Trinity Hall, Cambridge and St Peter's Hall, Oxford.[70] It proved

---

62. Millington, *Led by the Spirit*, pp. 14, 37-39.
63. Neill wrote that he was lecturing twelve times a week in the seminary. See Neill, Annual Letter to the CMS, 1932-33, CMS/G2 AL, CMS Archives, University of Birmingham.
64. Millington, *Led by the Spirit*, p. 13.
65. See Millington, *Led by the Spirit*, p. 34, and Neill, *God's Apprentice*, p. 139.
66. Millington, *Led by the Spirit*, pp. 34-35.
67. The only criticism Neill ever offered regarding Hollis was that 'he appears to be incapable of preaching about anything except justification by faith'. See Neill, Annual Letter to the CMS, 1935-36, CMS/G2 AL, CMS Archives, University of Birmingham.
68. Neill, Annual Letter to the CMS, 1933-34, CMS/G2 AL, CMS Archives, University of Birmingham.
69. In the Preface to *Builders of the Indian Church: Present Problems in the Light of the Past* (London: Edinburgh, 1934), Neill wrote that he was still at Oxford in April 1934.
70. In *God's Apprentice*, p. 131, Neill stated that initially he went to Cambridge but was asked to go to Oxford to speak at an Oxford Inter-Collegiate Christian

a productive time for Neill as he wrote and published three books and one article. The first book, *Annals of an Indian Parish*,[71] is essentially a collection of excerpts from his diary regarding his work as pastor of the Nazareth area churches. Details of Neill's daily schedule are provided. He discussed topics as diverse as the challenge of getting a good night's sleep to the endless quarrelling among Indian Christians. Neill provides an overview of his situation as a missionary in the book:

> The Church is a small island in a vast ocean of Hinduism. The village Christian is at all times breathing in through every pore non-Christian superstitions, non-Christian ideals, non-Christian standards, which corrupt and destroy the life that is within him. . . . Parish work in India is like pushing a heavy stone up a steep hill. The moment pressure is slackened, the stone begins to run down hill. Harm done by one year of neglect can hardly be repaired by ten years of labour.[72]

It appears from this quotation that Neill may have been anticipating an abysmal state of affairs upon his return to India and, indeed, this turned out to be the case. Upon his return to Nazareth he wrote, 'Naturally, everything had rather gone to pieces.'[73]

The second work Neill produced during his Oxford break was a pamphlet entitled *The Remaking of Men in India*.[74] This is a specialised study of mass conversions in India and the problems involved both for the converts as well as the missionaries looking after them. Mass conversions usually took place among the lowest castes. The 'remaking' referred to in the title shows Neill's belief that the Indians must be taught how to change. For example, Neill argued that they must move out of their conditions of 'extreme squalor' and 'learn to come clean to church . . . [as] cleanliness comes next to godliness'.[75] In this pamphlet, Neill also argued against the injustices of the caste system. Neill commented that the lowest castes *viewed themselves* as untouchables, something that was very difficult for them to

---

Union meeting and remained for the rest of his leave.
71. Stephen Neill, *Annals of an Indian Parish* (London: CMS, 1934). The inspiration for this 70-page volume came after friends in England read Neill's records of his parish work, prompting him to make them available in permanent form. See the Foreword to that work.
72. Ibid., p. x.
73. Neill, Annual Letter to the CMS, 1934-35, CMS/G2 AL, CMS Archives, University of Birmingham.
74. Stephen Neill, *The Remaking of Men in India* (London: CMS, 1934).
75. Ibid., p. 10.

4. An Educator in South India: 1928-39

overcome. Neill's solution was to send missionaries to them. However, the question of who would take on this sort of work and who would support it financially presented serious problems for Neill. The pamphlet concludes with a call for 'India's conversion':

> Early Church history shows us clearly that the Gospel tends to begin in the lower strata of society; it is indeed a message of life for the poor and the oppressed; but it tends to work upwards from below. I believe that this might happen also in India. . . . This caste movement is too new for us to speak of it in detail, but once the stream has begun to flow there is no reason why it should not grow into a mighty river. If it develops, . . . it will be the greatest event in the history of the Church in India. . . . It is a challenge to the great Churches to come to our help now in the day of God's opportunity, before it is called too late, in order that the Church may go forward to conquests on a far greater scale, and with the assurance that God is with her in all her warfare until the very end.[76]

The third work during his Cambridge-Oxford break, *Builders of the Indian Church*, was a great success.[77] According to Neill, 'For years it was the main text-book on Indian Church history in almost all the theological seminaries in India.'[78] *Builders of the Indian Church* was initially intended to be a larger history of Christianity in India but had to be cut short due to 'ceaseless demands' on his time.[79] Comprised of 160 pages, this book is a condensed history of Christianity in India from the early traditions of St Thomas to 1932. Neill admitted in the Preface that a more comprehensive history would have to wait.[80] The final chapter of the book emphasises Neill's belief that the mission era in India had produced many fruits and must continue. He concludes the book by asking the question, 'Does the Church in India still need and want the help of missionaries from the

---

76. Ibid., pp. 13-15.
77. By January 1938, four years after it was first published, this book was on its third impression.
78. Eleanor Jackson's personal collection, p. 230.
79. See the Preface to Neill, *Builders of the Indian Church*.
80. Neill would finally pursue his goal of a much larger history of Christianity in the last few years of his life. His death cut short his projected three-volume *A History of Christianity in India*, allowing for only the first two volumes that together covered the beginnings to 1858. Indian Christians hold to the belief that St Thomas, one of Jesus's twelve apostles, brought Christianity to India in the year AD 52.

West?' His answer is a resounding yes: 'the western missionary is still the indispensable pioneer. . . . [He] is a gift of immense value to his Indian fellow-workers.'[81]

The final work Neill produced during his leave of absence was a contribution to a book edited by Joe Oldham and entitled *The Modern Missionary*.[82] The opportunity to be associated with a name like Oldham was an honour for Neill. His chapter is entitled 'Rural Work in India'. In it, he discusses the state of Christianity in the villages of India and how the missionaries minister to the villagers.

By mid-1934 Neill was back in India, pressing the CMS for a new building from which to operate the seminary, 'our accommodation is ridiculously defective, and we could not possibly stay on in Nazareth for another year'.[83] Two factors stood in the way: first, the often difficult relations between the CMS and the SPG, which would handicap the much-needed fundraising; and, second, the dire financial state of the diocese. Initially, Neill suggested that the seminary merge with another one nearby, the United Theological Seminary at Pasumalai near Madras. However, this idea was defeated in late 1936 by the Pastoral Work Committee. The largely Indian membership of the committee preferred a site outside Nazareth and this carried the day. Neill reacted strongly to the decision:

> I can find no words to express my regret at this decision, and at the shameful methods by which it was reached. The little Nazareth clique managed, as usual, to lead the whole diocese by the nose and to get their own project carried. . . . Indians must work out their own salvation and we do not interfere, but often we are sufferers by the result. Anyhow a decision is a decision, and we have got now to try and give the diocese the best Seminary we can in a situation and on a site which are wholly unsuitable for the purpose.[84]

---

81. Neill, *Builders of the Indian Church*, pp. 150-52.
82. Joe Oldham, ed., *The Modern Missionary: A Study of the Human Factor in the Missionary Enterprise in the Light of Present-Day Conditions* (London: Student Christian Movement Press, 1935). Oldham was one of the most well-known figures of the Ecumenical Movement and was long-time Secretary of the International Missionary Council. See Oldham's biography by Keith Clements, *Faith on the Frontier: A Life of J.H. Oldham* (Edinburgh: T. & T. Clark, 1999).
83. Neill, Annual Letter to the CMS, 1935-36, CMS/G2 AL, CMS Archives, University of Birmingham.
84. Neill, Annual Letter to the CMS, 1936-37, CMS/G2 AL, CMS Archives, University of Birmingham.

4. An Educator in South India: 1928-39   107

Neill's own words reveal a striking personality trait. When he made a decision on a matter, he could not tolerate dissension and thus he fell into conflict with others. Neill's harsh words towards the committee's 'shameful methods' reveal his need to demonise his opposition ('the little Nazareth clique'). Neill's opinions were often inflexible.

Nevertheless, the SPG donated Rs. 30,000 for thirty acres of land and the new buildings[85] and the CMS contributed Rs. 16,000 and by June 1937 the seminary had been successfully relocated. The new name given to the seminary was 'Tirumaraiyur' or, in English, 'the village of holy revelation'.[86] There had been some nominal growth as there were by then 23 students training for ministry.

Around the time the seminary was being relocated, Neill was invited to give a series of lectures at the Kodaikanal Missionary Conference. Neill wrote that his audience consisted of about 200 missionaries.[87] He gave a series of lectures on the second half of the Apostles' Creed. There must have been a positive reception; Neill stated that afterwards 'they clamoured to have the lectures published'[88] and, indeed, they were, in 1940, as *Beliefs*.[89] A few years after that Conference, in 1941, Neill was again the keynote speaker at Kodaikanal and spoke on the first half of the Apostles' Creed. These were later published as *Foundation Beliefs*.[90]

A Context of War

'All the time the [international] political horizon was growing darker,' Neill wrote. 'We were unaware at the time of all the disasters that Hitler was cooking up for the world.'[91] Neill was always a voracious reader. Weekly, he received *The Spectator*, the *New Statesman* and *The Manchester Guardian*. He wrote, 'I reckoned that, if I had time to read

---

85. Neill, Annual Letter to the CMS, 1937-38, CMS/G2 AL, CMS Archives, University of Birmingham.
86. Ibid.
87. Neill, Annual Letter to the CMS, 1936-37, CMS/G2 AL, CMS Archives, University of Birmingham.
88. Ibid.
89. Stephen Neill, *Beliefs: Lectures Delivered at the Kodaikanal Missionary Conference, 1937* (Madras: Christian Literature Society for India, 1940).
90. Stephen Neill, *Foundation Beliefs* (Madras: Christian Literature Society for India, 1948). Timothy Yates describes the printed lectures as 'Two golden books on the Christian creed, compiled from addresses given to missionaries. . . . [They] deserve to be reprinted'; Yates, *Christian Mission in the Twentieth Century*, p. 144.
91. Neill, *God's Apprentice*, p. 147.

all three, I would know pretty well what was going on everywhere in the world.'[92] Gradually, Neill began to realise what was happening in Germany.

Several months before the war broke out, a German friend made Neill promise that Neill would come to visit him when the internment camps came into being.[93] Neill was caught off guard by the request. However, his friend's fears were not without substance. A letter of 3 August 1939 addressed to the National Christian Council in Nagpur reads: 'For the present it must be assumed that missionaries of enemy nationality would, on the outbreak of war, be immediately removed and detained, pending repatriation or such other action as may, in the interests of security, be found advisable.'[94] A month later, the internment camps were in operation.[95]

92. Eleanor Jackson's personal collection, p. 264. Neill's writings show a familiarity with issues unrelated to Christian missions. In his autobiography, Neill often went off on tangents describing things as various as the Spanish Civil War, the US stock market crash of 1929 and his cover-to-cover reading of George Eliot's *The Mill on the Floss* on a train ride. When travelling by train Neill always took the cheapest class.

93. Eleanor Jackson's personal collection, p. 266. For missionaries, internment camps were an unfortunate reality during both world wars, as Christians struggled with tension between loyalties to faith and to country. The phenomenon is usually referred to as 'orphaned missions', as the missionaries had to leave their mission stations for the camps. In 1939 1,700 German missionaries in Asia and Africa were cut off from their home support. Generally, after a brief internment and investigation by the governing (usually British) body, missionaries were released, albeit without support. After the beginning of the German *Blitzkrieg*, the invasion of the Netherlands, Belgium and France in 1940, most continental European Protestant mission points became orphaned. US mission organisations were extremely generous in assuming financial responsibility for many of the orphaned mission points in Asia and Africa; North American churches covered 90 per cent of total expenses. There is an excellent article in Neill, Anderson and Goodwin, eds, *Concise Dictionary of the Christian World Mission*, entitled 'Orphaned Missions', that deals with this topic. See also the important *World Christian Community in Action: World War II and Orphaned Missions* (New York: International Missionary Council, 1949) by K.S. Latourette and W. Richey Hogg. Similar things happened in World War I. See Richard V. Pierard, 'Shaking the Foundations: World War I, the Western Allies, and German Protestant Missions', *International Bulletin of Missionary Research*, Vol. 22, no. 1 (January 1998), pp. 13-19.

94. E. Conran-Smith to P.Z. Hodge, National Christian Council, Nagpur, 3 August 1939, Westcott Papers, Bishops Box 4, Special Collections, Bishop's College. 'Enemy' in this case referred to Germany, as German Lutherans had a long history of mission work in India.

95. Germany invaded Poland on 1 September 1939. Britain declared war on Germany on 3 September. Poland surrendered to Germany on 27 September.

4. An Educator in South India: 1928-39

The bishop of Nasik wrote a letter to the Metropolitan of India, describing the camps favourably: 'I went into the Camp last Friday. . . . They seem to be very comfortable there; but naturally they were eager to get let out.'[96] Although not oppressive, the camps did have rules, for example, no books or papers were to be admitted without heavy scrutiny. Before long, the internees were freed and family internment camps were established for those who for one reason or another continued to be incarcerated.[97] For example, a letter from the bishop of Nasik to Metropolitan Westcott, said that 'ten [internees] out of thirty-five had been let out' after they declared themselves 'anti-Nazi'.[98] Another letter discusses German nuns, having initially been required to report to the police station daily, now being permitted to report weekly.[99] Neill concurred that the internment camps were at least tolerable, 'If one has to be in captivity, it would be hard to imagine a more agreeable prison.'[100]

While there was undoubtedly a certain amount of unease, the mission work in South India continued. Neill summarises the climate at the time: 'It must not be supposed that we spent all our time brooding over our anxieties. For the greater part of the time we were able to go on unhindered with our work, though never with quite the same spontaneity that there had been over ten years earlier.'[101]

The CMS continually made it clear that missionaries were workers not for governments but for God. On 4 August 1939, the General Secretary of the CMS, William Wilson Cash, sent out a four-page letter marked 'Strictly Confidential' that advised the missionaries on the impending emergency.[102] The letter began by pointing out that the CMS was not a

---

96. Bishop of Nasik to Metropolitan Westcott, 23 November 1939, Westcott Papers, Bishops Box 4, Special Collections, Bishop's College. Westcott went to great lengths to help the German missionaries in the camps. In one letter he wrote to a German friend in the camps, assuring him that he was trying to get him released; Westcott to J. Stosch, 26 September 1939, Westcott Papers, Bishops Box 4, Special Collections, Bishop's College.
97. R.B. Manikam, Secretary, National Christian Council, 'Report of an Interview with Government of India', 24 April 1942, Westcott Papers, Bishops Box 4, Special Collections, Bishops College.
98. Bishop of Nasik to Metropolitan Westcott, 26 December 1939, Westcott Papers, Bishops Box 4, Special Collections, Bishop's College.
99. Bishop of Nasik to Metropolitan Westcott, 23 November 1939, Westcott Papers, Bishops Box 4, Special Collections, Bishop's College.
100. Neill, *God's Apprentice*, p. 174. The next chapter discusses Neill's years as bishop (1939-44). Issues involving World War II will be discussed there as well.
101. Neill, *God's Apprentice*, p. 147.
102. William Wilson Cash to 'Fellow-Missionary', 4 August 1939, Westcott Papers, Bishops Box 4, Special Collections, Bishop's College.

political organisation; it existed for 'the interests of the whole Kingdom of God'. Wilson Cash then urged each missionary to 'stick to his job as far as he possibly can'. He argued that those who had been ordained were not to become combatants, and, furthermore, lay missionaries were to 'relinquish their missionary work' if they chose to become combatants.

Neill and the Formation of the Church of South India

One event that occurred during Neill's time as Warden of the Nazareth Seminary would, in Neill's words, 'transform me from a private into a public figure'.[103] The Bishop of Tinnevelly asked Neill to represent the diocese at the General Council of the Church of India, Burma, and Ceylon. Meetings were held every three years in various cities across India. Neill was chosen as Clerical Secretary, a post which put him in touch with the influential leaders of the day. He served in this capacity for ten years and was 'continuously at the heart of things; little passed in the affairs of the Church that did not at one time or another come under my notice'.[104]

By far the most important subject that came before the committee was church union in South India. Discussions had been ongoing since 1919.[105] The first draft on the proposal was released in 1929. For many complicated reasons, the Church of South India (CSI) would not become a reality until the seventh draft was formally accepted in 1947.[106]

If discussions surrounding church union in South India had been discrete in the early years, the draft of 1929 made it a public issue. Many pamphlets were written to explain the situation, to condemn the proposal

---

103. Neill, *God's Apprentice*, p. 133. The year was 1935, p. 134.
104. Neill, *God's Apprentice*, p. 135.
105. The year 1919 is significant because this is the year of the 'Tranquebar Manifesto', the document drawn up by a group of about 30 mostly Indian ministers who had met to discuss Indian ministry and missions. The document is highly ecumenical. It begins, 'We believe that union is the will of God', quoted in Stephen Neill, *Brothers of the Faith* (New York: Abingdon Press, 1960), p. 62. Neill called this 'A master work', Eleanor Jackson's personal collection, p. 240. See also Bengt Sundkler, *Church of South India: The Movement Towards Union, 1900-1947* (Greenwich, CT: The Seabury Press, 1954). Sundkler's work is the recognised authority on the history of the CSI.
106. There were five Churches involved in the union: Congregationalists, Presbyterians, Reformed Christians, British Methodists and Anglicans. Such a union would not occur in the West until the United Church of Canada was formed in 1925 by 70 per cent of the country's Presbyterians, Methodists and Congregationalists. However, the Church of South India had episcopal representation, something with which the United Church of Canada did not have to deal.

4. An Educator in South India: 1928-39   111

or to herald the ecumenical progress.[107] One such pamphlet found a wide audience: *Why South India Churches Are Considering Union*.[108] The authors claimed that they were simply informing their readers about the situation. They thought it a terrible idea:

> hoever in England thinks of the South India United Church should chiefly keep in mind not big town congregations, but groups of humble, rather ignorant village folk gathered in mud-and-thatched sheds, for most of whom denominational questions are completely out of range. . . . Denomination in India is mostly a question of chance and geography, and not primarily of conviction.[109]

In contrast, those mainly British committee members who were involved with the union negotiations were described favourably, 'the proceedings of its Councils are conducted with decorum and reasonable efficiency'.[110] The authors continued their attack, explaining that Indians were entirely clueless about the history of the Church, thus they were bound to have no opinion on the matter of union whatsoever. One gets the striking sense that the united church movement in South India was more about Europeans healing their historical divisions than about Indian Christians negotiating a church for their future. For example, another pamphlet posed the question, 'Is the Scheme the expression of a desire of Indians for Union and have they had a share in working out this Scheme?'[111] The author's conclusion is very telling:

> It must be frankly admitted that inasmuch as the denominational differences among us have arisen largely because of European and American history, it is not strange that the movement to remove

---

107. Writing fifteen years later, Bishop A.T.P. Williams commented, 'The Scheme for Church Union in South India has already stirred a vigorous pamphleteering activity. . . . The subject is difficult and good men do not agree: it is therefore inevitable that most of the writing should be controversial.' See A.T.P. Williams, *Church Union in South India – A Reply to Mr. T.S. Eliot's 'Reunion by Destruction'* (London: SCM Press, 1944), p. 3.
108. Joseph Muir, G.E. Phillips, E.J. Palmer and W.J. Noble, *Why South India Churches Are Considering Union* (London: Hodder & Stoughton, 1929).
109. Ibid., pp. 10-11.
110. Ibid., p. 10.
111. *What About Church Union? Should the South India United Church Accept the Proposed Scheme of Union?* (Pasumalai: A.M. Lenox Press, 1933), p. 3. This pamphlet was issued under the authority of the South Indian United Church Committee on Union.

these divisions should have come originally from those who feel the sins of their forefathers rather than from the Indians whose forefathers had no part in these divisions.[112]

Stephen Neill was one who knew better than this. He knew that the entire process was begun by Indians but was quickly taken over by the Europeans. Later, in 1948, one year after the CSI was established, Neill would reflect:

> Since almost all those who met at Tranquebar [in 1919] and published the memorandum that set the whole process in motion were Indians, some have believed that the union movement grew spontaneously out of the consciousness of the Indian Church. . . . Since most of the negotiators were non-Indians, others have felt that this movement was one in which the Indian Church was not very much interested, and which was being imposed on it, in a form based on western experiences and far too complicated for India to understand, by missionaries from the West. There is some truth in both contentions.[113]

By 1932 negotiations had stalled over to the issue of episcopal ordination, an obstacle that would take fifteen years to resolve. The Presbyterians wanted a church government 'composed of ministers together with lay representatives'.[114] However, the episcopacy was an issue they would have to concede if there was to be church union at all.

Accepting an episcopal structure was even more alien to Congregational Christians. They preferred autonomy, whereby each congregation stood as its own authority. In the final years of negotiations, Congregationalists began to accept the inevitability of an episcopal arrangement. Sundkler recorded that, increasingly, Congregationalists were coming round to

---

112. *What About Church Union?*, p. 3. In reality church unity was every bit as much an Indian matter and many Indians were involved. Sundkler, *Church of South India*, p. 185, writes, '[Bishop] Azariah . . . was regarded, and indeed regarded himself, as the outstanding leader of South Indian church union.' Neill was equally aware of Azariah's contribution to union in south India. In *Brothers of the Faith*, Neill devoted an entire chapter to him, 'Bishop Azariah and the Call to Church Union'. This book is somewhat of an Ecumenical Hall of Fame, as Neill discussed eleven of the greatest leaders of the modern ecumenical movement: J. Mott, N. Soederblom, C. Brent, Azariah, Germanos, W. Temple, W. Paton, H. Kraemer, D. Bonhoeffer, D.T. Niles and John XXIII. On the Joint Committee was another distinguished Indian, A.J. Appasamy, an Oxford University DPhil.
113. Stephen Neill, *The Cross Over Asia* (London: Canterbury Press, 1948), p. 145.
114. *What About Church Union?*, p. 9.

4. An Educator in South India: 1928-39

the reality that, 'As fellowship increases, freedom must to a certain extent decrease.'[115] The Congregationalists clashed frequently with the Anglicans during the negotiations; however, most were committed to unity above all else.[116] Nevertheless, the chief reason that it took so long to establish the Church of South India was the obvious clash on the issue of the episcopate, which came up repeatedly and stultified the negotiations. Of the fifteen bishops who were appointed to the new CSI in 1947, three were from Congregationalist backgrounds, eight from Anglican, one from Presbyterian and three from Methodist.[117]

The Anglicans would not budge at all on this position because of the Church's claim to apostolic succession.[118] The solution to this paralysing dilemma was proposed by Bishop Western, Neill's predecessor in the bishopric of Tinnevelly, in a remarkable document, known to those involved as 'The Pledge'. It was edited several times before finally enabling the negotiations to move beyond the impasse at which they had stalled. The statement is quoted here in full:

> The uniting churches therefore pledge themselves and fully trust each other that the united church will at all times be careful not to allow any overriding of conscience either by church authorities or by majorities, and that it will not in any of its administrative acts knowingly transgress the long-established traditions of any of the churches from which it has been formed. Neither forms of worship or ritual, nor a ministry, to which they have not been accustomed or to which they conscientiously object, will be imposed upon any congregation; and no arrangements with regard to these matters will knowingly be made, either generally or in particular cases, which would either offend the conscientious convictions of persons directly concerned, or which would hinder the development of complete unity within the united church or imperil its progress towards union with other churches.[119]

---

115. Sundkler, *Church of South India*, p. 222.
116. Ibid., pp. 286-87.
117. Ibid., p. 341.
118. The pamphlet *What About Church Union?* clarifies here, p. 11: '"Apostolic succession" is that doctrine . . . which defines episcopacy as having a special grace bestowed upon the apostles by Christ Himself and transmitted by the apostles to the first bishops and from them to other bishops in direct succession from Christ even to the present day. That grace enables bishops to ordain men and to give them authority to celebrate the sacraments. Without that grace no man can be ordained or validly celebrate the Holy Communion.'
119. Sundkler, *Church of South India*, p. 259.

Stephen Neill later commented on the significance of this union, 'for the first time since the Reformation episcopal and non-episcopal Churches have become one, and a new type of Church has come into being, for which there is no earlier precedent'.[120] The end result was that the Church of South India (CSI) became an episcopal church, part of the Anglican Communion.

The formation of the CSI was watched closely by Christians around the world, particularly Anglicans.[121] T.S. Eliot, the poet and a well-known conservative Anglo-Catholic, joined the donnybrook with a pamphlet containing the barbed title, 'Reunion By Destruction'.[122] Like most critics, Eliot's misgivings revolved around the issue of apostolic succession:

> belief in the doctrine [of apostolic succession] is a belief that is binding on the whole Church. The situation is intolerable; unless his mind is as confused as those of the framers of the Scheme, he must either withdraw from that Church or recant. . . . [I]t is part of a fatal crack which runs through the Constitution . . . from top to bottom.[123]

Eliot's publication was one of many pamphlets, however his celebrity beckoned a reply from the then bishop of Durham, A.T.P. Williams, in a publication entitled *Church Union in South India: A Reply to Mr. T. S. Eliot's 'Reunion by Destruction'*. Williams' conclusion was that views like Eliot's would ruin hope of church unions anywhere but particularly in South India.

Stephen Neill was in the thick of all this. His intellectual gifts were useful for such a diverse gathering: several denominations, various countries involved, different theologies at work. Nevertheless, he was very much an Anglican. Bengt Sundkler records, 'Stephen Neill, a member of the Joint Committee from 1935 onwards . . . stated the Anglican standpoint with brilliant lucidity and had a capacity to understand other traditions which was of particular value.'[124]

---

120. Neill, *Anglicanism*, p. 379.
121. Stephen Neill wrote, 'The little group of men and women which met year by year in South India knew that they were like performers in the ring, lighted up by powerful searchlights, their every movement watched by a vast and unseen cloud of witnesses in every country of the world'; Stephen Neill, *Towards Church Union (1937-1952)* (London: SCM, 1952), p. 96.
122. T.S. Eliot, *Reunion by Destruction: Reflections on a Scheme for Church Union in South India: Addressed to the Laity* (London: Council for the Defence of Church Principles, 1943).
123. Ibid., p. 15.
124. Sundkler, p. 184.

4. An Educator in South India: 1928-39

Neill was not part of the inauguration of the CSI; he departed India in 1944.[125] However, he continued to voice his opinions on the matter. He was propelled to the centre of the maelstrom in 1947, the year the union occurred. By that year, Neill was lecturing at Cambridge and was an assistant bishop to the Archbishop of Canterbury. Neill corresponded with several people about the union that year and was clearly resistant to it in its current form. In one letter Neill recorded that, upon hearing what the final draft for union consisted of, he was 'simply horrified'. Clearly, the changeover in the Joint Committee had had an impact on the success of the union. Neill wrote that, when he was a part of the Committee, they:

> never even contemplated the possibility of such a radical separation of the new Church from the Anglican Communion. . . . It seems to me that we are drifting into a very serious and dangerous situation, and that matters of this kind must be cleared up before the new Church comes into existence. It is not clear to me what steps can, or should be taken at this point, but unless action is taken, we may find ourselves faced with a *fait accompli*.[126]

Neill was even encouraged to use his close proximity to the Archbishop to put the brakes on South Indian union. On 23 May 1947, one 'Max' wrote to Neill:

> What both Milford [Campbell] and I feel is that you as Assistant Bishop to the Archbishop should apprise him of the situation . . . [which] really is the most preposterous action. . . . I hope you will feel that you can get the Archbishop's ear about it sometime before you have to go to Canada.[127]

---

125. The union negotiations moved much faster after the stalwarts were removed from the process. This is one of the ironies of the history of the CSI; many of the great men who worked for decades for unity were only allowed to see that promised land from afar. Bishop Western (Neill's predecessor in the Tinnevelly bishopric) left India in 1938. Bishop Waller (also a former Tinnevelly bishop) died in 1942. The Metropolitan of India, Burma and Ceylon, Foss Westcott, died in 1949, having retired from active service in 1945. Bishop Azariah, the great voice of the Indians, died on 1 January 1945. The war years saw several others exit the negotiation process. See Sundkler, *Church of South India*, Chapter 13, 'The Beginning of the End', which begins with a discussion of the turnover on the Joint Committee.
126. Neill to 'My dear Max', 17 May 1947, CMS/G/Y/12/3/1, CMS Archives, University of Birmingham. Almost certainly, this 'Max' is Max Warren, General Secretary of the Church Missionary Society from 1942-62.
127. 'Max' to Neill, 23 May 1947, CMS/G/Y/12/3/1, CMS Archives, University of

Neill replied the following day, 'I think the right action is that they should demand immediately a special session of the General Council to clear up these matters before the Union takes place.' He commented on his attempts to reach the Archbishop: 'I was at Lambeth Palace yesterday, and tried to see the Archbishop, but two other Bishops got in front of me, and I had to come away.' Neill then wrote that he would try to see the Archbishop in a week's time.[128]

Apparently, Neill did get the Archbishop's attention, for in short order a widely read publication from the Archbishop was released entitled, *The South India Church: An Open Letter from the Archbishop of Canterbury to Bishop Stephen Neill*.[129] The Foreword explains the Archbishop's intent: 'As will be seen, this letter has been written from a detached and judicial point of view, and is designed to deal objectively with certain matters about which misunderstandings are frequent, in the hope that fears which spring from those misunderstandings may be allayed thereby.'[130] After explaining the union in some detail, it concluded, 'I hope that I have helped by this review to clarify the situation and to remove some uncertainties.'[131]

Neill was conflicted about the union in South India. He was attracted to the ecumenical dimensions but found it disconcerting in places. There were many on the Joint Committee who agreed with him. In retrospect, it is clear that, without the departure of those fiercely loyal to their denominations and creeds, such as Neill, the CSI never would have become a reality.

The history of the formation of the CSI was a topic that Neill returned to repeatedly throughout his writings. In no fewer than thirteen publications he discussed the event. In his 1948 book, His attitude toward the union can be seen as early as 1948, in his book, *The Cross Over Asia*. In that book, Neill describes his feelings on arriving at Madras, his first time back in India since his abrupt departure in 1944:

> Then I remembered almost with a shock that since I came away another great change had taken place. This is no longer an Anglican Church, it is a Church of South India. . . . For ten years I was engaged in the negotiations, long and sometimes wearisome. . . . At

---

Birmingham.
128. Letter from Neill to 'Max', 24 May 1947, CMS/G/Y/12/3/1, CMS Archives, University of Birmingham.
129. The Archbishop of Canterbury, *The South India Church: An Open Letter from the Archbishop of Canterbury to Bishop Stephen Neill* (Westminster: The Press and Publications Board of the Church Assembly, July 1947).
130. Ibid., p. 4.
131. Ibid., p. 15.

4. An Educator in South India: 1928-39   117

times it seemed that the effort was hopeless and had better be given up. . . . Every source of information open to me confirmed . . . that the inauguration of the new Church . . . gave . . . the feeling of deliverance and rebirth into a new life. . . . It seems to be agreed that a good start has been made. . . . Nevertheless I could sense deep anxiety in the formerly Anglican part of the church. . . . Criticisms of the scheme have been loud and severe. Utterances have been made suggesting that the Anglicans joining the new Church have lost entirely their previous status as Anglicans, and, so far from having gained a wider unity, have lost their part in the world-wide fellowship to which they had previously belonged. What is the truth of the matter? . . . In a few weeks we shall know.[132]

By 1950, Neill was giving approval to the union in unequivocal terms:[133]

After pondering the matter deeply for some years, I have come to the conclusion . . . that the Scheme of Church Union in South India, in spite of all its defects, is the best in all the world, since it alone faces with full frankness the facts of four centuries of division, and proposes a plan to overcome them. . . . I now believe that this is the plan which should everywhere be followed, when the division between episcopal and non-episcopal Churches is to be overcome, and that this method alone can lead in the end to full and unquestioned unity.[134]

Twenty years after the CSI had been formed, Neill was still thinking about it:

The Church of South India has been in existence for nearly twenty years, and its plan has proved itself to be at least workable, though, as we have recognized, not without certain internal and external difficulties. . . . The Church of South India was a monument to . . . ecumenical ideals. . . . Whatever misgivings there may have been, the infant Church soon gave ample indication of health and vigour.[135]

---

132. Neill, *The Cross Over Asia*, pp. 139, 144-47. 'In a few weeks' refers to the Lambeth conference of Anglican bishops that was to take place.
133. Neill delivered the 1950 CMS James Long lectures. These were published in 1952 in an important book by Neill, *Christian Partnership* (Gateshead: Northumberland Press).
134. Ibid., p. 105.
135. Stephen Neill, *The Church and Christian Union* (Oxford: Oxford University Press, 1968), pp. 365, 403.

Neill was a champion of ecumenism all his life. However, his ecumenism was tempered with a realistic understanding of theological difficulties between Churches. The early negotiators of the CSI were actually *too realistic* in their understandings of theological differences. What was needed to overcome the barriers to union in South India was *idealism*. Unsurprisingly, nearly the entire generation who began the South India negotiations had to either die or move out of India before unity finally occurred.

Neill, the CMS and the SPG

It is not surprising that, when Stephen Neill first became interested in affiliating himself with a missionary society, he chose the Church Missionary Society over the Society for the Propagaion of the Gospel. There were clear differences between the two at that time in India. Susan Harper summarises:

> Both [CMS and SPG] were voluntary societies for missions to non-Christians: the CMS expressed the 'low-church' Evangelical side of Anglican spirituality and the SPG expressed the 'high-church' Anglo-Catholic side. They worked side by side in Tinnevelly, where, despite their common evangelistic goals, they often fell prey to disagreements and rivalries. Thus, their growing congregations tended to identify themselves as 'CMS Christians' or 'SPG Christians'.[136]

There were various historical reasons for this division that had existed since the late eighteenth century.[137]

The CMS was founded in 1799 by Evangelicals from the Church of England.[138] As it grew, 'it attracted to itself almost all the "low Church" or Evangelical support for missions in the Church of England, leaving the SPG to be supported almost entirely by high churchmen'.[139] The result was that in South India one could discern whether a particular region was associated with the SPG or the CMS simply by attending a church service.

---

136. Susan Billington Harper, *In the Shadow of the Mahatma: Bishop V.S. Azariah and the Travails of Christianity in British India* (Grand Rapids, MI: Eerdmans, 2000), pp. 11-12.

137. M.E. Gibbs summarises these historical reasons well in *The Anglican Church in India, 1600-1970* (New Delhi: ISPCK, 1972), pp. 45-47. See also Grafe, *History of Christianity in India: Vol. IV, Part 2*, pp. 44-45.

138. See Ward and Stanley, *The Church Mission Society and World Christianity, 1799-1999*, p. 1.

139. Gibbs, *The Anglican Church in India, 1600-1970*, p. 46.

4. An Educator in South India: 1928-39

Neill was aware of these differences; his annual letters between 1929 and 1938 demonstrate this. His comments on the SPG and CMS illustrate that, while the two societies often worked conjointly, their relations remained frosty. For example, in Neill's Annual Letter to the CMS, 1933-34, he wrote about the Nazareth Seminary, where he was teaching at the time:

> Some of the SPG clergy are not at all content on having a CMS man in charge of the Seminary; and feel that the students are not being trained on the old SPG lines. This, of course, is quite true, and Hollis would heartily join with me in saying 'A very good thing too'. But it is as well to remember the task of bringing the CMS and SPG together; the diocese is only beginning, and is very far from having been successfully accomplished.[140]

Neill often compared the CMS with the SPG. Generally, in these cases, he would point to the superiority of the SPG, calling on his superiors in the CMS to step it up in certain aspects of the mission work. For example, in Neill's 1935-36 Annual Letter to the CMS, he wrote the following:

> I have now lived and worked for four years in an SPG station. This is not agreeable to me; and it is made more painful by the evident contract between the optimism, activity and progress which prevail in the SPG part of the diocese, and the discouragement, decay and collapse, which are manifest almost at every point of the CMS area. It appears to me that the SPG is superior to us in building, equipment, staffing organization and finance. We did once make the claim that we were far ahead of them in the spiritual life; I believe that this is still just true; but how long it will continue to be so, I do not know.[141]

Neill often made comparisons between the two, especially when he needed help in his work. On one occasion, he wrote: 'From the SPG, as usual, we have received more than twice as much help as from the CMS.'[142]

---

140. Neill, Annual Letter to the CMS, 1933-34, CMS/G2 AL, CMS Archives, University of Birmingham.
141. Neill, Annual Letter to the CMS, 1935-36, CMS/G2 AL, CMS Archives, University of Birmingham.
142. Neill, Annual Letter to the CMS, 1938-39, CMS/G2 AL, CMS Archives, University of Birmingham.

Neill's allegiance to the CMS came largely out of his evangelical commitments, and he wanted to increase the evangelical character of the Tinnevelly diocese: 'it has to be recognised that the Evangelical witness is still weak in the diocese'.[143] As bishop, Neill tried to change this.

Inklings of a Bishopric

It is uncommon that a man in his early thirties should be considered for a bishopric; yet that is what happened in 1933 when Neill was asked to consider accepting a bishopric in Western China. Only 32 years old at the time, an astonishingly young age for a bishop, Neill consulted his father on the matter and eventually declined.[144] Between 1933 and 1937 Neill received several invitations to serve as bishop in Rangoon (Myanmar/Burma), Mombasa (Kenya), Nagpur (near Bombay) and Colombo (Ceylon/Sri Lanka).[145]

In 1937 the General Secretary of the CMS wrote to the Archdeacon of the Tranvancore diocese, where Neill had served for a year while teaching in Alwaye, to suggest four possible candidates for that bishopric.[146] First on the list was an Indian listed as 'Archdeacon Jacob'. The CMS felt it was time to start appointing Indian bishops because of the tremendous success of Bishop Samuel Azariah in the Dornakal diocese. Neill's name was number two. George Selwyn, Neill's successor at Tinnevelly, was fourth. Neill did not want to leave Tinnevelly. In addition, he had no desire to move back to Kerala. He wanted to stay in the Tamil-speaking area, where he was fluent in the language. The General Secretary learned of Neill's desire to remain in Tamil Nadu and wrote: 'I know how important the Nazareth College is, but I cannot think that it is really as critically important as the diocese of Travancore. . . . I do hope you will not turn it down if the offer is made to you.'[147] Neill's mind was made up, however.[148]

While flattered by these prospects, Tinnevelly was home for Neill. He had poured himself into that place, knew the language and understood the

---
143. Neill to 'Geoff', 27 October 1943, CMS/G/AP7, CMS Archives, University of Birmingham.
144. Neill, *God's Apprentice*, pp. 153-54.
145. Neill, Annual Letters to the CMS, 1937-38 and 1938-39, CMS/G2 AL, CMS Archives, University of Birmingham.
146. General Secretary to Archdeacon Benjamin, 22 April 1937, CMS/G/Y/I5/3, CMS Archives, University of Birmingham.
147. General Secretary to Neill, 7 July 1937, CMS/G/Y/I5/3, CMS Archives, University of Birmingham.
148. Similarly, George Selwyn, Neill's successor as bishop of Tinnevelly, refused the Travancore bishopric when asked.

4. An Educator in South India: 1928-39

work of the Church there. If he were to become a bishop, then Tinnevelly is where he would serve. Neill recounts: 'Having had three mitres almost firmly placed upon my head and three others dangled not far from my nose, . . . I had come to the conclusion that my permanent state in the Church of Christ was that of presbyter. But then, as so often, the utterly unexpected happened.'[149] The story of Neill's rise to the Tinnevelly bishopric is told in the following chapter.

Neill worked hard as an educator in South India. He wrote, 'For eight and a half years theological teaching was my daily and hourly concern. The work was heavy and toilsome.'[150] He accomplished much during that time. He restored respectability to a fledgling seminary, he helped to produce dozens of Indian clergymen and he relocated the seminary to a better location. Seminary work was not his sole focus in those years, however. He helped with Megnanapuram High School and played a critical role in obtaining a new building for the school.[151] He kept the itinerancy campaigns alive, particularly in the north where evidence of the Church was thin on the ground. He published several books that were well received by the Christian public. He had taken a leadership role in the ecumenical discussions taking place. He was able to speak as well in Tamil as in English. The promoters of any large event related to the Church in India were almost certain to hope to put Neill's talent to use.[152] It is in this context that the famous Tambaram International Missionary Conference (IMC) of 1938 should be discussed.[153]

Neill had already accepted the bishopric of Tinnevelly, although he had not been consecrated, by the time the Tambaram Conference took place in December 1938.[154] At the time, this was 'The most widely representative meeting of the World Mission of the Christian Faith ever held.'[155] There

---

149. Neill, *God's Apprentice*, p. 154.
150. Ibid., p. 148.
151. Neill, Annual Letter to the CMS, 1937-38, CMS/G2 AL, CMS Archives, University of Birmingham.
152. In 1937 Neill was invited by the Tuticorin Church to give a series of lectures to non-Christians. This brought him great delight as his opportunities to speak to non-Christians were few and far between during his years at the seminary. The lectures were in Tamil for the most part and the audience was around 400 educated Indians. See his Annual Letter to the CMS, 1938-39, CMS/G2 AL, CMS Archives, University of Birmingham, and *God's Apprentice*, pp. 148-49.
153. Tambaram is located about eighteen miles south of Madras. Historical documents refer to the event as the 'Tambaram Conference' and the 'Madras Conference' interchangeably. The location of the conference was at the Madras Christian College in Tambaram.
154. The 1938 conference was originally to be held in China but the Japanese invasion thwarted the plans.
155. Stephen Neill, 'Madras', *Here and There with the CEZMS*, February 1939, p. 26.

Anglican Delegates at the famous 1938 Tambaram conference.
Neill in bottom row, second from right.

were 470 delegates present from 67 countries. Some of the more prominent figures on the world church scene were present, such as Bishop Azariah, historian Kenneth Scott Latourette, German missiologist Walter Freytag, Hendrick Kraemer and Professor H.H. Farmer of Cambridge. Perhaps the most notable presence was the great statesman of Christian missions, Dr John Mott, who presided and gave the opening address.[156] Mott was the leading figure at the first of these conferences in 1910 held in Edinburgh, the point at which most scholars agree the modern ecumenical movement was born. His authority and respectability in the worldwide church made him the natural choice to head the conference. By all accounts, John Mott knew how to chair a conference. Neill was amazed at the man's 'undiminished powers . . . he had a head start on everyone else'.[157] After the conference, Neill wrote a long letter to Dr Mott, essentially explaining his opinion that, 'Tambaram abundantly justified itself'.[158]

Neill received a personal invitation from William Paton, the organiser of the conference, to serve as chairman of the session 'On the Training of the Ministry'. This was the largest session at the conference and the

---

Neill wrote, 'This was the most international gathering held up to that point in the entire history of the Christian Church'; See Eleanor Jackson's personal collection, p. 276. The second IMC conference took place at Jerusalem in 1928. Tambaram was the third and most eagerly anticipated.

156. Neill, 'Madras', p. 26. Mott's assistant during the conference was William Paton, the eminent Scottish missionary.
157. Neill, *God's Apprentice*, p. 150.
158. Neill to Dr John Mott, 8 January 1939, RG 45, Box 51, Folder 1138, John Mott Papers, Special Collections, Day Missions Library, Divinity School, Yale University, New Haven, CT. Neill also discussed the conference in *God's Apprentice*, pp. 149-53.

4. An Educator in South India: 1928-39

diversity was extraordinary. When it came time to begin, Neill requested that the Lord's Prayer be said, each man in his own language. Neill recorded that there were 48 distinct forms of speech praying in unison.[159]

Years later Neill reflected on his role in that momentous gathering: 'Tambaram meant for me a rather sudden move from obscurity into a certain prominence in the affairs of the Church.'[160] Neill was now regarded as one of the world's foremost leaders in the burgeoning movement of ecumenical Christianity.

Neill's star was rising. His gifts were increasingly being recognised by the wider Church and, when the bishopric opened in his beloved Tinnevelly, he knew it was a task he must take up.

---

159. Neill, *God's Apprentice*, p. 152.
160. Ibid., p. 153.

Chapter Five
Neill's Years as Bishop of Tinnevelly: 1939-1945

Stephen Neill's six years as bishop of the diocese of Tinnevelly took place at a critical time in world history: World War II, the apogee of Indian nationalism and a decline in Western support for Christian missions. Britain was struggling for its own survival. Neill and his diocese were not immune from the tumultuous political events of that era, and, during this time of acute stress, some of Neill's character flaws and maladies would once again come to the fore. Suddenly, in 1944, Neill's diocese would be ripped out of his hands. It was an astonishing turn of events for this rising star of the Church and will be dealt with in detail in the next chapter.

Brief History of the Tinnevelly Bishopric: 1896 to 1939

When Stephen Neill ascended to the Tinnevelly bishopric in 1939, he was the sixth bishop and the fourth Cambridge scholar in a row to hold the position. None of the bishops between 1896 and 1939 disappointed. They were all strong leaders and they all maintained the trust and confidence of their community.

The Tirunelveli diocese looks to the year 1778 as its beginning.[1] That is the year in which 'Clorinda' – a Marathi Brahmin widow known today as

---
1. Muller, *The Tirunelveli Bishopric*, p. 1. Muller's work is the only known printed source devoted solely to the history of the Tinnevelly bishopric. Muller is from the Tinnevelly area and for many years was the official diocesan historian. He served in various academic posts during his long career in Tinnevelly. Prior to retirement he served as the Secretary at the Bishop Stephen Neill Study and Research Centre in Palayamkottai.

the founder of the church in Tinnevelly – was baptized by the missionary Christian Friedrich Schwartz. German missionaries, along with trained Indian clergy, established and nurtured the Tinnevelly area church until Christianity was a significant presence in the region. In the 1820s the CMS and SPG joined in the work that was previously Society for Promoting Christian Knowledge (SPCK) territory and both societies began to make significant progress. Throughout the nineteenth-century mission work flourished. The bishop of Madras supervised the Tinnevelly work until the year 1877, when two assistant bishops were appointed to oversee the Tinnevelly district: Robert Caldwell, representing the SPG, and Edward Sargent, representing the CMS.[2] Upon the deaths of these two men it was clear that a bishopric ought to be established. The mission work in the district had grown so immensely that Tinnevelly needed its own diocesan status.[3]

On 1 February 1894, a resolution proposed by the Metropolitan of India, Burma and Ceylon was passed in Palamcottah that effectively cleared the way for Tinnevelly to gain its first bishop. The new bishop was to be nominated by Bishop Gell of Madras.[4] W.W. Elwes, Gell's trusted archdeacon, received the appointment. He accepted initially but later refused when his wife became very ill.[5] The next choice was Samuel Morley. Morley had been a chaplain to Bishop Gell, but, perhaps most importantly, he was associated neither with the SPG nor the CMS. This would prevent the Tinnevelly Christians from accusing the diocesan leadership of siding with one particular mission society. Morley accepted and was consecrated in Madras on 28 October 1896.

Among the highlights of Morley's episcopate was his involvement in the formation of the Indian Missionary Society (IMS), inaugurated on 12 February 1903.[6] Morley was a strong supporter of the evangelistic band, the

---

2. There is an excellent discussion of the assistant bishoprics of Caldwell and Sargent in Muller, *The Tirunelveli Bishopric*, pp. 19-30.
3. Gibbs, *The Anglican Church in India, 1600-1970*, p. 293.
4. Bishop Frederick Gell was bishop of Madras from 1861 to 1899. See Gibbs, *The Anglican Church in India, 1600-1970*, Chapter 13, 'Bishop Gell and South India: 1861-1899'.
5. Muller, *The Tirunelveli Bishopric*, p. 32.
6. The IMS became an important organisation and made a significant impact through its slogan of 'Evangelizing India with Indian Personnel and with Indian Methods'. The first Indian bishop, V.S. Azariah (bishop of Dornakal from 1912 to 1945), served as its first Secretary. See Jason S. Dharmaraj, 'The Impact of the Indian Missionary Society in India', and M.G. Manickam, 'The Past, Present, Future of the Indian Missionary Society, Tirunelveli'. Both papers are at the IMS headquarters in Palayamkottai. They were presented in 2002 at the IMS

Itinerancy in which Neill later participated. Morley dedicated 26 churches during his time as bishop. During his tenure, he seems to have had a particular zeal for crushing any remnants of Hindu superstition among the Christians. He never learned Tamil, which limited his effectiveness. Notably, he voiced his concern that there were no indigenous bishops in India, although Africa did have some. Morley resigned in October 1903 because of his wife's deteriorating health.[7]

Arthur A. Williams succeeded Morley and served as the Tinnevelly bishop from 1905 to 1914. Williams took a keen interest in educating the blind and deaf. He built up the Tinnevelly Children's Mission. He was a careful keeper of records and his writings are a useful primary source for understanding the history of the diocese. He was an excellent speaker. Bishop Williams died suddenly of a heart attack on 30 June 1914 at Coonoor, the hill station. During the interregnum, Bishop Azariah of Dornakal oversaw the diocese, spending five months in residence there in 1915.[8]

On 28 November 1915 Edward Harry Mansfield Waller became the third bishop of Tinnevelly. Waller was more of an intellectual than his two predecessors. He held an MA from Cambridge and a doctorate of divinity from London College of Divinity when he arrived in India in 1897 as a CMS missionary. He served as principal of two theological colleges and, immediately prior to his bishopric, he had been Secretary for the CMS-India in London.[9]

Waller's work towards reconciliation between the CMS and SPG is the hallmark of his legacy. His most significant action in this reconciliation process occurred in 1917 when he convened a council of elected representatives from both groups to work towards a Tinnevelly diocesan council, rather than having a CMS council and a SPG council making separate decisions that inevitably came into conflict. He formed the Diocesan Trust Association which transferred funds and properties from the societies to the diocese. He left to become the bishop of Madras in 1923.[10]

Norman Henry Tubbs was elevated to the Tinnevelly bishopric in 1923. He was the Tinnevelly bishop when Neill arrived in India in 1924. Like

---

centenary celebration.

7. See Muller, *The Tirunelveli Bishopric*, p. 39. Muller points out that Morley never did effectively unite the CMS missionaries with those of the SPG. He notes that this may have had something to do with Morley's resignation. The conflict would continue for decades.
8. Muller, *The Tirunelveli Bishopric*, p. 45.
9. Ibid., p. 46. See pp. 46-51 for the chapter on Waller.
10. Neill wrote that from the 1820s to the 1870s the relationship between the CMS and SPG missionaries was 'congenial'. After that period the tension began to grow. See Neill, *A History of Christianity in India: 1707-1858*, p. 229.

Waller he was a Cambridge scholar and holder of a doctorate of divinity. He was the first bishop consecrated in Tinnevelly; Bishop Azariah of Dornakal preached the sermon.

Tubbs' work was hampered by continuing conflict emanating from CMS and SPG loyalties. In 1925 there arose a situation involving two dissident pastorates from Alvaneri and Sevel that insisted on the two missionary societies remaining separate.[11] These two pastorates, together consisting of about 10,000 Christians, refused to join the Tinnevelly diocese and insisted that they be placed under the bishop of Madras. They were successful in their demand.

During his time as bishop, Tubbs dedicated 70 churches, raised considerable funds for evangelism[12] and initiated a project to revise the Tamil Bible. Tubbs never achieved fluency in Tamil. In 1928 he was transferred to the see of Rangoon (in Burma, now Myanmar). As his successor the diocese elected Dornakal's Bishop Azariah, who declined the appointment. However, their second choice, Frederick Western, did accept.

Something of a trend was developing when Frederick James Western became bishop of Tinnevelly in 1929, for Western was the third Cambridge graduate in a row to lead the Tinnevelly diocese.[13] He was educated at Trinity College and did his clerical training at Westcott House, the same route taken by Stephen Neill. Like bishops Waller and Tubbs before him, Western was an academician.[14] He went to India around 1905 and served in various academic posts, excluding two years when he was involved in an ascetic group known as the 'Brotherhood of the Imitation of Christ'. Muller records:

> The rule of the Brotherhood was a very severe renunciation of all creature comforts. The members of the Ashram had to live within

---

11. See Muller, *The Tirunelveli Bishopric*, pp. 53-54, for details of this ordeal. See also George Selwyn to Metropolitan Westcott, 1 October 1938, Tinnevelly Box 2, Bishop's College. Selwyn discussed the 'schism' involving these two groups and how Tubbs and Western had worked to bring them back into the fold. The dissidents were 'now drawing nearer and nearer to the diocese' and were quite sorrowful that they were disallowed to participate in the election of a new bishop. There is also a discussion of the 'Alvaneri Schism' in Chapter 3 of the present work.
12. Muller, *The Tirunelveli Bishopric*, p. 54, records that during a 1924 furlough, Tubbs secured a grant from English churches who together promised 6,000 rupees a year solely for evangelism.
13. In the Bishop Stephen Neill Study and Research Centre in Palayamkottai there is a five-page 'Memoir of Bishop Western'. Muller includes the entire memoir in his account of Western, in addition to his own research; see *The Tirunelveli Bishopric*.
14. Muller, *The Tirunelveli Bishopric*, p. 62, discusses Western's academic prowess.

Rs. 5 each per month. The aims were to show our Lord to the Indian people by service rather than by preaching, and to achieve a closer contact with them by living among them. Western lived like a Hindu Sadhu, and for some time took his abode among the Hindu boys in the Hindu students' hostel.[15]

Western brought his ascetic approach into his bishopric where he initiated 'the self-denial offertory', aimed at raising funds for the diocesan evangelistic band, as well as other programmes geared towards propagating the faith. He was also a theological guard dog, occasionally reprimanding leaders for teaching 'wrong instructions and heretical teachings'.[16]

Stephen Neill described his predecessor in his autobiography: 'Frederick Western was of all bachelors the most completely bachelor.'[17] Neill was utterly shocked when a colleague announced in 1934, 'The Bishop is engaged to Grace New.' Neill replied tersely, 'Liar.' The wedding took place later that year. Unfortunately, tragedy struck in 1935 when Western and his pregnant wife were on holiday in the mountains. Both she and her unborn child died suddenly when she developed eclampsia, extreme hypertension during pregnancy that often leads to convulsions and coma. Bishop Western sank into deep despair. He took a leave of absence and returned to England in 1938 but never recovered from the devastation.[18] He chose to remain in England, creating the need for a new bishop.[19]

By 1938 the diocese had existed for over forty years, had been led by a total of five bishops and was in good shape. Its leadership consisted of a bishop, two British clergymen (Neill and George Selwyn), 34 Indian clergymen and over 1,300 lay workers.[20] There were many schools in the region.[21] To the relief of most, the SPG and CMS seemed, finally, to be

---

15. Ibid., p. 57.
16. Ibid., p. 61. See also the 'Memoir of Bishop Western', p. 4.
17. Neill, *God's Apprentice*, p. 154.
18. The tragic events of Frederick Western and his family are retold in Neill, *God's Apprentice*, p. 154.
19. Western resigned at some point before 23 June 1938. Metropolitan's Chaplain to George Selwyn, 23 June 1938, Tinnevelly Box 2, Special Collections, Bishop's College. This letter was written in response to a request by the diocese to be permitted to proceed with the election of a new bishop.
20. Church Missionary Society, *Annual Report of the Committee of the Church Missionary Society for Africa and the East, 1938-1939* (London: CMS, 1939), pp. 67-68.
21. According to the CMS Annual Report, 1938-39, there was a boys' college, many high schools, a training school, three boarding schools and a higher elementary day school. For girls there was the Sarah Tucker College, the Mary Sargent Boarding School, Ooliyasthanam St. T. Foundation School, the Elliott Tuxford School and

5. Neill's Years as Bishop of Tinnevelly: 1939-45

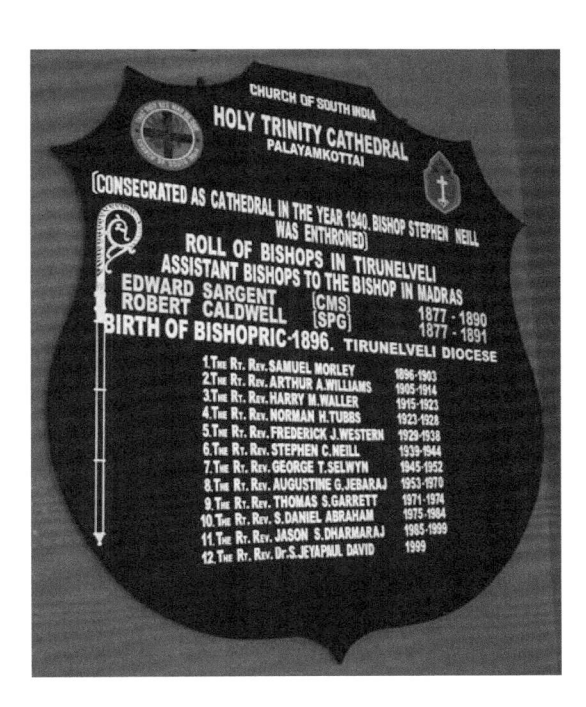

Wall plaque showing history of bishops in Tirunelveli up to 1999. Holy Trinity Cathedral, Palayamkottai.

cooperating. The diocesan council in Tinnevelly had taken control of the diocese, putting the decisions into the hands of the diocesan leaders rather than the SPG and CMS executives in England.

Too rosy a picture should not be painted, however. Bishop Western drew up a table (see below) comparing 1900 with 1937 that appeared in the CMS Annual Report of 1938-39. This table indicates that, while the mission was growing in members and resources, it was struggling to maintain clergy for the growing population of Christians because of a lack of emphasis on ministerial education in the diocese.

Category	1900	1937
Ordained missionaries	15	6
Indian clergy	87	93
Baptized members	80,400	115,000
Communicants	22,000	46,000
Local contributions	£4,150	£13,650

two boarding schools. There was a school for blind boys and girls, as well as a CEZMS school for the deaf and dumb, p. 118. Chapter 3 of the report includes a section on the history of the educational institutions in the Tinnevelly region.

The problems demonstrated in the graph were issues that Stephen Neill had been emphasising for years. Neill predicted that, if more resources were not apportioned towards educating the leadership of the diocese, the growing Christian community could could suffer from the shortfall. Now that Neill was about to become bishop, it would prove difficult to replace his competent leadership at the chief theological college of the Tinnevelly diocese, located in Tirumaraiyur, where Neill had been serving as principal.[22] In addition, the Tinnevelly diocese was also slipping in many of the categories used by the CMS for measuring effectiveness. In 1924, the year Neill arrived in India, Tinnevelly had led in many categories. Much had changed by 1938. The table below illustrates these marked changes.[23]

Category for 1938	Number	Rank (out of 30 mission points in Africa & the East)
Total Foreign Missionaries	16	25th (in 1924 it ranked 20th)
Total Native Workers	1,326	8th (in 1924 it ranked 7th)
Mission Stations	17	12th (in 1924 it ranked 2nd)
Organised Congregations	1,052	4th (in 1924 it ranked 1st)
Total Adherents	78,152	8th (in 1924 it ranked 3rd)
Total Baptisms	3,029	8th (in 1924 it ranked 5th)
Communicants	27,098	5th (in 1924 it ranked 3rd)

When 1924 (the year of Neill's arrival in India) is compared with 1938 (Neill's election to the bishopric), it can be seen that Tinnevelly had lost

---

22. The CMS Annual Report, 1938-39, p. 34, remarked on the predicament, 'The appointment of Rev. S.C. Neill to the bishopric of Tinnevelly deprives the college of a principal who has made a remarkable contribution in the past ten years.'
23. 'Statistical View of the Society's Missions', in CMS Annual Report, 1938-39; and 'Statistical View of the Society's Missions', in Church Missionary Society, *Annual Report of the Committee of the Church Missionary Society for Africa and the East, 1923-1924* (London: CMS, 1924), pp. xiii-xiv.

its once prestigious ranking in every major category when compared with the other 29 CMS mission points in Africa and the East. One chief reason is that, while the number of Christians in Tinnevelly was increasing, the number of Christian workers was in decline. Of these statistics, perhaps the most disappointing was the decrease in rank in organised congregations (from first to fourth) and mission stations (second to twelfth). There was a conflict of interest evident at the time of Neill's bishopric. Should the diocese devote its resources to preparing and supplying clergy? Or should it devote the majority of its resources towards bolstering its evangelisation programmes? Neill had his work cut out for him.

Neill's Rise to the Bishopric

When Neill heard of Bishop Western's resignation, he knew that he would 'very much like to be bishop of Tinnevelly'.[24] Neill was not sure, however, that he would win the election because 'we had all come to the conclusion that the time had come for the election of an Indian bishop'.[25] This issue led the Indian Christians in Tinnevelly into open conflict about who should occupy the bishopric.

A letter to the Metropolitan from 'The Poor Section of Christians in Tinnevelly District' indicates that at least some of them wanted a British bishop. It is clear that this group had grave reservations about the indigenous clergy. Excerpts from this insightful letter are included here:[26]

> Our Gracious Lord,
> ... We now understand that some of the Indian Priests who are graduates are now feverishly trying to occupy the seat of the Bishopric of Tinnevelly and are now running up and down to Calcutta and other places to influence people concerned. Christianity has already been spoiled, as everyone knows, by these so called Indian Clergy of whom, 98% we are sure, are purely worldly minded and are not fit to be called Servants of God. Some of these graduated Priests live very sumptuously in their comfortable Bungalows built by the ancient Missionaries and Bishops and do not stir out of such

---

24. Neill, *God's Apprentice*, p. 155.
25. Ibid.
26. The Poor Section of Christians in Tinnevelly District to Metropolitan Westcott, 6 June 1938, Westcott papers, Bishops Box 4, Special Collections, Bishop's College. The letter includes a postscript which reads, 'To avoid a split and displeasure among fellow members of the Church no names are given here please.'

Bungalows even to offer morning & evening prayers during week days, although they live very near to the Church. Generally they perform one service only on Sundays and festival days leaving the rest of the matters in the hands of the poor Catechist. With regard to the money matters of the Church these priests do what they like keeping under their pocket one or two rowdies of the place.

Now there is a strong rumour current that a Priest now living in the Bungalow of late Bishop Caldwell is trying to become the Bishop of Tinnevelly. If this is true he is a wolf under the skin of a lamb. Let not the choice fall up on him at all, we pray. Let the pious people of the Church of God ask only for a Bishop from England direct, if English Missionaries are not available in India.

Clearly, there were objections to an indigenous bishop in 1938. As the list of nominees narrowed, objections became louder.

On the other hand, there were also Indians who felt it was high time to elect an indigenous bishop. Mr Y. Samuel, the chief editor of *The Good Samaritan*, a South Indian journal published in Madras, wrote a letter to Metropolitan Westcott in Calcutta urging him to overrule the preliminary showings, and 'select an Indian regardless of the number of votes he has obtained'. He then accused Neill and Selwyn of influencing the vote to their advantage. He continued:

The Diocese has had the benefit of European Bishops for over 60 years and it is my firm belief and of a large section of the Christian community in Tinnevelly that it is high time to give a chance to an Indian. . . . It is a pity that the Tinnevelly Diocese which gave India the first Indian Bishop [Azariah of Dornakal] is still without an Indian Bishop.[27]

The rising tide of nationalism taking place during the 1930s was influencing some; however, the Tinnevelly Christians overall preferred European leadership in their diocese in 1938 and for years to come.

The time arrived for nominations for bishop. Tinnevelly's method for electing a bishop was described by Neill: 'any five members of the Diocesan Council, clerical or lay, could combine to nominate any bishop or priest of the Anglican Communion as a candidate for election to the vacant bishopric'.[28]

---

27. Mr Y. Samuel to Metropolitan Westcott, 11 October 1938, Westcott Papers, Bishops Box 4, Special Collections, Bishop's College.
28. Neill, *God's Apprentice*, p. 155.

5. Neill's Years as Bishop of Tinnevelly: 1939-45

Fourteen men were successfully nominated. Below is a table showing how many votes each candidate received.[29]

Nominee	Votes
J.S.C. Banerjee (Asst Bishop, Lahore)	5
A.B. Elliott (Asst Bishop, Dornakal)	5
A.J. Appasamy (Former Lecturer, Calcutta)	5
Michael Hollis (Former Lecturer, Nazareth)	5
W.P. Hares (Canon, Lahore)	5
G.T. Simeon (Priest, Madras)	15
George Selwyn (Principal, Palamcottah)	55
John Asirvatham (Chairman, Sachiapuram)	5
V. Gell Rajiah (Priest, Rangoon)	5
Thomas Sitther (Vice Principal, Calcutta)	5
D. Koilpillai (Chairman, South Church Council)	12
Stephen Neill (Principal, Tirumaraiyur)	35
J.R. Peacey (Principal, Calcutta)	10
R.A. Manuel (Canon, Madras)	5

It is interesting that in Neill's autobiography he got the count wrong. He wrote:

> When the list of persons nominated was printed and circulated, there were fifty signatures under my name. It was clear that Selwyn and I were going to divide the vote, and that there was no Indian candidate who had the confidence of any large section of opinion in the diocese.[30]

Neill was correct in his assertions that he and Selwyn would split the vote and that the results showed that no Indian candidate would be able to compete; however, he was wrong in his recollection of how many votes he received.[31] In fact, it was Selwyn with 55 votes, outnumbering Neill

---

29. P.A. Thangasamy, Chairman of the Diocesan Council, Certificate in the Election of Persons out of whom a Bishop will be Appointed, 29 September 1938, Tinnevelly Box 2, Special Collections, Bishop's College.
30. Neill, *God's Apprentice*, p. 155.
31. This mistake was uncharacteristic for Neill. He was generally very good with remembering facts and figures. Perhaps Neill was remembering one of the votes

by quite a margin. The voters were then asked to write down their top preference followed by their second preference.[32] Only three candidates qualified according to the percentage that had to be obtained: Neill, Selwyn and Sitther who was a distant third. Surprisingly, Neill finished with 80 'first preference' votes, while Selwyn ended up with 61.[33] The results of the ballots were sent to the Metropolitan who calculated the votes by a system in which a certain number of points was allocated for first and second preferences.[34]

In his autobiography Neill claimed he knew the day that the votes would be counted, 18 October 1938.[35] He figured the results would be sent out immediately and would arrive with him on 21 October.[36] Neill went to the chapel for prayer, listened to the reading of a passage in II Corinthians, 'My grace is sufficient for thee' and returned to his study, finding several letters on the table. One was from the Metropolitan, inviting Neill to accept the Tinnevelly see. Neill returned to his normal duties, delivered his lectures and later attended Evensong. It was there, 'by one of those astonishing coincidences that are so much more common in real life than in fiction, the second [Bible] lesson for the day was Acts 6, "They chose Stephen."'[37]

Neill was correct in his recollection of the dates for, in a letter from Neill to Metropolitan Westcott, dated 21 October 1938, he wrote:

---

from the later stages in the election process, or he was given false information about the results. However, after becoming bishop, Neill would have had access to all of the files. Whatever the case, it is unlikely that Neill intentionally misrepresented the numbers here.

32. Metropolitan Westcott took detailed notes of the precise procedure as to how the decision was made. Westcott, Recordings of Proceedings for New Tinnevelly Bishop, 12 October 1938, Westcott Papers, Bishops Box 4, Special Collections, Bishop's College.
33. There was a total of 214 ballots cast. Both Neill and Selwyn knew this sort of result might occur. Neill wrote that he stayed with Selwyn the night before the election and they prayed together about it. Neill claimed, 'On that one night in my life, I, who am a notoriously bad sleeper, laid my head on my pillow at 10 pm, fell instantly asleep, and slept like a child without moving until 6 o'clock the next morning'; Neill, *God's Apprentice*, p. 155.
34. Neill, *God's Apprentice*, pp. 155-56.
35. This was correct as his official appointment is recorded as having taken place on that day. Instrument of Confirmation of the Election of a Bishop, DS by the Bishops of India, Burma, and Ceylon, 30 November 1938, Neill papers, Tinnevelly Box 2, Special Collections, Bishop's College.
36. Neill, *God's Apprentice*, p. 156.
37. Ibid. Acts 6.5.

5. Neill's Years as Bishop of Tinnevelly: 1939-45

My dear Metropolitan,

I have to thank you for your kind letter, and to tell you that I am willing to accept the Bishopric of Tinnevelly.

As you say, there have been reasons which in the past have made me feel it right not to accept Bishoprics. For the last six months, I have been conscious of a great improvement in my health mental and physical, and I have felt that this might be not without a purpose. Then, as the affair of the election began to develop here, and it seemed likely that I might be asked, it gradually became clear to me that this time, I ought not to say No.

I need hardly say how much I feel the need of your prayers and those of the other Bishops in the province. I know a good deal of my own defects. Also something of the unimaginable grace of God, which makes me hope that He will make it possible for me to be of some use to Him as a Bishop in His Church.

Yours very sincerely,
Stephen Neill[38]

Privately, Neill's excitement was obvious in a letter two days later to an unidentified friend named 'Tommy' who lived in Calcutta:[39]

My dear Tommy,

You are a bad and disrespectful man, and I look forward to putting an episcopal curse upon you. But I was very glad to get your letter today, and very glad that you had opened and read my letter. . . .

I can't say in a letter what I feel about it all. I am probably the only person in the world who is genuinely surprised at the result; I always thought Tinnevelly was the one place in which I was certain never to be elected, being by nature a rather outspoken sort of chap, and having as many enemies as that sort of chap usually has. But there is a special joy and consolation in being chosen in a place where all one's faults and imperfections are so well known, and where one can hardly do worse than people fear, and may by divine grace do better than they expect. . . . It's not necessary to say Pray for me. I know you will. And keep the Metro [Metropolitan] up to scratch about fixing the date of consecration and such details; delay is bad for things. . . .

---

38. Neill to Metropolitan Westcott, 21 October 1938, Westcott papers, Bishops Box 4, Special Collections, Bishop's College.
39. Neill to 'Tommy', 30 October 1938, Neill papers, Tinnevelly Box 2, Special Collections, Bishop's College.

Just a few days later Neill received a letter from the Metropolitan concerning the arrangements for the consecration. Westcott's purpose was to enquire from Neill as to where and when he would like the ceremony to occur. Neill replied on 3 November 1938:[40]

> My dear Metropolitan,
> ... It has been in my mind to wonder whether we should take advantage of the unique assemblage of Bishops at the Tambaram Conference for this purpose. ... The programme will be very full, but there are two Sundays, Dec. 11 and 18, which might be thought of for the Consecration.
> ... Another suggestion, which seems to meet with favour in this diocese is that the Consecration should take place in connection with the Consecration of Dornakal cathedral, with which we here have such close connection. This seems not at all impossible; but there is the objection that only a very small number of Tinnevelly people would be able to be present. But in any case, I am willing to fit in with whatever suits you.

After dealing with matters related to the consecration in this letter, Neill reminded Metropolitan Westcott that his furlough was due the following year. Neill felt that, for his own health, a holiday in England seemed 'rather urgently necessary'.[41]

On the following day, 4 November 1938, Neill's appointment was published.[42] The bishop of Dornakal, V.S. Azariah, had by that time heard of the possibilities for Neill's consecration and he offered up his cathedral for the occasion.[43]

---

40. Neill to Metropolitan Westcott, 3 November 1938, Westcott papers, Bishops Box 4, Special Collections, Bishop's College.
41. Ibid.
42. G.E. Tucker to Bishop Azariah, 4 November 1938, Westcott papers, Bishops Box 4, Special Collections, Bishop's College. Tucker was an ordained minister who served on the Metropolitan's staff at Bishop's House, Calcutta.
43. Ibid. Neill held Bishop Azariah in high regard. He discussed him at many places in his autobiography, calling him in *God's Apprentice*, p. 157, one of 'the greatest men and greatest Christians that I have ever known'. Neill was largely responsible for the existence of Azariah's biography by Susan Billington Harper. She writes, 'The scholar who opened my eyes to Bishop Azariah's importance was the late bishop and historian, Stephen Charles Neill. Neill challenged me shortly before he died in 1984 to fulfill his own dream of producing a critical scholarly biography of Bishop Azariah. It has been a privilege to carry out his request.' Harper, *In the Shadow of the Mahatma*, p. xv.

5. Neill's Years as Bishop of Tinnevelly: 1939-45

Vigorous correspondence followed between Neill, Azariah and Westcott regarding the details of the consecration. It was decided that it should be held on 8 January 1939 at Dornakal Cathedral.[44] Neill's appointment was announced in *The Times* on 22 November 1938:

> Stephen Neill has been appointed to the See of Tinnevelly . . . in succession to Bishop Western, who resigned for ill health. Neill took a first class in Classical Tripos part II in 1922, and the Theological Tripos the next year and won many prizes. He was a fellow from 1924 to 1928. In 1928 he was ordained and accepted as a missionary in the CMS and served at Alwaye Christian College in Travancore for two years. Then he became Warden of the Bishop's Theological Seminary at Nazareth, where he has been assisted by a missionary of the SPG. He is a gifted linguist and learned Tamil.[45]

Neill's parents and his sister, Isabel, were present for his consecration.[46] Eight bishops took part, making it 'a great display of ecclesiastical pageantry'.[47] Selwyn, the runner-up to the bishopric, preached the sermon. The scriptures selected for the occasion were Acts 20:17-35 and John 21:15-17.[48] Several songs were sung including 'The Church's One Foundation' and 'Come Holy Ghost, Our Souls Inspire'.

After the great ceremony, Neill returned to Tinnevelly; jubilant crowds greeted him along the way to his mansion, Bishopstowe in Palamcottah. There is a reason why Neill was always so popular among the people; he was fluent in their language. Neill wrote, 'The last bishop who had been able to preach in Tamil was the old Assistant Bishop, Edward Sargent, who died

---

44. In *God's Apprentice*, p. 157, Neill recorded the date of his consecration as 6 January 1939. However, that is the day the Dornakal Cathedral was dedicated. The day of Neill's consecration was 8 January. See 'Order of Service at the Consecration of the Rev. Stephen Charles Neill, Bishop-Designate of Tinnevelly', 8 January 1939, Tinnevelly Box 2, Special Collections, Bishop's College.
45. *The Times*, 22 November 1938, p. 19.
46. Neill, *God's Apprentice*, p. 157. Isabel was working with Muslims in Coonoor.
47. Neill, *God's Apprentice*, p. 157. The bishops who participated in the consecration alongside Metropolitan Foss Westcott of Calcutta were: Azariah of Dornakal; Harry of Madras; Alex of Nagpur; A.B. Elliott; S.K. Tarafdar; John Guildford; W.J. Thompson of France; F.A. Aotearoa of New Zealand; T.S.C. Johnson; and J. Sandegren of Tranquebar. See 'Order of Service at the Consecration of the Rev. Stephen Charles Neill, Bishop-Designate of Tinnevelly'.
48. John 21:15-17 is a well-known passage which records an exchange between Jesus and Peter: 'Jesus said to Simon Peter, "Simon son of John, do you truly love me more than these?" "Yes, Lord," he said, "you know that I love you." Jesus said, "Feed my lambs."'

Stephen Neill, newly enthroned as Bishop of Tinnevelly, 1939.

in 1889.'[49] Neill's fluency in the language was and is widely known. The Tinnevelly Christians today still discuss his ability to speak the language without an accent. It was a shock to many when they first witnessed the phenomenon. It was a rare luxury for an Indian diocese to have this:

> All subsequent bishops [to Sargent] had preached by interpretation, standing on the chancel step. So, as I preached my first sermon as bishop, trying to share with my people my ideal of the servant church and the servant bishop, I knew that there were many among them who were glad to have a shepherd who could speak to them in their own language.[50]

A Brief Furlough in England

Neill had hardly been appointed bishop when he decided to take leave. There were several reasons why he needed to go but chiefly it was because he had been elected Hulsean Lecturer at Cambridge.[51] The appointment was announced in *The Times* on 1 December 1938: 'Stephen Charles Neill has been elected Hulsean Lecturer till the end of the Easter Term, 1940.'[52]

---

49. Neill, *God's Apprentice*, p. 158.
50. Ibid.
51. Ibid., p. 164.
52. See *The Times*, 1 December 1938, p. 8. There is a discrepancy in the dates here. Neill's diocesan letter dated July 1939 states Neill's 'hope to be back in time for Christmas'. Presumably, this meant Christmas 1939. However, *The Times* listed Neill as Hulsean Lecturer until the end of the Easter term 1940. It is unclear

5. Neill's Years as Bishop of Tinnevelly: 1939-45

This meant that Neill was scheduled to be in England during the latter half of 1939 and the first few months of 1940. He placed his friend George Selwyn in charge of the Tinnevelly diocese.[53]

Neill recorded that he left India on 10 July 1939.[54] Before heading to England he chose to take a holiday in the French Alps. As he travelled, it became clear to him that another war was inevitable. He wrote:

> Everyone over the age of thirty must have had vivid memories of the First World War; were there not still sufficient sane people about to guard us against the suicidal madness of a few? In any ordinary situation there would have been; we did not then realise that we were dealing with a maniac, who had managed to cast his evil and hypnotic spell on the best-educated and most intelligent people on the face of the earth.[55]

Arriving in England on 4 August, Neill set out for a month to visit friends and family all over Britain.

The war became a reality for Neill when he was in Aberdeen, drinking a glass of sherry with his great aunt. His cousin Willy burst in the door and said, 'They're bombing Warsaw.' Neill remarked in his autobiography, 'For the second time in my lifetime we were at war with Germany.'[56]

whether *The Times*' information was wrong or Neill foresaw his need to get back to India early, or perhaps another explanation. Neill had accepted an invitation to attend the Lambeth Conference of Bishops in July 1940. In *God's Apprentice*, p. 164, it appears Neill was trying to decide whether or not to stay for an extended time into 1940 or whether to go for a short time between 1939 and early 1940, go back to India and then head to England again for the Lambeth Conference, certainly an impractical schedule. Neill's Hulsean lectures at Cambridge were to be on 'The Forgiveness of Sins'. He was 'terrified' to give the lectures, as he felt, 'after living all these years in an Indian village, I am not at all fit to stand up in the midst of the great scholars of Cambridge to lecture'. Neill, *Letters to His Clergy*, July 1939, Bishop Stephen Neill Study and Research Centre, Palayamkottai. The annual Hulsean Lectures at Cambridge are in honour of John Hulse (1708-90), an English clergyman who graduated from Cambridge in 1728. He bequeathed a large part of his estate to Cambridge University upon his death, which serves to fund the lectureships. The recipient of the award is required to deliver four lectures, stipulated to be on the topic of either Christian evidence or Scriptural difficulties, although greater flexibility has been extended over the years regarding the topics.

53. Neill, *Letters to His Clergy*, July 1939, Bishop Stephen Neill Study and Research Centre, Palayamkottai.
54. Neill, *God's Apprentice*, p. 164. Neill recorded that he fell ill with a 'septic throat' during the journey back to Europe. Neill almost always became sick while on the sea.
55. Ibid.
56. Ibid., p. 166.

Bishop Stephen Neill in his prime, c. 1943.

The war had repercussions on Neill's visit. His first concern was getting back to India. Second, he went to Cambridge to enquire about the Hulsean Lectures. It was decided that they would be delayed until after the war. Now that the heavy preparation required for these lectures was off the itinerary, Neill was free to visit his relatives and friends. He recorded that his first visit was to his brother Gerald, who was serving as vicar near Gateshead, and then he went to see his father.[57] His father was vicar at St Keverne, Cornwall; Neill went southwest and served as his father's curate for several weeks.

Neill was able to book a Dutch ship sailing to India on 10 October 1939, cutting his furlough short.[58] After an awful journey – he fell ill at

57. Ibid., p. 165. He preached at his brother's church on 3 September.
58. Ibid., p. 166. Neill allowed a glimpse into his evolving ecumenical consciousness while sailing for India. He, a Dutch chaplain and a Dutch missionary planned a worship together; 'These were still pre-ecumenical days, and my colleagues were considerably surprised at such a suggestion coming from an Anglican bishop.'

sea – he arrived at Palamcottah on 24 November 1939.[59] Upon returning to India, Neill vowed to stay in good communication with his diocesan leaders: 'I have decided that in the future I will send out a letter each month to all the clergy.'[60]

Neill's Years in the Bishopric

The office of bishop in the Anglican Communion was a prestigious position to hold in Tinnevelly in the 1930s; it came with many perks. Neill wrote, 'I had to maintain what in England would appear to be a rather lordly establishment.'[61] Neill recorded that, while 'the average salary of an Indian priest was about 50 pounds a year',[62] the bishop received about £1,100 per year.[63]

Neill detailed the benefits that came with being 'kicked upstairs' to the bishopric.[64] First, he moved from 'a very small house with a tiny staff to a fair-sized mansion . . . with an adequate staff of servants'.[65] His staff included: a chaplain, who lived in a separate house on the Bishopstowe compound;[66] a clerk, who took dictation by typewriter, kept accounts

---

59. Neill to Metropolitan Westcott, 28 November 1939, Westcott Papers, Bishops Box 4, Special Collections, Bishop's College.
60. Neill, *Letters to His Clergy*, December 1939, Bishop Stephen Neill Study and Research Centre, Palayamkottai. These diocesan letters are the most important primary sources for Neill's bishopric.
61. Neill, *God's Apprentice*, p. 159.
62. Eleanor Jackson's personal collection, p. 318.
63. Bishop Frederick Western (Neill's predecessor to the Tinnevelly bishopric) to Metropolitan Westcott, 3 April 1933, Bishops Box 4, Special Collections, Bishop's College. It is conceivable that the bishop's salary would have been increased by 1939. The Colonial Bishoprics Fund provided half of Western's salary that year; it was £544. The CMS, SPG and Tinnevelly diocese provided the other half. The author was unable to find Neill's exact salary during his tenure as bishop, however, the annual cost of a bishop in India in 1945 (Neill's final year as bishop) was 8,400 rupees per year. The bishop would receive an additional 3,216 rupees were he to leave India on furlough or business. A house, furniture, car and typewriter were also provided. A bishop had to have served in India a total of fifteen years in order to be eligible for a pension upon retirement. Westcott Notes on Bishopric Costs, 28 October 1944, Westcott papers, Bishops Box 4, Special Collections, Bishop's College.
64. Eleanor Jackson's personal collection, p. 293.
65. Neill, *God's Apprentice*, p. 159.
66. Neill's first chaplain was R.V. Avirvadam. In 1941 Neill made him archdeacon, along with the following as canons: G. Selwyn, D. Koilpillai, S.S. Moses, M.V. John and I. Gnanayutham. Neill to Metropolitan Westcott, 25 April 1941, Bishops Box 4, Special Collections, Bishop's College. See *God's Apprentice*, pp.

and filed records; a driver for the new Chevrolet;[67] an office messenger who communicated messages from the bishop by bicycle, as there were no telephones; a butler; a cook; a sweeper; and two gardeners for the lavish, beautiful verdure.

Neill's life in his new position was very regimented.[68] At 6 a.m. early tea arrived. He would sit on the flat roof of the bishop's house and read an 'English weekly'. At 7 a.m. he would spend one hour in the little chapel on the roof. Work began in the office at 9 a.m. While in the office, Neill 'was always clad in a white cassock and pectoral cross'. At noon Neill, the chaplain and the clerk would pray in the small chapel on the roof. Lunch and rest would follow. Work in the office would resume until tea. Neill would then get some exercise, usually tennis or a walk, followed by a bath and Evensong in the chapel. Dinner followed, then reading with 'many cups of tea' concluded the workday.

Visitation of the Diocese

Once Neill had settled into a routine, it became clear to him that the only way to understand his diocese was to visit the churches, all 1,000 of them.[69] This would take considerable effort;[70] Neill predicted, 'This will probably take me three years, and will be a very heavy labour indeed.'[71] During the diocesan visits of 1940 Neill 'took 122 Confirmation services . . . and confirmed 3500 candidates myself, which meant sometimes taking three services in a day'.[72] Soon Neill realised his goal of getting round all the villages in three years was too ambitious. In his diocesan letter of January 1941 he reckoned it would take four.

159-60, for Neill's discussion of his staff and quarters.

67. It should be noted that a driver also had to be a mechanic, as it was common for breakdowns to occur in the countryside. The new car had been provided by the previous bishop.

68. See Eleanor Jackson's personal collection, pp. 298-99.

69. Neill wrote one letter per month to his clergy, beginning in December 1939. The letters were sent out regularly until number 47, dated 19 July 1944. Neill's bishopric can be closely followed through these letters. They are located at the Bishop Stephen Neill Study and Research Centre, Palayamkottai. Henceforth only the number and date for each diocesan letter cited will be documented.

70. In *God's Apprentice*, p. 185, Neill recorded that there were about 1,000 villages which he had planned to visit: 700 villages that had a minister and 300 that held services via a visiting minister.

71. Neill, *Letters to His Clergy*, no. 1 (January 1940).

72. Neill, *God's Apprentice*, p. 162. This is also recounted in *Letters to His Clergy*, no. 13 (January 1941).

5. Neill's Years as Bishop of Tinnevelly: 1939-45   143

Neill enjoyed being out in the villages. There were problems, however:

> As I go about the diocese, I become more and more concerned about the lack of genuine Christian life in our village congregations. . . . [T]he number of those who actually attend church with any regularity is very small, and, . . . private prayer and Bible reading are almost unknown. We have to aim at raising the whole standard of Christian life.[73]

Neill tried to remedy this situation by sending out teams of four into the villages to conduct 'eight-day missions'. These missions included daily Bible teaching, sectional meetings, games and sports and an evening worship service. They lasted from Sunday to Sunday and concluded with the partaking of Holy Communion.[74]

By August 1942 Neill began to doubt that he would be able to visit all the churches, due mainly to war-time restrictions, such as petrol rationing and infrequent trains.[75] The war endured for the rest of Neill's episcopate and his goal went unfulfilled. Later, when writing his autobiography, Neill reminisced: 'It has always been a matter of great regret to me that I was never able to finish my visitation. I still think that the plan was excellent; but the end of my service in India came before the visitation had been completed.'[76]

Confirmations

One of the primary responsibilities of a bishop is to perform confirmations. In 1940 Neill was proud to point out that he was responsible for performing 'the largest number of confirmations ever held' in Tinnevelly.[77] In January 1941 he decreed that he would not perform confirmations for fewer than

---

73. Neill, *Letters to His Clergy*, no. 23 (November 1941).
74. Ibid.
75. Neill, *Letters to His Clergy*, no. 32 (August 1942).
76. Neill, *God's Apprentice*, p. 186. Part of Neill's visitation project was to gather information in order to make maps of the diocese. In 1941 two of his *Letters to His Clergy* (nos 14 and 23) state that Neill would be coming around to look at the maps that had been created by the pastors of the particular regions. The maps were eventually completed. Related to the maps project, this project was trying to come to an assessment of how many Christians there were in the diocese. This was a very difficult task. Neill and his clergy worked hard to obtain statistics (which he claimed probably had a margin of error of fifteen per cent) for the diocese but precise numbers were never possible to obtain. Neill, *God's Apprentice*, pp. 185-86.
77. Neill, *Letters to His Clergy*, no. 13 (January 1941).

25 people at a time. This was increased to 40 in November and he could not be expected to exceed three confirmation ceremonies per day.[78] Neill was also fond of extensive and detailed documentation. In February 1941 he ruled that every pastorate was to maintain a confirmation register that was to include a considerable amount of information.[79]

The preparation Neill assigned for confirmation candidates was great. He split the candidates into two groups: literate and illiterate. While the illiterate had to learn substantial material, the agenda for preparation for those who were literate was heavy indeed. Neill required a preparation period of three to six months; candidates for confirmation were to have 'mastered the Prayer Book Catechism with explanations'; they had to pass an interview by the priest and be convincing in their pledge to maintain regular habits of prayer and Bible study; they were to possess a Bible, prayer book and lyric book prior to confirmation; they were to know the confirmation promises, 'not all the words, but the substance and meaning'; they were required to know the Pentecost story and to understand the Holy Spirit; they were to understand communion and attend regularly after their confirmation; and they had to be at least fourteen years old.[80] On some occasions when Neill thought the candidates were unprepared, he postponed the confirmations.[81]

Marriage and Divorce

A large proportion of the letters from Neill to his clergy dealt with marriage and divorce. One senses the frustration in Neill on these matters; in July 1940, *Letters to His Clergy* (number seven), he wrote:

> As you know, it is part of the cross which the Bishop carries that he is so much more concerned with unholy than with Holy Matrimony. . . . I like to associate myself with the people of the diocese in their times of special rejoicing. But such occasions are not very many, when compared with the immense number of difficulties, irregularities, and broken marriages, the news of which crowds my office table day after day.

---

78. Neill, *Letters to His Clergy*, no. 13 (January 1941) and no. 23 (November 1941).
79. Neill, *Letters to His Clergy*, no. 14 (February 1941).
80. Even this is not the extent of the regulations Neill laid down for his diocese. There is an appendix in his collected *Letters to His Clergy* that stipulates the confirmation rules, the precise duties to be followed on the confirmation day and a section on 'after confirmation'. In all there are 28 rules. See also *Letters to His Clergy*, no. 22 (October 1941).
81. Neill, *God's Apprentice*, pp. 162-63.

5. Neill's Years as Bishop of Tinnevelly: 1939-45

Neill was disturbed by rampant pre-marital sex taking place among the youth. Neill wrote sternly to the priests on this matter, encouraging them to teach that this is 'directly contrary to the teaching of the Bible and the Church'.

Neill authorised only ten minutes for the marriage address, an address that should always point 'directly to Christ'.[82] The marriage service should be 'carried out according to the Prayer Book and in no other way'.[83] Neill was aghast when he went to a marriage ceremony and found it so loosely structured: 'the tying of the *tali* was followed by the singing of a lyric. This is quite incorrect. The whole section, beginning with the words "With this ring," down to the end of the first blessing, must be said without a break of any kind.'[84]

Neill ordered that the local priest must visit all newlywed couples twice in the first three months of their married life.

Early in his episcopate, Neill had to deal with an 'unfortunate' situation – mixed marriages between Christians and Hindus: 'The chief point to remember is that all who have had anything to do with such a marriage have by that act cut themselves off from the fellowship of the Church, and are in the state of excommunicated people.'[85] Excommunication was based on the issue of idolatry, since Hinduism would be a part of the marriage ceremony and of the married couple's life.

Regarding divorce, Neill wrote, 'The Church of this province does not recognise divorce. It takes seriously the words of the marriage service that nothing but death can break a marriage solemnly made in the presence of God.' The problem, however, was that the law of the land did permit divorce. Neill's ruling was that, if divorce were to take place, it had to do so separately and apart from any clergyman and, Neill added, 'I will not in any circumstances give permission for the marriage of divorced persons in Church.'[86]

Other 'irregularities' with which Neill had to deal was the practice of a man marrying his deceased wife's sister and a woman marrying her deceased husband's brother, practices he allowed under certain conditions. Another marital anomaly that was not permitted by the Anglican Church was a man marrying his niece. It is clear from one of Neill's letters that, while he could

---

82. Neill, *Letters to His Clergy*, no. 7 (July 1940). According to this letter, since Neill never married, he generally spoke of the example of his parents during the marriage services he conducted.
83. Neill, *Letters to His Clergy*, no. 18 (June 1941).
84. Ibid.
85. Neill, *Letters to His Clergy*, no. 10 (October 1940).
86. Neill, *Letters to His Clergy*, no. 12 (December 1940).

not authorise such an arrangement, as it was illegal in the Anglican Church (but not in the Roman Catholic), he thought it a mistake to cut the people involved off from the church.[87]

A Difficult Case

On one occasion Neill had to address an incident involving a married, Indian minister named I.N.S. Ponnuswamy from the region of Sawyerpuram. Ponnuswamy was an intelligent man, fluent in English. A scandal had broken out in 1937 (before Neill became bishop) when a young widow named Nallathambi Chellammah charged that this man had made her pregnant during a pastoral visit ten months before. On 19 November 1937 Ponnuswamy wrote a sworn declaration that he was innocent of the charges and that his relationship with the woman was strictly that of 'pastor and a sheep'.[88] However, the woman wrote a sworn declaration days later on 26 November that was in direct contradiction.[89] She asserted that Ponnuswamy came to her house at midnight on one occasion and tempted her to the point of having intercourse. When she realised she was pregnant, he bought purgative pills for her to induce miscarriage. The pills failed and she gave birth, racking up 100 rupees of debt in the course of these events. The woman wanted compensation and continued payment, as she had been cast out by her family. For Ponnuswamy, his reputation and livelihood as a minister were at stake.

Initially, the matter was dealt with by Neill's predecessor, Frederick Western and the case went to the Bishop's Court for trial.[90] Ponnuswamy was found guilty unanimously by the Diocesan Consistory Court on 19 January 1938.[91] Bishop Western wrote to Ponnuswamy on 8 February 1938 to inform him of the decision, 'Guilty of the charge of having had carnal intercourse' with the woman.[92] Ponnuswamy's ministerial licence

---

87. Neill, *Letters to His Clergy*, no. 20 (August,1941).
88. I.N.S. Ponnuswamy, Sworn Statement, 19 November 1937, Tinnevelly Box 2, Special Collections, Bishop's College.
89. Nallathambi Chellammah, Statement of Events, 26 November 1937, Tinnevelly Box 2, Special Collections, Bishop's College.
90. Bishop Western to Ponnuswamy, 10 December 1937, Tinnevelly Box 2, Special Collections, Bishop's College.
91. George Selwyn, Ruling on Ponnuswamy Case, 19 January 1938, Tinnevelly Box 2, Special Collections, Bishop's College. It probably did not help Ponnuswamy that he had written an acrimonious letter to Selwyn in August 1937 completely unrelated to the events under discussion. I.N.S. Ponnuswamy to G.T. Selwyn, 19 August 1937, Tinnevelly Box 2, Special Collections, Bishop's College.
92. Bishop Western to Ponnuswamy, 8 February 1938, Tinnevelly Box 2, Special Collections, Bishop's College.

5. Neill's Years as Bishop of Tinnevelly: 1939-45 147

was immediately revoked and Western concluded, 'I think therefore that you will do better to give up the thought of returning to the work of a clergyman, and seek some other work.' Ponnuswamy promptly appealed. According to a letter from the Metropolitan's chaplain, dated 9 August 1938, 'The man's appeal failed.'[93]

Ponnuswamy's wife wrote to Metropolitan Westcott on 27 July 1940, begging for Westcott to reconsider the decision regarding her husband.[94] She felt three years' suspension was too harsh. By the time she wrote, her husband had completed nearly two years of his suspension. Her letter claimed that her family was unable to eat adequately and that her children were unable to pursue their education: 'We are almost ruined. We find it difficult to get our daily bread. So my Lord . . . I beg you to cancel the sentence and take him again. Our Bishop [by now Stephen Neill] says that he cannot meddle with the sentence pronounced by you.'

The Metropolitan's chaplain wrote back to Mrs Ponnuswamy to tell her that the decision was not made by the Metropolitan but by the ecclesiastical court, thus the Metropolitan could not overturn it.[95]

Two years later, on 7 July 1942, Mr Ponnuswamy wrote to Metropolitan Westcott, informing him that, while he was due to be reinstated on 4 August 1941, Bishop Neill and Reverend Selwyn had refused to resolve his case.[96] He claimed Selwyn had 'considerably prejudiced the mind of the bishop' against him. Ponnuswamy recorded the following regarding a conversation with Neill:

> I saw Bishop Neill and spoke to him on the 30th of June about my restoration. He told me that he consulted some people who advised him not to give me back ministerial work hereafter but to employ me as a catechist on a smaller salary. He is advised not only to reduce my status but asks to cut down my salary when he has already illegally extended the period of my suspension to one more year.

Westcott wrote back to Ponnuswamy on 15 July 1942 advising him, 'I think you would be wise to seek some other form of employment.'[97]

---

93. Metropolitan's Chaplain to Col. N.F. Barwell, 9 August 1938, Westcott Papers, Bishops Box 4, Special Collections, Bishop's College.
94. Mrs. I.N.S. Ponnuswamy to the Most Reverend Foss Westcott, 27 July 1940, Westcott papers, Bishops Box 4, Special Collections, Bishop's College.
95. Metropolitan's Chaplain to Mrs I.N.S. Ponnuswamy, 1 August 1940, Westcott papers, Bishops Box 4, Special Collections, Bishop's College.
96. I.N.S. Ponnuswamy to the Most Rev. Foss Westcott, 7 July 1942, Westcott papers, Bishops Box 4, Special Collections, Bishop's College.
97. Westcott to Ponnuswamy, 15 July 1942, Westcott papers, Bishops Box 4, Special

On 12 October 1943 Ponnuswamy sent a nine-page letter to Bishop Neill, retelling his side of the story. The letter is vitriolic in its tone:

> It is loathsome that you are wanting in regard for truth, humanity and social decorum. . . . Your conduct . . . is unworthy of a Bishop and a Gentleman. . . . You are the organ of the Rev. G.T. Selwyn; you have neither brain to think nor eyes to see but according to his direction. It is indeed most extraordinary, that a mind like yours, a mind richly endowed in many respects by nature, and highly cultivated by study and classical acquirements, a mind which has exercised considerable influence on the most enlightened people in England, should be utterly destitute of the power of discerning justice. . . . You act in the most unscrupulous, horribly immoral, murderously cruel and impeachably unjust manner, and it is melancholy to note how hopelessly you grope your way from blunder to blunder to camouflage the situation. I find in you a tyrant; not a small teasing tyrant, but an awful tyrant like an avenging angel. . . . You are deficient in a horrible way in the two great elements of all social virtues in which your pious father is reputed to be abundantly rich: in respect for the rights of others and in sympathy for the sufferings of others. . . . The wounds which you have inflicted on me are too deep to be effaced or even cannot be properly healed.[98]

Ponnuswamy sent a copy of the letter to Metropolitan Westcott, who replied essentially that it was entirely up to a bishop to consider a priest for employment.[99] Strangely, Neill seems never to have written about this incident.

Education

In Neill's monthly *Letters to His Clergy*, he scarcely mentioned the work in the schools. This is very odd, since education was Neill's job prior to his bishopric. The only explanation for the obvious omission in the *Letters* seems to be that the majority of his clergy would have had little need to understand the inner workings of the educational institutions. Neill did

---

Collections, Bishop's College.
98. Ponnuswamy to Neill, 12 October 1943, Westcott papers, Bishops Box 4, Special Collections, Bishop's College.
99. Westcott to Ponnuswamy, 28 October 1943, Westcott papers, Bishops Box 4, Special Collections, Bishop's College.

endeavour to bring the teachers up to par in their knowledge of theology with his 'Tinnevelly Theological Series' that contained four or five books published each year in Tamil during his reign. Neill recruited several clergy and missionaries to contribute volumes to the series while he wrote one book each year during his bishopric. One of his books was on the Eucharistic liturgies of the Church; another was on the Reformation. In 1939 the first of these books came out, on St Athanasius, the great defender of Trinitarianism against Arianism.[100] The contributors to the series were not paid and Neill did the editing.

Diocese of Tirunelveli printing press, initiated by Stephen Neill in 1942.

In addition to helping the Tinnevelly-area teachers in their theological understandings, the Tamil series of books gave birth to an important chapter in the Tinnevelly diocese: the acquisition of a diocesan printing press. Neill was determined to get a copy of the Tamil Bible into the hands of all of his people but there was a rather difficult practical problem to be surmounted: 'This was wartime; the stock of paper was in Calcutta, the

---

100. Eleanor Jackson's personal collection, p. 337. In Neill's 1941 report to the SPG, he wrote: 'I have found it quite impossible to continue my study of Tamil. Until I became Bishop, I had a teacher in for an hour every day that I was in headquarters and read with him. Since I became Bishop, I have hardly opened a Tamil book. This is a grievous loss, but one can't have everything. Each year I try to produce one book in Tamil for the Tinnevelly Theological Series, and have just finished a small book, historical, on Christianity and Islam.' See 'Diocese of Tinnevelly: Report for the year 1941', SPG E95, located at the Bodleian Library of Commonwealth and African Studies at Rhodes House, Oxford.

printing press in Madras, with a thousand miles between them and no means of bringing them together.'[101] Thus, Neill ventured to buy for the diocese its own printing press. The Tinnevelly Diocesan Printing Press was established by Neill in 1942 and to this day is an important part of the Church's activity in Tirunelveli. Based in Palayamkottai, the press enjoyed its 75th anniversary in 2017.

War

Neill's bishopric, 1939 to 1945, covers the exact years of World War II. It is curious that Neill does not mention the war in his *Letters* until January 1941: 'The work of God has gone forward, even in these troublous days of war, and we can say that the diocese is not weaker, perhaps even a little stronger than it was a year ago.'[102]

In March 1941, however, Neill devoted the majority of that month's clerical letter to condemning the raffles and lotteries invented by the British government to raise money for the war: 'The gambling instinct is strong in all men and is doing great harm among our people.'[103] Other than that, Neill's comments regarding the war are limited to discussing travelling restrictions.[104] All of that changed however in April 1942:

---

101. Neill, *God's Apprentice*, p. 178.
102. Neill, *Letters to His Clergy*, no. 13 (January 1941). Neill's writings highlight few significant changes in the mission work, noting only minor inconveniences and moments of anxiety. During WWII Christian missions to India suffered. Gibbs, *The Anglican Church in India, 1600-1970*, p. 378, notes, 'Mission institutions soon began to suffer, as any hope of sending new men from England or of raising new money was of course at an end, and this time all British laymen of military age were conscripted at once.'
103. Neill, *Letters to His Clergy*, no. 15 (March 1941).
104. Tirthankar Roy's study, *The Economic History of India, 1857-1947* (Oxford: Oxford University Press, 2000), points to some of the constraints placed upon all in India at the time. He writes, pp. 164-65, that 'the Second World War . . . led to a massive scarcity of food . . . and was thus a bad time for the labourer and labour-intensive occupations.' Neill orchestrated a cooperative store for the selling of grain during his bishopric. While Neill was preparing for a worst-case scenario in which hunger may have become a factor, the harvests remained good during his episcopate and food rationing was never a major concern in Tinnevelly. The idea behind the cooperative store was 'to purchase grain in large quantities and to sell it at as reasonable a price as we could manage'; Neill, *God's Apprentice*, p. 170. The cooperative store that he established still exists in Tinnevelly and is another of Neill's legacies. In a letter to the SPG dated 15 July 1940, Neill wrote: 'My great difficulty has been that no one in India has yet taken the war seriously. The general attitude has been "They won the last war and they will win this. Things may be difficult for a time, but all will come right in the end." Very few

5. Neill's Years as Bishop of Tinnevelly: 1939-45

It was the entry of Japan into the war that made our situation really serious. The war, which had been so distant, now was at our very doors. We read of one disaster after another. Singapore first, and then Rangoon; then, within a few weeks, the Japanese were at the gates of India. It was touch and go.[105]

Neill gave explicit directions to his clergy on what to do if the Japanese invaded South India. He figured it a real possibility that the Japanese would isolate South India and cut it off from the rest of the country, as well as from British control. In that event, the Church should not resist the invaders; this would lead only to 'useless bloodshed'.[106] He wrote that the Church had continued to function in China, despite the Japanese occupation. India would do the same.[107] Neill wrote in June 1942, 'I am not a prophet; but I believe that the Japanese have lost their chance, and that we shall hear no more of an invasion.'

---

indeed I think have realised the extreme gravity of the situation for the world and for the missions. The events of the last two months have at last begun to work deeply on the Indian consciousness. There is a real feeling of the seriousness of the war, a very wide spread feeling that India must take a greater part in it and some understanding of what it would mean if the enemy won.' Neill to the Overseas Secretary, SPG, 15 July 1940, SPG E95, located at the Bodleian Library of Commonwealth and African Studies at Rhodes House, Oxford.

105. Neill, *God's Apprentice*, pp. 168-169. Gibbs, *The Anglican Church in India, 1600-1970*, claims that Japan's threat to India came as early as December 1941 with the defeat of Singapore. She notes that the Japanese occupied all of Burma, murdered the archdeacon and forced the bishop to flee to India. She writes, 'The cathedral was desecrated and used as a brewery'; p. 378. Neill's 'Report for the year 1941' to the SPG begins thus, 'This year has been in many ways an exhausting and taxing one. The anxieties of the war and certain difficulties in the internal situation have added to the burden of the Bishop's work. But we have ended the year in a state of fair prosperity, and with most of the immediate difficulties overcome.' See 'Diocese of Tinnevelly: Report for the year 1941', SPG E95, located at the Bodleian Library of Commonwealth and African Studies at Rhodes House, Oxford.

106. Neill, *Letters to His Clergy*, no. 29 (April 1942).

107. Neill disclosed the reasons for his fears in *God's Apprentice*, p. 169. He claimed his anxieties were because the Japanese had bombed Colombo (in Ceylon/Sri Lanka) from the air and in early 1942 had led a military sweep across southeast Asia. In addition, there was a massive mix-up when the government sounded a signal to alarm the people that a Japanese fleet was sailing for Madras. This was only an exercise drill but many had no idea the signal was only precautionary.

Gibbs, *The Anglican Church in India, 1600-1970*, p. 379, notes that the Japanese threat really did not come to a permanent halt until 1944 when the battles of Kohima and Imphal in Assam, in northeast India, resulted in a decisive defeat of the invading Japanese army.

In his autobiography, Neill wrote that 'India itself was bitterly divided on the issue of the war'.[108] On the one hand, he noted, those who knew of Hitler and his doings knew that he must be stopped. On the other, there was a widespread opinion promulgated by the Congress Party that the war was between imperialist powers and that India could profit most if Britain were forced to relinquish India, hastening its independence.[109] Ultimately, Neill pointed out, India as a whole decided not to support the British government and not to support the war effort.[110] This did not seem to disturb Neill. He was more concerned with his flock than with the political situation, although he was always in tune with political developments.[111]

Neill's Writings

In spite of an exacting schedule, while he was bishop, Neill made time for research and writing. His first publication began as a series of addresses at a missionary conference in the city of Kodaikanal in 1937. Neill's lectures at that conference were on the second half of the Apostles' Creed.[112] In 1940 he published the lectures as *Beliefs*.[113] The success of *Beliefs* spawned a second volume entitled *Foundation Beliefs*, based on Neill's 1941 lectures

---

108. Neill, *God's Apprentice*, p. 170.
109. On the widespread opposition to the war effort by the All-India Congress Committee, see S.M. Burke and Salim Al-Din Quraishi, *The British Raj in India: An Historical Review* (New York: Oxford University Press, 1995). Of particular relevance is Chapter 17, 'World War II', pp. 333-60. The All-India Congress Committee (AICC) is the secondary decision-making body of the Indian National Congress. Members of the primary decision-making body, the Congress Working Committee, are elected from the AICC. For more on Indian political parties, see *The India Handbook* (Chicago: Fitzroy Dearborn, 1997).
110. The Indian National Congress resigned their offices as a sign of protest against Viceroy Linlithgow's declaration of India as a belligerent in the war against Germany. Sugata Bose and Ayesha Jalal's study *Modern South Asia: History, Culture, Political Economy* (Oxford: Oxford University Press, 1998), pp. 154-57, asserts: 'From the Indian nationalist point of view, the world war was a conflict between old and new imperialist powers. That Britain was fighting for freedom and democracy was simply not credible to its colonial subjects unless they too were given a taste of these values.'
111. Neill, *God's Apprentice*, p. 176.
112. Neill's lectures were on the following topics: 'I Believe in the Holy Ghost'; 'The Holy Catholic Church'; 'The Communion of Saints'; 'The Forgiveness of Sins'; and 'The Resurrection and the Life Everlasting'.
113. Neill, *Beliefs: Lectures delivered at the Kodaikanal Missionary Conference, 1937* (Madras: The Christian Literature Society for India, 1939). See Eleanor Jackson's personal collection, p. 362.

in Kodaikanal, dealing with the first section of the Apostles' Creed.[114] In his autobiography, Neill noted that both of these books – *Beliefs* and *Foundation Beliefs* – enjoyed 'long life' and were 'repeatedly printed'.[115]

Neill's third publication during this period was a scholarly article on the Danish theologian Søren Kierkegaard. It was published in *The National Christian Council Review* in April and May 1942.[116] The two-part article was based on a lecture Neill had delivered to a missionary conference in Bangalore in September 1941. Neill was fascinated by Kierkegaard's meditations on Christ's sufferings. He wrote, 'I do not know any other writer who portrays with equal penetration and depth of feeling, almost with personal agony, the death of Christ.'[117]

A fourth publication during Neill's bishopric owed its conception to another missionary convention which took place in May 1942 in the Nilgiri Hills.[118] Neill spoke on the book of Romans.[119] A small book resulted and was published in 1943 as *The Wrath and the Peace of God and Other Studies*.[120] This book, too, sold well. A fifth publication was based on Neill's lectures at Lahore Cathedral in northwest India (now Pakistan).[121]

---

114. Neill, *Foundation Beliefs: Lectures delivered at the Kodaikanal Missionary Convention, May 1941* (Madras: The Christian Literature Society for India, 1948). The chapters are entitled, 'Belief'; 'God Our Father'; 'Jesus Christ Our Lord'; and 'Crucified Under Pontius Pilate'. Neill had originally intended to contribute a third volume to this project on the Apostles' Creed. He did lecture on the remaining parts of the creed at one of the Kodaikanal conferences but these lectures were never published. See *God's Apprentice*, p. 187, and the Preface to *Foundation Beliefs*.
115. Neill, *God's Apprentice*, p. 187.
116. Stephen Neill, 'Søren Kierkegaard: Part I', *The National Christian Council Review*, Vol. 62, no. 4 (April 1942), pp. 165-70; and 'Søren Kierkegaard: Part II', *The National Christian Council Review*, Vol. 62, no. 5 (May 1942), pp. 191-98.
117. Neill, 'Søren Kierkegaard: Part I', p. 169. Neill wrote, 'In September, I gave four lectures at the United Theological College Bangalore on the Pastoral Ministry.... I have always found the students very friendly and this particular piece of bridge-building is not without its value for the whole church.' See 'Diocese of Tinnevelly: Report for the year 1941', SPG E95, located at the Bodleian Library of Commonwealth and African Studies at Rhodes House, Oxford.
118. The Nilgiri hills or Blue Mountains in English are near Ooty and Coonoor. This gathering was run by the Plymouth Brethren.
119. His four lectures were entitled: 'The Wrath and the Peace of God'; 'The Faith of Abraham'; 'Sin in the Believer'; and 'Life in the Spirit'.
120. Stephen Neill, *The Wrath and the Peace of God and Other Studies: Addresses Delivered at the Nilgiri Missionary Convention, May 1942* (Madras: Christian Literature Society for India, 1943).
121. At partition in 1947 this part of northeast India became part of Pakistan.

The series of lectures was given during Holy Week (18 to 25 April 1943) and was published a year later as *The Challenge of Jesus Christ*.[122] This book is an apologia for Jesus Christ as the saviour of the world and the crux of human existence. Its central feature is a chapter which discusses in detail the sayings of Jesus while hanging on the cross. It concludes with a discussion of resurrection and a reinforcement of Jesus as 'The Answer of Life'.[123]

Neill's final book published during his bishopric was *Ecclesia Anglicana*.[124] This book was written 'to those who are trying to make up their minds about Church Union and the position of the Anglican Church in relation to it'.[125] This book was written during Neill's holiday in 1943 in the Kashmir region.[126]

A final scholarly pursuit occupied Neill's time during his bishopric: 'I was also responsible for bringing upon myself the heaviest of all my extra-curricular burdens – participation in the revision of the Tamil Bible.'[127] The Tamil translation had been in existence since 1714. Tamil was the first Indian language to have a translation of the Bible.[128] There had been several revisions over the years, which had led to differences in practice. The Protestant churches, for the most part, used the Union Version of 1869. The exception to this was the Lutherans, who preferred the missionary Fabricius' translation of 1750. There was also the 'rather clumsy' Roman Catholic version which dated back to 1857.[129] Thus, in 1939 Neill set to work with a group of scholars under the leadership of Indian scholar L.P. Larsen to produce a new translation. The project outlasted Larsen and eventually came under the chairmanship of C.H. Monahan. By the time the work was complete in 1949, Neill had already left India. However, his contribution to the work in the early years was considerable. Neill described the breadth of their work:

---

122. Stephen Neill, *The Challenge of Jesus Christ* (Madras: SPCK in India, 1944).
123. Ibid. That is the title of the final chapter, Chapter 8.
124. Stephen Neill, *Ecclesia Anglicana: An Open Letter to the Clergy of the Diocese of Tinnevelly* (Madras: SPCK in India, 1943).
125. This quotation is from the Preface.
126. Neill, *God's Apprentice*, p. 192.
127. Ibid., p. 189.
128. For the history of the Tamil Bible, see Grafe, *History of Christianity in India, Vol. IV, Part 2*, pp. 248-59; and Michael Bergunder, 'The "Pure Tamil Movement" and Bible Translation: The Ecumenical Thiruviviliam of 1995', in *Christians, Cultural Interactions, and India's Religious Traditions*, ed. by Judith Brown and Robert Frykenberg (Grand Rapids, MI: Wm. B. Eerdmans, 2002), pp. 212-31.
129. According to Grafe, *History of Christianity in India, Vol. IV, Part 2*, p. 250, the Roman Catholic version was sponsored by the foreign missionaries of Paris and was a translation of only the four Gospels and the book of Acts. Neill called this a 'rather clumsy' version in *God's Apprentice*, p. 190.

5. Neill's Years as Bishop of Tinnevelly: 1939-45

> We had of course before us the Greek and the Hebrew, all the known Tamil versions, a wide range of English translations.... [T]he cognate Dravidian languages Telugu, Malayalam and Canarese, ... the Hindi, the Sanskrit... the Danish and Swedish.... To those must be added lexicons, and the most up-to-date commentaries in a variety of languages.[130]

Neill wrote that the group met together for about forty days each year. While Neill found it to be highly interesting and beneficial to the Tamil Church, 'It was certainly also the most exhausting work that I have ever undertaken.'[131]

Vacation in 1943

> We have now reached the year 1943. It was clear that I was becoming seriously overtired. I had been nine years in India with only ten weeks in England. Insomnia was becoming an increasingly harmful plague. It was difficult for me to get a real holiday in India, as work followed me to the hills, and it was almost impossible to refuse all the preaching and speaking engagements that crowded in upon me.[132]

By January 1943 Neill was writing to his clergy that he needed a break of at least four months. Not only was this break to be for his health but also so that he could prepare for the upcoming Lambeth Conference.[133] He departed for his holiday on 13 April 1943, heading first to Lahore for Holy Week and then to Kashmir to write.[134] In July he wrote to his clergy: 'I am enjoying the best holiday I have ever had in my life, and am eagerly looking forward to taking up work again refreshed in body and spirit.'[135]

Neill had never been to Kashmir before. He was struck with awe by its beauty, calling it 'the most beautiful country in the world'.[136] A young missionary named Gilbert Hort, the grandson of New Testament Greek scholar, Fenton John Anthony Hort, and some travel assistants accompanied him. During the week, Neill worked for five hours a day and

---

130. Eleanor Jackson's personal collection, p. 374.
131. Neill, *God's Apprentice*, p. 191.
132. Ibid.
133. Neill, *Letters to His Clergy*, no. 37 (January 1943).
134. Neill, *Letters to His Clergy*, no. 40 (April 1943).
135. Neill, *Letters to His Clergy*, no. 41 (July 1943).
136. Neill, *God's Apprentice*, p. 192. See pp. 192-95 for a discussion of this holiday.

during the late afternoon he would explore. Saturdays were exclusively for hiking; Sundays were for worship with local missionaries. On the trip back to Tinnevelly Neill deliberately stopped to visit with military men. In all, he visited eleven cantonments and held services for them. He returned to Tinnevelly in early September 1943.[137]

Upon his return Neill focused on the upcoming diocesan elections. He also had to deal with a serious falling out between two clergymen. One accused the other of misusing church funds. Somehow, according to Neill, issues of caste had entered into the fracas.[138] Neill dealt with the matter and imposed a light sentence on the accused party, although the man held staunchly to his innocence.

Another issue with which Neill had to engage was charges of immorality aimed at one of his clergymen. Although the charges were dismissed as 'non-proven', Neill had concerns about the clergyman involved. A third issue, about which Neill mentions almost nothing, is how, upon his return, 'one of those in whom I ought to have been able to repose the most complete confidence was in fact doing his best to undermine my position in the diocese'.[139] Tantalisingly, there is nothing more in Neill's writings to indicate the nature of the matter.

Overall, however, Neill felt the diocese to be in good shape. In his first diocesan letter after his return, he wrote, 'I am glad to find that all has gone so well in my absence.'[140]

It is at this point, however, that the records demonstrate a curious omission in Neill's monthly correspondence to his clergy. After hardly missing a clerical *Letter* since his bishopric began, between September 1943 and March 1944 Neill wrote only two letters: one upon his return in September and one in November. This omission is conspicuous

---

137. See Neill, *Letters to His Clergy*, no. 42 (August 1943) and no. 43 (September 1943).
138. See Neill, *God's Apprentice*, pp. 195-96. The precise nature of how caste entered into the quarrel is not explained by Neill.
139. Neill, *God's Apprentice*, p. 197. This enigmatic statement opens up many intriguing questions. One possibility is that George Selwyn, Neill's successor, was beginning to make his move towards the bishopric. Another possibility is that Neill was beginning to get on the wrong side of leading Indians in his diocese who were sympathetic with the movement towards nationalism. A third possibility is that Neill's chronology here is wrong and the person trying to undermine him was actually someone involved in the events which led to his downfall, recorded in the next chapter. In fact, in the paragraph immediately following this quotation, Neill wrote: 'for this period of my life alone I have difficulty in reconstructing the chronology.'
140. Neill, *Letters to His Clergy*, no. 43 (September 1943).

Photo of Neill as bishop, hanging in Bishopstowe, Palayamkottai.

indeed as it was out of character for Neill. The *Letters* had been such a regular part of his work and were the only way of communicating with his clergy *en masse*.

Neill's depression and insomnia were surfacing again, perhaps – or even probably – because he could sense trouble brewing.[141] This marked the

---

141. Neill's insomnia first became problematic for him when he was a student at Dean Close. He wrote, 'At this time I became aware of a problem which though not new had not previously forced itself so clearly on my attention, and which was to become a life-long affliction – difficulty in sleeping'; Neill, *God's Apprentice*, p. 44. His depression also first occurred during his Dean Close years: 'At about the same time I also became aware of another kind of trouble, more serious. . . . It was as though all the lights went out in the world. . . . I diagnosed this affliction as the malaise which often beset medieval monks, *daemonium meridianum*; later I learned to call it *accidie*. . . . [I]t was only in later years that I became fully aware of

beginning of a sequence of events that resulted in the fall of Tinnevelly's beloved bishop. It might have appeared inevitable to Neill that something serious was about to happen. However, he was not prepared for its magnitude.

Views of Neill's Bishopric

Bishop Stephen Neill Centre, Palayamkottai, India.

Interviews with some of Neill's former parishioners resulted in ambivalent descriptions of his episcopacy. Few doubted his genuine concern for his flock, his tireless devotion to the betterment of the diocese and the great accomplishments that continue to exist in Tinnevelly today because of him: the Diocesan Printing Press, the co-operative store, the Nazareth Seminary[142] and the many works of the evangelistic bands. When a new

---

the extent to which this misfortune can fall'; Neill, *God's Apprentice*, p. 45. In his autobiography, Neill lamented his frequent bouts of poor health, 'I have from time to time asked myself where I should have been and what I might have done if I had been gifted with better health. But this is a futile and meaningless question. . . . I would have been an entirely different person, and the story that follows would have been an entirely different story. At times I have been tempted to wish that there could have been a little less suffering on the way that I have trodden. . . . In any case, to look across the river and suppose that the grass is greener on the other side is an absurd and futile waste of time'; Neill, *God's Apprentice*, p. 46.

142. Neill moved the Nazareth Seminary to a spacious campus called Tirumaraiyur, as explained in Chapter 4. Eventually, the seminary was merged with the Tamilnadu Theological Seminary at Arasaradi, Madurai. See 'Tirunelveli Diocese: A Profile',

5. Neill's Years as Bishop of Tinnevelly: 1939-45

diocesan research facility was built, it was named the Bishop Stephen Neill Study and Research Centre.[143] At the same time, however, Neill acquired a reputation for being overly autocratic.

For example, the Rev. S.T. Paul Gnaniah, who was ordained deacon by Neill in 1943, showed deep ambivalence.[144] He vividly described the character of Neill's bishopric, first pointing out that Neill could be extremely generous:

> When Neill became Bishop, he was very concerned with the poor. They could not buy Bibles, which cost 2 Rs each. Neill wanted to give every house a Bible. He visited the Western countries and raised lots of money and had printed thousands of Bibles. He wanted to give one Bible to every house. He was successful in this. Buying a Bible was just not possible in those days, as people were too poor. He did not want to give it completely free, so he collected 75 paisa.

Gnaniah also pointed out that Neill cared deeply for Dalits. He tried to help them move up to a better livelihood. However, Gnaniah also expressed another side: 'Neill was a very hard man to deal with. He was very strict in many ways. He was a disciplinarian, an autocrat, imperialistic. Highly intelligent, he used to think very little of other people.'

Reverend R. Joseph, a former vice-chairman of the diocese, made similar remarks:

> Neill's touch is still all over the diocese. . . . [However] people said Neill was an imperialist when he was here. . . . [For example] at the run-down retreat centre at Pannerkulam, Neill once was leading a training session of catechists. An air plane flew by. They had never seen an air plane. Neill got angry and cancelled the training course for that particular group. . . . [But] the diocese would be in better shape had Neill been permitted to stay.[145]

Former bishop of Tinnevelly (1985-99) Jason Dharmaraj stated: 'Neill had an aggressive, dominating personality.'[146]

---

      pamphlet (ca. 1995), Bishopstowe, Palayamkottai.
143. The Centre came into being in 1992 on the campus of St John's College in Palayamkottai. It was relocated to a new building in the year 2000.
144. Rev. S.T. Paul Gnaniah, interview by author, transcribed and approved by interviewee, Palayamkottai, India, 14 February 2003.
145. Rev. R. Joseph, interview by author, transcribed and approved by interviewee, Palayamkottai, India, 16 February 2003.
146. Jason Dharmaraj, interview by author, transcribed and approved by interviewee,

Ambivalence about Neill's legacy in South India is rampant even today. Some argue that, while bishop, he completely disregarded the indigenous Indian Missionary Society, located in Tinnevelly. He never attended a single meeting, nor did he ever even acknowledge this important institution. This was offensive to the members of the society, as all Indian bishops, including former ones, were lifetime patrons of the IMS.[147]

At times, Neill pushed for the Indianisation of the diocese. For example, Neill was the one who initiated the change from Tinnevelly to Tirunelveli as the official name of the diocese. This can be dated to July 1940 in his eighth *Letter to His Clergy*. Neill recorded:

> You may be interested in the change of signature at the foot of this letter. I have always very much disliked the Anglicised form Tinnevelly, which is quite meaningless, and wished to bring my English signature into line with my Tamil signature. . . . I think the change will commend itself to most of our Indian Christians. We may consider later on changing the name of the diocese as well, but that is a slow process having to be carried out through the Provincial Council.

In another expression of solidarity with Indians, Neill often went barefoot: 'It has always amused me that, whereas I the foreigner always went to Church barefoot, [Bishop of Dornakal] Azariah, the Indian, always wore leather shoes.'[148]

Neill also abandoned the traditional practice of sitting above his clergy from a chair while they sat around him on the floor:

> I saw that, if I was to get anywhere I, like the prophet Ezekiel, must sit where they sat. After that, there was no more nonsense about putting a chair for the bishop. Some of the clergy did not like this, feeling that it was not dignified for the bishop to sit with everyone else on the floor.[149]

On the other hand, Neill's dealings with Indians could be condescending and exacting in his expectations. His *Letters* provide many examples. He chastised clergy for using plastic flowers.[150] He was fastidious when it came to punctuality. He reprimanded people for talking during church

---

      Palayamkottai, India, 18 February 2003.
147. Ibid.
148. Harper, *In the Shadow of the Mahatma*, p. 149.
149. Eleanor Jackson's personal collection, p. 341.
150. Neill, *Letters to His Clergy*, no. 9 (September 1940).

services. He told people to keep their babies quiet during church. He said members read services too quickly and too loud.[151] He was overbearing in his expectations for the Eucharist and the offering. He became upset at pauses during the singing of hymns: 'Let me add that if hymns are sung, they must be sung straight through, and not with long pauses. Nothing is more distracting and interrupting to prayer than pauses of uncertain length, determined by the caprice of the organist, punctuated by single verses of a hymn.'[152]

While there must have been some resentment towards Neill at the time, 'the barefoot bishop' is today described in mostly favourable terms:

> The people, even today, say Neill's bishopric was the Golden Age. Neill had control of the priests and the diocese. . . . I loved him. He was such a wonderful and intelligent man in spite of his weaknesses. . . . Neill came back in 1980 and the people still loved him. So many people loved him. . . . Neill had many ideas and goals. All was shattered when he left the diocese. Had he continued as the bishop, the diocese would be in a better position than it is now. He would never have allowed partisan politics, which are going on right now in the diocese. Neill had so much love for this diocese.[153]

All agree that Neill's leadership was strong, if at times draconian. However, his concern for the diocese was clear. Real progress was made by the diocese on his watch. It was devastating when he was forced to resign.

---

151. Neill, *Letters to His Clergy*, no. 33 (September 1942).
152. Neill, *Letters to His Clergy*, no. 39 (March 1943).
153. Gnaniah, interview by author.

Chapter Six
Loss of a Bishopric:
1944-45

In 1944 Stephen Neill became entangled in a scandal that led to his downfall as bishop, resulting in an abrupt end to his missionary service to India.[1] The blow began with a deterioration in Neill's physical health in late 1943. The Metropolitan of India, Burma and Ceylon, Foss Westcott, knew Neill's health was taking a bad turn. Neill's life began to break down in several other areas: mental health, ministry, relationships and emotional control. This breakdown also involved a curious episode over Neill's disciplining of an Indian schoolmaster.

The mental problems Neill had battled in the past rained down on him relentlessly during this period. Sexual anomalies came to a head during his bishopric as well, ultimately leading many to oppose his leadership. Neill refused to take the blame for the incidents that led to his downfall. To the end he felt he was the victim of a coup.

Indian Nationalism prior to and during Neill's Bishopric

Indian nationalism had been a factor in South India since before Neill's arrival in 1924;[2] missionaries noticed a widespread nationalist feeling in

---

1. Lamb writes, 'In 1945 came the breakdown that altered his career. The full nature and consequences of this event cannot yet be known. . . . [H]e had to resign his bishopric and leave India for good. He never held office in the Anglican Church again, nor was he given the academic responsibilities that his gifts deserved'; Lamb, 'Stephen Neill 1900-1984: Unafraid to Ask Ultimate Questions', p. 447.
2. In Chapter 5 Indian nationalism was alluded to. Nationalism was certainly

India as early as 1883.³ That is the year the Theosophical Society was established in Adyar, near Chennai. This became a 'strong base from which Hindu revivalists attacked missionaries'.⁴ Indian nationalism caught on and spread quickly. Alexander writes:

> The foundation of the Indian National Congress in 1885 was the first major step to organize and coordinate nationalist activities on an all-India basis. The spirit of nationalism spread to the Indian Church. Within the Christian community educated Indian Christians began to question the domination of the Indian Church by foreign missionaries. These growing trends caused a major shift of emphasis in missionary attitudes by the early years of the twentieth century.⁵

During the last decade of the nineteenth century and the first decade of the twentieth, a more radical form of nationalism was apparent and the notion of *swaraj*, or self-rule, became a familiar topic of conversation.⁶

---

a factor during Neill's entire time as bishop. However, there was a particular incident that occurred in the latter part of Neill's bishopric that shows just how complex the nationalistic climate could become. This incident serves as a crucial reason Neill had to leave Tinnevelly. Because of the important role that nationalism played in Neill's fall from the See, the discussion of nationalism has been postponed until now.

3. Elizabeth Susan Alexander, *The Attitudes of British Protestant Missionaries towards Nationalism in India: With Special Reference to Madras Presidency, 1919-1927* (Delhi: Konark Publishers, 1994). Most historians of nationalism in India consider the foundation of the Indian National Congress in 1885 a convenient beginning point for the movement. For an example of this, see Bose and Jalal, *Modern South Asia*, pp. 90, 107. However, nearly all historians of the period will point out ample examples of nationalistic tendencies percolating throughout the entire nineteenth century. One clear example of this is the 1857 revolt. Earlier examples are well-known, such as the Madras mutiny at Vellore in 1806 and the Bengal army mutiny in Java in 1815. See also Gerald Studdert-Kennedy, *Providence and the Raj: Imperial Mission and Missionary Imperialism* (Delhi: Manohar, 1998); Peter van der Veer, *Religious Nationalism: Hindus and Muslims in India* (Berkeley, CA: University of California Press, 1994); and Sumit Sarkar, *Modern India, 1885-1947* (New York: St Martin's Press, 1989).

4. Alexander, *The Attitudes of British Protestant Missionaries towards Nationalism in India*, p. 8. For the Theosophical movement's relationship to nationalism and opposition to Christian missions, see Kenneth Jones, *Socio-Religious Reform Movements in British India* (Cambridge: Cambridge University Press, 1989), pp. 165-85.

5. Alexander, *The Attitudes of British Protestant Missionaries towards Nationalism in India*, p. 8.

6. Bose and Jalal, *Modern South Asia*, pp. 106, 117.

The years of World War I showed Indians that the so-called 'Christian nations' were not so magnanimous, leading to a 'spurt in Indian nationalist agitation'.[7] There were many reasons for this. Most notably, the Indians had been loyal to Britain throughout the war and felt a debt was owed to them for their fidelity. India suffered 101,439 casualties and contributed around $100 million to the war effort. Indian nationalists argued that their country had earned their freedom.[8]

By 1919 Mohandas Karamchand Gandhi had secured his place as leader of the nationalist movement.[9] Under Gandhi, religious sectarianism seemed to take a back seat to the greater display of nationalist unity among people of different faiths.[10] Gandhi provided a leadership that had been lacking, resulting in 'widespread opposition against British Government action'.[11] Missionaries were caught in the fray and were anxious about their future.[12]

7. Alexander notes that Mrs Annie Besant of the Theosophical Society in Madras began a 'Home Rule Movement' that demanded self-government for India after the war. Her movement 'spread like wildfire from district to district'. Christian missionaries were critical of Mrs Besant. See Alexander, *The Attitudes of British Protestant Missionaries towards Nationalism in India*, p. 10.
8. Burke and Quraishi, *The British Raj in India*, pp. 148-57.
9. In 1919 a protest occurred that ended with the death of 379 Indians and 'a few British officials'. This was a major impetus for Gandhi's rise to a position of leadership. See Bose and Jalal, *The British Raj in India*, p. 138. Alexander writes, 'The events of the year 1919 . . . reflect an important stage in the growth of nationalism in the sub-continent. Indian nationalism had gained strength since the outbreak of World War I, and in the year 1919 the movement clearly entered a more forceful phase.' See Alexander, *The Attitudes of British Protestant Missionaries towards Nationalism in India*, p. 21.
10. Ibid., pp. 46-47: 'Educated Hindus who were not really affected by the Turkish Treaty, saw the distress of the Indian Muslims as an opportunity to unite and to strengthen their political demands. . . . The alliance of Indian nationalists with Muslim leaders concerned with a specifically Muslim cause, made the forces of opposition to the British Government potentially formidable.' The issues here revolved around Britain's opposition to the Muslim leadership of the Ottoman Empire. The Muslims of Turkey considered the Sultan to be the Caliph (Khalifa) of Islam, thus the religious and political ruler of the country. However, during World War I, the Turkish Emperor joined on the side of Germany. After the defeat of Germany, the Allies had planned to dismember Turkey and abolish the Caliphate. The Caliphate was abolished in 1923. See Burke and Quraishi, *The British Raj in India*, 'The Khilafat Question', pp. 215-26.
11. Alexander, *The Attitudes of British Protestant Missionaries towards Nationalism in India*, p. 45.
12. Ibid., p. 57.

6. Loss of a Bishopric: 1944-45

With the support of pro-Caliphate Muslims, Gandhi was able to win the leadership of the Indian National Congress in 1920.[13] His popularity steadily rose over two decades until the late 1930s when Indian nationalism began to split into various factions.[14]

During World War II, Britain was as strong as ever in its determination to hold onto its Indian empire. The fracture within Indian nationalist groups watered down the protest that at one point in time had seemed much more united. However, Indian opinions during the war years began to coalesce, forming, again, a more united resistance to British rule. Indian resources were depleted: cloth, kerosene oil and, most of all, food.[15] That, combined with more detentions of nationalists, created outrage. Gandhi's fasting was shaping public opinion in dramatic ways. At times, it seemed as though the Mahatma was on the verge of death and the outcomes typically went in his favour. The American missionary E. Stanley Jones, with whom Stephen Neill had worked in 1926, was intrigued by this radical move on the part of his good friend Gandhi:

> Mahatma Gandhi was an activist – a moral and spiritual activist. And fasting was one of his strategies of activism, in many ways his most powerful. For through his fasts the Mahatma accomplished almost as much as through his nonviolent passive resistance. . . . When Mahatma Gandhi was in the Yeravda jail, I raised this question with him as he sat on a cot in the open courtyard: 'Isn't your fasting a species of coercion?' 'Yes,' he said very slowly, 'the same kind of coercion which Jesus exercises upon you from the cross.' I was silent. It was so obviously true that I am silent again every time I think of it. He was profoundly right.[16]

---

13. See Bose and Jalal, *The British Raj in India*, Chapter 13, 'Gandhian Nationalism and Mass Politics in the 1920s', and Chapter 14, 'The Depression Decade: Society, Economics, and Politics'. Regarding Muslim assistance to Gandhi's cause, they write, p. 146, 'The Muslim League . . . offered co-operation against the British until 1937.'
14. In addition to the Gandhian approach, there were more radical, militant programmes, such as those led by Subhas Chandra Bose and Jawaharlal Nehru, and even religious-based organisations, such as the All-India Muslim League.
15. Bose and Jalal, *The British Raj in India*, p. 156. See Chapter 15, 'Nationalism and Colonialism during World War II and its Aftermath: Economic Crisis and Political Confrontation'; also p. 159: 'It was in the context of a deepening economic crisis that the major political confrontations between nationalists and the British colonial state occurred.' One important resource for delineating the impact that financial distress during World War II had on Indian nationalism and ultimately Indian independence is Tirthankar Roy's *The Economic History of India: 1857-1947*. See especially pp. 160-65.
16. Jones, *Gandhi: Portrayal of a Friend*, pp. 108-10. See Chapter 8, 'The Fastings of

Missionaries had mixed views of Gandhi; and Gandhi had mixed views of Christians. This interplay resulted in some interesting dynamics between Christians and Indians during this period. On one hand, Gandhi admired the teachings of Christ. On the other, Gandhi was averse to missions. Dr E. Stanley Jones, Mahatma's close friend, wrote a wonderful biography of him.[17] Dr Jones' Preface to the biography shows tremendous ambivalence:

> I have believed in and have loved Mahatma Gandhi through the years – in spite of differences. . . . But to try to interpret such a complex character as he was – well, it was beyond me. ... He was simple and yet very complex. . . . You thought you knew him, and then you didn't. It was intriguing. There was always something there that eluded your grasp, something that baffled you. And yet out of that many-sidedness which amounted to complexity, there arose simplicity, a unified character, simple and compelling. . . . There were deep disagreements. And yet, something held me to him amid those disagreements. I felt that he had a way of coming out on the right side of things. . . . Mahatma Gandhi . . . has taught me more of the spirit of Christ than perhaps any other man in East or West.[18]

Stephen Neill held strikingly similar views:

> That ambiguous and ambivalent man Mahatma Gandhi . . . made no secret of his devotion to Jesus Christ, and of his high regard for the Gospels. . . . He urged young Hindus to read the Gospels for themselves, and to find out what the teaching of Jesus really was. For the first time in the modern period, therefore, Hindu India was ready to listen to the voice of Jesus Christ. There is, however, another side to this picture. Mr. Gandhi made it quite clear that he never had been, and never intended to be, anything but a Hindu. He told his admirers that they could get from the Gospels everything he had got, without prejudice to their faith and to their standing as Hindus. Conversion was anathema to him, as disobedience to God; if God has caused you to be born as a Hindu, that is where it is your duty to stay.[19]

In another place, Neill recorded:

---

    the Mahatma'.
17. Ibid.
18. Ibid., pp. 5-8.
19. Neill, *God's Apprentice*, p. 101.

6. Loss of a Bishopric: 1944-45

> Between these two extremes of unconditional support and outright opposition [towards Gandhi] was to be found every line of the intervening spectrum. I found it exceedingly difficult to make up my mind. Like every missionary of my acquaintance, I regarded myself as pledged to work for India's political maturity and independence. But I was far from certain as to how this could best come about. I never met Mr. Gandhi, but I found it impossible to overcome a deep distaste for him and for all his methods.[20] On every occasion, up till 1947, in which Mr. Gandhi set in motion a campaign of non-violent non-co-operation, the result was outbreaks of violence all over the place; the dead did not come to life again when Mr. Gandhi disassociated himself from the violence which his campaign had let loose.[21]

By the time Neill became bishop in 1939, it was clear that Gandhi's movement was not going away:

> It was Gandhi who succeeded in turning himself into a legend in his own lifetime, and in swaying the hearts of the masses as probably no other man in the history of India has succeeded in swaying them. From about 1926 his influence was steadily on the increase, and in the end the independence of India was to be achieved by revolution and not by gradual progress.[22]

Neill often encountered Indian nationalism in his ministry. On one occasion, a few years before he became bishop, he encountered some nationalist students:

> I had become very friendly with a group of students from Kerala, all of them rip-roaring nationalists and supporters of Mahatma Gandhi. When I met them in Rangoon, they were all wearing smartly cut suits of Western style. I mocked them, saying, 'Is this your nationalism?' Next time I saw them they were looking much nicer in their graceful Indian dress; whereupon they seized me and said, 'Now you have got to wear it too.' I said, 'I am perfectly happy

---

20. Neill described an incident when an Indian crowd stormed a police station and set it on fire, killing 22 policemen. Neill claimed that, while Gandhi's movement clearly motivated the crime, Gandhi accepted no responsibility during the trial. See Neill, *God's Apprentice*, pp. 129-30.
21. Neill, *God's Apprentice*, p. 130.
22. Ibid., p. 128.

wearing Indian dress, but I haven't brought any; if you supply it I shall be delighted to wear it.' No sooner said than done; but there was only one difficulty; I had no sandals with me, and I very much object to wearing English shoes with Indian dress; so there was nothing for it but to go about barefoot. I learned later that this earned me an enormous and entirely undeserved reputation for holiness: 'This young *sannyasi* missionary, who has adopted our ways, even goes about barefoot.'[23]

Neill understood the difficulties involved, writing, 'It was impossible to remain unaffected by the rising tide of nationalism.'[24]

South India had entire castes that tended to resist Indian independence. British rule had worked rather well for some. Neill recorded:

> For the most part Indian Christians had been indifferent to politics; they came from the underprivileged classes, which had little or no instruction in Indian culture, and had been accustomed to servitude rather than to participation. British rule had meant to them a marvellous emancipation. Justice was not easy to secure; but there was at least a chance that before a British magistrate the poor man would not be overwhelmed by the bribery indulged in by the rich. Even to the outcaste there was now offered the possibility of education, and of employment in the police, in the armed forces and in other branches controlled by the government. People on this level had no desire other than that the British Raj should continue to the end of time. What they feared above all was the restitution of the rule of the Brahmans which from time immemorial they had experienced as unscrupulous, oppressive and corrupt. . . . British control had meant a world of opportunity and advancement, and they had little desire for a revolutionary change in the situation.[25]

Neill saw Indian independence on the horizon, yet he also knew that Christians in South India, for the most part, had benefited from British rule. Nonetheless, he could not fully support the Gandhian movement in all of its manifestations:

---

23. Ibid., pp. 126-27. Harper, in her biography of Bishop Azariah, refers to Neill as the 'barefoot bishop in Tinnevelly'. See Harper, *In the Shadow of the Mahatma*, p. 455.
24. Neill, *God's Apprentice*, p. 128.
25. Ibid., pp. 128-29.

6. Loss of a Bishopric: 1944-45

The younger supporters of 'the revolution' invariably demanded that the Church should line itself up behind the forces of revolution. In view of the many ambiguities in Gandhi's methods and his defence of them, many of us felt that this was not the way in which political freedom could best come to India and were therefore unable to enrol ourselves in the ranks of his supporters. This led to much painful misunderstanding with our Indian friends. Even those who believed themselves to understand the way in which the Western mind worked would tell us that, probably without our own knowledge, we were crypto-imperialists, and that we really believed in the innate inferiority of the Indian man. It was inconceivable to them that a foreigner could at the same time believe fervently in democracy and political progress and retain his right to be critical of the man who had succeeded in making himself the idol of large sections of the Indian people. This was an unpleasant time at which to be at work in India; and, the deeper one's affection for the Indian people, the more unpleasant it was certain to become.[26]

In concluding his thoughts on Mahatma Gandhi in his autobiography, Neill wrote: 'I still believe that on the whole British rule in India was beneficial.'[27]

The chief concerns of Western missionaries in India were evangelism, education and medical service. These three themes are the dominant ones in every single CMS Annual Report during the years 1936 to 1946; nationalism and Indian independence received negligible attention. An incident occurred, however, at some point in either late 1943 or early 1944 that would bring the issues of Indian independence and charges of imperialism to the Tinnevelly diocese and, in particular, to the Tinnevelly bishopric. Moreover, it had everything to do with Stephen Neill.

Earlier, we noted a curious and conspicuous omission in Neill's regular monthly correspondence to his clergy. Neill wrote only two letters between September 1943 and March 1944: one in September upon his return from holiday in Kashmir and one in November. What is clear is that Neill knew his health was taking a turn for the worse when he left for holiday

---

26. Ibid., pp. 130-31. Neill was not an admirer of Gandhi. He seemed to be comfortable with a strong British presence in India for the foreseeable future.
27. Ibid., p. 131. On Gandhian nationalism in South India, see Harper, *In the Shadow of the Mahatma*, Chapter 9, 'The Conflict with Gandhi and Political Nationalism'. Harper's account is intriguing because her subject, Bishop Azariah of Dornakal, was an Indian, however, he was also a committed Christian who was aware of the symbiotic relation between Indian Christianity and British rule.

in April 1943. His superior, Metropolitan Westcott, knew Neill's life had taken a bad turn in all areas: physical and mental health, his ministry, his relationships and emotional control. The breakdown centred on a curious incident when Neill physically disciplined one of his clergymen.

The Loss of a Bishopric: Contemporary Sources

Issues with Neill's Health

The first piece of circumstantial evidence in the historical records that points to something going wrong in Neill's life occurred in his letters to the clergy. Prior to Neill's holiday in Kashmir, he had never neglected this responsibility – 40 letters without missing one month. During his 1943 holiday to Kashmir, Neill was in good spirits. There is nothing to indicate that anything had gone wrong. The only sign that a breakdown might have been on the horizon was three months before the holiday, in January 1943, when he wrote to his clergy, 'I have to recognise that the strain of the last few months has told rather heavily.'[28] Yet in a letter to the Metropolitan on 24 March 1943 Neill made no mention of any impending breakdown or crisis. Furthermore, it is unlikely that Neill's major breakdown occurred prior to or during the holiday to Kashmir (April to September 1943). That means the breakdown must have occurred either in late 1943 or early 1944. The sporadic nature of Neill's *Letters to His Clergy* in late 1943 and early 1944, while not proving that anything had gone terribly wrong, at least hints at some rupture in his routine. However, Neill explained the infrequency of the letters in November 1943:

> With expenses increasing in every direction, I have had regretfully to come to the conclusion that I cannot meet so heavy a bill each month, and that, for the time being, these will have to be occasional letters, perhaps once a quarter, until better times come, and I am able to resume the regular monthly publication.[29]

Thus, there is a caveat that may indeed explain the infrequency of the letters. Perhaps the finances in the diocese would not allow for monthly letters. True to his word, Neill did not write another letter to his clergy until March 1944 and nothing in that letter exposed anything problematic. Nevertheless, a different letter, a confidential one that Neill wrote in the same month, points to something having gone awry.

---

28. Neill, *Letters to His Clergy*, no. 37 (January 1943).
29. Neill, *Letters to His Clergy*, no. 44 (November 1943).

6. Loss of a Bishopric: 1944-45

On 4 March 1944, Neill wrote a letter to Metropolitan Westcott.[30] In this letter Neill intimated that he was struggling and proposed a lengthy furlough for himself. He wanted to go to England in October and not return until April 1945. In that letter, Neill wrote: 'It is time that I should see my specialist in London. . . . [I]t is 10 years since I had the opportunity of consultation and treatment . . . and if necessary to get some treatment for my old malady.'[31] Metropolitan Westcott replied with the following:[32]

> I think your decision about taking leave is right and there are other reasons which I could add which lead me to think that that is so. You know of the thoughts that are in my own mind which lead me to think that your decision to go on leave next October is right.

Westcott was aware of Neill's 'old malady'. Neill described his problem in uncharacteristic detail in his autobiography. After discussing his chronic insomnia which plagued him from his youth, he wrote the following:

> At about the same time I also became aware of another kind of trouble, more serious, though at the time I had no premonition of the way it would determine the major part of my career. It was as though all the lights went out in the world. This could happen suddenly, like a bolt from heaven; or it could start as a grey patch somewhere on the horizon, which would gradually spread until the whole heaven was blotted out by this grey blankness. The experience was accompanied by a total lack of interest in anything. . . . Prayer became a mere formula, with no sense that it was being addressed to anyone in particular or that there was any possibility of its being heard.[33]

Neill speculated that he was suffering from *daemonium meridianum* or accidie.[34]

Westcott knew something else. There was much more to the story than a breakdown in Neill's health. Rather, Neill needed to get out of India *immediately* in order to escape a possible trial. Westcott must have worked

30. Neill to Westcott, 4 March 1944, Westcott Papers, Bishops Box 4, Special Collections, Bishop's College.
31. The 'old malady' that Neill had in mind here was related to his debilitating episodes of insomnia, depression, anxiety and mental imbalance that afflicted him during the years of his education.
32. Westcott to Neill, 31 March 1944, Westcott Papers, Bishops Box 4, Special Collections, Bishop's College.
33. Neill, *God's Apprentice*, p. 45.
34. Neill, *God's Apprentice*, p. 45.

hard to secure Neill a passage, as wartime travel restrictions were stringent. Westcott was told that Neill had to prove his medical condition was urgent before passage to England could be attained. Westcott sent an 'EXPRESS' telegram to Neill at Tinnevelly on 19 June 1944:

IN_ORDER_TO_GET_AIR_OR_SEA_PRIORITY_BISHOP_OF_ TINNEVELLY_MUST_APPEAR_BEFORE_PROVINCIAL_MEDICAL_ BOARD_AND_SEND_CERTIFICATE

Before leaving India Bishop Neill made his way to Calcutta to see Metropolitan Westcott. Once Neill arrived, Westcott wrote an urgent, confidential letter to all of the bishops of India, Burma and Ceylon, informing them of the shocking news that Bishop Neill was to resign under distressing circumstances. The letter is dated 28 June 1944 and is here quoted in full:

My dear Bishops,

I have the sad duty of conveying to you the news of the resignation of the Bishop of Tinnevelly under the most distressing circumstances.

At the time of the General Council he told me that he was anxious to go on leave this summer and later he wrote to me and said that he was anxious to go at as early a date as possible preferably by air if a passage was available as certain symptoms of a psychological neurosis from which he had suffered in 1933-1934 were coming into evidence. I wrote at once to the Secretary to the Government of India, Defence Department, urging that a priority passage be given him at a very early date. Early this month he wrote in fuller detail but said it was better that he should see me when he could explain more fully his condition.

Meanwhile I received a complaint from a Teacher in his Diocese that he had been violently assaulted by the Bishop. I had offered to meet the Bishop wherever convenient but on Sunday I received a wire from him saying that he expected to arrive in Calcutta at midday on Monday. He duly arrived and we talked matters over and it seemed to me right that I should not accept his resignation then but hold it in suspense till I received a report from the specialist in London regarding the possibility of a complete recovery and his ability to carry on his work. He assured me that the bulk of the godly people in his Diocese from whom he has had many letters, desired him to remain.

The next day shortly before the time he was due to leave, I received a petition signed by the lay and clerical Secretaries and the

6. Loss of a Bishopric: 1944-45 173

> Treasurer of the Diocesan Council and endorsed by the Deputy Chairman, the Rev. Canon Selwyn, citing a number of instances of violent assault of Clergy, laymen and teachers and adding that a petition had been prepared calling on me to summon an Episcopal Court under Rule 1 of Chapter XLI to try the charges which were being brought against the Bishop.
>
> Clearly it was right for me to accept the Bishop's resignation but he has earned long leave and I arranged with him that he should go on leave at once and his resignation would not take effect till the end of September 1944. The Archdeacon would act as his Commissary and it would be under the Rules and Canons of our Constitution possible for me to issue a Mandate for the election of a new Bishop before the actual resignation of Bishop Neill took effect.
>
> You will share with me in my deep grief that such an affliction should have overtaken the Bishop. It is due, I believe, to some conditions which he obtained in his early life and while there is every hope that under proper treatment he will recover full health again, it is clear that he should not return to India but I hope he may still by his writings render service to the Church of which he has been such a gifted member.[35]

Thus, Neill would have to stand trial in the Episcopal Court for charges of violent assault. This petition had been endorsed by 'lay and clerical Secretaries and the Treasurer of the Diocesan Council'.[36] However, most importantly, it had been endorsed by the deputy chairman of the Tinnevelly diocese, George Selwyn, Neill's former roommate in Tinnevelly and long-time acquaintance. This was quite likely the person by whom Neill felt most betrayed, prompting him to write in his autobiography:

> It came to my notice that one of those in whom I ought to have been able to repose the most complete confidence was in fact doing his best to undermine my position in the diocese. This rumour came to me first through Indian friends, but I was not prepared to listen to gossip . . . and took no notice of what had been told me. The evidence, however, continued to accumulate, and in the end reached a point at which it could be neither disputed nor denied. This hit me very hard.[37]

---

35. Westcott to the bishops of India, Burma and Ceylon, 28 June 1944, Westcott Papers, Bishops Box 4, Special Collections, Bishop's College.
36. Ibid.
37. Neill, *God's Apprentice*, p. 197.

One important revelation occurs here. In a letter from Westcott to a Mr Samuel, dated 29 June 1944, Westcott wrote: 'Rev. Canon Selwyn emphasised the need of the acceptance of his [Neill's] resignation and indicated that a case would be lodged in the Episcopal Court *if this was not done*.'[38] This shows that Neill was in the precarious situation of having to resign or else face the court. As Westcott mentions in this same letter:

> Clearly any such action would cause the most serious division in the Diocese and create great scandal. The Bishop himself was most anxious that I should accept his resignation and I have done so but it will not take effect till the end of September till which period he will be on leave.

Westcott claimed Selwyn's endorsement of the petition convinced him to accept Neill's resignation.[39] Selwyn entered India before Neill. He was a respected missionary and his opinion mattered.

Word spread quickly in the Tinnevelly diocese that Neill would soon resign. Copious telegrams poured into Westcott's office, both for and against Neill.[40] Most of the telegrams were adamant that Neill remain bishop. Below are some examples:

> Metropolitan Calcutta, Pray Refusal Bishop Neill resignation otherwise serious troubles.
> Pray Retain Bishop Neill Otherwise Apprehend Schism in Church.
> Office Bearers Do Not Represent Diocesan Views They Selfish In Motive We Want Bishop Neill.
> Pray Bishop Neill's Continuance for better spiritual life.[41]

Westcott defended Neill in some of his correspondence. For example, in a letter dated 1 July 1944, he wrote:

---

38. Westcott to Mr Samuel, 29 June 1944, Westcott Papers, Bishops Box 4, Special Collections, Bishop's College (my italics).
39. Ibid. 'When . . . the petition . . . was endorsed by the Rev. Canon Selwyn, the Deputy Chairman of the Diocese of Tinnevelly, the case for accepting his resignation seemed to me very strong.'
40. Ibid. 'I have received many letters both of complaint and also of appreciation of the various great gifts of the Bishop.'
41. Telegrams, 12-20 July 1944, Westcott Papers, Bishops Box 4, Special Collections, Bishop's College. There are many telegrams like this that press for Neill's continuance as bishop. They are dated between 12 July and 20 July, probably because that is when the diocese began to get word that Neill had in fact resigned.

> Remember I regard actions which he has committed as due to mental illness and he cannot be held responsible for them as though they had been done by a man in normal health. We do not hold a man physically ill as able to discharge the normal duties of his health and we do not blame him for his incapacity. The same is true in the case of actions due to mental illness.[42]

Westcott was not certain how to interpret the situation, however. In a letter written to Bishop Michael Hollis of Madras, who knew Neill well and shared a house with him at one point, Westcott wrote:

> I am trying to arrange to fly to Madras next Wednesday that I may take counsel with you as the one most in touch with that Diocese. From the conflicting telegrams and petitions which have reached me, it is very difficult to gauge the situation accurately. The petition which reached me signed by the Clerical and Lay Secretaries and Treasurer of the Diocesan Council indicated that there had been several incidents of this character. I showed the petition to the Bishop and he said that those who signed it were respectable people and trustworthy. He has since written to me a letter in which he says that there were inaccuracies in the statements made in the petition.[43]

Westcott then proposed that he would try to secure a seat on a flight to South India to investigate the situation for himself.

Meanwhile, letters continued to come to the Metropolitan. A letter dated 10 July 1944 claimed that the village of Sawyerpuram had become involved. The letter reads, 'A strong reaction against the treatment given to our Bishop by Sawyerpuram is gaining ground.' It continues with a plea that the Metropolitan refuse Neill's resignation. Interestingly, Sawyerpuram was home to Neill's victim.

In addition to letters and telegrams flooding Westcott's office, petitions began to arrive. One of these petitions is of particular significance. It was written by the 'Clergy and members of the Tinnevelly Diocese and the members of the Tinnevelly Diocesan Council'.[44] In detail, this petition recounts Neill's fifteen years of faithful service to the diocese:

---

42. Westcott to the Archdeacon of Tinnevelly, 1 July 1944, Westcott Papers, Bishops Box 4, Special Collections, Bishop's College.
43. Westcott to Michael Hollis, 7 July 1944, Westcott Papers, Bishops Box 4, Special Collections, Bishop's College.
44. Clergy and members of the Tinnevelly Diocese and the members of the Tinnevelly Diocesan Council to Westcott, undated, Westcott Papers, Bishops Box 4, Special Collections, Bishop's College.

> He was gifted with great intellectual powers. . . . His knowledge of Tamil language and literature and his talent for speaking the Tamil language with easy facility, as if to the manner born, is a great asset in his work among the villages of this diocese. . . . He has been untiring in his efforts to improve Biblical knowledge and scholarship . . . and has already published a series of books in Tamil for this purpose. His labours on the Tamil Bible Revision Committee are well known throughout South India. . . . In brief, the activities of the Bishop has [sic] touched and benefited every sphere of life of the Diocese.

The petition then offers a defence of the bishop's actions:

> The constant and indefatigable travelling done by the Bishop during these years has greatly affected his health. It is a fact that for some months past he has been in indifferent health and has been suffering from insomnia and other allied ailments. It is in these unfortunate circumstances that the incident of beating the schoolmaster occurred.

The petition concluded with a plea that the Metropolitan reconsider the matter, refrain from accepting Neill's resignation and grant Neill a long furlough.

Letter from a Young Clergyman

On 20 July 1944 a fascinating, well-written letter was sent to Westcott from Reverend Andrew Kurian, a man who claimed to be 'the youngest clergyman in the Tinnevelly Diocese'.[45] This letter is the most important personal letter written to the Metropolitan during the upheaval. The letter is eloquent and persuasive in its defence of Neill: 'Bishop Stephen Neill resigned his office at a time when his spirits were at the lowest. Physically he was suffering from insomnia. Mentally he was in a most perturbed condition.'

With frankness, the young clergyman addressed the core issue at hand:

> I must say a word about his striking. Whatever psychological explanation may be given, I know that the Bishop was made to believe that it did real good to some men. I can speak with authority because I happened to speak to him about it in 1938 and

---

45. Rev. R. Andrew Kurian to Westcott, 20 July 1944, Westcott Papers, Bishops Box 4, Special Collections, Bishop's College.

6. Loss of a Bishopric: 1944-45

he <u>definitely</u> gave it up. Only after this, he felt that he could be a Bishop. But, take it from me, your Grace, there are men who will go to him and ask to be thrashed! So, he has yielded now, we can be sure, he will not repeat if for a thousand pounds. So I leave this there.

The letter explains that Neill's resignation would only hurt the diocese. He suspected a conspiracy against Neill. Reverend Kurian points out that only six of the over-1,000 congregations in Tinnevelly were against Neill. He even urged the Metropolitan upon his visit to Tinnevelly to verify this fact. Further, he claimed that even in the six villages that were opposing Neill, 'there isn't a 100% opposition'.

The young clergyman's insightful letter discussed many of the political intricacies of the diocesan personnel that led several individuals to oppose Neill.[46] The young clergyman also developed Neill's response in the aftermath and gave his personal assessment:[47]

Coming back to the incident, the Bishop <u>has</u> made amends. He went to the houses of the aggrieved party and did what a Christian Bishop could do. In this, our Bishop is a great example to us. If I were in his shoes, I would have argued the other way. 'Why should I stoop to this? I can live anywhere. I can make a name for myself in England by accepting a professorship and writing books. Why should I care to apologise to these fellows?' That is how I would have argued. But the Bishop made a pilgrimage to that man's house and humbled himself. If the Diocese of which I am a part does not

---

46. In addition to the 'young clergyman', there is also a very helpful letter to Westcott from a lawyer who identified himself as being a member of the 'Nazareth Circle'. This lawyer's name is V. Ponniah, and he claimed to know Neill 'fairly well'. He defended Neill in the strongest of terms in his letter. With great detail, Ponniah described the prominent individuals who opposed Neill. The letter reads, 'It pains me to see that four persons [this list of four may include Selwyn] are propagating against the Bishop. One is a Priest! I am extremely sorry that there was an occasion when Bishop Waller ought to have weeded this Priest out of the Mission. . . . But My Lord, should this Priest create false Public opinion against Bishop Neill <u>consciously</u>? The second man is one who owes his Medical Education to our Mission. . . . The third man is a Lawyer. . . . The fourth man is one whom Rev. Evans elevated far above from the rank of a clerk. . . . I cannot know why these people should hate the innocent Bishop.' V. Ponniah to Westcott, 8 September 1944, Westcott Papers, Bishop's Box 4, Bishop's College.
47. Kurian to Westcott, 20 July 1944, Westcott Papers, Bishops Box 4, Special Collections, Bishop's College. This is the only written account from within the diocese that gives insight into Neill's handling of the matter.

> forgive him, we have no right to meditate on the 1st of the 7 words on the Cross, on Good Fridays. God forbid that our Diocese must be branded as an unforgiving Diocese.

In the strongest of words, the young clergyman asked the Metropolitan to intervene and save Bishop Neill from such humiliation.

Kurian explained that the older clergy who opposed Neill were 'a small minority, though influential and well organised'. He described George Selwyn as caught in the middle. Neill felt betrayed by Selwyn; however, the situation may have been that Selwyn had little choice: 'Can. Selwyn is ultra loyal. His innocent advice has not helped the Bishop in this, because he in turn was advised by others, about whom I have grave suspicions. These may be rectified if a fair chance be given.'[48]

> Finally, in prophetic words, the young clergyman of Tinnevelly concluded: 'If Bp. Neill left us, he will do so with a depression in his mind and it will haunt him throughout his life.' This young man was wise beyond his years. The incident did haunt Neill, both personally and professionally. He was, ultimately, forced to leave the land he loved. He was never offered another bishopric.

A Decision Is Made

In mid-July 1944 the Metropolitan flew south to Tinnevelly to investigate. The young clergyman was spot on: 90 per cent of the diocese wanted to retain Bishop Neill.[49] A resolution passed, postponing any formal action against Neill. In a letter the Metropolitan disclosed his personal feelings to the bishops:

---

48. Ibid. It is clear that Neill was having doubts about Selwyn. In a letter to Neill, Westcott wrote, 'I suppose [in your letter] you meant Selwyn. I was not altogether sure of him when I was down there. The fact of his attaching that kind of certificate to the petition which reached me from those three officials raised doubts in my mind.' Westcott to Neill, 12 August 1944, Westcott Papers, Bishops Box 4, Special Collections, Bishop's College. Regarding George Selwyn, there are a few possible scenarios. Perhaps Selwyn was set against Neill and managed to position himself in such a way that would not attract the wrath of Neill's supporters. Perhaps Selwyn was coerced or at least caught in the middle; or, perhaps, Selwyn had his eyes set on the bishopric. After all, he did become the next Bishop of Tinnevelly. The biography of Selwyn does not address these matters. However, it does mention that there was a 'feeling of unsettlement and uneasiness which existed after the resignation of Bp. Neill.' Neither does it address the events surrounding Neill's resignation or the election that allowed Selwyn to become bishop. See Sargunam, *Bishop Selwyn of Tirunelveli*.
49. Westcott to the Bishops of India, Burma and Ceylon, 21 July 1944, Westcott Papers, Bishops Box 4, Special Collections, Bishop's College.

6. Loss of a Bishopric: 1944-45

The impression I gained was that his [Neill's] own great ability made him reluctant to delegate any of his functions to others less gifted. The result was that he was greatly over-worked. . . . I spoke to the Bishop about this and suggested that he should have at least two Archdeacons. . . . The Bishop has appointed the Revd. Dr. Appasamy as his Commissary and there is every prospect that harmony will prevail.

Westcott had every intention that Neill would return after a long period of furlough, as long as the psychiatrist in England allowed. Neill was in Bombay with his sister, awaiting a passage back to England. Westcott wrote a letter to the Archbishop of Canterbury, William Temple, advising him that Neill would soon arrive to England.[50] The letter is dated 29 July 1944:[51]

My dear Archbishop,
Since I last wrote to you I have visited Palamcottah and met the leaders of the Church of the Diocese of Tinnevelly. . . . There is no question whatever as to the desire of the diocese to retain the services of their Bishop. The great bulk of the people are devoted to him. . . . I have received a great number of telegrams from people

---

50. Metropolitan Westcott to the Archbishop of Canterbury, 29 July 1944, Westcott Papers, Bishops Box 4, Special Collections, Bishop's College. Neill's account here follows exactly the account as constructed by Westcott's letters. See Neill, *God's Apprentice,* pp. 201-4.Neill knew of the communication between Westcott and Temple. 'One personal loss added to the mood of depression from which I was finding it hard to escape. The Bishop of Calcutta [Westcott] had written to William Temple, by now Archbishop of Canterbury, and I had received in Bombay an extremely friendly letter from William, telling me to come and see him as soon as I reached England. . . . Then, one afternoon, the lady who was occupying a flat in one corner of Barnwell Rectory called down the stairs, "I think you would wish to know that the Archbishop of Canterbury has just died." My heart stood still. William was only sixty-two, and still at the height of his powers. . . . He had been receiving my regular circular letters from India. . . . More than any other man in England, he was the one to whom I would have turned for help and guidance in those difficult days. . . . The first public occasion I attended after reaching England was the funeral of William Temple. . . . The next time that I was in Canterbury Cathedral was for the enthronement of Geoffrey Francis Fisher as the ninety-ninth Archbishop of Canterbury.' Neill, *God's Apprentice,* p. 206.
51. In addition to this letter, Westcott also sent a telegram to Temple on the same day. The telegram mentioned that the final decision on Neill must wait until after the psychiatrist's report. However, Westcott pointed out, 'Ninety percent of Christians want their Bishop back.' Telegram from Westcott to Temple, 29 July 1944, Westcott Papers, Bishops Box 4, Special Collections, Bishop's College.

in the diocese expressing their desire to retain his services, and the only one telegram I have received to the contrary effect was from the people who sent the petition.[52]

I shall be very grateful if you could keep in touch with the Bishop of Tinnevelly and in due course let me know what your own opinion in the matter is. . . . If, however, the Psychiatrist is of the opinion that in the interest of his own health it would be better for him not to be a resident in the climate of southern India that would alter the situation.

Westcott continued to communicate with Neill during his wait in Bombay. On 7 August 1944 Westcott wrote to Neill, telling him that he hoped Neill would be able to come back, 'You know how greatly I desire this.'[53] Westcott expressed this same opinion to others as well.[54]

Neill knew his future was uncertain. Much hinged on the report he was to receive from the psychiatrist. He was focusing on his mental health, fighting his lingering depression. His final letter to his clergy, dated 19 July 1944, and sent from Ootacamund while he was *en route* to Bombay, reads:

I want to send you my greetings and my thanks for your love and fellowship during the past five and a half years. And specially I want to thank you for your sympathy and prayers during these days of trouble. It has been hard at times not to lose heart; at times the sense of God's presence has been altogether withdrawn. . . . I do not know how many times during the sleepless hours of the night I have said the 23rd Psalm to myself. . . . I am sure that you will continue to pray for me during the days of uncertainty that lie ahead; ask only for one thing – that the will of God may be made plain, and may be accepted by us all.[55]

Metropolitan Westcott continued to receive letters urging him to give Neill time. Things were beginning to calm down. One letter to Westcott read:

---

52. Interestingly, Westcott had previously written to the Archdeacon of Tinnevelly (cited above, letter dated 1 July 1944) that he had received telegrams (plural) both in favour and in opposition to Neill. His letter to the Archbishop of Canterbury clarifies the matter.
53. Westcott to Neill, 7 August 1944, Westcott Papers, Bishops Box 4, Special Collections, Bishop's College.
54. See, for example, a letter from Westcott to Bishop Walsh of Coimbatore, 8 August 1944, Westcott Papers, Bishops Box 4, Special Collections, Bishop's College.
55. Neill, *Letters to His Clergy*, no. 47 (19 July 1944), Special Collections, Bishop Stephen Neill Study and Research Centre.

6. Loss of a Bishopric: 1944-45

'Now that everything has been made clear and that your Grace also has given an official announcement in the papers, everything is quiet in the Diocese. There are a few discontented people here and there and I hope their voice is not heard loudly in public.'[56]

The entire situation took a sudden and surprising turn when the Archbishop of Canterbury, William Temple, died on 26 October 1944. Westcott had been in communication with Temple and now a new Archbishop would have to hear the case.[57] To compound Neill's problems, in early 1945 Westcott announced his own resignation. In a sombre letter to Neill dated 7 February 1945, Westcott wrote:

> My dear Bishop,
> At the recent Episcopal Synod I consulted the 9 other Bishops who were present at Nagpur who advised me with regard to my own resignation. I had told my Diocesan Council that I proposed to resign but would consult the Episcopal Synod as to the exact date. . . . [T]hey agreed that I should send in my resignation now which will be accepted but would not take effect till some date within six months when my successor was appointed.
> He told me also that they had considered the question of your return to India and that it was their unanimous opinion that as much in your own interest as in that of the Church, you should not do so but should take up work in England. ... I said I would not give a definite answer to your letter of resignation to me till March. . . . I think it would be well for you to take into full consideration this expression of the Bishops' opinion and recognise that I am doubtful whether it would be right for me on the eve of my departure to decide contrary to the opinion of the Bishops.[58]

What had appeared to be a situation on the mend had quickly become a permanent separation between Neill and the Tinnevelly diocese.

One of Neill's fiercest opponents, a lawyer named P.A. Thangasamy, wrote to Westcott on 16 February 1945, reminding him that Neill's situation must be resolved.[59] Nevertheless, many letters continued to arrive

---

56. R.V. Asirvadam to Westcott, 9 September 1944, Westcott Papers, Bishops Box 4, Special Collections, Bishop's College.
57. This is discussed in a letter from Westcott to the Bishop of Nagpur, 25 November 1944, Westcott Papers, Bishops Box 4, Special Collections, Bishop's College.
58. Westcott to Neill, 7 February 1945, Westcott Papers, Bishops Box 4, Special Collections, Bishop's College.
59. P.A. Thangasamy to Westcott, 16 February 1945, Westcott Papers, Bishops Box 4, Special Collections, Bishop's College. Thangasamy will be discussed in the

in support of Neill and the diocese knew nothing yet of the psychiatrist's report.[60] However, on 28 April 1945 Westcott received the psychiatrist's report and it left open the door for Neill's return to India. Westcott was now in a pickle: the area bishops had unanimously agreed that Neill should not return to India; while the Tinnevelly diocese almost unanimously wanted Neill back. Clearly confused over what to do, Westcott sent a letter to the bishops of India, Burma and Ceylon: 'I should be glad to know what your opinion is as to his return in the light of this opinion [the psychiatrist's report] and of the fact that his return is desired as far as I can understand by the almost unanimous desire of the Diocese.'[61]

By 12 July 1945, Westcott had clearly decided officially to accept Neill's resignation, effective 31 August 1945.[62]

On 26 June 1945, Westcott wrote a long letter to Neill explaining why he had decided Neill should not return to India, despite the optimistic report from the psychiatrist:[63]

> My dear Bishop,
> It was with a heavy heart that I sent you the telegram accepting your resignation of the Bishopric of Tinnevelly which you had placed in my hands over nine months ago. . . . I believe the decision reached is in accordance with the will of God. . . . I have taken great pains to ascertain the position in the Diocese and unquestionably you have overestimated the proportion of those who desired your return. But I do not wish to dwell at length on that aspect of the situation as being the one that had the dominant influence on our minds.
>
> You have in writing to me laid great stress on the psychiatrist's report as providing you with a clean bill of health. I cannot say that I wholly agree with you in that view, but what has troubled me and your brother Bishops most, is the entire absence of any sense of repentance, or sorrow for the evil which has been committed. Making every allowance for the psychological trouble the causes for which you were not morally responsible, you must have realised

---

next section where this author's interviews from 2003 are examined.
60. R.V. Asirvadam to Westcott, 20 March 1945, Westcott Papers, Bishops Box 4, Special Collections, Bishop's College.
61. Westcott to the bishops of India, Burma and Ceylon, 28 April 1945, Westcott Papers, Bishops Box 4, Special Collections, Bishop's College.
62. Westcott to the Diocese of Tinnevelly, 12 July 1945, Westcott Papers, Bishops Box 4, Special Collections, Bishop's College.
63. Westcott to Neill, 26 June 1945, Westcott Papers, Bishops Box 4, Special Collections, Bishop's College.

6. Loss of a Bishopric: 1944-45

the scandal which your action had caused and serious injury to the Church and her work which they had entailed, but in not one of your letters has there been any acknowledgement of this fact, or expression of sorrow for having been the cause of it. I will not dwell further on this point but it has been a cause of surprise to me and led me to feel that it would not be right for you to return.

There are other reasons which confirmed me in this decision. I do not think that you should live and work in a climate so trying as that prevailing in Tinnevelly. . . . I also feel that in Tinnevelly you are in a large measure isolated from men of comparable intellectual gifts and though in your letter you spoke of having your sister to live with you if you returned, I do not know that she would have provided you with the intellectual fellowship which able men require.

I think you know I had hoped that you would have succeeded me as Metropolitan of this Province and brought to the discharge of the duties of that office, the great gifts in which I was so largely deficient. You have told me in your letters how much work has been given to you since you have been in Cambridge, for which you are so richly endowed, and I am sure that God will give you the work there He would have you do, and which in that environment both intellectual and physical you will be able successfully to achieve.

I know how deeply your heart was set on mission work in India, and while your return to India is I believe inadvisable, you will I hope still continue to serve the Church of India by your writings.

I realise what a disappointment my decision will be to you, and I believe you will realise how painful it has been to me to come to this conclusion, but I trust you will accept it as being the expression of God's will for which you and many others have earnestly prayed.

Two months later, on 25 August 1945, Westcott wrote a personal letter to Dr A.J. Appasamy, who had been put in charge of the Tinnevelly Diocese until a new bishop was appointed. This letter is significant for two reasons. First, it establishes that the accusations against Neill were widely known:

It is perfectly well known in the Diocese that charges were brought against Bishop Neill. ... I do not feel that I ought to enter into it in detail as the charges are well known. They were made to me confidentially by the Bishop himself and the less said about them the better.[64]

---
64. Westcott to Dr Appasamy, 25 August 1945, Westcott Papers, Bishops Box 4,

Second, this letter notes two significant dates: Neill's bishopric would officially end on 31 August 1945; and as early as January 1945 the bishops of the region (India, Burma and Ceylon) had voted unanimously that Westcott should accept Neill's resignation.[65]

By at least 10 July 1945 Neill faced the reality that his bishopric was indeed over. On that day *The Times* recorded: 'Bishop Stephen Neill has informed Metropolitan Westcott that he'll resign, effective August 31 this year.'[66]

On 12 July 1945, Westcott sent a letter to the Tinnevelly diocese (cited above), stating that Neill was requesting his 'Provident Fund Money'. The money was sent and arrived with Westcott on 6 September 1945.[67] The cheque for Neill was for Rs. 4,070.13. Neill bequeathed the money to the Endowment Fund of the Bishopric of Tinnevelly.[68]

Westcott resigned his own see about the same time Neill's resignation was accepted.[69] Westcott was succeeded by George Hubback, long-time bishop of Assam. It is not known whether the Neill case is what led to Westcott's resignation. However, it does not seem likely, as Westcott was already 82 years old and he lived for only four years after his retirement.[70]

Neill Interferes with the Election of a New Bishop

Around 2 July 1945 Westcott called an election for the Tinnevelly bishopric.[71] Various diocesan officials sent letters to Westcott, requesting

       Special Collections, Bishop's College.
65. A letter was sent from Michael Hollis, bishop of Madras, to Appasamy on 14 September 1945 (carbon copied to Westcott), claiming that, if the diocese was to elect Neill as the new bishop (again), the other bishops would not approve. This was important because the other bishops of a region or province had to approve any newly elected bishop. Michael Hollis (Neill's former roommate) was highly influential as the bishop of the distinguished see of Madras; he went on to serve as the first Moderator of the Church of South India. Hollis to Appasamy, 14 September 1945, Westcott Papers, Bishops Box 4, Special Collections, Bishop's College.
66. *The Times*, 10 July 1945, p. 6.
67. Tinnevelly treasurers to Westcott, 6 September 1945, Westcott Papers, Bishops Box 4, Special Collections, Bishop's College.
68. Metropolitan's chaplain to Appasamy, 17 September 1945, Westcott Papers, Bishops Box 4, Special Collections, Bishop's College.
69. The date of Westcott's resignation was between 25 August 1945 and 14 September 1945. It is likely that the resignation was official on 31 August, as it was common for resignations to take effect on the last day of the month. Westcott was 82 years old when he resigned. Gibbs, *The Anglican Church in India 1600-1970*, p. 380.
70. Ibid., p. 380. Westcott retired to St Paul's School, Darjeeling. He was buried in a garden on the school grounds. He was succeeded by George Hubback who had served as bishop of Assam for 21 years.
71. Appasamy to Westcott, 2 July 1945, Westcott Papers, Bishops Box 4, Special Collections, Bishop's College. This letter states, 'The Mandate for the election of a

6. Loss of a Bishopric: 1944-45

Neill's name to stand as a candidate. Metropolitan Westcott understood that, were Neill elected, his appointment would have to be approved by the bishops of the region, and this would be highly unlikely.[72] The following letter from a diocesan official to the new Metropolitan (George Hubback) sheds light on the issues at stake:

> There is a strong rumour afloat here that though a satisfactory medical report was received, the matter was taken to the House of Bishops in which it was decided not to recall Rt. Rev. S. C. Neill. May I request you to inform me: 1. What the nature of the Medical report was? 2. On what issues the matter was taken to the House of Bishops? 3. On what grounds it was decided not to recall Rt. Rev. S. C. Neill?[73]

Another letter from Appasamy, the commissary in charge of the Tinnevelly diocese, shows a certain strategy: by keeping Neill's name on the ballot, the pro-Neill faction could be pacified. However, realistically, the re-election of Neill was impossible.[74]

Neill was actively making things worse. The person in charge of the election was George Selwyn, the one who ended up winning the election. Selwyn received a cable from Neill expressing his willingness to return to Tinnevelly if a call were extended to him. Neill also wrote a letter published in the vernacular diocesan magazine making it clear that he would come back if asked.[75]

When the first ballots were cast, Neill was placed first, with 147 votes, George Selwyn second with 65 votes and Appasamy third, with 46 votes.[76]

The new Metropolitan, however, would not countenance Neill being elected. In an autocratic display, he immediately removed the possibility of Neill's name remaining on the ballot. His conclusion was to the point:

---

new Bishop for this diocese sent to me by registered post reached me this morning."
72. Westcott to Edward Raj, 3 August 1945, Westcott Papers, Bishops Box 4, Special Collections, Bishop's College.
73. G.G. Joshua to Metropolitan Hubback, undated, Hubback Papers, Bishops Box 5, Special Collections, Bishop's College. This letter was written after Hubback's ascension to the office of Metropolitan; it was likely to have been written in September 1945.
74. Appasamy to Hubback, 17 September 1945, Hubback Papers, Bishops Box 5, Special Collections, Bishop's College.
75. Appasamy to Hubback, 19 September 1945, Hubback Papers, Bishops Box 5, Special Collections, Bishop's College.
76. Hubback to the bishops of Travancore and Madras, 29 September 1945, Hubback Papers, Bishops Box 5, Special Collections, Bishop's College.

Stephen Neill should not return to India. Therefore, it rests with us to decide between the Rev. Canon G.T. Selwyn and the Rev. Dr. A.J. Appasamy.... While regretting that a national of this country has not secured a majority of the votes, it is my personal opinion that we should appoint the Rev. Canon G.T. Selwyn.[77]

The decision became official on 17 October 1945. George Selwyn was the new bishop of Tinnevelly.[78] It was only on 31 October 1945, when Selwyn was formally confirmed in office,[79] that the situation began to ease.

The Loss of a Bishropic: According to Interviews

Interview with Reverend S.T. Paul Gnaniah[80]
An important interview for understanding the incident surrounding Neill's dismissal was with Reverend Paul Gnaniah in South India in February 2003. At the time Gnaniah was the oldest living clergyman in the Tirunelveli diocese and the only living clergyman ordained by Neill. Ordained deacon in 1943 and priest in 1944, both by Neill, Gnaniah knew him very well.[81] More importantly, Gnaniah was active in the diocese when the scandal surrounding Neill occurred.

Gnaniah began his interview with the following words:

> Neill had human weaknesses. In spite of all goodness and greatness and good deeds, he had one main weakness. That weakness is what led him to leave Tirunelveli. Here is the weakness: when the pastors and evangelists would go to meet the bishop, he would take them

---
77. Ibid.
78. Metropolitan Hubback to the bishops of the Province of India, Burma and Ceylon, 17 October 1945, Hubback Papers, Bishops Box 5, Special Collections, Bishop's College.
79. Instrument of Confirmation of the Election of a Bishop, DS by the bishops of India, Burma and Ceylon, 31 October 1945, Bishop Selwyn papers, Tinnevelly Box 2, Special Collections, Bishop's College.
80. Rev. S.T. Paul Gnaniah, interview by author, 14-15 February 2003, transcribed and approved by interviewee, interviewee's home, Palayankottai.
81. Gnaniah served for twelve years as a parish priest. Then he served for ten years as General Secretary of the Indian Missionary Society. During his final fifteen or so years of active ministry, he served in a variety of positions including: parish priest, diocesan administrator, clerical secretary, vice-chairman of the diocese, the bishop's commissary, the moderator's commissary, manager of mission schools and superintendent of the Diocesan Press. He retired in 1976 and from 1976 to 2000 he worked as a coordinator for an associate evangelist to Billy Graham's work in India. In 2003 he was serving as Honorary Chaplain at Holy Trinity English Church in Tuticorin.

6. Loss of a Bishopric: 1944-45

in, listen to them, ask them what they did good, and then he would ask them what they did bad. Neill would almost force the person to say, 'Yes, I've done something wrong.' Neill would then say that punishment was necessary. If the person argued, Neill would leave them alone. If it was a submissive man, Neill would ask if they were prepared for punishment. The poor fellow would say yes. Then Neill would take them into a room where he had a table and a cane. The man would be asked to lie on the table, on his stomach. The clothes would be removed from the buttocks. Some poor fellows would get three, six or even twelve cuts on their buttocks. When they cried, Neill stopped. Neill did this all throughout his ministry, even as Bishop. Advice was given to him by his supervisors and friends, but he continued to do it. Neill would often beat young people, mainly teenagers. Normally, he would beat people aged 10 to 25 years. Older ones who were close to him were also beaten.

When asked about the method of the beatings, Gnaniah described them: 'Beatings were only on the buttocks, with a cane. This cane was made of a small kind of bamboo. It was not hollow but thick. It was very flexible and would not break easily.' Gnaniah then reflected: 'This one weakness in Neill brought him down. Many advised him to stop, but he just could not stop. Neill's weakness is a known fact in this diocese.'

When asked about the details of the situation that brought Neill down, Gnaniah provided an important, inside perspective to the situation:

In 1944 a similar thing happened. A teacher, named Paul Raj, was beaten and had a half-dozen cuts.[82] The young man was shy but his friends who were standing outside the Bishopstowe heard the beating. The young man came down and the friends said, 'What happened?' The people found out and became very angry. The people who became angry were from Sawyerpuram. The people of the village got against him [Neill]. The whole diocese came to find out. Some of the leaders in the diocese said, 'We don't want this kind of bishop.' I was at Nazareth at the time and had just been ordained by Neill.

At this point in the interview, Gnaniah paused to break the tension that was obviously involved in recounting the events. He laughed and spoke the following words in jest: 'No one was equal to Neill, as he was an intellectual

---

82. Rev. G. Stephen Lionel, the pastor of the Cathedral Church in Palayamkottai, also named the man involved as Paul Raj, interview by author, 16 February 2003, transcribed and approved by interviewee, interviewee's home, Palayamkottai.

giant. But he had this devilish weakness. Perhaps he had the theology of the Old Testament in his discipline. In his "theology of discipline" he must have been a Jew. Perhaps he had a "theology of caning".'

Gnaniah then continued with the story at hand:

> So the diocese had to decide about all of this. Some said, 'After all, he's a bishop and he's doing so much for the diocese.' But P.A. Thangasamy, a lawyer and the leader of the group, said Neill had to go. Those joining on Thangasamy's side were Rev. Canon S.S. Moses and Dr R. Vedabothakam, a medical doctor. These three men were three of the top men in the diocese and they didn't even like Neill before this incident.

It was at this point Gnaniah made comments about Neill's authoritarianism: 'Neill was a very hard man to deal with. He was very strict in many ways. He was a disciplinarian, an autocrat, imperialistic.'

Gnaniah then continued the story:

> Neill apologised to the man. But still some of the people wanted him to go. They were very adamant. So, the diocesan leaders got into two groups: Daniel Thomas, who later became a government minister – but he was a lawyer at the time, led a group who said that the bishop should be excused upon apology. We all make mistakes. God forgives. Why not forgive our bishop?

Once the line in the sand had been drawn, dividing supporters of Neill from those who opposed him, Metropolitan Westcott flew down south. Gnaniah described the meetings which took place:

> The diocesan executive committee met with Metropolitan Westcott, who came on the invitation of the diocese. He came from Calcutta. There were two groups. One group said Neill must go. The other group said he must stay. Those in favour of Neill staying were Daniel Thomas and Rev. R.G. Jesudason, and others. The majority of the people were with Daniel Thomas and wanted Neill to stay. Thomas was a leading criminal lawyer. The other lawyer, P.A. Thangasamy, was not as powerful. With regard to speech, Daniel Thomas was a powerful speaker.

Gnaniah then described the argument against Neill, summarised to the diocesan council by Thangasamy:

6. Loss of a Bishopric: 1944-45

(1) Thangasamy said, 'We don't want a beating bishop; we want a loving bishop.' It was no great secret that Neill used to beat people with a cane.
(2) At this time, nationalism was in the air. Thangasamy said, 'He thinks low of Indians, so he beats us. He doesn't beat Englishmen!' This was the argument that would eventually prevail and force Neill to leave India.
(3) Sadism. Thangasamy argued that this is a disease that cannot be cured – this getting pleasure from other people's pain.

Next, Gnaniah commented on Westcott's response:

> The Metropolitan did not want to take sides. He said, 'We'll give the bishop a long leave of six months.' The Metropolitan then appointed a commission. Appasamy was appointed. Appasamy was educated at Harvard. He was very wealthy and he was ordained. However, he was not working at the time. He didn't need to work. So Neill went on a long leave – nine months or so. The Metropolitan studied everything carefully and made the decision that Stephen Neill should not go back. The diocese then became vacant. Westcott was thoroughly upset about Neill. Neill and Hollis [Michael – bishop of Madras] were the two brilliant men of the day. The Metropolitan had a great opinion of these two, but he preferred Neill.

Gnaniah discussed the outcome of the new election:

> Neill's name came up again. I voted for him again, too. So many people voted for him. He came in first place in the election. Selwyn came in second, and Appasamy came in third. Appasamy thought he would become bishop. The people figured this out. And so Selwyn won. Neill won the vote, but he was not allowed to become bishop. At the discussion concerning the nomination papers, one man who was in support of Neill stood up and said, 'If you're going to get a knock on the head, it's better to get it from the bishop's gold ring than from an ordinary hand!' This was related to an ancient Tamil proverb and this man applied it to Neill.

Finally, Gnaniah contrasted Neill with his successor, George Selwyn: 'Neill was an imperialist, unlike Selwyn. Selwyn felt one with the people. Selwyn intermixed with the people. Selwyn was a wonderful man – very fatherly. He ate what others ate. But Neill . . . that man was an imperialist!'

Interview with Rt Reverend Jason Dharmaraj[83]

Another important interviewee about the incidents surrounding Neill's fall from the bishopric was Jason Dharmaraj, who served as bishop of Tirunelveli diocese from 1985 to 1999. The interview with Dharmaraj was significant not only because he was bishop of Tirunelveli for so long, but also because he was a relative of Paul Raj – the schoolmaster whom Neill purportedly beat, leading to his downfall. Paul Raj was his uncle.

Dharmaraj began the interview with detailed information on Paul Raj:

> Paul Raj was my mother's elder brother. He was a physical education instructor in a high school.[84] At first, he was with the diocesan school, then he went to the army in World War II. He was sent back in 1942 or 1943. When he returned, he was unemployed. He got an appointment at a Catholic school in Tuticorin. At the end of the year there was a vacancy at Pope Memorial Diocesan High School in Sawyerpuram. He got the job.

Dharmaraj then described the context wherein the beating incident occurred:

> There was a summer school for some of the teachers, and Neill was in charge of the conference. Paul was not beaten at Bishopstowe. My father was also at the conference. It was a three-week summer course. Neill was the main teacher. My father heard that it was well-known that Neill would beat people who did something wrong. My father heard and thought, 'What is this?'

Dharmaraj next recounted the beating incident itself:

> Paul Raj was asked to go to Neill around 7 p.m. My father, A. Simon Dharmaraj, accompanied Paul to Chaffter Hostel of St John's College in Palayamkottai. Uncle Paul went in. My father waited and waited at the entrance and suspected a beating which he only found out about a day before. He went up a few steps. He heard a sound of whipping and stopped on the stairs, as he was startled. Uncle Paul then came down. My father asked him what happened. Paul had received 12 lashes on the bare buttocks. My father was angry

---

83. Rt Rev. Jason Dharmaraj, interview by author, 18 February 2003, transcribed and approved by interviewee, interviewee's home, Palayankottai.
84. Rev. Stephen Lionel verified that Paul Raj was from Sawyerpuram and he taught physical education for students between grades 6 and 12, interview by author, 16 February 2003.

6. Loss of a Bishopric: 1944-45

because of this and because of the nationalistic feelings. My father openly told everyone at the summer school what happened. People told my father to calm down. My father and a few people went to Rev. Samuel, who was a senior man.[85] Rev. Samuel said calm down and he would meet the bishop next month. The following evening the summer course was complete.

With extraordinary insight, Dharmaraj was able to provide intricate details, such as the content of the conversation that led to Paul Raj's beating:

What did Paul do wrong? Neill asked, 'Why did you leave the diocese to join the army.' He replied, 'I could join the army and make a better salary.' Neill asked, 'So why did you leave the army?' Paul replied, 'I failed a physical and jumping exam.' Neill said, 'If you failed the exam, they would have given you opportunity to train and retake the exam. The other offer is that you could return and leave the army.' Paul said, 'I decided to come back.' Neill said, 'Why did you come back?' Paul said, 'It's a very hard life in the army, so I came back.'

The source of Neill's consternation was then revealed:

Neill then asked, 'So why did you then join a Roman Catholic school?' Paul replied, 'I needed a job as I have a family. I heard there was a job so I took it.' Neill said, 'So why did you rejoin the Anglican diocese?' Paul said, 'This job is very convenient for me because it is located in my own native village [Sawyerpuram] and I have a house there.'

Dharmaraj continued:

Neill said, 'First you left the diocese for more money. Then you left the army because you didn't want to work hard. Then, when you returned, you should have asked me for a job. But you didn't. You just went and joined the Catholic school. That shows you are worldly and only after money. And you didn't continue there – you left and joined here. So you are worldly, money-minded, and you did not serve in the army faithfully. So I feel you are liable to be punished.'

---

85. Dharmaraj described Rev. Samuel as 'the chaplain at Madras Christian College and priest in Tuticorin'.

Dharmaraj claimed that Paul agreed, 'Yes I should be punished.' Then, 'Stephen Neill had him lie down for lashing. After the lashing, Neill led a prayer.'

Dharmaraj's father decided that somebody must take action to stop this:

> Simon [Dharmaraj's father] said something must be done. He heard that there were others who had been beaten. However, he heard rumours that, if a person was beaten, he would be given preference and even a promotion. This was the rumour. Neill was very kind to people after they were punished. Simon strongly encouraged Paul to tell the people and to do something. Paul was persuaded by Simon.

Shortly thereafter, the people were roused to take action, according to Dharmaraj:

> In those days, the people in Sawyerpuram were from Burma. Sawyerpuram was a unique village. A.J. Thomas was the maternal uncle of Paul Raj. He was a municipal health inspector in a Rangoon corporation. He was a strong man. He was an Indian nationalist. He took the leadership of this problem with Neill. It was a respected, educated family. This was all propagated throughout the village. They had a big meeting. They called on Paul Raj to tell everything that happened in detail. He did. This was 1944 and the whole country was full of nationalism. Everyone got emotional. Villagers decided they would talk to the bishop.

Dharmaraj then explained the suspicions that some pro-nationalist Indians had towards Neill. On one occasion, Neill had publicly opposed Prime Minister and nationalist leader Jawaharlal Nehru. Dharmaraj recounted the event:

> Some leading lawyers in Palayamkottai were Congressmen – affiliated with nationalism. However, the Justice Party supported British rule as well as Neill. Both sides had a conflict, trying to decide what to do. This all went back to a secular meeting when Neill said, 'The first person we hate is Hitler, the second is Nehru.' In 1944, however, Nehru was loved by all of the people. In 1944, most felt India would soon get freedom. Thangasamy, a leading lawyer in Palayamkottai, said a person like Neill should not be bishop.[86]

---

86. It should be noted that Gnaniah and Dharmaraj both mentioned Thangasamy as one of the major opponents of Neill during the uproar. It is unclear why Neill

6. Loss of a Bishopric: 1944-45

Gnaniah also talked about the political dimension of the situation:

> Neill was a politician. Missionaries should not be politicians. On one occasion he gave a political address. In the speech, Neill said, 'Nehru is the third enemy of the world. First is Hitler, second is Mussolini and third is Nehru.' All of the papers condemned him for talking about politics. Nehru was a great leader and was, with Gandhi, fighting for independence. Neill finally apologised to the papers.[87]

Dharmaraj conjectured that Selwyn realised he was probably next in line for the bishopric and thus he took the position that Neill should leave.

According to Dharmaraj, a delegation from Palayamkottai – not including Neill – visited Sawyerpuram. They met with Thomas (Paul Raj's maternal uncle) to try to get him to relent from his strong opposition to Neill. However, he stood firm and maintained the position that Neill must leave the diocese. Some time later, according to Dharmaraj, Neill made his way to Sawyerpuram to apologise to the whole village.[88] The entire village discussed whether or not they would accept him. They all met in front of Jeevamani Kailpallai's house; this was the house of Dharmaraj's maternal grandfather. Meanwhile, Neill and other important people from the diocese went to meet with Paul Raj. Paul went outside the village to greet Neill. Immediately, they embraced.

Wearing only a white cassock and a cross, instead of the normal, more elaborate vestments of the bishop, Neill entered the village. Jason Dharmaraj said many in the village were crying. Neill placed Dharmaraj's young brother of five years on his lap. Paul stood next to Neill the entire time, his arm around him. Neill then spoke to Paul Raj's extended family, who had gathered. According to Dharmaraj, Neill said, 'I apologise for bringing great shame to your family. Now I'm returning to England. If I return to India, I'll visit your family.' Dharmaraj claimed that Neill was true to his word and came to visit Paul Raj when Raj was bedridden and close to

---

was so critical of Nehru. Nehru's irreligious or socialist beliefs may shed some light, although Neill never mentions these as factors. In fact, Neill does not speak strongly against Nehru in the few places where he mentions the Indian leader.

87. Neill did not record the incident in *God's Apprentice*. He only mentioned Nehru briefly, 'nationalism as represented by Mahatma Gandhi and Pandit Jawaharlal Nehru triumphed'. Neill, *God's Apprentice*, p. 128.

88. This story was also recounted by Rev. Lionel. However, he added a couple of details, 'Sawyerpuram obstructed Neill's path with thorny bushes and a pit. If he entered, he would fall into a pit. People advised him not to go, but he went anyway. He could have been attacked.'

death.[89] On that occasion, Dharmaraj stated, 'Neill went and prayed with Paul. Neill didn't speak much at all.' Raj died in 1974, a few months after Neill visited him.[90]

Confidential Interview at Cambridge

On 4 March 2003 I interviewed a person who attended Wycliffe Hall, Oxford, from 1983 to 1985. Neill served as Senior Scholar there from 1975 until his death in 1984. This individual did not wish to reveal his name. The reason this interview is important is because it reveals an example of Neill's beatings late in his life. This incident occurred shortly before Neill died, showing that the events that transpired in 1944 were closely similar to this event, which took place either in 1983 or 1984, the interviewee was unable to recall a precise date. It must be pointed out that this interviewee had no knowledge of the events that led to Neill's dismissal from Tinnevelly.[91]

The interviewee claimed that, while Neill was preparing his book *A History of Christianity in India: 1707-1858* for publication, he asked for help in organising the chapters before sending the manuscript to the press. Neill asked the interviewee to come up to his room to help him in this task. The individual went. At some point during the evening, Neill 'totally

---

89. Dharmaraj stated that Paul Raj lived from 1917 to 1974.
90. Neill only visited Tirunelveli on two occasions after he left the bishopric, although he did visit his sister in Ooty and Coonoor, South India, often. He visited in 1974 in order to speak at the centenary celebration of Bishop Azariah's birth in 1874. Regarding Neill's visit in 1974, Gnaniah claimed, 'I invited Neill back in 1974. He came. He received a very cordial welcome. Only one of the original opposition was still alive: Dr R. Vedabothakam. Neill had been invited through the IMS [Indian Missionary Society]. I was presiding at this event. Neill gave two talks. When it became known that Neill was coming, Vedabothakam said, "Neill? We've already sent him out!" Everyone voted for Neill to come. When they had the vote to elect Neill as the speaker for this occasion, Vedabothakam walked out of the meeting. . . . Neill spoke like a native. He had such fine, good Tamil. He had absolutely no repetition of words. He spoke so fluently. He talked in pure Tamil about Azariah, in 1974, for an hour. I said to him, "You didn't even repeat one word. How is that possible after a gap of so many years?" Neill replied, "You do not know the strain – German will come in, French will come in, then English. So many languages pressing me." Only the Lord knows why Neill was still so fluent. When he was here that time, there was a great demand for him.' Neill also visited in 1980 to celebrate the second centenary of the church as the year 1780 is recognised as the starting point for the history of the diocese. Gnaniah claimed, 'Neill came back in 1980 and the people still loved him. So many people loved him. Half of the crowd came to see him. They were all excited, saying, "Bishop Neill is coming!"'
91. Anonymous, interview by author, 4 March 2003, transcribed and approved by interviewee, Faculty of Divinity building, University of Cambridge.

6. Loss of a Bishopric: 1944-45

changed', in the words of the interviewee, and asked him to come to his lap. The individual then sat on Neill's knee. Neill then said the following, 'Now how about some punishment.' This person became 'exceedingly uncomfortable' and tried to get away because Neill was slapping him/her on the buttocks. Neill did not ask the individual to remove his pants.

At the time this individual was single and did not talk to people about the incident. He had been on friendly terms with Neill until the episode but afterwards 'started avoiding Neill to an extent'. In retrospect, this individual said, 'There was another side to the bishop. He was a real enigma.'

Events at Tinnevelly According to Neill

In his autobiography, Neill recorded that: 'for this period of my life alone I have difficulty in reconstructing the chronology, and cannot be certain that I am recording events exactly in the order in which they occurred.'[92] In Neill's discussion of the loss of his bishopric, he avoided some central issues. For example, he never mentioned striking other people. He tried to convey in his autobiography that his ill health was the central issue. In addition, he patently got some facts wrong.

In the autobiography Neill recorded that when he returned from his 1943 Kashmir holiday, he was 'called upon to breast a sea of troubles'.[93] Neill said he had to settle an argument between two clergymen involving caste and the misuse of church funds. However, in his September 1943 letter to his clergy, he wrote: 'I am glad to find that all has gone so well in my absence.'[94]

The next 'trouble' involved charges of immorality against one of Neill's old students. Neill claimed that he 'immediately appointed a commission of enquiry'. Ultimately, 'The charges were dismissed as "non-proven".'[95]

Next, Neill wrote that a person whom he trusted greatly 'was in fact doing his best to undermine my position in the diocese'.[96] Neill was hurt by this. He commented:

> This hit me very hard. I do not like fighting; but I am prepared on occasion to fight, and to fight hard, for what I believe to be right, provided that everything is above board, that there are no aces up

---

92. Neill, *God's Apprentice*, p. 197.
93. Ibid., p. 195.
94. Neill, *Letters to His Clergy*, no. 43 (September 1943), Special Collections, Bishop Stephen Neill Study and Research Centre.
95. Eleanor Jackson's personal collection, p. 392.
96. Neill, *God's Apprentice*, p. 197.

people's sleeves or extra cards hidden under the table. But anything done against me behind my back or without my knowledge, has always had the power to wound me very deeply.[97]

It may have been his good friend, George Selwyn.

The next 'trouble' with which Neill had to contend was his own health. He claimed the first of these was 'an agonizing whitlow on the third finger of my right hand'.[98] Neill believed the infection was due to exhaustion. Exhaustion seems to be a curious diagnosis here as Neill said he felt much rested upon his return from vacation. Nevertheless, Neill's whitlow became so problematic he went to the hospital to get his fingernail removed.

Neill wanted to stay in India but his health was threatening his career there. He had a few options open up to him, however. First, the CMS was searching for a new General Secretary to succeed Dr W.W. Cash.[99] Neill recorded that he had received requests from some of the leaders of the society, asking him to allow his name to go forward, but he refused. Max Warren succeeded Cash and served in that role for 21 years.

Neill's second offer was from E.W. Barnes. He was then the bishop of Birmingham and had asked Neill to return to England and serve as his archdeacon and assistant bishop. Neill again declined. The third possibility opened up when the bishop of Madras had a stroke and had to resign. Neill's name did go forward. However, Neill's old colleague Michael Hollis was elected and eventually served as the first moderator of the Church of South India. The fourth option was, Neill felt, that he would move to the more conducive climate of Bangalore, teach at the United Theological College and write books. With several options on the table, he felt he should resign, although, according to Neill, Metropolitan Westcott demurred:

> I . . . placed my resignation in the hands of the Metropolitan. What I received in return was almost a cry of horror. . . . Westcott therefore begged me not to make any decision in haste. . . . He now revealed to me that it was his desire and hope that I would succeed him. It is strange that I myself had never once considered this possibility. . . . I could see that there was quite a strong probability that I would be elected. . . . I still wonder whether I was not right, whether I should not have stuck to my own guidance rather than yielded to his. But

---

97. Eleanor Jackson's personal collection, p. 392.
98. Neill, *God's Apprentice*, p. 197.
99. Cash left the CMS to become the bishop of Worcester.

6. Loss of a Bishopric: 1944-45

it was hard to stand out against the wishes of so wise and generous a patriarch. So I put on one side for the time being the thought of resignation. There was plenty to occupy me in the diocese.[100]

This is a remarkable version of the story indeed. While it was a fact Westcott considered Neill his most worthy successor, it is clear that Westcott's misgivings would form shortly after the scandalous news reached him that Neill had caned a man. The scandal surrounding Neill would remove him from being seriously considered as a candidate for Metropolitan of all India, Burma and Ceylon.

At this point, Neill recorded, he returned to his work as diocesan bishop, largely occupied by discussions on the formation of the Church of South India. He claimed that it was during these sessions, of which he was chairman, he once lost his temper in public. He wrote, 'This was something that had never happened before, and I was determined that it must never be allowed to happen again. But it is not easy, as tiredness grows, to have everything under control.'[101] This is a strange assertion by Neill. He knew he struggled with his temper. It was a life-long battle for him.[102] In his autobiography, while writing about his teenage years, he wrote the following: 'My fierce temper, the outward expression of so many inward frustrations, began to come under control; though this was only the beginning of a long process, which perhaps will not be complete at the time of my death.'[103]

While the loss of his temper in public might have shown Neill that he had to seriously reconsider his own health, it was actually something quite trivial that Neill claimed was: 'The thing that finally convinced me that I could not go on [as bishop].' Seemingly, during a rainstorm, Neill's desk was thrown into disarray because of the strong winds that came through the windows. Furthermore, during that same storm, Neill's eyeglasses went missing and he had trouble replacing them because of war-time restrictions. Neill claimed it was this that forced him 'to take drastic action':

I wrote again to the Metropolitan, telling him that I was now convinced that I must return to England for an extended period

---

100. Neill, *God's Apprentice*, pp. 198-99.
101. Ibid., p. 200. It is possible that Neill turned some individuals against him because of this outburst.
102. See Pierard, 'Stephen Neill', p. 532; Moule, 'Foreword', in Neill, *God's Apprentice*, pp. 7-8; and Neill, *God's Apprentice*, p. 200.
103. Ibid., p. 36. It is not clear what Neill meant when he claimed this 'had never happened before'. Perhaps he meant he had never lost his temper *in public* prior to that point. As we have seen throughout the present work, this was a struggle with which Neill had dealt several times previously.

of rest. . . . I told him something of the darker shadows that were crowding in upon me, of which he already knew something . . . and that it would be better for me to resign. . . . The Metropolitan . . . secured for me first priority for appointment as temporary chaplain to troops, and that he had come regretfully to share my opinion that it would be wise for me to place my resignation in his hands.[104]

At this point, Neill discussed the fact that:

the Metropolitan found himself deluged by an avalanche of telegrams . . . which . . . said that I belonged to the diocese and must in no circumstances be separated from it; if the period of recovery proved to be long, the diocese would be perfectly willing to wait as long as need be for my return.[105]

Neill's facts were correct when he claimed that the Metropolitan flew down to Tinnevelly from Calcutta to judge the situation for himself. Neill claimed the plan was that the diocese would settle and wait for him to return from a trip to England.

Once in Britain Neill went to Barnwell, Northamptonshire, to assist his father who was rector there. Neill claimed that he 'had one duty, and one only – to recover my seriously shattered health and to return as soon as possible to a diocese which still urgently needed my services'.[106] He visited Westcott House, Cambridge (where he had studied for the ministry), and worked on his 'favourite subject, the history of Christianity in India'.[107]

In England Neill was not well. He wrote, 'recovery was very slow, and was not helped by long spells of insomnia again'.[108] Neill lamented the sudden death of the Archbishop of Canterbury, 'More than any other man in England, he was the one to whom I would have turned for help and guidance in difficult days.'[109]

Neill then wrote with surprising insight what the Metropolitan was having to deal with regarding the Tinnevelly diocese:

---

104. Ibid., p. 201.
105. Ibid. How Neill would have known this is unclear unless the Metropolitan told him. It is also possible that Neill reviewed Westcott's archives in Calcutta at some point over the years. This is not the only occasion when Neill seemed to know things that would otherwise have been kept from him.
106. Ibid., p. 205.
107. Ibid., p. 206.
108. Ibid.
109. Ibid.

6. Loss of a Bishopric: 1944-45

> During all these months medical reports of various kinds were going to India, and I could sense the increasing perplexity in which the venerable Bishop of Calcutta found himself caught up. I knew that he was exceedingly anxious for my return to India . . . even if the medical verdict was against my undertaking the additional strains involved in the position of Bishop of Calcutta and Metropolitan of the Church of India. On the other hand, he was being subjected to strong local pressure not to delay any longer, but to make provisions for the needs of the flock in South India by making provision for my replacement as Bishop of Tinnevelly. I had conscientiously left the decision in his hands.[110]

Neill understood that he would probably have to remain in England:

> Gradually I came to see quite clearly the way in which the decision would go. He was an old man, eighty years old, and lacked the vigour and decisiveness of his earlier years. He was headed off from further consultation with the diocese. ... He would listen to other voices, and to their opinion as to what was for the welfare of the Church of India.[111]

Neill was not surprised when Westcott's decision reached him: 'I received a cable from the Metropolitan, telling me that it was his considered judgment that I should not attempt to face again the rigours of the exacting climate of South India, and that I should find my place in the service of Christ in England.'[112]

Neill then had to face the fact that he was no longer a missionary in India:

> Although I had long foreseen this result, it was not altogether easy to accept. For twenty years I had lived India and breathed India and loved India; I had never had any other idea than that, when the time came, I would lay my bones there, as my parents and my elder sister have done. It was not easy to come to terms with the idea that I would once again have to take my place in a Western world from which I had grown away, and in which in many ways I no longer felt at home.[113]

---

110. Ibid., p. 207.
111. Eleanor Jackson's personal collection, p. 416.
112. Neill, *God's Apprentice*, p. 207.
113. Ibid.

Assessment

Richard Holloway, bishop of Edinburgh from 1992 to 2000, dropped a bomb when his review of Neill's autobiography was published in the *Church Times* on 8 November 1991.[114] His review, 'The Mystery in Stephen Neill', opened up a conversation that revealed information about Neill. Holloway began thus:

> This posthumously published autobiography by Bishop Stephen Neill has confronted me with a moral dilemma. At the heart of Stephen Neill's tragic yet productive life there lies an unresolved mystery, about which I know something. I can either use this review to maintain the conspiracy of silence that surrounded the career of this gifted man or I can use it to throw some daylight on the mystery, at the risk of offending members of his distinguished family. I have decided to follow the latter course, mainly because the editor of the present volume, Dr. E.M. Jackson, in a note at the end of the book, points out that serious allegations have been made against Stephen Neill that will have to be tackled by any future biographer. That note, I believe, opens the matter up, however unintentionally, and makes it impossible for me to review this book without reference to the matters hinted at.

Holloway noticed the obvious omission on Neill's part, that of bringing up the real reason he resigned his bishopric. Neill blamed his dismissal on depression and insomnia. However, Holloway, like few others, knew not only the real reason Neill was dismissed, but he also knew about Neill's 'mystery' firsthand.

Holloway discussed his relationship with Neill, how they met in 1958, how they were friends, how Neill loved the company of young men and how Neill backed off when Holloway married. Then Holloway opened up a discussion, that would not soon go away, with the following words:

> During those years I grew warily fond of him, but I came to realise that he had an obsession about punishment. At some point during one of his visits he would announce that it was time to find out how badly I had been behaving and a confessional interview would ensue. It gradually became obvious to me that these odd and uncomfortable sessions were meant to lead to some sort of punishment, for which he carried a small whip. I had read little psychology in those days

---

114. Holloway, 'The Mystery in Stephen Neill', p. 13.

6. Loss of a Bishopric: 1944-45

and was considerably overawed by the attentions of this famous scholar bishop, but I reached an untutored and compassionate realisation that, whatever its origins, he suffered from some version of controlled sadism. Now, reading this beautifully written memoir [*God's Apprentice*] that hides more than it discloses, I am able to find some meaning in the mystery of the man.

Holloway placed Neill's behaviour in the context of 'classic Victorian Evangelical' Christianity, 'heavy with all the pressures and unacknowledged neuroses that characterised some of the best-known clerical families'. He then offers an explanation:

An obsession with punishment is a well-known characteristic of this period.[115] . . . It is against that background that we can judge the heroic nature of the struggle he was engaged in with himself. He was a man with an overpowering sense of duty, endowed with a formidable intellect. He was from a stern Evangelical background with the dour blood of Scottish Ulster in his veins. Yet here he was, struggling with God knows what fantasies of punishment and pain. It is increasingly obvious to me that he handled the complex in two ways. There was the referred pain of insomnia and depression. How much of that was self-punishment for the fantasies that pursued him? Alongside his depression and self-disgust grew an almost insatiable appetite for praise. Again and again he tells us of assemblies he has brilliantly addressed and how wave after wave of applause rolled over him. But it never was enough to heal the sore place in his nature.

Holloway goes on to describe Neill's condition as 'psychosexual', and therefore probably 'intractable'. He writes:

The pain of disciplining the compulsions is notoriously fierce. How could an Evangelical bishop with a tyrannous conscience find an outlet for such urges? I suspect that he denied their existence on one level, and indulged them, to what extent I cannot tell, on another, by creating scenarios that appeared to justify the infliction of punishment.

Then Holloway comments on the incident in South India:

---

115. It is overwhelming to think that, if, indeed, there was an obsession with punishment during this period, how this would have played out in British colonies.

Something probably went badly wrong with his self-control in India in 1944, and he was banished from his beloved Tinnevelly; and he spent the rest of his life wandering the earth as a theological mercenary, serving the WCC, the German Church, the Church in East Africa, and just about every theological faculty in the world. Along the way he wrote many books, some of them marvellous, delivered many speeches and heard wave after wave of applause . . . in spite of a thorn in the flesh that brought him into the darkness.

The response to Holloway's comments was immediate. Just one week later, on 15 November 1991, the former Archbishop of Canterbury, Donald Coggan, wrote the following comments:

I have read with interest Bishop Holloway's review of Bishop Stephen Neill's posthumously published autobiography. So now all may know what some of us knew many years ago about Stephen Neill's thorn in the flesh. It was a hard decision for Richard Holloway – should he expose for all to see what Stephen Neill covered up and, in doing so, contribute to historical truth? Or should he abide by the kindly dictum – *de mortuis nihil nisi bonum*? He went for the former course. So be it.[116]

Coggan then almost reprimanded Holloway, 'But it seemed to me a pity that so much of the review was devoted to the sad side of a fruitful life and ministry.' He then praised the extraordinary brilliance of Stephen Neill, obvious in his corpus of truly great books.

In the same issue of the *Church Times* there is a letter to the editor from Canon Eric James.[117] James also had encountered this dark side of Neill:

I must be only one of many thankful for the costly honesty and compassion of Bishop Richard Holloway's review of Bishop Stephen Neill's autobiography. I saw something of Stephen Neill when I was a curate at St Stephen's, Rochester Row. He would

---

116. Coggan was Archbishop from 1974 to 1980. Donald Coggan, 'Stephen Neill's "thorn in the flesh"', *Church Times*, 15 November 1991, p. 9. Neill wrote of Donald Coggan in *God's Apprentice*, p. 320, 'Donald Coggan . . . set himself to preach for greatness. I have no doubt he will go down in history as a great archbishop. . . . Donald Coggan has received far less credit than he deserved. Single-handed, he saved the Lambeth Conference.'
117. Canon Eric James, letter to the editor, *Church Times*, 15 November 1991, p. 9.

arrive unannounced from Geneva and ask for safe lodging in our clergy house. I saw more of him when I was Chaplain of Trinity College, Cambridge, 1955-1959 – and came to know the tragic truth Bishop Holloway reveals.

James went on to issue a call for 'psychosexual understanding' and for members of the Church to 'examine the psychosexual basis of much that passes for theological conviction'.

Private Correspondence Regarding Holloway's Review
In 1991, shortly after he wrote his review of *God's Apprentice*, Holloway and Eleanor Jackson were in brief correspondence. On 19 November 1991 Holloway wrote to Jackson:

> Dear Dr. Jackson,
> Thank you very much for your letter about Stephen Neill. I wrote my piece with a certain amount of discomfort, not wanting to hurt anyone, including the memory of the dead, but feeling I had to tell what I knew. In the event, it has proved to be the right decision because it has led to an outpouring of reminiscence from people who knew Bishop Neill and had either been puzzled or wounded by him and were relieved to hear the truth spoken at last. I understand there has been criticism of the piece published in some quarters, but the only thing I've seen has been Bishop Coggan's slightly critical letter in the *Church Times*.[118]

Holloway's letter not only received the attention of scholars and clergy who had known Neill, but a member of Neill's family got involved. The executor to Neill's private papers, his nephew Charles Neill, wrote a letter to Eleanor Jackson shortly after the Holloway article was published.[119] This letter reveals Charles Neill's attitude to the infamous footnote regarding the reason Stephen Neill left India:

> Dear Dr. Jackson,
> Throughout the time you were working on my uncle's manuscript I made no attempt to communicate with you. I am

---

118. Holloway to Eleanor Jackson, 19 November 1991, Eleanor Jackson's personal collection.
119. Charles Neill to Eleanor Jackson, 18 November 1991, Eleanor Jackson's personal collection. Charles Neill was the copyright holder of the published autobiography, *God's Apprentice*, prior to his death in 1996.

writing now to thank you and to congratulate you on your editorial work. It seems to me that you have preserved the character of the original and its essential parts, at the same time reducing it, as was necessary. . . .

I wondered whether to protest about your now notorious note. I guessed that to leave it out would have seemed to compromise your integrity as an historian and involved you in the 'conspiracy of silence', and so I chose to let it pass. I thought and think that it was an invitation to Bishop Holloway to write as he did. I suspect that he or some other person might well have done so anyway. Lord Coggan's letter was good, I thought.

It is not my uncle's family, but his admirers who may have been embarrassed. I hope that in the end they may make a balanced appraisal of his life and work and that some good will ensue.

I wrote to Bishop Holloway in March 2003. On 8 April 2003:

> I met [Neill] in 1958 at an ecumenical conference in Accra, Ghana, where he collected me, as he frequently collected young friends. After I was ordained in Scotland, he visited me a couple of times, though we lost touch when I got married. It was well known that he was a brilliant man with a tragic flaw, sado masochism, which contributed to his departure from India. Understandably perhaps, he never really came clean about this in his autobiography, and maybe he never really admitted it to himself.[120]

The Holloway review elicited one other significant response. Bishop Lesslie Newbigin, a contemporary of Neill in South India, corresponded with Eleanor Jackson in 1991 regarding the Holloway review. On 21 November 1991 Newbigin wrote:

---

120. Another young friend to Neill, Rupert Higgins, said once he married, Neill backed off. In a letter to the author dated 4 April 2003, he wrote, 'It wasn't easy to get to know Stephen very well – he had a few favourites of which I was one for a while until I got married! Stephen's favourites were always single men. I have no evidence that Stephen was homosexual and my take on it is that he wasn't.' Hans Ruedi-Weber was another young, single man whom Neill befriended. He, however, stated to me his opinion that Neill was 'probably' a homosexual. While working together in Geneva at the WCC, Weber said Neill took him 'a little too much under his wing'. Weber resented it. He was much younger than Neill and could never feel at ease with the bishop. Hans-Ruedi Weber, interview with author, 12 October 2004, Geneva, Switzerland.

6. Loss of a Bishopric: 1944-45

Dear Eleanor,
Bishop Holloway has certainly taken the opportunity to publicise things which could have been left for some more time to the circle of Stephen's friends. I think I mentioned to you that I got Charlie Ranson to remove from his autobiography the details of the reasons for Stephen's leaving India, as I thought it did no one any good. I did not know, or ever imagine, that Stephen carried a whip around with him. . . . I am afraid I landed you with a very difficult job, but I did not think it would generate this kind of controversy. . . .[121]

I wish that Holloway's review had said more about Stephen's great achievements. I am no psychologist, but I dare say he is right in his analysis. It certainly increases one's sympathy with Stephen as he coped with these inner problems. I remember Visser 't Hooft telling me that the Zurich psychiatrist who treated Stephen told Wim [Visser 't Hooft's nickname] that he had never met such a severe case of manic depression. . . .

I hope that the controversy about S.C.N. won't bring you any bothers. You have done a splendid job and I know many will be grateful for what you have done.[122]

In a later letter to Jackson dated 27 April 1992, Newbigin made the comment: 'what Neill did was bad, but not as bad as rumour might make it'.[123]

Analyses from Other Researchers

Timothy Yates (who died in 2016) was a scholar who both knew and researched Neill. Yates believed that Neill's physical and psychological difficulties 'led him at times to the brink of suicide via insomnia and depression, the kind of personal cost known often to the superbly gifted and creative but outside the ken of many more ordinary mortals'.[124]

---

121. Charles Ranson knew about the allegations of Neill's inappropriate relations with others. Ranson had written a letter to Charles Long dated 7 September 1984. The letter states: 'Next to Bishop Azariah, Neill was the most outstanding figure in the Indian Church. He seemed certain to be the next Metropolitan. Then the blow fell. He was accused of improper relationships with boys. Dear old Foss Westcott, the Metropolitan, was devastated. He did his best, and largely succeeded, in preventing an open scandal; but Stephen had to resign and return to England. There began a new era in which his great gifts were recognised.' Ranson to Charles Long, 7 September 1984, RG 96, Box 1, Charles W. Ranson Papers, Special Collections, Day Missions Library, Divinity School, Yale University, New Haven, CT.
122. Newbigin to Jackson, 21 November 1991, Eleanor Jackson's personal collection.
123. Newbigin to Jackson, 27 April 1992, Eleanor Jackson's personal collection.
124. Yates, 'Stephen Neill: Some Aspects of a Theological Legacy', p. 161. Lamb also

Eleanor Jackson edited Neill's autobiography and she also knew him personally. She speculated on the possibility that Neill may have been gay:[125]

> Homosexuality was a crime in Britain until 1968, and certainly for one brought up in a strict evangelical household, a sin. There is no evidence that Neill ever admitted having a problem in this area. . . . In the end, it is impossible to say whether it was ill health, rumours of homosexuality, or his courageous criticism of colonial administrators that blocked his path to preferment after 1944.[126]

Jackson believes that Neill's autobiography could serve as something of a therapeutic tool for some. She writes:

> When all is said and done, the autobiography is an inspiration to all who wrestle with depression. However, it raises in acute form the question of who cares for the carers. Only once did Neill have a sympathetic bishop. Another told him to take some aspirin and pull himself together. He kept going through years and years of darkness until he found peace.[127]

Another biographical article on Neill is by the distinguished scholars Kenneth Cragg and Owen Chadwick, among the few who could be called Neill's intellectual equals.[128] They commented on the trauma Neill endured:

> In 1944 [Neill] went on furlough to England to get medical treatment. While he was there the Indian bishops met and decided to advise Neill to retire from his See. The advice came as a shock to

---

writes of Neill's suicidal contemplations. See Christopher Lamb, 'The Legacy of Stephen Neill', *International Bulletin of Missionary Research*, Vol. 11 (April 1987), pp. 62-67. Lamb writes, p. 62, 'At times he contemplated suicide but was protected from it, he reckoned later, by an inherited obstinacy and a deep-seated dislike of exhibiting such ingratitude to God. He knew no complete freedom from this malady until 1965.' In citing the date 1965, Lamb was referring to a passage in *God's Apprentice*, p. 46, where Neill wrote, 'It was not till 21 December 1965 that I received a further message that my healing had now reached such a point that I could begin to think of living a normal life. This was confirmed by a further word of healing on Christmas Eve, 1970, one week before I started on the writing of this book.'

125. Jackson, 'The Continuing Legacy of Stephen Neill', pp. 77-81.
126. Ibid., p. 80.
127. Ibid., p. 81.
128. Cragg and Chadwick, 'Stephen Charles Neill, 1900-1984', pp. 602-14.

him and his resignation was certainly the hardest decision he ever made. He loved India, and had a sense of a vocation to serve that country. He seemed to be destroying his past and the trauma of this decision remained with him to the end of his life.[129]

Cragg and Chadwick pointed out that during Neill's life he was prone 'to show signs of unbalance, and to cause anxiety to his colleagues'.[130]

These kinds of problems continued to plague Neill until the end of his life. Nevertheless, he pressed on and, in spite of the thorn in his flesh, his contributions to the Church became much more widely known when his services began to be utilised in the European context.

---

129. Ibid., p. 606.
130. Ibid., p. 606.

Chapter Seven
Return to Europe and Ecumenical Labour: 1944-62

Once safely arrived in Britain, Neill went to stay with his parents, in Barnwell, Northamptonshire, 'one of the most beautiful villages in England', and not far from Cambridge.[1] Neill had not seen his homeland in five years and his first morning back home was 'a glorious, still, clear September morning'. He did not know what to expect since the war had wreaked havoc for such a length of time. Neill 'realised that much had been taken, but much still remained. There was still an England to be lived and died for.'[2]

In his autobiography, Neill says that upon his return in 1944 he had 'one duty, and one only – to recover my shattered health and to return as soon as possible to a diocese which still needed my services'.[3] Neill remained under considerable strain for a solid year; George Selwyn would not be confirmed as the new bishop of Tinnevelly until 31 October 1945. While Neill's return to India became less and less likely as time went on, the final decision impacted him deeply. He fell into a deep depression and recovery

---

1. Neill, *God's Apprentice*, pp. 203-4. In the unpublished version of the autobiography (p. 411), Neill mentions that his father was 76 years old and was serving as rector of Barnwell. To my knowledge, the only complete copies of the unpublished autobiography are with me and with Bishop N.T. Wright. It was Wright who made a photocopy of the entire autobiography and graciously sent it to me. Wright and Neill were friends and had collaborated together on a book.
2. Ibid., p. 204.
3. Ibid., p. 205.

was slow. He was a lifelong insomniac, and it only worsened during this stressful period. Convinced he had brought dysentery with him back from India, he wrote in his autobiography, 'The winter of 1944-5 was terribly cold.' Indeed, in many ways, it was a very cold season for Neill.[4]

No Lack of Openings

With shattered health and a shattered career, Neill set about doing what he always did best – he buried himself in books at the University of Cambridge, specifically at Westcott House, a place he knew well. Among many other writing assignments, he contributed frequent book reviews for *The Spectator*.[5] After a short time he found employment 'combining full teaching work in the Faculty of Divinity at Cambridge with the somewhat exacting duties of a Chaplain at Trinity College', his *alma mater*.[6] According to Neill, it was not long before people realised he was 'on the market' and there were 'no lack of openings' for him to consider.[7] There was talk of Neill succeeding Charles Raven as Professor of Divinity but, at that particular time, Neill 'suffered from a grave lack of confidence' in his abilities to step into academia at such a high level.[8]

The truth as to why Neill did not survive long at Cambridge could be more complicated than Neill admitted. In 2007 and 2008 I was in communication with a man named Patrick Hamilton, who claimed to have inside knowledge about why Neill had to leave Cambridge in 1947. Hamilton first contacted me in April 2007 via an ominous email but one which I had every reason to believe to be true:

> Certain things [Neill] did have affected my whole life and now, at the age of 83, I still find him lurking in the dark places of my mind. I believe I am the one who reported what was happening and was probably responsible for his immediate removal from Trinity in about 1947. . . . I shall be glad to get it all off my chest – a kind of catharsis for which I shall be grateful to you.[9]

I emailed back with questions, which Hamilton tried to answer. He called it 'an exorcism for myself rather than of anything new for you'. After hearing

4. Neill, *God's Apprentice*, pp. 205-6.
5. Neill's unpublished autobiography, Section VII, 4, 'Among the Students', p. 152.
6. Ibid., p. 137. See also Neill's entry in *Crockford's Clerical Directory, 1965-66*. There he is listed as being chaplain at Trinity from 1945-47 and as lecturer at the University of Cambridge from 1945-47.
7. Neill, *God's Apprentice*, pp. 206-7.
8. Unpublished autobiography, p. 418.
9. Patrick Hamilton, email to author, 26 April 2007 and 28 April 2007.

my brief description of what Neill often did to other young men, he wrote, 'I dare say that all those you have talked to have much the same story to tell while their inner feelings and compulsions remain properly hidden. I have let some of mine out but you will know that what you have here is but the tip of an iceberg.'[10]

Hamilton claimed that his experiences with Neill impacted his life dramatically. He wrote:

> The inner turmoil cost me two more marriages and a constant pull into dark areas. This, at age 84, has now quietened down and I can see an underlying pattern that is actually something of a triumph with a happy fourth marriage and a conviction that nothing happens by accident.

Hamilton had an erratic life. In his emails he described being a journalist, a teacher and an oil executive at British Petroleum. He claimed he lived in London, Ghana, Nigeria and Aden in Yemen. He went into the publishing industry in his late forties and later realised he could paint and draw. These artistic gifts took him to Malta, Sicily and eventually to Florence, Italy, where he said he spent nearly twenty 'wonderful' years. He finally moved to London.[11]

Hamilton's story was eerily similar to others. Neill invited him to his private room, where there was a discussion of Hamilton's personal failings and need for correction. Neill punished him using his strange fetish of spanking. One distinction in his story was that Neill focused his line of interrogation much more on Hamilton's overly exhausting work schedule rather than on his spiritual condition.

Hamilton and I emailed back and forth a few times and in March 2008 I emailed to let him know I would be travelling to the United Kingdom and would like to meet up with him. My email bounced back to me. I knew Hamilton had not been in good health and in May 2007 he had undergone a medical procedure to repair an aortic aneurism. I looked online and found that he had died on 8 January 2008. His obituary appeared in the *Independent* on 5 February 2008.[12]

Stephen Neill's niece, Penny Golby, contacted me in January 2013 after reading one of my articles on Bishop Neill. In her email she wrote: 'I know that there was some kind of unacceptable behaviour when he was assistant to

---

10. Hamilton, email to author, 1 May 2007.
11. Hamilton, email to author, 1 May 2007.
12. Hamilton, email to author, 3 May 2007. For Hamilton's obituary, see James Hamilton, 'Patrick Hamilton: Itinerant writer and painter', *Independent* 5 February 2008, located at: https://www.independent.co.uk/news/obituaries/patrick-hamilton-itinerant-writer-and-painter-778050.html.

the Archbishop of Canterbury – but my parents did not want to discuss it so I never actually knew what happened.' Most likely Ms Golby was referring to Neill's painful interaction with Patrick Hamilton and its fallout.[13]

In April of 1946 a letter sent from Geneva caught Neill's attention. It was an invitation for him to participate in the formative conference of the World Council of Churches (WCC) in Amsterdam in 1948, with an invitation for him to take up residence in Geneva. Neill was unable to make the move to Switzerland until the summer of 1947 but he could do his work remotely in the meantime. Geneva colleagues agreed and thus Neill's long years as a professional ecumenist began in August 1946, although he was still living in England.[14] He would not relocate permanently to Geneva until 8 September 1947.[15]

Neill had several commitments that he needed to fulfil before he moved. One commitment was to give the prestigious Hulsean Lectures on the topic of 'The Forgiveness of Sins'. Neill had been supposed to give the lectures during his leave of absence in 1939 but the outbreak of war prevented him from doing so. It is certainly possible that Neill's chosen topic was an attempt to deal with the traumatic events that led to his downfall as Tinnevelly's bishop.

Another commitment was Neill's attendance at the 1947 International Missionary Council in Whitby, Ontario, Canada. The conference was organised by Dr Charles Ranson (1903-88), a veteran missionary to South India whose life was almost exactly contemporaneous to Neill's. The two men would cross paths frequently in coming years. Ranson picked Neill to give one of the major addresses. Neill spoke on 'The Church in a Revolutionary World'. His lecture discussed how 'the long-established domination of the West had finally come to an end', and argued that 'the Church is called to be wholly identified with the world in its *needs* but wholly independent of it in its *desires*'. Neill would later develop these thoughts further and publish them in 1952 in a book called *Christian Partnership*. Neill took primary responsibility for drafting the conference report, which was given the title 'Renewal and Advance'.[16]

---

13. Penny Golby, email to author, 13 January 2013.
14. Neill, *God's Apprentice*, p. 208. On p. 209 Neill reveals that he was employed part-time for his first year as an employee of the World Council of Churches (in process of formation). There is a good paper dealing with Neill's ecumenical thought written by Hyung Jin Park, written while he was a PhD candidate at Princeton Theological Seminary in Spring 2001 entitled 'A Study of Stephen Neill: The Ecumenical Visionary'. It was a term paper written for Professor Milan Opocensky.
15. *The Times*, 13 August 1947, p. 7. 'Bishop Stephen Neill, formerly Bishop of Tinnevelly, and now assistant Bishop to the Archbishop of Canterbury for relations with the continental churches and for liaison with the WCC, will move his headquarters from Cambridge to Geneva on September 8.'
16. Neill, *God's Apprentice*, pp. 211-13 (my italics). See Neill, *Christian Partnership*.

Shortly after the IMC conference in Whitby, Neill flew to Oslo for a post-war youth conference that, in Neill's opinion, went very badly, as opposed to the Whitby conference which went delightfully well. Neill felt the Oslo conference focused too much on politics. Neill preached for the diverse audience – 'from almost every country upon earth' – on the topic of Christ's sovereignty. Neill spoke about Christ having sovereignty 'in the world, in society, in the Church and in ourselves'. It is a theme that remained important in his own theology throughout the rest of his life, evinced in one of his final books, published the year of his death and entitled *The Supremacy of Jesus*.[17]

It was now September 1947 and Neill moved to Geneva to take up his work with the organisation that would become the World Council of Churches the following year in 1948. Neill came to appreciate his boss, the General Secretary Willem Adolf Visser 't Hooft, known as 'Wim' to his friends. Neill noticed Wim's gifts immediately: fluency in four languages, an outstanding speaker, a true intellectual, yet 'a limited sense of humour'. Neill, however, ever the critical thinker, also perceived some weaknesses in Wim, such as his autocratic tendencies. Neill thought Wim tended to appoint inferior and younger men so he could maintain his grip on control. This frustrated Neill and he soon noticed that talented people were coming and going with regularity, because of Wim's dictatorial approach to leadership. Neill viewed the WCC as 'chaotic' in those early days and, based on the first and second meetings of the executive committee in February and July 1949, he was not far off the mark.[18] It must have been exhilarating yet exceedingly challenging to be at the nexus of twentieth-century ecumenism.[19] Hans-Ruedi Weber described Neill's and Visser 't Hooft's relationship as 'not very close'.[20] Visser 't Hooft made only one brief mention of Neill in his memoirs.[21]

17. Neill, *God's Apprentice*, p. 214. See Stephen Neill, *The Supremacy of Jesus* (London: Hodder & Stoughton, 1984).
18. See WCC archives, Geneva, Box 38.0001, Executive Committee, full set of documents 1949-53, File 7 (1949-June 1951).
19. Neill, *God's Apprentice*, pp. 214-15. See also Neill's unpublished autobiography, p. 434.
20. Hans-Ruedi Weber, interview by author, 12 October 2004, Geneva. Weber knew Neill well. In 1963 they co-edited a WCC-sponsored book entitled *The Layman in Christian History* (Philadelphia, PA: Westminster Press, 1963). Another sign that Neill and Visser 't Hooft may not have been close is that in Visser 't Hooft's correspondence papers, kept at the WCC archives in Geneva, there is only one letter exchanged between the two of them. However, there are many letters exchanged between Wim and other colleagues such as Lesslie Newbigin. It is from Neill, thanking Wim for a letter and congratulating him on being appointed Honorary President of the WCC. The letter is dated 27 August 1968. See WCC archives, Geneva, 994.1.09, W.A. Visser 't Hooft General Correspondence, File 994.1.09/10.
21. W.A. Visser 't Hooft, *Memoirs* (London: SCM Press, 1973).

7. Return to Europe and Ecumenical Labour: 1944-62

Early WCC Staff: Sitting from left: Bishop Stephen Neill, Dr W.A. Visser't Hooft (Netherlands), Dr Henry Smith Leiper (USA). Standing from left: Dr R.C. Mackie (UK), Oliver Tomkins (UK), Frederick Nolde (USA).

Neill's first appointment in the WCC was as Co-Director of the Study Department and he was given a generous salary and a secretary named Dorothy Grose (later Mrs Laurie). He enjoyed his work, although he thought the working conditions of the entire staff needed improvement. Salaries were not entirely fair, colleagues were not happy with Wim's authoritarianism, there was insufficient focus on prayer and worship and there was almost no fellowship taking place outside office hours. Neill corrected all of this by inviting nearly everyone over to his small flat for a glass of sherry – five or six at a time over a course of six months. The coldness in the staff that greeted Neill began to thaw.[22]

The work of the WCC staff in 1947-48 was considerable, as they were planning the official formation of the WCC which would take place at a large assembly in Amsterdam in 1948 on the theme: 'Man's Disorder and God's Design'. The planning was split into four sub-sections: (i) the Universal Church in God's design; (ii) the Church's witness to God's design; (iii) the Church and the disorder of society; and (iv) the Church and the international disorder. Neill was in charge of planning section two.[23]

---

22. Neill, *God's Apprentice*, pp. 215-16. See also Neill's unpublished autobiography, p. 436. Hans-Ruedi Weber argued, however, that 'the early WCC men had no money. They worked for next to nothing.' Weber, interview with author, 12 October 2004. According to *Crockford's Clerical Directory, 1965-66*, Neill was Co-Director of the Study Department from 1947 to 1948.

23. See *Man's Disorder and God's Design: The Amsterdam Assembly Series* (New York: Harper & Brothers, 1949). It should be noted that in this book, Vol. 2, p. 12, Neill is described as having two official titles: Assistant Bishop to the Archbishop of Canterbury and Co-Director of the Study Department. The others in charge of the Study Department were Rev. Nils Ehrenström and Rev. Wolfgang

In understated terms, Vissert 't Hooft described the task of planning as 'difficult'. Typically, in much more flowery terms, Neill described the planning as 'a whirligig of chaos and chance'. The twelve-day assembly began on 22 August 1948. There were delegates representing 147 churches in 44 countries. Virtually all major denominations were present, with the exception of the Roman Catholic Church, after the papacy announced in June 1948 that no Roman Catholics would be permitted to attend.[24]

Planning for the first assembly of the WCC was not the sole focus of the staff. There was also the herculean and constant task of translation. If the WCC was to be a global organisation, then a staff of highly trained linguists was also necessary. Neill, one of the great polyglots of the twentieth-century Church, took a leading role here, as opposed to Wim, who 'never seemed to understand the harm done by inadequate or misleading translation'. A second important task that kept the WCC staff busy between 1946 and 1948 was handling a grant given to them by the Rockefeller Foundation to purchase the Château de Bossey, about sixteen miles from Geneva, for the training of laypeople from all over the world. The Bossey Ecumenical Institute is still active, issuing diplomas in conjunction with the University of Geneva.[25]

During the planning for the Amsterdam conference, it became apparent that the churches of Asia were poorly connected with one another and not well integrated into the world church. If the WCC was to succeed as a global institution, then Asia – home to more than half of the world's population – ought to be better connected to the wider Christian world and to the WCC. Visser 't Hooft chose Neill as the WCC representative to visit churches in several Asian nations, including India, Pakistan, Burma (now Myanmar), Indonesia, the island of Borneo (now divided between Brunei, Malaysia and Indonesia), Singapore (then part of Malaysia), Bali (then under Dutch control), Celebes (now called Sulawesi, part of Indonesia), the Philippines, Formosa (now Taiwan), China, Korea and Japan.[26] Neill

---

Schweitzer. See Lambeth Palace library archives, Fisher Papers, folios 157-61.

24. W.A. Visser 't Hooft, *The Genesis and Formation of the World Council of Churches* (Geneva: WCC, 1982), p. 63. For the Neill quotation, see *God's Apprentice*, p. 216. Neill travelled to Rome in 1949 and met with Father Boyer at the Ecumenical Institute, a man he believed to be 'the ecumenical link in Rome'. Neill also met with Father Herman of the Pontifical Oriental Institute. Neill felt Pope Pius XII was a very firm man who liked to keep things centralised. Nevertheless, Neill did sense great interest in the ecumenical movement in Rome. Their first concern, however, was the Eastern churches and after that the Anglican Church. See Lambeth Palace library archives, MS 3411, folio 184.

25. Neill, *God's Apprentice*, pp. 216-17. See also the Bossey website at: https://institute.oikoumene.org/en/about.

26. Neill, *God's Apprentice*, p. 219. See also Neill's unpublished autobiography, p.

left London on 31 January 1948 and was in Asia for a total of fourteen weeks. This kind of assignment suited Neill well. In his published account of this tour, he recounted the following:

> It is impossible to imagine anything more stable and confidence-begetting than a great aircraft cruising at speed on a fair day and at great height beneath a cloudless sky. . . . To travel at a great height over a country is as it were to share the experience of Christ, when the devil took Him up on an exceeding high mountain and showed Him all the kingdoms of the world in a moment of time. . . . From the Christian point of view, the thought is rarely absent that, though all these millions have been redeemed by the death of Christ, the great majority of them have never so much as heard His name. There is the challenge of the Church of Christ in the year 1948.[27]

Neill was at his best in this kind of situation and it did not go unnoticed. Just two years later, in 1950, he was commissioned to do a very similar tour of Africa. Neill's gifts were on full display as he spoke with many churches and at numerous gatherings, took meticulous notes and summarised his experiences with tremendous clarity. Neill published his recollections later that year in the fascinating book *The Cross Over Asia*.

Due to his international travels, linguistic prowess and life experience, Neill was quickly becoming one of the most important minds in the ecumenical movement. He had a breadth of vision that was rare for the time. During a conference in Manila on his Asia tour, Neill began to see the world as made up of eight cultural regions: East Asia, the South Pacific, sub-Saharan Africa, the Muslim world, the Orthodox world, Europe, North America and Latin America. He pressed for each region of the world to put together ecumenical offices and programmes that could serve to strengthen the global church. Neill envisaged regional assemblies occurring once per year and a great world assembly should occur once per decade.[28]

In Japan Neill met with the Emperor as well as with American General Douglas MacArthur, with whom he had a very memorable conversation, although 'MacArthur talked at us for a solid hour'. Indeed, Neill said he could 'reproduce whole stretches almost exactly in the words originally spoken' nearly a quarter of a century after it happened. In Korea Neill met with two more American generals as well as with numerous church leaders.

444.
27. Neill, *The Cross Over Asia*, pp. 15, 32.
28. Neill, *God's Apprentice*, p. 220.

Stephen Neill,
c. 1948.

Neill felt the churches were 'in a sad state of disunity, bitterly divided by the question who had and who had not collaborated with the Japanese'. In Singapore Neill had the busiest Easter Sunday of his life, 'starting at 6 a.m. with Mattins and Holy Communion in Tamil, and ending at 10 p.m. with a nice unhurried discussion with the Bishop on the future of the Anglican Communion'. In Shanghai Neill noted the nearly worthless Chinese dollar allowed him to purchase for himself 'a pair of gloves for $900,000 and two shirts at $500,000 each'. Neill then travelled to south India to visit his parents and sister, yet conspicuously had nothing to say about that visit. His next stop was Karachi where he met Liaquat Ali Khan, the Oxford-educated Prime Minister of the newly created nation of Pakistan. He was surprised to see Ali Khan drinking gin, which of course is prohibited for Muslims. Sadly, Ali Khan was assassinated just a few years later, in 1951, while in office.[29]

---

29. Ibid., pp. 220-21. See also Neill's unpublished autobiography, p. 447-51.

7. Return to Europe and Ecumenical Labour: 1944-62

Just before heading out on his journey to Asia in January 1948, Neill was appointed Assistant Bishop to the Archbishop of Canterbury by Archbishop Geoffrey Fisher.[30] The details of Neill's position were written up in *The Times* on 27 December 1947:

> Bishop Stephen Neill, formerly Bishop of Tinnevelly, has been appointed Assistant Bishop to the Archbishop of Canterbury. Bishop Neill will represent the Archbishop in affairs of Continental churches in Northern and Central Europe, especially in Germany, and will act as a liaison officer between the Archbishop and the World Council of Churches at Geneva. During the period of his appointment he will also be a vice-chairman of the Church of England Council on Foreign Relations. Until next June the Bishop's headquarters will remain at Cambridge. He will then move to Geneva.[31]

Neill's purview would be continental and ecumenical affairs, a position that allowed him to attend the Lambeth Conference in June 1948. The Archbishop was ambivalent about it at first, however, as he thought Neill was already overextended.[32] Fisher understood Neill well and he was fully cognisant of Neill's mental health struggles. Around that time, one Bishop Philip asked the Archbishop to appoint Neill Master of Abbey Gate House, St Albans. Archbishop Fisher refused since Neill was already stretched thin. Fisher wrote, 'Neill has immense gifts and, as you know, some weaknesses.' Fisher concluded that Neill was not quite yet 'fully stabilised' after the traumatic events of 1944-45. Bishop Philip wrote back that he understood because he too had 'doubts which were lurking in my mind' about Neill.[33]

---

30. See *The Cambridge Review*, 18 January 1947, A26. Neill appreciated Fisher, but 'clearly did not have as much respect for Fisher as for his predecessor William Temple'. See Jolyon Mitchell, 'Stephen Neill: A Traditional Communicator in an Age of Revolution', MA Thesis at St John's College, Durham, January 1993, p. 161.

31. 'Ecclesiastical News', *The Times*, 27 December 1947, p. 7.

32. In the minutes for the 1948 Lambeth Conference, Neill is listed as 'The Assistant Bishop of Canterbury'. See Lambeth Palace library archives, LC 172, Report of the Lambeth Conference, 1948. See especially 29 July 1948, folios 113, 133, 145, 206. Neill was busy, indeed, serving as: Assistant to the Archbishop on the Continent; Vice-Chairman of the Church of England's Council on Foreign Relations; and as 'Liaison Officer' between the Archbishop and the WCC in Geneva, helping to prepare for the 1948 WCC Assembly in Amsterdam.

33. Lambeth Palace library archives, Fisher Papers, v. 28, folio 380, letter from 17 December 1947. See Philip's response in a letter dated 19 December 1947. Kenneth Cragg said that eventually Neill became *persona non grata* to Fisher. Kenneth Cragg, interview with author, 26 June 2007, Oxford.

Before attending the Lambeth Conference, however, Neill needed a vacation, so he went to Prali, a Waldensian town high in the Alps, for five days with his friend Tullio Vinay. They worked together on building Vinay's dream, an international Agape centre for Christian youth, which the WCC helped to finance. Neill returned to the Agape centre several times over the years and Tullio Vinay became an internationally beloved figure for saving Jews from the Holocaust, for establishing Agape and for fighting the Mafia in Sicily. In later years Vinay was elected to serve as a senator in the Italian parliament.[34]

In summer 1948 Neill attended the Lambeth Conference, a gathering for all the Anglican bishops throughout the world. In that year the focus was on the formation of the Church of South India and Neill became an important voice at the conference because of his long years there, as well as his leadership in the CSI talks that were going on when Neill was dismissed from his bishopric. Discussions centred on whether the Anglican Communion could accept into its fold an ecumenical church consisting of Anglicans, Congregationalists, Methodists and Presbyterians. Neill was propelled to 'the very forefront of the battle' and discussed his deep acquaintance with the topic, the negotiations and the various personalities involved.[35] Regarding the row over CSI polity and organisation, Neill argued that episcopacy would eventually prevail and the intense worry over this matter was unnecessary. It was a heated debate and, in the end, the Church of England provided a 'modest commendation' of the CSI's founding – which actually took place the year before, in 1947, just a month or so after Indian independence was declared. Neill wrote extensively about those discussions in his autobiography, revealing his deep and passionate feelings about his beloved India.[36]

34. Neill, *God's Apprentice*, p. 222. *TIME* magazine published an article on Vinay's community called 'Religion: Village of Love'. The article actually mentions Stephen Neill ('who trundled wheelbarrows of stones') and Visser 't Hooft working there. See *TIME*, 27 August 1951.
35. Indeed, Neill was in many ways *the* point person in the discussions regarding church union in South India. In July 1947 the Archbishop of Canterbury, Geoffrey Fisher, published a widely read tract entitled *The South India Church: An Open Letter from the Archbishop of Canterbury to Bishop Stephen Neill* (Church House, Dean's Yard, Westminster: The Press and Publications Board of the Church Assembly, 1947).
36. Neill, *God's Apprentice*, pp. 223-28. Quotations are from pp. 224 and 228. Neill states on p. 228, 'What is certain is that our report was accepted by a substantial majority, and that the general opinion of the Anglican Communion, as represented by its bishops, was favourable to what had been done in South India.' See also Louis Haselmayer, *The Church of South India: Its Relationship to the Anglican Communion* (New York: Morehouse-Gorham Co., 1948);

7. Return to Europe and Ecumenical Labour: 1944-62

Indeed, in the unpublished version of Neill's autobiography, he wrote at even greater length and included a fascinating episode that illustrates Neill's state of mind at the time. Neill refers to it as a 'painful episode' that affected him deeply. While delivering the final speech on the topic of church union in South India, Neill said, 'You will understand that I would very much rather be there than here.' One of the bishops took 'grave exception' to the statement and castigated Neill for saying it. What followed illustrates Neill's open wounds from his abrupt dismissal from South India:

> I thought that everyone knew that my whole life had been broken in pieces by my inability to return to India, and I still cannot understand how my words could be twisted into an expression of disloyalty to the Church of England. There was a good deal of noisy applause from the less intelligent section of the American episcopate. I was about to leap to my feet, but George Cockin wisely held me down.

Neill would have walked out of the conference then and there, had it not been for his fellow Irishman Bishop Bloomer of Carlisle, who consoled him.

Reflecting on the incident, Neill wrote, 'I was in no condition to withstand an assault of this kind. My health at the time was extremely bad.' Surely what Neill had in mind was his mental health, as he had just travelled extensively across all of Asia for fourteen weeks and, in order to do so, must have been in excellent physical health. Nevertheless, Neill was exhausted by the end of the fourth week of the conference. In his autobiography, he wrote, 'I probably made too much of the episode.' Indeed, twelve years later Neill ran into the bishop who wounded him so deeply on that occasion and the man 'had no idea' of the incident, or how Neill was deeply pained by it. Neill, on the other hand, wrote, 'It was a very

---

Christianity in India: An Historical Summary Having Particular Reference to the Anglican Communion and to the Church of South India (New York: American Church Publications, 1954); and the definitive work on the topic, Sundkler, *Church of South India*. Neill wrote numerous works on the Church of South India, including but certainly not limited to: *Under Three Flags* (New York: Friendship Press, 1954); *Towards Church Union (1937-1952)*; *Christian Partnership*; and Chapter 10, 'Plans of Union and Reunion, 1910-1948', in *A History of the Ecumenical Movement 1517-1948*, ed. by Rouse and Neill. See Chapter 4 of the present work for Neill's extensive involvement in the formation of the Church of South India. Neill's contributions to the conference can be found in the Lambeth Palace library archives, LC 172, Report of the Lambeth Conference, 1948. See especially 27 July 1948, folios 26-27, 133-35.

long time before my equanimity was restored; I am not sure that I have ever quite recovered from the effects of this flagrant denial of Christian decency and charity.'[37] Clearly, Neill was not over South India. He never did get over it. It was where he always wanted to be.

Neill returned to Geneva and jumped right back into preparations for the inaugural assembly of the WCC, which began shortly after the Lambeth Conference. Then he moved on to Amsterdam for the WCC conference. Neill was irritated by the huge crowds that were present, delegates, alternates, journalists and tourists all over the city, causing it to slow to a standstill. Traffic was awful and restaurants were unable to meet demand.

Once the conference began, however, beauty in diversity emerged, as 'the most varied list of Christian Churches that had ever met together since the day of Pentecost' were gathered in one place. 'Almost everyone who was anyone in the ecumenical movement was there', from the youthful D.T. Niles to an aging John Mott. The great theologian Karl Barth was there, as was Emil Brunner, whom Barth had attacked in his famous book *Nein!* Neill hoped the fellowship of these two great men might be restored at the assembly, but unfortunately it did not happen; 'the wounds . . . were too many and too deep'. There were moments of 'real greatness', such as when the Archbishop of Canterbury officially declared the constitution of the World Council of Churches.[38]

Neill was one of the speakers and, although the three speeches before him 'reduced the Assembly to a state of coma', Neill's speech seemed to be very well-received. He felt like he had hit a home run, with 'wave upon wave of applause . . . this may have been the highest point of my career as an orator'.[39]

Neill was in charge of drafting the assembly's statement on evangelism but it did not go over as well as his speech did. In fact, Martin Niemöller tried to get Neill removed from his role as secretary of the committee that focused on evangelism.[40] Neill remained in the position, however, and spearheaded the writing of a text that featured some of the prominent

---

37. See Neill's unpublished autobiography, pp. 466-68.
38. Neill, *God's Apprentice*, p. 230-32.
39. Ibid., p. 231-32. The full quotation is only in his unpublished autobiography, p. 475.
40. Neill served on the Message Committee and he served as secretary of the section 'The Church's Witness to God's Design'. See W.A. Visser 't Hooft, *The First Assembly of the World Council of Churches* (London: SCM Press, 1949), pp. 224-25. Neill also served on the committee on 'The Unity of the Church'. See *The Lambeth Conference 1948: The Encyclical Letter from the Bishops; Together with Resolutions and Reports* (London: SPCK, 1948), p. 40.

Christian voices of the day, such as Paul Tillich, Hendrik Kraemer, Lesslie Newbigin and Emil Brunner. The study was titled 'The Church's Witness to God's Design' and, while not perfect, Neill thought it superior to the statement on evangelism produced during the second WCC assembly at Evanston in 1954.[41]

Amsterdam 1948 lives long in the ecumenical movement as the place where the World Council of Churches became a reality. In Neill's mind, it was a success for the most part. The Russians were not there, the Roman Catholics were forbidden from attending, the assembly was far too Western in its representation, conservative Evangelicals had misgivings but, all in all, it was 'a great event' that has gone down in church history as important, even pivotal. It put into place a central committee that would take charge until the next assembly.[42]

Neill's work was done. He had been hired to help prepare for, and see through, the Amsterdam assembly. When it was over, Neill was told that he was now employed as the Associate General Secretary of the WCC, with special responsibility for study and evangelism. Neill accepted, but reluctantly, partly because he did not know where his career was headed and he had no greater prospects in England. His heart was in India but that door was now closed.[43]

Neill was not happy with the way in which he was appointed to his new position at the WCC. No one discussed a job description or salary with him. He did not even receive a letter of appointment. This frustrated Neill and he felt it represented a very unfortunate change in how the WCC was run. No longer was he on an adventure, an uncharted course into the age of Christian ecumenism. Rather, the WCC was now a formal institution that had unfortunately 'fallen into the hands of the great American church administrators', who ran churches like they ran corporations and banks. Instead of a group of colleagues, Neill felt they were now employees, trapped inside a bureaucracy. 'This was something that I had not foreseen.' Neill regretted his decision to return to the WCC headquarters:

> I was not the only contributor to feel that the whole atmosphere of the WCC changed abruptly the very day after the end of the first Assembly. . . . I had come to Geneva as a colleague; I was to make the experiment of serving as an employee, and to find that it was an experiment which simply did not work out. I think that those of us who had lived through the pioneer period would have been wise to

---
41. Neill, *God's Apprentice*, p. 233.
42. Ibid., p. 237.
43. Ibid., p. 238.

resign as soon as the Assembly was over. . . . Those who stayed on too long paid a price for their loyalty. Others . . . simply had to get out in order to save their own souls.[44]

Geneva and All That[45]

After the Amsterdam assembly, Neill returned to Geneva and set to work editing and polishing the papers from that celebrated conference, both in English and German, and Neill took charge of the publication in both languages.[46] He also began work on the primary journal of the WCC, *The Ecumenical Review*. That important journal is still published today and stands proudly as one of the great achievements of those early days of the WCC. Neill was highly involved in the journal's production, serving on the editorial board alongside editor Visser 't Hooft and associate editors Nils Ehrenstrom and H. Paul Douglass. The first issue featured articles and reviews by and about some of the major players of twentieth-century ecumenism, including Ruth Rouse, Hendrik Kraemer, Henry P. van Dusen (whose recent book *World Christianity Yesterday, Today and Tomorrow* had just been published), Ernest Rupp, Nathan Söderblom, Archbishop Germanos of Thyateira, Patriarch Sergius of Moscow and All Russia, D.T. Niles, Bishop Charles Brent, Oliver Tomkins and Suzanne de Dietrich. Neill contributed a major article to that first issue entitled 'The Asian Scene' which serves as a helpful overview of what was happening on the Asian church scene. Neill's much more comprehensive book *The Cross Over Asia* was published the same year – 1948. Visser 't Hooft wrote the front page editorial, beginning with the following words:

44. Ibid., pp. 238-39.
45. The published version of Neill's autobiography, *God's Apprentice*, omits the next four chapters of Neill's unpublished biography. The chapters in the unpublished version are titled, 'Geneva and All That', 'Of Making Many Books', 'In Journeys Oft' and 'Among the Students'. In *God's Apprentice*, Eleanor Jackson, the editor, decided to cut all four of these chapters out. Thus, in the published version, there is a major gap in Neill's life, between 1948 (the end of the Amsterdam WCC assembly) and 1962 (when Neill moved to Hamburg, Germany, for a professorship). The material in the rest of this chapter has never been published before. Of course we must present it here in a very condensed form; otherwise the chapter would be extremely long, by far the longest in this book. Neill was extremely active in these years and in some ways they could be considered the heyday of his impressive career. Neill was at the height of his intellectual powers during this time, from the age of 47 to 61.
46. *Man's Disorder and God's Design: The Amsterdam Assembly Series* (New York: Harper & Brothers, 1949). See Neill's unpublished autobiography, Section VII, Ecumenical Developments, 1, 'Geneva and All That', p. 1.

> This Review is not an end in itself. Its one and only purpose is to help in the creation of true fellowship between the Churches. It is an instrument to be used by the Churches in order to give substance and reality to the new relationships between them which are implied in their participation in the World Council of Churches. The birth of the World Council can only be conceived as a point of departure – not as a point of arrival. Whether 'Amsterdam' will be recorded in history as one of the great failures of the Church or as a new beginning will not in the first place depend upon the utterances of the Assembly but on the decisions and actions taken by the Churches as a result of it. If 'Amsterdam' does not lead, however gradually, to further concrete steps in the relations of the Churches to each other, it will all have been in vain.

Visser 't Hooft's editorial points out that 'For several centuries the Churches have not been on speaking terms with each other.' The WCC was established as a herculean plan to ameliorate this situation.[47]

One would think that Neill would be excited, even proud, to be part of a team that was truly engaged in important work for the worldwide church. Neill, however, was not enjoying his job. In his autobiography he wrote, 'It was not long, however, before the suspicion began to dawn in my mind that there really was not a job for me to do.'[48] What went wrong?

Neill thought his jobs were ill-defined and that others at the WCC were capable enough to do them without his assistance. As Associate General Secretary, Neill was in charge of study and evangelism but there were two men leading those areas who were highly capable: Nils Ehrenstrom and the 'genius' J.C. Hoekendijk – whom Neill had actually recruited to work in the WCC.[49]

Neill worked on putting together a salary scale and connecting WCC employees to the Swiss national pension scheme. He took responsibility for corporate worship for all employees. The WCC was expanding rapidly and 'new departments seemed to be springing up all the time'. The Lutheran and Presbyterian world headquarters both moved in, causing a need for many more offices. Neill must have been a jovial presence, as he was always eager to meet new friends and host gatherings, such as a monthly fondue meeting that lasted several years for those interested in theology.[50]

---

47. *The Ecumenical Review*, Vol. 1, no. 1 (Autumn 1948).
48. Neill, unpublished autobiography, 'Geneva and All That', p. 1.
49. Ibid., p. 2.
50. Ibid., p. 3.

Serving as Assistant Bishop to the Archbishop of Canterbury on the continent of Europe, Neill naturally took great interest in the Anglican church in Geneva. He worked in both the Anglican church there, as well as the American Episcopal church just down the road. Neill thought it very odd that the two churches knew little of each other but he served them both, providing confirmations, sermons and all manner of pastoral work to the people – some of them illustrious – who passed through Geneva. He also travelled quite a lot on behalf of the Church of England.

It is curious that, when Neill arrived in Geneva to work at the WCC, nobody seemed to be aware of his linguistic gifts. He was competent in French, German, Italian, Spanish, Portuguese, Dutch and Swedish, as well as 'a smattering of several other languages'. He was also fluent in Tamil and could understand several other Indian languages, not to mention his very strong facility in biblical Greek and Hebrew. This meant that Neill was a tremendous asset to the WCC because he could understand the vast majority of the communications without an interpreter.[51] For example, during his Geneva years, Neill translated two major scholarly books by Giovanni Miegge from Italian to English for Oxford University Press.[52] He preached in several languages, including German, Tamil and, of course, French. (In 1962 he left Geneva to take up a professorship – lecturing entirely in German – at the University of Hamburg.) He preached often in French, for many and various occasions, including at the famous Taizé community in Burgundy, France. Of his time in Geneva, Neill reflected, 'I may be the only Anglican who has ever ventured to preach from Calvin's pulpit in a modest imitation of Calvin's tongue.' He also lectured often in German while in Geneva, although it took him longer to attain complete fluency. On one occasion he lectured at the University of Basel, with Karl Barth in the audience. Barth recommended that Neill's lecture be published, which it was.[53] Hans-Ruedi Weber stated that Neill 'was able to lecture at the drop of a hat in any language'.[54]

At WCC headquarters, Neill took charge when Visser 't Hooft was travelling – an occurrence that was not uncommon at all. He chaired the library committee. He helped out with the *Ecumenical Press Service* that capably broadcast global Christian news to the world. He lectured frequently at Bossey. He contributed scholarly articles often, especially to *The Ecumenical Review*. Despite all of these activities, Neill felt that 'a

---

51. Ibid., p. 12.
52. Giovanni Miegge, *Christian Affirmations in a Secular Age*, trans. by Stephen Neill (New York: Oxford University Press, 1958); also, *Gospel and Myth in the Thought of Rudolf Bultmann*, trans. by Stephen Neill (London: Lutterworth Press, 1960).
53. Neill, unpublished autobiography, 'Geneva and All That', pp. 12-13, 18-20.
54. Weber, interview by author, 12 October 2004, Geneva.

multiplicity of jobs do not amount to a job'. He was feeling 'very restless and discontented'. When planning for the second assembly of the WCC began, Neill decided that his time at the WCC should come to an end.[55]

A Survey of Theological Education in Africa in 1950

Before Neill left the WCC, he received an invitation from the International Missionary Council to conduct a survey of theological education in Africa, much like the one he had done two years before in Asia. It was now 1950 and Neill needed to get out of Geneva, partly to determine just what his future would be were he to step away from the WCC. He was delighted by the assignment and made the very most of it.[56]

From April to July 1950 Neill embarked on a sweeping tour of East and West Africa to assess the state of African theological education. He visited Egypt, Sudan and the six British territories in tropical Africa: Tanganyika,[57] Kenya, Uganda, Nigeria, Gold Coast (Ghana) and Sierra Leone. Neill was to head the project as a 'one-man team'.[58] The overall objective was to shed light on what could be done to improve the quality of theological education and the training of ministry in Africa. Neill produced a considerable amount of material during and after the trip, including a 120-page 'travel diary' as well as a 51-page confidential report.[59]

Arising out of the Whitby, Canada, World Missionary Conference of 1947 and spearheaded by Bengt Sundkler, Norman Goodall and Kenneth Scott Latourette, Neill's tour of East and West Africa was part of an ambitious attempt to understand the state of the African Church in the aftermath of the war. Reports on China and India had already been completed and a report on the Church in the Pacific was under way.[60]

---

55. Neill, unpublished autobiography, 'Geneva and All That', p. 23.
56. See Dyron B. Daughrity, 'Bishop Stephen Neill, the IMC and the State of African Theological Education in 1950', *Studies in World Christianity*, Vol. 18, no. 1 (April 2012).
57. Tanganyika included modern-day Rwanda, Burundi and Tanzania (minus Zanzibar).
58. Neill, unpublished autobiography, 'Geneva and All That', p. 25.
59. Eventually, Neill's report became the first of three for the IMC, 'Part I: Report of a Survey in East and West Africa, 1950'. The second, 'Part II: Report of a Survey in Angola, Belgian Congo, French West Africa, etc.' was undertaken by M. Searle Bates, Bengt Sundkler, F. Michaeli and C. G. Baeta. 'Part III: Report of a Survey in the Union of South Africa, South and North Rhodesia, and Nyasaland', by Norman Goodall and Erik W. Nielsen. (London and New York: International Missionary Council, 1950-53).
60. The China report was compiled by Luther Weigle and the India report was completed by C.W. Ranson.

Africa was the next region of focus and considered 'high priority' because of the explosive growth in the churches. In July 1948 Neill's name was put forward.[61] By March 1949 a decision had been reached. Latourette wrote, 'I am delighted that you have obtained Stephen Neill to head it.'[62]

Early communications proposed that Neill be joined by an unnamed African American, but Neill rejected the suggestion, saying in a letter to E.J. Bingle, 'You know the difficulty I feel about having an American Negro.'[63] Bingle responded by suggesting that Neill conduct the research trip alone.[64] This comment by Neill brings up questions about his views on race relations. In perhaps his most direct passage on this specific topic, in 1961, he wrote the following:

> We have had the mythology of the good white man and the bad black man – of the heroic missionary who never made a mistake and gave his life courageously in the service of Christ. This has been followed by the mythology of the good black man and the bad white man – of the missionary who never did anything but make mistakes and was at all times the victim of his own self-deception. The first mythology belongs to the childhood of a younger Church, the second to its adolescence. It is high time that all younger Churches moved out of both into the securer realm of adult responsibility. . . . The doctrine that the black man must always lead and the white man must always follow is as absurd as the earlier doctrine that the white man must always lead and the black man must always follow. We ought to be agreed by now that the man best qualified for the job will be called to it, regardless of his background or of the colour of his skin.[65]

---

61. See 'Report on the Research Work of the IMC for the Period Jan. 1 to July 31, 1948', by Bengt Sundkler, 31 July 1948. Located at Yale University, IMC archives, Box 263138.

62. Letter from K.S. Latourette to Dr Sundkler, 14 March 1949. See Yale University, IMC archives, Box 263138.

63. Letter from Stephen Neill to E.J. Bingle, 10 November 1949. Latourette thought it 'wise' to include an African American who was not Anglican. See letter from Latourette to Sundkler, 14 March 1949. This quotation raises many questions regarding Neill's view of race. However, Neill dodged the issue. In a document entitled 'Notes on Talk with Bishop Stephen Neill at Mansfield College, Oxford, September 8th, 1949', Neill is recorded as saying the 'WCC was not greatly interested in this question of Race Relations'. Both documents are located at Yale University, IMC archives, Box 263138.

64. Letter from Bingle to Neill, 15 November 1949, located at Yale University, IMC archives, Box 263138.

65. Stephen Neill, 'Foreword', in *The Sierra Leone Church*, by Raymond Samuel

Given Neill's long service with the Indian Church, it is difficult to conceive of him as a racist in the strictest sense, but his comment to Bingle raises serious questions.

Initially, the IMC laid out an exhausting itinerary for Neill that would have taken him all over Africa. It was revised several times and became much more manageable. Upon confirmation of his itinerary, Neill drew up a 'most formidable list of books' to digest in order to comprehend the context of each region he would visit.[66] He understood the great expectations being placed on him. E.J. Bingle, a former missionary to South India and the Acting Research Secretary of the IMC, described this project as being 'vitally important for the well-being of the Church in Africa'.[67] A flurry of international correspondence demonstrates the anticipation of all parties involved. Several commented that Neill was uniquely poised for the task. Several media outlets wrote about the upcoming trip, including the *Church Times*, *The Christian*, *The Guardian* and the *Ecumenical Press Service*.[68]

By early January 1950, Neill was producing long letters and papers displaying an impressive knowledge of history, missions and theological education within an African context. His previous experience (1930-39) as warden of a theological college in India proved useful in preparing for the trip.[69] Neill knew the questions to ask. He understood patterns in mission history. He represented a remarkable combination: he was a seasoned missionary, a respected academic and he comprehended the unique challenges of theological education in the younger churches. While Neill was no expert on the African context, all parties involved were confident in his abilities.

Neill kept a travel diary during his journey that ended up covering over 120 single-spaced pages.[70] The diary entries are classic Stephen

---

Foster (London: SPCK, 1961).

66. Letter from Bingle's assistant to Neill, 6 December 1949, located at Yale University, IMC archives, Box 263139 (Files 1-12).

67. Letter from Bingle to IMC Secretaries, *et al.*, November 1949, located at Yale University, IMC archives, Box 263138. Neill reveals that it was Bingle who came up with the theme for the second WCC assembly in Evanston, Illinois, in 1954. See Neill's unpublished autobiography, 'Geneva and All That', pp. 41-42.

68. See 'Future of the Ministry in Africa', 27 January 1950, 'Paragraphs inserted in religious papers'. See also 'Durrant's Press Cuttings', 27 January 1950. Both located at Yale University, IMC archives, Box 263139 (Files 1-12).

69. See Daughrity, *Bishop Stephen Neill: From Edinburgh to South India*.

70. The diary is organised into thirteen long entries. Partial or complete copies can be located in the Rhodes House manuscripts at the Bodleian Library in Oxford, USPG X1047; Yale University, IMC archives, Box 263138; WCC archives in

Neill: impeccably written, engaging, highly informative and, above all, opinionated. The first diary entry reads: '"Travel by air, if you have time." This cynical saying was once again proved true, as my aircraft was eighteen hours late, an inauspicious beginning to a long tour.'[71]

Neill covered a great deal of ground on the first leg of his journey. He began by paying a visit to the Greek Patriarch in Cairo. They discussed whether Muslims and Christians could join together against communism. Neill cited the 'specifically Christian basis of the World Council' which refers to 'Jesus Christ as God'.[72] Thus, while cooperation with Muslims is possible, Christian conviction must not be diluted.

Neill then visited the Coptic Patriarch who, somewhat surprisingly, offered him a Coca-Cola. Neill conjectured how this ubiquitous and American staple had become 'the national drink of Egypt'.[73] Afterwards, Neill visited the Coptic theological seminary and had little good to say, for example, 'We looked into the library – a strange collection of junk.'[74]

Neill provided fascinating insights into the Egyptian Church. He discussed the sheep-stealing which led Copts to be very suspicious of Roman Catholics and Evangelicals: 'Almost all the pastors of the Evangelical Church are of Coptic origin.'[75] His assessment of the seminary of the Evangelical Church in Cairo was pessimistic. He criticised the teachers for their aloofness and claimed students were left to their own devices when it came to social life and pastoral care.

Neill described the mood in Egypt as being generally unhappy because of several factors, notably the mass disillusionment within the greater Arab world after surprising defeats by Israel. The majority of Egyptians believed Israel would soon collapse since the terrific level of financial support from outside could not be sustained. Post-colonial hopes in a Koranic Dar al-Islam were fading fast. The inspiration of the early ummah pulled the Muslim world backward into the seventh century instead of ushering them into the modern age. In Neill's observation, the rich were getting richer and the poor poorer in newly liberated Egypt; what was needed was a true social revolution anchored by the Sermon on the Mount.[76]

      Geneva, Reference Code: 26.31.38, 'Survey of the Training of the Ministry in Africa: Files of Sundkler and Bingle'; and the archives of the Centre for the Study of World Christianity at the University of Edinburgh.

71. Neill's Travel Diary, Entry No. 1 (31 March 1950), 1. Henceforth, Diary.
72. Diary No. 1, 1.
73. Diary No. 1, 1.
74. Diary No. 1, 2.
75. Diary No. 1, 4. In truth, virtually all Christians in Egypt have a Coptic background. The Coptic Christians originated in the first century AD.
76. Diary No. 1, 5.

7. Return to Europe and Ecumenical Labour: 1944-62

At the end of his Egyptian stop, Neill spent a delightful few hours in Alexandria, or, what he termed, 'the city of Athanasius'. He described the famous city as standing up 'like a dream city from its lagoon'.[77]

From Alexandria, he travelled 'a thousand miles up the Nile' to Khartoum, where his narrative begins with a bang:

> There are I suppose some fervent opponents of 'imperialism', who hold that the white man should never in any circumstances interfere in the affairs of the black. But one who considers the contrast between the abject misery in which the Sudan lay in the days of slavery and the steady progress and prosperity which it has enjoyed in the last fifty years may be forgiven if he doubts whether the generalisation holds in every case.[78]

Neill noted the growing nationalism in Sudan and doubted whether a united church could ever occur there.

Neill discussed the complexity of Bible translations. He pointed out that many Christians supported the use of Arabic in the Church, a language he labelled 'great and glorious'. He believed Arabic was the only language that could unite Christians in the Muslim world. This posed a dilemma, however, because by endorsing Arabic as the common language, Christians were more susceptible to an increased Islamic influence. In addition, the Arabic language has ossified in Islam and the same could happen were Christianity to adopt it. He concluded this discussion by asking 'Do people ever really absorb the Gospel except in their own language, do they ever really pray except in the language that they use at home?'[79]

From Khartoum Neill travelled to Dar-es-Salaam, where he learned that the local theological school had recently collapsed as a result of a row over teacher salaries. There he also met the famed Frank Laubach who was involved in 'one of his endless literacy campaigns' and who advised Neill that 'the only people who were really tackling the problem of literature for the African were the Seventh Day Adventists'.[80]

Next Neill visited a Lutheran seminary at Lushoto, Tanganyika, and was pleased to discover that the Lutheran missions in East Africa were finally waking up to the need for indigenous clergy.[81]

---

77. Diary No. 1, 6.
78. Diary No. 1, 6.
79. Diary No. 1, 8.
80. Diary No. 2 (8 April 1950), 4.
81. Diary No. 2, 5.

In Morogoro, Tanganyika, Neill met with some missionaries who emphasised the importance of rural education – for example, how to prevent soil erosion and better cultivate the land. His impression was that Africans were generally suspicious of these endeavours, seeing them as 'a scheme . . . to keep [the African] down and to withhold the blessings of Western knowledge'.[82]

Neill then travelled by road to Kenya, accompanied by an African Pentecostal teacher who viewed Neill's tobacco pipe as the mark of the beast.[83] In Kenya Neill visited several places, providing illuminating insights into the world of 1950. On race relations, he wrote:

> At one end are the European settlers, who still dream of a great white dominion stretching from Kenya to the Cape; these people are still living in the world of Cecil Rhodes. . . . At the other end is the party of Jomo Kenyatta, which would like to see the last European depart from the land.[84]

He marvelled at the Kikuyu people whose first baptism was in 1906 and by 1950 could claim tens of thousands of Christians.[85] He admired the 'quasi-military' ethos of the Salvation Army theological training school in Nairobi which, he claimed, was 'excellent for Africans at that stage of development'.[86] He praised the Canadian Pentecostal mission at Nyangore as an 'admirable organisation'.[87]

Neill observed that English was fast becoming the Kenyan language for theological training due to the number of tribes that did not speak Swahili. He conjectured that: 'As the African is educated, he is growing away from his tribal background.'[88] Since Africa was changing so quickly, he argued, it was 'anachronistic' for the Church to take the tribal background too seriously.

In Neill's visits to various Kenyan Bible schools, he remarked that 'All are in the general sense of the term fundamentalist', and many of them were 'first generation converts'.[89] He was relieved to learn that female circumcision was being abandoned in the missions, although male circumcision was retained on hygienic grounds and as an initiation

---

82. Diary No. 2, 9.
83. Diary No. 3, 4-5.
84. Diary No. 4 (24 April 1950), 1.
85. Diary No. 4, 2.
86. Diary No. 4, 3.
87. Diary No. 4, 9.
88. Diary No. 4, 5.
89. Diary No. 4, 7-8.

7. Return to Europe and Ecumenical Labour: 1944-62

rite into Christianity.[90] Neill was overjoyed to get out of this 'rarefied' environment and into a CMS mission where he could freely smoke his pipe.[91]

In Uganda the Roman Catholic and Anglican Churches were growing faster than clergy could be provided. He grumbled that the indigenous Catholic priests were 'not allowed to do a single thing without consulting their Italian overlords'.[92] After picnicking at Lake Victoria, the source of the Nile, he travelled to Kampala, where he discovered tensions between locals and the Indian population. He wrote about the 'Indian menace', remarking that Indians had outmanoeuvred Africans to the point that they were in control of 'almost all of the immensely profitable sugar and cotton estates'. He reasoned that, had the British not intervened, Indians might have gained complete control of the place.[93]

The growth of Christianity in Uganda was spectacular. Neill pointed out that 75 years before there was 'not a Christian in the area'; however, by 1950 there were over half a million. The local bishop characterised Christianity's growth as 'simply miraculous'.[94] There was a downside, however. The work was understaffed and Christianization was superficial. Neill was critical of the local kings and chiefs for being 'polygamous as the German Lutheran princes in the sixteenth century; and the rank and file tend to follow the example of their leaders'.[95]

Neill's visit to Bishop Tucker Theological College in Mukono, Uganda, caused him to reflect on 'the dreadful dearth of Christian literature' both in English and in the vernacular.[96] This could be considered a passing observation were it not for Neill's subsequent work in Geneva after his African tour. He gave the next decade of his life to addressing this problem.

After Mukono, Neill visited Martyr's Cross – where fourteen boys had been burned to death in the 1880s. The boys were heard singing praises to Jesus as they courageously died. Neill's tour guide for this moving experience was Ham Mukasa, who had been a pageboy to King Mwanga at the time of the persecution.[97]

---

90. Diary No. 4, 8.
91. Diary No. 4, 10.
92. Diary No. 5 (28 April 1950), 3.
93. Diary No. 5, 5.
94. According to Neill, the miraculous success was due mainly to the work of the CMS.
95. Diary No. 6 (6 May 1950), 1.
96. Diary No. 6, 4.
97. Diary No. 6, 6.

From Uganda Neill flew back to Nairobi to attend his cousin's wedding, 'Elizabeth Crabbe, the younger daughter of the Bishop of Mombasa'.[98] His tour of East Africa was done. He now headed west, stopping at Tripoli for a few days en route to Nigeria.

Neill's first stop in West Africa was Kano, Nigeria. His immediate impression was that West Africa was 'much more African than the East'. He took notice of the men's Muslim-style long white robes and the near-nakedness of the women with their brightly coloured headcloths.[99] He characterised the Muslim influence as being 'everywhere dominant'.[100]

In Kano, missionaries of the Sudan Interior Mission took care of Neill. He characterised the SIM as naïve and arrogant, yet having 'astonishing success in getting in where everyone else has failed'. In his view, these 'fundamentalist missions . . . are doing nine-tenths of the pioneer missionary work in the world'.[101] He resented their insularity, however: 'They might have heard that some people called Episcopalians existed and were rather like Roman Catholics, but that would be about all.'[102]

His next destination was the city of Jos. While speaking at a conference there, a sudden and deafening storm interrupted his lecture: 'At one point I had just got out the words, "Speaking frankly as Christian brethren", when the heavens opened and it became impossible to speak either frankly or as Christian brethren.'[103] Neill was deeply moved at that conference: 'I felt the deep creative movement of Christian fellowship among us, and I have rarely been so conscious of a meeting being wholly under the direction of the Holy Spirit.'[104]

In the 'damp and steamy' climate of Enugu, Nigeria, Neill wondered how European missionaries managed to keep their health.[105] He wrote of 'bursts of that tropical rain about which you read in books.'[106] He applauded the Americans for taking much better care of their missionaries than the Europeans. He wrote of the diverse student body at St Paul's College in Awka, necessitating instruction exclusively in English. This was a fundamental problem because the boys had to minister in their own languages when they returned to their tribal communities. Complicating matters was that graduates often acquired the ambition to move to the UK or the US. Then there were the political complexities:

98. Diary No. 6, 7.
99. Diary No. 7, 1.
100. Diary No. 7, 1.
101. Diary No. 7, 2.
102. Diary No. 7, 2.
103. Diary No. 7, 7.
104. Diary No. 7, 7.
105. Diary No. 8 (19 May 1950), 1.
106. Diary No. 8, 5.

7. Return to Europe and Ecumenical Labour: 1944-62

> Nigeria does not really exist. It is an entity created entirely by European occupation. . . . The two main races of the South, the Yoruba in the West and the Ibo in the East, very much dislike one another. Both are intensely disliked by the finer and on the whole more civilised, though educationally less advanced, people of the North. The question of whether Nigeria can hold together at all is one that cannot be readily answered.[107]

After these matters were explained to Neill by Miss Stewart – an Irish SCM missionary there – he began to feel depressed, questioning whether 'deep character development' was really taking place in Africa. He was reminded of an African leader who once made the statement, 'You Europeans are always talking about sin; sin is an idea in which Africans are not very much interested.'[108]

At St Paul's College the staff became defensive at Neill's scathing criticism. He pointed out that they could not produce one graduate capable of serving on staff. He blasted them for being 'segregated from the life of the Church in their immense mission compound . . . not speaking any African language . . . largely unaware of the changes taking place in the life of the Church'.[109] He bemoaned the lack of an agreed standard of admission to the theological college and urged higher academic standards. He noticed the utter absence of theological books in local languages and suggested a 'series of short books' dealing with Christian doctrine should be undertaken.[110] Neill addressed this problem upon his return to Geneva.

Neill resented the flourishing work of the 'Rivals in the Field' – the Roman Catholic Church in Nigeria – describing their strategy as a 'gold rush':

> The Roman Catholics are trying to stake out their claim in every village by putting up a church or founding a school; when that is done, it is too late for other people to come in. Almost every ship brings a fresh load of Irish priests and sisters. . . . I cannot pretend to think that Irish Roman Catholicism, as it presents itself on the West Coast of Africa, is of the highest type of Christianity.[111]

---

107. Diary No. 8, 3.
108. Diary No. 8, 4.
109. Diary No. 8, 7.
110. Diary No. 8, 8.
111. Diary No. 8, 9-10.

After Awka, Neill reflected on the many obstacles to Christian unity in West Africa: 'nonsensical' political boundaries, tribal affiliations, language differences and denominational loyalties.[112] Neill saw the only possible solution to be membership of the World Council of Churches.[113]

The next stop was Benin City in Nigeria, where he had a pleasant time looking at art, listening to music and experiencing the local culture. While touring the public library, a young man remarked, 'We lack books.'[114] Neill listened.

While in Benin City, Neill visited an unfinished but impressive church building. It had been built by King Oba Akenzua II (1933-78) as a temple for a new religion he created to merge Christianity, Islam and paganism. The king, however, converted to Anglicanism and the church was abandoned.[115] Neill thought Christianity was in its infancy in Benin: 'the old paganism has been driven only a very short distance below the surface'.[116]

From Benin City Neill made his way to a centre for the training of fiancées and young wives in Akure. This prompted him to ruminate on family life in Nigeria. In Neill's mind, polygamy led to a 'second-class type of Christianity' and should be rooted out of the Church. In his view, Nigerians 'simply do not know what Christian marriage means' since they had grown up with low moral standards, polygamous surroundings and young fathers/husbands who might go to England for a three-year stretch.[117] One cannot help but wonder what Neill, a lifelong bachelor, really knew about family life – especially in a culture he was encountering for the first time.

Neill's next stop was Ogbomosho, 'the centre of the Southern Baptists'.[118] He was to be hosted by Dr Pooh, prompting Neill to remark: 'We were uncertain whether we should be welcomed by a China-man or a bear. When we finally got there, we discovered Dr Pooh was neither, rather he was a Texan.'[119] As it turned out, Neill's instructions were wrong and the man's actual name was Dr Pool. Neill gave rare commendation to the Baptist academy at Ogbomosho with its six full-time faculty: 'This is the one adequately staffed theological school that I have seen in Africa.'[120]

---

112. Diary No. 9 (28 May 1950), 2.
113. Diary No. 9, 2.
114. Diary No. 9, 7.
115. Diary No. 9, 7. I cannot help but to think that the 'Chrislam' phenomenon in Nigieria may somehow be related to King Oba Akenzua's movement. For more on Chrislam, see Public Broadcasting Service (PBS) 'Religion & Ethics' at: http://www.pbs.org/wnet/religionandethics/episodes/february-13-2009/chrislam/2236/.
116. Diary No. 9, 8.
117. Diary No. 9, 10.
118. Diary No. 9, 10.
119. Diary No. 9, 10.
120. Diary No. 9, 11.

7. Return to Europe and Ecumenical Labour: 1944-62

Next was Ibadan, 'the largest purely African city in the world'.[121] Neill was fascinated by the city, if a little perturbed when the children kept calling him 'O-imbo', which literally translates as 'peeled man', due to his white skin.[122] Ibadan was around 50 per cent Muslim, 30 per cent pagan and 20 per cent Christian in Neill's estimate. He visited the new University of Nigeria and was impressed by its department of religious studies. He preached at the university with 230 in attendance and later met with the students. They were very interested in his views on polygamy.

In Ibadan Neill attended another conference that was mainly attended by Africans. They discussed how Africans who are taught in English develop two 'almost unrelated zones' in their minds.[123] Several attendees confessed to having great difficulty preaching in Yoruba because their training had been in English. Neill remarked: 'In this meeting . . . the Africans were not talking to us; they were allowing us to listen in as they thought aloud, and we were deeply grateful for the privilege.' Neill was moved. 'From my point of view, I felt that my tour had been worthwhile for this experience alone.'[124]

His next visit was to the Gold Coast (now Ghana), where his brother had taught for years. He reckoned about half the population was nominally Christian. He spoke at the new University College of the Gold Coast, opened in 1948. In just over a year it had assembled a staff of 60, of whom nine were African.

Neill described the Gold Coast as being educated and prosperous. The excellent education system was developed by missionaries with government aid.[125] Yet he derided the man who would become Ghana's first Prime Minister and President – Kwame Nkrumah – who happened to be in jail at the time. Neill described Nkrumah's emerging self-rule movement as 'extremist', 'irresponsible', yet very popular. Neill questioned one acquaintance, 'When these friends have got self-government, have they any idea of what to do with it?'[126]

Next Neill made his way to Akropong, where the Church of Scotland had inherited the work of the Basel Mission: 'Another great merit of the Basel Mission is that all over the world they have taught their Christians to sing.'[127] He met with Colin Forrester-Paton, a famous Church of Scotland missionary who was later appointed chaplain to Queen Elizabeth.

121. Diary No. 9, p 12. Ibadan was one of the largest cities in Africa at the time, perhaps after Cairo and Johannesburg. Neill estimated the population at 300,000 to 400,000.
122. Diary No. 10 (3 June 1950), 1.
123. Diary No. 10, 4.
124. Diary No. 10, 4.
125. Diary No. 11 (10 June 1950), 3.
126. Diary No. 11, 3.
127. Diary No. 11, 5.

On his drive to Abetifi Neill ruminated on politics:

> Colonialism is a phase of the world's history that is passing away. It is the fashion of today to vilify it in every possible way. But I wonder whether the final verdict of history will be quite the same. It seems to me that the British have remarkably little to be ashamed of in their service to the Gold Coast. Many mistakes have been made. But the country has been opened up . . . the people given peace, unity and security of life, property and land tenure, such as they had never known before, contact with the outside world, education and unimaginable wealth. . . . When the Gold Coast attains self-government, as it very soon will, the country will be handed over to the people in excellent working order.[128]

Next was Kumasi, 'the Klondyke of the Gold Coast'. Money just poured into the city and people became rich. He found the Anglican service quite formal: 'Apparently here, as in the USA, to become an Episcopalian marks a sense of having taken a step up in the social scale.'[129] After the service, he was 'a little taken aback' when they served whisky, sherry and beer, since it was only 11.15 a.m. 'Apparently, here, as in Korea, it is expected that the good Anglican will smoke and drink, to make it quite clear that he is neither a Methodist nor a Presbyterian.'[130]

At Kumasi Neill visited several theological training schools and a Methodist centre for training women and girls. At nearby Mampong he visited a group of Sisters of the Holy Paraclete who ran a secondary school, a college and a maternity clinic. He confided in his diary that they were known troublemakers.

From Kumasi Neill travelled to Ho, in British Togoland, and visited a co-educational teacher training college. He frowned upon the experiment of educating boys and girls together, 'I don't regard this as progress, but there are some who think otherwise.'[131]

Next was Accra, where he met with the Executive Committee of the Christian Council of the Gold Coast. A controversy broke out which Neill attributed to 'intense suspicion felt by the African': 'What the African wants to learn is Latin and things like that, to show that he is as good as the European, and to learn the secret of the Europeans' power.'[132] He

---

128. Diary No. 11, 6.
129. Diary No. 12 (22 June 1950), 1.
130. Diary No. 12, 'confidential extracts', 1.
131. Diary No. 12, 8.
132. Diary No. 12, 10-11.

7. Return to Europe and Ecumenical Labour: 1944-62   237

continued, in frustration, 'I have felt countless times, especially since I came to the Gold Coast, that the curse of British West Africa is that in everything it has followed so closely the English model, even down to tweed suits.'[133]

Neill's tour ended in Sierra Leone, 'the Canterbury, the Mother Church, of West Africa'. He described Freetown as 'somewhat ramshackle . . . one of the most backward areas in Africa'.[134] He claimed the policies of the CMS in Sierra Leone should 'serve as an awful warning as to how missionary work should not be done'.[135] However, he commended the work of the United Evangelical Brethren who had grown to become the largest Protestant body there.

Neill was outraged by the racially divided churches. He remarked that this 'may seem strange to some of my readers but it will be easily intelligible to those who come from the southern States'.[136] He made reference to South Africa, how blacks and whites would eventually have to reach a 'happy integration'.[137]

At Freetown Neill visited Fourah Bay College and gave glowing praise, 'I doubt whether any single Christian institution has exercised a wider or more beneficent influence on a great area of the earth's surface.'[138] He then enjoyed a swim with Cyril Bowles of Cambridge and Reverend Roberts, the Principal at Fourah Bay. They had a candid discussion on mission work in Africa. Neill wrote, 'We all agreed that the Church in Sierra Leone is much more awful than anything we have met with elsewhere. . . . Even after a century, Christianity is terribly formal and superficial.'[139] They discussed how 'fetishism' was rampant, even among the clergy. Neill argued that Europeans tended to show little sensitivity to the changing context of African Christianity.[140]

Neill's diary ends here. The 'Finis' is worth quoting entirely:

> And so my Odyssey comes to an end. All being well, tomorrow the Wayfarer will take me from Freetown to Dakar, and on Saturday morning I should be in New York. It has been a long and complicated journey, but it is wonderful how one thing has fitted

---

133. Diary No. 12, 11.
134. Diary No. 13 (28 June 1950), 1-2.
135. Diary No. 13, 'confidential extracts', 1.
136. Diary No. 13, 5.
137. Diary No. 13, 3.
138. Diary No. 13, 7. Fourah Bay College has produced great leaders such as Bishop Samuel Ajayi Crowther and Sir Milton Margai – the first Prime Minister of Sierra Leone.
139. Diary No. 13, 'confidential extracts', 2.
140. Diary No. 13, 'confidential extracts', 2.

in with another, and the way has been smoothed before me. I have not had a single day's illness. I have often been tired, but never worse than I often am in Geneva. I have not missed a single engagement through ill-health or overtiredness. I look back with gratitude on memories of an uncounted host of friends, African, missionary and government, who have made me welcome, taken me into their homes, cared for my needs, shared their problems with me, and showered upon me unmeasured kindness and affection. Their names are written in the book of life. But the deepest gratitude lies elsewhere. 'I being in the way, the Lord led me.'[141]

Neill condensed his diary to a 51-page report for the IMC entitled 'Survey of the Training of the Ministry in Africa'. It was published in 1950 and read carefully by many. Responses were mixed. Some thought Neill's report to be very helpful in understanding not only the situation of theological education in Africa, but even larger issues pertaining to the younger churches in general.[142] Others decried it. For example, CMS chief Max Warren criticised it on several points, particularly Neill's self-assured attitude. He thought some of Neill's views to be 'sheer nonsense' and some of his perspectives 'unrealistic'.[143]

While some cheered and others jeered, it is clear that Neill spent considerable time and energy on this project. He accomplished a tremendous amount of work in a very short period of time and it took a heavy toll on him. He visited nearly all of the institutions that prepared candidates for ordination along with many Bible schools. He met with myriad groups in many capacities, although never with a Catholic institution. He participated in several conferences, most of which had been organised specifically for his visit. He addressed many different audiences: churches, national Christian councils and clergy gatherings. He met individually with scores of high-ranking church officials and made time for countless students. He walked the compounds of many and diverse mission stations.[144]

---

141. Diary No. 13, 12.
142. See W.V. Stone, 'The Dark Ages and Twentieth-Century Africa: A Comparison in Churchmanship', *Scottish Journal of Theology*, Vol. 8, no. 2 (1955). Neill also published his findings in an article, 'African Theological Survey', *International Review of Mission*, Vol. 39, no. 154 (1 April 1950), pp. 207-11.
143. Letter from Max Warren to Rev. N. Goodall, 3 July 1950, CMS Archives, University of Birmingham, CMS/OSD AFg O27/6. Other papers related to Neill's tour of Africa are located in the same archive at: CMS/G59/AD 5 1950.
144. See Stephen Neill, *Survey of the Training of the Ministry in Africa* (London: International Missionary council, 1950), 1. The full text of the 51-page report is located in the CMS Archives, University of Birmingham, at: CMS/OSD AFg

7. Return to Europe and Ecumenical Labour: 1944-62

Quite predictably, after this period of intense work, Neill had a serious breakdown in health. While he was able to finish his findings, reports and summaries in a punctual manner, the Africa tour left him utterly spent and his colleagues knew about it. Those who commissioned the tour even apologised to him for the weight of the assignment. Once Neill settled back down in Geneva, it was clear that he was having 'a very serious breakdown of a form which precludes his being able to exercise a normal ministry'. Another wrote that Neill had been 'reduced to inaction'. As usual, Neill gave everything to his work, without counting the cost, even the cost it placed on his own health.[145]

Nevertheless, he was determined to finish what he had started. He prepared several versions of his conclusions for various audiences ranging from the 51-page report to a four-page 'brief summary' consisting of two sections: General Recommendations and Area Recommendations.[146] Under General Recommendations, Neill argued the following points:

1. 'The standards of living of the servants of the Church need to be raised.'
2. There should be a greater focus on youth, especially in recruiting ministry candidates.
3. More conferences should be held dealing with all manner of Christian education: from catechist training to higher education.
4. English should be the language of theological education; however, greater attention should be paid to understanding how 'the African mind actually works'.

O27/6.

145. See, for example, a letter from Bingle to Neill, dated 17 October 1950. Bingle mentions that Neill is 'under doctor's orders' for 'some extended form of treatment'. He apologised to Neill, 'I should also like to say how deeply sorry I am personally that you should have been reduced to inaction at this time. We of the IMC have placed very great burdens on you during the past year and we can never be grateful enough.' Located at Yale University, IMC archives, Box 263139 (Files 1-12). See also letter from M.A.C.W. to T.F.C.B., undated, entitled 'Christian Literature – Bishop Stephen Neill – and all that'. The letter states, 'Bishop Neill, as you may know, has had a very serious breakdown of a form which precludes his being able to exercise a normal ministry.' In all likelihood the letter dates to late 1952 as plans were coming together for Neill to begin his new job working for the IMC on his World Christian Books project. This letter is located in the CMS Archives, University of Birmingham, CMS/OSD AFg O27/6.

146. See 'The Training of the Ministry in Africa, brief summary', 15 November 1950, CMS Archives, University of Birmingham, CMS/OSD AFg O27/6.

5. Pedagogy must change. The dictation of notes is insufficient. Teachers must use the tutorial method.
6. Theological education will be more effective in community. Provisions and accommodations should be made for the families of students.
7. There is a severe dearth of good textbooks in Africa. This must be addressed immediately.

Perhaps Neill's top priority was to see a Christian college in East Africa and the language for instruction should be English.

In so many ways Neill's survey of African theological education can be criticised from the vantage point of over 70 years later. However, his efforts to address the problems he identified are admirable indeed; he devoted the next chapter of his life to a publishing venture, sponsored by the IMC, called World Christian Books, with heavy support from Cambridge professor Charles Raven and the backing of the IMC and WCC.[147] During the 1950s and 1960s Neill oversaw the publication of 60 books in 35 languages. The chief goal was to produce 'good simple literature' that would be widely available to younger church leaders.[148] He wrote seven books for the series and devoted the next fifteen years of his life to taking on the problems he had witnessed first-hand in his African tour. Much later, in 1969, he moved to Africa and founded the Department of Philosophy and Religious Studies at the University of Nairobi, which exists today as one of the most prestigious departments of religion in all Africa. He worked there for four years before semi-retirement in Oxford.

Clearly and unambiguously, the tour of Africa impacted Stephen Neill deeply. Indeed it changed him; it completely altered the direction of his professional life.

A Long Break with the WCC

Officially, Neill's term with the WCC lasted from December 1947 to March 1950.[149] However, he continued to work for the organisation on an

---

147. 'Our first Chairman, Professor C.E. Raven, was taken from us on 8th July 1964. . . . More than any other single man he was the creator of World Christian Books.' See Stephen Neill, 'World Christian Books, Newsletter No. 18', January 1965, WCC Archives, Geneva, Box 26-18-03, IMC Archives, Christian Literature, File: Christian Literature Newsletters, 1956-1965.
148. See Dyron Daughrity, 'The Literary Legacy of Stephen Neill', *International Bulletin of Missionary Research*, Vol. 32, no. 3 (July 2008), p. 151.
149. *The Times*, 18 March 1950, p. 8. In a letter from Eleanor Kent Browne to Mr James Best, dated 15 May 1953, Browne writes, 'Bishop Neill has not been

informal basis, specifically, in spearheading a project to write the history of the ecumenical movement. That project, and others that came along on occasion, kept Neill in the WCC orbit until 1954.

As noted above, Neill was exhausted after his four-month trip in Africa. In his unpublished autobiography he wrote:

> By this time it had become clear that I must make a radical change in my way of living. My health was steadily deteriorating and, though I was still capable of a great deal of work, it had become obvious that I must become more fully master of my own time.[150]

Owen Chadwick, in his biography of Neill in the *Oxford Dictionary of National Biography*, revealed that Neill was actually hospitalised after the Africa trip and in February 1951 Archbishop Fisher asked him to resign fully his various positions and tasks underneath the direct supervision of the Archbishop of Canterbury.[151]

The 'excessively boring endless committees' of the WCC were becoming onerous to Neill and his chronic insomnia was haunting him again. Neill needed a change but 'It was not readily clear where I could fit in. Then the solution came clearly but unexpectedly.' That solution, which became clear in 1947, was that Neill would work on a comprehensive, much needed

---

officially on the staff of the World Council for well over a year in any capacity. As you know, of course, he had to resign as Associate General Secretary because of a nervous breakdown. During the past few months he has been helping Ruth Rouse with *The History of the Ecumenical Movement*. He is receiving no salary from the World Council for this work, however.' WCC archives, Geneva, Stephen Neill file. According to *Crockford's Clerical Directory, 1965-66*, Neill was Associate General Secretary from 1948-51.

150. Neill's unpublished autobiography, 'Geneva and All That', pp. 46-47.
151. Owen Chadwick, 'Neill, Stephen Charles (1900-1984)', in *Oxford Dictionary of National Biography* (Oxford University Press, 2004). It is difficult to discern in the records precisely when Neill resigned, and which post or posts he resigned and at what time. It appears that in March 1950, just before his tour of Africa, Neill resigned his appointment as representing the Archbishop in North and Central Europe. However, he continued in other capacities until asked to fully resign his position as Assistant Bishop to the Archbishop of Canterbury. See *The Times*, 18 March 1950, p. 8, which states that as of 31 March 1950 Neill would resign his appointment (from the Archbishop) working with Northern and Central Europe. See also Neill's entry in *Crockford's Clerical Directory, 1957-58*. There he is listed as being Assistant Bishop to the Archbishop of Canterbury from 1946-49. There may be discrepancies in the historical record here.

history of the ecumenical movement alongside Ruth Rouse. After much discussion, they decided they should cover the period from 1517 (the beginning of the Reformation) to 1948 (the Amsterdam assembly).[152]

Miss Ruth Rouse, a prolific ecumenist, was asked to be the General Editor of the project.[153] She was 75 years old and, among other important offices, had served as President of the Young Women's Christian Association (YWCA) between 1938 and 1946. Neill described Rouse as 'remarkable . . . she seemed to know personally half the Christian world'. She was full of 'restless and indomitable energy', even at the age of 75. However, Neill felt that she was also 'inordinately, almost pathologically, shy and in need of assurance'.[154]

Everything went well for a time. Neill was quite impressed by Rouse's incredible work ethic as she attended conferences and recruited authors, compiling an enormous collection of materials along the way, all in a short time. Neill was assigned a chapter on church union because of his expertise on the formation of the Church of South India. However, Neill notes candidly, 'It was at this point that our difficulties began.'[155]

The WCC committee in Geneva that was in charge of the project began to realise that the project was moving too slowly. The money – in fact, $10,000 – that had been donated to the project by the Disciples of Christ was running out. Only two chapters had been submitted when many more had been expected. The committee approached Neill and asked him to help, which he agreed to do, although with much trepidation. Neill figured this would amount to 'three years' slavery', and in retrospect he wrote, 'My worst fears were more than justified by what I went through'. It was not chiefly the work that concerned Neill; rather, it was his colleague. He wrote, 'It was quite clear that Ruth Rouse was very conscious of her position as editor, and was in no way inclined to divest herself of any of her authority.'[156] Rouse's biographer, Ruth Franzen, had a different take on the conflict. She thought Rouse's attitude was 'responsible', given that Neill 'was in bad health and needed medical treatment', which is entirely accurate.[157]

---

152. Neill's unpublished autobiography, 'Geneva and All That', pp. 46-47.
153. The authoritative biography of Ruth Rouse is by Ruth Franzen, *Ruth Rouse among Students: Global, Missiological, and Ecumenical Perspectives* (Uppsala: Swedish Institute of Mission Research, 2008). For a condensed version, see Ruth Franzen, 'The Legacy of Ruth Rouse', *International Bulletin of Missionary Research*, Vol. 17, no. 4 (October 1993), pp. 154-58.
154. Neill's unpublished autobiography, 'Geneva and All That', p. 47.
155. Ibid., p. 48. Neill channelled much of the research on this chapter into a book that he published immediately, *Towards Church Union (1937-1952)*.
156. Neill's unpublished autobiography, 'Geneva and All That', p. 49.
157. Email message from Ruth Franzen to Dyron Daughrity, 15 May 2008.

During the work on *A History of the Ecumenical Movement*, one of the contributors, Cambridge professor Norman Sykes, asked for an increased word limit, to which Rouse readily agreed. Neill was very irked by this because it ended up being far too long. So he decided to edit the chapter down to a reasonable size and then took upon himself the responsibility of explaining to Professor Sykes why the changes were necessary. In response, Neill received 'a series of letters in which all the vials of his wrath were poured out on my unoffending head. If I had kidnapped the heir to the throne I could have hardly come in for worse.' Neill claimed he tried not to put 'too much blame on my aged and eminent colleague', but he received from Rouse 'a growl in return'.[158]

After more funding, the volume finally came to fruition and was published in 1954, perfectly timed to precede the second assembly of the WCC in Evanston, Illinois. It was dedicated to the Disciples of Christ, 'whose untiring ecumenical spirit has once again been manifest in the generous provision of the funds which have made possible the writing and publication of this *History of the Ecumenical Movement*.'[159]

Neill, however, once again, was physically obliterated. His insomnia was in full steam. He had tussled with authors and with Miss Rouse for several years now, from 1948 to 1953 (the *History* manuscript was due in March of that year). At one point during the final proofing stages, Neill exploded at Rouse, banged his fist on a table and really told her off, blaming it on 'the extremity of exhaustion to which I had been reduced, not least by her excessive demands'.[160] He desperately needed 'a complete change of scene and work', which, thankfully, arrived in a timely fashion when a group of twelve young, male theology students from the University of Geneva asked him to teach them for three weeks at a chalet in the Rhône valley. It was therapeutic for Neill, providing him with 'delirious and adolescent joy', although upon his return to Geneva he started seeing a woman psychiatrist.[161]

However, before returning to Geneva, Neill needed to escape to a place where nobody would find him. He ended up at a bed-and-breakfast converted from a farmhouse near Divonne, France, about thirteen miles from

---

158. Neill's unpublished autobiography, 'Geneva and All That', pp. 55-56.
159. Neill's unpublished autobiography, 'Geneva and All That', p. 49. Rouse and Neill, eds, *A History of the Ecumenical Movement 1517-1948*; the authors of the chapters are John Thomas McNeill, Martin Schmidt, Norman Sykes, Georges Florovsky, Don Herbert Yoder, Henry Renaud Turner Brandreth, Ruth Rouse, Kenneth Scott Latourette, Tissington Tatlow, Stephen Neill, Nils Karlström, Nils Ehrenström, Nicolas Zernov, Oliver Tomkins and Willem Adolf Visser 't Hooft.
160. Neill's unpublished autobiography, 'Geneva and All That', pp. 68-69.
161. Ibid., pp. 61-65.

Geneva. It offered freedom and paradise to Neill so he could recover from a long string of exacting work. He told his friends he would be 'somewhere in France'. He read voraciously, including Augustine's *Confessions* in Latin and 'a good deal of Dante'. He 'drank beer in little country inns' and hiked often. On Sundays he attended a little Protestant church in Drôme. After some time he moved to Troinex, outside Geneva and very close to the French border. Here again, Neill sequestered and recovered, although he was only four miles from the WCC headquarters, which caused him some stress.[162]

Neill's emotional collapse and subsequent 'deep vale of depression' lasted for eighteen months, but it finally began to break after this long period of rest. He bought a motor scooter which allowed him to tour the area and take in wonderful sites. Indeed, he took 'four journeys from Geneva to London and back and four expeditions over the Alps' on that scooter, which he lovingly named François.[163]

In September 1954 *A History of the Ecumenical Movement* was published to wide acclaim and Neill 'had no further regular appointment with the World Council'. He stuck around, however, often as a pastor to the people constantly coming and going both from the WCC as well as this international city. He lectured frequently at Bossey and wrote articles for *The Ecumenical Review*. He took a leading – though unofficial – role in integrating the International Missionary Council into the WCC, which finally happened in 1961.[164]

In the aftermath of his work on *A History of the Ecumenical Movement*, Neill did not fully recover his health and setbacks caught up to him frequently. He missed the Evanston 1954 WCC assembly because he was undergoing treatment at the Hospital for Tropical Diseases in London. However, he certainly had opinions about the assembly. In his view, it was at the Evanston assembly where the 'greatest mistake of recent ecumenical history was made', namely, that Visser 't Hooft did not resign from the position of WCC General Secretary. As a matter of fact, Visser 't Hooft stayed in position until 1966 and even after retirement remained closely connected to the WCC, continuing to exert his influence and unique power to shape it until well into the 1980s. Neill was convinced the WCC needed a new direction and new leadership and he believed 1954 was the time to do it. The old guard had done the Church a great service by bringing the WCC into being. However, it was time for the ecumenical movement to listen to fresh voices. Neill was always of the opinion that 'The World

---

162. Ibid., pp. 75-79.
163. Ibid., pp. 80-81.
164. Ibid., pp. 88-90. It should be noted that Neill was honored with an honorary DD (doctorate of divinity) in June 1961. See *The Times*, 24 June 1961, p. 2.

Council of Churches was nothing but the Student Christian Movement grown up'. There was much truth to this perception. With Visser 't Hooft in charge – he was a former YMCA and SCM man – little was going to change. Neill had almost nothing positive to say about the WCC, especially the general assemblies, during the 1950s and 1960s, precisely when Visser 't Hooft was at the helm. Neill felt that the 1968 assembly at Uppsala 'dragged itself along . . . enlivened only by the incursions and improprieties of the young, and condemned by the defects of its organisation to almost total futility'. Neill wondered whether another WCC assembly would ever be held after what he perceived to be the almost utter failure of Uppsala 1968. Clearly, Neill believed that, had the dictatorial Visser 't Hooft retired in 1954, the WCC would not have descended into the unfortunate pattern that it did. Furthermore, when Visser 't Hooft finally stepped down in 1966, his replacement – American Eugene Carson Blake – was a mere 'transitional appointment'. Indeed, according to Neill, 'a decision had not been made . . . [it] had simply been postponed'. Blake served as General Secretary until 1972, guaranteeing, in Neill's mind, that 'nothing very exciting would happen in the world of the Council'. Neill's final verdict on the WCC was that it 'failed to live up to our hopes and ideals for it'.[165]

World Christian Books . . . and More Books

Once free from that 'terrible incubus' of *A History of the Ecumenical Movement*, Neill swore he would never edit again. 'But the Lord thought otherwise' and Neill faithfully edited books for the next fifteen years.[166]

At the third International Missionary Conference at Tambaram, India, in 1938, Neill and the other attendees identified a dearth of theological books in the younger churches as being one of the most significant impediments to theological training in Africa and the East. The books used in those seminaries were of Western origin and often had very little relevance in the Global South. By the early 1950s little had changed.

In 1952 Cambridge theologian Charles Raven flew to Geneva to discuss a major book project with Neill that would provide helpful, 'reasonably simple' theological resources, in English, to the younger churches. The

---

165. Neill's unpublished autobiography, 'Geneva and All That', pp. 105-6, 112-13, 115-16. YMCA is the Young Men's Christian Association. SCM is the Student Christian Movement. Hans-Ruedi Weber said that one major contribution that Blake made was that he 'repaired many of the financial problems with the WCC. Wim [Visser 't Hooft] was not interested in money.' Weber, interview with author, 12 October 2004, Geneva.
166. Neill's unpublished autobiography, Section VII, 2, 'Of Making Many Books', p. 1.

key idea was that these texts could then be translated, without too much difficulty, into many different languages. The series would enable pastors and educated laypeople in the Global South to 'build up a library' and increase their theological knowledge. Raven thought Neill would be the perfect person to oversee such a task. Support would be provided by the IMC and publication would be provided by Lutterworth Press and the United Society for Christian Literature. Neill enthusiastically agreed to serve as General Editor as well as a frequent translator. Indeed, Neill was eager to get to work on it. A series was put together, with Professor Raven and George Appleton – the General Secretary of the Conference of British Missionary Societies – in charge. The project was to be called World Christian Books and they would publish around four per year. They were to avoid theological jargon as much as possible and use good, plain English. The texts would hover around 80 pages each (25,000 to 30,000 words) and authors from the younger churches would be particularly encouraged to contribute.[167]

---

167. Ibid., p. 2. See also 'Confidential' letter from George Appleton, Secretary of the Christian Literature Council, CBMS, 4 September 1952. The letter is entitled 'Basic Christian Books: A Tentative Plan for an International Christian Library', WCC Archives, Geneva, Box 26-18-03, IMC Archives, Christian Literature, File: World Christian Books Circulars and Advertising. The letter states that Neill would be able to devote 'two-thirds of his time during 1953, and subsequently his whole time, to some such creative task as this'. Book writers were paid a £25 honorarium. Neill wrote a similar letter in response, 'World Christian Books: Bishop Neill's Plan', 20 November 1952. By May 1962 authors for the series were from the following backgrounds: British (20 volumes), Indian (three volumes), German (five), American (six), Ceylonese (two), Italian (one), Japanese (two), Dutch (one), Canadian (one), Persian (one) and Swedish (one). By 1962 there were also already 300 translations of the books in print. In 1961 the funding for the project passed from the IMC to the WCC Commission on World Mission and Evangelism, as the IMC joined the WCC in that year. See Stephen Neill, 'World Christian Books. Newsletter No. 14', May 1962. There is conflicting data about who exactly supported WCB. In the early phases it appeared it would 'be financed jointly by the Christian Literature Council of the Conference of Missionary Societies of Great Britain and Ireland, and the Committee for World Literacy and Christian Literature of the Division of Foreign Missions of the National Council of Churches in the U.S.A., with the IMC providing funds, if necessary, for secretarial travel, such funds to be taken from the Carnahan Literature Fund'. See 'History of Project', 8 July 1953, by Glora M. Wysner. This is part of the correspondence between 'all members of the Ad Interim Committee'. Questions were directed to C.W. Ranson. On 30 March 1953 George Appleton wrote a 'Plan of Action'. Others who became involved in the correspondence are Alfred D. Moore and Norman Goodall, WCC Archives, Geneva, 26-18-03, IMC Archives, Christian Literature, Correspondence 1922-

7. Return to Europe and Ecumenical Labour: 1944-62

It should be pointed out, however, that not everyone was enthusiastic about Stephen Neill being in charge of the project. In a 'Confidential' letter from Norman Goodall (London secretary of the IMC) to Dr G.M. Wysner, on 15 October 1952, Goodall wrote:

> Despite the present fluidity of the plan, the fact remains that it crystallizes around a particular person – Stephen Neill – whose services have become available in circumstances which justify serious consideration. Neill may or may not prove to be the right man for the job. . . . [Neill is] a person whose merits and demerits are known to us. . . . You have expressed misgivings about Stephen and of course I fully understand those, and to a large extent share them. I think personally that, subject to safeguards which I will touch on, the risk is worth taking in connection with this particular proposal. . . . Do the terms of your letter signify that Neill's association with the plan will kill it from the beginning as regards the possibility of North American support?[168]

Despite serious misgivings about Neill, the final decision was that he would serve as General Editor of World Christian Books. There were other concerns, however, such as the fact that Westerners were organising a project to represent the 'Younger Churches'. The conclusion was that:

> The younger churches are not producing their own vernacular writers of basic books on theology, personal devotion, Christian conduct, etc. This series would not be a substitute for original work in the vernacular which we all want to see, but in the meantime it might help to stimulate such work as well as do a little towards filling the gap which its absence at present creates.[169]

Neill's editorship became official on 13 October 1953 at the meeting of the Executive Committee of World Christian Books at Edinburgh House, London.[170]

1965, File: Christian Literature, World Christian Books Correspondence.
168. WCC Archives, Geneva, 26-18-03, IMC Archives, Christian Literature, Correspondence 1922-1965, File: Christian Literature, World Christian Books Correspondence.
169. 'Confidential' letter from Goodall to Wysner, 15 October 1952; WCC Archives, Geneva, 26-18-03, IMC Archives, Christian Literature, Correspondence 1922-1965, File: Christian Literature, World Christian Books Correspondence.
170. Minutes of the Executive Committee, 13 October 1953, WCC Archives, Geneva, Box 26-18-03, IMC Archives, Christian Literature, File: IMC Committee on

Stephen Neill, 1953.

Neill sat down in the summer of 1953 and quickly whipped out the first volume in the series, *The Christians' God*, which promptly sold 30,000 copies in just a few years and was translated into 30 languages.[171] Neill avoided theological abstractions and stuck to biblical concepts such as 'God is light, God is life, God is love, and God is Spirit'. It was a smashing success. Neill tried to stick to *TIME* magazine's mantra, which at that time prohibited a sentence from having more than eighteen words.[172]

The next book published was *Christian Giving* by the famous south Indian bishop, V.S. Azariah, although the author had died several years before in 1945. It, too, became a big bestseller and 'has been translated into more languages than any other' book in the series. Neill wrote a brief

---

Christian Literature Minutes 1953-1960.
171. Stephen Neill, *The Christians' God* (London: Lutterworth Press, 1954). By October 1954 it had sold 21,432 copies. Second was *Christian Giving* with 17,164 copies sold. See Stephen Neill, 'World Christian Books, Newsletter No. 1', January 1956, WCC Archives, Geneva, Box 26-18-03, IMC Archives, Christian Literature, File: Christian Literature Newsletters, 1956-1965. By 30 June 1957 *The Christians' God* had sold 24,177 copies. *Christian Giving* had sold 20,990 copies by that time. See Stephen Neill, 'World Christian Books, Newsletter No. 4', September 1957. By 31 March 1961 *The Christians' God* had sold 30,901 copies and *Christian Giving* had sold 27,011. These two books remained the bestsellers, although Neill's *The Christian Character* was close on their heels. See Stephen Neill, 'World Christian Books, Newsletter No. 12', May 1961.
172. Neill's unpublished autobiography, 'Of Making Many Books', pp. 3, 11.

biography of Azariah for the book. Neill and Azariah knew each other well; they had served the Church together for many years in south India as colleagues and eventually as bishops.[173]

Next Neill approached Eduard Lohse to contribute a volume on Mark's gospel; then he commissioned Professor Reginald Fuller of Chicago to write a book on Luke's gospel. He recruited a geographer, Denis Braby, to write *Palestine and the Bible*, a book that Neill absolutely loved. He secured a Dutch scholar, Professor Hermann Ridderbos, to write a book on Matthew's gospel. Neill translated Ridderbos' book from Dutch; indeed, he translated many of the texts from their original language into English, writing, 'There were times when I wished that they would all write in French or Italian, so that I might myself make them talk the language that I thought their readers would be able to understand.'[174]

Neill wrote seven volumes for the series, including *Who Is Jesus Christ?*, written during his long vacation in 1955 while staying in an undergraduate room at his *alma mater*, Trinity College, Cambridge. His old friend, Professor C.F.D. Moule, offered feedback on each chapter. Neill wrote an excellent little book on *Paul to the Galatians* while at the Agape retreat centre that Neill frequented high in the Italian Alps. He had no books with him to rely upon other than his Greek New Testament, which suited him just fine. He also wrote a book on St John Chrysostom – *Chrysostom and his Message* – that is still quite useful for understanding this great Church Father. Between 1954 and 1963 Neill wrote seven books for the series: *The Christians' God* (number one), *The Christian Character* (number six),

---

173. Ibid., p. 4. It is interesting to note that the most important biography of Azariah was written at Neill's request. Susan Billington Harper, in her magisterial book *In the Shadow of the Mahatma: Bishop V.S. Azariah and the Travails of Christianity in British India*, writes: 'The scholar who opened my eyes to Bishop Azariah's importance was the late bishop and historian, Stephen Charles Neill. Neill challenged me shortly before he died in 1984 to fulfill his own dream of producing a critical scholarly biography of Bishop Azariah. It has been a privilege to carry out his request.' See p. xv. Neill wrote about Azariah in numerous places in his large corpus on Indian Christianity. He wrote a touching tribute to Azariah upon his death in 1945. He wrote, 'There is a prince and a great man fallen this day in Israel.' Neill described him as 'far and away the most outstanding of Indian Christians, and one of the most eminent Church leaders in the world. By sheer ability and simple Christian devotion he had risen from the poverty and obscurity of his father's country parsonage in Tinnevelly to be the first Indian Bishop of the Anglican Church . . . above all, Azariah was a man of God, and no one who met him could ever forget this.' See Stephen Tirunelveli, 'Bishop Azariah of Dornakal', *The Student Movement* (London: Student Christian Movement), Vol. 47, no. 4 (1945), p. 84.

174. Neill's unpublished autobiography, 'Of Making Many Books', pp. 4-6, 11.

Who Is Jesus Christ? (number fourteen), *Paul to the Galatians* (number 25), *What Is Man?* (number 36, published in the United States as *Man in God's Purpose*), *Chrysostom and His Message* (number 44) and *Paul to the Colossians* (number 50).[175]

Neill admitted they had trouble finding authors from the younger churches but they managed to secure a few. They had the posthumous volume from Azariah. D.T. Niles, from Sri Lanka, contributed two books to the series. Norimichi Ebizawa brought together a group of five Japanese authors to pen *Japanese Witnesses for Christ*. However, there was certainly not an abundance of non-Western authors, a striking fact considering the goals early on.[176]

Overall, Neill was pleased with how World Christian Books worked out. Eventually, 60 volumes were produced and translated into over 40 languages, including all common European languages, several Indian and African languages, Japanese, several smaller languages in Burma, Arabic, Persian and more.[177] All told, a million copies were disbursed around the world. Neill felt that, of the 60, about 20 of them could be considered 'minor masterpieces'. Over time, however, sales began to falter.[178] While the project was sponsored by the IMC and, later, the WCC (which the IMC had become part of in 1961), the budget did not allow for much advertising and World Christian Books was driven out of the market by large publishing houses.[179] Neill served as Honorary Director of the project after he began his professorship in Hamburg. John Goodwin, a close friend and colleague of Neill, took over the general editorship in October 1962.[180]

During this same era Neill spearheaded two dictionaries that were aimed at a similar audience as the World Christian Books series: *The Concise Dictionary of the Bible* and *The Concise Dictionary of the Christian*

---

175. Ibid., pp. 6-7. See also Daughrity, 'The Literary Legacy of Stephen Neill', pp. 150-54.
176. Neill's unpublished autobiography, 'Of Making Many Books', pp. 10-11.
177. See Neill, 'World Christian Books, Newsletter No. 4', September 1957, WCC Archives, Geneva, Box 26-18-03, IMC Archives, Christian Literature, File: Christian Literature Newsletters, 1956-1965.
178. Some of the accounts for World Christian Books survive. See WCC Archives, Geneva, Box: IMC Archives, Christian Literature, File: World Christian Books Minutes 1957-1961.
179. Neill's unpublished autobiography, 'Of Making Many Books', pp. 11-14. The million copies reference comes from Neill's obituary in the *Daily Telegraph*, 24 July 1984.
180. See Neill, 'World Christian Books, Newsletter No. 15', October 1962; see also 'Newsletter No. 14', May 1962, as it announces the upcoming changes, WCC Archives, Geneva, Box 26-18-03, IMC Archives, Christian Literature, File: Christian Literature Newsletters, 1956-1965.

World Mission.[181] Neill thought the first one entered a saturated market, though it was translated into several languages. The second made Neill very proud and really filled a gap in the scholarship, as its only rival – the *Encyclopedia of Missions* – had been out of print for many years. The *Concise Dictionary of the Christian World Mission* was later at the centre of a lawsuit. The co-editors of the volume were Stephen Neill, Gerald H. Anderson and John Goodwin. When the volume was translated into German, however, Neill and a German professor were the only ones listed as editors. Gerald Anderson hired a lawyer to sue the publisher and the publisher capitulated. Anderson asked that the remaining copies be printed with an apology and any future advertisements for the volume must show all three of the original editors. The publishing house paid Anderson's legal fees. Anderson approached Neill about this situation later and Neill said he was unclear about how the omission of his co-editors had happened.[182]

In the late 1950s and through the 1960s Neill wrote a number of books. These continued to escalate in sophistication when he moved into academia at the University of Hamburg in 1962. Prior to that, however, his mission was to produce good, readable books for pastors and educated laypeople. He wrote a bestseller, *Christian Faith Today*, for Penguin in 1955 that was based on some 'open lectures' he gave in 1945 at the University of Cambridge.[183] In 1957 he published *Seeing the Bible Whole*, a 'pathfinder through the jungle', intended to help people understand the Bible's general trajectory and major themes.[184] That same year he published *The Cross in the Church*, an interesting little book that delves into the meaning of that subject in some detail.[185]

Also in 1957 Neill published his chief missiological treatise, *The Unfinished Task*. Although dated and no longer in demand, it is a sophisticated analysis of the mission situation in the midst of colonial

---

181. See the initial proposals for these WCB dictionaries (to be published by Lutterworth Press) at the WCC Archives, Geneva, 26-18-03, IMC Archives, Christian Literature, Correspondence 1922-1965, File: Christian Literature, World Christian Books Correspondence. See letter from Neill to Rev. R.K. Orchard, 23 June 1959.
182. Neill's unpublished autobiography, 'Of Making Many Books', pp. 15-16. Gerald Anderson, interview with author, Port Dickson, Malaysia, 5 August 2004. Anderson stated that Neill conceived the dictionary, Anderson was joint editor and Goodwin was the manager of the project.
183. See p. 12 of this work for context of his lectures.
184. Neill's unpublished autobiography, 'Of Making Many Books', p. 23. Stephen Neill, *Seeing the Bible Whole* (London: The Bible Reading Fellowship, 1957).
185. Stephen Neill, *The Cross in the Church* (London: London Missionary Society/ Independent Press, 1957).

decline. Neill's global purview is obvious. In this text he clearly emphasises the younger churches, what he terms 'the dynamic minority'. As time has shown, however, the days of the younger churches being in the minority were numbered. Neill was one of the first to see clearly the trend of Christianity 'moving south'. *The Unfinished Task* sold well and kept Neill firmly on the missions lecture circuit for the rest of his life. It also prompted his next book, *Creative Tension* (1959), based on his Duff Lectureship of 1958. In this follow-up Neill focused his sights on missionary strategy by covering four themes: the approach to non-Christian religions, rising nationalism, the partnership of the older and younger churches and 'approach to mission'.

Bishop Stephen Neill next to U. Kyaw Than (Burma) associate general secretary of the East Asia Council and two unidentified Asian delegates. International Missionary Council Assembly, Accra, Ghana, 28 December 1957 - 8 January 1958.

During this period of tremendous literary output, Neill produced one of his best-selling books, *Anglicanism* (1958), a classic introductory text that warmly introduces the Anglican way. Many Anglicans still cut their teeth on it, which has led to many print runs and at least four editions. Neill's passionate devotion to his denomination comes through clearly in the text and he later observed, 'Of all my many books this was perhaps the one which it was easiest to write.'[186] By all accounts, it is a great book, written by one of the most Anglican of churchmen in the twentieth century. It was written in 1957 and published by Penguin the following year with hopes that the 1958 Lambeth Conference would generate some interest. Neill wrote much of the book during the summer while a guest in the home of his doctor friend, Hugh Thomlinson, in Kensington Court. He used the library at Sion College, containing 'one of the best collections of Anglican books in the world'. He wrote 2,500 words per day.[187]

---

186. Neill's unpublished autobiography, 'Of Making Many Books', p. 24.
187. Ibid., pp. 25-27.

In 1959 Neill published *A Genuinely Human Existence: Towards a Christian Psychology* with Doubleday.[188] More than any of his 70 plus books, this one seems out of place, even for Neill's rather wide-ranging corpus. Neill was no stranger to psychotherapy and he had counselled hundreds of people during his pastoral career. However, he was no expert. He did, however, read enough to make himself competent on the more recent literature and he combined that with his biblical knowledge to create a kind of Christian psychology, just as the subtitle says. Neill argued that people are all unique, so there really is no 'normal' psychology. However, the life of humanity is best epitomised in Jesus Christ – God's incarnation for the benefit of humankind. Neill realised this book was not his best work but it did minister to many: 'Quite a number of friends regard it as the most important of all my books.' Surely these were the people who knew Neill best and realised his struggles with his mental health. Oddly for Neill, the book 'never became a best seller' and it eventually went out of print. It was translated into German but, still, it never achieved a second edition, much to Neill's disappointment.[189]

In 1961 Neill's *Twentieth Century Christianity: A Survey of Modern Religious Trends by Leading Churchmen* was published.[190] This edited volume drew together significant names from across the ecumenical spectrum, including Roger Aubert, Robert Handy, Vasil Istavridis, D.T. Niles and Max Warren. It shows Neill's remarkable ability to put his finger on the pulse of Christian happenings in the world. That ability was on full display when in 1960 he launched a major, critical evaluation of the world's religions and Christianity's place in that world.

Over time Neill became something of an expert on comparative religions and at least two of his books dealt with interreligious dialogue from a Christian perspective. One was originally Neill's Moorhouse Lectures, delivered at Melbourne in 1960 and published the following year as *Christian Faith and Other Faiths: The Christian Dialogue with Other Religions*.[191] Clearly, his missionary years had equipped him for understanding the religions of India, including Islam. In these lectures, however, he covered other world religions

---

188. Neill had been thinking about a Christian psychology since at least 1949 when he first lectured on 'A Christian Approach to Psychology' for the Guild of Pastoral Psychology, which published it as Guild Lecture No. 62 (London: Proberts Printers Ltd, 1949).
189. Neill's unpublished autobiography, 'Of Making Many Books', pp. 33-37. In Switzerland Neill often attended the British clinic, in the Montana municipality, for psychotherapy.
190. Stephen Neill, ed., *Twentieth Century Christianity: A Survey of Modern Religious Trends by Leading Churchmen* (London: Collins, 1961).
191. This book was revised and published again in 1984, just weeks before Neill's death, under the title *Crises of Belief*.

as well, for which he had undertaken new, extensive study. He was no doubt assisted by his passion for taking on new subjects, mixed with chronic insomnia and his lifelong state of bachelorhood. His discussions of the world's religions are sympathetic and thoughtful, rather than apologetic. Neill's timing for this book was prescient; he had a remarkable ability to anticipate the next hot topic and the book sold very well: 'a reprint was called for within a year of publication'. It was used widely in seminaries and departments of religion and helped to pave the way for his professorship in Kenya in 1969 when he established a department of religious studies. He became one of the early proponents of a Christian model for interreligious dialogue.[192]

Years later, Neill's second major work on interreligious dialogue appeared, *Salvation Tomorrow* (1976), which had a more missiological focus. It was based on Neill's Chavasse Lectures at Wycliffe Hall, Oxford. To understand this book best, the theme of the fifth assembly of the WCC, at Nairobi in 1975, should be kept in mind: 'Confessing Christ Today'. Neill's ability to speak about interreligious dialogue, missions and ecumenism in a unified manner is striking. He made his thesis explicit in the subtitle: *The Originality of Jesus Christ and the World's Religions*. Neill's Christology remained firm – some would say uncompromising – until the end of his life. This belief was explicitly reinforced in 1984, the year of his death, when *The Supremacy of Jesus* was published. Neill's profound commitment to Jesus Christ was evident in his final declaration that Jesus was, in his view, 'The Central Point of History'.[193]

In 1962 Neill was invited to deliver the Firth Lectures at the University of Nottingham. His topic was the New Testament, Neill's 'first field of expert theological study'. To prepare, Neill 'pulled together much that I had read and thought about all that had happened in the field of New Testament study in the century between 1861 and 1961'. He chose 1861 because that was the year that J.B. Lightfoot was promoted to the Hulsean professorship at Cambridge, a pivotal moment in the history of biblical criticism according to Neill. He chose 1961 because it was the last full year on record.[194]

Neill's admiration for and acquaintance with the New Testament was sincere and profound. In his unpublished autobiography, he wrote:

> No book in history has ever been torn apart, dissected, weighed and studied from every conceivable angle as has the New Testament over the last 150 years. There have been many blind alleys; many theories confidently put forward have had to be abandoned or

---

192. Neill's unpublished autobiography, 'Of Making Many Books', p. 40.
193. This is the title of the Introduction; see also p. 155.
194. Neill's unpublished autobiography, 'Of Making Many Books', pp. 40-41.

radically modified when the glamour of newness has been replaced by the sobriety of mature consideration. But almost every great mind that has busied itself with this most important of all studies had made some contribution to knowledge and understanding, and even those who have been wrong at almost every point have at times made a contribution by stimulating those who knew that they were wrong but could not immediately say why.[195]

However, his book 'committed the unpardonable fault of criticising the Germans – this is just not allowed' and, as a result, was not translated into the language. Neill did respect German scholarship but he held the 'increasingly important' contributions of the Americans, the scholarship of Britain and Roman Catholic scholarship in nearly equally high esteem. The result was a masterpiece, *The Interpretation of the New Testament: 1861-1961*, and was used as an introduction to New Testament criticism for many years, and even still reads quite well.[196]

For a person who wrote so many books, Neill has repeatedly stated that he disliked writing them. To write well requires a heavy time commitment, an exacting schedule, an exhausting level of concentration and endless re-reading. Of the enterprise of making books, Neill wrote:

By the time that the printed copies of a book reach me, I have usually lost interest in it, and have no particular desire to look again at what I have said. . . . When a book is done, I like to let it go. . . . I have very little awareness of what happens to my books after they have been published. . . . While writing I am very conscious of potential readers . . . eager to carry the reader along with me. But when the book is published, this sense of contact ceases.[197]

The Aeroplane and the Ecumenical Movement

'One of these days someone will write a doctoral dissertation on "The Aeroplane and the Ecumenical Movement".'[198] Air travel's popularity was ascending just as Neill's star was rising in the ecumenical world. Aeroplanes took him to the far reaches of the world and made him one of the early examples of a true 'world Christian'. Neill was somebody who understood well the booming indigenous churches of sub-Sahara, the ancient Thomas

---

195. Ibid., p. 43.
196. Ibid., pp. 44-46.
197. Ibid., pp. 62-63.
198. Neill's unpublished autobiography, Section VII, 3, 'In Journeys Oft', p. 65.

Christians of India, the emptying cathedrals of Western Europe and the hillside village gatherings of South Americans. He was everywhere. He loved travelling and, even more, he loved the opportunity to learn, to preach and to teach anywhere in the world. He made thousands of friends along the way. However, there were obvious downsides to the post-war proliferation of ecumenical globetrotting:

> Far too many people are travelling for far too few reasons. The movement has produced a generation of ecumenical experts, always on the move, hurrying from conference to conference at which nothing will be decided, halting briefly by the way, disrupting the routine of their hosts, delivering everywhere the same dull speeches, never staying anywhere long enough to gather more than superficial impressions of delicate situations, and gradually becoming unemployable in any settled form of existence.[199]

Stephen Neill was one of those travellers but somehow managed to exclude his own endless itineraries from the preceding critique.

For Neill, travelling was a joy partly because it enabled him to get things done. On one eleven-hour bus ride from Durban to Umtata (Mthatha) he had the time to 'not merely see a great deal of the country, but also to ponder all my sins, to pray for all my friends, to prepare several lectures, and to engage in some discursive meditation'.[200] He used his time wisely and, having travelled to 66 countries by the time he was 72 – that number increased 'considerably' in his final twelve years – Neill became quite an expert. He bundled tasks together to make the most of a journey, learned much about the Church in a particular region, always made time for old friends and he welcomed down time when he could read and write.[201] Indeed, at one point Neill expressed his near-religious passion for travel:

> I will admit unashamedly that I love travel – to see new scenes, to see places which I have long known in the imagination but had never before visited, to renew contacts with old friends and to make new ones, and especially to be drawn so easily into the fellowship of people of entirely different race and background, where oneness in Christ makes all differences fade into insignificance and the fellowship of the Spirit rules over all.[202]

---

199. Ibid., p. 65.
200. Ibid., pp. 65-66.
201. Ibid., p. 67.
202. Ibid., p. 132.

7. Return to Europe and Ecumenical Labour: 1944-62 257

For Neill, travel revealed the ecumenical nature of Christ's church and engaging with Christians globally provided unique insight into God's vast work building His kingdom.

Perhaps the most common reason for Neill's unceasing travels was to deliver important lectures, such as the Carnaham Lectures in Buenos Aires in July 1958. The Carnaham Lectures were published in 1960 as *Christian Holiness*.[203] Neill always made time for detours that could add to his understanding of the worldwide church; thus, on this occasion, he stopped off in the 'beautiful city of Bogota', the 'dazzling city of Lima', the 'astonishing city' of Santiago de Chile. While breath-taking in their natural environs, the architecture of Latin American capital cities reminded him of 'German cities half repaired after the devastation'. Neill viewed Latin America as a 'Continent of endless problems but also of hope and promise'.[204]

After lecturing in Argentina, Neill travelled to Venezuela, Puerto Rico, Cuba and, finally, Mexico City. Since the vast majority of Latin Americans are Roman Catholic, Neill often felt the seminaries and churches he visited seemed somewhat abandoned and lonely. Neill sensed this from the students and he felt it himself, especially while in Mexico. His sense was that virtually all of the teachers in these seminaries were working at other jobs and only fitted their seminary work in where they could, just here and there.[205]

Neill noticed the 'thrust of the Pentecostal Church' all over Latin America. He had encountered its great ability to work amongst the most depressed classes while he was a missionary in India. Neill realised that it was accomplishing great things among similarly disenfranchised people in Latin America. Indeed, the Pentecostal Church had instigated a 'social revolution': it persuaded people to stop drinking alcohol, save their money instead of wasting it and send their children to school, thereby producing 'a sober, diligent, thrifty and educated Protestant middle class'. Just a few years after Neill visited Latin America, some Pentecostal churches from the Continent were admitted into the WCC.[206]

---

203. In Britain the lectures were published by Lutterworth Press. As often the case, an American company published the work for North American audiences. In this case it was Harper and Brothers in New York. The book was published in both Spanish and English. See Neill's unpublished autobiography, 'In Journeys Oft', pp. 79, 86. Yet another example of prestigious lectures gave were the Gallagher Memorial Lectures in 1967, which were published as *Ecumenism: Light and Shade* (Toronto: Ryerson Press, 1969).
204. Neill's unpublished autobiography, 'In Journeys Oft', pp. 72-73, 75.
205. Ibid., pp. 84-85.
206. Ibid., p. 76.

Neill found Latin American Protestants, or 'Evangelicos' as they are known there, as being rather 'anti-ecumenical', particularly in Brazil. He reasoned this was because of American missionaries and their preoccupation with all things being categorised as either 'liberal' or 'conservative'. The conservative Protestants planted a fundamentalist kind of Christianity in Latin America that did not lend itself to the worldwide ecumenical consciousness that was developing. 'Anything that could by any stretch of the imagination be called "liberal" was immediately suspect as destructive to the faith.'[207]

Neill's 1958 three-month-long Latin American journey ended with him stopping for rest at the Episcopal seminary in Austin, Texas, where he was a guest on several occasions. He spent his time returning correspondence, writing articles for various publications and devouring the French version of Teilhard de Chardin's *The Phenomenon of Man*.[208]

Mission to Students

Neill had a 'good deal of experience' conducting missions to students during the years covered in this chapter, 1944 to 1962. He saw himself in the tradition of Dwight L. Moody and William Temple, who had made tremendous impacts on the student bodies of Cambridge and Oxford in the nineteenth and twentieth centuries, respectively.[209]

In January 1947 Neill was living in Cambridge, still recovering from the trauma of severance from Tinnevelly, teaching and doing chaplaincy work at Trinity College.[210] Although England was home to him, it had changed markedly in the twenty years he had been away, especially the youth culture. He was invited to conduct a mission at the University of Oxford, for eight evenings, from Sunday to Sunday. This was a big deal. On 1 February 1947 *The Times* publicised the event:

> From to-morrow until February 9 the Rt. Rev. Stephen Neill, late Bishop of Tinnevelly and now special assistant to the Archbishop of Canterbury, will conduct a mission in the University of Oxford. At 8.15 p.m. each evening (except February 9, at St Mary's Church) there will be a mission meeting in the Sheldonian Theatre at which Bishop Neill will give the address. He will be helped by almost 40 assistant missioners.[211]

---

207. Ibid., p. 79.
208. Ibid., p. 86.
209. Neill's unpublished autobiography, Section VII, 4, 'Among the Students', pp. 133-34.
210. An extract from the *Toronto Globe*, 12 July 1947, stated Neill was 'of Trinity College, Cambridge' while he was attending the IMC conference in Whitby.
211. *The Times*, 1 February 1947, p. 6.

7. Return to Europe and Ecumenical Labour: 1944-62 259

These were not church services; rather, they were aimed at non-Christians, with the hope that Christian students would turn out and provide much needed support for the lectures. There would be no worship, hymns or prayers. Neill had no idea whether anyone would show up from 'this strange and unknown audience'. As a Cambridge man, he knew little about the Oxford campus culture. Nevertheless, he accepted the invitation. When the time came, he nervously took the podium, only to realise this was not an ordinary audience of university students:

> [M]ost of the men and women were older than the average since so many of them had come back from unimagined strains in far parts of the warring world, tired, disillusioned, perplexed, yet not unwilling to think, to believe that there might be a better way. . . . I knew in that moment that we should be friends.

The first night a full thousand students turned out. By the final evening that number was up to 1600 and the top administrators even took their seats to witness what was happening. Neill was in his element, 'enjoying every minute'. He credited the success of the mission to the prayers of those who planned it.[212]

In no time Neill was on an aeroplane headed to the University of Toronto to conduct a similar campaign on a similarly sized, but very different, audience. Neill wrote, 'I have always got on extremely well with Canadian students; less brash than Americans, they are simpler and more straightforward in their reactions than the British.' As usual, Neill charmed and impressed but his favourite aspect of university work was always meeting with students in smaller groups around a dinner table: 'Nothing in the world gives me greater pleasure than a face-to-face encounter of this kind with the young.'[213]

The word was now out. Neill was an excellent speaker for this kind of venue and he promptly received an invitation from Americans to do a kind of one-month university mission tour to Yale, Harvard, Princeton and the University of California. While he knew something of the Ivy League universities – all very different from each other – California was 'simply an unknown jungle'.[214]

The Yale mission went off without incident. It was successful and began a long-standing relationship between Neill and that great university in New Haven, Connecticut. Neill's visit to Harvard was different. For one thing, Neill's invitation to Yale was for five days, but Harvard only wanted him for

---
212. Neill's unpublished autobiography, 'Among the Students', pp. 137-40.
213. Ibid., pp. 142-45.
214. Ibid., p. 150.

two and a half days. Neill found the audience at Harvard to be smaller in number – around 300 – but extremely attentive. Neill was most impressed by Princeton, 'the best teaching system of any University in the States'.[215]

Finally, after a thirteen-hour flight across the Continent, Neill arrived at the University of California at Berkeley, 'with its 22,000 students, brash, gay and adventurous and not as revolutionary as it has since become'. It was 'as different as could be imagined from the sober Ivy League universities, with their almost British traditions'. At Berkeley, Neill was formally prepped for what he might encounter:

> I was told that many students would come, but that if they did not like the speaker, they would just get up and walk out; and that if I went on till the clock struck twelve, they would all get up and go, and neither the President of the University nor the President of the United States could stop them. The meeting had been sponsored by the Interfaith Committee of Catholics, Protestants and Jews, and nothing must be said to offend any of them.[216]

Neill found the situation nearly impossible as, 'There is a state law against religious propaganda on the campus. And then one is invited to get up and preach the Gospel.' Nevertheless, nearly 6,000 students turned up; 'I suppose the largest audience I have ever addressed.' However, 'fervent appeals for surrender and conversion' simply did not happen, as it did in Toronto.[217]

Neill spoke at many other colleges in the United States over the years, such as Carleton College in Minnesota and Westmont College in California – 'one of the most beautiful places it has ever been my good fortune to visit'.[218] On one tour he spoke at Smith College – a women's college, Amherst College and Williams College, all in Massachusetts.[219] When giving the Moorhouse Lectures in 1960 in Melbourne, he spoke at three Australian universities and encountered 'callow but extraordinarily open-hearted students'. These were all opportunities for Neill to share the Gospel with young adults but also to learn something about university life outside Europe. For instance, he wrote, 'Why is it that all over the States music is so superbly excellent, leaving the greater part of Britain standing far out in the cold?'[220] During a mission to Colorado, Neill spoke at Colorado College in Colorado Springs,

---

215. Ibid., pp. 150-57.
216. Ibid., pp. 152-58B.
217. Ibid., pp. 158-60.
218. Ibid., p. 155.
219. Ibid., p. 161.
220. Ibid., pp. 162-64, 168.

7. Return to Europe and Ecumenical Labour: 1944-62

at the University of Denver and at the University of Colorado-Boulder. On one of these occasions he debated with an agnostic professor of philosophy who was considered 'the local champion of unbelief'. Neill was unprepared for the format as the agnostic ripped into religion for nearly half an hour. Neill claimed he actually lost his temper he was so irritated but he managed to rebound, to preach the Gospel and all worked out in the end with a warm handshake between the two men.[221]

In 1954 one Disciples of Christ school in Missouri – Culver-Stockton College – presented Neill with an honorary doctorate for his *History of the Ecumenical Movement*. Neill was particularly impressed by the students there: there were no hippies, they were unpretentious and they were eager to welcome a foreigner like him. Neill was surprised to learn that few of them had ever seen the ocean. However, he declared, 'This is the America in which elections are determined, and it is vitally important that those who are not Americans should understand something of this [small, church-affiliated down-to-earth college] world.'[222]

Neill came to understand and appreciate the small liberal arts colleges that dot the American landscape: 'The best of them are very good indeed.' They provide an intimacy that the mammoth institutions simply cannot. Many of them have truly great professors who resist the pull and higher salaries of the research schools. The students at these small colleges are fortunate, as, perhaps a little surprisingly, they provide 'some of the best education in the world'.[223]

Neill's university missions were not limited to the Western world, either. One of his most successful was to Makerere University College in Uganda, a place to which he would return time and again. These missions set up the scene for the remaining years of Neill's life, as he was employed by universities from 1962 until his death in 1984.[224]

During the 1940s, 1950s and 1960s Neill became a mainstay on the university scene. At heart, he was an evangelist. It must be remembered that he had lost his missionary career in India and the university missions met a very deeply felt need within him. However, they were not all successful. He wrote, 'Out of every ten University missions, seven are in reality failures.' He felt that his mission to the University of New Brunswick in 1961 was a complete failure and that the universities of North Dakota and of Texas at Austin were unhealthy places for a mission because of the jealous denominationalism of the Christian scene.[225]

---

221. Ibid., pp. 172-74.
222. Ibid., pp. 174-76.
223. Ibid., pp. 178-79.
224. Ibid., p. 180.
225. Ibid., pp. 185-88.

Overall, however, Neill thought the university missions were an important enterprise and he was happy he spent so much of his life invested in them. In 1973 he wrote:

> I am inclined to think that the University mission is not yet played out; and that, given the right ideas as to what is to be achieved, the necessary measure of careful preparation, and a speaker who knows how to get on the wave-length of his hearers, there are still useful jobs to be done.[226]

Indeed, Neill's university work was about to begin in a full-time capacity, as he had decided to take a professorship at the University of Hamburg.[227]

Conclusion

The years 1944 to 1962 were extremely productive for Neill but they were also turbulent, as he held numerous positions, took on a hodge-podge of different jobs, wrote many books on various topics and travelled all over the world – literally – to deliver lectures and investigate what was happening in the world church. It would be an extremely impressive array of accomplishments for anybody but, ultimately, it can be seen as being somewhat sad, as this most competent and gifted person fought constantly with his demons. His breakdowns of health, both mental and physical, were frequent and occasionally severe. Neill's brilliance and talents seemed to be matched with an equal propensity to hit rock bottom in his personal life as well as in his mental health.

One thing was certain, however. Neill was a gifted scholar. Trinity College, Toronto, recognised his gifts by awarding him Honorary Doctor of Divinity in 1950. The University of Hamburg awarded him Honorary Doctor of Theology in 1957. The University of Glasgow awarded him Honorary Doctor of Divinity in 1961.[228]

Neill's publications during these years are so numerous that they are difficult to keep up with. He published at least 28 books during this eighteen-year period of his life:

---

226. Ibid., p. 195.
227. Neill was acquainted with the University of Hamburg; he had served as 'Visiting Professor of Missiology' at some point during part of the 1956-57 academic year. See Neill's entry, *Crockford's Clerical Directory, 1965-66*.
228. Additionally, the University of Uppsala awarded him Honorary Doctor of Theology in 1965. *Crockford's Clerical Directory, 1965-66*. This honorary doctorate was also mentioned in *The Times*, 24 June 1961, p. 2.

7. Return to Europe and Ecumenical Labour: 1944-62

1944– *The Wrath and Peace of God and Other Studies: Addresses Delivered at the Nilgiri Missionary Conventions May 1942* (Madras: Christian Literature Society for India)
1944 – *The Challenge of Jesus Christ: Addresses Delivered in the Cathedral of the Resurrection, Lahore, April 18-25, 1943* (Madras: SPCK in India)
1948 – *Christ, His Church and His World* (London: Eyre & Spottiswoode)
1948 – *The Cross Over Asia* (London: Canterbury Press)
1952 – *On the Ministry* (London: SCM Press); published in the United States as *Fulfill Thy Ministry* (New York: Harper and Brothers, 1952)
1952 – *Christian Partnership* (London: SCM Press)
1952 – *Towards Church Union (1937-1952)* (London: SCM Press)
1952 – *The Christian Society* (London: Nisbet)
1954 – *The Christians' God* (London: Lutterworth Press)
1954 – *A History of the Ecumenical Movement 1517-1948* (London: SPCK)
1954 – *Under Three Flags* (New York: Friendship Press)
1955 – *The Christian Character* (London: Lutterworth Press); published in the United States as *The Difference in Being a Christian* (New York: Association Press, 1955)
1955 – *Christian Faith Today* (Harmondsworth: Penguin)
1956 – *Who Is Jesus Christ?* (London: Lutterworth Press)
1957 – *The Cross in the Church* (London: Independent Press)
1957 – *Seeing the Bible Whole* (London: The Bible Reading Fellowship)
1957 – *The Unfinished Task* (London: Lutterworth Press)
1958 – *Paul to the Galatians* (London: Lutterworth Press)
1958 – *Christian Affirmations in a Secular Age*, trans. by Neill, written by Giovanni Miegge (New York: Oxford University Press)
1958 – *Anglicanism* (Harmondsworth: Penguin)
1959 – *A Genuinely Human Existence: Towards a Christian Psychology* (New York: Doubleday)
1959 – *Creative Tension* (London: Edinburgh House)
1960 – *What is Man?* (London: Lutterworth Press); published in the United States as *Man in God's Purpose* (New York: Association Press, 1961)
1960 – *Christian Holiness* (New York: Harper and Brothers)
1960 – *Brothers of the Faith: The Story of Men Who Have Worked for Christian Unity* (New York: Abingdon)
1961 – *Christian Faith and Other Faiths: The Christian Dialogue with Other Religions* (London: Oxford University Press)
1961 – *Twentieth Century Christianity* (London: Collins)
1962 – *Chrysostom and His Message* (London: Lutterworth Press)

Neill's articles and reviews during this period of his life are virtually impossible to track down in any complete or systematic way. Neill was an incessant writer during these years, contributing to dozens of journals, papers and projects.

Over these same years Neill was also invited to give many prestigious lectures at Oxford, Cambridge, Dublin, Buenos Aires and Melbourne. His sermons all over the world will never be fully known, as there were countless of them, many lost to history.[229] Neill mentored many younger men during these years, many who went on to great accomplishments, such as Tullio Vinay, Hans-Ruedi Weber, and David Barrett – the celebrated author of the *World Christian Encyclopedia*.[230]

The famous Persian bishop Hassan Barnaba Dehqani-Tafti spoke glowingly of Neill's mentorship and timely pastoral care, which began in 1947 at a youth conference in Oslo:

> I've had an up-and-down life. The right person always appeared. If I had not met Neill, I don't know what would have happened. I had psychological issues. Neill was the only one who understood me. I was almost broken. Neill made me one person again. He was a father figure to me.[231]

In his autobiography, Dehqani-Tafti discusses Neill's words of wisdom which he preserved from one of Neill's letters to him:

> God does not waste His material: if He gives a special vocation of suffering He gives a special reward in special opportunities of service. I think some men have to fight against these temptations to despair all their lives, but if they are sure that God is leading them all the time they win through. Others are set free from them completely. . . . Yes! Everyone in the world needs to be broken-hearted at some time or other – with some it comes before

---

229. For example, Neill preached four times for the Chicago Sunday Evening Club, in 1950, 1956, 1961 and 1962. In email correspondence from a representative, the club let me know that it does not have the manuscripts for those sermons. Email message from CSEC Mailbox to author, 7 October 2003.
230. On Neill's mentorship of Barrett, see Gina Zurlo, 'The Legacy of David B. Barrett', *International Bulletin of Mission Research*, Vol. 42, no. 1 (2018), pp. 29-39.
231. Bishop Hassan Dehqani-Tafti, telephone interview with author, 27 June 2007. The famous scholar of Islam, Kenneth Cragg, said, 'Dehqani was a recipient of Neill's spiritual discipline.' Cragg described Neill and Dehqani-Tafti's relationship as like 'an uncle and nephew'. Kenneth Cragg, interview with author, 26 June 2007, Oxford.

> conversion, with others after but no Christian can escape this experience. . . . Never make any promise. Simply say to yourself each day: 'Now today, if I am faithful to God and trust Him, He will keep me from evil.' We can't live more than one day at a time.[232]

Bishop Dehqani-Tafti said that, during his deep distress, Neill recommended reading Psalms and Job in his mother tongue, Persian. Neill had a very calming presence for the bishop. He wrote:

> Recalling those vital meetings now, I do not remember Bishop Neill saying anything that someone else could not have said. The crucial factor in my whole experience stemmed, I am sure, from who he was: the grace, wisdom and gentleness of his whole persona. He had a brilliant mind, excelling in all things academic. . . . Yet this great man's generous openness to me was, for me, a soul-transforming example of pastoral self-giving, for which I am eternally grateful to God. He took me beyond all my sadness, hidden grief and into an acceptance of my life and vocation.[233]

Perhaps, as Bishop Dehqani-Tafti notes, anyone could have given him this sage advice but Neill had lived much of his life at the point of despair. Timothy Yates, who knew Neill, noted that Neill's 'great turmoil, very great physical and psychological difficulties . . . led him at times to the brink of suicide via insomnia and depression, the kind of personal cost known often to the superbly gifted and creative'.[234]

Jolyon Mitchell rightly pointed out that Neill often used 'euphemisms to avoid embarrassment' when discussing his intense periods of crippling depression. In order to express his own pain and inner turmoil, Neill masterfully researched the great authors on this topic – Kierkegaard and Dante – and used them 'as windows onto his own feelings'. This deep soul-searching culminated in one of Neill's most important books, *A Genuinely Human Existence*, a book that shows how Neill tried to integrate modern psychology into his Christian worldview. Indeed, that book was 'an attempt to come to terms with his own shadows'.[235]

---

232. H.B. Dehqani-Tafti, *The Unfolding Design of My World: A Pilgrim in Exile* (Norwich: Canterbury Press, 2000), pp. 118-19.
233. Ibid., pp. 119-23.
234. Yates, 'Stephen Neill: Some Aspects of a Theological Legacy', p. 161.
235. Neill, 'Søren Kierkegaard: Part I', pp. 165-71 and 'Søren Kierkegaard: Part II', pp. 191-98. See Mitchell, 'Stephen Neill: A Traditional Communicator in an Age of Revolution', pp. 143-47.

Chapter Eight
A Professorship in Hamburg: 1962-68

It has been argued that Neill's long years in Geneva can be defined by three primary roles: ecumenist, writer and apologist – a defender of the faith to his many audiences.[1] That may well be, and Neill certainly continued serving in all three of these roles to varying degrees for the remainder of his life. However, in 1962 he turned over a new leaf by moving to Hamburg to work as a university professor, specifically as an historian.

Called to Hamburg

Neill loved the city of Hamburg, calling it 'a very great and a very proud city' because of its magnificent Hanseatic League heritage; it was part of a confederation of guilds that controlled the trade of modern Europe from the twelfth to the sixteenth centuries. It dominated both the North Sea as well as the Baltic and became a cosmopolitan, open-minded place.[2]

Neill first visited Hamburg in 1947, around the time he attended the Oslo youth conference, where he was the main speaker. In those days he was still serving as the Assistant Bishop to the Archbishop of Canterbury. Some

---
1. See Mitchell, 'Stephen Neill: A Traditional Communicator in an Age of Revolution', p. 160.
2. Neill's unpublished autobiography, Section IX, 'Professor in Germany', p. 35.

of what Neill observed in post-war Germany made a lifelong impression on him. The people were 'pale, undernourished, and ill-clothed'. There were thousands of refugees there. He recorded:

> Driving through these broken towns, we could not help wondering whether even the Germans, with their noted diligence, would ever be able to put them together again. Even three years after the end of the war, homeless and parentless children were still living in the bunkers, disorderly, apparently unassimilable, and keeping themselves alive by stealing. . . . The devastation was terrible. Whole blocks of houses had simply disappeared and were represented simply by piles of rubbish in the street. . . . And yet about these people there was an unmistakable sense of determination. Now the time had come to build.

Hamburg had been badly damaged by sustained British bombing because the city's port had been home to the deadly German submarine force, and the post-war occupying forces were there to ensure 'nothing like this would ever be allowed again'.[3]

Over the years, Neill returned to Germany often and he noticed what has been dubbed 'the German miracle', which was a period full of rapid progress and quick recovery from massive destruction. Neill wrote, 'If that first post-war generation had not worked its fingers to the bone, its children and grandchildren would not have had the wonderful country which they have inherited today.'[4]

Always a student, Neill grappled seriously with the years leading up to World War II and, as an historian, he understood Hitler's rise, all the hope and rebuilding that came with it. Hitler represented a Germany that was regaining its confidence after a humiliating defeat in World War I. 'It was not long however before doubts began to arise. The horror of the concentration camps began to be known, but not by any means to the whole of the German population.' It soon became clear to the members of the Confessing Church that what Hitler was doing had absolutely nothing to do with the Christian Gospel, and some church leaders like Bonhoeffer began to catch on. Unfortunately, around a third of the Protestant clergy came to accept the Aryan myth and around half of them remained in 'a confused and rather unhappy state, believing that loyalty to Hitler and loyalty to Christ were not necessarily in conflict with one another'. Most of the Roman Catholic priests 'just went along', but there were some courageous Catholics

---

3. Ibid., pp. 8-9, 19. See also Neill, *God's Apprentice*, p. 240.
4. Neill's unpublished autobiography, 'Professor in Germany', pp. 19-20.

who stood up for right.[5] Neill's understanding of the German Church during Hitler's Third Reich went this way: 'The German Christians were rather like liberals in England, committed to the basic truths of Christianity, yet aware that the expression of these truths must vary from age to age, and that the possibility of new sources of revelation is not to be denied.'

Neill's cards are shown in this comment regarding biblical interpretation. This comment also shows his anti-Bultmann bias. Bultmann's demythologisation was all the rage in Germany from the early 1940s to the 1970s, and Neill had grave misgivings with it, for example, when he asked, 'What is the preacher to say, if he is called to preach on Ascension Day?'[6]

There was another option to Bultmann, however. It was Martin Niemöller, the 'former submarine commander turned pastor', who was uncompromising in his opposition to Hitler and spent nearly a decade in a concentration camp because of it. Neill admired the famous pastor but felt him to be a *Krisemann* – one who is only at home in a crisis and, if no crisis exists, he is rather inclined to create one. On one occasion Neill proposed the idea that the WCC build a major ecumenical centre in West Germany but Niemöller opposed the idea, effectively killing it, on the premise that he refused to see West Germany become a colonial territory. Neill thought Niemöller's decision was a huge mistake as it caused the West German Church to turn inward, rather than looking outward towards greater ecumenical cooperation.[7]

Not only was Neill familiar with the city of Hamburg prior to moving there in 1962, he was already quite acquainted with the university, as he had served there as Visiting Professor of Missiology during the 1956-57 academic year, filling in for missions professor Walter Freytag.[8]

It is interesting how Neill fell into that temporary position. He was invited to speak in Hamburg. While there, he paid a visit to Freytag and during the conversation Freytag announced, unexpectedly, that he had been asked to tour many mission points all around the world on behalf of several missionary societies, similar to Neill's work in Asia and Africa in 1948 and

---

5. Ibid., pp. 21-22.
6. Ibid., pp. 11, 22. Bultmann argued that as modern people we need not accept the highly spiritual and miraculous world of the New Testament. His central claim was that the myths – in his reading so common in the New Testament – should be examined from a modern perspective and 'demythologized'. In other words, *meaning* should be sought from New Testament texts rather than a straight acceptance of the texts as scientifically or historically accurate. Neill was not a fundamentalist, but he certainly took the worldview and the claims in the New Testament more literally than Bultmann did.
7. Ibid., pp. 22-24.
8. See Neill's entry, *Crockford's Clerical Directory, 1965-66*.

8. A Professorship in Hamburg: 1962-68 269

1950. Freytag asked Neill, 'Would you like to come and replace me here for a semester?' Neill was surprised, partly because he did not think his German was good enough. Freytag reassured him and set Neill's temporary appointment into motion. Later in the year the dean of the faculty wrote to Neill, asking 'Are you coming?' Neill found no reason not to and thus, 'The die was cast; against my expectation and against my will, I was to become a German professor.'[9] Thus, Neill served as Visiting Professor of Missiology at the University of Hamburg from November 1956 to February 1957. During that semester he utilised his already stellar linguistic skills, became a polished speaker of the German language and never looked back.

For that four-month period Neill stayed in the mission house on Mittelweg – the perfect location for an Anglican bishop who taught the *via media*. He was housed in the same building as the Freytags, who were kind and generous to him and helped him learn the ropes. Professor Freytag's younger son, Justus, befriended Neill and they went for beer weekly. Neill was given Freytag's office as well as the services of the secretary, Fräulein Ebert, who was brilliantly helpful.[10]

In an interview in the year 2000 Justus confirmed that Neill stayed with them during that semester. Justus said he spent a lot of time with Neill and attended his lectures. He said Neill struggled as a teacher, however:

> Neill had difficulty understanding the German 'scene'. He struggled with the 'seminar' approach and couldn't quite figure out how the students thought. He wanted feedback from me on how he was teaching. He taught in German but used English texts. This was difficult for his students. He wouldn't change it, though.[11]

Justus remembered Neill teaching 'turbulent and volatile' topics in that semester, such as 'liberation, revolution and anti-colonialism'. However, when Neill came back to Hamburg in the 1960s for a full-time appointment, he focused more on interreligious dialogue and Christianity's relationship to other religions. Neill confirmed as much in his autobiography.[12]

During Neill's 1956-57 appointment he taught an English class that was well attended. It should be noted that English was not well entrenched in West Germany at the time. Neill quickly recognised that, while a few of

---

9. Neill's unpublished autobiography, 'Professor in Germany', p. 35.
10. Ibid., pp. 36-37. For 'four months', see p. 53. Justus was a sociology postgraduate student during most of the time of Neill's Hamburg professorship.
11. Justus Freytag, interview with author, 2 October 2000, Hamburg.
12. Freytag, interview with author, 2 October 2000. Neill's unpublished autobiography, 'Professor in Germany', p. 63.

his colleagues could read English, none of them could speak it readily. He was also surprised to learn that the students, and much of the faculty, were almost completely oblivious to the scholarship taking place outside the German world. Indeed, West Germany had some important scholars at the time, particularly in the field of biblical studies, such as Ernst Käsemann and Joachim Jeremias. However, in Neill's view, 'The years of isolation had resulted in woeful ignorance of anything outside the limits of German theology.' They had heard of Reinhold Niebuhr, but more for his political views than his theology.[13]

In addition to English, Neill taught a class in German on the Epistle to the Hebrews that he felt did not go well. He lectured through his book *The Unfinished Task* that was published in 1957 in English but did not appear in German until a few years later.[14] It is a somewhat scholarly book on what the Church must do to move closer to worldwide evangelisation. Neill also led a seminar each week – it happened to be his favourite class – that dealt with one of his specialities: the global history of church unity movements. This last class had sixteen students in it. Finally, Neill led a seminar for the faculty that dealt with 'the problem of episcopacy', although Neill would have had very little to offer that was problematic about the institution.[15]

While at Hamburg in 1956-57 Neill also had the opportunity to meet Helmut Thielicke, Hamburg's most famous theologian. Although he was somewhat under-appreciated in West German theological circles, his sermons made him well known in the English-speaking world. Later on, in 1962, Thielicke published his extraordinarily successful book, *A Little Exercise for Young Theologians*. That book hit the English market just as Neill joined the faculty on a more permanent basis. Neill thought highly of Thielicke for a variety of reasons: he was a 'really great preacher', he spoke with great clarity and precision, he was extremely well-read, he was in touch with current events and he dressed handsomely – as opposed to the stereotypical, slovenly-dressed German professor. Thielicke preached each Saturday at 5 p.m. in St Michael's Church to a packed house of 2,000 attendees. These sermons fascinated Neill, as they were marvellously delivered and would last exactly 52 minutes each time. Despite some of the tall tales that were told, Neill, nevertheless, was thoroughly impressed by them.[16]

One issue that Neill noted amongst the students, in particular, was their preference to Bultmann over Barth. While Barth seemed to be the theological giant of a previous era, Bultmann was read with great enthusiasm among

---

13. Ibid., pp. 44, 48.
14. Neill, *The Unfinished Task*.
15. Neill's unpublished autobiography, 'Professor in Germany', pp. 39-41.
16. Ibid., p. 42-43.

younger people. Barth spoke to those who lived through World War I, whereas Bultmann's relevance was more obvious in a post-World War II era. In fact, 'the students had read little of Barth; and when they did read him, he seemed to speak from very far away, from a world which for them had simply never existed'. They could not get enough of Bultmann, however, as 'he spoke in a language which they felt that they could understand'. Neill was very interested by this situation, which surprised him a little.[17]

Neill was not confined to Hamburg in 1956-57. He ventured north to teach at the University of Kiel, as well as east to the Kirchliche Hochschule in Berlin, where he lectured on ministry in the younger churches of the Global South – a topic that the students knew nothing about.[18] Neill ventured into East Berlin on a few occasions, as 'the infamous wall had not yet been erected', but crossing into East Berlin was 'to pass from one world to another. . . . As soon as one crossed the frontier, one entered a world of silence, of apprehension, of anxious and troubled people.'[19]

Neill was utterly fascinated by what he learned from the theological students at the Kirchliche Hochschule, as information was already extremely limited for those who crossed into East Berlin. Guards at the border were especially zealous to confiscate any periodicals or newspapers coming from the West. Neill was extremely impressed by the East German students and perceived them to be 'fresh, lively, open and interested'. Neill spoke to them in German, as they knew no English and were learning Russian. Neill noted that escape was possible in those years; the border had not yet been sealed and the Berlin Wall was not erected until 1961. The students had no desire to escape, as they believed they were in East Germany for a reason, and 'if staying meant trouble and affliction, God would give them grace to see it through'. Neill greatly admired these young people but he also sensed that a more profound division between East and West was on the horizon. Neill noted with some surprise that the East German students were already becoming 'harshly critical' of the Western Church. They said, 'You do not recognise your enemy and have therefore been lulled to sleep. . . . You have failed to see that the god you worship is really mammon and not the God of the Bible.' Whether it was immersion in Soviet ideology, or the result of having a different perspective, the East German students felt the Western world had become 'unbelievably hierarchic, stiff and pompous'. Neill predicted that, when the Berlin Wall fell, it would 'by no means be a case of two long separated brothers falling on one another's necks and rejoicing; there would be suspicion, misunderstanding, and an infinity of

---

17. Ibid., p. 48.
18. The school was located in Dahlem and was founded by Martin Niemöller.
19. Neill's unpublished autobiography, 'Professor in Germany', p. 49.

difficulties to be faced and overcome'. Neill died in 1984 and therefore missed the opportunity to see that amazing moment, a moment that would have fascinated him.[20]

At the end of his teaching appointment in February 1957, the dean of the faculty at the University of Hamburg telephoned Neill to let him know that he had, by a unanimous vote, been awarded an honorary Doctor of Theology degree, indicating how much the community appreciated his work there and respected his scholarship. They had a ceremony with gowns and procession, with speeches, all in Neill's honour, and he considered the occasion 'one of the best moments of my life'. He then delivered his final lecture for that visiting appointment, on 'Anglicanism and the Ecumenical Movement'.[21]

Thus, when Neill entered the Hamburg academic scene full-time in 1962 – four years after his visiting professorship – he entered a friendly place where people thought highly of him. His German-speaking skills were very strong. He had made a few good friends. The title they gave him was Professor of Missions and Ecumenical Theology.[22] He noticed that the West Germans had a particularly warm feeling towards the British when compared to the other three nations that occupied their nation in the aftermath of World War II. According to Neill, the West Germans viewed the Soviets like they did the Mongol hordes who swept across Europe seven centuries before – 'a swarm of locusts, without principles, without compassion, and without civilization'. The French they perceived as being 'harsh but not unjust'. Their French occupiers tended to think that what West Germany needed was a 'strong injection of French culture'. West Germans liked the Americans very much but viewed them as being 'tragically naïve and simple'. The Brits, however, were 'the best of the lot', according to Neill. They were 'constantly illogical and inconstant', as opposed to the extremely rational Germans. However, they clearly 'wanted to get the [West] German people on their feet again'.[23]

It was a good omen. In West Germany Neill finally felt warmly accepted after long years in Geneva, where he had seemed like something of an outsider, always working independently – or nearly independently – on writing projects, and travelling to far off places, completely alone. Just perhaps, beginning in Hamburg in 1962, Neill had finally found his place.

20. Ibid., pp. 50-51.
21. See Neill's entry, *Crockford's Clerical Directory, 1965-66*. See also Neill's unpublished autobiography, 'Professor in Germany', pp. 52-53.
22. For Neill's title, see WCC Archives, Geneva, letter from Neill to 'My dear Victor', on World Christian Books letterhead, 27 December 1963. Neill was still serving as General Editor of World Christian Books, as indicated on the letterhead. The letter was written while Neill was on Christmas break in Switzerland.
23. Neill's unpublished autobiography, 'Professor in Germany', p. 6.

Professor Neill

When Neill finished up his visiting professorship at the University of Hamburg in 1957, he had no idea that he would move there full-time in 1962. In fact, it was under extremely unfortunate circumstances that he ever took the job. Walter Freytag, Neill's good friend, died suddenly on 24 October 1959, creating the opening that Neill eventually filled. Freytag and Neill were only one year apart in age. Freytag had died unexpectedly of a heart attack at the age of 60; Neill wrote, 'This good, wise and gentle man was taken from us.' Moreover, while technically Neill took his place, the truth was that 'No man has ever quite taken the place which Walter Freytag occupied in Germany, and in the ecumenical movement. If his quiet wisdom had continued, the later history might have been very different from what it became.'[24]

The most logical successor to Freytag was Jan Hermelink, a promising scholar in his late thirties who had been mentored by Freytag. However, just a couple of years after Freytag died, Hermelink was accidentally killed when he veered off the road. He was on his way to a Protestant church gathering. Driving alone at night, he fell asleep at the wheel and collided with a tree.[25]

Hermelink was killed in July 1961. Neill had actually just spent a month in the early part of the summer lecturing in Hamburg. When Neill heard of Hermelink's death, he thought he might be asked to come to Hamburg since the faculty was in desperate need of a professor; Freytag's position had been vacant for two years. Sure enough, the faculty voted unanimously to invite Neill to come in 1961. However, Neill was scheduled to teach at two North American institutions for the upcoming months: at Colgate-Rochester Seminary in Rochester, New York; and at Wycliffe College, Toronto. The Hamburg faculty agreed to wait on him and in May 1962 Neill finally severed his long connection with Geneva.[26]

Neill had never imagined he would live in Geneva for fifteen years. It is not as if he did not like the city; rather, he did, especially since it was the world's 'centre of ecumenical activity'. However, Neill was not happy with the direction of the WCC, a fact he mentions several times in his memoirs. As he was no longer connected to the WCC in any formal capacity, he felt no reason to stay in Geneva. He knew he would miss regularly seeing the WCC staff; he went to the campus each day to join them for tea. The only things anchoring him to Geneva were his writing projects

---

24. Ibid., p. 54.
25. Ibid., p. 56.
26. Ibid., p. 57.

and, most importantly, his editorial work with World Christian Books. In reality, however, he could do his editorial work from anywhere and, after approaching the Executive Committee, the members had no objection to him running WCB from Hamburg. So, after fifteen years as a globetrotting ecumenist based in Geneva, Neill made the move to Hamburg to join the faculty as Professor of Missions and Ecumenical Theology.

Thanks to his time at the multilingual WCC and his semester lecturing in Hamburg in 1956-57, Neill's German-speaking skills were already in excellent shape when he arrived in the spring of 1962. His first public lecture in the German language had occurred in the mid-1950s when he was asked to lecture in the city of Erlangen on the topic of ecumenism in South India. He shut himself away for three hours with a German-English dictionary and prepared a 50-minute speech. After delivering it a German friend said the only mistake that was noticeable was that he made the word *Bach* – which is the word 'stream' or 'brook' in English – a neuter term, rather than masculine. Ever since then, Neill had lectured occasionally in the German language and he had often dealt with German on the written page working in book publishing.[27]

It cannot be said that Neill greatly admired the German language. He thought it was full of 'musty obscurity which so often clouds utterances in the German language'. Of one of his German colleagues, Neill wrote, 'He spoke too often and too readily. He was always good to listen to; and yet, if one asked oneself even a few hours later, "What was he really talking about?", it could be extraordinarily difficult to remember.'[28] Another language problem that Neill encountered but solved rather quickly, was how to address Germans in conversation. Neill never liked the American habit of 'slinging around Christian names at a first meeting'. He learned quickly that, with Germans, it is better to 'err on the side of formality'.[29]

It was a 'religious experience' – certainly a fortuitous one – that culminated in Neill's move to Hamburg in 1962.[30] It seemed that all of the stars aligned for this position to work out for him. The language barrier was almost non-existent, he had already worked there for a time, he had made some good friends and he had already built up for himself an excellent reputation within the faculty and local churches.

---

27. Ibid., pp. 33-34. Neill also published reviews of German books he read, including his review of *Theologie und Kirche in Africa* (Stuttgart: Evangelisches Verlagswerk, 1968), ed. by Neill's friend Horst Bürkle, in the *Journal of Ecumenical Studies*, Vol. 7, no. 1 (1970), pp. 150-51.
28. Neill's unpublished autobiography, 'Professor in Germany', pp. 25-26. Neill was here referring to Hanns Lilje.
29. Ibid., p. 26.
30. Neill, *God's Apprentice*, p. 240. Neill wrote most of his autobiography in 1973. See also Neill's unpublished autobiography, 'Professor in Germany', p. 1.

8. A Professorship in Hamburg: 1962-68

Neill's office was located at: Zimmer (room) 1261, Evangelische Theologische Fakultät, Von-Melle-Park 6, Hamburg 13, Germany.[31] His predecessor, Professor Freytag, Neill had met at the famous Tambaram mission conference of 1938[32] and had come to know him and his family extremely well when he filled in for Freytag for a semester. Although Neill considered Freytag a less-than-stellar scholar, he, nevertheless, considered him a 'remarkable man'. Freytag was a Moravian Christian with a deeply pietistic understanding of faith. Neill referred to him as having a 'delicate and sensitive spirit'.[33]

One thing that Freytag had done exceedingly well over the years: he had 'gathered round himself a quite remarkable group of young men, whom he was grooming for responsibilities in the world of German missions'. These included: Horst Bürkle, Hans Margull, Dr Viening, Dr Wagner and Jan Hermelink. All of these men (except Jan Hermelink, whose career was sadly cut short) went on to accept important academic positions in the world of German missions. Freytag was also very gifted in 'creating around him an attitude of goodwill and bringing together men who were likely to be able to work together in harmony'. For example, the faculty gathered monthly in one of their homes for fellowship, wine and cigars; one of them would read a paper that would then be discussed by the group. Neill thoroughly enjoyed those times. He remembered one, in particular, in 1963, when the phone rang and they heard those horrible words: 'Kennedy has been shot.' They immediately joined in prayer. There was also an outing which occurred once a year, when the entire university faculty met at the banks of the Elbe, ten miles from Hamburg, to spend the day in fellowship and in discussion of some important academic topic.[34]

Shortly after his move to Hamburg, Neill learned of his employment terms at a dinner party with colleagues. For many months Neill had assumed he would simply take Professor Freytag's place. However, that evening at the party, Neill was in for a shock. He was handed his contract which made it clear that he was not replacing Freytag. In Germany the highest level of professor is the professor ordinarius. In the English world this position is usually referred to as university professor with a chair. It is a very exclusive group of people who ever attain this position. In Germany the ordinarius position is much higher than a typical professorship, as these

---

31. See Neill's entry, *Crockford's Clerical Directory, 1965-66*.
32. See Hans-Werner Gensichen, 'The Legacy of Walter Freytag', *International Bulletin of Missionary Research*, Vol. 5, no. 1 (January 1981), pp. 13-18.
33. Neill, *God's Apprentice*, p. 241. Neill's unpublished autobiography, 'Professor in Germany', p. 11. Gensichen, 'The Legacy of Walter Freytag', p. 13.
34. Neill's unpublished autobiography, 'Professor in Germany', pp. 37, 41.

elite professors are the ones who confer degrees and honorary degrees on behalf of the university. Further, 'When a professorship falls vacant, it is the Ordinarii who decide whom to call to fill the vacant place.'[35]

Neill was extremely disappointed to learn that he would not be appointed ordinarius. He wrote, 'If I had known this earlier I would not have accepted the appointment.' Unfortunately, Neill had left the matter of negotiating his terms to his colleague, Hans Margull. This proved to be disastrous for Neill, as many of the perks that he had anticipated were not extended to him, partly because he was a foreigner, partly because he was too old and partly due to reasons that he never fully understood.[36]

When he arrived to Hamburg in May 1962, Neill was 61 years old. However, to qualify for ordinarius, one has to be no more than 58, since he must retire at age 68 and therefore work for a full decade before qualifying for full pension. Thus, Neill regarded his position as 'anomalous', stating that he 'was given full charge of the missionary and ecumenical department with the status of professor, but I was not a member of the inner circle of the Ordinarii'. This situation 'weighed most heavily' on Neill for several reasons. First, Neill would have no formal connection to Professor Freytag's Mission Academy – a theological institute in the city aimed at training future missionaries.[37] The Mission Academy was located about eleven kilometres west of Neill's office at the University of Hamburg. Neill had assumed that, when he came to work at the university, he would – like Freytag before him – serve as director of the Mission Academy and spend roughly equal amounts of time at both. However, this was not the case at all and, since Neill did not have the rank of ordinarius, he was unable to change the situation. His sense was that some of the staff at the Mission Academy kept him at a distance because he was not German and he was not a Lutheran. However, Neill never fully understood why he was given the cold shoulder by the academy staff.[38]

---

35. Ibid., pp. 59, 62.
36. Ibid., p. 59.
37. The Mission Academy was founded in 1954 by Walter Freytag who was at the time the chairman of the German Evangelical Mission Council. Support for the Mission Academy came from the Lutheran World Federation and the International Mission Council. In 1955 it was recognised as a 'Mission Academy at the University of Hamburg' by the Senate of the University of Hamburg. The academy was meant to be ecumenical, meaning it was to serve all German mission societies. Over time its purpose has changed. It is now 'aimed at promoting foreign students. More than 100 scholarship holders from Asia, Africa, and Latin America have successfully completed their doctoral or master's degrees in the Mission Academy. Many of them now work in responsible positions in their home countries and churches.' The current address for the Mission Academy is Rupertistrasse 67, in Hamburg.
38. Neill's unpublished autobiography, 'Professor in Germany', pp. 60-61.

8. A Professorship in Hamburg: 1962-68 277

In fact, Neill had initially planned to secure a home near the Mission Academy, since it was far enough away from the university campus that rents were much cheaper. However, 'when it became clear that I was to have very little to do with that institution, I widened my gaze and looked in other directions also'.[39]

These developments struck at the heart of Neill's plans for his position in Hamburg, as mentoring young missionaries was extremely important to him. Teaching in the university would be fine but mentoring people who were preparing for mission work was Neill's passion. He cherished being in the position of father figure to young people, especially those with interest in missions. The rug was pulled out from underneath his feet, however, and from his earliest days in Hamburg he felt that everything got off on the wrong footing. It was a terrible development for him and he never quite got over it during his years in West Germany.

One of Freytag's former students, Horst Bürkle, recognised that there was a problem and tried to come to the rescue by providing an opportunity for Neill to spend one evening per week with a group of six young pastors who had come to the Mission Academy for missionary or ecumenical training. Neill thoroughly enjoyed working with this small group of students that came and went. However, it wasn't long before Bürkle moved to Africa to take up mission work, and Bürkle's replacement didn't see the need for Neill's services at the academy.[40]

Because Neill was denied the rank of ordinarius, there was nothing he could do to change the frustrating situation at the academy. Neill wrote, 'So here was I, a professor but not a member of this sacred conclave. As a result I knew nothing whatever of what was going on. When a new professor was added to the faculty, I learned of the event through the public press.'[41]

Since Neill was not very welcome at the Mission Academy, he had to focus his attention on his work at the university, in the Institute for Mission, Ecumenical and Religious Studies.[42] His department, however, had troubles of its own. In Neill's words, 'the situation in my own department was confused and unsatisfactory'. Neill blamed the disorderly situation on the lack of leadership in the department due to Freytag's death – and the leadership vacuum that followed. Freytag's assistant was left in charge but he was still working on his doctoral dissertation. Eventually, that man finished his studies and was replaced by a young man named

---

39. Ibid., p. 71.
40. Ibid., pp. 61-62.
41. Ibid., pp. 62-63.
42. Institut für Missions, Ökumene und Religionswissenschaften, Abteilung für Religionswissenschaft und Theologie der Religionen.

Rolf Christiansen, who got on very well with Neill. The only problem was that Christiansen had a serious heart condition that 'gravely hindered his work'.[43]

One of Neill's first goals was to build up the theology department's library, especially English resources, which he did rather quickly. However, in Neill's opinion the students did not appropriately utilise the books he worked so hard to obtain. They could read English but avoided it if there was a resource available in German. He also ordered subscriptions to many papers and periodicals, hoping they would plug themselves into modern developments in the Church. Again, language proved to be a barrier.[44]

Neill's personal library, however, was another story. When he moved to Geneva in 1947, he left his huge collection of books with his brother Gerald, in Gateshead, near Newcastle upon Tyne, northeast England. Neill had arranged for a company to box them up and ship them from Cambridge to his brother's place. However, one of the two shipments never made it and by the time that Neill moved to Hamburg, fifteen years had passed, and it was much too late to try to recover that second shipment. Neill was devastated by this loss of books:

> So I found myself deprived of a number of valuable and in some cases irreplaceable books. . . . What is a scholar without his books? . . . Books have a history and a personality of their own. Some had been painfully saved up for, when I was a boy; some had come as gifts or prizes; the whole history of a lifetime is recorded on the shelves. There are losses to which one never becomes reconciled; these aching gaps in my wealth diminished permanently the pleasure I was able to take in my new and carefully planned home; I could not look at the shelves without being aware of the books that ought to have been there and were not.[45]

For a bibliophile like Neill, this was a catastrophic, irrecoverable loss.

Neill was committed to providing a first-rate, rigorous course of study for students. In his words, it was 'very hard and exacting'. Coming from Neill, who was a workaholic, there can be little doubt that the students had plenty to do. Neill required them to study Greek, Hebrew and Latin. He also immersed them in the study of the Bible, at a time when Germans were already nearly wholly ignorant of what was in the scriptures. Neill was so irritated by their 'extensive ignorance' – especially of classical languages

---

43. Neill's unpublished autobiography, 'Professor in Germany', pp. 63-64.
44. See ibid., p. 65.
45. Ibid., p. 76.

and biblical content – that it caused him to reconsider his stringent requirements; luckily, 'Philip Melanchthon had laid it down in 1530 that all candidates for the ministry must be learned in Greek and Hebrew, and no change could be made in this divinely inspired edict.' Neill's arduous standards for his students were no doubt propelled by his exasperation at them: 'Students in Germany criticize their professors and make fun of them behind their backs, as students do all over the world.' Seemingly the only exception to this tendency was the close relationship that often developed between a doctoral candidate and his supervisor.[46]

While students took written tests, there was a special emphasis on the oral examination. This was the traditional German approach. Neill was not fond of this system, as it 'put a tremendous strain on both professors and candidates'. It put students with less self-esteem at an obvious disadvantage. In the end, Neill felt that 'many lame dogs were helped over many stiles'.[47]

Neill was also surprised by the students' lack of awareness of what was happening around them in the Christian world – readily available in the daily newspapers. For example, in their exams, Neill often asked students what they knew about the developments occurring in Rome at the Second Vatican Council. They had no idea. He also asked them basic questions about the World Council of Churches. Again, they had no clue. Neill was routinely struck by how little they kept abreast of current events in the Christian sphere.[48]

After carefully observing his students for a few years, Neill came to the conclusion that university students (at least in West Germany) had passed through a series of phases after the disaster of World War II. Neill tried to put his finger on these 'phases' in his autobiography.

The first phase was one of shock in the aftermath of a traumatic era that ended in the disaster of the war itself. West German students were 'defeated, hungry, emaciated, and cold . . . studying in drafty and windowless classrooms, taught by professors who had emerged from the cellars or even the concentration camps'. They simply waited and hoped for a better day.[49]

The second phase was a non-political one – *ohne mich* ('without me'). Students refused to become engaged with affairs going on around them. They could not trust society very well because there were so many changes going on. Germany moved from a starving Weimar Republic, to a proud and powerful society under Hitler, to near-complete destruction saved only by the mercy of the nations which defeated it. Neill was surprised by

---

46. Ibid., pp. 65-66, 70-71.
47. Ibid., p. 68.
48. Ibid., p. 68.
49. Ibid., p. 103.

the students who were proving themselves to be fairly resilient. He wrote, 'What astonished me was not that they were neurotic, but that they were as normal as they were.'[50]

The third phase, Neill observed, was that the students of West Germany 'seemed to become violently political'. It caught Neill by surprise, as it seemed to happen 'almost overnight'. Upon reflection, Neill began to realise it had everything to do with the problem of East Germany, the German Democratic Republic. 'The West German government tried to pretend that it did not exist, that there was only one Germany and that, if this pretence was kept up long enough, the problem would just get up and walk away.' Neill's analysis of this 'violently political' turn in the West German student is complex. He believed that when split families met together – in the years before the Wall – news began to leak out that East German students were doing quite well. They had trenchant criticism for what they saw in the West – a society that was 'antique, ossified, and unbelievably hierarchical in its constitution'. While East Germans did not have political freedom, they believed they were living 'in a much freer society . . . a great deal nearer to genuine democracy than their kinsman in the West'. Thus, it was clear to Neill that students on both sides of the border were ambivalent, yet frustrated by global circumstances that they could not fully comprehend – which led to suspicion and occasionally aggression.[51]

What eventually happened was that two very different Germanys began to emerge. East German students had become extremely different in culture and ethos from their West German counterparts. According to Neill, the East German students simply 'endured' the 'long hours of Marxist indoctrination'. However, they did not wholly accept Marxism. In the words of Neill, the Soviet occupation 'had singularly little effect on their minds'. However, East Germans certainly did not have 'unqualified admiration' for the West. Rather, they were in a state of suspended judgement.[52]

West German students were conflicted during this third phase. They were hearing criticism from their East German, separated friends that maybe they were simply pawns. Were West Germans merely puppets for the United States in its relentless Cold War? Had West Germany become an 'inbred and self-indulgent society', as the Soviet world proclaimed? Perhaps it was time for revolution in the West as well? Some West German students – Neill estimates perhaps two per cent, but a very loud, boisterous and fanatical two per cent – seemed determined to 'destroy everything that existed, without any idea of the nature of the new institutions by which

---

50. Ibid., p. 103.
51. Ibid., p. 104-5.
52. Ibid., p. 106.

8. A Professorship in Hamburg: 1962-68

they planned to replace the old'. These 'violently political' students preyed on the frustrations of other students and made 'every undesirable situation a tool of which they could make use'.[53]

Eventually, the situation became serious. Beginning in 1966 and culminating in 1968 students across West Germany began to revolt, some of them violently. Extremely vocal students with fanatical views managed to intimidate more sensible majorities. These radicals refused to listen to anybody, they publicly shamed professors and they vilified anyone in authority. At the University of Hamburg, they occupied entire departments. In Neill's estimation, they aspired to 'destroy all semblance of order in the University'. Neill's colleague, the distinguished and respected theologian Helmut Thielicke, tried to speak out against the revolutionaries, only to get brutally pilloried by them as merely 'another stalwart of the old and moth-eaten order'.[54]

One of Neill's former students at Hamburg, Darrell Guder, remarked that these revolutionary actions in the German university were particularly distressing for Neill, who was 'comfortable in that older model, [where] a professor is semi-divine'. Guder himself said that he witnessed the student revolutions of 1967-68 but left Germany for Los Angeles 'just as it began to explode'.[55]

Neill was shaken by the anarchy going on in the German universities and the demands that students were making upon entire faculties – such as that students should play a major role in choosing new professors. In Neill's mind, the German university was burning. Academics had become secondary to political affiliation. Neill bemoaned what he viewed as a sudden collapse when he wrote, 'I got out of the German University situation just at the right moment.'[56]

Contributions to Knowledge

One of Neill's friends in Hamburg stated that Neill 'would stay up all night reading and writing'. This is a theme that comes up throughout Neill's lifetime. People who knew him realised that he was an insomniac but few of them understood the toll it took on his health. Neill worked compulsively – for example, there is even a claim that he read while shaving in the morning. Whether stories such as these are understood as legend

---

53. Ibid., pp. 107-8.
54. Ibid., pp. 109-10.
55. Darrell Guder, phone interview with author, 15 July 2020. Also, email from Guder to author, 16 July 2020.
56. Neill's unpublished autobiography, 'Professor in Germany', p. 110.

or truth – or somewhere in between – there is no reason to doubt the substance of them: that Neill accomplished extraordinary amounts of work throughout his life, wherever he happened to be stationed.[57]

Lesslie Newbigin once judged that: 'Stephen Neill was at heart a historian.'[58] There is truth to this observation, as Neill spent much of his life – going way back to his college days – engaged in the task of writing history. During the final 22 years of his life – 1962 to 1984 – he produced piles of it, some of it extremely impressive scholarship that transformed his reputation – from a gifted churchman to a world-renowned historian. It was while he was in Hamburg that Neill 'made that series of contributions to knowledge which in seven years brought him election to the British Academy'.[59]

Between 1962 and 1968 Neill published no less than nine books and eleven scholarly articles. The books written during his Hamburg years include:

1962 – *Chrysostom and His Message* (London: Lutterworth Press)
1963 – *Paul to the Colossians* (London: Lutterworth Press)
1963 – *The Eternal Dimension* (London: Epworth)
1963 – *The Layman in Christian History* (Philadelphia, PA: Westminster Press)
1964 – *The Interpretation of the New Testament: 1861–1961* (London: Oxford University Press)
1964 – *A History of Christian Missions* (Harmondsworth: Penguin)
1966 – *Concise Dictionary of the Bible* (London: Lutterworth Press)
1966 – *Colonialism and Christian Missions* (London: Lutterworth Press)
1968 – *The Church and Christian Union* (Oxford: Oxford University Press)[60]

---

57. Freytag, interview with author, 2 October 2000. It is possible that Justus knew a great deal about Neill's darker side, as he admitted to hearing that 'Neill hit a clergyman in India'.
58. Newbigin wrote this to Timothy Yates in a personal letter. See Yates, 'Stephen Neill: Some Aspects of a Theological Legacy', p. 157.
59. Cragg and Chadwick, 'Stephen Charles Neill, 1900-1984', p. 610. *The Times* mentioned Neill's election to the British Academy on 12 July 1969, p. 10.
60. It should be noted that there are bound to be more articles written by Neill during this time. The articles for which I have a copy are: 'Charles Henry Brent', *Canadian Journal of Theology*, Vol. 8, no. 3 (July 1962), pp. 153-71; 'Threatened Christendom', *The Empire Club Addresses*, 22 February 1962; 'Theology 1939-1964', *The Expository Times*, October 1964, pp. 21-25; Chapter 2, 'Western Europe', in *The Prospects of Christianity Throughout the World*, ed. by M. Searle Bates and Wilhelm Pauck (New York: Charles Scribner's Sons,

8. A Professorship in Hamburg: 1962-68

Indeed, five of these books were significant contributions to ecclesiology and missiology and it is difficult to understand how Neill produced five books of such a high quality within a short period of time, given that he took no sabbatical, was almost constantly teaching and preaching, producing many other works during this period and was often conducting his tasks in a foreign language. These five excellent books will be discussed briefly.

In 1963 Neill and Hans-Ruedi Weber co-edited *The Layman in Christian History*, a compelling study of the laity that was sponsored by the WCC department on the laity. It claimed to be 'the first book ever to present a history of the place of laymen in the life of the Church from the earliest times until today'.[61] The book claimed to fill a gap in knowledge: 'It is time that some kind of memorial was raised to these forgotten saints, in the firm conviction that "Their seed shall remain forever and their glory shall not be blotted out" (Eccles 44.13).' The book was a Who's Who of Christianity in 1963, including such well-known figures as George Huntston Williams, William H.C. Frend, R.W. Southern, E. Gordon Rupp, Jan Grootaers and several others.[62]

Hans-Ruedi Weber was much younger than Neill and he looked to Neill as a father figure, stating that Neill, 'took me in a fatherly, episcopal way under his wings and gave me confidence'. However, Neill could be difficult to work with, as Weber recounted:

> The collaboration for *The Layman in Christian History* (what an insensitive, male title!) was sometimes a bit difficult. I did the whole planning and administration of the study and writing project on this theme and Neill did the main editorial work. He

---

1964); 'An Anglican in a Lutheran Atmosphere', *Lutheran World*, Vol. 12, no. 3 (1965), pp. 238-47; *Christianity Today* (Singapore: Student Christian Movement University Lectures, approx. 1965); 'The Church: An Ecumenical Perspective (An Attempt at Definition)', *Interpretation*, Vol. 19, no. 2 (1965), pp. 131-48; 'The Anglican Communion and the Ecumenical Council', in *The Councils of the Church: History and Analysis*, ed. by Hans Margull, trans. by Walter Bense (Philadelphia: Fortress Press, 1966); 'The Church of the Future, Reunion and the Ecumenical Movement', *The Modern Churchman*, Vol. 10, no. 1 (1966); *Rome and the Ecumenical Movement* (Grahamstown: Rhodes University, 1967); 'Intercommunion Today', *The Churchman*, Vol. 82 (1968), pp. 285-89. Throughout his career, Neill also wrote many book reviews and this practice continued during his Hamburg years. One example is his review of *George Bell: Bishop of Chichester*, by Ronald C. D. Jasper (New York: Oxford University Press, 1967), in the *Journal of Ecumenical Studies*, Vol. 6, no. 2 (Spring 1969), pp. 261-63.

61. The quoted words are from the volume's dust jacket.
62. Quotation from *The Layman in Christian History*, p. 12.

wrote for instance the rather self-congratulatory introduction and I was reticent to co-sign it with him, but he insisted that we sign together.

While Weber admired Neill, he was always cognisant of the fact that 'I always remained very much the junior', which was part of the reason they never developed a deep friendship.[63]

Also in 1963 Neill published a classic text, *The Interpretation of the New Testament: 1861-1961*. This book's quality was explained well by Richard Pierard:

> Although Neill is generally remembered for his studies on mission history, many regard his most thoughtful and useful work to be a historical account of the trends in New Testament studies during modern times, *The Interpretation of the New Testament: 1861–1961*. This was a [Firth] lecture series given at the University of Nottingham [in 1962] which Oxford University Press published in 1964 and reissued in 1988 with an update by Tom Wright that covered the period 1861-1986. It is one of the most informative one-volume surveys of the topic available. It reflects a commitment to the inspiration of the New Testament, an evangelical understanding of its meaning (including the existence of a historical Jesus and the need for personal salvation), and a willingness to deal critically with the various interpreters. Neill's focus on the personalities of the scholars involved in the debates over New Testament criticism, depth of knowledge of their works in the major European languages, and balanced assessment of their contributions make the book absorbing reading.[64]

Another wrote the following about Neill's *Interpretation of the New Testament*: 'The breadth of his reading is staggering, especially as many of the books he cites were not yet translated into English.'[65]

The Interpretation of the New Testament was written for 'the non-theologian'. However, it quickly became a favourite for students being introduced to biblical criticism in college or seminary. Neill seemed to have a knack for drawing attention to people and issues which have 'permanent

---

63. Email communication from Hans-Ruedi Weber to the present author, 19 July 2003.
64. Pierard, 'Stephen Neill', p. 537.
65. Mitchell, 'Stephen Neill: A Traditional Communicator in an Age of Revolution', p. 186.

significance'. Part of what makes this book fascinating is that Neill knew many of the scholars he discussed: 'I am moved to find how many of these scholars I have been privileged to know personally during the forty years since I first devoted myself to the intensive study of the New Testament.'[66] Indeed, Neill's first two published works were on the study of the Bible. His first published book was *How Readest Thou? A Simple Introduction to the New Testament* (SCM Press, 1925), and *The Gospel According to St John* (Cambridge University Press, 1930).

Neill's next major work, *A History of Christian Missions*, was one of those rare books that everyone in a particular field reads. It was Neill's bestselling book.[67] According to Cragg and Chadwick, this book 'could have been written by no one else of his generation'.[68] Neill's 600-page masterpiece was volume six in the prestigious Pelican History of the Church series, which placed him in the company of Henry Chadwick, Owen Chadwick, Alec Vidler, R.W. Southern and Gerald Cragg. When asked how long it took him to write it, Neill responded, 'The answer could be either four months or forty years.'[69] This book, more than any other, established Neill as an important, authoritative scholar. Almost instantly, he became established as one of the chief historians of the expansion of Christianity. This masterpiece continues to be used in university and seminary courses. It is actually the first volume in a trilogy by Neill on the academic study of Christian missions.[70]

Neill's follow-up to *A History of Christian Missions* was a trailblazing tome entitled *Colonialism and Christian Missions*. In a highly favourable review, one scholar wrote:

> A thousand books have surely been written on the history of missions, but this one seems to be the first of its kind. . . . A number of articles and a few books have been written on some aspects of the subject, but they have not been surveys of the whole missionary enterprise in its relationship to colonialism. . . . There seems, actually, to be hardly anything of value which Neill has not examined in his researches for this history. . . . The materials have not mastered him, but he has mastered them, and the book, as a consequence, masters the reader.[71]

66. Neill, *The Interpretation of the New Testament: 1861-1961*, pp. v-vi.
67. Neill's unpublished autobiography, 'Of Making Many Books', p. 52.
68. Cragg and Chadwick, 'Stephen Charles Neill, 1900-1984', p. 610.
69. Neill's unpublished autobiography, 'Of Making Many Books', p. 51. The book was actually written when Neill was in Hamburg.
70. The other two are *Colonialism and Christian Missions* and *Call to Mission*.
71. Sigurd F. Westberg, 'An Evaluation of Stephen Neill's *Colonialism and Christian Missions*', *The Covenant Quarterly*, Vol. 27 (August 1969), pp. 37-41.

Strikingly readable, this book takes a genuinely global approach. It was meant to tackle, head on, the mythologies that have become standard interpretation in the university:

> Colonialism was the worst thing that has ever happened in the history of the world. Colonialism was wholly evil. Missionaries were in the service of the colonial powers and identified their interests entirely with that of the colonial government. Missionaries were therefore wholly evil and did nothing but harm in the countries in which they worked.

Unfortunately, according to Neill, 'Mythology grows much more rapidly than history' and historians must work overtime to counter grossly one-sided claims. Moreover, while colonialism can certainly be criticised – most certainly – it also 'practically eliminated cannibalism, female infanticide and twin murder'.[72] Neill's conclusion to that book is balanced, as he pointed out some of the major gains for colonial nations such as the introduction of Western education, religious freedom and economic improvement. He was equally determined to point out the tragic flaws in the colonial enterprise: 'The injury done to the minds and wills of proud and sensitive peoples by a sense of colonial subjugation and inferiority can hardly be expressed in words; there is no doubt whatever that the wounds went very deep.' His conclusion is clear: 'Whether the advantages gained compensate for the injustices suffered is a debate that could be carried on to the end of time.'[73]

In *Colonialism and Christian Missions* Neill revealed he was as acquainted with Japanese and Russian colonial rule as he was with British and Portuguese. His writings illustrate a voracious appetite for devouring books in many languages. His familiar descriptions of historical figures almost gives one the sense that Neill knew these people. His penchant for highlighting obscure events in history enlivens what could have been mundane. One reviewer called it a 'masterpiece from the pen of a man whose writings have become well known in the missionary constituency'.[74]

There was one major irony about Neill's writings on colonialism and mission that haunted him repeatedly throughout the years. Many who knew him thought of him as the quintessential colonialist. One of his students stated:

---

72. Neill's unpublished autobiography, 'Of Making Many Books', p. 53-54.
73. Neill, *Colonialism and Christian Missions*, pp. 422-23.
74. G.W. Peters, Review of Neill's *Colonialism and Christian Missions* in the journal *Bibliotheca Sacra*, Vol. 124, no. 495 (Jul-Sept 1967), pp. 275-76.

Neill was a colonialist. He was a part of the reconsideration of colonialism, but he was an example of how not to do it. He was an Irish Anglican who fancied himself as a part of the British nobility, of the old aristocracy. He had all of his academic hoods for his honorary doctorates hanging in his closet, and he delighted in showing them off and talking about them.[75]

Similar critiques of Neill, almost verbatim, were made by his colleagues and students in both India and Africa.

The fifth major contribution to knowledge during Neill's Hamburg years were his 1964 Bampton Lectures published by Oxford University Press in 1968 as *The Church and Christian Union*. This work 'represents Neill's most rigorous work on ecclesiology . . . [and] reflects not simply his work in Hamburg as professor of Ecumenics, but also his considered reflections on forty years of active involvement within the ecumenical movement'.[76] The book masterfully draws together Neill's many years working actively to unite the global Church of Jesus Christ. One would be hard pressed to find someone more fit to write the history of Christian unity, as Neill had not only published numerous works on the topic, he had also tremendous practical experience, such as his work on the WCC and his long tenure on the committee that worked to create the Church of South India. Max Warren, long-time General Secretary of the Church Missionary Society, wrote glowingly of this book in a personal letter to his son-in-law, Roger Hooker:

> This is a superb bit of writing. I'm getting you a copy. For I know you'll enjoy it. Stephen is at heart a missionary and the whole book is one superb vindication of the missionary enterprise. I don't mean that he applauds it in all its forms. He doesn't. But he provides a *theology* of mission which is incomparably the best and most thorough thing attempted of which I am aware.[77]

As General Secretary of the CMS for over two decades (1942-63), Max Warren's perspective is important and judicious. For him to say Neill's theology of mission was 'incomparably the best and most thorough' means that it probably was.

---

75. Guder, interview with author, 15 July 2020.
76. Mitchell, 'Stephen Neill: A Traditional Communicator in an Age of Revolution', pp. 193-94.
77. Graham Kings, *Christianity Connected: Hindus, Muslims and the World in the Letters of Max Warren and Roger Hooker* (Zoetermeer: Boekencentrum, 2002), pp. 211-12.

The Church and Christian Union is perhaps Neill's most complicated book. One reviewer wrote, 'What emerges is a history and contemporary assessment of most of the important questions that have been asked about the Church, theological, pastoral and sociological.'[78] He ruminates on the nature of history, he analyses numerous examples of church union and he theologises more in this book than perhaps any of his others. In the end, however, he succeeds in arguing that unity is 'dangerous'. Indeed, 'We cannot be assured that the days of divisiveness in the Church are finally at an end' because the new ecumenical consciousness has also led to a 'strengthening of denominational consciousness'. Discussions of unity are also dangerous because they 'may lead to sharp differences of opinion within denominations, and possibly even to new divisions'. Thus, ecumenism is, ironically, prone to backfire and potentially cause proliferation. It is a counterintuitive risk that those who have participated in this kind of work realise all too well. Neill concludes that we must attempt unity anyway because Christ desires it. He argues that unity requires courage and a desire for the Church to be made well. The problem is that denominations have so much invested in their distinct identities: 'what holds them apart is in large measure the deep-seated love of separate existence, pride in valued traditions, and the sense of superiority enjoyed by those who feel themselves to have been endowed with a special portion of the truth'.[79]

According to the two distinguished historians Kenneth Cragg and Owen Chadwick, it was while working as a professor in Hamburg that Neill 'made that series of contributions to knowledge which in seven years brought him election to the British Academy'.[80] It could also be stated that, after his astonishingly productive years in Hamburg, Neill could no longer be considered just a missionary, just a bishop, just an ecumenist or just a prolific writer and editor. His incredible output of high-quality scholarship during the Hamburg years propelled him to being, without question, one of the greatest minds in the twentieth-century Church. His mastery of

---

78. Review by Anthony Nye, S.J., in *New Blackfriars*, Vol. 49, no. 576 (May 1968), pp. 436-37.
79. Neill, *The Church and Christian Union*, pp. 401-2. Not everyone agreed with Neill's understanding of unity. Max Warren once wrote about Neill, 'Altho' he and I belong to the same wing of Anglicanism we differ fundamentally in our conception of unity. Scratch Stephen and you shall come to a rigid Episcopalian who can only think in terms of organic unity – whereas I believe we haven't done justice yet to the federal concept of unity.' This quotation actually comes from Norman Goodall's unpublished personal journal, in a passage where he is discussing what Warren said about Neill. See Graham Kings, *Christianity Connected*, p. 109, fn. 101.
80. Cragg and Chadwick, 'Stephen Charles Neill, 1900-1984', p. 610.

many fields of knowledge, his competence in well over a dozen languages, his extraordinary gifts of communication and his grasp of other religions and cultures meant that Stephen Neill was firmly established as one of the great intellectuals of modern Christianity.

Life outside Academia

Life in Hamburg was good for Neill. When he first arrived, he rented two rooms from an elderly widow for several months but knew he needed his own place. Eventually he found a two-room flat that was brand new and came with a cellar and an attic. He could catch the tram nearby. There was a lovely canal flowing on the other side of the highway that he frequented because of its wonderful gardens. Neill was very happy with his residence; it became 'a real home'. It had a very large living room where he could host groups, which he often did. He wrote, 'I had provided myself with a dwelling larger than I needed for myself in order to be able to entertain, and entertain I would.' Neill was quite the entertainer, always prepared with ample alcoholic drinks and cigars. His favorite guest was Helmut Thielicke, whose robust conversation could go on for hours without pause. To help him stay on top of things at home, he hired a lady who came in twice a week to clean, launder and run errands for him.[81]

Neill had a flourishing spiritual and church life in Hamburg. He quickly signed up to be one of the university preachers and was a little surprised when he – an Anglican – was welcomed onto the roster.[82] He also surprised many students when he ended the social gatherings at his house with a Compline devotional service, complete with prayers and scripture reading. Even for theological students, 'this always took them by surprise'.[83]

Naturally, the Anglican Church in Hamburg – named after St Thomas à Becket – became a refuge for Neill. That congregation was centuries old in Hamburg, with a continuous presence in the city since 1615, when English sea merchants were allowed to conduct English-only services – so as not to corrupt the German Lutherans. Neill connected with the chaplains who served the parish and 'took over a good deal of the preaching'. As an honorarium at the end of each year, the church would present Neill with a gift made of silver, such as candlesticks or a beautiful jug. Neill was most pleased with these gifts; he relished anything made of silver.[84]

---

81. Neill's unpublished autobiography, 'Professor in Germany', p. 73-74, 76-78.
82. Ibid., pp. 69-70.
83. Ibid., p. 79.
84. Clearly evident in the archives at St Thomas à Becket Church in Hamburg, it was a regular annual occurrence that the church would officially thank Neill. See

Neill became a core part of St Thomas à Becket. After services, he hosted visitors who were passing through. He led services often, participated in clergy gatherings and attended parish meetings regularly, although he noted that they were – as in England – 'attended mainly by elderly women, who would listen courteously to anything that was said but whose minds had taken on such a fixed patter that it was unlikely that any new idea could penetrate their heads'. It delighted Neill to expose the West Germans to the beauty of the Church of England – 'a Church which appears to Roman Catholics to be all too Protestant, and to Protestants to be all too Catholic'. Neill noticed that West Germans knew almost nothing about Anglicanism, due partly to the fact that, even by 1973 when Neill wrote his memoirs, there was 'no satisfactory book on Anglicanism in German'.[85]

Never just a professor, Neill was ever the student and in West Germany he studied the people and the culture carefully. He was curious about why the West German churches were so wealthy and realised it was because of taxation. The churches benefitted from huge amounts of tax income each year. The downside to this, however, was that 'the [West German] pastor, being assured of his social and financial position whether anyone comes to church or not, may be less than enthusiastic in the fulfilment of his duties'. Neill also noted that, because of their relatively minor colonial operations overseas, they tended not to spend much money on people and causes outside their own nation. This was slowly changing while Neill was living in Hamburg and, by the time he wrote his memoirs in 1973, the West German approach to the Third World was dramatically different to what it had been in the years following World War II: 'When all criticisms have been made, and all human imperfections allowed for, the emergence of the West German churches as benefactors on this great scale is one of the most important things ever to emerge in the relationships between the richer and the poorer nations.'[86]

On a more personal note, Neill's health improved during his Hamburg years, which is doubtlessly one of the reasons his scholarly output skyrocketed. In an important letter addressed to 'Victor', dated 27 December 1963, Neill gave an update about his personal life and health. Neill moved to Hamburg in May 1962, so he had been there well over a year and a half. To catch a glimpse of the personal, candid, unfiltered

---

the annual 'Report on the Proceedings of the Annual General Meeting held by the church community' of 12 April 1967, 25 April 1966, 3 May 1965 and 28 April 1964. See also Neill's unpublished autobiography, 'Professor in Germany', pp. 81-83.
85. Ibid., pp. 86, 91.
86. Ibid., pp. 99-102.

Neill during his early Hamburg years, there is no better source than this letter, which was actually written while he was in Switzerland during the Christmas holidays. Neill wrote:

> My dear Victor,
> Your two letters have brought me very much interesting news, I am sorry that I have been slow in answering. Between July and November I went right round the world, and came back to extremely heavy work; correspondence has got into arrears. . . . During my stay in Coimbatore [India] with my sister, I was able to learn much of the state of the C.S.I., and also to meet many old friends from Tinnevelly who are now in that area. I would very much like to see Tinnevelly again, but, though at least 90 per cent of our Christian friends would give me the most loving welcome, there are still a few who would be made unhappy by my coming, and I have not yet received permission from on high to visit the old places again. I was glad to find that I can still speak Tamil quite fluently. . . .
> About three years ago I was able to get special treatment for my insomnia. It is very hard to get ordinary doctors to take insomnia seriously; I have known for a long time that there was a physical cause for this affliction, but was never able to persuade a doctor that this was so. Then I found a woman in Geneva who gives special treatment for this kind of trouble; I am not completely cured, but I have greatly improved, and have been able almost entirely to leave off the drugs which I had to use for many years in order to get enough sleep to carry on with my work. I am very grateful indeed for this improvement in my health. . . . I trace the cause of the insomnia back to a severe illness when I was 15, which was never diagnosed at the time, but which I think affected the special glands which control the body's relation to temperature and pressure, and so to sleep. Even in Cambridge days I was troubled by lack of sleep. It is wonderful after so many years to be so much freer from a trouble that has hindered me throughout the whole of my adult life.
> I am not sure whether you know that I am now serving as Professor of Missions and Ecumenical Theology in the University of Hamburg. This is a very important centre, and there is a great work of interpretation to be done between the German- and the English-speaking worlds. I find that I get on very well with the young people in Germany; they are very anxious to know the truth

about the past, and are very unmilitary in their point of view. My students work hard; I hope that a number of them will find their way into the work of the Church overseas.

During November and December I was extremely tired – lecturing in German is still something of a strain; so I have come away to Switzerland for a little rest. On Christmas night, in the mountains, we had 150 in Church for English carols, and then just 100 for Holy Communion. I go back to Hamburg on Jan. 1. Next year I have to give eight lectures in Oxford, called the Bampton lectures, the subject will be the Church, the Churches and Christian Union. I think that I am the first Cambridgeman to be elected since 1886. These lectures have to be published. I still keep alive the hope of writing a big book on the History of Christianity in India – but I do not seem to have time at present to do more than plan a book, which, if written, will have to be the fruit of a number of years of labour.

This brings you all best wishes for 1964. Perhaps I shall be able to pay a visit to Tinnevelly in 1966 – if the Lord opens the way, and gives me the clear indication that it is his will.

    All good wishes,
      Yours very sincerely,
        +Stephen Neill[87]

The tone of this letter is heartfelt, warm, and revealing. Neill was bravely fighting through his medical issues, he was thinking often about his true love – India, he was mindful of his students and he was juggling a number of travels and scholarly commitments. The 'big book' on Christianity in India was published in two volumes in 1984 and 1985, the year of his death and the year after. The third volume, planned but not written, tragically never appeared.

Winding Down

Neill's original contract at the University of Hamburg was to end in May 1967. Neill wanted to collect a Germany pension, however, so he needed to remain until 1968. He asked permission to stay for longer and this was seemingly granted when the dean announced to the faculty that 'the ecumenical bishop' would have his contract extended. However, 'administrative complications set in'.[88]

---

87. WCC Archives, Geneva, letter from Neill to 'My dear Victor', on World Christian Books letterhead, 27 December 1963.
88. Neill's unpublished autobiography, 'Professor in Germany', pp. 110-11.

8. A Professorship in Hamburg: 1962-68

Technically, Neill's position was always supposed to be temporary and would eventually be filled by a German. When Walter Freytag died, the replacement was supposed to be a German with the rank of ordinarius, which Neill never was offered. They always denied him that opportunity. Neill seemed to know these facts but he held out hope that perhaps he could manage to stay on in his position, somehow. When two prominent Germans, Horst Bürkle and Hans Margull, became available, the university was obliged to hire one of them. Neill was a bit relieved when Bürkle was recruited from Makerere College in Uganda in order to return to his homeland to work at the University of Munich.[89]

Hans Margull was another story, however. Margull was the one who had negotiated Neill's terms before Neill moved to Hamburg. During his Hamburg years, Neill was always curious as to why he was never given the title of ordinarius. It would have protected his employment, would have given him more prestige and perks and would have placed him in the inner circle at the university so he could be involved in determining which professors should be hired. What Neill originally perceived as an oversight on Margull's part became far more complicated when it became clear that Neill aspired to stay on in the faculty at Hamburg.

Margull worked for several years in Geneva at the WCC before moving to Japan for a time. When Neill's contract was up, the university reached out to Margull to replace Neill. Margull, however, would technically be replacing Freytag, since Neill was only a temporary appointment. In the end, Margull was hired – at the rank of ordinarius. They kept Neill on the faculty for six more months – until July 1968 – so he could 'look around' for another position elsewhere, but the decision that he must leave had been made. Neill was disturbed that all of the hiring conversations occurred 'without my knowledge, and this was painful to me, but was an inevitable consequence of the system of the tight-knit ring of Ordinarii . . . to which I did not belong'.[90]

Justus Freytag revealed that Neill hoped to achieve the rank of ordinarius and that Neill was caught off-guard when he was ultimately let go from the university. Justus also explained that it was basically understood by all – perhaps with the exception of Neill – that a qualified German would come back to the department one day, meaning Neill would have to leave. Margull fulfilled all of the requirements for the position and was invited back, meaning Neill had to move on. It was no surprise to the faculty members involved.[91]

---

89. Ibid., pp. 111-13.
90. Ibid., pp. 111-13.
91. Justus Freytag, interview with author, 2 October 2000. See also 'Hans Jochen Margull' in *International Review of Mission*, Vol. 71, no. 283 (July 1982), p.

One other issue that may or may not have been at play in Neill's dismissal from Hamburg was his old demon – spanking, or disciplining people whom he came to know rather intimately. I asked Darrell Guder about this, as Guder was a student at Hamburg in those days and came to know Neill fairly well. Guder responded, 'I know that Prof. Thielicke was aware of Neill's "fetish" and that the leadership of the faculty were alerted to ensure that there would be no re-occurrence. I suspect that Margull also knew.'[92]

Very rarely in his 1,500-plus-page autobiography did Neill show contempt for a person. However, in this case he did, when he discussed his 'friend' Hans Margull:

> Hans-Jochen Margull, to my infuriation, had gone to Geneva as Secretary of the Department of Evangelism. There, as I foresaw, he travelled widely and attended many conferences giving the same address over and over again. He wrote nothing of any theological value and diminished rather than enhanced his reputation in the theological and in the ecumenical world.[93]

Neill was utterly shocked when it became clear that he could not stay. In his view, he 'could not afford to stop working'.[94]

Having spent a career in several different countries, Neill's retirement income was next to nil. He was entitled to a small Swiss pension from his years at the WCC but as far as he knew there was nothing else. Neill was 'perplexed', even forlorn. However, divine intervention arrived in the form of a letter from Nairobi: 'We are thinking of starting a Department of Religious Studies in the University College here. Could you come for three months, as visiting professor of religions . . . and to draw up the feasibility study which the University requires before such a department can come into existence?'

---

394. According to Freytag, Margull (1925-82) was eminently qualified, as he completed a doctorate as well as the habilitation. He was educated in Germany and the United States, was ordained, had served in Japan as a missionary-professor and had worked in the WCC for several years. While Neill had little use for the 'Geneva nonsense' (as Neill called the later work of the WCC, see *God's Apprentice,* p. 272), Margull poured himself into that work and accomplished a lot. After Margull died, his position was filled by Professor Theodor Ahrens. Theodor Ahrens, interview with author, Hamburg, Germany, 2 October 2000.

92. Darrell Guder was a member of the faculty at Princeton Theological Seminary from 2001 until 2015 and served as Dean of Academic Affairs between 2005 and 2010.

93. Neill's unpublished autobiography, 'Professor in Germany', pp. 111-13.

94. Ibid., p. 113.

8. A Professorship in Hamburg: 1962-68

Neill responded, without hesitation: 'I could, and would.' Neill would soon move to Africa – 'a continent which I had often visited, but in which I never expected to reside'.[95]

Divine intervention made its way into Neill's life again at his going away party, which he hosted at his house in November 1967. Neill mentioned that he was heading to Nairobi and needed to work anyway since he was not entitled to a pension for his years of service in Hamburg. Some of the younger faculty members felt this was unfair and promised to look into it. What they found out ended up helping Neill financially: seemingly 'anyone who has served the University in an academic position for five full years is entitled to proportionate pension'. Neill was overjoyed to learn that this pension from Germany:

> is related not to what my salary was at the time of my retirement but to what it would be if I had remained in service till the present time. This grant has saved me from all anxiety as to the future. . . . I shall have enough to live on in modest comfort to the end of my days.[96]

Neill's church in Hamburg, St Thomas à Becket, was particularly sad to see Neill move on. In the 'Chairman's Report, 1968' it is recorded: 'Two of our greatest losses of course have been felt in the departure of Bishop Neill, whose many years in Hamburg and whose many admirable sermons will be fresh in your memories.'[97]

This little Anglican congregation in Hamburg had made good use of Neill's extraordinary preaching abilities during his time there, and it would have been very difficult to see someone of his talent and stature depart. Neill kept in touch with this little church, even offering to send them free copies of the books he wrote on Bible reading and spirituality aimed at laypeople.[98]

Neill wrapped up his lectures and recruited his lawyer friend, Hans Bender, also a member of the congregation at St Thomas à Becket, to take over his flat. Hans Margull – who was to take over Neill's position – offered

---

95. Ibid., pp. 113-15.
96. Ibid., pp. 114-15.
97. See the St Thomas à Becket Archives, Hamburg, 'Chairman's Report, 1968'.
98. St Thomas à Becket Archives, Hamburg, letter from Ian Thomas, Director of the Bible Reading Fellowship (148 Buckingham Palace Rd, London) to the Rev. R. Precious, English Church of St Thomas à Becket, Hamburg, 20 January 1969. The book that was being discussed in this letter was Neill's *One Increasing Purpose* (London: Bible Reading Fellowship, 1969). First published in 1969 with 10,000 copies, it was printed again (10,000 copies) in 1971.

to drive Neill to the airport at an ungodly hour in the morning. Neill rose and waited in the freezing cold but got let down again by Margull, who never showed up. Neill was lucky enough to find a taxi. When he arrived to the airport just in time to catch his flight, Margull turned up with the news that his secretary had given him the wrong address.[99]

Neill had deep appreciation for all that he experienced in Hamburg. He made some close friends from the church, from the faculty and from the students that passed through during his years there. It was a difficult six years for him but he 'held the fort'. In retrospect, he was pleased with the faculty's decision to appoint Margull. He held no hard feelings that can be discerned from his autobiography. Furthermore, while Neill was never entirely comfortable in West Germany, he 'never regretted spending the last six years of my ordinary working life in that Free and Hansa City'.[100]

---

99. Neill's unpublished autobiography, 'Professor in Germany', p. 116.
100. Ibid., p. 116.

Chapter Nine

The Nairobi Years: 1969-73

Neill was no rookie when he moved to Africa. He had visited numerous times, conducted a major research project there in 1950, was external reviewer for St Paul's Theological College in Limuru in Kenya and in the past had participated in an ecumenical church history conference in Nairobi with Owen Chadwick. At one point, in 1936, Neill was even invited to serve as Bishop of Mombasa, which he turned down. Neill was no stranger to Kenya. In fact, the idea of him starting a department of philosophy and/or religion in Nairobi had been kicked around by several people for several years before it finally came to fruition.[1]

In 1968 Neill 'was ready to leave Hamburg' but he wanted to keep working. When the invitation came from University College, Nairobi, the timing seemed perfect.[2] Neill was invited to serve as Visiting Professor of Religion for three months, and his salary would come from the Church. The first of his responsibilities was 'to get the idea of the Department widely known' by lecturing on the world's religions and basic issues in the scientific study of religion. As predicted, Neill's

---

1. Neill's unpublished autobiography, Section X, 'Last Phase: East Africa', pp. 121, 125.
2. When Neill first began talks with University College, Nairobi, it was part of the University of East Africa. In 1970 the University of East Africa was split into three entities: University of Nairobi (Kenya), University of Dar es Salaam (Tanzania) and Makerere University (Uganda).

lectures attracted attention and in short order the idea of a department of philosophy and religious studies began to morph from an idea into a possibility.[3]

Neill submitted a feasibility study to the university authorities in February 1968. It was not without a fair amount of opposition. The local churches in Nairobi thought the department would be too liberal, while university people thought a department of religion was inappropriate for a secular college. There was a long period of waiting, until Neill was informed that University College, Nairobi would be unable to fund the department because its budget was planned every five years and the deadline had passed. Thus, if the Department of Philosophy and Religious Studies were to come about, it would have to be paid for by private donors or organisations until the next official budget was approved in 1973. Thus, Neill and others beat the bushes and came up with funding from several Christian and Hindu organisations. The result was . . . more waiting . . . for over a year. Neill spent some of his time lecturing and researching in the United States, although he was based in England during those 'idle and tedious months'. Finally, at long last, Neill received a letter offering him the position. He readily indicated his acceptance but the official letter of offer was, once again, badly delayed, causing Neill to wonder whether the position had fallen through. Finally, in mid-August 1969, he received an urgent letter stating that the first day of classes was 22 September and they needed him to relocate to Nairobi as soon as possible. He arrived on 10 September, eager to start his new career.[4]

Nairobi – A New World

While Nairobi was not entirely unfamiliar to Neill, in many ways it was 'a new world'. Kenyans achieved their independence in December 1963, so the colonial past was still visible in the rear view mirror, including the Mau Mau uprisings (also known as 'The Emergency') against the British in the 1950s that led to the death of tens of thousands of East Africans. President Jomo Kenyatta (in office from 1963-78) emerged as a reconciler who opposed retaliation against the British. Yet he was determined to make Kenya 'unmistakably and unconditionally an African country'.[5]

There was tension in East Africa, however, as various people and groups jockeyed for political power. The famous leader of the Luo people – Oxford-educated Tom Mboya – was assassinated in broad daylight in Nairobi. In

---

3. Neill's unpublished autobiography, 'Last Phase: East Africa', pp. 121, 127-28.
4. Ibid., pp. 129-33.
5. Ibid., pp. 133-34.

Neill's view, Kenya appeared tranquil on the outside, but 'there was the feeling of deep discontent not far below the surface'.[6]

Despite the political pressures, Neill loved the city, writing, 'Nairobi must be one of the most beautiful cities in the world.' However, he also noted the crushing poverty there, for example, the time he went to a man's house for tea and found his family of eight crammed into one room without electricity or running water.[7] This grave lack of basic services for many residents of Nairobi lent itself to a very high crime rate that tended to keep the foreigners in a state of alarm. There was 'a constant fear of robbery and theft'. Cars were stolen with regularity and cars were burgled on a scale that baffled Neill. According to Neill, this kind of crime is 'more frequent in Nairobi than can be imagined by anyone who has not lived there'. On one occasion, Neill had two suitcases stolen out of his car which contained a brand new suit he had bought in London, his gold pectoral cross that he had used for more than three decades, a ring, golden cufflinks gifted to him by St Thomas à Becket Church in Hamburg and a set of his episcopal robes – which were thrown out and quickly found by police.[8]

Nairobi had other challenges as well, many of which are common to any rapidly expanding megalopolis. The traffic was awful and could become dangerous, especially at the confusing roundabouts all over the city. Neill found Nairobi to be hopelessly bureaucratic, especially at the airport where on one occasion he waited in line for four hours just to get his passport stamped. Neill found this inefficiency to be deflating and oppressive, an 'enormous wastage of time involved in these formalities that wore one down'.[9]

When Neill first arrived at the university, he found that 'nothing had been arranged' for him. Instead of a proper office, he was given a 'cubbyhole . . . with partitions which did not reach the ceiling', no telephone, an incompetent secretary and no colleagues. For one of the first times in his life, Neill found himself completely unprepared for the task ahead – his courses would start in ten days and he was expected to teach both religion and philosophy courses. That first term did not go well and Neill felt his lectures were very bad. In fact, Neill was generally overworked throughout his Nairobi years, at times even reaching 'the absurd point of being in the classroom eighteen periods a week'. Neill commented, 'to give so many bad and unprepared lectures is a soul-searing experience, which I do not wish

---

6. Ibid., p. 135.
7. Ibid., pp. 135-36.
8. Ibid., pp. 171-72.
9. Ibid., pp. 172-74.

ever to repeat'.[10] In addition, he was frustrated by the pace of progress, writing: 'Anyone who lives in Africa soon discovers that it takes five times as much energy to get anything done in Africa as it does in Europe.'[11]

He felt much better about his flat – very low cost, less than a mile from the university and about half a mile from the Anglican cathedral. The two bedrooms meant Neill had a quiet study to work and another room for guests.[12]

A middle-aged man was hired to work as Neill's servant, but proved to be 'a thorn in my side'. The man worked hard and was exceedingly neat and great at cleaning but he tended to be 'sullen and scowling'. Neill was accustomed to 'smiling Indian servants' from his years in India but this man had a mind of his own. Neill wrote, 'If I looked into the kitchen to give him his order for the day, quite often he would not even look up from what he was doing.'[13]

Neill was able to build a library quickly, as the British government was generous in donating funds for books. Each department was allotted £1,000 per year but, due to budgetary reallocations he made, Neill was able to secure £1,300 per year and acquired many of the essential texts for his budding department.

He also began to build a core team of teachers. Dr Jacobs taught African indigenous religions. An excellent American teacher arrived, Dr Malcolm McVeigh, who had experience working in Angola and Zaire. An Englishman – whom Neill chose not to name – took over the philosophy course but, unfortunately, half of the students fell away. Neill lectured on biblical studies, Greek, philosophy of religion, the Old Testament and religion in the modern world. Neill was also shouldering all of the administrative burden when, unexpectedly, a professor arrived who would prove extremely helpful to Neill. His name was T. Cuyler Young. He had been a missionary in Iran and he had headed the Middle Eastern Department at Princeton. Neill was able to put Old Testament studies into his hands, which, Neill stated, 'just saved my life'. On the other hand, Neill was forced to accept the appointment of an Arabist – Said Hamdun – who did not have the degree that he claimed. Neill was shocked and 'unhappily carried this secret in my inner consciousness' for three years. Hamdun was unable to complete his degree while teaching and therefore the university cancelled his contract. This situation left Neill very stressed and with 'a hole of nearly £10,000 in our finances, with not very much to show for it'.[14]

---

10. Ibid., pp. 142-43, 150, 192.
11. Ibid., p. 149.
12. Ibid., p. 143.
13. Ibid., pp. 144-45.
14. Ibid., pp. 146-47. Neill did not mention Hamdun's name, however, he tells the story in detail in ibid., p. 141.

9. The Nairobi Years: 1969-73

Neill arranged several public lectures to try and build momentum for his department and also to reach out to the community. That first year, the lecturers were Cuyler Young, John Mbiti – who attracted audiences of nearly 300, Taran Singh and Neill himself. These lectures opened doors to the public and helped people to understand a bit about what was happening in the up-and-coming Department of Philosophy and Religious Studies.[15]

While Neill clearly worked tirelessly to establish the new department, he very quickly developed a reputation as a colonialist while in Nairobi, and it was due largely to his own methods and need for control. In a candid letter to his niece, Neill exposed his deep frustration about his work in Nairobi:

> At the moment I am driven mad by examinations; our system here is absurdly complicated; some of my colleagues have not understood the system, and I am trying desperately to get their marks into the proper arrangement for submission to the Arts Faculty Board early next week; I don't see how I can possibly get it done, but if one puts one's mind to a thing, it usually does get done on time. What wears me out here is the necessity of keeping an eye on every blessed thing; to say that something is to be done does not necessarily mean that it will be done, unless one watches with lynx eyes and sees to every blessed thing oneself. . . . But it means that I am very tired and looking forward very much to some leave.[16]

Neill was now an elderly man, past the age of retirement for most Europeans, and he felt it. He blamed it on the hot weather, although Nairobi is nearly 6,000 feet above sea level and thus rarely gets above 26 degrees Celsius. However, the altitude took a toll on him and he could rarely work in the evenings, often being 'too tired even to listen to music'. This 'useless idleness' was yet another source of irritation for Neill in Nairobi as he was used to working late into the evenings in his home office.[17]

Neill's old enemy – insomnia – also returned to haunt him due to what he thought was the stillness of the evenings combined with the intense humidity. Neill started taking sedatives again just to catch a bit of 'artificial sleep'. The predictable result was physical and mental exhaustion. As a result, Neill felt he made 'many mistakes' in dealing with colleagues. He provoked unnecessary opposition and alienated people who could have become his friends.[18]

---

15. Ibid., p. 148.
16. Neill to Penelope (Penny) Neill Golby, 17 March 1973. A scanned copy of this letter was sent from Golby to the author.
17. Neill's unpublished autobiography, 'Last Phase: East Africa', p. 151.
18. Ibid., p. 152.

The second year saw the addition of 'a most excellent colleague' named J.G. Donders (1929-2013), a Dutch 'White Father', a Roman Catholic priest-missionary. Father Donders was a highly capable professor who got on well with everybody. Neill also started hiring Kenyans, such as Joseph Nyasani, a brilliant scholar with degrees from Rome (BA), England (Diploma in Social Ethics), Germany (JD) and a PhD from the University of Cologne. Unfortunately for Neill, Nyasani promptly left Nairobi in 1971 to serve in the United Nations offices in New York. From 1973 to 1974 he served as an Associate Professor at the City University of New York, only finally to return to the University of Nairobi (as University College, Nairobi became in 1970) just after Neill left. A philosophy professor named Henry Odera Oruka arrived with the rank of 'Special Lecturer' – despite having a doctorate in hand. According to Neill, he showed 'considerable originality and enterprise'. Neill was also able to secure the services of John Mbiti – an outstanding scholar at the University of Makerere – as the external examiner. Neill was delighted when all of the department's students passed the annual examinations.[19]

One day Father Donders remarked to Neill that Western notions of 'logic' seemingly did not register in the African mind. This prompted Neill to assert that: 'The African still tends to think in pictures and Western abstract terms have little meaning for him; he can learn them by heart and use them, but they will still continue to be foreign bodies in his mind.' These ideas prompted Neill to wonder aloud about 'the really fundamental question – How does the African think, and is there such a thing as African philosophy?' He continued:

> The African does not think in abstract terms of being, but of vital force, what a thing does or can do. This vital force can be diminished or augmented. . . . Part of our problem is that it is really Europe which has created Africa, just as it was the British who created India. . . . African unity is now a basic part of the creed of every educated African; this tends to make him overlook the vast differences which separate the culture of one African people from another. . . . The culture of the Kikuyu is largely based on the rite of circumcision . . . This has been extended to include

---

19. Ibid., p. 153. See also email from Jesse Mugambi to the author, 6 June 2010. Nyasani's CV is online at: https://profiles.uonbi.ac.ke/nyasani/files/cv_nyasani_2013_latest.pdf. For 'Special Lecturer' and for details on Odera, 'the real pioneer Kenyan philosopher when he joined the department . . . on May 1st, 1970', see Anke Graness and Kai Kresse, *Sagacious Reasoning: Henry Odera Oruka in Memoriam* (New York: Peter Lang, 1997), pp. 233-34.

> female circumcision, a barbarous, brutal and senseless mutilation . . . which has become as the ark of the covenant to the Kikuyu. . . . The neighbouring tribe, the Luo, on the other hand, being Nilotic, have never known circumcision and regard it with a mixture of dislike and contempt. But such differences ought not to hide from us the fact that there is a real unity, of which the Africans have every right to be proud.

Neill was indebted to Dr Henry Odera's lectures and research on African history and philosophy; they enlightened him immensely in understanding the varied contexts of his students and he gave credit to Dr Odera in his autobiography. However, Odera was deeply frustrated by Neill's conviction that 'Africans . . . could not think in a straight logical fashion as required by the discipline. . . . Africans were not made to and could not be philosophers. . . . African modes of thought were deeply grounded on their mythical representations of reality.'[20]

The third year saw the arrival of Reverend Dr Terence Day, a CMS missionary from India. He was able to take over the lectures dealing with Asian religions. However, Dr Day had to surmount a number of problems that stemmed from the fact that he was Asian: at that time in East Africa Asians and Africans did not typically get on well with each other. Neill described it as a situation of apartheid in the student body, much of it stemming from a difference of religion, as the Asians were rarely Christian. Additionally, Indians had for years dominated the commercial scene in East Africa and, once independence was gained in 1963, the Indians living there lost many of their rights. Neill wrote, 'Even for Kenyan citizens there was no real security; the Kenyan government, like most other African governments, made no secret of its view that no one in Africa has any real rights, except the born black African.'[21]

In Neill's fourth year at Nairobi – the academic year 1972-73 – his department saw a fourth straight annual increase in students, now up to 144. In that year, the Roman Catholic Church sent Reverend Reginald Fuller to work in the department and he proved to be a great help. Hugh Pilkington was another who arrived that year. Pilkington was a wealthy philanthropist who eventually became a renowned scholar of Ethiopic, completing his doctoral dissertation at the University of Oxford in 1979. His estate was used to establish the Windle Trust which is still very active. Pilkington

---

20. Neill's unpublished autobiography, 'Last Phase: East Africa', pp. 157-58. For quotations related to Odera, see Graness and Kresse, *Sagacious Reasoning*, pp. 233-34.
21. Neill's unpublished autobiography, 'Last Phase: East Africa', pp. 177-79.

was also a licensed pilot and owned a four-seater aeroplane. He flew Neill to several places on safari, flew all across East Africa, visited remote lakes, feeling 'thoroughly colonial' as they had up, close and personal moments with wild animals. Neill greatly appreciated these excursions away from 'the torrid zones of overwork and tiredness'.[22]

During that fourth year, Neill decided to offer a course on Christianity in Africa. He had asked the History Department to do so but they refused Neill's request more than once. Thus, Neill offered it, knowing full well that there were big holes in his curriculum. At that time, in 1972-73, Neill stated that one of the most difficult aspects of teaching Christianity in Africa was that there was simply no textbook yet written on the topic. Furthermore, Neill felt that his students had fallen under the spell of the anti-missionary myth, which he found particularly offensive. He wrote:

> The anti-missionary myth runs roughly as follows: African society was practically perfect, until the missionaries came along and ruined everything.... The most evil thing that has ever existed on the face of the earth has been white colonialism. The missionaries were inescapably part of the colonial system; therefore it was impossible for them to do any good, and in point of fact they did a great deal of harm.

Obviously, as a famous colonial missionary, Neill found this perspective to be questionable, at best, and patently false, at worst. As Neill argued in his important work, *Colonialism and Christian Mission*, the truth is somewhere in between. Furthermore, since careful, scholarly studies of Christianity in East Africa were practically non-existent in 1973, Neill felt it would 'be a long time before mythology is overtaken by the march of the scientific study of history'. For the present time, however, Neill felt that most East Africans held onto 'an almost wholly imaginary idealisation of the past and a nostalgic desire to return to the womb of tribal existence'.[23]

Neill's course on Christianity in Africa had fifteen students and he knew that, as a white man, he 'would have to walk very warily'. He determined not to show his cards so that he would not lose the confidence of the class. He wrote, 'My method was simply to help them to see that the history was far more complicated than they had been led to suppose.' Neill's topics still hold up well today: the uniqueness, resiliency and antiquity

---

22. Ibid., pp. 193-94. On the Windle Trust, see https://windle.org.uk/history.
23. Neill's unpublished autobiography, 'Last Phase: East Africa', pp. 194-96. Neill did note that West Africa, Nigeria in particular, had two scholars who were doing such research: Professor Ajaya and Professor Agendele.

9. The Nairobi Years: 1969-73

of the Ethiopian Church; Muslim-Christian interactions; the Protestant missionary societies; the Roman Catholic 'White Fathers'; and the African prophets William Wade Harris and Simon Kimbangu--as well as the movements those two charismatic leaders spawned. They also discussed hot topics such as polygamy. Neill adopted the German 'seminar' format for this course, which meant that each student had to prepare a factual paper and present it in class for discussion and debate with his or her peers.[24]

Neill thought that his fourth year in Nairobi would be his last; however, the university asked him to extend his stay for a few months into the fifth year, as a few problems had popped up. The first was that the academic calendar had changed. Instead of beginning in September, the new academic year would begin in July. Neill's contract would keep him in Nairobi until September 1973. Thus, Neill was asked to lead the department for a few extra months.

The second problem was more significant. A new faculty of education had been opened in the university and had admitted hundreds of students who would have to do their preliminary studies in the arts faculty, meaning the Philosophy and Religious Studies Department would have an increase in students from 144 to 312. In addition, some members of the faculty were leaving and would have to be replaced. An Ismaili professor came on board, as did Reverend M.W. Mathews from the CMS. Dr Day moved back to Canada. An American professor named Waetjer arrived from California to come and volunteer. Hugh Pilkington, who had just won a prestigious prize from Oxford, 'signed on for another year, and was prepared to teach almost any language under the sun'. Neill and the department made it work, but it was very difficult and they were unable to cultivate personal relations with the students as they had done in the past; there were just too many.[25]

A third problem was much bigger. It had to do with 'the so-called moratorium on missionaries in the third world', which suddenly put Neill and many other foreigners onto the chopping block. Neill felt that, were the foreigners to leave, the philosophy side would be okay, since 'A group of young Kenyan philosophers was growing up, on whom we should be able to draw as posts had to be filled'. The situation with the religious studies side of the department was not so clear, as there simply were not enough high-quality candidates to fill the professorships. Pressure was increasing on the entire university to 'Kenyanise as quickly as possible'. Neill referred to the anti-foreigner sentiment as 'tribalism' and felt that this tribalism had

---
24. Neill's unpublished autobiography, 'Last Phase: East Africa', pp. 196-98.
25. Ibid., pp. 213-14.

won the hearts and minds of the vast majority of Kenyans. It was becoming clear to Neill that he was no longer welcome. It was not personal, it was just the power of the vast winds of change blowing through Kenya at that time.[26]

The Christian Scene

Christianity was growing by leaps and bounds in East Africa during Neill's tenure there. He discussed one report that said the church had 'doubled itself in less than eight years', and was growing at a rate of around ten per cent each year. There were problems with this explosive growth, for example, the tendency for entire tribes to join one church, as the Kikuyu had with the Presbyterian Church. However, this situation was no better than 'the old days . . . [where] every CMS missionary had been absolutely supreme in his own area'. Neill was particularly dismayed by the 'widely divergent principles' of organisation he saw happening in the Anglican Church episcopacy there: 'The combination in an African bishop of the worst features of the old CMS missionary, of the naturally autocratic tendencies of a great African chief and of a concept of episcopacy which seemed to me thoroughly un-Anglican.'[27]

Neill realised he was hired to teach in a completely secular way in the university; however, a missionary at heart, Neill was most concerned with matters pertaining to the kingdom of God. While the student body was around 75 per cent 'Christian' – largely Protestant – there were still a fair number of Hindus, Sikhs and Muslims. During Neill's time there, 1969 to 1973, the university doubled in size to around 4,000 students. Neill remarked, 'We had a considerable parish on our hands.'[28]

There was an array of ministries in Nairobi, beginning with the students' worship service held every Sunday morning in St Andrew's Church, which routinely attracted nearly 400 students. Neill preached there several times a year. Another ministry, the Christian Union, consisted primarily of evangelical students who were of a conservative bent; Neill made friends with many of them. The Kenya education system also has what are called Harambee (self-help) schools which were established all across the country under Jomo Kenyatta. Neill was invited to speak at them from time to time, which gave him great joy and often proved to be an escape from the city. On one occasion he travelled 300 miles to speak at one and had a delightful time learning about people in the remote parts of Kenya. Neill

---

26. Ibid., pp. 214-19.
27. Ibid., pp. 136-38.
28. Ibid., p. 158a.

was even asked to fill in at a Baptist church for a month on one occasion, an invitation that greatly surprised him. Neill thought that the Baptists at that church were 'the most thoughtful Christians in Nairobi' at the time.[29]

The Anglican Church made good use of Neill during his years in East Africa. He chaired the Provincial Commission on Training for the Ministry, which caused him some heartache; he was appalled by the inferior standards, the lack of interest in Anglican ministry and the 'horrifying picture of confusion' due to an 'almost complete lack of planning and foresight'.[30] Neill was also asked to help out with the creation of a constitution for the Anglican Church in Kenya. He was dismayed by the supreme power of the bishops in Kenya and realised the situation must be changed. Neill thoroughly enjoyed his time on that committee, calling it 'one of the best bodies I have ever sat on. . . . I hope that some of the drafts that I wrote may remain in the Constitution of the Church of the Province, and may perhaps be the most lasting memorial of my work in this part of the world.'[31]

One area where neither Neill nor any other Christian could make much progress was in evangelising the Asian population. Very few Indians in East Africa are Christian and the ones who are were already Christian when they arrived to do business there. The Southern Baptists from the United States did have a little success here and there, but by and large 'Indian converts in Kenya are a rare species indeed'. Even Dr Day, an Indian national, had no success in penetrating the 'closed world' of the Indians in Nairobi.[32]

Neill had a fascination with the Maasai people and he was ecstatic to learn that, after years proving to be 'an almost solid wall of resistance to the acceptance of the Gospel', they were now, at long last, responding to the message of Christ. Neill took two trips to Isinya, 58 kilometres south of Nairobi, where there was 'an excellent Maasai development centre'. He also conducted services amongst Maasai communities on occasion, usually in Swahili – which is not their native tongue but is slowly catching on. Neill never mastered Swahili but he was learned enough to conduct a church service in the language and often did so when outside the city.[33]

In Neill's final few months in Nairobi, he began to sense that foreigners were being shown the door and this was as true in the churches as it was in the university. Neill was sad about this development, as he had never

---

29. Ibid., pp. 158a-64. For a good article on Harambee schools, see Kilemi Mwiria, 'Kenya's Harambee Secondary School Movement: The Contradictions of Public Policy', *Comparative Education Review*, Vol. 34, no. 3 (August 1990), pp. 350-68.
30. Ibid., p. 165.
31. Ibid., pp. 169-70.
32. Ibid., pp. 179, 182.
33. Ibid., pp. 199-204.

thought that tribalism was the answer in an age of global Christianity. Neill had seen this sentiment before, in his final years in India, just before Gandhi led the nation to independence. Neill wrote candidly about this development in Nairobi:

> When colour, racism, anti-foreign prejudice, ambition and intrigue enter in the life of a Church, the cause of Christ is bound to be grievously wounded, and to suffer serious set-backs. It looks as though the next twenty years might be for the Kenyan Churches a period of introversion, of opportunities lost because not observed, and of impoverishment rather than enrichment in the life of the Spirit. I had little time for the consideration of such problems, since my period of service in Kenya was drawing to a close.

Neill was now 72 years of age and this was the kind of battle that could not be won. If Kenyanisation was the collective will, then foreigners could rarely if ever succeed in making a case to stay.[34]

Neill's close colleague, Father Donders, said this controversy was actually caused by Neill himself when the bishop stated that, 'for the good of African Christianity a constant flow of foreign missionaries would be necessary'. Kenyan Christians, however, argued that their churches needed to indigenise so that they could become independent from the West. They needed to be the shapers of their own identity and destiny. Thus, there was a strong belief that all foreigners should leave so that Kenyans could chart their own course, 'at least for a time'.[35] Neill was obviously uncomfortable with these ideas, challenging them as being 'tribalistic'.

By the end of Neill's time in Nairobi, he had developed some fairly strong opinions about Kenyan culture. He wrote a letter to his niece in England in March 1973, providing a short commentary on the state of affairs in Kenya:

> For the time being Kenya is an oasis of peace in troubled Africa; there is a vast amount of discontent under the surface; the Kikuyu are getting a stranglehold on the whole life of the country; no one loves them, but they have got themselves into a very strong position and this may lead to great trouble later on. But for the time being all is peaceful; getting less and less efficient through

---

34. Ibid., p. 219.
35. Joseph G. Donders, 'My Pilgrimage in Mission', *International Bulletin of Missionary Research*, Vol. 36, no. 2 (April 2012), pp. 96-99.

too rapid Africanisation, and getting rid of the Asians is doing the country no good – more rabid racialism even than South Africa! But we are thankful to be able to get on with our jobs in peace.[36]

Clearly Neill had, or thought he had, caught himself up on the politics of Kenya by the end of his time in Kenya and as usual his opinions were not hidden.

Neill's Scholarship in Nairobi

Despite Neill's inability to get much done in the evenings and the fact that he felt exhausted much of the time, his scholarly output was remarkable. During his Nairobi years (1969-73) Neill published seven books and numerous articles. Again, it must be kept in mind that he was also preaching often, lecturing in various places when invited, travelling regularly, carrying out all of the responsibilities of a professor, as well as heading a new academic department. The books that Neill published during these years were:

1969 – *One Increasing Purpose* (London: Bible Reading Fellowship)
1969 – *Ecumenism: Light and Shade* (Toronto: Ryerson Press)
1970 – *Call to Mission* (Philadelphia, PA: Fortress Press)
1970 – *Bible Words and Christian Meanings* (London: SPCK)
1970 – *The Story of the Christian Church in India and Pakistan* (Grand Rapids, MI: Eerdmans)
1970 – *What We Know about Jesus* (London: Lutterworth Press)
1970 – *Concise Dictionary of the Christian World Mission* (London: Lutterworth Press), with Gerald Anderson and John Goodwin

The groundbreaking nature of his scholarship was not as obvious in Nairobi because of a number of factors. Library resources were not nearly as strong in Nairobi as they were in Hamburg and Geneva. His work load was significantly more onerous in Nairobi than in Hamburg, as developing and administering a new department that was growing prolifically would have been extremely taxing. Finally, for most of his Nairobi years, Neill was a man in his seventies. He was not able to work deep into the evenings as he once did. As mentioned, he was never able to sleep well in Nairobi, he became dependent upon sedatives to put him to sleep and the muggy nights seemed to bother him. In spite of all this, Neill produced a fairly impressive corpus of writing. Two books a year would be stellar for most academics but, compared to Neill's years in Hamburg, for him it represents a decline in productivity.

36. Neill to Penelope Golby, 17 March 1973.

Neill's first book during his Nairobi years was *One Increasing Purpose: Lenten Meditations*. Not an academic work, this little book came from the pen of a bishop, a pastor committed to building up the faithful. First published in 1969, the book's Foreword was written by Donald Coggan, then Archbishop of York, 1961-74, and later Archbishop of Canterbury, 1974-80. Archbishop Coggan's perspective on Neill's writings are about as accurate as any could be:

> It is always good news to hear that Bishop Stephen Neill has produced a new book – whether it be a stout volume of Bampton Lectures or a slim book like this to help us in the understanding of the Bible. We can be sure of scholarship, of spirituality, and of lucidity – and that is a good trio.

Coggan described the book: 'The readings will serve not only as a guide for their readers during Lent, but as something of an introduction to an understanding of the Bible and its dominant themes.'[37]

Neill's second Nairobi book was *Ecumenism: Light and Shade* and was also published in 1969. This book was a publication of Neill's 1967 Gallagher Memorial Lectures in Canada. The Reverend Dr W.J. Gallagher, who died in 1964, was for twenty years the General Secretary of the Canadian Council of Churches. Neill's lectures were the first to be given in commemoration of Gallagher and they took place in the cities of Toronto, Vancouver, Edmonton, Montreal and Halifax, respectively.[38] In this book Neill argued that the modern ecumenical movement arose out of the explosion of Protestant missions in the nineteenth century, a thesis that has since been broadly accepted. Tellingly, Neill wrote that the first time he had visited Canada two decades earlier, things were very different. In the 1940s, he wrote, 'we were all younger, and still living in the brief period of relief and exhilaration which followed upon the end of the Second World War'. However, Neill noted, the 1950s and 1960s had been full of disasters, and the only course for the Christian's life was to realise that 'Jesus Christ alone is hope for the Church and for the world'.[39]

The third book published during Neill's Nairobi years was actually the third instalment of his missions trilogy (the previous two being *A History of Christian Missions* and *Colonialism and Christian Missions*). It

---

37. Stephen Neill, *One Increasing Purpose: Lenten Meditations* (London: Bible Reading Fellowship, 1969), p. 5.
38. Stephen Neill, *Ecumenism Light and Shade: The Gallagher Memorial Lectures 1967* (Toronto: Ryerson Press, 1969), p. v.
39. Ibid., p. vii-viii.

was a slender volume produced in 1970 entitled *Call to Mission*. It was vintage Neill. He took the complicated, scholarly material from the two former books and re-presented it for a larger audience. Neill knew that many laypeople had a deep interest in missions. More than most leaders, Neill knew that Christians without higher education needed to know what was going on in mission studies. Such a perspective governs this fascinating, 113-page practical guide. Simple chapter titles say it all: 'Why Missions?', 'What the Missionaries Did Wrong', 'What the Missionaries Did Right' and 'Where Do We Go from Here?' This was Neill at his best – communicating an enormously complicated subject in a way the average layperson could comprehend. Precisely this skill prompted Gerald Anderson to describe Neill's literary genius as '*Encyclopedia Britannica* in *TIME* Magazine form'.[40]

Neill's fourth Nairobi book was *Bible Words and Christian Meanings*. It was the second of five books he published in 1970 and designed for reading groups who wanted to learn more about the basics of their faith. Neill organised the book into twelve chapters, which were meant to be studied a week at a time. The chapters were organised according to the following 'Bible words': Creation, Light, Life, Sin, Sacrifice, Grace, Faith, Reconciliation, Peace, Hope, Love and Glory. The book ends with a reflection upon the book of Revelation and with the following words of encouragement from Neill, 'The aim of Revelation is not to terrify us but to assure us that the one who is Ruler and Judge of all the ages is also our friend, the Friend of sinners, and that his aim, from Alpha and Omega, is to make us partakers of his victory and his peace.'

The fifth book published by Neill during the Nairobi years was *The Story of the Christian Church in India and Pakistan*. Published in 1970 by Eerdmans, it was part of a series called *Christian World Mission Books*. It is a fast-moving and concise (183 pages) work wherein Neill discusses his true passion. It no doubt set the stage for his mammoth two-volume *A History of Christianity in India*, which was published in 1984 and 1985 – the year of his death and the year after. It is interesting to note that scholars of Christianity in India read this earlier book but were aware that Neill had long aspired to write a major, definitive work on the topic. Therefore, this work proved to be something of a disappointment to some. One reviewer concluded with these words:

> There is a great deal of work to be done in the field of Indian church history and one can only hope that the more extensive work

---

40. Gerald Anderson, interview by author, Port Dickson, Malaysia, 5 August 2004.

in the area, which the good Bishop has promised his readers in the future, will be more original and 'pioneering' than the present volume.[41]

Indeed, in the Preface of this book, Neill wrote that he found this somewhat slim volume to be frustrating to write, because he had to omit large amounts of information that he and his more informed readers would certainly know about and expect to be present in a history. Yet, while Neill defended himself repeatedly in the Preface by saying 'I have done my best', he promised a better product in the future, 'I have already planned a work on Indian church history on a far more extensive scale, in which I can promise such readers that they will find all the information that they could desire.'[42]

Neill's sixth Nairobi book was a slender, 84-page volume called *What We Know about Jesus*. Neill wrote several books specifically on Jesus: *The Gospel According to St John* (1930); *The Challenge of Jesus Christ* (1944); *Christ, His Church and His World* (1948); *Who Is Jesus Christ?* (1956); *What We Know about Jesus* (1970); *Jesus Through Many Eyes* (1976); and *The Supremacy of Jesus* (1984). *What We Know about Jesus* asks intriguing questions such as 'Why did people ever write gospels?' and 'What did Jesus think about himself?' Clearly meant for a popular audience, the book has the hallmarks of a series of lectures meant to build up the body of Christ.

The final book published during Neill's Nairobi years is the wonderful, helpful volume entitled *Concise Dictionary of the Christian World Mission*. It was edited by Neill, Gerald Anderson and John Goodwin and was part of Neill's *World Christian Books* project. At nearly 700 pages, the book is a major contribution to knowledge in the field of mission studies. The editors believed that they had accomplished something unprecedented, and the Preface begins with big promises:

> Only rarely is it possible for authors and editors to claim that they have done something that has never been done before. The editors of this Dictionary, however, believe that this is a claim they are entitled to make. . . . Here for the first time an attempt has been made to provide in dictionary form somewhat comprehensive

---

41. David C. Scott, 'Review of *The Story of the Christian Church in India and Pakistan*', *Journal of Ecumenical Studies*, Vol. 9, no. 4 (Fall 1972), pp. 899-900.
42. Stephen Neill, *The Story of the Christian Church in India and Pakistan* (Grand Rapids, MI: Eerdmans, 1970), pp. 9-10.

information as to the entire process through which in the last five centuries Christianity has grown from a western to a universal religion.[43]

With more than 200 contributors and over 1,000 articles, the book is a masterpiece and is still useful 50 years later. Beginning with Neill's entry on Abdul Masih, 'the first Indian clergyman of the Church of England in India', and ending with an entry on Samuel Marinus Zwemer, a missionary to Muslims who later taught at Princeton Seminary, this book succeeds on many levels. It is extremely well written, largely due to Neill's strong desire to produce readable scholarship rather than complicated writing aimed exclusively at the academically inclined.

Concise Dictionary of the Christian World Mission was reviewed widely and well-received, with the exception of the valid criticism that it gave insufficient attention to Catholic missions. Reportedly 80 per cent of the articles were written by Protestant authors about Protestant themes. However, one Jesuit reviewer did note that:

> Normally Protestants know more about Catholic mission history and theology than Catholics know about Protestant mission. . . . Though the articles on Catholic mission are fewer, one can readily retort that hardly any Catholic books on mission give proportionately as much attention to Protestant mission history and theology.[44]

One reviewer, David L. Lindberg, noticed that Neill wrote one fifth of the articles, which would be more than 40 entries. Nevertheless, he concluded, 'We have here, therefore, an authoritative source book of basically western mission material and bibliography not available elsewhere except through the indices and footnotes of . . . others.'[45]

Among the dozens of articles, chapters, lectures and reviews that Neill wrote during the Nairobi years, there are several that stand out.[46] In 1969

---

43. Stephen Neill, Gerald Anderson and John Goodwin, eds, *Concise Dictionary of the Christian World Mission* (New York: Abingdon Press, 1971), pp. v-vi.
44. George A. Mueller's review of *Concise Dictionary of the Christian World Mission* in *The Catholic Historical Review*, Vol. 59, no. 3 (Oct. 1973), pp. 505-6. See also Jesuit Francis X. Clark's review of the same book in *Philippine Studies*, Vol. 20, no. 2 (Second Quarter 1972), pp. 345-46.
45. Lindberg's review of *Concise Dictionary of the Christian World Mission* is in *Church History*, Vol. 40, no. 4 (December 1971), p. 506.
46. Jolyon Mitchell writes that during Neill's Nairobi years, he lectured or researched in Malawi, the United States, Canada, England and numerous Asian nations. See Mitchell, 'Stephen Neill: A Traditional Communicator in an Age of Revolution', p. 215.

he published a curious chapter entitled, 'The Participation of Indian Christians in Political Affairs', in which he made the important observation that: 'It was only by chance that the declaration of the independence of India and the inauguration of the Church of South India came about in the same month of the same year.'[47]

In 1970 he published 'The History of Missions: An Academic Discipline', a very useful piece of missions historiography that summarises the history and present state of missiology as an academic field in its own right.[48] Also in 1970 Neill published a daily devotional for the month of February that combined insights from the book of Acts with insights from the WCC's 1948 Amsterdam assembly.[49]

In 1971 Neill published a weighty article for the scholarly journal *Review and Expositor* entitled 'Syncretism and Missionary Philosophy Today'. This piece interacts with modern critical reviews of Christian missions, coming both from inside and outside the church. Neill's long conclusion, spanning four pages, is beautifully summarised in a couple of sentences: 'A Christian faith which is not quite sure of itself tends to be harsh, dogmatic, and aggressive. If we really believe Jesus Christ to be the truth, we can go very far in the direction of openness to others.' Moreover, while Neill points out there are 'certain dangers' in practicing interreligious dialogue, he concludes that: 'it is a method that needs to be carefully considered; and in a world which is becoming increasingly hostile to anything in the way of direct proclamation, it is perhaps the only method of Christian witness open to us'.[50]

Perhaps the best articulation of Neill's pneumatology is found in his little-known article from 1971 entitled 'The Holy Spirit in the Non-Christian World'.[51] This article has been analysed carefully by Jolyon Mitchell. He writes that this article is:

---

47. This chapter is in Sigbert Axelson, *The Church Crossing Frontiers: Essays on the Nature of Mission, In Honour of Bengt Sundkler* (Lund: Gleerup, 1969), pp. 67-82.
48. This is a chapter in G.J. Cuming, ed., *The Mission of the Church and the Propagation of the Faith: Papers Read at the Seventh Summer Meeting and the Eight Winter Meeting of the Ecclesiastical History Society* (Cambridge: Cambridge University Press, 1970).
49. In *Word for the World, Book 1: January to March* (London: Bible Reading Fellowship, 1970). Neill wrote the daily devotionals for the month of February. January was written by Suzanne de Dietrich and March was written by Philip Potter. Potter became General Secretary of the WCC in 1972, just two years after this volume was published.
50. Stephen Neill, 'Syncretism and Missionary Philosophy Today', *Review and Expositor*, Vol. 68, no. 1 (February 1971), pp. 65-80. Summary is from p. 77.
51. Stephen Neill, 'The Holy Spirit in the Non-Christian World', *Church Quarterly*, Vol. 3, no. 4 (1970/71), pp. 301-11.

highly significant . . . for understanding Neill's perception of the part which the Holy Spirit played in the communication of the Gospel. . . . His reading of the New Testament leads him to conclude that the 'Spirit now means the Spirit of the risen Jesus'. As the Spirit is located primarily within the Christian community, then writers should avoid using 'Spirit' in a wider more inclusive and universalistic context. . . . Therefore, [Neill] makes the contentious identification of Jesus with Spirit and appears to confine the work of the Holy Spirit to a narrow context. . . . He also has little time for those who make 'undiscriminating use of the term Christ' and who say that 'we do not go to take Christ with us; we go to find him where he has already gone before'. In other words, Neill implicitly identifies the Spirit's work more closely with Jesus the Saviour than God the Creator. . . . [Neill's] Conclusion makes it clear where he believes the Holy Spirit primarily works. On the basis of past activity [Neill] argues that it has 'almost always been through the presence of the Church, through an uncompromising witness to Jesus Christ, through humility and service . . .' that the Holy Spirit has been able to break the hardness of the human heart.

Mitchell concludes that Neill's pneumatology is in fact couched in a Christocentric model: 'It is as if the stone of Christ drops into the pool of history and ripples out by the Spirit through the Church to the non-Christian world.'[52]

Neill believed that the Spirit does indeed work outside the borders of the Christian Church but it is nearly impossible to know for certain where exactly that work is taking place. Neill's interest in African traditional religions, and his decision to include them in the teachings of the Department of Philosophy and Religious Studies, illustrate his belief that 'the Spirit was working universally'.[53]

Also in 1971 Neill reflected upon his WCC book series in an article for *International Review of Mission*, the WCC's flagship journal. The article was entitled 'World Christian Books: A Venture of Faith'.[54] It is a good historical overview of how Neill and his team of editors and authors managed to churn out 60 books with a total of nearly 5,000 pages, and what contributions to the Church that they were able to make with the series. Neill's conclusion was that:

---

52. Mitchell, 'Stephen Neill: A Traditional Communicator in an Age of Revolution', pp. 218-27.
53. Ibid., p. 226.
54. Stephen Neill, 'World Christian Books: A Venture of Faith,' *International Review of Mission*, Vol. 60 (1971), pp. 478-89.

> We failed to solve the problem of literature for the younger churches. But no one else has solved it either. . . . All that can be said is that in certain corners a certain amount of ploughing and sowing has been going on. . . . we take our wages and are gone, we pass on the teas to others with our best wishes, and hope that they may be led into greater achievements than we were able to encompass in our day.[55]

One gets the sense that Neill felt a bit disappointed in what they accomplished, despite the fact that they had indeed accomplished much in that major book series.

In 1972 Neill published a scholarly article called 'The Necessity of Episcopacy: Anglican Questions and Answers' for the journal *Concilium*.[56] Neill's perspective in the article is balanced. He is willing to criticise the office of bishop but ultimately defends it: 'Episcopacy has often broken down and failed to fulfil its proper functions; but no more satisfactory form of church organization has ever yet been devised'. In the end, Neill showed his colours when he urged that, if Anglican Churches were to get involved in schemes for Church union, the episcopacy is the one sacred cow that they must preserve at all costs.[57] That same year, Neill published another look at episcopacy, yet with a more narrow focus, in his article 'The See of Canterbury'. In the article he praised William Temple, Archbishop of Canterbury from 1942 to 1944, with the following words: 'Perhaps the greatest Christian of the century. . . . The Romans have had no man as learned as William Temple.'[58]

Neill had strong opinions about the position of Archbishop of Canterbury, as he had served as Assistant Bishop to the Archbishop in the late 1940s. In a 1972 article in *The Times* Neill was highlighted as one pushing for an 'international election' of the Archbishop of Canterbury. Neill pointed out that the pontificate has a kind of international election process via the College of Cardinals and argued that the Church of England should take a similar approach. Neill argued that, while recent popes had been influential, recent archbishops had been rather impotent.[59]

---

55. Ibid., p. 489.
56. See Stephen Neill, 'The Necessity of Episcopacy: Anglican Questions and Answers', *Concilium*, Vol. 80 (1972), pp. 87-96.
57. Ibid., p. 96.
58. Stephen Neill, 'The See of Canterbury', *The Churchman*, Vol. 86, no. 3 (Autumn 1972), pp. 198-200.
59. 'Anglican from abroad could head church', *The Times*, 23 December 1972, p. 2.

In 1973, Neill's last year in Nairobi, he wrote at least three major scholarly articles. The first one was a careful look at 'The Nature of Salvation' for the upcoming fifth assembly of the WCC that was eventually held in Nairobi in 1975.[60] He also published a major lecture on the missionary David Livingstone entitled 'Livingstone Reconsidered'. He delivered this 'Livingstone Memorial Lecture' on 30 April 1973 at Chancellor College Hall, Blantyre, Malawi. Despite Neill's opening, 'Is it possible to say anything new about David Livingstone? The answer is almost certainly, No', he did manage to provide enough for 20 single-spaced pages of print, as usual studded with insights. A third article that Neill wrote while in Nairobi in 1973 was 'Salvation Today?' for the journal *Churchman*.[61] This article was an analysis of the Bangkok assembly of the Commission on World Mission and Evangelism and was almost thoroughly critical.

Assessments of Neill's Time in Nairobi

Professor Jesse Mugambi, an acclaimed theologian from Kenya, was at the University of Nairobi during Neill's years there. He was gracious enough to grant me a series of interviews over the years, both in person and by email, beginning in early 2003. Mugambi has taught religion at the University of Nairobi since 1971. His perspective of Neill, the university and Neill's Nairobi years has been crucial to my own understanding. Mugambi's observations and impressions are valuable, as they are amongst the last surviving eyewitness perspectives of Neill during his years in Kenya.

One of the first things Mugambi emphasised was the nature of Neill's relationship with East Africans. He was responding to my letter, in which I mentioned that, after lecturing about Neill at the University of Cambridge, some of the members of the audience commented that 'The African Christians were scared to death of Bishop Neill'. Mugambi explained:

> I think 'scared' is perhaps not the right adjective. The point is that he did not 'interact' with Africans. I got quite close – but only as close as a mature undergraduate African lay student could get to a British Anglican Bishop, a retired professor working in a foreign country of which he had little regard or respect.... To the university administration he was not one of the 'popular' professors.[62]

---

60. Stephen Neill, 'The Nature of Salvation', *Churchman*, Vol. 89, no. 3 (1975).
61. Stephen Neill, 'Salvation Today?', *Churchman*, Vol. 87, no. 4 (1973), pp. 263-274.
62. Email from Jesse Mugambi to the author, 10 March 2003.

Mugambi stated that Neill 'interacted mainly with British missionaries in Kenya, who have since returned to the UK, and some have already passed away'.[63]

Jesse Mugambi was apparently one of the few Africans who managed to get to know Neill somewhat. Actually, he came to know Neill even before the department was launched. Mugambi sat in some of Neill's classes and 'interacted with him at several levels'. Then, thirteen years after Neill left in 1973, Mugambi filled the position that Neill had once held when he became chairman of the department, from 1986 to 1990.[64]

Mugambi pointed out that Neill did not establish the Department of Philosophy and Religious Studies on his own. Planning had been ongoing since the 1960s. His retirement from Hamburg occasioned the invitation that led to his being hired in Nairobi: 'His long missionary career and reputation, coupled with his marital status (single) and personal income – these were important considerations when he was invited.'[65]

First impressions go a long way, and the impression Neill made on Mugambi was that he 'had a "bloated ego", very much like many Britons of his age and status'. Neill may have had the idea that he had come to 'civilize' Africans, as many Westerners did. This perception was nurtured by the imperial legacy under which he trained, 'and of which he became a luminary representative!' Neill was 'autocratic'. Neill was puzzled when Africans told him 'No' to his face. As a former bishop, he was not used to this kind of behaviour. 'He had been used to being obeyed without question', especially in the Church and, when 'African bishops would not let him have his way', he was extremely surprised.[66]

One of the important points Mugambi wanted to make in our correspondence was that 'Neill knew nothing about African religion and culture, and he was not interested. I know this as a fact, because we challenged him on this point in his lectures!' Mugambi then pointed to the contrast between Neill and his successor in the Chair, Father Donders – also a Westerner but a person much more sympathetic towards African religion and culture. Mugambi wrote that Donders 'has written at least a dozen books, all inspired by his fifteen years in Kenya!' Neill, however, often displayed 'racism and arrogance' and 'sometimes seemed to enjoy it'. Mugambi continued:

Neill belongs to a generation of British imperialist intellectuals who believed that the British Empire made the twentieth century,

---

63. Email from Mugambi to the author, 4 March 2003.
64. Ibid.
65. Email from Mugambi to the author, 31 March 2003.
66. Ibid.

very much like many of the American elite today believe that the twenty-first century will be shaped by the USA. They were grossly mistaken . . . but their error greatly affected their actions, sermons, lectures and writings.

Mugambi then discussed the historiographical climate during Neill's time in Nairobi:

There was a big debate at that time between British and African historians. The former believed that there was no 'African History' prior to colonization of the continent by European powers. Africans pointed out that the first modern University, long before Bologna, Paris, Halle, Oxford and Cambridge, was in Timbuktu, in present day Mali. They pointed out that the pyramids were built by negroid Africans, not by Europeans and Asians.

Thus, while due credit should go to Neill for helping to establish the department, and serving as the first chairman – no easy task, his imperialist tendencies came through quite clearly. Even Neill's inaugural lecture was offensive in the way 'he talked AT people, not WITH them'.[67]

In Mugambi's mind, Neill never fully understood his role – that he was a guest. His sense of 'indispensability' was off-putting to Africans, and he should have known that it was his job to train a successor and then get out within four years at the most. Neill was not sensitive to the African way of doing things and 'only wanted to order his way about'. He had a 'bullyish etiquette, especially when he lost his temper over matters requiring bureaucratic procedures'.[68]

Indeed, Neill was exploitative to the people around him, Mugambi continued: 'Racism is a very dangerous disease. Neill suffered incurably from it.' In retrospect, Mugambi argued: 'Neill himself ought not to have come to Africa, and if he came, he ought not to have taken that role of leadership before learning about the African culture and religious heritage. It was English nepotism that brought him to Kenya. [He was] an exploiter of Africa.'

Mugambi then criticised Neill for never becoming fluent in an African tongue. Neill actually defends himself on this matter. Apparently, he tried to use Swahili in church services but never attained fluency. Moreover, for one who was able to learn Tamil in a few months, he was surely capable. However, as Mugambi argued, 'Neill had no appreciation of the African

---

67. Ibid. Mugambi's capitals.
68. Ibid.

cultural and religious heritage. From that perspective, he was a tragic failure as a missionary. I think he perceived this failure at the end of his term in Nairobi.'

Mugambi then compared Neill to Lesslie Newbigin, the beloved bishop of South India who enjoyed great popularity amongst members of the younger churches, including Mugambi. Neill was very different, however. 'Neill remained an expatriate missionary and imperialist until he left.' Mugambi then mentioned the 'moratorium debate' which was sparked by John Gatu, a Kenyan Presbyterian leader who argued that missionaries from the Western world should return to their home countries. Neill finally did return to England in 1973 after four years in Nairobi but he left some hard feelings in his wake.[69]

In another letter, Mugambi wrote, 'Neill mentions very few Kenyans, and gets the spelling wrong on several of them! This shows how little he interacted with nationals.' He explained that Neill seemed to be regretful of his years in Nairobi. He paints a negative picture of them. In contrast, Father Donders did the opposite. He was inspired by his years in Africa.

Despite misgivings, Mugambi was quick to point out the talents that Neill possessed as well, although by no means could the gifts make up for the seeming disregard for African culture:

> [Neill] was very articulate – never repeated himself. Although he wrote his addresses, he eloquently delivered them orally. You would not notice it if he was reading his notes. He also delivered lectures on the National Radio, covering various topics, but I do not think they were preserved. He had a very high opinion of himself, and a very low opinion of Africans. He was a typical representative of the British Empire (and knighted for it!), considering Africans as people with neither religion nor culture worthy of respect.[70]

Clearly, if this is what other African students thought of Neill, then it makes sense that he left after only four years. He was replaced by a Westerner, Father Donders, who lasted much longer as head of department than Neill and seems to have been much more in sympathy with the East Africans. According to Mugambi, Donders was in the Chair from 1973-81 and stayed in Nairobi for a total of sixteen years, from 1968 until 1984.[71]

---

69. Ibid.
70. Email from Mugambi to the present author, 6 June 2010. Mugambi was talking about a radio programme called 'The Voice of Kenya' that frequently featured Neill.
71. Email from Mugambi to the author, 31 March 2003. See also Donders, 'My

9. The Nairobi Years: 1969-73

Mugambi said that Neill's time in Nairobi was a missed opportunity. 'He became a role model for hardly anybody among both staff and students.' Once, when Mugambi asked Neill to be patron of Open Forums, Neill agreed, and covered the cost of promoting the events that Mugambi had organised. However, Neill was more patronising than he was patron, in that his relations with Africans were 'puzzling'. He continued: 'He had come to "help" Africans, but he could not relate amicably with them. . . . Neill's relationship is a dramatic illustration of the pervading and persistent institutional relationship between North Atlantic "benefactors" and African "beneficiaries".'

Mugambi emphasised, however, that:

> Neill's attitude was not unique. It was pervasive among 'experts' on Africa, and this attitude still lingers on among North Atlantic 'experts' on Africa. Books that are being published today by North Atlantic Africanists are replete with this attitude, presupposing that Africans can neither 'name' nor 'explain' themselves. They can only be 'named' and 'explained' by others. Neill was a child of his time. He was a child of the British Empire. Neill was condescending towards Africans, but his attitude was representative of most missionaries and expatriate personnel working in Africa at that time. He may have been extreme, but other expatriates were on the same wave-length with him, even though they would have been less explicit in their prejudices.

According to Mugambi, little has changed in the way Westerners believe themselves to be competent on a topic after little or no experience in a context, especially when it comes to Africa:

> It was a common view among expatriate personnel that decolonisation had come too soon, if it should have come at all. Again, this attitude lingers on. . . . Kenyans have become immune to uninvited and unsolicited lectures from self-appointed expatriate 'experts' about every thinkable topic. The validation and accreditation of that expertise is almost always non-existent. Under normal circumstances Neill would not have qualified for a Professorial Appointment in Philosophy and Religious Studies in an African university, having not conducted any research on Africa. But he was neither the first, nor the last of such expatriates in Africa. They keep coming!

Pilgrimage in Mission', pp. 97-98.

However, once again, Mugambi was willing to give credit where credit was due. Neill was indeed gifted but, due to his perceived arrogance, he struggled to make friends with the people around him, especially while living in Africa. Despite this flaw, Mugambi wrote, 'We must learn to appreciate both the strengths and weaknesses of other people. We can achieve this only if we are able to appreciate our own limitations.'[72]

When I asked Mugambi about Neill's seeming inability to conceal his temper – which likely pushed people away – his perspective was balanced:

> Neill's personality trait is not unique. . . . Some clerical and lay leaders are hot tempered. . . . Perhaps Neill's prolific output is a manifestation of his passion for rigour. We find such manifestation among famous artists and composers. St Paul was pious, but he was also hot tempered. . . . Jesus was pious, but in a rage he drove money-changers out of the temple, calling them thieves.

I also asked Mugambi about Neill clashing with a female lecturer named Dr Louise Pirouet at Nairobi. I had learned about their clash from the famous world Christianity scholar David Barrett, who had mentioned their tense relationship to me in an interview. Father Donders also brought up this situation but explained it away by saying, 'Neill had difficulties with women.'[73] Mugambi had not heard of the clash but did provide illumination, nonetheless:

> Dr. Louise Pirouet . . . was the first woman to be employed on the teaching staff of the Department of Philosophy and Religious Studies under Neill. Her doctoral research was on African Evangelists in Uganda. The Thesis was published as 'Black Evangelists' (London: Rex Collings, 1978). It is understandable that she and Neill would clash, because she was appreciative of African initiatives in religion, while Neill had the opposite attitude. Neill was also a 'male chauvinist', while Louise Pirouet in her time could be described as a 'feminist'. If Neill clashed with Pirouet, I would attribute the clash more to the differences of character disposition than to gender conflict.[74]

---

72. Quotations in this paragraph are from an email from Mugambi to the present author, 13 July 2010.
73. Donders, telephone interview by author, 3 June 2005.
74. For information on Pirouet, see 'Noteworthy', *International Bulletin of Missionary Research*, Vol. 37, no. 3 (July 2013), p. 147. See also her entry in the *Dictionary of African Christian Biography*, located at: https://web.archive.org/

9. The Nairobi Years: 1969-73   323

It was clear that Neill's years in Nairobi were full of interpersonal strife, as such clashes seemed to greet him at every turn. Surely after four years Neill realised that his time in Nairobi must soon come to an end?

However, for all of the criticisms of Neill that Mugambi has offered over the years, there is a persistent respect that comes through. In 2012 he wrote:

> Neill was a very perceptive thinker, a faithful citizen of the British Empire, and a committed servant of the Church of England. Whatever his shortcomings as an individual, he put his whole heart and mind onto any task assigned to him. He was not a Team Player, and that, perhaps, was his greatest weakness. His greatest strength was his brilliant mind.[75]

Hardly a more accurate description could be made of Neill.

David Barrett (1927-2011) was another person who interacted with Neill during his Nairobi years. Barrett held a PhD from Columbia University (1965) in the sociological study of religion and became famous in missiological circles for his influential *World Christian Encyclopedia* that was first published in 1982. He devoted much of his latter career to religious demography and essentially gave birth to that academic field. He was an ordained Anglican priest and spent many years in Kenya. Barrett was deeply impacted by the life and ministry of Bishop Neill and considered him his mentor. It was Neill's lectures on 'the call of the unevangelised millions' that filled him with an urgency to go overseas for mission work, leading to his move to Kenya in 1957. He lived and worked there in various capacities until he finally left Nairobi in 1985 because of 'disagreements with African Anglican church authorities over the scope of [his] research'. He and his family relocated to Richmond, Virginia, where he remained until his death in 2011.[76]

In an interview that took place just a year before his death, Barrett answered questions about his relationship with and observations of Stephen Neill. Barrett's take on Neill's time in Nairobi was that it all 'depends upon

---

web/20161010212434/http://www.dacb.org/stories/uganda/cm--pirouet.html. My interview with David Barrett occurred by phone on 8 July 2010. Quotations in this paragraph from Mugambi are from an email from Mugambi to the author, 13 July 2010.

75. Email from Mugambi to the author, 13 March 2012.
76. Zurlo, 'The Legacy of David B. Barrett', pp. 29-39. See p. 32 for the quotation. For 'mentor', see p. 33. See also Zurlo's article in the *Dictionary of African Christian Biography*: https://dacb.org/stories/kenya/barrett-david/.

one's point of view'. Neill did have some important achievements while in Nairobi, however, there is the other side. Some people did not appreciate him, such as the local bishops. Barrett said, 'His relationship with African bishops was puzzling.' This was an interesting statement coming from Barrett, who had also experienced the ire of the African bishops while he was living in East Africa. However, Neill's dealings with the local bishops seemed to be far more confrontational. Barrett stated: 'He was really lording it over black bishops. He was criticised for his view that African bishops were being appointed too soon. Some say Neill was anti-African.' Barrett noted that 'Neill was brilliant in some things but disregarded indigenous clergy' throughout his career. For example, after reading Neill's *History of Christianity in India* in 1984 and 1985, Barrett thought, 'This is the old stuff.' Neill seemed to understand Christianity almost exclusively from the colonial perspective rather than the indigenous, a perspective he held to the end of his life.[77]

Barrett was one of several who led the charge to get Neill to come to Nairobi after his time in Hamburg came to an end. The archbishop of East Africa at the time was Leonard Beecher. Bishop Beecher approached Barrett one day and said, 'I heard you are trying to get Neill as professor. Ramsay [Archbishop of Canterbury, 1961-74] wrote a letter opposing this.' Barrett asked to see evidence but Beecher refused to produce the letter. Eventually Barrett and other Neill supporters managed to invite Neill, but not without a fight. According to Barrett, Bishop Beecher was sceptical of Neill because of rumours about what had happened with Neill in India years earlier. With a sense of satisfaction, Barrett said, 'Eventually we got Neill.'[78]

True to Neill's reputation for disregarding African indigenous religions, Barrett said Neill 'dismissed' them. Instead, upon arrival in Nairobi, Neill set his mind on organising the 'parochial archives', meaning the archives of the Church. Barrett stated that Neill took them over, trying to get them into a respectable shape. Clearly, Neill's focus was on the Church and Christianity and he held little regard for anything unrelated.[79]

Regarding Neill's personality, Barrett noted that Neill had quite the temper. 'He lost his temper, slammed the door, and pushed me out' one time. Neill was reviewing the minutes of a meeting and was irritated by the distraction. He noted that people seemed always to develop strong feelings about Neill: 'You either loved him or couldn't stand the sight of him.' He mentioned Neill's confrontation with Dr Pirouet as well as yet another memorable example. In defence of Neill, however, Barrett stated that 'the

---

77. Barrett, telephone interview by author, 8 July 2010.
78. Ibid.
79. Ibid.

9. The Nairobi Years: 1969-73

situation in Africa was really quite a mess' when Neill arrived. As Neill detailed in his autobiography, he was not allowed into Kenya until just a couple of weeks before he had to start lecturing and the scaffolding of the department that he was supposed to establish was in absolute disarray. This placed enormous strain upon Neill, who was nearly 70 years old at the time.[80]

However, much of the problem was Neill's nature. He expected others to rally around him and came across as quite selfish at times. For instance, Barrett said that he read through the entire manuscript of Neill's *History of Christian Missions* before it was published in 1964, carefully vetting all footnotes and offering feedback, but 'Neill never said thanks'. Barrett also noted that once Neill was speaking to a group of CMS missionaries in Nairobi and their overall impression was that Neill had 'an inflated ego'. Barrett, who at one point was strongly in Neill's camp, opined about that day, 'He probably deserved it.'[81]

However, Barrett noted that Neill's brilliance shone through every time he lectured: 'Every lecture was good. Everybody drank in every word.' This perspective was ironic because the precise word that Neill used to describe his lectures in Nairobi was 'bad'. Neill was a perfectionist when it came to his lectures and writings, so it is quite possible that the frenetic context within which he was working led him to have an overly critical view of his performance during that strained period in the beginning. Barrett also pointed out that Neill 'did an excellent job organising the department in Nairobi'.[82]

Before Neill arrived in 1969 there was no Department of Philosophy and Religious Studies in Nairobi. When he left in 1973 there was a world-class Department of Philosophy and Religious Studies; and the standard that Neill set has remained exceptionally high for decades, to the present day. That is no small accomplishment. Moreover, perhaps hiding in plain sight is the fact that Neill was, after all, hired to establish that department. He did it and with flying colours. The task that Neill set out to do was a difficult one. Whether or not one agrees with Neill's personal quirks, he always did what he was tasked to do – and his standards were high, extremely high. They were so high that it caused him a lot of broken relationships along the way, particularly if Neill sensed that his high standards were being threatened or compromised. Neill was no compromiser. He was not good at negotiation. However, he was extremely gifted at getting things done and with the highest attention to detail. That

---

80. Ibid.
81. Ibid.
82. Ibid.

cannot be taken from him. Neill's legacy in Nairobi is that department, which still stands – proudly – as a testament to his exacting standards for academic excellence.[83]

At the end of the interview, Barrett noted, 'We were up against mediocrity.' But Neill's perspective won. He refused to compromise with mediocrity. He used his connections to bring in world-class people – many of whom went on to achieve outstanding careers and great accomplishments. Neill had an eye for talent. However, as many have noted, Neill's shadows were ever present. The very last words Barrett said about his former mentor were the following: 'Neill lost his temper at me when I told him that many Africans were converting to Islam. He was very typical in his views that Christians were sweeping Africa and Muslims were declining.'[84]

Barrett seemed hurt by Neill's harsh and hurtful tone four decades earlier. Unfortunately, like many others, Barrett's comments signified a common theme: Neill's stellar gifts seemed to be eclipsed, or at least overshadowed, by his deep and persistent personal shortcomings – especially with people who risked getting close to him.

A third interview that shed tremendous light upon Neill's years in Nairobi was with Neill's successor, Father Joseph Donders (1929-2013). Donders took over the leadership of the department after Neill left in 1973 and he remained chair of the department until 1980 or 1981.[85]

Father Donders began his interview by discussing Neill's living quarters, 'a very humble flat', with an African servant. Then, immediately, Donders began discussing Neill's tendency to find trouble. He first mentioned Neill's row with David Barrett, although he said, 'I don't know why they fell out.' Apparently Neill was involved in Barrett's research for a while but that did not last long.[86]

Donders then discussed how Neill was already a 'very old man' at the time of his arrival, although in fact Neill was only 68 years old. Donders described Neill as an 'old kind of Daddy, clumsy, and not very well-dressed'. Perhaps Neill's personality and disposition caused him to appear older than he was, as Donders said, 'Anglicans thought of him as an old colonial.' He added the following: 'Henry Odera, Joseph Nyasani . . . Neill was not keen on his African colleagues. He was an old English colonialist.' While revered for his scholarship, Donders continued, Neill 'was a strange kind of person,

---

83. Ibid.
84. Ibid.
85. Father Donders told me he was in the chair until 1980. However, Mugambi told me Donders was chair until 1981. It could be that the position was vacant for a period, leading to the confusion.
86. Donders, telephone interview by author, 3 June 2005.

9. The Nairobi Years: 1969-73   327

a bit of a relic of the old colonial type. . . . He had no respect for African religion. To Africans, he did not take them seriously. They felt that. He was framed by his colonial environment.'[87]

Donders next talked about Neill's 'personal assistant', Hugh Pilkington (1942-86). This came as a surprise to me because, although I had heard about Pilkington, I never imagined him to be Neill's personal assistant. Donders stated that Neill always seemed to have young men around him, helping him out, a recurring view of Neill. Donders verified that Pilkington owned a personal airplane and would fly Neill to exciting and exotic places.[88]

As an extremely wealthy philanthropist, Pilkington lived in the desirable, picturesque area of the Ngong Hills just outside Nairobi. His family had made a fortune in the glass industry, which afforded Hugh great opportunities; he was conversant in ten languages and became a world-renowned expert in Ge'ez, an ancient Semitic language found mainly in Ethiopia today. Donders said Pilkington often walked his dogs in that scenic place and had to contend with wild animals on those walks. On one occasion Pilkington's dog attacked a buffalo. The buffalo then charged at Pilkington, leaving him badly injured to the point that he could not walk, surrounded by 'vultures waiting for him to die'. Pilkington saw a small group of tourists in the distance and 'waved his handkerchief'. The tourists scrambled to the police, who rescued him. 'He was saved, but had to get extensive therapy', according to Donders. He had been violently gored in the groin. Donders emphasised that Pilkington was very 'accident prone'. Indeed, Pilkington died in Canada when he was hit by a car while 'jogging just before dawn'. He had been touring Canadian universities, speaking and raising awareness of the plight of African refugees. He was only 44 years old and had just two years earlier defeated hepatitis, an experience, he said, that 'rid me of all my fear of death'. In his obituary in *The Times* he was described as a 'very remarkable and unusual man'. Yet he was also a man who proved to be 'a rare and prominent example of man's will to improve the human condition through individual effort. . . . His deep spirituality was his source of energy. . . . He arranged for scholarships for hundreds of refugees. He was their counsellor and friend.'[89]

---

87.   Ibid.
88.   Ibid.
89.   Ibid. See 'Obituary of Dr Hugh Pilkington', *The Times*, 20 October 1986. Also Jesse Mugambi, interview with author, 26 July 2010, University of Nairobi, Kenya. For his jogging death, see Michael Valpy, 'An unusual man is given his due', *Toronto Globe and Mail*, 3 December 1986.

On the one hand, Donders, too, recognised the soaring brilliance of Neill, how he lectured effortlessly on the *Bhagavad Gita*, assembled an outstanding, truly world class faculty and devoted himself tirelessly to the work of the Church and church organizations, such as the Navigators. He may have had a nervous streak, as he was a 'rampant scribbler', constantly taking notes at meetings and throughout the day, but inevitably he would use these notes marvellously and strategically in his preaching, teaching and writing.[90]

On the other hand, Donders, perhaps more than anybody in Nairobi, had a clear-eyed view of Neill's struggles. Neill struggled to get along with the African church officials. He was an insomniac, which enabled him to get a lot more done than virtually anyone else. However, this high level of productivity and giftedness gave him 'a high idea of himself' that was off-putting to others. Neill often hosted gatherings at his home but, on one occasion, Neill 'held a big party for himself that was catered' but, surprisingly to Donders, 'not very many came'.[91]

When asked about Neill's more controversial side, Donders said he would 'not be surprised if he was gay'. However, the evidence did not point to that. There were certainly rumours floating around – Donders had heard them – but there was 'no sexual connotation'. It was just obvious that Neill enjoyed being around young men. When I asked Donders about the physical punishment often associated with Neill, he stated, 'Beating people in Kenya? Corporal punishment was normal.'[92]

Donders said Neill was still adventurous, willing to take on new things, willing to take risks, even as an elderly man. For example, while in Nairobi, 'Neill got his driving licence for the first time.' Neill wrote about this in his memoirs, always with a bit of trepidation due to the chaotic traffic in Nairobi. The truth is that Neill never fully mastered driving, according to Donders: 'He was not a very good driver. People would not go with him.' Neill was an avid traveller because he was always being invited to give lectures, which kept him in touch with the world church, meeting new faces at every turn. Donders said Neill aspired to write a mystery novel but it never came to be. Also, at one point Neill tried to climb Mount Kilimanjaro but 'had to turn back'. He was not happy about it, however, saying, 'You are looking at a defeated person.'[93]

There is some evidence, too, that Neill was more open-minded than the people around him gave him credit for. The problem was that his pride

---

90. Donders, telephone interview by author, 3 June 2005.
91. Ibid.
92. Ibid.
93. Ibid.

prevented him from admitting that his adversaries might have something to teach him. However, here and there, over the span of his lifetime, Neill showed signs of personal growth, at times in altogether surprising corners of his mind. For example, in a long and wide-ranging interview with Reverend William Gilbert in Toronto in August 1971 – while on break from his work in Nairobi – Neill showed signs of change on the issue of women's liberation, as well as on the indigenisation of African Christianity.[94]

On the issue of women, Neill admitted that he was probably old-fashioned, as at the time of the interview he was 70 years old, but he had moderated his views somewhat throughout the course of his life. In the interview, he opined that the women's liberation movement seemed to have fallen into a state of confusion. He stated, 'Woman is not liberated by becoming a man.' He continued:

> Women must have the fullest support and develop their own special gifts. Some people think I'm terribly old-fashioned but I'm not sure it's such a good thing in the school age for boys and girls to be educated together. . . . What did God mean when He made them male and female? . . . In the women's liberation movement there seems to be a certain tendency to think that women will be free when they can do all the things that men can do and do them in the same way as men do them. This would seem to me to be an appalling impoverishment of the human race. . . . I wonder whether I'm simply the victim of age-long prejudices. I can't say I have any enthusiasm for the ordination of women. And, in the churches where it has been practiced it has not been altogether a success. But I suspect that this is just prejudice on my part and I try to be honest. I certainly don't feel as strongly against the ordination of women as I did thirty years ago.

In that same interview, Neill also showed signs of opening up his perspective on African Christianity. While reflecting on the state of missions in 1971, Neill made the following remarks conveying a perspective that most Kenyans seemed not to notice in him:

> Basically, the primary quality for a missionary is humility. [The missionary] has got to understand that he comes as a guest to people in an alien culture. He has to submit himself to their ways of thinking, not necessarily accept them, but understand them and

---

94. William Gilbert interviewed Neill in Toronto in August 1971 and sent a transcript of the interview to the author.

understand that for them these ways are valid. And, as the church grows, the missionary more and more has to come to understand himself as the servant of the church. He's not there to boss. He's not there to put over Western ways of doing things. He is to be, as St Paul says, 'the helper of their joy and not the Lord of their faith' (2 Cor. 1:24).[95]

Clearly, Neill was not completely averse to reconsidering hot-button issues. He was a man of his times, struggling to keep pace with the changes happening all around him. Perhaps his attempt to keep pace was hopelessly slow. Nonetheless, there was movement, perhaps ever so little. In some ways it would be unfair to expect an elderly man born in the year 1900 to be able to think like the much younger people around him. For better or for worse, this inability proved his undoing time and time again.

At 70 years old Neill also had some obvious physical problems. He had allowed himself to become 'totally overweight'. According to Donders, he was 'not a healthy person'. He also had major trouble with his drooping eyelids that required multiple surgeries. He was beginning to face his own mortality in Nairobi and read the obituaries in *The Times* every single day, observing his generation dying off. In some ways he was living in the past, often reminiscing to those around him about India and the WCC.[96]

Search for a Successor

The Department of Philosophy and Religious Studies would soon need a new leader so Neill began advertising for the position and gave a six-month notice of his leaving in September 1973. The administration asked for Neill's shortlist of candidates to replace him and Neill immediately offered two: John Mbiti and Father Donders. Mbiti was the clear choice of the faculty. He was Kenyan, had a PhD from Cambridge, was ordained an Anglican priest and had served for some years as head of the Department of Religious Studies at Makerere University in Uganda. He was also by then a well-known scholar in the field of African religion and philosophy. Father Donders was a Dutch White Father, a Roman Catholic priest-missionary, who had basically headed the philosophy side of the department, while Neill tended to focus on the religious studies side of things. Father Donders, Neill speculated, probably did not want the job, as he enjoyed his professorial work and would rather not have to deal with the 'burdens

---

95. Gilbert interview of Neill in Toronto, August 1971.
96. Donders, telephone interview by author, 3 June 2005.

9. The Nairobi Years: 1969-73 331

and frustrations that weigh so heavy on . . . the head of a Department'. However, Donders' interviews went exceptionally well, making him a very strong candidate.[97]

Nevertheless, the position was clearly Mbiti's for the taking, a fact that Neill 'did not like' according to Donders.[98] A major problem suddenly arose with Mbiti's candidacy, however. At the same time as Mbiti was offered the chair of the department in Nairobi, he was also invited by the WCC in Switzerland to become Director of the Ecumenical Institute at Bossey. It was a near-impossible decision for him to make; although Mbiti longed to return home to Kenya, the position in Geneva meant that he would become world-renowned – an exceedingly rare opportunity extended only to the greatest of talents in the world Christian scene. Ultimately, Mbiti decided to move to Geneva.[99]

Father Donders accepted the position and served as chair for six years. Reflecting upon that period in his life, Donders wrote the following in 2012, just a year before his death:

> Stephen Neill retired in Britain in 1973, and I was appointed his successor. Up to that time I had been mainly involved in the philosophy side of the department, but now I represented also the religious studies part of it. It brought me more in contact not only with my colleagues in religious studies but also with the great variety of local Muslim, Eastern, and African religious leaders in Kenya. It was an experience that made me discover as never before that those 'others' walked with God.[100]

Donders was a very different leader to Neill and, despite being a Westerner, he still managed to lead the department through a turbulent era. It was a herculean task that speaks very highly of Donders' sensitivity to what was happening around him. Jesse Mugambi wrote that, when Donders took over in 1973, 'the situation was completely reversed within the following five years. . . . Expatriates left, and Kenyans took over.'[101]

In March 1973 Neill was visiting England and wrote a letter to his niece, Penny, explaining his future. He was scheduled to fly back to Nairobi

---

97. Neill's unpublished autobiography, 'Last Phase: East Africa', pp. 220-21.
98. Donders, telephone interview by author, 3 June 2005.
99. Neill's unpublished autobiography, 'Last Phase: East Africa', pp. 221-22. See also 'John Mbiti, 87, Dies; Punctured Myths About African Religions', *New York Times*, 24 October 2019.
100. Donders, 'My Pilgrimage in Mission', pp. 96-99.
101. Email from Mugambi to the author, 13 July 2010.

on 22 June. He would finish up his work in August but then 'go eastwards, visiting a lot of countries, looking up old friends and seeing places that I have never been to before'. He planned to spend several months in early 1974 in the United States, lecturing to various audiences. His plan was to return to England around May 1974. However, Neill had concerns about where he would live out his remaining years. He wrote:

> I don't know where I shall finally settle; house prices are so fantastic in Britain that I begin to wonder whether I shall be able to settle there at all, and whether I may not have to think of India as Aunt Isabel is doing; I think she will settle there for good, it is much cheaper than England, though much more expensive than it was; and one can get servants which is a great consideration as one gets older and is not married. But the only thing to do is to take each thing step by step, and in a wonderful way the decisions seem to be made for one, before one reaches the point at which decisions have to be taken; like my coming here; I never had any idea of coming to Africa, but I did want to go on working after I left Hamburg and this came along at just the right moment.[102]

Writing in August 1973, less than a month before he was to leave Africa, Neill reminisced, almost with a sense of melancholy:

> I do not regret having given the last four years of my fully active life to an African University at a crucial stage of its development. But I have come to the conclusion that I have the wrong kind of memory. I remember and feel as vividly and acutely as though they were happening today all the fears and anxieties, the frustrations and failures, the absurdities and contradictions, the feelings of exasperation and near despair. I do not forget the occasional successes and achievements, the moments of happiness in which it has seemed as though something really had got done that was worthwhile; but these things come to me with far less immediacy and vividness than the others. As a result I tend to take a rather dark view of the past.

He realised his years in Africa were not unproductive. He had achieved the founding of a university Department of Philosophy and Religious Studies. Student enrolment increased year on year. The churches in the area appreciated Neill's ever-present eagerness to work with them.[103]

102. Neill to Golby, 17 March 1973.
103. Neill's unpublished autobiography, 'Last Phase: East Africa', p. 223.

9. The Nairobi Years: 1969-73

Neill concluded this chapter in his autobiography thus:

> In seventeen days I shall leave this flat which has been my home for nearly four years. . . . Six days after that, my contract will be at an end, though I shall continue to lecture for four more days to round off the term. And just one month from now . . . I hope to set out on the long journey through South-east Asia and across the Pacific which in the end will bring me to America, and then to England.
>
> I have no intention whatever of retiring in the ordinary sense of the term. In fact I hope to settle down again to serious work, after the constant interruptions attendant on eleven years of university work. There are a number of books which I still hope to write. If I manage to complete in ten years all that I have in mind to do, I may then perhaps sit down to write my autobiography, and that would be a far more difficult and exacting task than the setting down of these somewhat random recollections of grace abounding to the chief of sinners over a period of rather more than seventy years.
>
> Nairobi.
> August 1973.[104]

After this entry, Neill did not touch his autobiographical recollections again for ten years. In 1983 he picked up his pen one last time and wrote 'A Last Chapter', which would indeed be the last, as he died the following year.

---

104. Ibid., pp. 224-25.

Chapter Ten
Final Years in Oxford: 1973-84

In 1973, writing from Nairobi just days before he left, Neill ended his sweeping autobiography: 'If I manage to complete in ten years all that I have in mind to do, I may then perhaps sit down to write my autobiography.'[1]

True to his word, in 1983 Neill sat down once again, ten years later, and picked up where he left off, writing, 'When I brought my narrative to a conclusion in the year 1973, I little thought that I should be given another ten years of active and varied life.' Thus, the last chapter of his autobiography was written in 1983. He lived one more year and died suddenly on 20 July 1984 at the age of 83.[2]

After Nairobi

Neill claimed that, when he left Nairobi, his plan was to travel a lot and eventually settle in England. However, it took a while for him to return to England and settle. His life before settlement was decidedly unsettled, as he kept up a bustling schedule of teaching, preaching, research and writing on several different continents and in numerous countries.

Neill's first task was to help a professor friend by filling in for him for six months at another African University: the University of Durban-Westville,

---

1. Neill's unpublished autobiography, 'Last Phase: East Africa', pp. 224-25.
2. Neill's unpublished autobiography, 'A Last Chapter', p. 1. For the date of his death, see *The Decanian*, no. 264, January 1985.

10. Final Years in Oxford: 1973-84

in South Africa, which was a successor to the Indian University College that was established in 1961. That university is now part of the University of KwaZulu-Natal. Neill filled in for Gerhardus Cornelius Oosthuizen, a South African scholar of African Christianity who eventually became one of the more prominent and widely read authors in that academic field.[3]

Always a student of his surroundings, Neill became acquainted with the South African approach to university education in the 1970s. They had five universities for non-whites: three for blacks, one for 'coloureds' (mixed race) and one for Asians – mainly Indians at that time. In this section of his autobiography, Neill gave his perspective on apartheid:

> The principle of separate education for various communities is one that does not appeal to me, but the provision of such universities is bound to lead in time to the rise of highly educated non-white elite, which will become increasingly vocal in the demand for equality and a full share in the government of their country. While serving in Natal, I became convinced that the only hope for peace in South Africa would be the development of something resembling the Swiss solution, of many small sovereign authorities, with a central government so planned that no one section should be able to dominate the whole. . . . [A] solution in any other direction would seem to spell only disaster.[4]

Neill's expectation for the nation did not come to pass and in 1994 Nelson Mandela was elected South Africa's first black president.

Neill then took a 'leisurely journey across the Pacific' and spent some time in Papua New Guinea, greater Melanesia and Tahiti. At that time of political emancipation, it was impacting the churches directly by giving them much more independence from denominations based in the West, such as the Lutheran and Anglican Churches. Neill noticed that the bishops in that part of the world were being selected from the local people rather than from the Churches in the West, a fact that he neither praised nor bemoaned in his autobiography.[5]

Neill continued his journey east to Ontario, Canada, where he conducted Christmas services in 1973. He was without his normal vestments and had to borrow from his hosts. Neill was very particular with his ecclesiastic

---

3. Neill's unpublished autobiography, 'A Last Chapter', p. 1. See also Johannes Smit and P. Pratap Kumar, eds, *The Study of Religion in Southern Africa: Essays in Honour of G.C. Oosthuizen* (Leiden: Brill, 2005).
4. Neill's unpublished autobiography, 'A Last Chapter', pp. 1-2.
5. Ibid., p. 2.

raiment and was quite peeved when he learned they had not made it across the ocean. His next stop was Boston. His bishop garments finally caught up with him after he had been in North America about a month. Neill's autobiography says almost nothing about his time in North America. He skips right up to his arrival back in England and provides no dates other than the Christmas 1973 reference. In one place in his autobiography he points out that he did not finally settle in England until he was 75 years old, which means the year of his arrival must have been 1976.[6]

Neill had no plans for his return to England. He entered negotiations with a lady for a flat in North London. He wanted to be near the British Library, specifically the library of the India Office, so he could write his magnum opus. Neill was reluctant to make the move because he was not excited about attending the local church there and he knew nobody in that part of London. The matter settled itself when the negotiations over the price of the flat broke down. Neill wrote: 'my possible maximum could not be made to agree with her minimum'.[7]

Then, suddenly, almost out of nowhere, Neill was invited by Jim Hickinbotham, the Principal of Wycliffe Hall, Oxford, to deliver the first annual Chavasse Lecture series. Neill agreed and brought up the fact that he was without a home at that time. Wycliffe Hall offered Neill a guest suite for the entire six weeks that he was to lecture on the topic of the mission of the Church. Neill had previously spent a term there in 1933 while on furlough from India. Neill felt at home there, 'in the atmosphere of an English theological college'. Before the six weeks were over Neill and Hickinbotham had come to an agreement that Neill would spend the rest of his days there in retirement, living in a flat that was designated for married students, but they allowed Neill to take residence there. Most pleasing to Neill in this new arrangement was that he would spend his final years with students and he would have access to the Indian Institute Library at the Bodleian in order to complete his life's work on the history of Christianity in India.[8]

Shortly after finally settling at Oxford Neill attended a conference at the University of Lancaster, where Professor Ninian Smart was all the rage in the world of comparative religion. Neill was asked to introduce Smart

---

6. Ibid., p. 3. For the year 1976, see p. 13. In his book, *Salvation Tomorrow*, Neill wrote: 'I owe a special debt of gratitude to Wycliffe Hall, where the lectures [for this volume] were first given, and which has since become my home. *Oxford 1976.*' See p. vii. The lectures to which he refers were the Chavasse Lectures which Neill delivered at Wycliffe Hall, Oxford.
7. Neill's unpublished autobiography, 'A Last Chapter', p. 3.
8. Ibid., pp. 4-5.

and he did so using a humorous limerick, much to the surprise of all in attendance who were caught off guard; perhaps they were much more comfortable with boring academic introductions that pour out praise on the speaker. Neill described the moment as 'highly amusing'. While at that conference, Neill attended a lecture on South Indian Hinduism with one problem – the lecturer did not show up. Fortuitously, Neill had just published a book on the topic called *Bhakti: Hindu and Christian*, so he filled in and spoke on the topic 'without notes and without preparation', much to the delight of the audience who had come to be enlightened. After that lecture, one of the members of the audience, Professor Norvin Hein of Yale University Divinity School, struck up a conversation with Neill. Sometime later, Professor Hein wrote to Neill offering him a position at Yale as a 'visiting fellow'. Neill took full advantage and travelled to Yale for a portion of each year to work in the Day Missions Library, which 'ranks as one of the best missionary libraries in the world – there is nothing in England to touch it'.[9]

Much had changed between 1933 and the mid-1970s. When Neill was at Wycliffe Hall in 1933, virtually all of the students were from Christian, mainly clerical, homes. They were thoroughly Christianized from birth. However, in the 1970s, it was very different. The vast majority of the students were 'new believers', meaning they came from completely secular homes or 'at best a rather meaningless Anglican conformity'. They were zealous in their new-found Christian faith. Many of them had very little understanding about Christianity, other than the fact that they had been converted in late high school or in college. Neill noticed that each of them 'would speak without hesitation of "my conversion", and in most cases could date the occurrence, and identify the circumstances in which it took place'. The students were rather 'rigid' and 'conservative' in their understanding of Christianity and had almost no experience with liturgical worship – nor had they a desire to practise it in that way. Neill was up for all of the challenges that faced him as he entered into the life of yet another academic institution, yet this time on his home turf.[10]

Jim Hickinbotham was Principal of Wycliffe Hall from 1970 until 1978. He and his successor, Geoffrey Shaw (who died in 2011 at age 84), worked together to secure Neill's retirement in Wycliffe Hall, believing Neill

---

9. Stephen Neill, *Bhakti: Hindu and Christian* (Madras: Christian Literature Society, 1974). Neill's unpublished autobiography, 'A Last Chapter', pp. 5-6. Gerald Anderson also confirmed that Neill spent part of each winter at Yale during the 'last six or seven years of his life'. Anderson, interview with author, Port Dickson, Malaysia, 5 August 2004.
10. Neill's unpublished autobiography, 'A Last Chapter', pp. 7-8.

would be a great asset for the college's atmosphere. At the time, Shaw was transitioning from Oak Hill College in northern Oxford to Wycliffe Hall, where he served as Principal from 1978 to 1988. Shaw's obituary reads, 'He recruited qualified and enthusiastic staff, and was also helped by retired eminent clergy such as Bishop Stephen Neill.' Shaw knew of Neill's great gifts; he had hosted Neill as a guest speaker at Oak Hill in 1977 or so.[11]

Principal Geoffrey Shaw and Arthur Moore – the Vice President of Wycliffe Hall from 1970 to 1983 – stated that Neill came back from Nairobi completely homeless. As Neill intimates in his autobiography, Wycliffe Hall was a godsend for him. Neill was 'not easy to work with', however. Shaw and Moore quickly came to realise that 'the church hierarchy was suspicious of him'. They found that Neill put up 'a kind of shield around himself', and therefore they did not get to know him well. He was older than everyone there but, even still, there were 'bits of Neill that he kept hidden'. Moore stated, 'Everybody knew of him, but nobody knew him.'[12]

Nevertheless, Shaw and Moore shared some fascinating insights into Neill's final years, for example, his very specific tastes when it came to food and drink. 'Neill was a wine man, not a whisky man.' He would routinely send back the wine at restaurants.[13] He was equally fastidious about good coffee, which he described as: 'Black as sin. Strong as death. And hot as Hell!' Neill's strong preferences did not translate into an overly assertive personality at Oxford. They both agreed, 'We saw nothing of his assertiveness. . . . He never entered into debate in those years.' This may have been a case of declining powers in those final years, as they also noted that: 'Students quit going to his lectures. It was awkward. They voted with their feet. His lectures were too anecdotal. They wanted to make the most of their time.' Neill was a 'showman' in younger years, 'When you went to see him, he had four honorary doctorate hoods.' However, by the end 'he was in decline . . . like a man in an old people's home'.[14]

---

11. Geoffrey Shaw, phone interview with author, 1 June 2007. See 'Obituary: Canon Geoffrey Norman Shaw', *Church Times*, 23 March 2011, located at: https://www.churchtimes.co.uk/articles/2011/25-march/gazette/obituary-canon-geoffrey-norman-shaw.
12. Geoffrey Shaw and Arthur Moore, interviews with author, Kingham, Oxfordshire, 28 June 2007.
13. Neill's nephew, Rev. Charles Neill, wrote, 'He was, perhaps, just a little naughty in his readiness to send back the bottle on the merest suspicion that the wine was corked.' *The Decanian*, no. 264, January 1985, p. 51.
14. Shaw and Moore, interviews with author, 28 June 2007. Rupert Higgins also stated that Neill's course was 'very much his own experiences and the events surrounding his involvement in various church movements'. Rupert Higgins, email to the author, 4 April 2003.

10. Final Years in Oxford: 1973-84

In point of fact, Neill must have been somewhat modest on those occasions when showing off his hoods, as the distinguished historian, Owen Chadwick, wrote in his biographical entry on Neill in the *Oxford Dictionary of National Biography* that Neill actually held eight honorary degrees, in addition to the doctorate of divinity that he took at Cambridge at the age of 79. Neill's earned and honorary doctorates were just the icing on the cake, however, as he had already been elected a fellow of the British Academy a decade prior, in 1969. The British Academy was the highest form of recognition he could have received by his fellow countrymen.[15]

Shaw and Moore did not seem to think that the students' lack of enthusiasm dented his confidence, however, as 'Neill knew he was a man of stature. He enjoyed it. Why wouldn't he?' Neill was a celebrity in the Anglican world. His college missions in the late 1940s were hugely successful and students all over England converted to Christ because of those powerful and moving sermons delivered by Neill shortly after his devastating loss of his career in missions. Neill's resilience was remarkable. Whereas most people would have been beset in mere recovery mode after such devastation, Neill progressed from strength to strength during those years. He overcame and built for himself new identities. From a missionary to a bishop, to an evangelist, to an ecumenist, to a writer, to a professor and finally to a convergence of all of his various identities – and he excelled at every phase. Moore said, 'In my schoolboy days he was a hero.'

When Neill first arrived at Wycliffe Hall, he was still a very powerful man. Wycliffe Hall was 'privileged to have him. . . . Very few colleges had a man of his stature.' He had this stellar reputation as a bishop and as a top-shelf, world-famous scholar, yet he was also full of 'warmth' and 'deep spirituality'. The most common word used for Neill was 'brilliance'. Nevertheless, the word 'enigmatic' also comes up frequently. Shaw said: 'In a way, such brilliance is a handicap. You must always be striving for perfection that you're never quite attaining. Cutting off people by your brilliance. Some people you never want to offer your opinion for fear of what they might think about it.'

Shaw and Moore were ecstatic to have Neill on board but quickly realised his gifts pulled him in a number of different directions: the Middle East to advise clergy, North America to research and lecture, the Church of England to exercise his calling as a priest and bishop, his vast array of scholarly pursuits and, of course, his ministry at Wycliffe Hall.[16]

---

15. Chadwick, 'Neill, Stephen Charles (1900-1984)'. Also located at: http://www.oxforddnb.com/view/article/31491, accessed 30 May 2007.
16. Shaw and Moore, interviews with author, Kingham, 28 June 2007.

Early on, one of Neill's immediate ambitions was to be a pastor to the students. He was zealously focused on the spiritual development of those who placed themselves underneath his mentorship. Indeed, Neill was 'very methodical' about the students' spiritual growth. He created a system of spiritual progress that consisted of ten levels and he expected the students to work through those levels in a grading type of system. Neill would often order 'check-ups' to measure whether the students were proceeding in the right direction, spiritually.[17]

Neill offered a course each year on twentieth-century Christianity – a topic on which he was uniquely prepared to speak with authority. He preached with frequency. He counselled many students in informal ways at his house over coffee. He became, in his words, a 'grandfather in residence' at Wycliffe Hall. Alister McGrath said Neill's official title was 'Scholar in Residence', although Shaw and Moore thought it was 'Senior Scholar'. Either way, Neill was never a paid member of staff. He was provided with a room and meals. He enjoyed being aloof yet also a part of the life of the college. He travelled often, even during the year of his death in 1984.[18]

Religion in England had changed dramatically during Neill's lifetime. It was not at all the England that he experienced in the 1920s as a student, nor the England of the 1930s while he was on paid leave of absence from India, nor was it the England of the 1940s while he served as Assistant Bishop to the Archbishop of Canterbury. Neill was now living in a much more secular England, what he termed, 'an increasingly un-Christian England'. There was an overall aura of 'gloom and despondency'. Theological colleges were being closed or combined with others. Exactly the same situation was happening with churches. Church authorities were unable to pay what was needed to support so many parishes and were thus insisting on fewer ordinations per year. The financial situation in the Church was grim. In Neill's words, 'Many people had come to the conclusion that there was little if any future for the Church of England.'[19]

Amidst this depressing situation Neill found great hope in the leadership of Donald Coggan, the Archbishop of Canterbury from 1974 to 1980. For a time the ethos of the Church changed, due largely to Coggan's great gifts, his 'quiet tenacity' and his great hope that the Church could turn

---

17. Ibid.
18. Neill's unpublished autobiography, 'A Last Chapter', pp. 9-10. Alister McGrath, interview with author, Harris Manchester College, Oxford, 27 June 2007. Geoffrey Shaw was the Principal of Wycliffe Hall when Neill was there and preached at Neill's funeral. Shaw and Moore, interviews with author, Kingham, UK, 28 June 2007.
19. Neill's unpublished autobiography, 'A Last Chapter', pp. 9-11, 14.

itself around and prosper again. Indeed, Neill noted, the Church began to increase slowly in places. The evangelical colleges, in particular, were growing in noticeable ways, with the more progressive institutions not far behind. Neill remarked, 'I have no doubt that Donald Coggan will go down to history as one of the great archbishops of Canterbury.'[20]

Neill made himself available to the diocese and was gratified to be appointed Assistant Bishop in the Oxford diocese by Bishop Patrick Rodger, which gave him the opportunity – one he relished – to perform regular confirmations. He was invited by Christopher Lamb to serve as chairman of a committee that was to explore how to reach out to the 'steady influx' of immigrants from India, Pakistan and East Africa. Neill was, of course, well-prepared for this task after having spent much of his life in South Asia and part of it in East Africa.[21]

Neill found Oxford to be an 'exciting' place in the 1970s and 1980s. 'Every Sunday' the four large evangelical churches and main Roman Catholic church were all crowded to the doors. College students were fairly well represented and many of them were baptized during their college years. Neill worked extensively with Canon Michael Green (1930-2019), rector of St Aldates, to reach out to these students. Neill estimated that around two thirds of the people in England still had their babies baptized in the Church, which provided some opportunities to interact with those who rarely attended church. All in all, however, England was becoming a 'dechristianized' society and 'No one as yet seemed to have discovered the way to emerge from the steadily narrowing Christian ghetto.' There was a sense of despondency amongst many Christians that the faith of England's past was receding rapidly.[22]

Neill fitted in well into the atmosphere of Wycliffe Hall. His colleague Alister McGrath said Neill would attend chapel every single day and always sat at the extreme right-hand corner of a raised set of pews. He took his meals at Wycliffe Hall and became a fixture for much of the year. He held frequent meetings with students, especially young men, according to McGrath.[23]

Indeed, Rupert Higgins, former senior associate minister of All Souls Church, Langham Place in London, said something very similar to McGrath. He wrote:

20. Ibid., p. 11.
21. Ibid., pp. 13-16.
22. Ibid., pp. 17-19.
23. McGrath, interview with author, Harris Manchester College, Oxford, 27 June 2007. Alister McGrath stated: 'While at Wycliffe Hall, Neill loved to be with young men.' This was not to imply anything sexual. Indeed, Neill was deeply appreciated at the college and there was even established a Stephen Neill Memorial Scholarship Fund for students from Asia and Africa.

It wasn't easy to get to know Stephen very well – he had a few favourites of which I was one for a while until I got married! Stephen's favourites were always single men. He used to invite a few of us out for dinners and they were always great fun with Stephen playing the role of 'wise sage with his pupils'. We would play along too and enjoy his company. We also got regularly asked up to his flat for coffee and quizzed about our reading habits and sometimes our love lives too! Stephen was always adamant about making sure we read a lot and very widely. He produced a sheet of book titles every clergyman should read.[24]

Visits to North America

Each year during Neill's semi-retirement in Oxford he would travel to the United States, usually to anchor down at Yale Divinity School so he could work on the history of Christianity in India. One year he went to Union Theological Seminary in New York instead, in order to work in the Missionary Research Library. These visits to the States normally lasted about two months. Neill enjoyed the distinguished history of Yale: home of the Revised Standard Version of the Bible – Neill's favourite; the place where K.S. Latourette wrote his famous history of world Christianity; and where H. Richard Niebuhr had laid the foundations for Christian ethics and Christian sociology.[25]

While Yale emerged relatively unscathed from the student rebellions of the 1960s and 1970s, institutions in New York did not get off so easy. Cornell and Union Seminary suffered badly. Students made their demands known, such as equal male and female student bodies and equal numbers of black and white students. Robert Handy (1918-2009) did make progress with the students at Union but much damage had been done and, in Neill's view from the early 1980s, Union was struggling to regain its once prestigious reputation.[26]

Yale University did have some inner turmoil, however. The Women's Liberation movement 'sometimes appeared to go to the length of denying that men have any rights at all'. Neill noted that Yale's 'gay caucus' distorted the meaning of the word 'gay'. He wrote, 'Has there ever been in history so complete a distortion of the meaning of a word?'[27]

---

24. Rupert Higgins, email to the author, 4 April 2003. Higgins mentioned that David Urquhart, current Bishop of Birmingham in the Church of England, was also involved in these dinners and would have much to say about them.
25. Neill's unpublished autobiography, 'A Last Chapter', pp. 19-20.
26. Ibid., pp. 20-21.
27. Ibid., p. 21.

10. Final Years in Oxford: 1973-84   343

While at Yale, Neill integrated himself into the life of the institution quite effectively. Every Wednesday night he attended Eucharist at St Luke's Chapel. On one occasion, in March 1975, Neill celebrated his 50-year jubilee of being ordained into the priesthood. He preached regularly and took one meal per day in the cafeteria so he could interact with students. He invited students to his home for coffee as he had done over the years.[28]

One of those visits resurrected old demons in Neill's life that followed him wherever he went: his bizarre fetish for spanking younger men. In a 2007 interview with a former Yale divinity student, I learned that Neill still struggled with this bizarre routine nearly to the last, yes, even at the ripe old age of 78. The person involved was Jerry Jones, a minister in the Churches of Christ denomination and a college lecturer, including at my own institution, Pepperdine University, in California. He also served as a pastor in England for eighteen years. He currently serves in France as a missionary. Jones was willing to share his experience with me and granted me permission to use his name.[29]

Jones happened to attend a lecture on Neill that I gave in 2007 specifically on the topic of Neill and why Neill was dismissed from the Tinnevelly Bishopric in 1945. After my lecture, Jones approached me and stated that he had known exactly what I was going to say, as he had witnessed something very similar from Neill and had never really understood what that episode was all about. He had little reason to revisit the strange experience until he attended my lecture and learned more about the pattern in Neill's life. He approached me and offered a few details about what he saw. I told him his experience was precisely what I had heard about over the years. I asked him if he would sit down to do a detailed interview with me, which we did not manage to do until the summer of 2020.

This interview with Jerry Jones is crucial, as he was an eyewitness. Jones knew Neill both at Yale and at Oxford, as Jones studied at both institutions. Jones was at Oxford on two different occasions but this particular experience with Neill happened at Yale in the autumn term of 1979 while Jones was completing his Master of Divinity. Jones had already met Neill at Wycliffe Hall, Oxford, during a year of study there in 1977-78. Jones frequently attended daily chapel services, as did Neill, and they became acquainted. When Jones returned to the United States in 1978 he married in June. He also resumed his studies at Yale and was pleased to see Bishop Neill on Yale's campus and they conversed several times.

Jones understood Neill to be a retired and well-known bishop, although he did not fully comprehend the details of Neill's prolific and fascinating life. He said Neill was excited to meet with 'the ordinands', those who were

28.   Ibid., pp. 22-24.
29.   Jerry Jones, Zoom interview by author, 30 July 2020.

studying for ordained ministry. Jones and several others were invited by the bishop to come to his place in the graduate dormitory, which they did on two occasions. The first gathering went well. Clearly, Neill was a learned pastor, eager to share his wisdom with younger men who were preparing for ministry.

Shortly thereafter, Neill invited them for a second devotional, again at his place. There were either four or five young men participating on this particular evening. Jones was the only married one. Neill led them in a devotional that was interesting and helpful. The young men had a time of confessing sin. However, at some point, the topic of Neill's devotional thoughts began to go in the direction of paying a price for our sins, as the apostle Paul had discussed in I Corinthians 9:27, 'I strike a blow to my body and make it my slave so that after I have preached to others, I myself will not be disqualified for the prize.' Neill discussed the Christian tradition of 'beating the body' or flagellation. He emphasised the importance of corporeal punishment for spiritual discipline. He discussed some of the historical aspects related to this teaching, including prayer postures. In this case, however, Neill indicated he wanted to do the disciplining and he wanted to do it on the young men present at the devotional.

When Neill asked for volunteers, Jones opted not to participate. However, two or three of the young men agreed. They approached Neill and turned their backsides to him and he spanked their buttocks. Nobody removed their trousers. Neill spanked them on top of their trousers. Jones said Neill emphasised that this was all very valuable as a spiritual discipline. Neill spanked at least two if not three of the men. Jones continued:

> Neill did not groan or do anything gross. He did not appear sexually excited. He was a pro at it. He spanked with the open hand. He did not use an object.[30] It was not a hard spanking. He was an old man at that time. It was not a 'beating'. His hand was open. It was not a tap, but it was not hard, either. It was somewhere in the middle. We prayed afterwards. He said physical discipline was of spiritual value. Nothing said during the lecture was weird at all. He talked about bad language, cursing, and listed a bunch of sins. Then he

---

30. This is important, as Bishop Holloway recounted that Neill always kept a whip with him for such punishments. The account that Jones gave and the account that Bishop Holloway gave in 1991 are remarkably similar in all other details. See Holloway, 'The Mystery in Stephen Neill', p. 13. It is also interesting that, while Jones saw little to characterise as sexual in the punishments, Holloway thought it was definitely psychosexual, or 'controlled sadism'.

10. Final Years in Oxford: 1973-84

went into 'I beat my body' from Paul. He said, 'I should spank you to make sure you are not getting off without punishment.' He related the beneficial aspect of it.

As a student of the Bible, however, Jones realised that Paul was talking about beating his own body, not the bodies of others.

As they were leaving, Jones turned to one of the others and asked, 'Was that weird or what?' One of the boys said he was going to talk to someone about what had just happened. Jones thought this other student either went to a dean or to the head of the college. Quite possibly he went to Harry Adams. Indeed, the word got out, and Jerry was contacted by Rowan Greer, a patristics scholar. Greer told Jones, 'Don't go back. We have made the decision that students should not meet privately with Neill.'

There would be no third devotional gathering, as 'Neill was told not to have any more private meetings with students.' Jones did run in to Neill several more times but they just said hello. Jones reflected, wondering, 'How did the devotional get to that point?' He could not remember a transition in Neill's devotional thoughts. Everything was running along just fine and then, the next thing you know, Neill was spanking some of the young men. Jones was glad that it was stopped, although he asserted that 'Neill didn't do anything "wrong" but it was weird. It was obviously for his jollies.' Jones realised that this sort of thing should not be happening. It just felt wrong, although it was hard to put it into words. Jones continued:

> He didn't put his hand on us or grab us or anything like that. It was weird, but it could have been much worse. He didn't talk dirty. He didn't even know us! It was weird partly because we had just gotten to know him. Nobody had any sin problem that would be improved by being spanked. He was trying to be a spiritual mentor, but he ruined it. No one wanted to go back.

Jones speculated that perhaps Neill gained some kind of pleasure from disciplining people: 'Very clearly, he combined a biblical teaching with a practice that gave him pleasure. Clearly, it made him feel good in some way.'

Jones was emphatic that this was not about sex. There was no evidence whatsoever that anything sexual was going on. Sexual thoughts did not even seem to be involved. Jones reasoned, 'Somebody probably did this to Neill. Somebody spanked him in the past, I'm sure.'[31]

---

31. Jones, Zoom interview by author, 30 July 2020. Rupert Higgins, who was at Wycliffe Hall with Neill in the early 1980s and was one of Neill's 'young men'

Jones ended the interview by directing me to read about the scandals related to Bishop Peter Ball (1932-2019), who had been jailed for similar behaviour, although presumably of a much more overtly sexual nature than Neill's offences. The strange urge to control younger men was eerily similar, however.

Stephen Neill's niece stated that the Neill family knew about his fetish. They always thought it was 'sado-masochistic tendencies', although she admitted she 'had no idea it was so entrenched – so sad – for him, and for his victims'.[32] It is clear that Neill was unable to gain control over this vice he had, even in his old age. Whether he was in India or Britain or America, he eventually succumbed to the pull of needing physical control over young men who had placed themselves under his mentorship.

Over time, Neill's frequent trips to the US led him to ruminate about the nature of the Americans. He came to believe that: 'Americans, like Spaniards, tend to have every virtue except that of moderation.' This plays out especially in the religious world. America is a culture divided between liberals, who have 'tended to go so far as almost to exclude the ideas of divine revelation', and conservatives, who have become equidistant from the centre because they have fallen into an obscure fundamentalism, 'in which the defence of every syllable of the Bible as inspired Scripture was a basic article of the faith'. Writing in 1983, Neill wrote that: 'It is hard for English readers to realise the intensity of the conflict' in America between liberals and conservatives. It had become painful and divisive in virtually every major denomination and university. The nation's institutions were polarising, with everyone forced to choose a side. The situation birthed a flourishing evangelical movement that has drawn in multitudes of young people from the mainline, liberal denominations which are in a staggering, statistical decline. Neill felt no desire to get caught in these 'local controversies', although he was aware that the conservative seminaries tended to use his books more.[33]

Neill genuinely made friends with many of his students. He was by this point an elderly scholar with perhaps some of the hubris that Kenyans noticed in him starting to recede. When in the United States he was delighted to speak at churches and colleges and seminaries. One year he spent a month lecturing at Gordon-Conwell Theological Seminary, near

---

also denied that Neill was homosexual. He wrote, 'I have no evidence that Stephen was homosexual and my take on it is that he wasn't. I know of no one at Wycliffe Hall who was subject to any "disciplining" although, if there was, I guess I wouldn't have known.' Higgins, email to the author, 4 April 2003.

32. Penny Golby, email to author, 9 February 2013.
33. Neill's unpublished autobiography, 'A Last Chapter', pp. 24-26.

Boston, and noticed their priority towards educating African American students. While he was there he also had Michael Ford – the son of then-President Gerald Ford – in his class. On several occasions Neill was invited to lecture at the conservative Asbury Theological Seminary in Kentucky. He guest lectured at Concordia Seminary in Exile – also known as Seminex – in St Louis during the fall semester of 1974.[34] The quite conservative Southern Baptists – the largest Protestant denomination in the United States – hosted Neill at four of their seminaries, which utterly surprised Neill because of his strong views in favour of infant baptism and their firm rejection of it. Nevertheless, their reception of him was always 'effusive'. One year the Southeastern Baptist Theological Seminary in Wake Forest, North Carolina hosted Neill for a full seven weeks, although they had wanted him for an entire semester.[35]

Neill was also a frequent guest at the OMSC – Overseas Ministries Study Center – which was based in Ventnor, New Jersey from its foundation in 1922 until 1987 when it relocated close to Yale Divinity School.[36] According to Gerald Anderson, former executive director of the Center, Neill visited in March 1984 (the year of his death) and provided a series of lectures that were filmed and published. The evening before Neill's scheduled lectures, Neill asked Anderson, 'What is my topic for tomorrow?' Anderson said the topic was to be 'How my mind has changed about mission'. Neill immediately quipped, 'Well, you know Gerald, my mind really hasn't changed.' Anderson said Neill could lecture on any subject imaginable, with about fifteen minutes' notice. He was '*Encyclopedia Britannica* in *TIME* magazine form'. Anderson stated: 'Neill was one of the most brilliant men I was ever associated with.'[37]

Naturally, the American Episcopal seminaries hosted Neill frequently, as he was something of a legend in their ranks. Neill had worries about the future of the Episcopal Church in America, however, as it had become a 'ghetto of the upper middle class, mainly composed of prosperous white Anglo-Saxons' and little else. Their membership was declining rapidly in America, yet, 'No

---

34. John Groh, 'Ecumenism's Past and Future: Shifting Perspectives. An Interview with Bishop Stephen C. Neill', *Christian Century*, Vol. 92, no. 21 (1975), pp. 568-72. The date of 1974 is revealed in an article by Stephen Neill, 'Great World Mission Conferences – At an End or Just Beginning', *Currents in Theology and Mission*, Vol. 2 (April 1975), pp. 61-64.
35. Neill's unpublished autobiography, 'A Last Chapter', pp. 27-30.
36. The OMSC has moved again. Since the beginning of the 2020-21 academic year the OMSC has been based at Princeton Theological Seminary.
37. 'Stephen Neill', in *The Christian Catalyst Collection from the Twentieth Century* (two tapes, CAT #4325, Worcester, PA: Vision Video, copyright OMSC, 1984). Also, Anderson, interview with author, Port Dickson, Malaysia, 5 August 2004.

one seemed very much worried.' The priesthood had lost its power, as it was composed largely of draft dodgers who lacked real conviction and merely took a graduate degree in theology to avoid going to Vietnam.[38]

Neill was pleased to see the charismatic movement gaining popularity in America in the 1970s and 1980s, largely because it showed itself uniquely competent at reaching all ethnicities, especially African Americans. They were accomplishing unbelievable acts of social improvement among African American communities. Neill was also excited to see John Stott's growing popularity in America, with his strong concern for evangelism.[39]

A Decade of "Uninterrupted" Writing

When Neill retired in 1973, he anticipated having an 'uninterrupted period of writing', although that period was not quite as uninterrupted as he had hoped.[40] He did produce a respectable corpus during that decade that included seven books:

1974 – *Bhakti: Hindu and Christian* (Madras: Christian Literature Society)
1976 – *Salvation Tomorrow: The Originality of Jesus Christ and the World's Religions* (London: Lutterworth Press; and Nashville, TN: Abingdon)
1976 – *Jesus Through Many Eyes: Introduction to the Theology of the New Testament* (Philadelphia, PA: Fortress)
1984 – *The Supremacy of Jesus* (London: Hodder & Stoughton)
1984 – *Crises of Belief: The Christian Dialogue with Faith and No Faith* (London: Hodder & Stoughton); published in the United States as *Christian Faith and Other Faiths* (Downers Grove, IL: Intervarsity Press). This book, in both UK and US editions, was a revision of Neill's 1961 book, *Christian Faith and Other Faiths*
1984 – *A History of Christianity in India: The Beginnings to AD 1707* (Cambridge: Cambridge University Press)
1985 – *A History of Christianity in India: 1707-1858* (Cambridge: Cambridge University Press)

During Neill's final decade, it is clear he gave considerable thought to the world's religions. When considering Neill's theological understanding of non-Christian religions, most scholars have tended to put Neill in a middle-of-the-road category. Neill is not a radical exclusivist, meaning all non-

---

38. Neill's unpublished autobiography, 'A Last Chapter', pp. 32-33.
39. Ibid., p. 33.
40. Ibid., p. 38.

10. Final Years in Oxford: 1973-84

Christian religions are worthless, and he is certainly not a pluralist. Other religions offer something to their subjects, just not the ultimate truth. Paul Knitter, in his classic study, *No Other Name?*, a critical survey of Christian attitudes towards world religions, placed Neill in the 'Mainline Protestant Model' which he defined as believing that 'Salvation is only in Christ'. In a section on Neill and Lesslie Newbigin – who were actually very similar both in career and in theology – Knitter characterises their beliefs thus: 'Unless one knows Christ, one cannot know the one, true God.' Knitter's perspective was not too far off the mark.[41] As Neill wrote in his first volume of the history of Christianity in India, what was at stake in the encounter of Christians with the surrounding cultures of India, was truth. Christians persisted in India, despite tremendous opposition, because they believed that 'the truth would in the end prevail and that the darkness of centuries would be brought to an end by the penetration of the light of Christ'. This may have been offensive to non-Christians but it was the conviction of centuries of Christians, and it was the ultimate conviction of Neill and the justification of his life's work.[42]

Neill did not completely write off other religions but he did point out that the apostle Paul considered other religions to be 'refuse' when compared to Christ. In a letter to Max Warren, Neill wrote:

> We have a big battle to fight; it seems to me that so many theologians, having encountered the other religions for the first time, John Hick, Macquarrie, etc., have really sold the pass. What was it that made Saul of Tarsus who had all that the best religion in the world could offer, treat all things as refuse in comparison with the knowledge of Christ? It seems to me that those brethren simply will not face this phenomenon. And we do desperately need a study of conversion in the third world, very few converts say what according to these friends they ought to say – to nearly all of them the old world was a dark world, out of which they have been delivered by Christ, and not a bright world to which Christ has added just a little more brightness.[43]

However, Neill was also capable of seeing Bhakti Hinduism – a kind of devotional-oriented faith that focuses on God's grace and His ability to offer salvation to all – as 'a possible field of encounter and dialogue'. Christianity and Hinduism's potential points of contact are precisely why Neill published his excellent study, *Bhakti: Hindu and Christian* in 1974.[44]

---

41. Paul Knitter, *No Other Name?* (Maryknoll, NY: Orbis, 1985), pp. 97, 109.
42. *A History of Christianity in India: The Beginnings to AD 1707*, p. 252.
43. Kings, *Christianity Connected*, p. 384.
44. See Oliver Scallan, 'The Supremacy of Christ: Inter Religious Dialogue in the

Neill's final seven books, published between 1974 and 1985, delved deeply into the world of non-Christian religions. Even Neill's introduction to the New Testament, entitled *Jesus Through Many Eyes*, included some fascinating perspectives on how 'the Gentile world' related to Christian faith in the Early Church. The rest of the books during his final decade dealt at length with non-Christian religions, even Neill's two histories of Christianity in India. They discuss the history of Islam and Hinduism throughout, of course in the context of Christianity's development in the subcontinent.

In addition to the books, Neill wrote numerous other pieces during his final decade as well, including two articles meant to counter a book edited by John Hick entitled *The Myth of God Incarnate*.[45] Hick's book made a splash in England in 1977. Theologian Michael Green, an evangelical, decided to put together a roster of respected authors who could challenge Hick and company and re-assert *The Truth of God Incarnate* – which served as the title of their book.[46] Neill authored Chapters Two and Three: 'Jesus and Myth' and 'Jesus and History'. This debate made headlines. In *The Times* Neill and his co-authors were referred to as 'the five champions of orthodoxy' who 'have stepped forward to pick up the gauntlet'.[47]

Similarly, in 1981, Neill published a chapter in a book called *No Alternative: The Prayer Book Controversy*. It, too, was taking a stand for something, in this case a stand against the new Alternative Service Book for use in Anglican churches. While Neill's chapter was primarily an historical survey, his intentions were clear: he did not like the new prayer book. His conclusions, at the end of his essay, illustrate his perspective:

> English prose rhythm is a very delicate thing; only those with a sensitive and well-trained ear can handle it successfully. From what they have produced, it does not seem that any member of either the English or the American team had such an ear. . . . Surely there are people about who have the necessary gifts and could be brought in

---

      Writings of Bishop Stephen Neill', MPhil thesis, University of Dublin, 1987. See especially Chapter 5, which deals with Bhakti and the potential for interreligious dialogue with Christianity.

45. John Hick, ed., *The Myth of God Incarnate* (London: SCM Press, 1977). The authors were Maurice Wiles, Frances Young, Michael Goulder, Leslie Houlden, Don Cupitt, Dennis Nineham and John Hick.
46. Michael Green, ed., *The Truth of God Incarnate* (London: Hodder & Stoughton, 1977). The authors were Green, Neill, Christopher Butler, Brian Hebblethwaite and John Macquarrie.
47. Clifford Longley, 'Challenge to "myth" view of the Incarnation'. *The Times*, 18 August 1977, p. 1.

to help in matters of style and diction. We may not have a Cranmer today; we should at least have some who can hear his rhythms and understand the brilliance of his workmanship.

He had more substantial criticisms in that essay, too, for example, that the prayer book should tap into the rich liturgical traditions found in Eastern Christianity. Neill's final words in that essay reveal a bit about his mindset just three years before his death:

So there is plenty to be done in the next ten years. I fear it is unlikely that I shall be there to greet the year 1991. But I hope that that year may bring us a bright and shining new Prayer book, worthy of our past, relevant to our present and full of promise for our future.[48]

Clearly, Neill was becoming more conscious of time's limitations and aware of his imminent demise. In his autobiography he admitted that by this point in his life he was decidedly a conservative, a 'faithful old-timer', whose ideas should be considered, but 'must not be allowed to stand in the way of progress'.[49]

His ideas kept coming, however, as he travelled, wrote and spoke prolifically all the way to the end of his 83 years. Even during Neill's final months, at the age of 83, 'he delivered thirty-six wide-ranging lectures on Twentieth-Century Church History in the United States'.[50] He conducted numerous interviews, as a kind of victory lap for a life well-lived, for example, a wonderfully illuminating discussion on the state of ecumenism in 1975.[51] The Fifth General Assembly of the World Council of Churches was held in Nairobi in 1975 and several publications asked Neill to write a piece for them, usually associated in some way with the ecumenical movement.[52]

---

48. David Martin and Peter Mullen, eds., *No Alternative: The Prayer Book Controversy* (Oxford: Blackwell, 1981). Authors included Neill, Martin, I.R. Thompson, Margaret Doody, Rachel Trickett, Roger Beckwith, Geoffrey Shepherd, David Cockerell, Tom Paulin, Margot Lawrence, Dorothy Parker, Mullen, Chris O'Neill and others. Neill wrote the first chapter, entitled 'Liturgical Continuity and Change in the Anglican Churches', pp. 1-11. (See review of *No Alternative*, by Laurence Lerner, in *The Modern Language Review*, Vol. 80, no. 4 (October 1985), p. 896.) Quotations here are from p. 11. For 'Eastern Christianity', see Neill's unpublished autobiography, 'A Last Chapter', p. 45.
49. Ibid., p. 42.
50. Mitchell, 'Stephen Neill: A Traditional Communicator in an Age of Revolution, p. 257.
51. Groh, 'Ecumenism's Past and Future: Shifting Perspectives. An Interview with Bishop Stephen C. Neill', pp. 568-72. See also Stephen Neill, 'Some Realism in the Ecumenical Illusion', *Churchman*, Vol. 89, no. 3 (1975), pp. 235-40.
52. See, for example, Neill, 'The Nature of Salvation', in ibid., pp. 225-34.

Journals routinely consulted Neill to carry on exchanges on a variety of topics in their pages, for example, his well-documented opposition to recent Anglican liturgies. In one of those journals Neill wrote, 'I have come to the conclusion that the English Rite of 1662 is incomparably the best Eucharistic service in the world.'[53] For the journal *Expository Times* Neill wrote an excellent article called 'Conversion' in 1977.[54] Also in 1977 he wrote an article on 'Myth and Truth' for *Churchman* – one of his favourite avenues for quick publication of his ideas.[55]

To prepare for the Lambeth Conference of 1978 Neill was asked to write the lead article in the preparatory document. Neill was an obvious choice for the task as the author of the bestselling book, *Anglicanism*. On this occasion his article was entitled 'On Being Anglican'.[56] In 1979 Neill published an article entitled 'Missions in the 1980s', a topic on which he was seen as the living authority.[57]

In 1983 Neill published the lead chapter in the book, *When Will Ye Be Wise? The State of the Church of England*. His article was entitled 'The Church of England: has it a future?'[58] Also in 1983 he published one of his sermons entitled 'To Think the Way God Thinks: Philippians 2:1-18'.[59] In his final year, 1984, Neill published his long article, or 'Comment', on the Lambeth Quadrilateral, an official articulation of Anglican faith.[60] He did an interview for a book in 1984 entitled *Between Peril and Promise* which revealed the fact that: 'Bishop Neill's mind and enthusiasm have never waned.'[61] One of Neill's final journal articles was a long review of

---

53. Stephen Neill, 'Liturgical Excogitations', *Anglican Theological Review*, Vol. 57 (July 1975), p. 334.
54. Stephen Neill, 'Conversion', *Expository Times*, Vol. 89, no. 7 (April 1978), pp. 205-8.
55. Stephen Neill, 'Myth and Truth', *Churchman*, Vol. 91, no. 4 (1977), pp. 309-17.
56. Stephen Neill, 'On Being Anglican', in *Today's Church and Today's World with a Special Focus on the Ministry of Bishops: The Lambeth Conference 1978 Preparatory Articles* (London: CIO Publishing, 1978).
57. Stephen Neill, 'Missions in the 1980s', *Review and Expositor*, Vol. 82, no. 2 (1979), pp. 181-84. This article was also published by the *International Bulletin of Missionary Research* in January 1979.
58. Stephen Neill, 'The Church of England: Has It a Future?', in *When Will Ye Be Wise: The State of the Church of England*, ed. by Anthony Kilmister (London: Blond & Briggs, 1983), pp. 4-18.
59. This article gives the title of Neill's position as 'Resident Scholar, Wycliffe Hall, Oxford'. Stephen Neill, 'To Think the Way God Thinks: Philippians 2:1-18', *Faith and Mission*, Vol. 1, no. 1 (1983), pp. 71-74.
60. Stephen Neill, 'Comment', *Historical Magazine of the Protestant Episcopal Church*, Vol. 53 (1984), pp. 111-28.
61. James R. Newby and Elizabeth Newby, *Between Peril and Promise: Fifteen*

10. Final Years in Oxford: 1973-84

the massive, highly touted *World Christian Encyclopedia*, first published in 1982 but now in its third edition. The editor of the encyclopedia was Neill's old friend David Barrett and Neill is listed as one of the consultants for the volume. Neill's review is mainly positive, but he had words of high praise for Barrett. He wrote: 'The work has been completed with the help of many friends and collaborators, whose names are duly listed; but essentially everything has depended on one brain and one iron will – that of the editor David Barrett.'[62] In that article Neill also called for the creation of:

> a well-equipped centre of Christian research, in which study of the changing situations can be continuously carried on, in which data from all the world can be assembled, sifted and made available to students, and in which even now preparation can be made for the publication of a second and more perfect edition of the *World Christian Encyclopedia*.

It is interesting to note that Barrett and others took Neill's advice. A research and study centre was established by Barrett in Richmond, Virginia in 1985. It was moved to Gordon-Conwell Theological Seminary in 2003 where it is now called the Center for the Study of Global Christianity. It is headed by Professors Todd Johnson and Gina Zurlo. A second edition of the encyclopedia was published in 2001 and a third edition in 2019. This important encyclopedia is widely acknowledged as the most reliable source for statistical data on the world's religions.[63]

One of Neill's many posthumous works, a book review of Jacques Desseaux's *Vingt siècles d'histoire oecuménique*, was published in the fall of 1984, a few months after his death. In a postscript to Neill's review, the editor wrote: 'Bishop Neill wrote this review for the *Journal of Ecumenical Studies* in March 1984, from Yale Divinity School while he was in the U.S. for a visit. He died later in 1984 at Oxford.'[64] However, Neill's most important posthumous writing, by far, was the second volume of his history of Christianity in India.

Neill's grand ambition, since 1930, had been to write a magnum opus on the history of Christianity in India. He did not want it to be a history of missions, although some claimed that is essentially what he produced. He wanted it to be scientific history, written by one who understood India,

---

Christian Thinkers Share their Vision for the Church (New York: Thomas Nelson, 1984), pp. 100-9.

62. Stephen Neill, 'A World Christian Encyclopedia', *Missiology*, Vol. 12, no. 1 (1984), pp. 5-19. Quotation is on p. 5.

63. Todd Johnson and Gina Zurlo, *World Christian Encyclopedia*, Third Edition (Edinburgh: Edinburgh University Press, 2019).

64. Stephen Neill, 'Review of *Vingt siècles d'histoire oecuménique* by Jacques Desseaux', *Journal of Ecumenical Studies*, Vol. 21, no. 4 (Fall 1984), p. 770.

who understood the Church there, who comprehended Indian religions and was familiar with Indian languages. A task of this size also needed to be taken on by one who could review sources in many Western languages, as that is where most of the Christian records are found. Neill was one of the few who had the 'good fortune to read without difficulty the six Western languages in which many of these sources are to be found – Latin, English, French, German, Italian and Spanish'. Neill was also able to make headway in Portuguese and Dutch. His knowledge of Norwegian, Swedish and Danish was strong enough 'to read extensively' in their primary sources.[65]

Neill began putting together his great history of the Indian Church in 1974. He later realised he was extremely lucky to end up living in Oxford, with access to the Indian Institute Library – housed on the top floor of the Bodleian. Neill had only vaguely known about this immensely rich storehouse of Indian records before moving there. If that library fell short, he went to the London Library, the India Office library in London, the archives of various missionary societies located around England, or else he placed a special order at Holden Books in Oxford for anything that he needed to order from overseas. Of course, he spent two months each year in the Day Missions Library at Yale University which is a magnificent resource.[66]

Initially, Neill drew up plans for five volumes but the publishers would only agree to three. Neill was frustrated by this reality, as colour and 'picturesque detail' would have to be jettisoned. Neill desired an annotated bibliography that would help future researchers. He wanted his history to be readable and interesting. When he finished his first volume, which covered the beginnings to 1707 – the year of the first Protestant mission in India – the anonymous peer reviewer panned it. Neill wrote, 'I was not pleased.' He had worked for four years using research from many countries. However, Neill quickly found a publisher in Cambridge University Press, one of the, perhaps the, most prestigious academic press in the world. Neill was extremely satisfied by his decision to publish with 'this noble firm' that represents 'all that publishers ought to be'. After finishing the first volume in four years, Neill worked for another two years to bring the story up to 1858 – when the United Kingdom essentially took over responsibility for India. Neill was working hard on a third volume when he died in 1984. It was planned to cover the years 1858 to 1947, the year India achieved independence. He noted in his autobiography that his history was becoming unwieldy because of all of the various missionary societies entering the picture, as well as the indigenisation of many Indian churches.[67]

---

65. Neill's unpublished autobiography, 'A Last Chapter', pp. 46-49.
66. Ibid., pp. 49-51.
67. Ibid., pp. 49-54.

10. Final Years in Oxford: 1973-84

Neill never finished that third volume, partly because he was in his ninth decade finding it more and more difficult to write – a task he always did by hand. Neill tried dictating into recording machines but never enjoyed that approach. He was also ultra-sensitive to deadlines fixed by publishers and journals, which as a seasoned editor he always tried to honour. When Neill's writing projects were finished, he would 'rarely look at it again'. Even in his eighties, and after writing numerous bestsellers, Neill claimed that he always experienced 'a little surprise that anyone should want to read what I write'.[68]

Another reason Neill never finished that third volume was that Neill did not enjoy writing in what he calls his 'declining years'. Despite writing so many books, the task was laborious for him. He thoroughly enjoyed lecturing in the university atmosphere, especially while using the German seminar method – an approach he even used in India as a young man. However, writing, as an old man with tired hands, became more and more difficult.[69]

Neill's second volume of *A History of Christianity in India* was published posthumously, in 1985. Thankfully, after Neill died in 1984, Alister McGrath devoted 'two months of work' to bringing the disorganised manuscript to press. McGrath was a new lecturer at Wycliffe Hall, having only arrived in August 1983. McGrath said that, while the manuscript was 'fairly complete', there were many 'jottings and notes not in the text' and the page numbers were inconsistent. It was a labour of love, however, as McGrath deeply appreciated and admired Stephen Neill, even devoting one of his books to Neill's memory: *Christianity's Dangerous Idea*. The following 'Editorial Note' was published in the second volume of Neill's magnum opus:

> Bishop Stephen Neill's *A History of Christianity in India: The Beginnings to 1707* was published by Cambridge University Press in February 1984. He had substantially completed the present volume at the time of his death. The Press wishes to record its thanks to the Reverend Dr Alister McGrath of Wycliffe Hall, Oxford for the inestimable help he has given in finalizing the typescript.[70]

McGrath did a great service by making sure Neill's second volume came to fruition.

---

68. Ibid., pp. 55-56.
69. Ibid., pp. 56-57.
70. Alister McGrath, interview with author, Harris Manchester College, Oxford, 27 June 2007. See Alister McGrath, *Christianity's Dangerous Idea: The Protestant Revolution from the Sixteenth to the Twenty-First Century* (New York: HarperOne, 2007), dedication page. See the 'Editorial Note' in Neill's *A History of Christianity in India: 1707-1858* (Cambridge: Cambridge University Press, 1985).

Unfortunately, by the 1980s, Neill's approach to history was already being viewed as dated at best and deeply colonial at worst. However, Richard Pierard wrote, Neill's history of Christianity in India 'received favorable treatment in the Western press'. However, it did not fare nearly as well in India: 'The time had passed when one lone individual could carry out a task so massive as writing the full story of Christianity in the subcontinent.' The review in the *Indian Church History Review* was 'extremely critical', pointing to numerous mistakes and stating that it overlooked more recent research on Indian Christianity and lacked direction. One Indian reviewer, the renowned church historian M. Mundadan, wrote that Neill's history was written in 'the traditional, somewhat paternalistic, missionary style'. It should be seen as an 'apologia' for Western missions and for British rule in south Asia.[71]

Other reviewers were more balanced. For example, Jesuit historian Joseph Wicki noted some of Neill's mistakes while keeping the bigger picture in mind: 'These are small details in comparison with the extraordinary value of this volume, the fruit of a labor of decades of reading, study, and personal experience on Indian soil – all synthesized objectively.' Esteemed Indian scholar Susan Visvanathan criticised Neill's history for being 'one-dimensional and unproblematic' and 'facile'. However, she praised certain sections, such as Neill's 'very vivid' discussion of the Portuguese missions and early Roman Catholic era beginning in the late 1490s. She credits Neill's works for being 'carefully researched with an extensive review of literature'. She notes that Neill wrote 'in the old style', meaning it was not technical and overly scholarly. Neill knew how to tell a story. However, she boldly acknowledged, Neill's histories were most obviously 'written by an Englishman!'[72]

America's foremost historian of Indian Christianity, Robert Frykenberg, described Neill's two volumes as being 'monumental', placing Neill in the company of the 'towering scholars of his generation', including Roland Bainton and Kenneth Scott Latourette. Frykenberg noted that Neill fully understood that Christianity was not a Western faith. Rather, it was from

---

71. Pierard, 'Stephen Neill', p. 546. The 'favorable' reviews Pierard cites are P.J. Marshall in *Time Literary Supplement* (May 4, 1984), p. 501 and (April 18, 1986), p. 426; G. Ernest Long, *The Expository Times*, Vol. 96 (November 1984), p. 60; John Pollock, *The Churchman*, Vol. 98, no. 3 (1984), pp. 266-67; and Klaus K. Klostermaier, *Pacific Affairs*, Vol. 58 (Summer 1985), pp. 352-53. See also M. Mundadan, C.M.I., in *Indian Church History Review*, Vol. 24 (June 1990), pp. 87-90.
72. Wicki's review is in *Catholic Historical Review*, Vol. 71, no. 3 (1985), pp. 458-60. Visvanathan's review is in *The Indian Economic and Social History Review*, Vol. 23, no. 1 (1986), pp. 117-18.

the Middle East. Of course Neill understood well that 'Christianity is no more inherently European (or Western) than it is Indian (or Eastern).' However, Neill was more of a 'forerunner' to the scholars of the late twentieth and early twenty-first centuries, who gave greater privilege to indigenous perspectives. Neill kept very high standards in his history, he was balanced in his judgements and sympathetic in his appraisals. 'We can all strive to emulate' him in these aspects. However, he was a bridge to the more recent scholars who more effectively provided an indigenous framework to the history of Christianity in India, scholars such as Susan Bayly, Dennis Hudson, Judith Brown and G.A. Oddie.[73]

One could not criticise the amount of work Neill had put into his histories of Christianity in India. The bibliographies for the two volumes add up to over 70 pages. There are over 150 pages of extensive and detailed endnotes. Notably, Neill published no books between 1976 and 1984. The reason for this lacuna in his bibliography was that he was researching and writing his history of Christianity in India.

Scholars often struggle to make time to research and write, especially when employed as a teacher, when married, with children and so on. Neill had no wife or children but, still, he was far busier than most due to his church duties, lecturing, pastoring and travelling. How did he find the time to write so much? One of Neill's missionary friends, Roger Bowen, once conveyed to me Neill's advice about making time to write: 'Allocate two hours every evening of the week, when you do nothing but work on your book. Then, when you have read and absorbed enough, decide it is time to write. Resist the temptation to keep on reading and researching – that way you will never get anything written.'[74]

Stephen Neill was one of the most prolific Christian writers of the twentieth century. His books were relevant, they contributed to the ongoing conversations of the day, they were often cutting-edge but, perhaps more than anything else, they were so readable. Even today, most of Neill's books read well. They are organised, insightful, informative and

---

73. Robert Eric Frykenberg's review is in *The Journal of Asian Studies*, Vol. 46, no. 1 (Feb. 1987), pp. 195-97.
74. Email from Roger Bowen to the author, 3 April 2003. Bowen was ordained in the Church of England in 1961, served in Tanzania from 1965-76 and in Kenya from 1976-80, and therefore would have known Neill during the Nairobi years. He wrote that Neill 'was not popular in Nairobi'. Similarly, he wrote that Neill 'had made himself very unpopular with his colleagues in Hamburg, as he was never available to play his part in necessary activities which fell between 7 and 9 p.m.! But his advice was excellent!' Bowen went on to teach at St John's College, Nottingham from 1980-95 and finally as General Secretary of Crosslinks, London, until 2000.

often quite enjoyable, which is hard to achieve as a writer. In a word, Neill was supremely *effective* as a writer. Historian Richard Pierard opined that Neill's effectiveness as a writer was because he 'captured the vision of a global faith and sought to communicate this to his fellow believers'. He continued:

> Although he spent much time in the libraries, his real workshop was in the world. He was more than an intellectual: he was an equipper of the saints. He was truly a striking and gifted personality with a versatile mind, a prolific pen, and a compassionate heart. After confronting the life and works of Stephen Neill, no one can dare say that Christianity is merely a Western religion. He has ensured that we will understand Christianity as a faith which is at home in all cultures and all lands. As a global Christian he has modeled a global faith.[75]

Indeed, Neill was a global Christian, or, a 'worldly Christian', not only in his work but also in his extremely broad understanding of the kingdom of God on earth.

Welcome Distractions

One of Neill's welcome distractions during his last decade was to help his old friend, Anglican President Bishop Hassan Dehqani-Tafti of Iran. In 1977 Neill was invited to serve as an adviser to his friend, who was called to lead the Anglican province of the Middle East. This was a turbulent period in the Middle East, as the Islamic Revolution broke out in 1979. An Anglican priest was murdered, many were arrested and church properties were confiscated. In October 1979 Dehqani-Tafti was extremely lucky to escape an assassination attempt one night that included four shots at point blank range; all, miraculously, missed him. The intruder did manage to shoot the bishop's wife, Margaret, in the hand. The bishop's son, Bahram, was brutally murdered in May 1980. The family was compelled to leave Iran and move to England, conducting their tireless work from afar. Neill was honoured to assist his old friend in various capacities.[76]

---

75. Pierard, 'Stephen Neill', p. 547.
76. Neill's unpublished autobiography, 'A Last Chapter', pp. 58-60. See also Mark Ellis, 'Bishop's wife took bullet to save her husband's life', *God Reports*, 11 November 2016, located at: http://blog.godreports.com/2016/11/bishops-wife-took-bullet-to-save-her-husbands-life/. See also John Clark, 'Margaret Dehqani-Tafti', *Church Times*, 9 December 2016, located at: https://www.churchtimes.co.uk/articles/2016/9-december/gazette/obituaries/margaret-dehqani-tafti.

Another welcome distraction was Neill's sister's decision to retire to India. She had worked as a missionary in India for decades but then retired to England. She quickly regretted it, as she felt India was her home. So Neill helped his beloved sister relocate to Coonoor, located way up high – over 6,000 feet – in the Nilgiri Hills of Tamil Nadu. Neill and his sister, named Isabel, bought 'two three-roomed apartments at a very reasonable price'. This spacious arrangement enabled Isabel to look after her now-married adopted daughter Anwari and gave her enough room to host guests, including her brother. In his autobiography, Neill wrote, 'Anwari is technically the owner of our Indian home' in order to conform with Indian property law.[77]

Neill visited his sister every two years. On one occasion in the 1970s he was invited to Tirunelveli, his old diocese. There was to be a centenary celebration of the birth of V.S. Azariah, the first Indian Anglican bishop. On that occasion Neill was invited to do some confirmations in a village where he had once baptized 250 people during one afternoon. Neill had some trepidation, as 'the ghosts of departed bishops can be a great nuisance'. In 1980 he was invited again to Tirunelveli diocese for celebrations and, on this occasion, was the main preacher, with an audience Neill estimated to be 5,000. On that trip, Neill participated in an enormous, unforgettable immersion-baptism ceremony of some 500 people. With obvious nostalgia, Neill wrote, 'When I am in South India, I feel that these are my own people; I do not regret any of the years spent in their service.'[78]

After launching into a wonderful summary of the state of Christianity in the early 1980s, as well as much insight into Indian politics, Neill began to wind down his autobiography with words of satisfaction and peace. He noted that his days were rather monotonous for the most part. He meditated often and focused on 'the inner life'. His niece, Penny Golby, wrote:

> My husband and I and the children visited him when he was living in Oxford in his later years. . . . He seemed to have found peace and no longer had the grand airs that he used to have. . . . I do believe that there was a depressive streak in the family. . . . My father and Uncle Stephen came from a dysfunctional family in which I do not think much tenderness was shown to children – as was standard for those times.

It is to be hoped that Stephen Neill in his final years was able to overcome the pain of neglect. Golby wrote that Stephen and her father 'had a series of nannies and governesses until they settled in Cheltenham and went to prep school'.[79]

---

77. Neill's unpublished autobiography, 'A Last Chapter', pp. 60-61.
78. Ibid., pp. 61-64.
79. Golby, email to author, 5 February 2013.

Stephen Neill's final decade of church work was a labour of love. He thoroughly enjoyed his role as Assistant Bishop in the Oxford diocese, although he was a bit disturbed by the downgrading of the sacrament of confirmation in the West. 'The baptism of infants cannot be defended' without it, he argued. He found himself being invited to preach in country churches, college chapels and in schools. If anything, his pastoral work with individuals increased: 'There are many people, young as well as old, who feel the need to talk to an older friend about the many troubles which beset both believers and non-believers in these anxious days.' He relished these labours of love for God's people but, ultimately, they prevented him from completing that third volume on Indian church history that he and the world of scholarship wanted so desperately to see.[80]

The final paragraph of Neill's autobiography is worth quoting in full:

> So the days pass by for the most part peacefully. I find myself enormously rich in friends – of all ages, in many parts of the world, and of many different avocations. When they turn up to see me or write, I am delighted. If they do not make contact, I find that more time each day is given to praying for them. As years pass, I find less and less need to pray for myself. All I ask for really is courage – to carry out the duty as long as it is required, not to grow impatient, to work as long as I can while it is day before the night comes when no man can work – but after all there is no night time but, as John Donne was tireless in insisting, only the unchanging radiance of an everlasting day.

Neill knew he would not finish volume three. The history was getting too complicated and his legendary powers were fading. Indeed, in his autobiography he tacitly admitted he would not be able to complete the mammoth project when he wrote that the third volume 'was planned to cover the period from 1858 to 1947'. Those were the plans but they would not come to fruition. Neill was now well into his eighties; he would reluctantly abandon his lifelong ambition.

Death and Tributes

Gerald Anderson, a long-time friend of Neill, was supposed to fly from the United States to Oxford in 1984; he had scheduled an evening dinner with Neill upon arrival. However, shortly before Gerald departed, he was shocked to see Neill's obituary in the paper. Nevertheless, Anderson made

---

80. Neill's unpublished autobiography, 'A Last Chapter', pp. 69-71.

10. Final Years in Oxford: 1973-84   361

the trip and made it a point to record Neill's funeral service, which was used by BBC Radio in their broadcast shortly after Neill's death.[81]

On Neill's last day, he had met with an American student for dinner, then returned to his house in Wycliffe Hall. He was found dead, seated in an armchair, with a slight smile on his face. It was on a Friday, 20 July 1984. Neill was 83 years old.[82]

Alister McGrath, the well-known theologian who was friends with Neill, said Neill's housekeeper, Elizabeth Harris, went to clean Neill's rooms but Neill failed to answer the door.[83] She entered and found Neill sitting in a chair and 'couldn't rouse him'. She stepped out to get help and returned to Neill's flat with Rupert Higgins, former senior associate minister of All Souls Church, Langham Place, London. Higgins explained the scene:

> I was in fact the first person, along with Wycliffe Hall's housekeeper (who has [since] died), to find Stephen. Elizabeth Harris couldn't rouse him so got me. It was out of term time and I was living in a flat under the library with my (then!) new wife. So very few people were around. Stephen was indeed in a chair and had died very peacefully reading *The Economist* which I clearly saw just laid down on his lap. To me, it looked like he had been reading and then nodded off during which he died. A doctor was summoned and in the meantime I was asked to cover his body.

Higgins noted that: 'Stephen had slowed down a lot during the weeks before his death and had 'aged' markedly.'[84]

---

81. Anderson, interview with author, Port Dickson, Malaysia, 5 August 2004. David Lawrence produced the BBC Radio special on Neill. I am unsure of the precise date, although it states on the broadcast that Neill died 'last Saturday' indicating the 'Special Tribute' must have been broadcast not long after his death. BBC Radio gives credit to OMSC (Overseas Mission Study Center) as well as the Oxford Centre for Mission Studies at the end of the recording.

82. Douglas Hunt, former assistant to the chancellor at University of North Carolina at Chapel Hill, phone interview by author, 22 August 2002. For date of death, see *The Decanian*, no. 264, January 1985. There is a discrepancy in the exact date of Neill's death. Geoffrey Shaw, in his funeral sermon about a week after Neill passed, said Neill was found dead on a Saturday morning. Sources are not entirely clear whether Neill died on Friday or on Saturday morning. It is probable that he died on Friday night and was found on Saturday morning.

83. Alister McGrath, interview with author, Harris Manchester College, Oxford, 27 June 2007.

84. Higgins, email to the author, 4 April 2003. There is a discrepancy about what Neill was reading the moment of his death. Neill's nephew, Rev. Charles Neill, wrote: 'Late in the evening of July 20th, as he sat in his rooms in Wycliffe Hall

Neill was cremated at Oxford Crematorium and his ashes were given to Reeves and Pain funeral directors, in Oxford. On Monday, 6 August 1984, he was interred in the churchyard at St Giles' Church, Oxford. The stone is somewhat hidden, although with persistence can be found 'in the row nearest to the East window'. The reference for finding Neill's memorial stone is CH9.[85]

There were actually two memorial services for Neill: one in Oxford shortly after his death and one in Westminster on Halloween, about three months later. Reverend Geoffrey N. Shaw – the Principal of Wycliffe Hall when Neill was there – preached the sermon for the first one. It was held in Oxford on Thursday, 26 July 1984, about a week after Neill passed away. The location of the service was Christ Church Cathedral, Oxford. Shaw's funeral sermon was entitled 'Reserved in heaven for you' and was based on 1 Peter 1:3-5.[86]

Stephen Neill's grave marker, churchyard of St Giles, Oxford, location: space CH9.

The manuscript of Shaw's sermon contains much insight on Neill's life during his final decade. Shaw's sermon began thus:

---

reading the life of Rutherford, sleep came to him at last and found him and claimed him for the last time. May he rest in peace and rise with Christ in glory.' *The Decanian*, no. 264, Jan. 1985. I have opted to trust Higgins' version of events as he was an eyewitness.

85. Quotation from Anne Dutton, St Giles' Parish Office, email to the author, 5 May 2009. See also email from Sue Killoran, librarian at Harris Manchester College, Oxford, to the author, 3 July 2007.

86. Shaw and Moore, interviews with the author, Kingham, 28 June 2007. Also, Shaw, phone interview with author, 1 June 2007. The sermon manuscript was given to the present author by Geoffrey Shaw at our physical meeting in June 2007. The sermon can also be found in *The Decanian*, no. 264, January 1985, pp. 2-3.

> For the past 9 years, Wycliffe Hall has been a home for Bishop Stephen. My predecessor, Dr. Jim Hickinbotham invited him to be our Resident Scholar and as grandfather of our community we have benefitted from his learning, friendship, counsel and sanctity of life. It has been an immense privilege to have him as part of the Wycliffe family and when I was asked to speak at this service I gladly accepted the honour. You could regard it as a small way of discharging a large debt!

Shaw continued:

> This is not a tribute to the Bishop as such. That must be left for a later occasion when many more of Stephen's friends and associates can be brought together. I wish simply to try and express the thanksgivings of all of us for Stephen's life and ministry. This approach we trust will be worthy of the Lord whom he loved and served so faithfully, would rejoice Stephen's own heart, and will comfort those of us who will most miss him in the coming days. Missed he certainly will be.

Shaw described how Neill would be missed by his brothers and his sister, his nephew, Charles, also an Anglican priest, and the Wycliffe Hall community.

Shaw mentioned Neill's 'often frail' health, yet, despite this, Neill made himself available for church responsibilities, for his countless chapel talks and especially his ministry of informal pastoral counselling. He said Neill had 'a constant stream of visitors to his flat from those who needed their doubts resolving or their faith strengthening'. Shaw mentioned Neill's ambitious travel schedule and that you never knew whether he was heading to Cairo, Jerusalem, Cypress, India or to some Baptist seminary in the United States. Shaw told a funny story of how he went to do research in the great library at Yale University and came across a desk which had a notice on it which said, 'Reserved for Bishop Neill'. Shaw then referred to Neill's magnum opus:

> It was at that desk that much of the research was done which has now given us the first volume of his *A History of Christianity in India*. Fortunately volume two is almost ready for the printers. Volume three alas we shall not now see from Stephen's own hand. But with these and all his other writings he has left a legacy which will enrich the world wide church for many years.

Shaw then made a brilliant connection between that desk, which was reserved at Yale for Neill, and I Peter 1:5, 'kept, reserved in heaven for you, and certain reserved in heaven for Stephen Neill'. He then focused his attention on the 'living hope' that this passage in I Peter offers the one who trusts in Christ.

Shaw referred to Neill's belief in the 'supremacy of Jesus' which was the title of a book Neill published that very year.[87] He emphasised Neill's fervent belief in the actual, physical resurrection of Christ. He referred to Neill's belief in Christian conversion, 'a turning in repentance and faith to the Lord who loved us and gave Himself for us'. He pointed out that Neill was many things: a missionary statesman, prolific writer, teacher, lecturer and thinker. Indeed, 'He was all these things and more but he never ceased to be at heart an evangelist.' Shaw discussed how many of his peers came to Christ through Neill's famous missions in the universities, when he held thousands of undergraduate students spellbound with the message of Jesus Christ, at the world's greatest institutions, such as Cambridge, Oxford, Yale, Harvard, Princeton and Berkeley.[88]

The sermon closed with a story about how Lord Coggan, former Archbishop of Canterbury, had led a retreat at Wycliffe Hall the previous semester. During one of his lectures, he was searching for just the right translation of a particular Greek text and, seeing Neill at the back of the chapel, he asked whether the word he had chosen was accurate, to which Neill replied, 'I think it will do.' Reverend Shaw then wove those words into the conclusion of his funeral sermon:

> It seems to me that as Stephen rose and dressed and sat in his favourite armchair last Saturday morning, he could have used the same words, 'I think it will do.'[89] And so he slipped away from this life to experience a greater and more glorious life. But he was able to have such a hope because of Another who said, 'It will do', 'finished', from the Cross of redeeming love.

It was a beautifully worded conclusion to a most appropriate funeral sermon and surely would have made Bishop Stephen Neill very proud.

---

87. Neill, *The Supremacy of Jesus*.
88. Cecil Northcott, 'Bishop Stephen Neill', *Contemporary Review*, Vol. 209, no. 1207 (1966), p. 63.
89. As mentioned earlier, there is a discrepancy about whether Neill died on Friday or Saturday. There is a similar discrepancy about whether he was found on Friday or Saturday.

10. Final Years in Oxford: 1973-84

The second memorial service for Neill took place on Wednesday, 31 October 1984, at 11.30 a.m. It was held at St Margaret's Church, Westminster, London.[90] Neill's younger brother, Gerald Monro Neill, was there, as were prominent churchmen and academicians, such as Michael Hollis, Owen Chadwick, former Archbishop Lord Coggan and Alister McGrath.[91]

The choral music before the service was by Bach. The description of his life included several notable facts: (i) that he received a doctorate of divinity from Cambridge University in 1980; and (ii) that he served as 'Chaplain of Trinity College and lecturer in faculty of theology' from 1945-47. Strangely, it omitted his years as a professor in Nairobi.

The Order of Service opened with the rector of St Margaret's, Canon Trevor Beeson, reading 'The Bidding' about Neill's life and work. Neill's great erudition was acknowledged and the scripture selected was II Corinthians 5:17, 'If any man be in Christ, he is a new creature: old things are passed away; behold all things are become new.' The first hymn was 'Ye choirs of new Jerusalem, Your sweetest notes employ'. The lesson was the Great Commission, Matthew 18:16-20, and was read by Stanley Hoare, a nationally recognised hockey player who devoted much of his life to Dean Close School, which Neill attended as a youth.[92] Psalm 91 was also read. Reverend Robert Atwell, chaplain of Trinity College, Cambridge, Neill's *alma mater*, read an extract from one of Neill's books, *A History of Christian Missions*, which notably included a passage that might have been written for the occasion, 'For all their unfaithfulness and imperfection, God is willing to use his people and do great things through them. Indeed, it is hard to say which is more to be wondered at – that men should be so unfaithful, or that God should be able so marvellously to work through their unfaithfulness.'

The next hymn was 'Let there be light!', which begins, 'Thou, whose almighty word Chaos and darkness heard, and took their flight.' The Address was delivered by the Right Reverend Leslie Brown. The Prayers of Thanksgiving and Commendation were led by Reverend Charles Neill, the nephew to Bishop Neill. Next was the Anthem that featured words from a John Donne sermon. The Prayers of Intercession were led by Bishop Oliver Tomkins (1908-92) – a cleric who had a career similar in some ways to

---

90. 'A Service of Thanksgiving for the Life and Work of Stephen Charles Neill 1900-1984', pamphlet located in the archives of Trinity College, Cambridge.
91. *The Times*, 1 November 1984, p. 18.
92. See article on Hoare in Cheltenham Local History Society, Newsletter No. 72, March 2012, located at: http://btckstorage.blob.core.windows.net/site765/NewsletterMarch2012pdf.pdf.

that of Neill: from Cambridge, he became an Anglican bishop, worked as a secretary to the World Council of Churches and was a popular author of many religious books.

Another hymn was sung, with the lyrics, 'For all the saints who from their labours rest, Who thee by faith before the world confessed, Thy name, O Jesu, be forever blest. Alleluia!' Finally, everybody was asked to kneel for the blessing, given by the then Archbishop of Canterbury, Robert Runcie (in office 1980-91). Then all stood as the procession left the church to the ringing of the church bells. The recessional music was another Bach composition: his Prelude and Fugue in E flat, 'St Anne'.

Neill's death generated many obituaries and tributes. It is hard to find a singular interpretive thread connecting them all, other than the obvious one: his tremendous intellectual gifts. However, they went in different directions. *The Times* published, 'Beneath the eloquence and dynamism was a mind of singular power and range. . . . An unusual gift with words. . . . A facility and vividness of style and a range of erudition that were rarely found in such harmonious combination.'[93] Tim Yates wrote, 'He was a kind of *stupor mundi* [wonder of the world] in the breadth of his erudition and of his intellectual and theological interests.'[94] Many also mentioned the pastoral gifts possessed by Neill, perhaps best summarised by John Ferguson, 'Bishop Stephen Neill was a man of rich humanity, a challenging speaker, an outstanding scholar and a wise church leader. He gave himself first to the community of the church in pastoral leadership, and will always be associated with the church in India.'[95]

BBC Radio featured a 35-minute special on Bishop Neill shortly after his death. On that recording, several people were interviewed with reflections about Neill. One stated that Neill 'had been very distinguished, even from his school days'. He outlined the details of his life and gave special attention to his 1947 mission to the students of Oxford, which was extremely successful and 'thrilling', as Neill made Christian faith relevant to his hearers. 'It had a profound effect', as many young men put themselves on the path to ordination because of those nightly sermons. The young men had come back from the war and were trying to figure out what they believed and what they would do with their lives. One interviewee from Penguin books said, 'Neill was the model author to deal with. Always punctual with his script and accurate to an uncanny

---

93. Obituary, 'The Right Rev. Stephen Neill, Missionary work in India', *The Times*, 24 July 1984.
94. Tim Yates, 'Stephen Charles Neill (1900-1984): An Appreciation', *Anvil*, Vol. 1, no. 3 (1984), p. 198.
95. John Ferguson, 'In Memoriam', *Mission Studies*, Vol. 2, no. 2 (1985), p. 90.

degree. The only difficulty with Stephen was if you ever thought he was in the least bit wrong about anything because that he was rather loathe to admit.'[96]

The BBC tribute made much of the fact that Neill was a professor in West Germany, 'which is a thing that was almost unprecedented for an Anglican – we mustn't say Englishman because he wasn't English, he was Irish.'

According to the BBC tribute, Neill was 'sought after the world over'. They discussed some of his most important books. They also listed some of his visiting professorships, including Colgate Rochester Crozer Divinity School, New York, Wycliffe College, Toronto, Drew University, Durban, and Union Theological Seminary in New York. 'It was, by anyone's standards, a full life.' However, it was clear by his final years that he had mellowed, which was a sign of 'grace' in his life.

In a fascinating part of the BBC tribute, Gerald Anderson was interviewed, recounting his first meeting with Neill. It was an occasion in Singapore and Neill invited Anderson up to his room. Almost immediately upon arriving at Neill's room, Neill said, 'Tell me about your spiritual life, Gerald.' Anderson noticed a pastoral concern in Neill, especially for his 'younger friends'. They kept up a very close acquaintance up to the end of Neill's life. When Gerald became leader of the OMSC in New Jersey, he invited Neill annually. 'Neill was generous with younger scholars like myself.' Anderson added, 'He was an extremely able lecturer. . . . He was a giant intellectually. . . . Apart from his intellectual stature, he was such an articulate and interesting lecturer, that one simply had to marvel at it.' Anderson went on to opine that Neill was 'The senior missionary statesman of our time. . . . [W]idely respected . . . he was viewed with appreciation as he had a grasp of the roots and fruit of the ecumenical movement. . . . [H]e was a pastor to many of us, . . . a father figure in the faith."

Canon Michael Green, Neill's friend and colleague, was also interviewed for the BBC tribute and remarked: 'Many theologians live in ivory towers and have very little to say to the ordinary man. That could never be said of Stephen Neill.' Green worked at Lutterworth Press at one point and was amazed that a man of Neill's stature wrote short, simple books about Christianity for the ordinary, average person in the third world. He had 'an astonishing gift' where he could take important and complex ideas and make them very simple.

When asked about Neill on a more personal level, Green responded:

---

96. David Lawrence, BBC Radio, 'Memorial Tribute to Bishop Stephen Neill', undated, but refers to Neill's death having occurred 'last Saturday'. Parts of two interviews with Neill, one by Anderson and one by Lawrence, were featured in the tribute.

> I loved him. . . . He was warm, shrewd, and spiritual. . . . Each year people would come through Oxford to come and sit at the feet of Stephen Neill. . . . His greatest gift was speaking in the exceedingly difficult venue of a college chapel. . . . The conversations around the room would eventually die out, as Stephen Neill would hold court in this sort of Areopagus situation with very, very clever people from all sorts of disciplines. And gradually, he would show the relevance of the Lord he loved to the discipline in which they laboured. It was absolute education. There's nobody quite like that left in Oxford to do that now.

The BBC tribute concluded with a moving reading from Neill's book, *The Supremacy of Jesus*, then just published, and a recording of the closing music from Neill's funeral.

Perhaps more than any other book that Stephen Neill wrote, his motivation and purpose are clearly revealed in that one, *The Supremacy of Jesus*. As Neill finished that book, he must have realised his course was near complete when he wrote the following, a disclosure of his innermost, most sacred convictions:

> So we have come to the end of our journey, and we find that all roads lead to Jesus of Nazareth. . . . In this book, we have tried to see and hear something of the good and the great of many traditions. We have admired the courage of Muhammad. . . . We have been drawn by the tranquil beneficence of the Buddha. . . . We have watched Moses as he climbs the mountain and enters the darkness where God is. We have listened to the sages of Greece, and found that they had strange foreshadowings of the Christ. . . . Each has shown us something that is of great value; but to each in turn we have found ourselves obliged to say, 'You are not he.' Each points to one beyond himself, in whom the best that he has to offer is transcended, fulfilled, perfected. . . . Jesus always goes before us – we never quite catch up with him. . . . Not one of us can ever know him completely; but we do find that, as we touch the hem of his garment, however blindly and uncertainly, we are touching life. And we have the promise and the assurance that we shall be able to comprehend, *with all the saints*, the breadth and length and depth and height, and to know the love of Christ that passes knowledge. Could we possibly ask for more than this?[97]

---

97. Neill, *The Supremacy of Jesus*, pp. 164-65 (Neill's italics).

Afterword

I chose to give this biography of Neill the title *A Worldly Christian* in acknowledgement of the often uneasy relationship between the worldly and the Christian aspects of his life and legacy. He prayed without ceasing, elevating his thoughts often to the source of his strength. Yet he knew what a good wine should taste like, and he was not averse to sending it back if it was lacking. He could offer sublime confirmation services to dozens of people at a time, only to sink into crippling depression when alone. He could gently comfort a young minister with grace and compassion, only to lose his temper badly with a colleague when feeling slighted. He could preach to crowded auditoriums and win them over with such skill and remarkable ease, yet fail to win the confidence or the friendship of those with whom he worked closely on a daily basis.

In addition, what is now well-established is that Neill's treatment of young clergymen was wrong. Whether Neill realised it at the time, behaviour like this has caused enormous damage to people, to institutions, and to the Christian religion in general. Some people seem to have moved on fairly well after encountering Neill, whereas others became haunted by his misdeeds. As recent history has shown, churches far and wide, both Catholic and Protestant, are still reeling from the consequences of exceedingly inappropriate actions by some clergy.

In his autobiography, Stephen Neill referred to himself as 'the chief of sinners'. We will probably never know what exactly he had in mind when he wrote those words, which were an obvious reference to the apostle Paul's self-designation in 1 Timothy 1:15. It is unclear whether Neill ever fully realised the severe and painful consequences of the disciplinary sessions that he inflicted on young clergymen wherever he went. Even to the end of his life he exhibited this routine.

Stephen Neill had many flaws: a volatile temper, a colonial mentality, and an occasional tendency towards arrogance. However, he could be very tender-hearted, self-sacrificial, and fiercely loyal to people. He was extremely pious in his Christian faith, working long hours throughout his life, trying to win people for Jesus and encourage the family of God. When he preached, he did so with all his might, often to the point of tears. His scholarly output was vast, but his heart was that of an evangelical Christian who understood well the meaning of God's grace – in the words of John Bunyan, 'grace abounding to the chief of sinners'.

Neill's evangelical upbringing would have confirmed this truth: we are all broken. In Christian theology, the preferred expression is that we are fallen. Some choose to say that all humans are depraved, and our only hope is through the work and sacrifice of Jesus Christ.

Stephen Neill's story is often painful to read. There are chapters in his life, however, that are thoroughly inspiring. Such is the nature of a human life, perhaps most notably in the case of our personal heroes. They are incredible examples of the heights that human beings can attain, yet often tragically punctuated by mistakes, missteps, and upon closer inspection, flat out failure.

As the global church continues to face a massive reckoning with the ongoing repercussions of clergy scandals, I can only assume that Neill's story will be yet another example of an extremely flawed pastor in the church who meant well, yet could not stop doing the things he knew he should not do. As St. Paul, the other chief of sinners, wrote in Romans chapter 7 (NIV): 'I do not understand what I do. For what I want to do I do not do, but what I hate I do. . . . For I have the desire to do what is good, but I cannot carry it out. For I do not do the good I want to do, but the evil I do not want to do – this I keep on doing. . . . Although I want to do good, evil is right there with me. . . . What a wretched man I am! Who will rescue me? . . . Thanks be to God, who delivers me through Jesus Christ our Lord.'

Recently, at the end of an academic term, one of my students made this rather profound comment: 'It is said, people rarely leave your presence neutral. They leave engaged or depleted.' I suspect Stephen Neill did a lot of both. His life was both tragic and inspiring, often at the same time. This worldly, Christian man could leave you in stitches after an evening of fabulous conversation with exotic tales of traveling the world. Yet he could also leave people confused and wounded.

May Stephen Neill, the chief of sinners, rest in peace. May those he hurt find relief and peace, even as some of them struggle mightily to make sense of the pain he caused them. May stories such as Neill's bring the church to repentance, and provide a glimmer of hope that improvement is on the horizon.

Appendix

On 27 January 2021, just before going to press with the present work, I received another email from the United Kingdom regarding Stephen Neill's strange behaviour with young adult men. This man's encounter with Neill occurred in 1972, while Neill was a professor in Nairobi. This incident was much like the others I had heard about over the years, with details I had not received before. What was more important, however, was the email's attachment. It was a statement of this man's experience with Neill that he had recently submitted to church authorities upon their request.[1]

The man reached out to me because one of his superiors had encountered some of my research, and asked him to contact me to learn if his experiences fit Neill's well-established pattern. Indeed they did. He asked me specifically about Neill's dismissal from the bishopric of Tinnevelly in 1945. He explained that he had met Neill a few times, beginning in 1972, in Nairobi, Kenya. He described one encounter with Neill that was 'more than bizarre'. He sensed that his encounter 'was not unique'. He requested some of my publications on Neill so that he could find out whether other people's experiences matched his own.

I replied to the man and asked if he could Zoom with me that very day. He agreed, and we met by video just hours after our email exchange. I explained to him that his experience with Neill was not unique at all.

---

1. The author of this letter gave me permission to include his story and his typed testimony, but requested anonymity.

Appendix

Indeed there was a well-established pattern that Neill followed for decades. He asked me what I knew about these episodes and I told him some stories, particularly the one about Patrick Hamilton, discussed in chapter seven of the present work. As described in that chapter, Hamilton told me that his experiences with Neill left him emotionally and psychologically damaged, and sent him into a massive tailspin in his personal life.

My 2021 interviewee, however, had no such emotional trauma. Rather, he said his strange encounter with Neill came up in conversations over the years and he would laugh about it. While it was certainly a bizarre moment in his life, he refrained from taking it all that seriously. We discussed why people handled these kinds of encounters in very different ways. Some people were able to move on seamlessly, while others were emotionally haunted.

Importantly, my 2021 interviewee was able to confront Neill a few years later when Neill tried to get him alone again. He told Neill how inappropriate it was to spank a grown man. Neill was flummoxed. My interviewee felt that, looking back, perhaps this confrontation helped him to feel that he had overcome the strange episode. However, he admitted, during the years between the bizarre spanking in 1972 and his confrontation of Neill in 1977, he did not really think much about the episode. Rather, he dismissed it as weird, and dealt with it by making light of it in conversations with friends.

In fact, it was in the context of my interviewee's retelling of the story in 2020 with a senior church administrator that he was urged not to consider the incident a laughing matter. Rather, he was urged to report it. He thought this reaction was strange because he had told the story many times before, usually to surprise and laughter. However, the senior official covered his ears and said my interviewee should carefully write everything down in a kind of deposition for Anglican Church authorities to have on file. They discussed the fact that there was a growing file on Stephen Neill, and they needed to know what had occurred in this situation.

What had changed so much in the last few years to cause the incident to be taken so seriously? My interviewee mentioned the 2015 film *Spotlight* and stated that many stories of clergy abuse had been coming to light in the aftermath of that film. Of course people had reported clergy abuse before the film, but *Spotlight* caused people to come forward more readily. The film was widely praised and in fact won the Academy Award that year for Best Picture. It dealt with clergy abuse in the Roman Catholic Church, but it was only a matter of time before the shrapnel from that bombshell would reach into other ecclesiastical bodies, in this case the Church of England.

My 2021 interviewee said his encounter with Bishop Neill 'lay dormant for many, many years', without an adverse emotional toll. However, diocesan officials urged him to write it down so they would have it on record. He made it very clear that he had 'no desire to rubbish Bp Stephen. He was, undeniably, a remarkable Christian teacher – but like so many, he clearly had some flaws. And maybe sharing my story might be of help to some others? Who knows?'[2]

What follows is that interviewee's report, dated 11 July 2020, which he graciously shared with me, and allowed to be included in my publications, under the condition of anonymity:

A STATEMENT concerning an encounter with
RT REVD STEPHEN NEILL circa June/July 1972.

A few months ago I was enjoying an informal lunch and relaxed conversation with _____ [withheld, for confidentiality]. During our chat I began to tell _____ [withheld, for confidentiality] of my slightly strange encounter with The Rt Revd Stephen Neill former Anglican Bishop of S. India. [His] demeanour rapidly changed, and he explained very clearly that I needed to make a formal statement about my experience; that statement now follows:

During the course of 1971 – 1972 I was an overseas volunteer working in Kenya, East Africa under the auspices of the Church Mission(ary) Society – CMS. Towards the end of my time in Kenya I was pleased to have met Bishop Stephen Neill when he visited the church I was helping to run in _____ [withheld, for confidentiality], near Nanyuki, in central Kenya.

Bishop Stephen was a retired Anglican Bishop who had served for much of his active ministry in the Church of Southern India but at the time I met him he was on the staff of Nairobi University. He was an internationally recognised authority on church history and a very gifted scholar, with a significant number of published books bearing his name.

Whilst talking with Bishop Stephen in _____ [withheld, for confidentiality] he explained that he occupied a 'grace-and-favour' apartment in Nairobi and, should the need ever arise, I was very welcome to stay with him were I to have cause to visit the nation's capital.

A few months later (I am guessing maybe June or July of 1972) I took Bishop Stephen up on his kind invitation and arranged to pay him an overnight visit. He was already aware of the fact that although I was still a young man (21) I was considering offering myself for ordination in the Anglican Church. Bishop Stephen was very keen to encourage my

---

2. Email to the present author, 27 January 2021.

sense of vocation and after an evening meal together he invited me into his study with the express intention of discussing in detail the nature of my calling.

He explained that his practice with would-be ordinands was to ask a series of simple questions and from the answers given to determine which areas in their lives might need encouragement, development, elaboration, or expansion etc.

Bishop Stephen, with my agreement, began by asking a series of gentle questions and, depending on my answers, he jotted down a 'score' out of ten for each of the questions.

I cannot recall the exact sequence, but they ran along the lines of....

'Do you pray regularly?' – 'Yes' – 'Let's give that eight of ten. . .'

'Do you read Scripture? – 'Yes' – 'Let's give that nine out of ten. . .'

'Do you like writing letters? – 'Yes' – 'Let's give that eight of ten. . .'

'Do you get on well with other people? – 'Yes' – 'Let's give that nine of ten. . .' etc, etc.

Then, quite unexpectedly, during these seemingly very appropriate questions he said, '. . . do you masturbate?' I was clearly flummoxed by the unexpected nature of this question and I momentarily struggled to give a coherent reply. 'Not to worry', said Bishop Stephen, '. . . we'll score that, maybe, a three of ten?'

He then carried on with a dozen or so more questions without missing a beat. At the end of the process Bishop Stephen looked at my 'results' and in a very matter-of-fact way drew my attention to the fact that I appeared to have a low score when, to use his phrase, I was 'not in charge of my own body'. He then explained that if any young man is wrestling with the issue of masturbation then this is clearly a 'little boy's problem' – and the way to treat naughty little boys is to 'spank their bottoms'.

He then, again in a very matter of fact way, explained that it would help me a great deal if I would drop my trousers and underpants, bend over, and he would then spank me hard to deal with this little boys' problem. I have a clear recollection of him opening a drawer in his study desk and pulling out a short length of knotted white rope which was there, I assume, for the purpose of beating, and beating alone.

Bishop Stephen began to smack me, but after a very short while I felt increasingly uncomfortable (no pun intended) and I stood up and explained that I felt things had gone on quite long enough – but that I was grateful for his 'ministrations'.

Bishop Stephen remained fully clothed during this encounter, but I have a sneaking suspicion that he found the experience arousing. <u>I certainly did not.</u>

At the time I guess I was somewhat in awe of a bishop, but I also felt humiliated and that I had been taken advantage of.

Knowing that it would not be long before I was due to return to the UK and, because I clearly felt 'uncomfortable' about the whole issue and experience, I explained there and then, that I thought it might be a good idea to discuss the matters the bishop had raised with my own parish priest when I returned to England. This clearly unsettled Bishop Stephen and, to use the classic phrase, he said the matter was *'strictly confidential, and [I] should speak to no-one about what has taken place and what had been discussed'*.

By a strange quirk in or around early 1977 Bishop Stephen was invited to address students at _____ [withheld, for confidentiality], where I was, at the time, in the final year of studying for a degree in theology.

Bishop Stephen stayed in the college, overnight, and invited me to his room, after college supper, just to 'catch up'. I recall meeting with him briefly in his room, but as soon as he began to allude to our encounter in Nairobi some five or so years earlier I felt it appropriate to stand up to him and explain that I felt his behaviour at the time (in Nairobi) was clearly inappropriate and that I did not wish to discuss anything of a personal nature with him at any stage. I sensed he was slightly taken aback by my confrontational response, but I felt very satisfied that I was able to rebut him.

At one level I do not feel I was particularly 'damaged' by the encounter. But it clearly was, for me, a humiliating experience, and not one I would ever wish to repeat.

Bishop Stephen died in 1984 and therefore is of no threat nor danger to anyone any longer. But I offer this statement just in case there have been other people who have encountered Bishop Stephen in not dissimilar circumstances and perhaps have been far more troubled by his somewhat eccentric behaviour.

Given my own nature and outlook on life, over the years, I have shared this tale with a few close and trusted friends, often with a sense of levity and light-heartedness on my part. But I am grateful to _____ [withheld, for confidentiality] for explaining that there may be a darker side to this tale and that my willingness to make a statement may be of help to others.

I am very willing to be contacted should any interested or appropriate person wish to discuss any details of the above statement.

11th July 2020

Bibliography

Stephen Neill: Books

Anglicanism, 4th edn (Oxford: Oxford University Press, 1982 [1958])
Annals of an Indian Parish (London: CMS, 1934)
Beliefs: Lectures Delivered at the Kodaikanal Missionary Conference, 1937 (Madras: Christian Literature Society for India, 1940)
Bhakti: Hindu and Christian (Madras: Christian Literature Society, 1974)
Bible Words and Christian Meanings (London: SPCK, 1970)
Brothers of the Faith (New York: Abingdon Press, 1960)
Builders of the Indian Church: Present Problems in the Light of the Past (London: Edinburgh House, 1934)
Call to Mission (Philadelphia, PA: Fortress Press, 1970)
The Challenge of Jesus Christ (Madras: SPCK in India, 1944)
Christ, His Church and His World (London: Eyre & Spottiswoode, 1948)
The Christian Character (London: Lutterworth Press, 1955); published in the United States as *The Difference in Being a Christian* (New York: Association Press, 1955)
Christian Faith and Other Faiths: The Christian Dialogue with Other Religions (London: Oxford University Press, 1961; repr. 1999)
Christian Faith Today (Harmondsworth: Penguin, 1955)
Christianity Today (Singapore: Student Christian Movement University Lectures, approx. 1965)
Christian Holiness (London: Lutterworth Press, and New York: Harper and Brothers, 1960)
Christian Partnership (Gateshead: Northumberland Press, 1952)
The Christians' God (London: Lutterworth Press, 1954)

The Christian Society (London: Nisbet, 1952)
Chrysostom and His Message (London: Lutterworth Press, 1962)
The Church and Christian Union (Oxford: Oxford University Press, 1968)
Colonialism and Christian Missions (London: Lutterworth Press, 1966)
Creative Tension (London: Edinburgh House, 1959)
Crises of Belief: The Christian Dialogue with Faith and No Faith (London: Hodder & Stoughton, 1984); published in the United States as *Christian Faith and Other Faiths* (Downers Grove, IL: Intervarsity Press, 1984); this book, in both UK and US editions, was a revision of Neill's 1961 book, *Christian Faith and Other Faiths*
The Cross in the Church (London: London Missionary Society/Independent Press, 1957)
The Cross Over Asia (London: Canterbury Press, 1948)
Ecclesia Anglicana: An Open Letter to the Clergy of the Diocese of Tinnevelly (Madras: SPCK in India, 1943)
Ecumenism: Light and Shade: The Gallagher Memorial Lectures 1967 (Toronto: Ryerson Press, 1969)
The Eternal Dimension (London: Epworth, 1963)
Foundation Beliefs (Madras: Christian Literature Society for India, 1948)
A Genuinely Human Existence: Towards a Christian Psychology (Garden City, NY: Doubleday, 1959)
God's Apprentice: The Autobiography of Bishop Stephen Neill, ed. by Eleanor Jackson, with a Foreword by C.F.D. Moule (London: Hodder & Stoughton, 1991)
The Gospel According to St John (Cambridge: Cambridge University Press, 1930)
A History of Christianity in India: The Beginnings to AD 1707 (Cambridge: Cambridge University Press, 1984; repr. 2004)
A History of Christianity in India: 1707-1858 (Cambridge: Cambridge University Press, 1985; repr. 2002)
A History of Christian Missions (Harmondsworth: Penguin, 1964; rev. London: Penguin, 1986)
How Readest Thou? A Simple Introduction to the New Testament (London: Student Christian Movement, 1925)
The Interpretation of the New Testament: 1861-1961 (London: Oxford University Press, 1964)
The Interpretation of the New Testament: 1861-1986, 2nd edn, rev. by N.T. Wright (Oxford: Oxford University Press, 1988)
Jesus Through Many Eyes: Introduction to the Theology of the New Testament (Philadelphia, PA: Fortress Press, 1976; repr. Cambridge: James Clarke & Co., 2002)
Livingstone Reconsidered (Zomba, Malawi: Livingstone Centenary Committee, 1973)
One Increasing Purpose: Lenten Meditations (London: Bible Reading Fellowship, 1969)
On the Ministry (London: SCM Press, 1952); published in the United States as *Fulfill Thy Ministry* (New York: Harper and Brothers, 1952)
Out of Bondage: Christ and the Indian Villager (London: Edinburgh House, 1930)
Paul to the Colossians (London: Lutterworth Press, 1963)
Paul to the Galatians (London: Lutterworth Press, 1958)
The Remaking of Men in India (London: CMS, 1934)
Rome and the Ecumenical Movement (Grahamstown: Rhodes University, 1967)

Bibliography

Salvation Tomorrow: The Originality of Jesus Christ and the World's Religions (London: Lutterworth Press; and Nashville, TN: Abingdon, 1976)
Seeing the Bible Whole (London: Bible Reading Fellowship, 1957)
The Story of the Christian Church in India and Pakistan (Grand Rapids, MI: Eerdmans, 1970)
The Supremacy of Jesus (London: Hodder & Stoughton, 1984)
Survey of the Training of the Ministry in Africa (London: International Missionary Council, 1950)
Towards Church Union (1937-1952) (London: SCM, 1952)
Ed., *Twentieth Century Christianity: A Survey of Modern Religious Trends by Leading Churchmen* (London: Collins, 1961)
What is Man? (London: Lutterworth Press, 1960); published in the United States as *Man in God's Purpose* (New York: Association Press, 1961)
What We Know about Jesus (London: Lutterworth Press, 1970)
Who Is Jesus Christ? (London: Lutterworth Press, 1956)
The Wrath and the Peace of God and Other Studies: Addresses Delivered at the Nilgiri Missionary Convention, May 1942 (Madras: Christian Literature Society for India, 1943)
Under Three Flags (New York: Friendship Press, 1954)
The Unfinished Task (London: Lutterworth Press, 1957)

Co-edited volumes

Neill, Stephen, John Goodwin and Arthur Dowle, eds, *Concise Dictionary of the Bible* (London: Lutterworth Press, 1966; repr. 2004)
Neill, Stephen, Gerald Anderson and John Goodwin, eds, *Concise Dictionary of the Christian World Mission* (New York: Abingdon Press, 1971)
Neill, Stephen, and Hans-Ruedi Weber, eds, *The Layman in Christian History* (Philadelphia, PA: Westminster Press, 1963)

Translations

Miegge, Giovanni, *Christian Affirmations in a Secular Age*, trans. by Stephen Neill (New York: Oxford University Press, 1958)
———, *Gospel and Myth in the Thought of Rudolf Bultmann*, trans. by Stephen Neill (London: Lutterworth Press, 1960)

Articles and chapters in volumes (this list is not exhaustive)

'African Theological Survey', *International Review of Mission*, Vol. 39, no. 154 (1 April 1950), pp. 207-11
'The Anglican Communion and the Ecumenical Council', in *The Councils of the Church: History and Analysis*, ed. by Hans Margull, trans. by Walter Bense (Philadelphia, PA: Fortress Press, 1966)
'An Anglican in a Lutheran Atmosphere', *Lutheran World*, Vol. 12, no. 3 (1965), pp. 238-47
'Bishop Azariah of Dornakal', *The Student Movement* (London: Student Christian Movement), Vol. 47, no. 4 (1945)

'Charles Henry Brent', *Canadian Journal of Theology*, Vol. 8, no. 3 (July 1962), pp. 153-71

'The Church: An Ecumenical Perspective (An Attempt at Definition)', *Interpretation*, Vol. 19, no. 2 (1965), pp. 131-48

'The Church of England: Has It a Future?', in *When Will Ye Be Wise: The State of the Church of England*, ed. by Anthony Kilmister (London: Blond & Briggs, 1983), pp. 4-18

'The Church of the Future, Reunion and the Ecumenical Movement', *The Modern Churchman*, Vol. 10, no. 1 (1966)

'Comment', *Historical Magazine of the Protestant Episcopal Church*, Vol. 53 (1984), pp. 111-28

'Consecrated – Satisfied', *Here and There with the CEZMS*, December 1933, pp. 245-46

'Conversion', *Expository Times*, Vol. 89 (April 1977), pp. 205-8

'Conversion', *Scottish Journal of Theology*, Vol. 3, no. 4 (1950), pp. 352-62

'A Curriculum for a Theological School', a paper written for *The National Christian Council Review*, May 1933 (Mysore: Wesley House Press and Publishing House, 1933)

Daily devotionals for February, in *Word for the World, Book 1: January to March* (London: Bible Reading Fellowship, 1970)

'Foreword', in *The Sierra Leone Church*, by Raymond Samuel Foster (London: SPCK, 1961)

'Great World Mission Conferences – At an End or Just Beginning', *Currents in Theology and Mission*, Vol. 2 (April 1975), pp. 61-64

'The History of Missions: An Academic Discipline', in *The Mission of the Church and the Propagation of the Faith: Papers Read at the Seventh Summer Meeting and the Eight Winter Meeting of the Ecclesiastical History Society*, ed. by G.J. Cuming (Cambridge: Cambridge University Press, 1970)

'The Holy Spirit in the Non-Christian World', *Church Quarterly*, Vol. 3, no. 4 (1970/71), pp. 301-11

'India To-day and To-morrow', *Here and There with the CEZMS*, November 1933, pp. 215-17

'Intercommunion Today', *Churchman*, Vol. 82 (1968), pp. 285-89

'Jesus and Myth' and 'Jesus and History', Chapters 2 and 3, respectively, in *The Truth of God Incarnate*, ed. by Michael Green (London: Hodder & Stoughton, 1977)

'Liturgical Continuity and Change in the Anglican Churches', in *No Alternative: The Prayer Book Controversy*, ed. by David Martin and Peter Mullen (Oxford: Blackwell, 1981), pp. 1-11

'Liturgical Excogitations', *Anglican Theological Review*, Vol. 57 (July 1975), p. 334

'To Think the Way God Thinks: Philippians 2:1-18', *Faith and Mission*, Vol. 1, no. 1 (1983), pp. 71-74.

'Madras', *Here and There with the CEZMS*, February 1939

'Missionaries and the Vernacular', *The National Christian Council Review* (formerly *The Harvest Field*), Vol. 49, no. 11 (November 1929), pp. 598-603

'Missions in the 1980s', *Review and Expositor*, Vol. 82, no. 2 (1979), pp. 181-84; also published by the *International Bulletin of Missionary Research* in January 1979

'Myth and Truth', *Churchman*, Vol. 91, no. 4 (1977), pp. 309-17

'The Nature of Salvation', *Churchman*, Vol. 89, no. 3 (1975), pp. 225-34

'The Necessity of Episcopacy: Anglican Questions and Answers', *Concilium*, Vol. 80 (1972), pp. 87-96

'On Being Anglican', in *Today's Church and Today's World with a Special Focus on the Ministry of Bishops: The Lambeth Conference 1978 Preparatory Articles* (London: CIO Publishing, 1978)

'The Participation of Indian Christians in Political Affairs', in *The Church Crossing Frontiers: Essays on the Nature of Mission, In Honour of Bengt Sundkler*, by Sigbert Axelson (Lund: Gleerup, 1969), pp. 67-82

'Plans of Union and Reunion, 1910-1948', in *A History of the Ecumenical Movement 1517-1948*, ed. by Ruth Rouse and Stephen Neill (London: SPCK and Philadelphia, PA: Westminster Press, 1967)

'Review of *George Bell: Bishop of Chichester*, by Ronald C. D. Jasper (New York: Oxford University Press, 1967)', *Journal of Ecumenical Studies*, Vol. 6, no. 2 (Spring 1969), pp. 261-63

'Review of *Theologie und Kirche in Africa*, ed. by Horst Bürkle (Stuttgart: Evangelisches Verlagswerk, 1968)', *Journal of Ecumenical Studies*, Vol. 7, no. 1 (1970), pp. 150-51

'Review of *Vingt siècles d'histoire oecuménique* by Jacques Desseaux', *Journal of Ecumenical Studies*, Vol. 21, no. 4 (Fall 1984)

'Rural Work in India', in *The Modern Missionary: A Study of the Human Factor in the Missionary Enterprise in the Light of Present-Day Conditions*, ed. by Joe Oldham (London: Student Christian Movement Press, 1935)

'Salvation Today?', *Churchman*, Vol. 87, no. 4 (1973), pp. 263-74

'The See of Canterbury', *Churchman*, Vol. 86, no. 3 (Autumn 1972), pp. 198-200

'Some Realism in the Ecumenical Illusion', *Churchman*, Vol. 89, no. 3 (1975), pp. 235-40

'Søren Kierkegaard: Part I', *The National Christian Council Review*, Vol. 62, no. 4 (April 1942), pp. 165-70

'Søren Kierkegaard: Part II', *The National Christian Council Review*, Vol. 62, no. 5 (May 1942), pp. 191-98

'Syncretism and Missionary Philosophy Today', *Review and Expositor*, Vol. 68, no. 1 (February 1971), pp. 65-80

'Theology 1939-1964', *Expository Times*, October 1964, pp. 21-25

'Threatened Christendom', *The Empire Club Addresses*, 22 February 1962

'To Think the Way God Thinks: Philippians 2:1-18', *Faith and Mission*, Vol. 1, no. 1 (1983), pp. 71-74

'Western Europe', Chapter 2, in *The Prospects of Christianity Throughout the World*, ed. by M. Searle Bates and Wilhelm Pauck (New York: Charles Scribner's Sons, 1964)

'World Christian Books: A Venture of Faith', *International Review of Mission*, Vol. 60 (1971), pp. 478-89

'A World Christian Encyclopedia', *Missiology*, Vol. 12, no. 1 (1984), pp. 5-19

Film of lecture series

'Stephen Neill', in *The Christian Catalyst Collection from the Twentieth Century* (two tapes, CAT #4325, Worcester, PA: Vision Video, copyright OMSC, 1984)

Other source works

Aldrich, Richard J., *School and Society in Victorian Britain: Joseph Payne and the New World of Education* (New York: Garland Publishing, 1995)

Alexander, Elizabeth Susan, *The Attitudes of British Protestant Missionaries towards Nationalism in India: With Special Reference to Madras Presidency, 1919-1927* (Delhi: Konark Publishers, 1994)

Anonymous, '"Bishop, Scholar, Missionary", Review of *God's Apprentice*, by Stephen Neill', *Expository Times*, no. 103 (April 1992)

The Archbishop of Canterbury, *The South India Church: An Open Letter from the Archbishop of Canterbury to Bishop Stephen Neill* (Church House, Dean's Yard, Westminster: The Press and Publications Board of the Church Assembly, July 1947)

Balasundaram, Franklyn J., *Dalits and Christian Mission in the Tamil Country* (Bangalore: Asian Trading Corporation, 1997)

Barabas, Steven, *So Great Salvation: The History and Message of the Keswick Convention* (Westwood, NJ: Fleming H. Revell, 1952)

Bebbington, D.W., *Evangelicalism in Modern Britain: A History from the 1730s to the 1980s* (London: Unwin Hyman, 1989)

Berger, Peter, Brigitte Berger and Hansfried Kellner, *The Homeless Mind: Modernization and Consciousness* (New York: Random House, 1973)

Bergunder, Michael, 'The "Pure Tamil Movement" and Bible Translation: The Ecumenical Thiruviviliam of 1995', in *Christians, Cultural Interactions, and India's Religious Traditions*, ed. by Judith Brown and Robert Frykenberg (Grand Rapids, MI: Eerdmans, 2002), pp. 212-31

Bose, Sugata, and Ayesha Jalal, *Modern South Asia: History, Culture, Political Economy* (Oxford: Oxford University Press, 1998)

Brown, Judith, and Robert Frykenberg, eds., *Christians, Cultural Interactions, and India's Religious Traditions* (Grand Rapids, MI: Eerdmans, 2002)

Bugge, Henrietta, *Mission and Tamil Society: Social and Religious Change in South India* (Richmond: Curzon Press, 1994)

Burke, S.M., and Salim Al-Din Quraishi, *The British Raj in India: An Historical Review* (New York: Oxford University Press, 1995)

Carmichael, Amy, *Gold Cord: The Story of a Fellowship* (London: SPCK, 1932)

———, *This One Thing: The Story of Walker of Tinnevelly* (London: Morgan & Scott, 1916)

Chadwick, Owen, *Michael Ramsey: A Life* (Oxford: Clarendon Press, 1990)

———, 'Neill, Stephen Charles (1900-1984)', in *Oxford Dictionary of National Biography* (Oxford University Press, 2004).

Christianity in India: An Historical Summary Having Particular Reference to the Anglican Communion and to the Church of South India (New York: American Church Publications, 1954

Church Missionary Society, *Annual Report of the Committee of the Church Missionary Society for Africa and the East, 1938-1939* (London: CMS, 1939)

Clark, Francis X., 'Review of *Concise Dictionary of the Christian World Mission*', *Philippine Studies*, Vol. 20, no. 2 (Second Quarter 1972), pp. 345-46

Clements, Keith, *Faith on the Frontier: A Life of J.H. Oldham* (Edinburgh: T. & T. Clark, 1999)

Cragg, Kenneth, and Owen Chadwick, 'Stephen Charles Neill, 1900-1984', *Proceedings of the British Academy*, Vol. 71 (1985), pp. 602-14
Crockford's Clerical Directory (London: Oxford University Press)
Curtis, S.J., *History of Education in Great Britain* (London: University Tutorial Press, 1968)
Daughrity, Dyron B., *Bishop Stephen Neill: From Edinburgh to South India* (New York: Peter Lang, 2008)
——, 'Bishop Stephen Neill, the IMC and the State of African Theological Education in 1950', *Studies in World Christianity*, Vol. 18, no. 1 (April 2012)
——, 'The Literary Legacy of Stephen Neill', *International Bulletin of Missionary Research*, Vol. 32, no. 3 (July 2008)
Dehqani-Tafti, H.B., *The Unfolding Design of My World: A Pilgrim in Exile* (Norwich: Canterbury Press, 2000)
Dharmaraj, Jason S., 'The Impact of the Indian Missionary Society in India', paper presented at the IMS centenary celebration, 2002, held at IMS headquarters in Palayamkottai
Donders, Joseph G., 'My Pilgrimage in Mission', *International Bulletin of Missionary Research*, Vol. 36, no. 2 (April 2012), pp. 96-99
Eliot, T.S., *Reunion by Destruction: Reflections on a Scheme for Church Union in South India: Addressed to the Laity* (London: Council for the Defence of Church Principles, 1943)
Elliot, Elisabeth, *A Chance to Die: The Life and Legacy of Amy Carmichael* (Grand Rapids, MI: Fleming H. Revell, 1987)
Elwin, Verrier, *The Tribal World of Verrier Elwin: An Autobiography* (Oxford: Oxford University Press, 1964)
Fenn, John Eric, *Learning Wisdom: Fifty Years of the Student Christian Movement* (London: SCM Press, 1939)
Ferguson, John, 'In Memoriam', *Mission Studies*, Vol. 2, no. 2 (1985)
Franzen, Ruth, 'The Legacy of Ruth Rouse', *International Bulletin of Missionary Research*, Vol. 17, no. 4 (October 1993), pp. 154-58
——, *Ruth Rouse among Students: Global, Missiological, and Ecumenical Perspectives* (Uppsala: Swedish Institute of Mission Research, 2008)
Frykenberg, Robert Eric, *History and Belief: The Foundations of Historical Understanding* (Grand Rapids, MI: Eerdmans, 1996)
——, 'Review of *A History of Christianity in India*', *The Journal of Asian Studies*, Vol. 46, no. 1 (Feb. 1987), pp. 195-97
Gensichen, Hans-Werner, 'The Legacy of Walter Freytag', *International Bulletin of Missionary Research*, Vol. 5, no. 1 (January 1981), pp. 13-18
Gibbs, M.E., *The Anglican Church in India, 1600-1970* (New Delhi: ISPCK, 1972)
Girling, M.A., and Sir Leonard Hooper, eds, *Dean Close School: The First Hundred Years* (Oxford: Holywell Press, 1986)
Goodhew, David, 'The Rise of the Cambridge Inter-Collegiate Christian Union, 1910-1971', *The Journal of Ecclesiastical History*, Vol. 54, no. 1 (January 2003), pp. 62-89
Grafe, Hugald, *History of Christianity in India: Vol. IV, Part 2: Tamilnadu in the Nineteenth and Twentieth Centuries* (Bangalore: Church History Association of India, 1990)

Graness, Anke, and Kai Kresse, *Sagacious Reasoning: Henry Odera Oruka in Memoriam* (New York: Peter Lang, 1997)
Green, Michael, ed., *The Truth of God Incarnate* (London: Hodder & Stoughton, 1977)
Groh, John, 'Ecumenism's Past and Future: Shifting Perspectives. An Interview with Bishop Stephen C. Neill', *Christian Century*, Vol. 92, no. 21 (1975), pp. 568-72
Guha, Ramachandra, *Savaging the Civilized: Verrier Elwin, His Tribals, and India* (Chicago: University of Chicago Press, 1999)
Harper, Susan Billington, *In the Shadow of the Mahatma: Bishop V.S. Azariah and the Travails of Christianity in British India* (Grand Rapids, MI: Eerdmans, 2000)
Haselmayer, Louis, *The Church of South India: Its Relationship to the Anglican Communion* (New York: Morehouse-Gorham Co., 1948)
Hick, John, ed., *The Myth of God Incarnate* (London: SCM Press, 1977)
Hoefer, Herbert E., ed., *Debate on Mission* (Madras: Gurukul Lutheran Theological College, 1979)
Holloway, Richard, 'The Mystery in Stephen Neill', *Church Times*, no. 6717 (8 November 1991)
Houghton, Frank, *Amy Carmichael of Dohnavur* (London: SPCK, 1953)
Hudson, D. Dennis, *Protestant Origins in India: Tamil Evangelical Christians, 1706-1835* (Grand Rapids, MI: Eerdmans, 2000)
Hunter, Ian, *Malcolm Muggeridge: A Life* (Nashville, TN: Thomas Nelson, 1980)
The India Handbook (Chicago: Fitzroy Dearborn, 1997)
Jackson, Eleanor, 'The Continuing Legacy of Stephen Neill', *International Bulletin of Missionary Research*, Vol. 19, no. 2 (April 1995)
———, *Red Tape and the Gospel: A Study of the Significance of the Ecumenical Missionary Struggle of William Paton (1886-1943)* (Birmingham: Phlogiston, 1980)
James, William, *Varieties of Religious Experience* (London: Longmans, Green & Co., 1903)
Jayakumar, Samuel, *Dalit Consciousness and Christian Conversion: Historical Resources for a Contemporary Debate* (Chennai: Mission Educational Books, 1999)
Jeyakumar, D. Arthur, 'Amy Carmichael of Dohnavur 1867-1951', *Indian Church History Review*, Vol. 36, no. 1 (2002), pp. 5-11
Johnson, Todd, and Gina Zurlo, *World Christian Encyclopedia*, 3rd edn (Edinburgh: Edinburgh University Press, 2019)
Jones, Kenneth, *Socio-Religious Reform Movements in British India* (Cambridge: Cambridge University Press, 1989)
Jones, E. Stanley, *The Christ of the Indian Road* (London: Hodder & Stoughton, 1925)
———, *Gandhi: A Portrayal of a Friend* (Nashville, TN: Abingdon, 1948)
———, *A Song of Ascents: A Spiritual Autobiography* (Nashville, TN: Abingdon Press, 1968)
'Jones, E. Stanley', *New 20th Century Encyclopedia of Religious Knowledge*, 2nd edn, ed. by J.D. Douglas (Grand Rapids, MI: Baker Book House, 1991)
Kanagaraj, P., 'Tirunelveli Diocese: A Spiritual Laboratory in the Evolution of Bishop Stephen Neill', research paper, Bishop Stephen Neill Study and Research Centre, Palayamkottai

Kings, Graham, *Christianity Connected: Hindus, Muslims and the World in the Letters of Max Warren and Roger Hooker* (Zoetermeer: Boekencentrum, 2002)

Knitter, Paul, *No Other Name?* (Maryknoll, NY: Orbis, 1985)

Kommers, J. Hans, *Triumphant Love: The Contextual, Creative and Strategic Missionary Work of Amy Beatrice Carmichael in South India* (Durbanville: AOSIS, 2017)

Lamb, Christopher, 'The Legacy of Stephen Neill', *International Bulletin of Missionary Research*, Vol. 11 (April 1987), pp. 62-67

———, 'Stephen Neill 1900-1984, Unafraid to Ask Ultimate Questions', in *Mission Legacies: Biographical Studies of Leaders of the Modern Missionary Movement*, ed. by Gerald Anderson, Robert Coote, Norman Horner and James Phillips (Maryknoll, NY: Orbis Books, 1994)

The Lambeth Conference 1948: The Encyclical Letter from the Bishops; Together with Resolutions and Reports (London: SPCK, 1948)

Latourette, K.S., and W. Richey Hogg, *World Christian Community in Action: World War II and Orphaned Missions* (New York: International Missionary Council, 1949)

Lerner, Laurence, 'Review of *No Alternative: The Prayer Book Controversy*', *The Modern Language Review*, Vol. 80, no. 4 (Oct. 1985)

Lewis, C.S., *Surprised by Joy: The Shape of My Early Life* (New York: Harcourt, Brace & World, 1955)

Lindberg, David L., 'Review of *Concise Dictionary of the Christian World Mission*', *Church History*, Vol. 40, no. 4 (December 1971)

Long, Charles Henry, 'Review of *God's Apprentice*, by Stephen Neill', *Anglican Theological Review*, Vol. 75, no. 3 (Summer 1993)

Manickam, M.G., 'The Past, Present, Future of the Indian Missionary Society, Tirunelveli', paper presented at the IMS centenary celebration, 2002, held at IMS headquarters in Palayamkottai

Man's Disorder and God's Design: The Amsterdam Assembly Series (New York: Harper & Brothers, 1949)

McGrath, Alister, *Christianity's Dangerous Idea: The Protestant Revolution from the Sixteenth to the Twenty-First Century* (New York: HarperOne, 2007)

McNeile, R.F., *A History of Dean Close School* (Shrewsbury: Wilding, 1966)

Metcalf, Thomas R., *Ideologies of the Raj* (Cambridge: Cambridge University Press, 1998)

Millington, Constance M., *Led by the Spirit: A Biography of Bishop Arthur Michael Hollis, Onetime Anglican Bishop of Madras, and Later First Moderator of the C.S.I.* (Bangalore: Asian Trading Corporation, 1996)

Mitchell, Jolyon, 'Stephen Neill: A Traditional Communicator in an Age of Revolution', MA Thesis, St John's College, Durham, January 1993

Mott, John R., *The Decisive Hour of Christian Missions* (New York: Student Volunteer Movement for Foreign Missions, 1910)

Mueller, George A., 'Review of *Concise Dictionary of the Christian World Mission*', *The Catholic Historical Review*, Vol. 59, no. 3 (Oct. 1973), pp. 505-6

Muggeridge, Malcolm, *Chronicles of Wasted Time – Number 1: The Green Stick* (London: St James's Place, 1972)

Muir, Joseph, G.E. Phillips, E.J. Palmer and W.J. Noble, *Why South India Churches Are Considering Union* (London: Hodder & Stoughton, 1929)

Muller, George, *The Birth of a Bishopric: Being the History of the Tirunelveli Church from Early Beginnings to 1896* (Palayamkottai: Diocesan Offset Press, 1980)

———, *The Tirunelveli Bishopric: A Centenary Survey* (Palayamkottai: Diocesan Offset Press, 1996)

Mundadan, M., 'Review of *A History of Christianity in India*', *Indian Church History Review*, Vol. 24 (June 1990), pp. 87-90

Murray, Jocelyn, 'Book Review: *God's Apprentice: The Autobiography of Bishop Stephen Neill*', *International Bulletin of Missionary Research*, Vol. 17, no. 3 (July 1993)

———, 'The Role of Women in the CMS, 1799-1917,' in *The Church Mission Society and World Christianity, 1799-1999*, ed. by Kevin Ward and Brian Stanley (Grand Rapids, MI: Eerdmans, 2000)

Mwiria, Kilemi, 'Kenya's Harambee Secondary School Movement: The Contradictions of Public Policy', *Comparative Education Review*, Vol. 34, no. 3 (August 1990)

Neill, Dr C., 'Some Ranaghat Jottings', *Mercy and Truth: A Record of CMS Medical Missions*, no. 11 (1907), pp. 176-78

Newby, James R., and Elizabeth Newby, *Between Peril and Promise: Fifteen Christian Thinkers Share their Vision for the Church* (New York: Thomas Nelson, 1984)

Northcott, Cecil, 'Bishop Stephen Neill', *Contemporary Review*, Vol. 209, no. 1207 (1966)

Oldham, Joe, ed., *The Modern Missionary: A Study of the Human Factor in the Missionary Enterprise in the Light of Present-Day Conditions* (London: Student Christian Movement Press, 1935)

Park, Hyung Jin, 'A Study of Stephen Neill: The Ecumenical Visionary', a term paper for Professor Milan Opocensky, written while he studied for his PhD at Princeton Theological Seminary in Spring 2001

Pierard, Richard V., 'Shaking the Foundations: World War I, the Western Allies, and German Protestant Missions', *International Bulletin of Missionary Research*, Vol. 22, no. 1 (January 1998), pp. 13-19

———, 'Stephen Neill', in *Historians of the Christian Tradition: Their Methodology and Influence on Western Thought*, ed. by Michael Bauman and Martin Klauber (Nashville, TN: Broadman Holman, 1995)

Pollock, John, 'Amy Carmichael', in *Concise Dictionary of the Christian World Mission*, ed. by Stephen Neill, Gerald Anderson and John Goodwin (New York: Abingdon Press, 1971)

———, *The Keswick Story: The Authorized History of the Keswick Convention* (London: Hodder & Stoughton, 1964)

Porter, Andrew, 'Trusteeship, Anti-Slavery, and Humanitarianism', in *The Oxford History of the British Empire: The Nineteenth Century*, ed. by Andrew Porter (Oxford: University Press, 1999), pp. 198-221

Rouse, Ruth, 'Voluntary Movements and the Changing Ecumenical Climate', in *A History of the Ecumenical Movement 1517-1948*, ed. by Ruth Rouse and Stephen Neill (London: SPCK and Philadelphia, PA: Westminster Press, 1954)

Rouse, Ruth, and Stephen Neill, eds, *A History of the Ecumenical Movement 1517-1948* (London: SPCK and Philadelphia, PA: Westminster Press, 1954)

Roy, Tirthankar, *The Economic History of India, 1857-1947* (Oxford: Oxford University Press, 2000)

Sargunam, M.J., *Bishop Selwyn of Tirunelveli: A Biography of the Rt Rev. George T. Selwyn, Faithful Missionary and Bishop of Tirunelveli, 1945-53* (London: Christian Literature Society, 1966)
Sarkar, Sumit, *Modern India, 1885-1947* (New York: St Martin's Press, 1989)
Scallan, Oliver, 'The Supremacy of Christ: Inter Religious Dialogue in the Writings of Bishop Stephen Neill', MPhil thesis, University of Dublin, 1987
Scott, David C., 'Review of *The Story of the Christian Church in India and Pakistan*', *Journal of Ecumenical Studies*, Vol. 9, no. 4 (Fall 1972), pp. 899-900
South Indian United Church Committee on Union, *What About Church Union? Should the South India United Church Accept the Proposed Scheme of Union?* (Pasumalai: A.M. Lenox Press, 1933)
Smit, Johannes, and P. Pratap Kumar, eds, *The Study of Religion in Southern Africa: Essays in Honour of G.C. Oosthuizen* (Leiden: Brill, 2005)
Stone, W.V., 'The Dark Ages and Twentieth-Century Africa: A Comparison in Churchmanship', *Scottish Journal of Theology*, Vol. 8, no. 2 (1955)
Studdert-Kennedy, Gerald, *Providence and the Raj: Imperial Mission and Missionary Imperialism* (Delhi: Manohar, 1998)
Sundkler, Bengt, *Church of South India: The Movement Towards Union, 1900-1947* (Greenwich, CT: The Seabury Press, 1954)
Tatlow, Tissington, *The Story of the Student Christian Movement* (London: SCM Press, 1933)
'Tirunelveli Diocese: A Profile', pamphlet (ca. 1995), Bishopstowe, Palayamkottai
Tucker, Ruth, 'Biography as Missiology: Mining the Lives of Missionaries for Cross-Cultural Effectiveness', *Missiology: An International Review*, Vol. 27, no. 4 (October 1999), pp. 429-40
Vahl, Anneliese, 'Stephen C. Neill: Im Einsatz für die Ökumene', in *Ökumenische Gestalten: Brückenbauer der einen Kirche*, ed. by Günter Gloede (Berlin: Evangelische Verlagsanstalt, 1974), pp. 275-83
Veer, Peter van der, *Religious Nationalism: Hindus and Muslims in India* (Berkeley, CA: University of California Press, 1994)
Visser 't Hooft, W.A., *The First Assembly of the World Council of Churches* (London: SCM Press, 1949)
———, *The Genesis and Formation of the World Council of Churches* (Geneva: WCC, 1982)
———, *Memoirs* (London: SCM Press, 1973)
Visvanathan, Susan, 'Review of *A History of Christianity in India*', *The Indian Economic and Social History Review*, Vol. 23, no. 1 (1986), pp. 117-18
Ward, Kevin, '"Taking Stock": The Church Missionary Society and Its Historians', in *The Church Mission Society and World Christianity, 1799-1999*, ed. by Kevin Ward and Brian Stanley (Grand Rapids, MI: Eerdmans, 2000)
Ward, Kevin, and Brian Stanley, eds, *The Church Mission Society and World Christianity, 1799-1999* (Grand Rapids, MI: Eerdmans, 2000)
Westberg, Sigurd F., 'An Evaluation of Stephen Neill's *Colonialism and Christian Missions*', *The Covenant Quarterly*, Vol. 27 (August 1969), pp. 37-41
Wicki, Joseph, 'Review of *A History of Christianity in India*', *Catholic Historical Review*, Vol. 71, no. 3 (1985), pp. 458-60
Williams, A.T.P., *Church Union in South India – A Reply to Mr. T.S. Eliot's 'Reunion by Destruction'* (London: SCM Press, 1944)

Wolffe, John, ed., *Evangelical Faith and Public Zeal: Evangelicals and Society in Britain, 1780-1980* (London: SPCK, 1995)

Yates, Timothy, *Christian Mission in the Twentieth Century* (Cambridge: University Press, 1994)

———, 'Stephen Charles Neill (1900-1984): An Appreciation', *Anvil*, Vol. 1, no. 3 (1984)

———, 'Stephen Neill: Some Aspects of a Theological Legacy', *Anvil*, Vol. 5, no. 2 (1988), pp. 151-61

Zurlo, Gina, 'The Legacy of David B. Barrett', *International Bulletin of Mission Research*, Vol. 42, no. 1 (2018), pp. 29-39

Archives and Special Collections

Bishop's College, Kolkata, India
Bishop Stephen Neill Study and Research Centre, Palayamkottai, Tamil Nadu, India
Church Mission Society, University of Birmingham, United Kingdom
Centre for the Study of World Christianity, University of Edinburgh, United Kingdom
Day Missions Library, Divinity School, Yale University, New Haven, CT, United States
Dean Close School, Cheltenham, United Kingdom
Gurukul Lutheran Theological Seminary, Chennai, India
St Thomas à Becket Anglican Church, Hamburg, Germany
University of Cambridge, United Kingdom
World Council of Churches (WCC), Geneva, Switzerland
Wren Library, Trinity College, Cambridge, United Kingdom

Index

Accidie, 44, 157, 171
Adams, Harry, 345
African religions, 234-5, 300, 303, 315, 318, 320, 322, 324, 327, 330-1
Agnosticism, 261
Air travel, 159, 172, 215, 228, 255-8, 259, 296, 304, 327
Akenzua II, Omo n'Oba n'Edo Uku Akpolokpolo, 234
Alighieri, Dante, 51, 244, 265
Ali Khan, Liaquat, 216
Alvaneri schism, 61, 127
Amherst College, 260
Amsterdam, 211, 213-4, 217, 220-3, 242, 314
Anderson, Gerald H., 251, 309, 311-3, 347, 360, 367
Anglicanism, 252, 263, 352
Angola, 300
Angus, Franklin, 45, 55
Annals of an Indian Parish, 104
Anwari, 359
Apartheid, 237, 303, 335
Apostolic succession, 113-4
Appasamy, Aiyadurai Jesudasen, 133, 179, 183-6, 189

Appleton, George, 246
Arabic, 229, 250
Archbishop of Canterbury, 8, 39, 53, 115-6, 179-81, 198, 202, 211, 213, 217-8, 220, 224, 241, 258, 266, 310, 316, 324, 340-1, 364, 366
Argentina, 257, 264
  Bogotá, 257;
  Buenos Aires, 257, 264
Arianism, 149
Asbury Theological Seminary, 347
Asirvatham, John, 133
Assault, 79, 172-3, 176, 187, 189-92, 194-5, 210, 219, 328, 343-5, 370, 372
Athanasius of Alexandria, 149, 229
Aubert, Roger, 253
Augustine of Hippo, 244
Australia, 17, 56, 260
  Melbourne, 253, 260, 264
Azariah, Vedanayagam Samuel, 80, 112, 115, 120, 122, 125-7, 132, 136-7, 160, 169, 194, 205, 248-50, 359
Bainton, Roland, 356
Ball, Peter, 346

Bampton Lectures, 287, 292, 310
Banerjee, J.S.C., 133
Barnes, Ernest William, 196
Barrett, David, 264, 322-6, 353
Barth, Karl, 220, 224, 270-1
Basel Mission, 235
Basil of Caesarea, 54
Bayly, Susan, 357
Beecher, Leonard, 324
Beliefs, 7, 107, 152-3
Bentley, James, 19
Bentley, Richard, 19
Between Peril and Promise, 352
Bhagavad Gita, 328
Bhakti: Hindu and Christian, 348-50
The Bible, 16, 19, 27, 30, 38, 52, 76, 88, 99-100, 127, 134, 143-5, 149, 154, 159, 176, 229-30, 238, 249-51, 263, 271, 278, 282, 285, 295, 309-11, 342, 345-6
　The Acts of the Apostles, 134, 137, 154, 314
　Colossians, 250, 282
　Corinthians, First Epistle to the, 344
　Corinthians, Second Epistle to the, 4, 134, 330, 365
　Ecclesiastes, 283
　Ezekiel, 160
　Galatians, the Epistle to the, 75, 249-50, 263
　Hebrews, the Epistle to the, 270
　John, the Gospel of, 87, 101, 137, 285, 312
　Luke, the Gospel of, 249
　Mark, the Gospel of, 86, 249
　Matthew, the Gospel of, 249, 365
　Peter, First Epistle of, 362, 364
　Philippians, the Epistle to the, 352
　Revelation to John, 311
　Romans, the Epistle to the, 153
Bible Words and Christian Meanings, 309, 311
Bingle, E.J., 226-7, 239
Bishop Stephen Neill: From Edinburgh to South India, 15
Blake, Eugene Carson, 245
Bloomer, Thomas, 219

Bonhoeffer, Dietrich, 112, 267
Bossey Ecumenical Institute, 214, 224, 244, 331
Bowen, Roger, 357
Bowles, Cyril, 327
Braby, Denis, 249
Brazil, 248
Brent, Charles, 112, 222
British Raj, *see* United Kingdom, British colonialism
Brotherhood of the Imitation of Christ, 127-8
Brothers of the Faith: The Story of Men Who Have Worked for Christian Unity, 110, 112, 263
Brown, E.E., 40
Brown, Judith, 357
Brown, Leslie, 365
Brunner, Emil, 220-1
Builders of the Indian Church, 51, 105-6
Bultmann, Rudolf, 268, 270-1
Bürkle, Horst, 275, 277, 293
Burma, 13, 52, 110, 115, 120, 125, 127, 134, 151, 162, 172-3, 178, 182, 184, 186, 192, 197, 214, 250, 252
　Rangoon, 120, 127, 133, 151, 167, 192
Caldwell, Robert, 88, 125, 132
Call to Mission, 7, 285, 309, 311
Cambridge, 8, 14-7, 19, 21-3, 25, 29, 33, 36, 43-8, 50-6, 71-3, 78, 82, 84, 86-90, 95-96, 101, 103, 105, 115, 122, 124, 126-7, 138-40, 183, 194, 198, 203, 208, 209, 211, 217, 237, 240, 243, 245, 247, 251, 254, 258-9, 264, 278, 291-2, 317, 319, 330, 339, 354, 355, 364-6
　Cambridge Inter-Collegiate Christian Union (CICCU), 52
　Cambridge Missionary Band, 52
　Trinity College, 8, 19, 43-6, 48, 51-6, 71-3, 88, 103, 127, 203, 209, 249, 258, 262, 365
　Gonville and Caius College, 19, 36, 45
Campbell, Milford, 115

Index 391

Canadian Council of Churches, 310
Caning, 32, 66, 76, 79, 82, 187, 188-9, 197
Cappadocian Fathers, 54
Carleton College, 260
Carmichael, Amy, 8, 10, 13, 58, 61-72, 74-77, 79-82
Carnaham Lectures, 257
Cash, William Wilson, 88, 109-10, 196
Ceylon, 13, 53, 58-60, 65, 110, 115, 125, 134, 151, 162, 172-3, 178, 182, 184, 186, 197, 246
Chadwick, Henry, 285
Chadwick, Owen, 5, 50, 98, 207, 241, 285, 288, 297, 339, 365
The Challenge of Jesus Christ, 154, 263, 312
Chardin, Pierre Teilhard de, 258
Chavasse Lectures, 254, 336
Chellammah, Nallathambi, 146-8
Cheltenham, 8, 16, 23-7, 29-31, 45, 359
Chile, *see* Santiago de Chile
The Christian, 227
Christian Affirmations in a Secular Age, 263
The Christian Character, 249, 263
Christian Faith and Other Faiths: The Christian Dialogue with Other Religions, 9, 253, 263, 348
Christian Faith Today, 251, 263
Christian Giving, 248-9
Christian Holiness, 257, 263
Christianity's Dangerous Idea, 355
Christian Partnership, 211, 219, 263
Christiansen, Rolf, 278
The Christians' God, 248-9, 263
The Christian Society, 263
Christian World Mission Books, 311
Chrysostom and His Message, 249-50, 263, 282
Chrysostom, John, 249
Church of Christ, 343
The Church and Christian Union, 287
Church of England, 30-1, 49, 53, 65, 88, 110, 113-8, 141, 145-6, 154, 216-9, 224, 231, 234, 236, 252, 288-90, 306-7, 313, 316, 323, 326, 337, 339-40, 342, 350-2, 357, 370
Church of England Zenana Missionary Society (CEZMS), 65, 100, 129
Churchman, 317, 352
Church Missionary Service (CMS), 8, 20, 23-4, 59-63, 72, 74, 78, 81-4, 87-90, 92-7, 99-100, 102-3, 106-7, 109, 118-120, 125-31, 137, 141. 169, 196, 231, 237-8, 287, 303, 305-6, 325, 371
Church of Scotland, 235
Church of South India (CSI), 7, 60, 91, 110-8, 184, 196-7, 218-9, 242, 287, 314
Church Times, 200, 202, 227
Church unity, 8, 110-8, 216, 234, 270, 287-8
Circumcision, 230-1, 302-3; Female circumcision, 230, 302-3
Civil Disobedience Movement, 51, 165, 167
Clorinda, 124-5
Close, Francis, 29-31
Cockin, George, 219
Coggan, Donald, 202-4, 310, 340-1, 364-5
Cold War, 7, 280-81; *See also,* Germany, East Germany; *and* Russia
Colgate-Rochester Seminary, 273, 367
Colonialism, 1, 7, 9, 16, 34, 141, 152, 165, 201, 206, 228, 232-3, 236, 251-2, 268-9, 285-7, 290, 298, 301, 304, 310-1, 319, 321, 324, 326-7, 356
Colonialism and Christian Missions, 7, 16, 282, 285-6, 310
Colorado College, 260
Colorado Springs, 260
Commission on World Mission and Evangelism, 246, 317
Communism, 228; *See also* Cold War, Russia, Marxism, *and* East Germany
Concentration camps, 267-8, 279
The Concise Dictionary of the Bible, 16, 250, 282

Concise Dictionary of the Christian World Mission, 6, 16, 108, 251, 309, 312-3
Concordia Seminary in Exile, 347
Confirmations, 38-9,142-4, 224, 341, 359-60
Congregationalism, 110, 112-3, 218
Connecticut, 7, 259
Coptic church, 228
Cornford, Francis, 45
Crabbe, Elizabeth, 232
Cragg, Gerald, 285
Cragg, Kenneth, 5, 98, 206-7, 217, 264, 285, 288
Creative Tension, 252, 263
Crises of Belief: The Christian Dialogue with Faith and No Faith, 253, 348
The Cross in the Church, 251, 263,
The Cross Over Asia, 116-7, 215, 222, 263
Crowley, Brian, 96
Culver-Stockton College, 261
Danish, 155, 354
Dar-es-Salaam, 229, 297
Day, Terence, 303, 305
Dean Close Memorial, 8, 16-7, 22-33, 35-36, 39-45, 47-50, 55-6, 79, 157, 365
The Decanian, 40-2, 47
Daemonium Meridianum, 44, 157, 171
Dehqani-Tafti, Bahram, 358
Dehqani-Tafti, Hassan Barnaba, 264-5, 358
Dehqani-Tafti, Margaret, 358
Denominationalism, 111-2, 116, 214, 234, 252, 261, 288, 335, 346
Depression, 3-4, 13, 34, 43-4, 98, 157, 171, 178-80, 200-1, 205-6, 208, 233, 244, 265, 340, 359
Dharmaraj, A. Simon, 190-2
Dharmaraj, Jason, 159, 190-4
Dietrich, Suzanne de, 222, 314
The Difference in Being a Christian, see *The Christian Character*
Disciples of Christ, 242-3, 261
Discipline, 29, 32, 66-7, 79, 170, 187-8, 191-2, 194-5, 200-1, 210, 328, 344-5

Divorce, 19, 144-6
Dohna of Scholodin, 62
Dohnavur Mission, 8, 13, 57, 59, 61-82, 90, 101
Donders, Joseph Gerald, 302, 308, 318, 320, 322, 326-8, 330-1
Donne, John, 360, 365
Douglass, Harlan Paul, 222
Drew University, 367
Dublin, 264
Duff Lectures, 252
Dutch, 140, 214, 224, 246, 249, 302, 330, 354
East India Company, 59
Ebizawa, Norimichi, 250
Ecclesia Anglicana, 154
The Economist, 361
Ecumenical movement, 4-6, 8-10, 14, 28-9, 52-3, 91, 99, 106, 110-2, 116-8, 121-3, 140, 204, 208-66, 268, 272-4, 276-7, 287-8, 291-2, 294, 297, 309-10, 331, 339, 351, 353, 367
Ecumenical Press Service, 224, 227
The Ecumenical Review, 222, 224, 244
Ecumenism: Light and Shade, 257, 309-10
Edinburgh, 8, 15, 19, 22-3, 28, 45, 122, 200, 247
Egypt, 225, 228-9; Alexandria, 229; Cairo, 228, 235, 363
Ehrenstrom, Nils, 213, 222-23, 243
The Elbe, 275
Eliot, Thomas Stearns, 114
Elizabeth II, Queen of the United Kingdom, 235
Elliot, Elisabeth, 63-70, 72-80
Elliott, Anthony Blacker, 133, 137
Elwes, W.W., 125
Elwin, Verrier, 32-3, 36-7, 39, 41, 48-51
Encyclopedia of Missions, 251
English, 8, 14, 19, 59, 68, 74, 79, 95, 100, 107, 121, 142, 146, 153, 155, 160, 194, 222, 224, 230-2, 235, 239-40, 245-6, 249, 257, 269-71, 274-5, 278, 284, 289, 291-2, 346, 350, 354

Index

Episcopacy, 112-3, 218, 270, 306, 316
Episcopalianism, 232, 236, 288
The Eternal Dimension, 282
Ethiopia, 304-5, 327
Evangelicalism, 8, 19, 24-31, 39, 49, 52, 61, 64, 102, 114, 118, 120, 201, 206, 221, 228, 237, 258, 276, 284, 306, 337, 341, 346-7, 350-1
Evangelism, 28, 49, 65, 82-6, 90, 96, 100, 118, 125, 127-8, 131, 158, 169, 186, 220-1, 223, 246, 261, 270, 294, 307, 317, 322-3, 339, 348, 364
Evanston, 221, 227, 243-4
Executive Committee of the Christian Council of the Gold Coast, 236
Expository Times, 352
Fabricius, 154
Farmer, Herbert Henry, 122
Ferguson, John, 366
Fetish, 210, 237, 294, 343, 346; See also assault, caning, discipline, sadism, *and* spanking
Firth Lectures, 254, 284
Fisher, Geoffrey, 179, 217-8, 241
Flecker, James Elroy, 42
Flecker, William Herman, 31-3, 40, 47-8
Ford, Gerald, 347
Ford, Michael, 347
Forrester-Paton, Colin, 235
Foundation Beliefs, 7, 107, 152-3
France, 41, 56, 108, 137, 139, 224, 243-4, 272, 343
Francis, Carey, 52
Franzen, Ruth, 242
Freetown, 237
French, 8, 23, 36, 43, 194, 224, 249, 258, 354
Frend, William Hugh Clifford, 283
Freytag, Justus, 269, 282, 293
Freytag, Walter, 122, 268-9, 273, 275-7, 293
Frykenberg, Robert Eric, 1, 356
Fulfill Thy Ministry, see *On the Ministry*
Fuller, Reginald, 249, 303
Fundamentalism, 28-9, 31, 52, 100, 230, 232, 258, 268, 337, 346-7

Gallagher Memorial Lectures, 257, 310
Gallagher, W.J., 310
Gambling, 150
Gandhi, Mohandas Karamchand, 1, 60-1, 83, 164-9, 193, 308
Gatu, John, 320
Gell, Frederick, 125
Gender inequality, 4, 18, 34, 322, 329, 342
General Council of the Church of India, Burma, and Ceylon, 110
Geneva, 7-9, 15-16, 43, 203-4, 211-4, 217, 220-5, 231, 233, 238, 242-5, 266, 272-4, 278, 291-4, 309, 331
A Genuinely Human Existence: Towards a Christian Psychology, 34-5, 253, 263, 265
German, 8, 14, 43, 51, 194, 222, 224, 246, 251, 253, 270-2, 274, 278, 290-2, 354
Germanos, Strenopoulos, 112, 222
Germany:
  Berlin, 19, 43, 271
  Berlin Wall, 271
  East Germany, 271, 280
  Erlangen, 275
  German nationals, 62, 122, 125, 202, 231, 255, 276, 278, 289, 293
  Germany in the World Wars, 39-40, 42, 108-9, 139, 152, 164, 267-8
  Mittelweg, 269
  West Germany, 7, 9, 217, 268-70, 272, 275, 277, 279-81, 290-1, 295-6, 302, 367
  See also, Hamburg
Ghana, 25, 210, 225, 235-7; Accra, 204, 236, 252; Akropong, 235; Kumasi, 236; Mampong, 236; University College, 235
Gibson, Sumner, 38-9
Gilbert, William, 329
Global South, 9, 245-6, 252, 271
Gnaniah, S.T. Paul, 159, 186-9, 192-4
God's Apprentice, see Neill, autobiography of
Golby, Penny, 210-1, 331-2, 359
Gold Coast, *see* Ghana

Goodall, Norman, 225, 246-7, 288
Goodwin, John, 250-1, 309, 312
Gordon-Conwell Theological Seminary, 346-7, 353
The Gospel According to St John, 87, 285, 312
The Great Commission, 365
Greek, 8-9, 19, 24, 36, 43, 45, 51, 87-8, 99-101, 155, 224, 228, 249, 278-9, 300, 364
Green, Michael, 341, 350, 367-8
Greer, Rowan, 345
Gregory of Nazianzus, 54
Gregory of Nyssa, 54
Grootaers, Jan, 283
Grose, Dorothy, 213
The Guardian, 227
Guder, Darrell, 281, 294
Hamburg, 5, 9, 15-6, 222, 224, 250-1, 262, 266-97, 299, 309, 318, 324, 332, 357
  Mission Academy, 276-7
Hamdun, Said, 300
Hamilton, Patrick, 209-11, 370
Handy, Robert, 253, 342
Hanseatic League, 266
Hares, Walter Pullin, 133
Harris, Elizabeth, 361
Harris, William Wade, 305
Harrison, Ernest, 45
Harvard University, 43, 189, 259-60, 364
Hebrew, 3, 8, 19, 36, 43, 51, 100, 155, 224, 278-9
Hein, Norvin, 337
Hermelink, Jan, 273, 275
Hick, John, 349-50
Hickinbotham, Jim, 336-8, 363
Higgins, Rupert, 204, 338, 341-2, 345-6, 361-2
Hindi, 155
Hinduism, 9, 38, 49, 60, 66, 71, 83, 85, 87, 92, 94-5, 97, 100, 102, 104, 126, 128, 145, 163-4, 166, 298, 306, 337, 348-50
Historiography, 6-7, 9-12, 94, 105, 116, 194, 198, 241-5, 282-8, 292, 311-5, 319, 324-5, 336, 342, 349-51, 353-8, 360, 363, 365, 371
A History of Christianity in India: 1707-1858, 10, 105, 198, 292, 311, 324, 336, 342, 348-50, 353, 355-7, 363
A History of Christianity in India: The Beginnings to AD 1707, 10, 105, 194, 198, 292, 311, 324, 336, 342, 348, 350, 353, 355-7, 363
History of Christian Missions, 7, 282, 285, 310, 325, 365
History of the Ecumenical Movement 1517-1948, 6, 9, 241-5, 261, 263
Hitler, Adolf, 107, 152, 192-3, 267-8, 279
Hoare, Stanley, 365
Hoekendijk, Johannes Christiaan, 223
Holland, Mary, 92
Holland, Michael, 92
Holland, Willy E., 86, 89-90, 92, 96
Hollis, Michael, 101-3, 119, 133, 175, 184, 189, 196, 365
Holloway, Richard, 10, 200-5, 344
The Holy Spirit, 28, 87, 144, 232, 314-5
Homosexuality, 4, 32-5, 204, 206, 346
Hooft, Visser't, 205, 212-4, 218, 222-4, 243-5
Hooker, Roger, 287
Hopwood, Edith, 75
Hort, Fenton John Anthony, 155
Hort, Gilbert, 155
Houghton, Frank, 62, 64, 66-9, 75, 77-9
Housman, Alfred Edward, 45, 48, 56
How Readest Thou? A Simple Introduction to the New Testament, 71, 285
Hubback, George, 184-5
Hudson, Dennis, 357
Hulsean Lectures, 138-40, 211
Ibo, 233
Icelandic, 8
Illinois, *see* Evanston
India:
  Aluva, *see* Alwaye
  Alwaye, 73, 87-93, 95-6, 100, 120, 137

Bombay, 120, 179-80
Calcutta, 21, 89, 131-3, 135-7, 149, 172, 174, 179, 188, 198-9
Caste, 2, 60-2, 65, 75, 83, 85-6, 94, 97, 104-5, 156, 168, 195
Congress Party, 152, 192
Coonoor, 11-2, 27, 76, 100, 126, 137, 153, 194, 359
Dalits, 2, 60, 86, 159, 168
Indian Church History Review, 356
Indian Missionary Society, 125-6, 160, 186, 194
Indian National Congress, 152, 163, 165, 192
Indian nationalism, 1-2, 99, 124, 132, 152, 156, 162-9, 189-93
Indian University College, *see* University of KwaZulu-Natal
Justice Party, 192
Kashmir, 154-5, 169-70, 195
Kolkata, *see* Calcutta
Nilgiri Hills, 11, 75, 153, 359
Outcaste, *see* Dalits
Sachiapuram, 97, 133
Sawyerpuram, 146, 175, 187, 190-3
St John's College, 89, 92, 159
St Paul's College, 89
Suviseshapuram, 74-5, 80
Tamil Nadu, 11, 16, 96-7, 120, 359
Tirumaiur, 8
Tirumaraiyur, 107, 130, 133, 158
Tirunelveli, *see* Tinnevelly
Villages, 11, 20, 71, 74, 77, 83-5, 92-4, 97-8, 104, 106-7, 111, 139, 142-3, 175-7, 187, 191-3, 359
Infant baptism, 347, 360
Inflation, 216
International Missionary Council, 106, 121-2, 211, 225, 244-5, 252, 276
International Review of Mission, 315
Internment camps, 108-9
The Interpretation of the New Testament, 1861-1961, 9, 255, 282, 284-5
Interreligious Dialogue, 228, 253-4, 269, 314, 350
Islam, 12, 60, 75, 92, 97, 137, 149, 164-5, 215-6, 228-9, 232, 234-5, 253, 264, 305-6, 313, 326, 331, 350, 358
Islamic Revolution, 358
Istavridis, Vasil, 253
Italian, 8, 51, 218, 224, 231, 246, 249, 354
Itinerancy, 65, 82-6, 91, 96-8, 101, 121, 125-6
Jackson, Eleanor, 4, 12, 15, 34, 36, 51, 61, 71, 81, 88, 200, 203-6, 222
James, Eric, 202-3
Japan, 65, 121, 151, 214-6, 246, 250, 286, 293-4
Japanese Witnesses for Christ, 250
Jeremias, Joachim, 270
Jesudason, R.G., 188
Jesus of Nazareth, 14, 28, 60, 71, 78, 105, 137, 153-4, 165-6, 212, 228, 231, 249-50, 253-4, 263, 284, 287, 309-10, 312, 314-5, 322, 348, 350, 364, 368
Jesus Through Many Eyes: Introduction to the Theology of the New Testament, 312, 348, 350
Johnson, Todd, 353
Joint Committee, 112, 114-6
Jones, Eli Stanley, 83-4, 90, 97, 165-6
Jones, Jerry, 343-6
Joseph, R., 159
Journal of Ecumenical Studies, 353
Käsemann, Ernst, 270
Kennedy, John Fitzgerald, 275
Kentucky, 347
Kenya, 7, 120, 225, 230, 254, 297-333, 346, 357, 369, 371
  Christian Union, 306
  Isinya, 307
  Limuru, 297
  Nairobi, 5, 7, 9, 15, 230, 232, 240, 254, 294-5, 297-334, 338, 351, 357, 365, 369-73
  Nanyuki, 371
  St Paul's Theological College, 297
  University College, 294, 297-333
Kenyatta, Jomo, 230, 298, 306
Keswick movement, 28, 64-5
Khartoum, 229

Kierkegaard, Søren, 153, 265
Kikuyu, 230, 302-3, 306, 308-9
Kilimanjaro, 328
Kimbangu, Simon, 305
Kirchliche Hochschule, 271
Knitter, Paul, 349
Kodaikanal Missionary Conference, 107, 152-3
Koilpillai, D., 133, 141
Korea, 214-6, 236
Krisemann, 268
Kurian, Andrew, 176-8
Laity, 8, 53, 59, 86, 150, 173, 214, 246, 251, 282-3, 295, 311
Lambeth Conference, 117, 139, 155, 202, 217-20, 252, 352
Lambeth Quadrilateral, 352
Larsen, Lars Peter, 154
Latin, 8, 24, 43, 45, 236, 244, 278, 354
Latourette, Kenneth Scott, 122, 225-6, 243, 342, 356
Laubach, Frank, 229
The Layman in Christian History, 212, 282-4
Leiper, Henry Smith, 213
Letters to His Clergy, 141-5, 148, 150, 155-7, 160, 169-70, 180, 195
Libya, *see* Tripoli
Lightfoot, Joseph Barber, 254
Lima, 257
Lindberg, David L., 313
Literacy, 95, 144, 229, 246
A Little Exercise for Young Theologians, 270
Littlejohn, Ruth, 19
Livingstone, David, 317
Lohse, Eduard, 249
Luo, 298, 303
Lutterworth Press, 246, 257, 367
Maasai, 307
MacArthur, Douglas, 215
Mackie, R.C., 213
Macquarrie, John, 349-50
Mainline Christianity, 8, 53, 78, 82, 258, 268, 298, 346, 349

Makerere University College, 261, 293, 297, 302, 330
Malawi, 313, 317
Malayalam, 8, 89, 91, 96, 155
Mali, 319
Man in God's Purpose, see What Is Man?
Mandela, Nelson, 335
Manuel, R.A., 133
Margull, Hans, 275-6, 293-6
Marriage, 4, 11, 17, 19, 21, 34, 70, 85, 99, 101, 103, 144-8, 200, 204, 210, 234, 332, 336, 342-4, 357, 359
Martin, Clifford, 52
Martyrdom, 231
Marxism, 45, 280
Masih, Abdul, 313
Massachusetts, 260
Mathews, M.W., 305
Mau Mau uprisings, 298
Mbiti, John, 301-2, 330-1
Mboya, Tom, 298
McGrath, Alister, 10, 340-2, 355, 361, 365
McVeigh, Malcom, 300
Megnanapuram High School, 101, 121
Melanchthon, Philip, 279
Melanesia, 335
Methodism, 30, 64, 110, 113, 218, 236
Metropolitan of India, Burma, and Ceylon, 13, 109, 115, 125, 131-2, 134-7, 147-8, 162, 170-2, 174-86, 188-9, 196-9, 205
Mexico, 257
Miegge, Giovanni, 224, 263
Mission hospitals, 20-1, 23, 27, 68, 98, 169, 177
Mission schools, 12, 57, 59-60, 68, 74, 76, 82-3, 89-90, 94, 97-8, 100-1, 121, 128-9, 148, 169, 186, 190-1, 230, 233-4, 236, 238
Mitchell, Jolyon, 265, 314-5
The Modern Missionary, 106
Monahan, C.H., 154
Monro, Charles, 20-1
Monro, Daisy, 8, 12, 20-8, 61, 64, 72-5, 77, 79-80, 90, 137, 145, 199, 208, 211, 216

Monro, James, 19-20
Monro, Jessye, 20, 23
Moody, Dwight Lyman, 52, 258
Moon, Philip E., 40
Moore, Arthur, 338-40
Moorhouse Lectures, 253, 260
Moravian Church, 275
Morley, Samuel, 125-6
Moses, S.S., 141, 188
Mott, John, 28-9, 112, 122, 220
Moule, Charles Francis Digby, 4-6, 17, 98, 249
Mugambi, Jesse, 10, 317-23, 326, 331
Muggeridge, Malcom, 33, 52, 67, 73, 92
Mukasa, Ham, 231
Mundadan, A.M., 356
Mussolini, Benito, 193
Mwanga II, Danieri Basammula-Ekkere Mukasa, 231
Myanmar, *see* Burma
The Myth of God Incarnate, 350
Nairne, Alexander, 51, 71, 87-8, 101
Napier, Francis, 63
Nationalism, 1-2, 99, 124, 132, 152, 156, 162-5, 167-9, 189, 191-3, 229, 252, 305-8
Nazareth Seminary, 91, 97-107, 110, 119-20, 133, 137, 158-9, 177, 187
Nehru, Jawaharlal, 165, 192-3
Neill, Charles, father of Stephen C. Neill, 8, 12, 17-28, 35-6, 43, 45, 53-4, 56, 61, 64, 72-80, 90, 120, 137, 140, 145, 148, 199, 208, 211, 216
Neill, Charles, nephew of Stephen C. Neill, 203-4, 338, 361-3, 365
Neill, Eric James, 22, 26, 36
Neill, Gerald Monro, 21-2, 36-7, 54, 140, 278, 365
Neill, Henry Christopher, 21, 24-6, 36-7, 41-2, 44-5, 47-8, 57
Neill, Henry James, 17-19
Neill, Isabel Ruth, 8, 12, 22, 67, 72, 75-6, 137, 179, 183, 194, 199, 216, 291, 332, 359, 363
Neill, Marjorie Penelope, 10, 21
Neill, Stephen Charles:

Amy Carmichael, conflict with, 74, 76-82
Appointment as bishop, 124, 131-38
Conversion of, 36-9
Dismissal from bishopric, 163-209
Death of, 360-8
Early life of, 17-28
Education of, 29-56
Furloughs of, 87-90, 96, 136, 138-141, 171, 176, 179, 206, 336
Health of:
 Mental health, 2-6, 8, 11, 13-4, 17, 19, 34-5, 43-4, 98, 135-6, 157, 162, 170-72, 175-6, 178-180, 200-1, 205-6, 208, 217, 219, 233, 244, 253, 262, 265, 301, 359, 370
 Physical health, 2, 4-5, 9, 11, 22, 34, 44, 98, 135-6, 155, 158, 162, 169-71, 175-6, 180, 182, 195-8, 206, 208-10, 219, 238-9, 241-2, 244, 262, 281, 290-1, 330, 363
Insomnia, struggles with, 3-4, 13, 34, 43, 84, 98, 155, 157, 171, 176, 198, 200-1, 205, 209, 241, 243, 254, 265, 281, 291, 301, 328
Missions to college students, 258-62
Ordination of, 22, 53, 86-88
Oxford, last years at, 5,10, 194-5, 240, 335-370
Professorship in Hamburg, 267-297
Professorship in Nairobi, 298-334
Scholarships, 43-5, 47-8, 50-2
Sexuality of, 4, 32-5, 162, 189, 201-4, 206, 210, 294, 328, 341, 343-6
Tour of Africa, 225-38
Tour of Asia, 214-6
World Christian Books, 9 239, 245-50, 274, 315-6
World Christian Council, 7-9, 202, 204, 211-4, 217-8, 220-7, 234, 240-5, 250, 254, 257, 268, 273-4, 279, 283, 287, 293-4, 314-5, 317, 330-1, 351, 366
New Jersey, 7, 347, 367
New Testament criticism, 6, 52, 71, 78, 82, 254-5, 284

Newbigin, Leslie, 204-5, 212, 221, 282, 320, 349
Niebuhr, Reinhold, 270, 342
Niemöller, Martin, 220, 268, 271
Nigeria, 210, 225, 232-5, 304
  Awka, 232-4
  Benin City, 234
  Enugu, 232
  Ibadan, 235
  Jos, 232
  Kano, 232
  Ogbomosho, 234
  St Paul's College, 232-3
Niles, D.T., 112, 220, 222, 250, 253
Nkrumah, Kwame, 235
No Alternative: The Prayer Book Controversy, 350-1
No Other Name?, 349
Nock, Arthur Darby, 43, 47, 55
Nolde, Frederick, 213
North Carolina, 7, 347, 361
Norwegian, 354
Nyasani, Joseph, 302, 326
Oddie, G.A., 357
Odera Oruka, Henry, 302-3, 326
Officers Training Corps (OTC), 41-2
Old Decanian Society (ODS), 48-9
Oldham, Joe, 106
On the Ministry, 263
One Increasing Purpose: Lenten Meditations, 295, 309-10
Oosthuizen, Gerhardus Cornelius, 335
Ootacamund (Ooty), 65-7, 75-6, 153, 180, 194
Ordinarius, 275-7, 293
Oslo, 212, 264, 266
Out of Bondage: Christ and the Indian Villager, 27, 87-8, 93-5
Overseas Ministries Study Center, 347
Oxford, 47-50, 54, 92, 104-5, 216, 258-9, 264, 292, 298, 303, 305, 319
  Hereford College, 101-2
  Last Years at, 5,10, 194-5, 240, 335-370
  St Peter's Hall, 103
  University Press, 224, 284, 287

Wycliffe Hall, 10, 194, 254, 273, 336-41, 343, 345-6, 355, 361-4
Oxford Dictionary of National Biography, 241, 339
Padfield, Richard, 26, 47
Pakistan, 153, 214, 216, 309, 311, 341
Palestine and the Bible, 249
Papua New Guinea, 335
Parry, John, 88
Paton, William, 52-3, 112, 122
Paul to the Colossians, 250, 282
Paul to the Galatians, 249-50, 263
Peacey, John Raphael, 133
Pelican History of the Church, 285
Pensions, 20, 141, 223, 276, 292, 294-5
Pentecostalism, 230, 257
Pepperdine University, 343
Peru, *see* Lima
The Phenomenon of Man, 258
Pierard, Richard, 3-4, 34, 61, 284, 356, 358
Pilkington, Hugh, 303-5, 327
Pirouet, Louise, 322, 324
Plotinus, 54
Pluralism, 314, 348-9
Polygamy, 49, 231, 234-5, 305
Ponnuswamy, I.N.S., 146-8
Portuguese, 8, 224, 286, 354, 356
Postwar economic miracle, 267
Poverty, 94, 105, 131-2, 159, 168, 228, 249, 290, 299
Presbyterianism, 52, 64, 110, 112-3, 121, 218, 223, 236, 306, 320
Race relations, 95, 226, 230, 233, 237, 239, 256, 304-9, 335
Racism, 28, 95, 226-7, 230, 233-4, 236-7, 239, 302-303, 308, 317-23, 335
Ragland, Thomas Gajetan, 84, 97
Raj, Paul, 187, 190-4
Rajamanian, David, 72, 74, 76, 78, 81
Rajappan, 76, 81
Rajiah, V. Gell, 133
Randle, A.P., 102
Ranson, Charles, 205, 211, 225, 246
Raven, Charles, 209, 240, 245-6

Index

The Remaking of Men in India, 104-5
Rhenius, Charles Theophilus Ewald, 62-3
Rhodes, Cecil, 230
Ridderbos, Hermann, 249
Robertson, Donald, 45
Rockefeller Foundation, 214
Rodger, Patrick, 341
Roman Catholicism, 54, 146, 154, 190-1, 214, 221, 228, 231-3, 238, 255, 257, 260, 267-8, 290, 302-3, 305, 313, 330, 341, 356, 370
Rouse, Ruth, 9, 222, 241-3
Runcie, Robert, 366
Rupp, Ernest Gordon, 222, 283
Russia, 30, 41, 221-2, 271-2, 280, 286
Sabbath, 52
Sadhu, 128
Sadism, 189, 201, 344; See also assault, caning, discipline, fetish, *and* spanking
Salvation, *see* soteriology
Salvation Army, 230
Salvation Tomorrow: The Originality of Jesus Christ and the World's Religions, 16, 254, 336, 348
Samuel, Y., 132
Sannyasi, 168
Sanskrit, 8, 51, 87-8, 95, 155
Santiago de Chile, 257
Sargent, Edward, 74, 82, 125, 137-8
Schwartz, Christian Friedrich, 125
Scotland Yard, 20
Second Vatican Council, 279
Seeing the Bible Whole, 251, 263
Segregation, 233, 237, 303, 335
Selwyn, George Theodore, 82-3, 86, 90, 120, 127-8, 132-4, 137, 139, 141, 146-8, 156, 173-4, 177-8, 185-6, 189, 193, 196, 208
Sergius I, 222
Seventh Day Adventism, 229
Shanghai, 216
Shaw, Geoffrey, 337-40, 361-4
Sierra Leone, 225, 237
Simeon, G.T., 133
Sin, 55, 101, 206, 233, 311, 338, 344-5

Singapore, 151, 214, 216, 367
Singh, Taran, 301
Sitther, Thomas, 133-4
Smart, Ninian, 336-7
Smith College, 260
Soames, Arthur Lancelot, 24
Socialism, 193, 235, 271, 280
Society for Promoting Christian Knowledge (SPCK), 125
Society for the Propagation of the Gospel in Foreign Parts (SPG), 60-1, 101-2, 106-7, 118-9, 125-9, 137, 141, 149-51
Söderblom, Nathan, 222
Soteriology, 67, 154, 254, 284, 315, 317, 349
South Africa, 237, 309, 335
The South India Church: An Open Letter from the Archbishop of Canterbury to Bishop Stephen Neill, 116, 218
Southeastern Baptist Theological Seminary, 347
Southern Baptist Convention, 234, 307, 347
Southern, Richard William, 283, 285
Sovereignty of Christ, 154, 212, 254, 310, 315, 364, 368
Spanish, 8, 224, 257, 354
Spanking, 67, 210, 294, 343-5, 370-2, *see also* caning
The Spectator, 107, 209
Spotlight, 370
Sri Lanka, *see* Ceylon
St Louis, 347
St Thomas à Becket Anglican Church, 9, 16, 289-90, 295, 299
The Story of the Christian Church in India and Pakistan, 309, 311-2
Stott, John, 348
Stragorodsky, Ivan Nikolayevich, *see* Sergius I
Student Christian Movement (SCM), 51-3, 233, 245
Student protests, 280-1
Sudan, 225, 229, 232
Sudan Interior Mission (SIM), 232
Suffolk Hall, 24

Sundkler, Bengt, 110, 112, 114, 225
The Supremacy of Jesus, 212, 254, 312, 348, 368
Swahili, 8, 14, 230, 307, 319
Swaraj, 163
Sweden, *see* Uppsala
Swedish, 155, 224, 246, 354
Sykes, Norman, 243
Tahiti, 335
Tambaram International Missionary Conference (IMC) of 1938, 121-3, 136, 245, 275
Tamil, 6, 8, 12, 14, 59, 63, 65, 72, 75-6, 83-4, 86-8, 91, 96-7, 100, 103, 120-1, 126-7, 137, 149, 154-5, 160, 176, 189, 194, 216, 224, 291, 319
Tanganyika, 225, 229-230
Telugu, 59-60, 88, 155
Telugu Mission, 59-60
Temple prostitution, 65
Temple, William, 14, 39, 53, 112, 179, 181, 217, 258, 316
Thangasamy, P.A., 181, 188-9, 192
Theological education, 8, 14, 53, 225, 227, 230, 233, 236, 238-40
Theosophical Society, 92, 163-4
Thielicke, Helmut, 270, 281, 289, 294
This One Thing, The Story of Walker of Tinnevelly, 68
Thomas, A.J., 192-3
Thomas the Apostle, 105, 255-6
Thomas, Daniel, 188
Thomlinson, Hugh, 252
Tillich, Paul, 221
Timbuktu, 319
TIME, 218, 248, 311, 347
The Times, 5, 49, 73, 137-8, 184, 217, 258, 316, 327, 330, 366
Tinnevelly, 6, 8, 58-65, 68, 71-2, 75-6, 81-2, 84, 91, 96-7, 102, 110, 113, 118, 120-1, 123-162, 163, 169, 172-86, 194-5, 198-9, 202, 208, 211, 217, 249, 258, 291-2, 343, 369
Tinnevelly Children's Mission, 126
Tinnevelly Diocesan Printing Press, 149-50, 158
Togoland, 236

Tomkins, Oliver, 213, 222, 243, 365-6
Towards Church Union (1937-1952), 242, 263
Tribalism, 230, 232-4, 304-8
Trinitarianism, 86-7,149, 314-5
Trinity College, Toronto, 262
Tripoli, 232
The Truth of God Incarnate, 350
Tubbs, Norman Henry, 59, 86, 126-7
Twentieth Century Christianity: A Survey of Modern Religious Trends by Leading Churchmen, 253, 263
Uganda, 225, 231-2, 261, 293, 297, 322, 330
  Kampala, 231
Under Three Flags, 263
The Unfinished Task, 16, 251-2, 263, 270
Union Christian College, 73, 89, 91-2
Union Theological Seminary, 342, 367
United Nations, 302
United Kingdom, 7, 10, 91, 108, 124, 139, 198, 208, 210, 255, 257, 259-60, 300, 331-2, 336, 346, 354, 369
  British Academy, 7, 9, 282, 288, 339
  British Missionaries, 124, 128, 131, 246, 287, 317-23
  Colonial enterprise, 1-2, 20, 64, 98, 108, 111, 124, 128, 150-2, 164-5, 168-9, 192, 201, 225, 231, 236, 237, 286-7, 298, 302, 317-23, 356
  Legislation, 206
  Public education, 29
  World War I, 41
  World War II, 108, 150-2, 164-5, 267, 272
United Society for Christian Literature, 246
University of California, Berkeley, 259-60
University of Colorado, Boulder, 261
University of Denver, 261
University of Durban-Westville, *see* University of KwaZulu-Natal
University of Glasgow, 262
University of Hamburg, 9, 224, 251, 262, 266-97

University of Kiel, 271
University of KwaZulu-Natal, 335
University of New Brunswick, 261
University of North Dakota, 261
University of Nottingham, 254, 284
University of Texas, Austin, 261
University of Toronto, 259-60
Uppsala, 245, 262
Urdu, 8
Van Dusen, Henry Pitney, 222
Vedabothakam, R., 188, 194
Victoria, Queen of the United Kingdom of Great Britain and Ireland, 19-20
Vidler, Alec, 285
Vietnam, 348
Vinay, Tullio, 218, 264
Vingt siècles d'histoire oecuménique, 353
Visvanathan, Susan, 356
Wake Forest, 347
Walker, Thomas, 63-5, 67-8, 81
Waller, Edward Harry Mansfield, 61, 115, 126-7, 177
Warren, Max, 115, 196, 238, 253, 287-8, 349
Warren Trust, 90, 101
Weber, Hans-Ruedi, 204, 212-3, 224, 245, 264, 283-4
Weimar Republic, 279
Westcott, Foss, 13, 71, 109, 115, 132, 134-7, 147-8, 162, 170-85, 188-9, 196-9, 205
Westcott House, 22, 53, 55, 127, 209
Western, Frederick James, 96-7, 113, 115, 127-9, 131, 137, 141, 146-7
Westminster Abbey, 88
Westmont College, 260
What Is Man?, 250, 263
What We Know about Jesus, 309, 312
When Will Ye Be Wise? The State of the Church of England, 352
White-Thomson, Leonard, 88
Who is Jesus Christ?, 249-50, 263, 312

Why South India Churches are Considering Union, 111
Wicki, Joseph, 356
Wigram, E.F.E., 72, 78, 87, 89, 93, 96
Williams, Arthur Acheson, 126
Williams, A.T.P., 111, 114
Williams College, 260
Williams, Garfield, 88
Williams, George Huntston, 283
Wilson, Robert, 64
Wim, *see* Visser't Hooft
Winckler, P.C.F., 62
World Christian Books (WCB), 9 239, 245-50, 274, 315-6
World Christian Encyclopedia, 264, 323, 353
World Christianity, Yesterday, Today, and Tomorrow, 222
World Council of Churches (WCC), 7-9, 202, 204, 211-4, 217-8, 220-7, 234, 240-5, 250, 254, 257, 268, 273-4, 279, 283, 287, 293-4, 314-5, 317, 330-1, 351, 366
World War I, 39-42, 49, 164, 271
World War II, 107-110, 124, 139-41, 150-2, 165, 190, 215-6, 267-8, 271-2, 279-80, 290, 310, 366
The Wrath and the Peace of God and Other Studies, 153, 263
Wright, Nicholas Thomas, 15-6, 208, 284
Wyatt, J.C., 88
Wycliffe College, 273, 367
Wysner, Glora M., 247
Yale University, 259, 337, 342-3, 347, 353-4, 363-4
Yates, Timothy, 7, 39, 107, 205, 265, 366
Yoruba, 233, 235
Young, T. Cuyler, 300-1
Young Women's Christian Association (YMCA), 242
Zaire, 300
Zurlo, Gina, 353
Zwemer, Samuel Marinus, 313